AI and Emotional Intelligence for Modern Business Management

Bhawana Bhardwaj
Central University of Himachal Pradesh, India

Dipanker Sharma
Central University of Himachal Pradesh, India

Mohinder Chand Dhiman
Central University of Himachal Pradesh, India

A volume in the Advances in Logistics, Operations, and Management Science (ALOMS) Book Series

IGI Global
PUBLISHER of TIMELY KNOWLEDGE

Published in the United States of America by
IGI Global
Business Science Reference (an imprint of IGI Global)
701 E. Chocolate Avenue
Hershey PA, USA 17033
Tel: 717-533-8845
Fax: 717-533-8661
E-mail: cust@igi-global.com
Web site: http://www.igi-global.com

Library of Congress Cataloging-in-Publication Data

Names: Bhardwaj, Bhawana, editor. | Sharma, Dipanker, 1982- editor. | Dhiman, Mohinder Chand, 1967- editor.
Title: AI and emotional intelligence for modern business management / edited by Bhawana Bhardwaj, Dipanker Sharma, Mohinder Chand Dhiman.
Description: Hershey, PA : Business Science Reference, [2024] | Includes bibliographical references and index. | Summary: "This book addresses the operational, managerial, and contemporary business management issues to provide thoughtful insight and stimulate discussion and debate amongst industry stakeholders and academicians about the role of artificial intelligence and emotional intelligence in modern business management"-- Provided by publisher.
Identifiers: LCCN 2023033715 (print) | LCCN 2023033716 (ebook) | ISBN 9798369304181 (hardcover) | ISBN 9798369304198 (paperback) | ISBN 9798369304204 (ebook)
Subjects: LCSH: Industrial management. | Management--Technological innovations. | Artificial intelligence. | Emotional intelligence.
Classification: LCC HD31.2 .A5 2024 (print) | LCC HD31.2 (ebook) | DDC 600--dc23/eng/20230828
LC record available at https://lccn.loc.gov/2023033715
LC ebook record available at https://lccn.loc.gov/2023033716

This book is published in the IGI Global book series Advances in Logistics, Operations, and Management Science (ALOMS) (ISSN: 2327-350X; eISSN: 2327-3518)

British Cataloguing in Publication Data
A Cataloguing in Publication record for this book is available from the British Library.

Advances in Logistics, Operations, and Management Science (ALOMS) Book Series

John Wang
Montclair State University, USA

ISSN:2327-350X
EISSN:2327-3518

Mission

Operations research and management science continue to influence business processes, administration, and management information systems, particularly in covering the application methods for decision-making processes. New case studies and applications on management science, operations management, social sciences, and other behavioral sciences have been incorporated into business and organizations real-world objectives.

The **Advances in Logistics, Operations, and Management Science** (ALOMS) Book Series provides a collection of reference publications on the current trends, applications, theories, and practices in the management science field. Providing relevant and current research, this series and its individual publications would be useful for academics, researchers, scholars, and practitioners interested in improving decision making models and business functions.

Coverage

- Production Management
- Operations Management
- Computing and information technologies
- Marketing engineering
- Information Management
- Finance
- Networks
- Political Science
- Decision analysis and decision support
- Risk Management

The Advances in Logistics, Operations, and Management Science (ALOMS) Book Series (ISSN 2327-350X) is published by IGI Global, 701 E. Chocolate Avenue, Hershey, PA 17033-1240, USA, www.igi-global.com. This series is composed of titles available for purchase individually; each title is edited to be contextually exclusive from any other title within the series. For pricing and ordering information please visit http://www.igi-global.com/book-series/advances-logistics-operations-management-science/37170. Postmaster: Send all address changes to above address.

Titles in this Series

For a list of additional titles in this series, please visit: www.igi-global.com/book-series

Innovation Capabilities and Entrepreneurial Opportunities of Smart Working
Beatrice Orlando (Department of Economics and Management, University of Ferrara, Ferrara, taly)
Business Science Reference • © 2024 • 300pp • H/C (ISBN: 9781799887973) • US $240.00

Integrating Intelligence and Sustainability in Supply Chains
Badr Bentalha (National School of Business and Management, Sidi Mohammed Ben Abdellah University, Morocco) Aziz Hmioui (National School of Business and Management, Sidi Mohammed Ben Abdellah University, Morocco) and Lhoussaine Alla (National Schools of Applied Sciences, Sidi Mohammed Ben Abdellah University, Moocco)
Business Science Reference • © 2023 • 330pp • H/C (ISBN: 9798369302255) • US $275.00

Global Perspectives on Soft Power Management in Business
Kannapat Kankaew (Burapha University International College, Thailand)
Business Science Reference • © 2023 • 360pp • H/C (ISBN: 9798369302507) • US $275.00

Strategies and Applications of Islamic Entrepreneurship
Ahmad Rafiki (Universitas Medan Area, Indonesia) Alfatih Gessan Pananjung (Bahrain Institute of Banking and Finance, Bahrain) and Muhammad Dharma Tuah Putra Nasution (Universitas Pembangunan Panca Budi, Indonesia)
Business Science Reference • © 2023 • 313pp • H/C (ISBN: 9781668475195) • US $250.00

Entrepreneurship Ecosystems and Their Opportunities and Challenges
Mohammed El Amine Abdelli (University of Brest, France) Shajara Ul-Durar (University of Sunderland, UK) and Hala Wasef Hattab (British University in Egypt, Egypt)
Business Science Reference • © 2023 • 337pp • H/C (ISBN: 9781668471401) • US $250.00

Climate Change Management and Social Innovations for Sustainable Global Organization
Sumita Dave (Amity University, Raipur, India) Monica Sainy (Amity University, Raipur, India) Disha Sharma (Amity University, Raipur, India) and Anupam Singh (University of Stirling, UK)
Engineering Science Reference • © 2023 • 313pp • H/C (ISBN: 9781668495032) • US $250.00

Technological Innovation Driving Sustainable Entrepreneurial Growth in Developing Nations
Nana Yaw Asabere (Accra Technical University, Ghana) Glenn Kwabena Gyimah (Accra Technical University, Ghana) Amevi Acakpovi (Accra Technical University, Ghana) and Florence Plockey (Accra Technical University, Ghana)
Business Science Reference • © 2023 • 452pp • H/C (ISBN: 9781668498439) • US $250.00

IGI Global
PUBLISHER of TIMELY KNOWLEDGE

701 East Chocolate Avenue, Hershey, PA 17033, USA
Tel: 717-533-8845 x100 • Fax: 717-533-8661
E-Mail: cust@igi-global.com • www.igi-global.com

Editorial Advisory Board

Table of Contents

Detailed Table of Contents

The disruptive VUCA environment affects both the organizations as well as the leaders. To survive in this unruly environment, and to find new solutions to this problem organizations need leaders with strong mental and emotional competencies. Prior research contends that a leader's emotional intelligence favorably promotes leadership effectiveness; however, the relationship is only studied superficially and not considering the VUCA circumstances. Furthermore, there is scant literature on the relationship between emotional intelligence and leadership effectiveness with mental health and happiness at work as mediators. Also, a thorough understanding of the influence of EI on positive psychology concepts remains elusive. From the authors' perspective, the ability of aspiring leaders and their effectiveness in handling this challenging environment will be greatly influenced by their emotional intelligence, mental health, and happiness at work. This study utilizes an integrative literature review methodology and attempts to theoretically link prior literature to fill the void.

This study aimed to investigate the association between the job satisfaction experienced by hospital nurses in Jaipur and their level of emotional intelligence. The triumphs and accomplishments of a person are directly proportional to their level of intelligence. In Jaipur, a correlational research study was carried out. For the study, one hundred registered general nurses were recruited from three private hospitals in Jaipur (50 females and 50 males). Both emotional intelligence and work contentment were evaluated using the Schutte self-report emotional intelligence inventory and the job contentment survey. Both of these surveys were administered online. The research showed a significant positive association between nurses' emotional intelligence and job satisfaction. In addition, the findings did not point to any substantial gender disparities in terms of emotional intelligence or happiness with one's place of employment.

Conventionally, intelligence has typically been associated solely with cognitive and logical abilities. Nevertheless, this conventional perspective on intelligence overlooks the wide range of other inherent faculties within the human mind. Human behavior emerges from an individual's inherent qualities, encompassing a diverse spectrum of actions and behaviors, especially in their interactions with others. Emotional quotient (EQ) delves into a person's capacity to effectively respond and react within diverse situations involving people. Meanwhile, spiritual quotient (SQ) forms the foundational basis not only for intelligence quotient (IQ) but also for emotional quotient (EQ). The present narrative study delves into how the fusion of emotional and spiritual quotients can empower a leader to make informed and

According to Business Wire, the e-commerce market in India is expected to reach US$107.3 billion in 2023 and attract more players in online retailing. E-commerce is essentially backed by technology, and it can be assumed that e-commerce users are tech savvy, seek solutions in technology. VR is one of the important components of artificial intelligence transforming online retail experience to a large extent. The chapter explores the transformative effects of VR on consumer behavior. The chapter begins with the introduction and rise of VR in mitigating the limitations of online shopping and explains how VR is substituting physically examining of products, and how it empowers consumers to make more informed purchasing decisions. Later, the role of AI in virtual e-commerce is discussed followed by shopping convenience for e-commerce users and the future of VR in e-commerce. The findings of this chapter reveal that VR significantly impacts consumer behavior by fostering a sense of presence, interactivity, and immersion. At last, a conclusion is presented.

Artificial intelligence (AI) offers both opportunities and difficulties. In addition to significantly enhancing industrial efficiency, these technologies also have mixed or adverse influences on employee well-being. Understanding the influence of AI on employee well-being is essential given the increasing use of these technologies across HRM domains. This study raises a crucial question: Does artificial intelligence influence employee well-being? Job satisfaction, stress, overall health, and job security are considered essential dimensions of well-being. This study suggests that, even though AI can improve employee well-being, caution can be taken to address concerns and ensure a positive work atmosphere in organizations. Managers and leaders can utilize their agency significantly by influencing working conditions, technological adoptions, and AI in the interest of employee welfare. Organizational support and training programs can be relevant in reducing the negative effects of AI on employee well-being.

AI is a revolutionary force that could disrupt several sectors. This chapter addresses key questions about AI's impact on banking. It examines natural language processing, machine learning, and predictive analytics in finance. The study aims to elucidate how AI can enhance the banking experience for customers by exploring its role in personalized services, customer support, and fraud prevention. Further, it offers a comprehensive analysis of the pros and cons of utilizing AI in banking operations, illuminating the

Foreword

In the ever-evolving landscape of modern business management, two distinct yet interrelated forces have emerged as pivotal players in shaping the way organizations operate and succeed: artificial intelligence (AI) and emotional intelligence (EI). This book sets out to investigate the dynamic potential of these two domains; it is critical to recognize their tremendous influence on the way businesses work and grow in today's fast-paced, data-driven world, full of diverse minds and emotions.

Artificial intelligence has challenged traditional business models due to its astonishing capacity to handle massive quantities of data, make predictions, automate operations, and even replicate human-like cognitive capabilities. AI-powered technologies, ranging from chatbots to complicated machine learning algorithms, are reshaping decision-making processes, improving consumer experiences, and optimising operations in ways that we could only have envisioned a few years ago.

Emotional intelligence, on the other hand, is sometimes referred to as the human touch in business and comprises the ability to recognise, comprehend, manage, and harness emotions—both one's own and those of others. It has long been acknowledged as an important aspect in good leadership, teamwork, and customer interactions. In the age of artificial intelligence, emotional intelligence (EI) serves as a powerful counterweight, reminding us that the core of business is profoundly entrenched in human connections, empathy, and the capacity to connect on an emotional level.

The role of AI and EI in modern corporate management is a fascinating phenomena, as described in this book. While AI can analyse data to identify patterns, make suggestions, and optimise processes, EI offers the critical insight and nuance required to understand and act on that knowledge in a way that is consistent with human values and emotions. They have the ability to generate a harmonious synergy that results in more educated, sympathetic, and effective decision-making, leading in long-term and sustainable corporate development and success.

In this thought-provoking exploration, the authors delves into the multifaceted dimensions of the role that both AI and EI play in modern business management. The editors have done a good job in examining how AI-driven analytics can offer valuable insights into customer preferences, market trends, and operational efficiencies, while also recognizing that EI remains integral in building trust, fostering innovation, and nurturing relationships with employees, customers, and stakeholders.

Through a series of insightful empirical, conceptual, descriptive, and other studies, this collection aims to shed light on the evolving landscape of business management, where the chemistry of technology and emotional intelligence can lead to more resilient, adaptive, and compassionate organizations. I am sure that these perspectives will serve as a guiding beacon for business leaders, executives, professionals, and researchers seeking to navigate the intricate tapestry of AI and EI in today's dynamic corporate world.

As the book embarks on this journey, I congratulate all the prolific authors and the dynamic editors namely; Dr Bhawana Bhardwaj, Prof. Dipanker Sharma and Prof. Mohinder Chand Dhiman for this exemplary contribution to the world of research.

Best Wishes,

Sat Prakash Bansal
Central University of Himachal Pradesh, India

Preface

The field of modern business management is at the forefront of transformation, driven by the relentless waves of technological innovation and changing paradigms in the corporate landscape. The Fourth Industrial Revolution, characterized by the pervasive influence of technology and data, has ushered in a new era of management practices. As editors of this reference book, *AI and Emotional Intelligence for Modern Business Management*, we embark on a journey to explore and illuminate the pivotal roles played by Artificial Intelligence (AI) and Emotional Intelligence (EI) in shaping the dynamics of contemporary business management.

The integration of AI into business operations has revolutionized how organizations function, introducing automation, optimization, and unprecedented scalability. Yet, with the remarkable strides in AI, questions have arisen about its potential impact on human employment and the ethical implications surrounding its application. Simultaneously, Emotional Intelligence, the ability to recognize, understand, and manage emotions, has emerged as a linchpin for effective leadership, teamwork, and communication within the corporate world. The interplay between AI and EI is a vital juncture that demands exploration, discussion, and careful consideration.

Our aim in this comprehensive reference book is to bridge the gap between AI and EI, providing readers with insights into how these two distinct yet interrelated aspects of human and artificial intelligence converge and coexist in the realm of modern business management. We aspire to equip researchers, practitioners, educators, students, industry leaders, and innovators with a profound understanding of the multifaceted roles AI and EI play in driving innovation, productivity, and success in contemporary business settings.

This book is structured to delve into a myriad of facets within the purview of business management, catering to a diverse audience. It delves into topics such as the significance of emotional intelligence in leadership, the impact of AI on decision-making, the implications of EI on organizational culture, and the ethical considerations of AI adoption. With a hands-on approach, we aim to provide a balanced exploration of AI and EI, shedding light on their practical applications, methodologies, and best practices.

The chapters in this book are meticulously crafted to provide valuable insights into AI and EI's roles in diverse areas such as employee engagement, customer service, innovation, and digital transformation. Whether you are a seasoned professional, a budding researcher, an educator, or a student, this reference book offers a comprehensive guide to navigate the complex and ever-evolving landscape of modern business management.

Chapter 1 explores the dynamics of AI and Emotional Intelligence (EI) in contemporary business performance. It emphasizes the need for a managerial orientation that balances EI and AI to sustain business performance effectively.

Chapter 2 delves into the influence of personality traits and emotional intelligence on investors' attitude towards financial risk (ATFR), using the Big-Five personality model. It sheds light on how understanding personality traits can inform financial product design and investment decision patterns.

Focusing on the role of emotional intelligence in nurturing creativity and innovation for entrepreneurial success, chapter 3 constructs a conceptual framework using insights from a literature review. It emphasizes how emotional intelligence can drive creativity and successful initiatives.

Chapter 4 explores the interconnectedness of emotional intelligence and effective leadership, particularly in the context of the post-COVID-19 era. It analyzes bibliometric data to depict trends and themes, highlighting the role of emotional intelligence in shaping future work environments.

Chapter 5 synthesizes existing literature to integrate AI and green HR practices to achieve sustainable organizational goals. It lays the groundwork for further research by proposing a conceptual framework that explores the augmentation of AI to green HR practices.

Chapter 6 reviews existing literature to understand the relationship between emotional intelligence, work performance, and psychological well-being. It aims to develop a descriptive model to aid in the design of human resource management policies based on situational contexts.

Chapter 7 delves into how emotional intelligence impacts decision-making and leadership in the corporate world. It highlights the significance of training and development in enhancing emotional intelligence among executives for organizational success.

Chapter 8 employs an integrative literature review methodology to theoretically link emotional intelligence with leadership effectiveness, considering mental health and happiness at work as mediators. It emphasizes the crucial role of emotional intelligence in leadership effectiveness.

Chapter 9 investigates the association between emotional intelligence and job satisfaction among hospital nurses in Jaipur. It presents research findings that highlight a positive relationship between emotional intelligence and job satisfaction.

Chapter 10 explores how the fusion of Emotional and Spiritual Quotients can empower leaders to make informed and empathetic decisions, propelling organizations towards elevated levels of success. It delves into various facets encompassing both dimensions.

Chapter 11 elucidates the interconnection between emotional intelligence and employee engagement, emphasizing how emotional intelligence positively impacts emotional productivity within organizations.

Chapter 12 addresses the research gap in AI's role in human resource management through bibliometric content analysis. It highlights prominent themes and future directions, focusing on AI's impact on building frameworks, machine learning applications, decision making, and recruitment processes.

Chapter 13 explores how artificial intelligence is transforming the landscape of behavioral finance. It discusses challenges and the potential impact of AI on investment decision-making, providing insights into creating efficient and unbiased investment strategies.

Chapter 14 studies the potential impact of artificial intelligence on employment, emphasizing its potential positive influence on economic growth and the importance of policies that address concerns related to AI's societal impact.

Chapter 15 explores how AI significantly impacts customer behavior in e-commerce, focusing on AI's role in addressing common customer service challenges. It emphasizes the importance of utilizing AI to improve customer satisfaction and overall business health.

Chapter 16 explores diverse AI techniques used for stock market prediction, categorizing them into traditional ML, deep learning, and sentiment analysis. It provides insights into the effectiveness of various models in forecasting market trends.

Chapter 17 explores the transformative effects of Virtual Reality (VR) on consumer behavior in e-commerce. It highlights how VR impacts consumer decision-making and empowers informed purchase choices, presenting future possibilities of VR in e-commerce.

Chapter 18 examines the influence of AI on employee well-being, encompassing dimensions such as job satisfaction, stress, overall health, and job security. It suggests measures to mitigate potential negative effects on employee welfare.

Chapter 19 explores the transformative impact of AI on the banking industry, focusing on customer service enhancement and operational optimization. It examines AI-driven tools and their roles in fraud prevention, client support, and personalized financial guidance.

Chapter 20 provides a comprehensive exploration of the integration of AI in data analysis and business intelligence. It showcases how AI techniques decipher complex datasets and enhance business intelligence platforms for informed decision-making.

Chapter 21 reviews the literature on AI and AR in tourism marketing using bibliometric methods, providing insights into research status, development, and growth. It also discusses the potential of AI and AR in sustainable tourism and proposes strategies for marketing techniques in the tourism sector.*

In closing, we express our gratitude to the contributors who have lent their expertise to shape this reference book. Their collective knowledge and commitment have been instrumental in the creation of a resource that we believe will inspire thoughtful discussions, spur innovation, and guide the future of business management.

We invite you to embark on this journey with us, exploring the intertwined worlds of Artificial Intelligence and Emotional Intelligence in the context of modern business management. May this book serve as a beacon, guiding you through the exciting possibilities and challenges that lie ahead.

Bhawana Bhardwaj
Central University of Himachal Pradesh, India

Dipanker Sharma
Central University of Himachal Pradesh, India

Mohinder Chand Dhiman
Central University of Himachal Pradesh, India

Chapter 1
Artificial Intelligence vs Emotional Intelligence: Unraveling the Companionship and Paradoxes

Bhawana Bhardwaj
https://orcid.org/0000-0002-0564-2964
Central University of Himachal Pradesh, India

Dipanker Sharma
https://orcid.org/0000-0003-0501-1473
Central University of Himachal Pradesh, India

Mohinder Chand Dhiman
https://orcid.org/0000-0002-8174-0013
Central University of Himachal Pradesh, India

ABSTRACT

In today's dynamic world, businesses are witnessing various transformational challenges. AI has played a critical role in facilitating managerial performances and has become a buzzword. AI-driven functions and decision-making are quickly becoming the norm in today's digital world. However, the role of emotional intelligence in managerial and business success must be addressed. AI also needs human intervention support. AI supports business success by increasing work efficiency and customer satisfaction, reducing overall business costs and allowing for a more rapid expansion, customer segmentation, and better consumer insights. The adoption of AI globally has increased 2.5 times in the last five years. In 2017, 20% of respondents accepted adopting AI in at least one business area. This figure now stands at 50%. This chapter examines the role of AI vs EI in contemporary business performances. The authors discuss the need for a new managerial orientation of balancing EI and AI for sustainable business performance.

DOI: 10.4018/979-8-3693-0418-1.ch001

1. INTRODUCTION

"If your emotional abilities aren't in hand, if you don't have self-awareness, if you are not able to manage your distressing emotions, if you can't have empathy and have effective relationships, then no matter how smart you are, you are not going to get very far"—Daniel Goleman

Emotional Intelligence (EI) is considered a vivacious success component in the workplace. Connecting and observing empathy provides a distinct edge in society and organizations (Back & Libert, 2017; Prentice et al., 2020; Bhardwaj & Kalia, 2021). People with high EI better comprehend context, relate to people, and persuade us to view their preferred option as our darker square. They enjoy life satisfaction, better personal and social relationships, and career success (Coetzee & Harry, 2014). EI also enhances job performance, employee engagement, job satisfaction, performance organizational commitment, and customer satisfaction (Prentice, C.,2016). It is also related to other dimensions of intelligence, such as social and cultural Intelligence (Bhardwaj,2021).

It has been observed that 95 percent of people believe they are self-aware, but in reality, only 10-15 percent have self-awareness (Eurich, 2018). People with high EQ can earn around $29000 more than people with less EQ.95% of HR managers and 99% of employees feel that EI is a must-have talent for every employee(Schwantes,2020). Furthermore, EI is a skill that cannot be computerized. However, it can be assisted with digital technology. With the advancement of technology and the role of artificial intelligence (AI) in altering every aspect of business, people have begun to speculate about the role of AI over EI. The ability of a computer programme or machine to think and learn is referred to as artificial Intelligence. John McCarthy, an American Computer scientist, coined the term artificial Intelligence. AI is multidisciplinary as it seeks the involvement of varied disciples such as computers, psychology, neuroscience, mathematics, linguistics, and philosophy. "artificial intelligence" generally refers to a programme that mimics human cognition.

Computers can perform various functions which are traditionally associated with human minds, such as learning and problem-solving, though in a different manner than we do (Budhwar et al., 2022). Machine intelligence exhibited by humanoid or non-humanoid robots that behave like people; can be employed in organizations to increase and enhance operational efficiency (Russell & Norvig, 2016). The adoption of AI globally has become 2.5 times in the last five years. In 2017, 20 per cent respondents reported adopting AI in at least one business area, whereas today; this figure now stands at 50 per cent, though it peaked higher in 2019 at 58 per cent (Mckinsey, 2022). There has been an increase in investment in AI from 40% in 2018 to 52% in 2022. The inclusion of AI in business operations has saved costs and increased profitability.

On contrary, emotional intelligence is a type of personal intelligence, whereas artificial Intelligence is machine intelligence. In this article, we discuss the role of EI in the era of digitalization and AI. We also uncover AI and EI's conflicting and collaborating part in modern business dimensions. AI is rapidly augmenting business functions and replacing human interventions in business. However, this paper explores and discusses how EI remains essential. The optimum use of AI tools requires the right balance of emotional quotient (Serrat,2017). This study is based on secondary information and provide formative basis for future studies.

Through this article we suggest that AI will replace most repetitive and manual labour duties. At the same time, humans will thrive at soft skills such as creative communication and relationship-building. Furthermore, AI can assist human resources in doing better work by helping them improve their emotional intelligence, soft skills, and interpersonal communication skills (Limon & Plaster, 2022). Future researchers can undertake research by linking the role of AI with contemporary issues such as skilled migrations (Bhardwaj & Sharma, 2022; Bhardwaj, 2017) and women's advancements other gender-related issues (Bhardwaj, 2013) and employee engagement (Kalia &Bhardwaj, 2019; Bhardwaj et al, 2024). This paper is divided into various subsections; Section 2 discusses the role of EI in contemporary business situations. Section 3 highlights the role of AI across multiple business functions. Section 4 elaborates on the part of AI vs EI. Section 5 discusses the role of EI vs AI; Sections 6 and 7 discuss and conclude the findings, respectively.

2. EMOTIONAL INTELLIGENCE IN CONTEMPORARY BUSINESS:

EI has been identified as a critical ability for workplace and organizational effectiveness. Emotional Intelligence is essential for effective team leadership and developing a positive work culture (Foltin,2012). Daniel Goleman coined this term in his book *Emotional Intelligence: Why It Can Matter More Than IQ*. EI is a concept based on science, but it is a soft skill also that can be measured and improved (Goleman, 2004). Understanding how emotions broaden our self-control and understanding our feelings and those of others empowers us to behave proactively. This can also help us in work and professional life. It helps to understand and control one's emotions and those of others. Managers with higher emotional Intelligence are better able to understand the requirements of their team, develop relationships, and motivate their team (Watkin et al.,2017). As a result, they create a positive work environment and are more equipped to deal with difficulties. Emotional Intelligence is an essential skill set for individuals and organizations in the modern business world. It positively impacts leadership, decision-making, communication, teamwork, customer relations, stress management, conflict resolution, adaptability, employee engagement, and organizational culture. Companies that prioritize and develop emotional Intelligence among their employees are likely to achieve higher success and employee satisfaction.

Self-awareness, self-management, social awareness, and relationship management are considered four components of emotional intelligence (Nurul et al., 2017). Understanding one's feelings and motivations and controlling them successfully is self-awareness. The ability to regulate one's impulses, handle stress, and maintain a positive attitude is referred to as self-management. Understanding and empathizing with others, recognizing others' feelings, and responding correctly are examples of social awareness. Finally, relationship management is defined as the ability to establish and sustain connections, communicate effectively, and handle issues. Figure 1 exhibits that EI has four major components. Understanding these dimensions facilitates managing employees, and recognizing their emotions.

1. **Self-Awareness:** Refers to recognizing our emotions and how our thoughts, feelings, and behaviour impact others. It helps managers understand and control their emotions and behaviour, improving relationships and communication. It allows them to be mindful of their words and actions, leading to managerial effectiveness (Nurul et al., 2017, Goleman, 2004).
2. **Self-Management:** This describes an ability to manage emotions, actions and behaviour. It also involves working on the feelings of others. Self-management skills help managers to remain calm in difficult and stressful situations. Self-management is essential for recognizing strengths and weaknesses and developing them to be successful effectiveness (Nurul et al., 2017, Goleman, 2004).

3. **Social Awareness:** Social awareness is the ability to understand and interpret the emotions of people around us. This involves understanding emotions with verbal and nonverbal cues. Understanding others' feelings can make us respond to them appropriately effectiveness (Nurul et al., 2017, Goleman, 2004). This creates an environment of mutual trust and eliminates the probability of potential conflicts. Managers may be sensitive to how their decisions and actions will affect the emotions of those around them, thus; ensuring positive relationships with employees and customers.
4. **Relationship Management:** This refers to understanding and sustaining relationships with others. These skills can help managers to establish long-term relationships with a team effectiveness (Nurul et al., 2017, Goleman, 2004). It influences stakeholder engagement, networking, conflict resolution, customer relations, negotiation, team building, mentoring, crisis management, vendor relations, and workplace culture. Developing and prioritizing relationship management skills can lead to stronger partnerships, better customer relations, and overall business success.

Figure 1. Dimensions of emotional intelligence
Sources: Created by Authors in line with literature

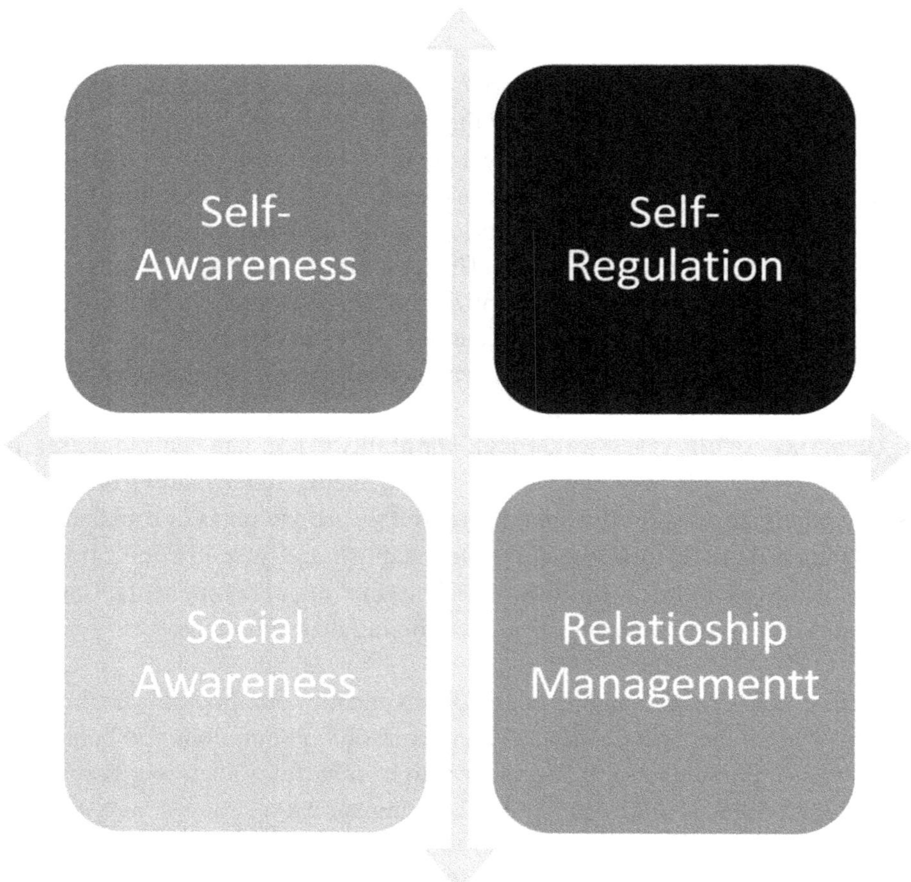

Managers who master these four elements of emotional Intelligence can become better leaders and create a productive work environment. Various forms of Intelligence, such as Social Intelligence, Cultural Intelligence (Bhardwaj, 2021) and Emotional Intelligence, can predict an individual's personal and professional success. However, EI has a vast role in supporting the advancement towards academic and professional success, improving relationships, boosting communication etc. Individuals can become more productive and successful at what they do by growing their emotional intelligence, and they can also assist others become more productive and successful(Krén and Séllei, 2021). Many components known to alleviate stress – for individuals and hence organisations — in the process and outcomes of emotional intelligence development include moderating conflict, enhancing understanding and relationships, and encouraging stability, continuity, and harmony. Last but not least, it is deeply associated with the ideals of love and spirituality. Figure 2 recognizes some of the benefits of EI at the workplace-

Figure 2. Role of EI at the workplace
Sources: Created by Authors in Line with existing literature

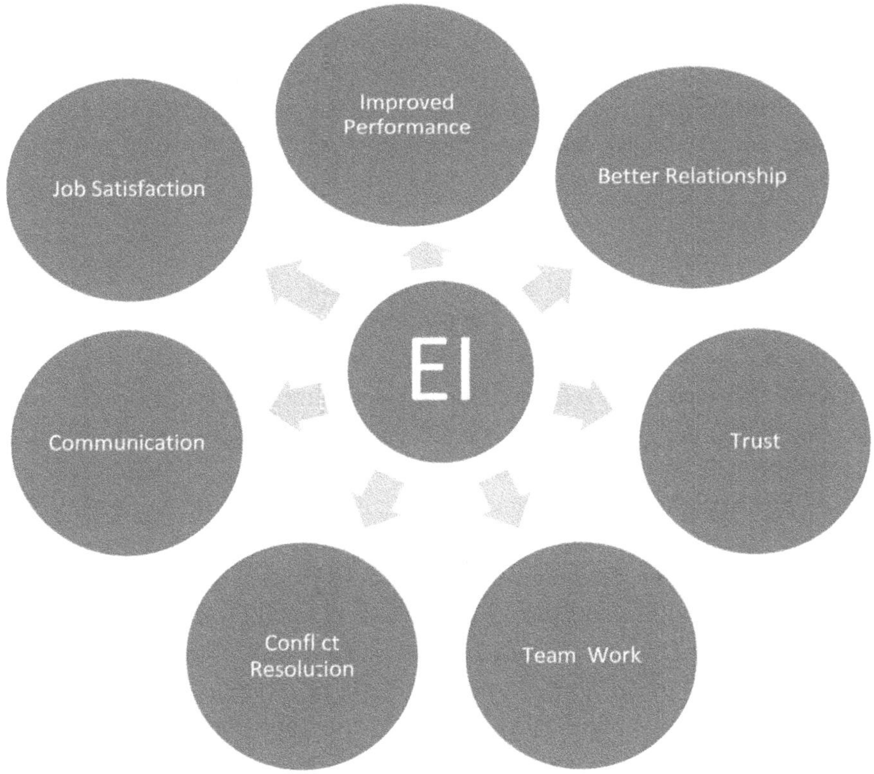

Emotional Intelligence has a profound impact on everything a person accomplishes. It is increasingly appreciated and sought after by organizations and individuals(Cote, 2014). It is a method of thinking and acting that allows us to be more aware and understanding of those around us, resulting in better and more positive behaviours and interactions. An increase in EI can significantly impact business, academics, and personal life. It remains a necessary skill for effective leadership and team management. It enables leaders to promote a healthy work culture, build strong connections, and successfully manage problems, ultimately leading to improved team performance and overall organizational success. Emerging Area of Artificial Intelligence in Business Enterprises: The concept of Intelligence has evolved from IQ (Intelligence quotient) to EQ (Emotional Quotient) and SQ (Social Quotient)

3. EMERGING ROLE OF ARTIFICIAL INTELLIGENCE IN MODERN BUSINESSES

Businesses use Artificial Intelligence (AI) in numerous ways to improve efficiencies, save time, and save costs. According to analysts, deploying artificial intelligence (AI) on a broader scale might add up to $15.7 trillion to the global economy by 2030 (De Cremer& Kasparov,2021). It is becoming a more helpful resource for businesses across industries. A Forbes Advisor poll of 600 business owners on how firms employ AI (Haan, 2023) revealed that AI impacts various business dimensions, such as cybersecurity, fraud management, content development, advisability, and customer service. Around (97%) of business owners believed that ChatGPT will benefit their organisation.AI is permeating nearly every function of organizations. It improves customer experience through instant messaging, emails, personalized services, text messages, personalized advertisements, website content and phone calls. AI also helps improve business performance by saving costs, reducing the risk of errors, streamlining job processes, increasing sales, reducing response time, improving customer relationships and streamlining business processes(Hann, 2023).

4. ARTIFICIAL INTELLIGENCE VS EMOTIONAL INTELLIGENCE: UNLOCKING THE PARADOX

Organizations have recognized EI's well-established role in improving managerial functions' efficacy. When working with individuals, their emotions and understanding are crucial. However, with the advancement of technology, AI is playing a pivotal role and permeating all management activities (Budhwar et al.,2022). Thus, people speculate that AI will also take over the part of EI. There is a debate over whether artificial intelligence (AI) or emotional Intelligence (EI) is more significant. If you are looking for a machine to do a job that requires precision and no emotion, then AI is the better choice. However, if you need something done that requires understanding human emotions and motivation, then EI would be better. With the rise of artificial Intelligence (AI), many people wonder how this will impact emotional Intelligence (EI). There are two schools of thought; some believe AI will make EI obsolete, as machines can replicate and surpass human emotions(Cremer & Kasparov, 2021). Others believe AI will only enhance EI, as human intervention will still be needed to interpret and understand machine-generated data. Thus, the question is will AI make EI obsolete or enhance it? The answer is both. As AI continues to develop, it will no doubt have an impact on EI. Intelligent technologies are displacing humans in manufacturing, service delivery, recruitment, and the finance industry, relegating human workers to lower-paying jobs or rendering them unemployed.

Figure 3. Role of AI in business functions
Sources: Created by authors in line with existing literature

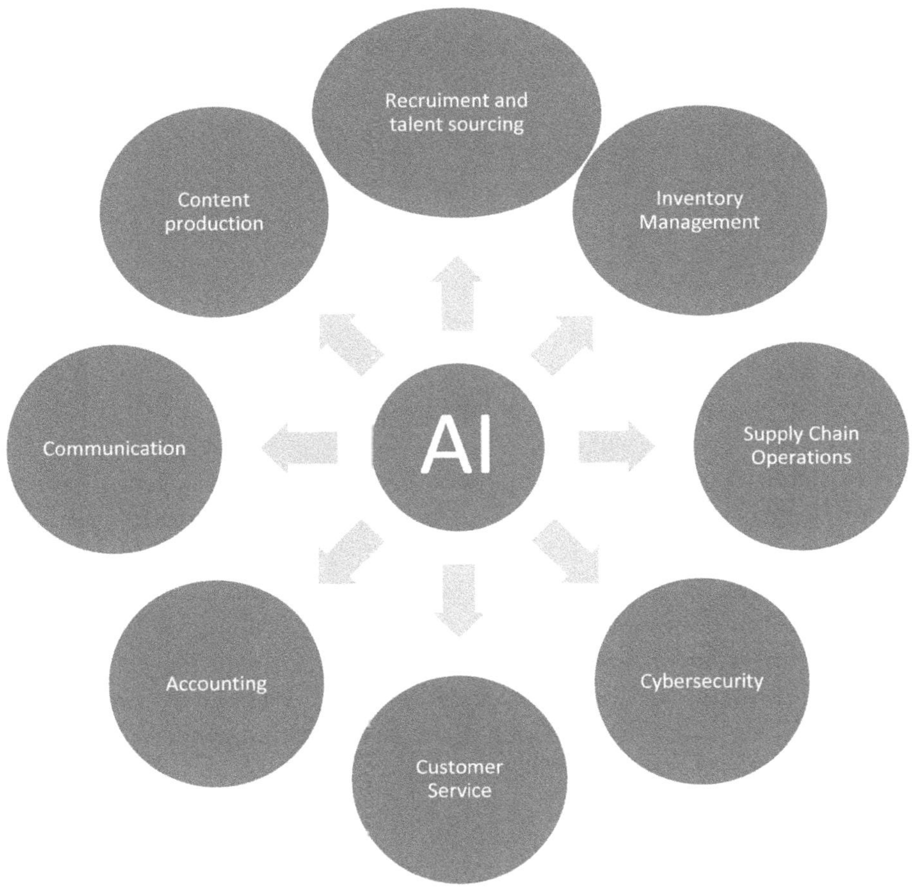

However, there are other characteristics of EI that robots will never be able to mimic, such as empathy, compassion, and others. AI can only enhance EI, as humans will still be needed to interpret and understand machine-generated data. Artificial intelligence technology assists in diagnosing and responding to human emotions. Recognizing facial expressions and body language, comprehending tone of voice, and extracting meaning from text are all examples. Emotional Intelligence enabled by AI can assist firms in automating customer care duties such as reacting to queries and giving support. For example, by understanding client wants and pain spots, emotional Intelligence can be leveraged to better marketing efforts. Thus, it can be used for providing customized customer solution and improve their satisfaction. The act of training a computer to make decisions for itself is known as artificial Intelligence (AI). The ability to recognize and control emotions is called emotional Intelligence (EI). AI and EI are both vital in their ways.AI excels at making rational data-driven conclusions. A computer, for example, can be programmed to play chess. It will consider all possible movements and select the one most likely to result in a win.

Usage of AI has a variety of applications in different business spheres, including medicine, customer services, trading, advertising, hand detection, language translation, music composition, artwork and much more.

However, with all these applications it has challenges associated with it-

- Risks and ethical concerns
- Resource consumption
- Concerns regarding using AI
- Technology Dependence
- Technical skills
- Human Resource Reduction
- Privacy Concerns
- Malicious Use
- Mis-communication and lack of Emotional Intelligence:

Thus, emotional Intelligence is beyond cognitive skills as it also includes other components, such as social skills, self-awareness, empathy, and self-regulation, which are difficult to replicate. However, understanding emotions can be augmented through AI. It is believed that more dependence on machine intelligence will further increase the importance of EI. Moreover, emotional Intelligence can also help deal with ambiguity and transformation. AI has its limitations in dealing with unexpected situations. E.g. a machine may be programmed to the cheapest option for a travel plan. Hence, it may not consider a last-minute change due to weather or other unexpected situations. A human with emotional Intelligence would make better decisions and perform in such cases. In conclusion, while AI has a lot of potential benefits, it cannot replace emotional Intelligence entirely.

5. ROLE OF AI IN AUGMENTING EMOTIONAL INTELLIGENCE

AI can play a significant role in enhancing and supporting Emotional Intelligence (EI) in various ways (Kaur and Sharma, 2021). While AI does not possess emotions or consciousness, it can assist individuals in developing and practising emotional intelligence skills(Back and Libert, 2017. Here are some ways AI can contribute to EI:

1. Virtual Emotional Assistants: AI-powered virtual assistants can be designed to interact with users in emotionally intelligent ways. These assistants can be programmed to recognize emotions through voice tone or text analysis and respond appropriately with empathy and understanding(Chiu, 2020). This interaction can help individuals feel heard and supported, even when communicating with a machine. This can also be used to provide personalized customer care service.
2. Emotion Recognition and Analysis: AI can analyze facial expressions, body language, and speech patterns to recognize emotions in others(Marechal et al., 2019).This technology can be used in various contexts, such as customer service, educational settings, or therapy, to understand the feelings of others better and respond with appropriate empathy. Thus, this component of AI can enhance the EI of an individual.

3. Emotional Coaching and Feedback: AI applications can be developed to provide feedback and coaching on emotional responses and behaviours. For example, in social skills training or public speaking, AI can analyze interactions and give suggestions to improve emotional communication.
4. Stress and Emotional Management: AI can monitor physiological indicators like heart rate, skin conductance, and facial expressions to detect anxiety or emotional distress signs. Based on this data, AI systems can suggest stress management techniques, meditation exercises, or relaxation strategies to help individuals cope with their emotions better. Also, communication and expression of feelings can be great stress relievers; EI can help in this aspect(Lin et al.,2021).
5. Mental Health Support: AI-powered chatbots or apps can offer mental health support and interventions by providing a safe space for individuals to express their emotions and concerns. These AI-based tools can offer resources, coping strategies, and referrals to professional help when needed.
6. Personalized Emotional Support: AI can analyze data from individuals' interactions, social media, or other sources to create personalized emotional support systems. AI can tailor recommendations and interventions to address specific emotional needs by understanding an individual's emotional patterns(Lin et al., 2021).
7. Emotional Awareness Training: AI can be used in gamified applications or simulations to help individuals develop emotional awareness and recognition skills. These applications can present scenarios where users can practice identifying emotions in themselves and others(Narimani et al., 2021).

In the context of EI, it is essential to emphasize that AI should be used as a complementary tool and not a replacement for genuine human connection and emotional support. While AI can aid in certain aspects of EI, fundamental emotional understanding and empathy often require human interaction and emotional connection. The responsible and ethical development of AI for EI purposes should prioritize user privacy and consent and ensure that AI interventions are sensitive to cultural and individual differences in emotional expression and understanding.

6. DISCUSSION

Emotional intelligence is treated as importance organizational variable affecting individual and organizational effectiveness(Krén and Séllei, 2021; Goleman, 2004). AI has emerged as important and contemporary concept affecting almost every function of an organization. Artificial Intelligence (AI) and Emotional Intelligence (EI) are two contrasting paradigms rooted in technology and human psychology. Their role in managerial contexts prompts whether they complement each other or represent divergent necessities in modern leadership. On the one hand, AI showcases automation prowess and efficiency, making it an attractive managerial tool. Its ability to analyze vast datasets, make data-driven decisions, and automate repetitive tasks boosts productivity and streamlines operations. AI's predictive modelling and natural language processing capabilities offer insights and communication advantages previously unattainable. As industries increasingly rely on data-driven strategies, AI becomes a necessity of the hour for forward-looking managers seeking to gain a competitive edge.

Emotional Intelligence emerges as a crucial asset for effective leadership and fostering meaningful relationships. Managers with high level of EI can understand and empathize with their team members, cultivating trust and building cohesive work environments. EI enables leaders to navigate conflicts with sensitivity, communicate authentically, and inspire collaboration. In the face of organizational challenges, EI proves instrumental in nurturing resilient teams and ensuring employee well-being.

The key lies in recognizing the symbiotic relationship between AI and EI. Rather than being at odds, these paradigms can reinforce each other. Integrating AI-driven insights with emotionally intelligent decision-making yields powerful outcomes. AI can assist managers in understanding employee sentiments, allowing for targeted EI interventions. Moreover, AI can offer data-backed feedback on leadership practices, aiding in EI development for managers. It is not a question of AI versus EI but a call for managerial orientation towards a harmonious fusion of both. Leaders with AI capabilities grounded in Emotional Intelligence can navigate complexities with more remarkable finesse, inspiring growth and resilience in the modern workplace. They embrace the synergy between AI and EI and position managers at the vanguard of progressive and human-centric leadership.

7. CONCLUSION

This paper presents the role of AI and EI in the current business environment. It is speculated that AI will replace EI. Recent issues such as COVID-19 and Russia- Ukraine war have reinforced the role of empathy and emotions (Sharma et al., 2022). However, our article asserts that machines can never wholly replace human emotions. It cannot be denied that AI has taken over various cognitive functions. However, EI still holds a vital role in business and managerial success. AI cannot replace EI; instead, it can facilitate EI through recognizing facial expressions, gestures and body language (Jarrahi & Newlands,2022),it can also help assessment of EQ which can help in personal development.

However, with the AI age's transformational change, we must also transform EI, which requires a difference in the organization's and leader's mindset. We cannot think of developing EI for the AI age until we set the right attitude. Instead of fearing AI taking over human roles, we need to understand AI can support EI. Organizations have invested a lot in adopting digital, and AI technology but their leaders and workforce are still in the analogue age. This created a lot of fear and apprehension due to fear of being replaced by AI. A competent leader will focus on EI as well as AI development(Budhwar et al, 2022).

Digital and AI mindsets are developed by understanding the essence of the transformation required by understanding the actual impact on customers, staff and stakeholders in your sector and by genuinely appreciating the necessary change to realize the full potential. A pilot doesn't need to understand the workings of a jet engine to fly a plane; however, the pilot does need to understand the plane's capabilities, power, and strengths/weaknesses in different environments. Detailed technical knowledge of the jet engine would not allow a pilot to fly the aircraft competently. Just like the pilot, leaders don't need to know the inner workings of AI or the latest emerging technology. However, they must understand its capabilities and the opportunities it could create for the organization. Adopting the right mindset is essential, although often overlooked by leaders; it is the magic sauce needed to ensure the digital or AI transformation will succeed. People with high EI naturally have empathy, which allows them to comprehend our context better, relate to us, and persuade us to view their preferred option as our darker square.

REFERENCES

Beck, M., & Libert, B. (2017). The rise of AI makes emotional Intelligence more important. *Harvard Business Review*, *15*(1-5).

Bhardwaj, B. (2013). Women empowerment: Cracking glass ceiling at the workplace. *International Journal of Management*, *4*(2), 267–272.

Bhardwaj, B. (2017). Migration vulnerability: Role of digital media and internet in stimulating and inhibiting brain drain. *International Journal of Advances in Management and Economics*, *6*(6), 24–32.

Bhardwaj, B. (2021). *Short-term foreign trips correlate with the four factors model of cultural Intelligence*. Rajagiri Management Journal. doi:10.1108/RAMJ-01-2021-0008

Bhardwaj, B., & Kalia, N. (2021). *Contextual and task performance: role of employee engagement and organizational culture in the hospitality industry*. Vilakshan-XIMB Journal of Management. doi:10.1108/XJM-08-2020-0089

Bhardwaj, B., & Sharma, D. (2022). Migration of skilled professionals across the border: Brain drain or brain gain? *European Management Journal*. ttps:// doi:10.1016/j.emj.2022.12.011

Bhardwaj, B., Kalia, N., Chand, M., & Sharma, D. (2023). Engaged Organizational Culture as a precursor to job performance: An evidence from the hospitality industry of Himachal Pradesh. *International Journal of Hospitality and Tourism Systems*, *16*(4), 48–57.

Budhwar, P., Malik, A., De Silva, M. T., & Thevisuthan, P. (2022). Artificial intelligence–challenges and opportunities for international HRM: A review and research agenda. *International Journal of Human Resource Management*, *33*(6), 1065–1097. doi:10.1080/09585192.2022.2035161

Chiu, P. S., Chang, J. W., Lee, M. C., Chen, C. H., & Lee, D. S. (2020). Enabling intelligent environment by the design of emotionally aware virtual assistant: A case of smart campus. *IEEE Access : Practical Innovations, Open Solutions*, *8*, 62032–62041. doi:10.1109/ACCESS.2020.2984383

Coetzee, M., & Harry, N. (2014). Emotional Intelligence as a Predictor of employees' career adaptability. *Journal of Vocational Behavior*, *84*(1), 90–97. doi:10.1016/j.jvb.2013.09.001

Côté, S. (2014). Emotional intelligence in organizations. *Annual Review of Organizational Psychology and Organizational Behavior*, *1*(1), 459–488. doi:10.1146/annurev-orgpsych-031413-091233

De Cremer, D., & Kasparov, G. (2021). AI should augment human intelligence, not replace it. *Harvard Business Review*, *18*, 1.

Eurich, T. (2018). What self-awareness really is (and how to cultivate it). *Harvard Business Review*, 4.

Foltin, A., & Keller, R. (2012). Leading change with emotional intelligence. *Nursing Management*, *43*(11), 20–25. doi:10.1097/01.NUMA.0000421675.33594.63 PMID:23086169

Goleman, D. (2004). What makes a leader? *Harvard Business Review*, *82*(1), 82–91. PMID:10187249

Haan, K. (2023). *How Businesses Are Using Artificial Intelligence In 2023*. https://www.forbes.com/advisor/business/software/ai-in-business/

Jarrahi, M. H., Lutz, C., & Newlands, G. (2022). Artificial intelligence, human intelligence and hybrid intelligence based on mutual augmentation. *Big Data & Society*, *9*(2). doi:10.1177/20539517221142824

Kalia, N., & Bhardwaj, B. (2019). Contextual and Task Performance: Do Demographic and Organizational variables Matter? *Rajagiri Management Journal*, *13*(2), 30–42. doi:10.1108/RAMJ-09-2019-0017

Kaur, S., & Sharma, R. (2021). Emotion AI: integrating emotional intelligence with artificial intelligence in the digital workplace. In *Innovations in Information and Communication Technologies (IICT-2020) Proceedings of International Conference on ICRIHE-2020, Delhi, India: IICT-2020* (pp. 337-343). Springer International Publishing. 10.1007/978-3-030-66218-9_39

Krén, H., & Séllei, B. (2021). The role of emotional intelligence in organizational performance. *Periodica Polytechnica Social and Management Sciences*, *29*(1), 1–9. doi:10.3311/PPso.15879

Limon, D., & Plaster, B. (2022). *Can AI Teach Us How to Become More Emotionally Intelligent?* https://hbr.org/2022/01/can-ai-teach-us-how-to-become-more-emotionally-intelligent

Lin, Q., Li, T., Shakeel, P. M., & Samuel, R. D. J. (2021). Advanced artificial intelligence in heart rate and blood pressure monitoring for stress management. *Journal of Ambient Intelligence and Humanized Computing*, *12*(3), 3329–3340. doi:10.100712652-020-02650-3

Marechal, C., Mikolajewski, D., Tyburek, K., Prokopowicz, P., Bougueroua, L., Ancourt, C., & Wegrzyn-Wolska, K. (2019). Survey on AI-Based Multimodal Methods for Emotion Detection. *High-performance modelling and simulation for big data applications, 11400*, 307-324.

McKinsey. (2022). *Five years in review: AI adoption, impact, and spending*. Author.

Narimani, A., Khaleghi, A., Haedar, H., & Semnani, F. (2021). The use of gamification in evaluating children's emotional intelligence. In *Internet of Things, Infrastructures and Mobile Applications: Proceedings of the 13th IMCL Conference 13* (pp. 806-813). Springer International Publishing. 10.1007/978-3-030-49932-7_75

Nurul, H., Redzuan, M., Hamsan, H., & Noor, H. (2017). Emotional intelligence (self-awareness, self-management, social awareness and relationship management) and leadership behavior (transformational and transactional) among school educator leaders. *International Journal of Educational Studies*, *4*(2), 37–47.

Prentice, C., Dominique Lopes, S., & Wang, X. (2020). Emotional Intelligence or artificial Intelligence– an employee perspective. *Journal of Hospitality Marketing & Management*, *29*(4), 377–403. doi:10.1080/19368623.2019.1647124

Russell, S. J., & Norvig, P. (2016). *Artificial Intelligence: A modern approach*. Pearson Education Limited.

SchwantesM. (2020). Retrieved from https://www.inc.com/marcel-schwantes/research-says-you-can-earn-way-more-money-by-boosting-your-emotional-intelligence-here-are-4-ways-to-do-it.html

Serrat, O (2017). Understanding and developing emotional intelligence. *Knowledge solutions: Tools, methods, and approaches to drive organizational performance*, 329-339.

Sharma, D., Chaudhary, M., Jaswal, N., & Bhardwaj, B. (2022). Hiding Behind The SWOT: Gender Equality and COVID-19. *Journal of Positive School Psychology*, 730–740.

Watkins, D., Earnhardt, M., Pittenger, L., Roberts, R., Rietsema, K., & Cosman-Ross, J. (2017). Thriving in complexity: A framework for leadership education. *Journal of Leadership Education*, *16*(14), 148–163. doi:10.12806/V16/I4/T4

Chapter 2
Influence of Personality Traits and Emotional Intelligence on Attitude Toward Financial Risk:
Evidence From Indian Investors

Amit Kumar
https://orcid.org/0000-0002-1686-3279
Eternal University, India

Ekam Riar
Eternal University, India

Anupriya Kaur
Jaypee University of Information Technology, India

Yashpal Azad
https://orcid.org/0000-0003-2957-8917
Eternal University, India

ABSTRACT

Investment is crucial to everyone's existence in the modern world. The way investors invest and their attitude toward financial risk are both influenced by a number of factors. The current study has explored the influence of personality traits using the big-five personality model and emotional intelligence on investors' attitude towards financial risk (ATFR). The research was conducted in the Delhi NCR region with the convenience sample of 190 investors. The findings revealed that the personality traits such as extraversion, agreeableness, openness, and emotional intelligence significantly influence investors ATFR, whereas neuroticism and conscientiousness had non-significant effect on investors ATFR. Additionally, the demographic variables demonstrate differential effects in context of personality traits, emotional intelligence, and ATFR. A better understanding of personality traits may offer an opportunity to financial institutions to appropriately design financial products and policies and identify the investment decision pattern of investors and their attitude toward financial risk.

DOI: 10.4018/979-8-3693-0418-1.ch002

1. INTRODUCTION

Investment has been a fundamental practice throughout human history. Investment dates back to ancient civilizations, when individuals would invest in various endeavours such as agriculture, trading trips, or real estate to build wealth and success. A financial investment is a financial commitment made with the hope of making a profit. The word 'investment' has several meanings in finance and economics. Economists speak of a real investment (such as a machine or house), whereas financial economists speak of a financial asset, such as money placed in a bank or the market and subsequently utilised to purchase a real asset (Lipe, 1998). Financial investment entails putting money into a variety of assets, including gold, bonds, real estate, and stocks. The goal of investing is to organize funds or resources in order to attain certain financial results (Dhiman & Raheja, 2018). Depending on their exclusive aims and conditions, investors pursue a variety of objectives. Capital appreciation is a frequent goal, in which investors seek investments that will improve in value over time, with the goal of selling them at a greater price later. Another goal is income creation, with investors seeking assets that pay out regular payments such as dividends or interest and wealth protection, which focuses on protecting capital from degradation caused by inflation or economic concerns. By establishing clear investment objectives, investors can align their decisions with their desired outcomes and work towards achieving their financial goals. Recent economic expansion as a result of globalization has increased household wealth while also providing a plethora of investment opportunities. Over time, investment practices have evolved and become more sophisticated. Financial markets, institutions, and investment vehicles have emerged to facilitate investment activities.

Nowadays, investments span a wide range of assets, including stocks, bonds, real estate, commodities, mutual funds, and more. The investment options differ in terms of risk and return basis (Nandan & Sourabh, 2016). Classification of investment options according to the risk level associated with them is presented through the investment risk pyramid in Figure 1.

An investment decision and behavior of an investor in the financial market is a process which is based on a combination of multiple factors such as demographic, psychographic and personal characteristics (personality trait) (Subrahmanyam, 2008). Early investment theories suggest that investors are rational and their decisions are majorly based on maximizing returns and limiting the risks (Joo & Durri, 2015). However, recent theories challenge these assumptions (DeBondt et al., 2010). They stated that the human mind does not always think rationally and neither do the markets always perform efficiently. According to Nandan and Sourabh (2016), humans make decisions using their social, emotional, and human brain. People do not always do intricate statistical computations before making a choice; instead, they depend on easy heuristics that can accurately forecast the values of the outcomes (Baker et al., 2021). According to many previous studies (Nga and Yien, 2013; Gokhan and Mutlu, 2019; Sadiq and Khan, 2019) psychographic features play a decisive role in determining an individual's investment behavior. Another important aspect to consider is that every investment opportunity entails a certain amount of risk. The set of personality traits exhibited by an individual is one of the elements that influence investors' risk perception (Muradoglu & Harvey, 2012). The psychological traits of individual investors are examined by Kasemsap (2015), who also identifies how emotions may prevent a successful investing approach from working. The process that an individual investor goes through while making financial investment decisions is frequently disregarded in the field of finance research. A behavioral paradigm must be developed in order to study the influencers of investors' financial decision-making processes (Bikas et al., 2013).

Figure 1. Investment risk pyramid
Source: Compiled by author

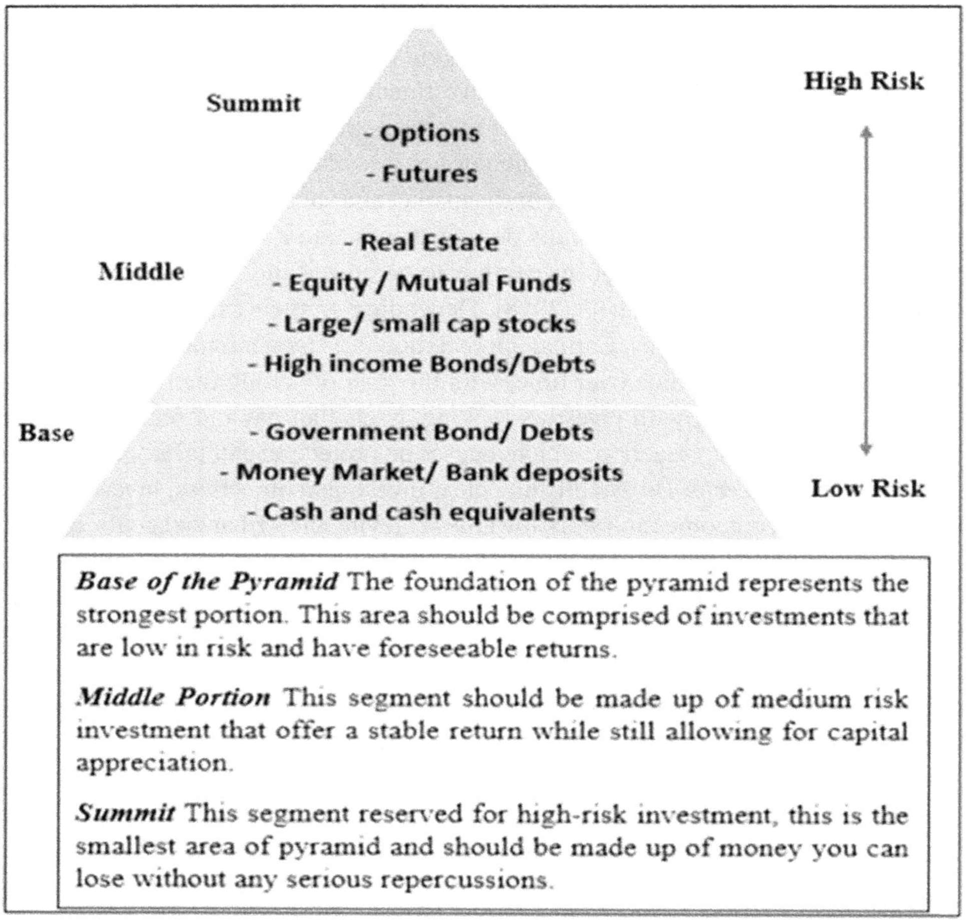

In the investment decisions, an investor's risk-taking propensity may vary depending on their personality. Although there is vast literature on financial decision making and the factor affects individuals' financial decision making, few of them have explored the effect of personality traits on investment behavior (Behavioral Finance) and other important factors such as emotional intelligence (EI) in context of investors' financial behavior and their attitude toward financial risk (ATFR). Considering this, the current study aims to investigate how investors' ATFR are influenced by their personality traits (the Big-five personality model) and EI. The research findings of this study can give crucial insights for the financial institutions in designing their financial products by better understanding of investors personality traits and their investment behavior particularly their ATFR.

2. BACKDROP, CONCEPTUAL FRAMEWORK, AND HYPOTHESES DEVELOPMENT

The linkages between behavioral finance, personality, EI, and ATFR are discussed in this section, which led to the formulation of hypotheses that are investigated in the next section. At the end of this section, a review of a few selected studies that investigated the relationship between personality traits and investment behaviour is offered.

2.1 Behavioural Finance (BF)

Investment is the process by which investors put their surplus money to work in order to generate a larger return. There are numerous aspects that influence an investor's investment decision. These factors could include the expertise in the financial field, personality attributes, and family & friends influence. The majority of financial theories are built on the assumption that everyone is logical and that everyone considers all relevant information before making a financial decision, which is not the case in reality (Brooks & Williams, 2021). During the 1980s, financial economists began to investigate the idea that some market participants acted irrationally. The finance literature that analyses psychological characteristics to explain market participants' behavior formed a separate branch of research in the 1990s, called BF (Kapoor & Prosad, 2017).

The term BF refers to financial ideas that are based on psychology (Subrahmanyam, 2008). The emerging field of BF combines classic economic and financial theory with behavioural and cognitive psychological theory to understand why people make irrational financial decisions (Bouzguenda, 2018). It is often used for investment decisions in stock markets all around the world. It explains why people buy and sell stocks and other securities without conducting basic research and making irrational financial decisions. Traditional finance remains the main focus of BF, but the behavioral facets of psychology also play a significant role as driving forces in this area of research. In traditional finance, each person is rational in their pursuit of wealth maximization, but emotions and irrational decisions frequently impact rationality (Sewell, 2007). The next part of the discussion focuses on the link between personality traits, EI and ATFR.

2.2 Linkage Between Personality Traits (Big-Five Model), Emotional Intelligence, and Attitude Toward Financial Risk

2.2.1 Personality Traits (Big-Five Model)

A person's personality is the characteristic or combination of characteristics that distinguishes them from other people. Every person is different based on their characteristics. A person's investing behaviour would differ depending on their personality type (Becker et al., 2012). A person's personality traits are a collection of emotional, cognitive, and motivational factors that affect how they respond to their surroundings and how they make decisions under different conditions. Allport and Olbert (1936) firstly started to work on personality traits and prepared a list of 4500 personality traits. Their work has provided the basis for many other psychologists who explored the phenomenon of personality. McCrae and Costa (2008) later worked for the validation of this model and the final version of model what we are using today developed with five traits i.e., openness, conscientiousness, extraversion, agreeableness, neuroticism and termed it as 'Big-Five model'. Description of these traits are presented in Figure 2.

2.2.2 Emotional Intelligence (EI)

It is the ability to recognize, understand, and control one's own emotions as well as those of other people. It calls for the capacity to adapt to shifting social contexts and make effective use of emotions to influence perception and behavior (Dulewicz & Higgs, 2000). EI is usually seen as a crucial component of both personal and professional success since it may affect how well people are able to handle social situations and relationships. These are the four components of EI:

Self-awareness: Recognizing and understanding one's own emotions, strengths, weaknesses, and values.

Self-management: Regulating one's own emotions, thoughts, and behaviors in order to achieve goals and cope with stress.

Social awareness: Recognizing and understanding the emotions and needs of others, as well as the dynamics of social situations.

Relationship management: Using emotional intelligence to communicate effectively, build relationships, and resolve conflicts with others.

Figure 2. Description of big-five personality traits
Source: Compiled by author

Openness (O)	*• Measures how creative, curious, and open to new experiences a person is. Individuals with high openness tend to be creative and courageous, whereas individuals with low openness may be more conventional and cautious*
Conscientiousness (C)	*• Defines how organized, responsible, and self-disciplined a person is. High conscientious people are often trustworthy and diligent, whereas low conscientious people may be more impulsive and disorganized*
Extraversion (E)	*• Measures a person's friendliness, assertiveness, and energy. A high extraversion personality tends to be gregarious and communicative, whereas a low extraversion personality may be quieter and more introverted*
Agreeableness (A)	*• Indicate a person's degree of friendliness, empathy, and cooperativeness. Those with high levels of agreeability are frequently kind and courteous, whilst those with low levels may be more competitive and pessimistic*
Neuroticism (N)	*• Measures a person's susceptibility to emotional instability and stress. People with high neuroticism frequently exhibit anxiety and irritability, whereas those with low neuroticism may be more emotionally stable*

2.2.3 Attitude Towards Financial Risk (ATFR)

Risk may be described as the extent to which a person is willing to engage in activities where the likelihood of a favorable outcome is very low. The readiness of an individual to accept an additional risk that might lower their future wealth can be viewed as financial risk (Nandan & Sourabh, 2016). Investors have a negative ATFR when they prefer much safer, certain and affordable financial investment options. On the other hand, a positive ATFR consists of investors preferring to invest in the stock options where the level of risk and return are high (Davies & Brooks, 2014). Considering the integral role of investors' ATFR in their financial decision making, it is important to explore the same. Xiao et al. (2014) asserts that while human behavior is complicated, financial behavior is even more. Environmental as well as human factors can have an impact on a person's financial decisions. The interest rate, the cost of living, access to financial services, and market norms are all environmental influences. While personal factors include a person's general attitude, personal financial situation, and psychology.

Individuals respond differently to these variables. These personal factors have an impact on the person's emotions and financial decision-making (Hira, 2012). Personality traits such as openness may be associated with a higher willingness to take risks, while conscientiousness with a lower willingness to take risks. Neuroticism, on the other hand, may be with a greater aversion to risk. People with higher emotional intelligence may be more willing to take risks whereas investors with low emotional intelligence prefer to go with safer or less risky options.

Investors' ATFR is also influenced by their perception of the potential gains and losses associated with an investment. People with a positive ATFR tend to focus more on potential gains, while those with a negative ATFR are more focused on potential losses. Overall, the linkage between personality traits, EI, and investor ATFR is complex and multifaceted. Understanding of these linkages could be insightful for investors as well as financial institutions that could lead to effective financial decision making. The literature review of a few chosen research that investigated the association between personality and financial behaviour is covered in the following section.

2.3 Review of Literature

Table 1 provides a snapshot of literature based on few selected studies on personality traits and their relationship with financial decision making.

2.4 Proposed Research Model

A conceptual framework (Figure 3) was developed based on the conceptual perspective and review of literature. The constructive purpose of this study is to empirically investigate that whether personality traits and EI influence investors ATFR and to examine the differential effects of demographic factors in context of investors personality traits, EI and ATFR.

Based on the discussion in this section following hypotheses are proposed for the study.

H_1: There is a statistically positive significant influence of openness on investors attitude towards financial risk.

H_2: There is a statistically positive significant influence of conscientiousness on investors attitude towards financial risk.

Table 1. Review of selected studies

S. no.	Author (s) and Year	Variables Studied	Key Findings
1.	Sarwar et al. (2020)	Big five personality traits and risk aversion	The authors found that all personality factors are statistically significant, with risk aversion and investors' intention to invest serving as the two most important predictors. Openness to experience, conscientiousness, extraversion, agreeableness, and risk are found to be significant and favourably connected with investment intention, in contrast to neuroticism, which was found to have a negative impact on investment intention.
2.	Akhtar and Das (2020)	Psychological biases, financial risk tolerance, financial overconfidence	It has been discovered that an investor's perceived level of investment performance, their level of financial risk tolerance, and their level of financial overconfidence are all related to their personality. A negative correlation exists between perceived investment success and both financial risk tolerance and overconfidence. The mediation study also demonstrated that personality traits completely mediate the relationship between psychological elements and investment success.
3.	Gokhan and Mutlu (2019)	Big-five personality traits	The authors discovered that personality characteristics like extraversion and agreeableness had a substantial association with perceived investment performance, but conscientiousness, openness to experience, and neuroticism do not.
4.	Nandan and Saurabh (2016)	Big-five personality traits, short term investment intention, long term investment intention, attitude toward financial risk	Individuals' short-term investment intentions are not directly influenced by neuroticism, openness to experience, or extraversion traits, rather they are influenced by their attitude towards financial risk. Financial risk attitude is the ideal mediator between each personality trait and a person's inclination to make short-term investments.
5.	Dhiman and Raheja (2018)	Big- five personality traits, emotional intelligence, risk tolerance	They found that relationships between risk tolerance, emotional intelligence, and personality attributes are statistically significant. Emotional intelligence has a greater impact on investors' risk tolerance than personal characteristics.

Source: Compiled by author

H_3: There is a statistically positive significant influence of extraversion on investors attitude towards financial risk.

H_4: There is a statistically positive significant influence of agreeableness on investors attitude towards financial risk.

H_5: There is a statistically positive significant influence of neuroticism on investors attitude towards financial risk.

H_6: There is a statistically positive significant influence of emotional intelligence on investors attitude towards financial risk.

H_7: The selected variables (openness, conscientiousness, extraversion, agreeableness, neuroticism, emotional intelligence and ATFR) are significantly varying in terms of demographic factors (gender, age, qualification, occupation, income and marital status).

Figure 3. Conceptual framework
Source: Compiled by author

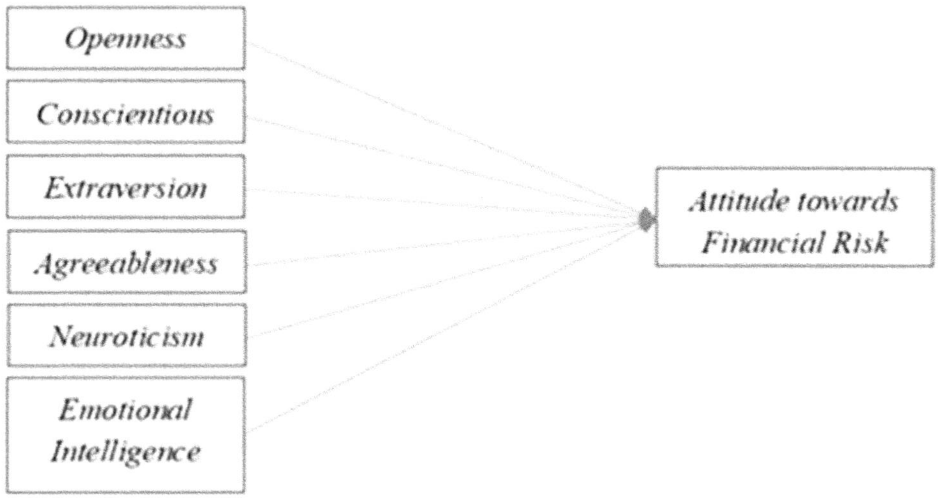

3. RESEARCH METHODOLOGY

3.1 Data Collection

A survey instrument (consisting of two parts) was developed for data collection. The first part consisted of the demographic information of the respondents. The second part consisted of statements related to variables such as openness, conscientiousness, extraversion, agreeableness, neuroticism and emotional intelligence to examine the investors ATFR. The current study gathers data through a survey at Delhi NCR region. A 35 items scale was considered to measure the construct. A questionnaire was given to 200 respondents out of which 190 responses were found complete, the same is considered for the final study. Convenience sampling was used for the study.

3.2 Measures

The measurement of variables was based on established scales. A brief description of the measures adopted is as follows: openness (6 items), conscientiousness (6 items), extraversion (5 items), agreeableness (4 items), neuroticism (5 items), attitude toward financial risk (4 items) taken from Nandan & Sourabh (2016) and emotional intelligence (5 items) taken from Dhiman & Raheja (2018). All the scale items were on a *"five-point Likert scale on which 1 represented strongly disagree and 5 strongly agree"*. The consistency of the scale was assessed through Cronbach's alpha (α). According to Hair et al. (2010) the Cronbach's alpha value above 0.6 is considered acceptable. Cronbach's alpha value for all the variables were found above the threshold value of 0.6 and hence inferred that the scale used in the study was reliable (Refer Table 3).

3.3 Demographic Profile of the Respondents

The demographic profile of the respondents includes information related to gender, age, qualification, occupation, income, marital status of respondents. Table 2 presents the respondent's profile. The majority of the respondents were female (51%) in the age group of 31–40 years (41%) have qualified on graduation level (51.6%). Most of the respondents were in private jobs (42.1%) and from the income group of 5,00,001–10,00,000 (33.2%) and most of them were unmarried (53.2%). Detail of the respondent's demographic information is given in Table 2.

Table 2. Demographic profile of the respondents (n= 190)

Demographic Characteristics	Frequency	Percentage
Gender		
Male	*93*	*49.0*
Female	*97*	*51.0*
Age (in Years)		
Up to 30 years	*70*	*36.8*
31- 40 years	*78*	*41.0*
41- 50 years	*26*	*13.7*
Above 50 years	*16*	*8.5*
Qualification		
Post Graduate	*70*	*36.8*
Graduate	*98*	*51.6*
Intermediate	*22*	*11.6*
Occupation		
Government Job	*38*	*20.0*
Private Job	*80*	*42.1*
Business	*38*	*20.0*
Others	*34*	*17.9*
Income		
Less than 2,50,000	*46*	*24.2*
2,50,001- 5,00,000	*51*	*26.8*
5,00,001- 10,00,000	*63*	*33.2*
More than 10,00,000	*30*	*15.8*
Marital Status		
Married	*89*	*46.8*
Unmarried	*101*	*53.2*

Source: Field Survey (2022)

3.4 Data Analysis

The statistical analysis of the data was accomplished through IBM SPSS version 25. Initially descriptive analysis was computed which follows the calculation of multiple regression to describe the rapport amongst a dependent (ATFR) and multiple independent factors (personality traits and EI) in this study. Further, multivariate analysis of variance (MANOVA) has been performed to explore the differential effects of demographic factors such as gender, age, occupation, experience and education on the selected factors of employee retention in this study.

4. RESULTS AND DISCUSSION

4.1 Descriptive Statistics

The descriptive statistics of the variables are presented in Table 3. The mean and standard deviation (S.D.) values of the variables demonstrate the level and variation in the respondent's score. In the study, the respondents show higher mean values for emotional intelligence (4.06) agreeableness (3.75), extraversion (3.74), attitude towards financial risk (3.58), openness (3.53), and conscientiousness (3.48) in comparison of neuroticism (2.99).

Table 3. Descriptive statistics

Code	Variables	Mean	Standard Deviation	Cronbach's Alpha (α) Value
Openness		**3.53**	**1.117**	
O1	Usually, relates to the designs in the sculpture and nature	3.58	1.139	
O2	Frequently try new and foreign products	3.36	1.275	
O3	Have slight attention in gambling on the nature of the world or the social condition	3.58	1.062	**0.713**
O4	Frequently enjoy living with the concepts or abstract ideas	3.35	1.147	
O5	Usually, carry conversation to a higher level	3.63	1.119	
O6	Have a lot of knowledgeable curiosity	3.70	0.961	
Conscientiousness		**3.53**	**1.139**	
C1	Usually, keep my things neat and clean	3.76	1.280	
C2	I am quite decent about stride myself so as to get work completed on time	3.70	1.292	
C3	Waste lot of periods before setting down to the effort	3.36	1.206	**0.928**
C4	Sometimes not as loyal or reliable as I should be	3.40	1.107	
C5	Never seem to be able to get organised	3.40	1.044	
C6	I am always dependable and organised	3.58	0.907	

continues on following page

Table 3. Continued

Code	Variables	Mean	Standard Deviation	Cronbach's Alpha (α) Value
Extraversion		**3.74**	**1.188**	**0.827**
E1	Really enjoy speaking to people	3.60	1.278	
E2	Often sense as if I am overflowing with liveliness	3.63	1.288	
E3	I am cheerful, excited person	4.06	0.971	
E4	I am very lively person	3.95	1.048	
E5	Usually make friends easily	3.45	1.358	
Agreeableness		**3.75**	**1.084**	**0.879**
A1	Frequently get into the quarrel with my family and friends	3.80	1.116	
A2	Some individuals believe, I am arrogant	3.66	1.099	
A3	Some persons think, I am cold and calculating	3.71	1.043	
A4	Generally, attempt to be thoughtful and kind	3.81	1.081	
Neuroticism		**2.99**	**1.370**	**0.843**
N1	I often feel inferiors to others	2.66	1.377	
N2	Under enormous anxiety and burden, sometimes feel like I am going into pieces	3.06	1.436	
N3	Often feel tense and nervous	3.05	1.345	
N4	Sometimes feel completely unimportant	3.11	1.290	
N5	Usually, when things go incorrect, I get dejected and sense like dropping	3.08	1.405	
Emotional Intelligence		**4.06**	**0.885**	**0.768**
EI 1	Usually, handle myself well in upset situation	3.93	0.954	
EI 2	Usually, calm myself in the adverse situation	4.00	0.843	
EI 3	I am very sensitive towards other's feeling	4.26	0.799	
EI 4	Usually, get along with others easily	3.93	0.880	
EI 5	Usually, I set my own aims and work hard to achieve those aims	4.20	0.953	
Attitude towards Financial Risk		**3.58**	**1.033**	**0.872**
ATFR 1	I am non eager to get hold of risk when selecting a fund or an investment	3.61	1.165	
ATFR 2	I desire a little risk/high returns investment with a stable performance over an investment that suggestions advanced risk/higher returns	3.58	0.979	
ATFR 3	Usually, prefer old investment strategy rather than taking risk in investing in new strategy, even new strategy has great return	3.58	1.046	
ATFR 4	Usually tend to avoid risk in the investment at any cost	3.56	0.945	

Source: As per author's calculation

4.2 Multiple Regression Analysis

In order to check the influence of selected personality traits and EI on investors ATFR multiple regressions was used. A multiple regression model is typically employed to investigate the impact of a group of independent factors on a single dependent variable. ATFR is a dependent variable in this study, while personality traits and emotional intelligence are independent factors. Table 5 shows the model summary of multiple regression. The results reveal that the R-square value which determines the proportion of variance in dependent variable is 0.534 or 53.4 per cent. Which means that 53.4 per cent of the variance is explained by the combination of independent variables on the dependent variable. The F-ratio measures whether the model as a whole has statistical significance or not. The F–ratio (49.08) and ($P< 0.05$) indicated that the model was statistically significant and had a good predictive power. Therefore, it can be inferred that the personality traits and EI have a considerable influence on investors ATFR.

Table 4. Model summary of multiple regression

Model		Adjusted	*F* Ratio	*P* Value
I	0.534	0.516	49.08	0.003

Note: Significance at 5% level
Source: As per the author's calculation

Next, the standardized Beta value is assessed to examine which independent variable (personality traits and EI in this study) accounts for the strongest contribution to explaining the dependent variable i.e., ATFR. The Beta value of each variable has been considered for individual variable analysis. From the results in Table 6, it was found that four variables in our study i.e., extraversion (0.167), agreeableness (0.348), openness (0.120), emotional intelligence (0.312) had a significant relationship as $P<0.05$. Another two variables neuroticism (0.089) and conscientiousness (0.050) have insignificant relationship with ATFR. Hence H_1, H_3, H_4, H_6 were accepted and H_2 and H_5 were rejected.

Table 5. Coefficients in multiple regression.

Independent Variables	Dependent Variable - ATFR			
	Beta	Coefficient Std. Error	T	Sig.
Openness	0.120	0.058	1.866	0.040
Conscientiousness	0.050	0.048	0.986	0.385
Extraversion	0.167	0.072	3.012	0.001
Agreeableness	0.348	0.082	5.196	0.000
Neuroticism	0.089	0.063	1.036	0.262
Emotional intelligence	0.312	0.042	5.483	0.000

Source: As per the author's calculation

The variable agreeableness has the highest coefficient value, indicating that it strongly influences investors' ATFR. People who are cooperative, dependable, and respectful of others' opinions and recommendations tend to be agreeable. A one-point rise in agreeableness causes a 0.348 points positive change in ATFR. Another variable that has a strong influence on ATFR is EI. Investors with greater EI know how to stay positive under pressure and take on greater risk than investors with less EI. The ATFR is positively affected by 0.312 points for every single point increase in the EI. Extrovert investors prefer spending time with people that are enthusiastic and happy. Investors that are more outgoing take on greater risk. A one-point rise in extroverts results in a 0.167 points improvement in ATFR. Investors that are highly open express a great preference for novel experiences. They readily take on fresh market knowledge and routinely adjust their investment portfolio in response to change in the circumstances. One point rise in openness results in a 0.120 points improvement in ATFR.

The personality traits such as conscientiousness (0.050) and neuroticism (0.089) have no significant influence on ATFR. Conscientious investors who have a certain degree of confidence and carefulness tend to have certain investment goals. Conscientious investors have negative ATFR. Neurotic investors are emotionally reactive. They are more inclined to perceive everyday events as risky and minor dissatisfaction as impossibly challenging. The results also gain support from the previous studies (Bashir et al. 2013; Nandan & Sourabh, 2016; Dhiman & Raheja 2015; Chavali & Mohanraj, 2016; Parameshwari & Krishnan, 2015).

4.3 MANOVA Analysis

Next, to determine significant differential effects in investors personality traits, EI and ATFR in terms of demographic variables (gender, age, qualification, occupation, income and marital status) multivariate analysis of variance (MANOVA) was used. Results of the MANOVA test are summarized in Table 7.

In case of gender, results of MANOVA analysis reveal that male and female investors display differential effects (Wilks' $\lambda = 0.843$; F= 2.241; P = 0.016; $\eta2 = 0.114$). Partial eta squared (0.114) evidence that gender explains 11.4 per cent of variance in context personality traits, EI and ATFR. Furthermore, from the mean analysis, it was found that male investors reported comparatively higher degrees for agreeableness, conscientiousness. However, females have higher degrees for neuroticism, extraversion, openness, emotional intelligence and ATFR. With regard to age, results for MANOVA analysis reveal that age displays a differential effect (Wilks' $\lambda = 0.709$; F = 1.180; P = 0.004; $\eta2 = 0.187$). Partial eta squared (0.187) evidenced that age explains 18.7 per cent of variance context personality traits, EI and ATFR. Furthermore, from the mean analysis, it was found that investors up to 30 years age groups reported comparatively higher degree of extraversion. However, investors in the age group of 31-40 years show higher degrees for openness, conscientiousness and ATFR. The investors of the 41-50 years age group show higher degrees for neuroticism, agreeableness and emotional intelligence.

Considering qualification, it was found that qualification also displays differential effects (Wilks' $\lambda = 0.849$; F = 2.142; P = 0.002; $\eta2 = 0.140$). Partial eta squared (0.140) indicating that qualification explains 14 per cent of variance in context personality traits, EI and ATFR. Furthermore, from the mean analysis, it was found that post graduate investors reported a comparatively higher degree of extraversion, openness, emotional intelligence and ATFR. However, graduate's investors display higher degree of agreeableness, conscientiousness and the investors qualified on intermediate level reported higher degree for neuroticism.

With regard to occupation, it was found that government jobs, private jobs, business and others display differential effects (Wilks' $\lambda = 0.883$; F = 3.360; P = 0.001; $\eta^2= 0.159$). Partial eta squared (0.159), indicating that occupation explains 15.9 per cent of variance in context personality traits, EI and ATFR. From the mean analysis, it was found that government job investors reported comparatively higher degrees for conscientiousness, openness and ATFR. However, investors in private jobs have higher degrees for neuroticism, agreeableness and self-employed investors have higher degrees for extraversion and emotional intelligence. Next, the results of MANOVA for income, reveals that income displays differential effects (Wilks' $\lambda = 0.860$; F = 2.604; P = 0.002; $\eta^2= 0.098$). Partial eta squared (0.098) evidenced that income explains 9.8 per cent of variance in context personality traits, EI and ATFR. From the mean analysis, it was found that investors having income between 2,50,001-5,00,00 reported comparatively higher degrees for neuroticism, extraversion. However, investors having income between 5,00,001–10,00,00 have higher degrees for conscientiousness, ATFR and investors having income of more than 10,00,000 reported higher degrees of agreeableness, openness and emotional intelligence.

Table 6. MANOVA results for socio-demographic profile of respondents

Category	O	C	E	A	N	EI	ATFR
Gender							
Male	3.58	3.62	3.72	3.75	2.95	3.99	3.56
Female	3.70	3.45	3.96	3.67	3.03	4.29	3.66
Wilks' $\lambda = 0.843$; $F = 2.241$; $P = 0.016$; $\eta^2 = 0.114$							
Age							
Up to 30 years	3.63	3.15	4.24	3.70	3.05	4.11	3.87
31 – 40	4.10	3.60	4.20	3.85	3.12	4.32	4.37
41 – 50	2.82	3.33	3.85	4.00	3.40	4.40	3.54
Above 50 years	2.12	3.00	3.50	3.25	1.10	4.20	3.43
Wilks' $\lambda = 0.709$; $F = 1.180$; $P = 0.004$; $\eta^2 = 0.187$							
Qualification							
Post Graduate	3.90	3.28	4.00	3.36	2.54	4.21	3.84
Graduate	3.47	3.72	3.79	3.87	3.08	4.10	3.45
Intermediate	3.83	3.23	3.71	3.82	3.22	3.91	3.80
Occupation							
Government job	3.94	3.72	3.87	3.75	2.33	4.13	3.91
Private job	3.71	3.64	3.78	3.81	3.15	4.17	3.57
Business	3.53	3.25	4.20	3.44	3.04	4.20	3.72
Others	3.55	3.47	3.77	3.68	2.87	4.09	3.58
Wilks' $\lambda = 0.883$; $F = 3.360$; $P = 0.001$; $\eta^2 = 0.159$							
Income							
Less than 2,50,000	2.98	3.43	3.76	3.69	3.08	4.16	3.64
2,50,001 – 5,00,000	3.53	3.66	4.05	3.96	3.36	4.02	3.39
5,00,001 – 10,00,000	3.64	3.74	3.75	4.12	2.60	4.20	3.93
More than 10,00,000	3.73	3.70	3.84	4.70	1.60	4.36	3.90
Wilks' $\lambda = .860$; $F = 2.604$; $P = .002$; $\eta^2 = 0.098$							
Marital Status							
Married	3.54	3.71	3.12	3.64	2.48	4.40	3.55
Unmarried	3.78	2.28	4.16	3.72	3.13	4.08	3.87
Wilks' $\lambda = .704$; $F = 3.122$; $P = .002$; $\eta^2 = 0.226$							
Note: O-openness; C-conscientiousness; E-extraversion; A-agreeableness; N-neuroticism; EI-emotional intelligence; ATFR-Attitude toward financial risk; η^2- partial eta square							

Source: As per the author's calculation

Lastly, from the results of MANOVA for marital status, it was found that married and unmarried investors display differential effects (Wilks' $\lambda = 0.704$; $F= 3.122$; $P = 0.002$; $\eta^2 = 0.226$). Partial eta squared (0.226) evidenced reasonable effect size, indicating that marital status explains 22.6 per cent of variance in context personality traits, EI and ATFR. Furthermore, from the mean analysis, it was found that married investors reported comparatively higher degrees for conscientiousness and emotional intelligence. However, unmarried investors have higher degrees for neuroticism, extraversion, agreeableness, openness and ATFR. Overall, it was discovered that diverse effects of demographic characteristics can be seen in relation to an investor's personality, EI, and ATFR. Hence H7 was accepted.

5. CONCLUSION

This study explored the influence of Big-five personality traits and emotional intelligence on investors' attitudes towards financial risk. The current study may be among the few which has integrated the Big-five personality traits model with emotional intelligence to measure investors' attitude towards financial risk. Additionally, the relationship between Big-five personality traits, investors' attitudes towards financial risk, and demographic variables such as (gender, age, qualification, occupation, income, and marital status) is also examined. Among the personality traits openness, agreeableness, extraversion and emotional intelligence have significant influence on attitude toward financial risk. Whereas conscientiousness and neuroticism have insignificant influence on attitude toward financial risk. Out of the significant personality traits, agreeableness and emotional intelligence are the most influencing variables of investors' attitude towards financial risk. Personality traits (openness, conscientiousness, extraversion, agreeableness, neuroticism), emotional intelligence and investors' attitudes towards financial risk are significantly varied across the socio-demographic variables. In India, a developing nation with little studies in this field, this research adds to the expanding body of knowledge concerning investors' personality traits and investing behaviour. The findings may aid policymakers in financial planning, selecting and educating relevant investors for their products/programs. The finance/investment companies should design investment avenues based on investor personality traits since it gives them a chance to comprehend how each investor makes investment decisions. They should also design investment products based on the risk-taking capacity of investors.

6. LIMITATIONS AND FUTURE RESEARCH

Like most studies, this study is also having some limitations. It focused on the north Indian sample which somewhat limits the overall generalization of the results in a diverse country like India. Current study has examined only big-five personality model out of numerous personality traits that influence investors attitude toward financial risk. Future studies should explore the wider set of personality traits and their effect on investors decision. The scale used in this study can also be validated with diverse and greater sample size.

REFERENCES

Akhtar, F., & Das, N. (2020). Investor personality and investment performance: From the perspective of psychological traits. *Qualitative Research in Financial Markets, 12*(3), 333–352. doi:10.1108/QRFM-11-2018-0116

Allport, G. W., & Odbert, H. S. (1936). Trait-names: A psycho-lexical study. *Psychological Monographs, 47*(1), i–171. doi:10.1037/h0093360

Baker, H. K., Kumar, S., & Goyal, N. (2021). Personality traits and investor sentiment. *Review of Behavioral Finance, 13*(4), 354–369. doi:10.1108/RBF-08-2017-0077

Bashir, T., Azam, N., Butt, A. A., Javed, A., & Tanvir, A. (2013). Are behavioural biases influenced by demographic characteristics & personality traits? Evidence from Pakistan. *European Scientific Journal, 9*(29), 277–293.

Becker, A., Deckers, T., Dohmen, T., Falk, A., & Kosse, F. (2012). The relationship between economic preferences and psychological personality measures. *Annual Review of Economics, 4*(1), 453–478. doi:10.1146/annurev-economics-080511-110922

Bikas, E., Jurevičienė, D., Dubinskas, P., & Novickytė, L. (2013). Behavioural finance: The emergence and development trends. *Procedia: Social and Behavioral Sciences, 82*, 870–876. doi:10.1016/j.sbspro.2013.06.363

Bouzguenda, K. (2018). Emotional intelligence and financial decision making: Are we talking about a paradigmatic shift or a change in practices? *Research in International Business and Finance, 44*, 273–284. doi:10.1016/j.ribaf.2017.07.096

Brooks, C., & Williams, L. (2021). The impact of personality traits on attitude to financial risk. *Research in International Business and Finance, 58*, 101501. doi:10.1016/j.ribaf.2021.101501

Chavali, K., & Mohanraj, M. P. (2016). Impact of demographic variables and risk tolerance on investment decisions–an empirical analysis. *International Journal of Economics and Financial Issues, 6*(1), 169–175.

Davies, G. B., & Brooks, P. (2014). Risk tolerance: Essential, behavioural and misunderstood. *Journal of Risk Management in Financial Institutions, 7*(2), 110–113.

DeBondt, W., Forbes, W., Hamalainen, P., & Gulnur Muradoglu, Y. (2010). What can behavioural finance teach us about finance? *Qualitative Research in Financial Markets, 2*(1), 29–36. doi:10.1108/17554171011042371

Dhiman, B., & Raheja, S. (2018). Do personality traits and emotional intelligence of investors determine their risk tolerance? *Management and Labour Studies, 43*(1-2), 88–99. doi:10.1177/0258042X17745184

Dulewicz, V., & Higgs, M. (2000). Emotional intelligence–A review and evaluation study. *Journal of Managerial Psychology, 15*(4), 341–372. doi:10.1108/02683940010330993

Gokhan, O. Z. E. R., & Mutlu, U. (2019). The effects of personality traits on financial behaviour. *Journal of Business Economics and Finance, 8*(3), 155–164.

Hair, J. F., Black, W. C., Babin, B. J., & Anderson, R. E. (2010). *Multivariate Data Analysis* (7th ed.). Pearson.

Hira, T. K. (2012). Promoting sustainable financial behaviour: Implications for education and research. *International Journal of Consumer Studies*, *36*(5), 502–507. doi:10.1111/j.1470-6431.2012.01115.x

Joo, B. A., & Durri, K. (2015). Comprehensive review of literature on behavioural finance. *Indian Journal of Commerce and Management Studies*, *6*(2), 11–19.

Kapoor, S., & Prosad, J. M. (2017). Behavioural finance: A review. *Procedia Computer Science*, *122*, 50–54. doi:10.1016/j.procs.2017.11.340

Kasemsap, K. (2015). The role of psychological factors in behavioural finance. In *Handbook of Research on Behavioural Finance and Investment Strategies: Decision Making in the Financial Industry*. IGI Global. doi:10.4018/978-1-4666-7484-4.ch006

Lipe, M. G. (1998). Individual investors' risk judgments and investment decisions. The impact of accounting and market data. *Accounting, Organizations and Society*, *23*(7), 625–640. doi:10.1016/S0361-3682(97)00065-2

McCrae, R. R., & Costa, P. T. Jr. (2008). The five-factor theory of personality. In O. P. John, R. W. Robins, & L. A. Pervin (Eds.), *Handbook of Personality: Theory and Research*. The Guilford Press.

Muradoglu, G., & Harvey, N. (2012). Behavioural finance: The role of psychological factors in financial decisions. *Review of Behavioral Finance*, *4*(2), 68–80. doi:10.1108/19405971211284862

Nandan, T., & Saurabh, K. (2016). Big-five personality traits, financial risk attitude and investment intentions: Study on Generation Y. *International Journal of Business Forecasting and Marketing Intelligence*, *2*(2), 128–150. doi:10.1504/IJBFMI.2016.078154

Nga, J. K., & Ken Yien, L. (2013). The influence of personality trait and demographics on financial decision making among Generation Y. *Young Consumers*, *14*(3), 230–243. doi:10.1108/YC-11-2012-00325

Parameshwari & Krishnan J. (2015). Personality Traits and Risk Profile Influencing Attitude of Investor. *Paripex – Indian Journal of Research*, *4*(5), 86–89.

Sadiq, M. N., & Khan, R. A. A. (2019). Impact of personality traits on investment intention: The mediating role of risk behaviour and the moderating role of financial literacy. *Journal of Finance and Economics Research*, *4*(1), 1–18. doi:10.20547/jfer1904101

Sarwar, D., Sarwar, B., Raz, M. A., Khan, H. H., Muhammad, N., Azhar, U., & Kasi, M. K. (2020). Relationship of the big five personality traits and risk aversion with investment intention of individual investors. *The Journal of Asian Finance. Economics and Business*, *7*(12), 819–829.

Sewell, M. (2007). *Behavioural finance*. London: University College London.

Subrahmanyam, A. (2008). Behavioural finance: A review and synthesis. *European Financial Management*, *14*(1), 12–29.

Xiao, J. J., Ahn, S. Y., Serido, J., & Shim, S. (2014). Earlier financial literacy and later financial behaviour of college students. *International Journal of Consumer Studies*, *38*(6), 593–601. doi:10.1111/ijcs.12122

Chapter 3
Emotional Intelligence for Entrepreneurial Success:
Mapping Inferences From Literature Review

Saloni Devi
University of Jammu, India

Vinay Chauhan
University of Jammu, India

Sonali Vaid
University of Jammu, India

ABSTRACT

Emotions affect creativity and innovation. An entrepreneur who is emotionally intelligent encourages the team members to think out of the box whenever the situation is not on the good of the organization. This leads to higher levels of creativity and results in successful initiatives, and idea sharing is best which results in the achievement of goals in the organization. The present study is based on the inferences of literature review mainly collected from important databases like Scopus and Web of Science. The aim of this study is to construct a conceptual framework to explore the role of emotional intelligence in nurturing creativity and innovation for entrepreneurial success.

1. INTRODUCTION

Organizations are improving in the crucial areas, and 78 percent of respondents say their company has handled the crisis effectively, according to a McKinsey study (Emmett et al., 2020). Over the past 25 years, emotional intelligence (EI) has gained recognition as a critical factor in emotional adjustment, personal wellbeing, interpersonal connections, and general achievement in a variety of contexts of daily life (Fernandez-Berrocal & Ruiz, 2008). According to studies by Fernando-Berrocal and Extrem-

DOI: 10.4018/979-8-3693-0418-1.ch003

era (2006) and Schutte, Malouff, Thorsteinsson, Bhullar, and Rooke (2007), it has a favorable relationship with traits including empathy, verbal intelligence, extroversion, openness to feelings, self-esteem, and life satisfaction. Additionally, it has been discovered that emotional intelligence is linked to better outcomes, among other things, in the domains of job and academic achievement (Boyatzis, 2006). Emotional intelligence (EI) is a fundamental aspect of engagement and interpersonal communication. It comprises the ability to recognize and grasp one's own emotions as well as the ability to empathically detect and understand the emotions of others. EI is crucial for establishing and sustaining meaningful connections because it enables individuals to manage social situations with compassion, responsiveness, and tact. This involves the capacity to resolve conflicts, actively listen, and accurately interpret non-verbal cues like posture and facial expressions. Self-awareness, self-motivation, empathy abilities, and social skills make up emotional intelligence. The ability to identify and convey emotions, emotional adjustment, and using emotions to motivate oneself and others are all parts of emotional intelligence (EI) (Mayer and Salovey, 1989). Weinberger (2002) provided a summary of the research work conducted in the area of emotion including emotional intelligence. The summary broke down the study of emotion from three disciplines – a) Sociological domain, b) Psychological domain, c) Human Resource Development. No matter where a person falls on the cognitive intelligence scale, emotional intelligence can help leaders maximize their leadership potential, according to Stein and Book (2011). People can improve their productivity and success in their careers, as well as the productivity and success of others, by increasing their emotional intelligence. The process and results of developing emotional intelligence also include a number of components that are known to lessen stress for both individuals and organizations through conflict management, relationship building, and stability, continuity, and harmony. Not to mention, it has deep connections to ideas about love and spirituality (Seerat, 2017). The link between emotional intelligence training and effective leadership was clearly demonstrated (Smith et al., 2018). EI is defined as the capacity to notice and integrate emotion to assist thought, understand and regulate emotion to enhance human growth (Mayer and Salovey, 1997). It is further acknowledged that EI contains four distinct categories of ability. According to Extremera et al. (2018), EI treatments can raise engagement, which in turn can raise work satisfaction. According to earlier research, an emotionally intelligent entrepreneur inspires their team to think creatively and innovatively and results in higher levels of innovation and creativity. Innovation (IN) is crucial right now and is the main force behind growth (Hungund & Kiran, 2017). Novelty and Initiation are its two main components, and it is an innovative continuous process in a particular organization (Cheung et al., 2011). Every novel concept, approach, or objective adopted by an entrepreneur generates innovation, which is then put into practice on the market to ensure its success. Entrepreneurs who are less fearful and possess less ego are better able to think creatively and collaborate with others in a non-competitive environment. Consequently, when emotions are controlled, pleasant outcomes and creativity follow. When a circumstance is not favorable to the company, an emotionally intelligent entrepreneur inspires fellow team employees to think creatively. An entrepreneur with high levels of EI will be able to inspire, support, and ignite creativity among staff members. Additionally, they will take the necessary actions to offer their followers the confidence, optimism, and enthusiasm to effortlessly embrace creativity irrespective of how and when it may present itself (Zhu and George, 2003). The focus of the current study is on EI as a significant predictor of their followers' creativity. Knowing how emotional intelligence can enable entrepreneurs to be inventive by leveraging their emotions is crucial because innovation (IN) is a critical success factor in entrepreneurship. Entrepreneurs need to have strong emotions in order to accept the challenges that their stakeholders, including their employees, clients, suppliers, the government, agencies, and a long list of others, present to them every day. According to a Statista poll conducted in 2019, 36% of CEOs believe that emotional intelligence is a necessary ability. According to Ahmedtouglu et al. (1997), entrepreneurship is more than just starting a firm; it also refers to a collection of behaviors or activities that entrepreneurs engage in. According to a popular theory, business owners with high EI are more likely to have diverse performance expectations. According to Cross and Travaglione (2003), entrepreneurial success (ES) is the benchmark that entrepreneurs use to assess the success of their companies. According to Ahmedtouglu et al. (1997), entrepreneurship is more than just starting a firm; it also refers to a collection of behaviors or activities that entrepreneurs engage in. According to a popular theory, business owners with high EI are more likely to have diverse performance expectations. As a result, those with high EI are better at controlling their emotions and problem-solving (Bahadori, 2012).Owners who started their firm were shown to be emotionally more secure and autonomous than owners who took over from their parents or other relatives (Statter, 1997).Additionally, it was discovered in the preliminary results that managerial styles do have a direct impact on organization performance, while an entrepreneur's EI does not (Yitshaki and Rothsein, 2011). Successful entrepreneurs must possess a blend of analytical, creative, and practical intelligence. Further research by Ahmetouglu et al. (2011) revealed that people with high EI tend to be more effective, which fosters innovative tendencies. The study further stressed that an entrepreneur can only be successful when they are having their emotional high points. By finding, creating, and stimulating opportunity, entrepreneurship frequently exudes enthusiasm, energy, and inventiveness. Achieving emotional intelligence requires having a high degree of empathy for the needs, emotions, and general circumstances of other people. Therefore, a driven entrepreneur will be better able to develop goods or services that satisfy the demands of future clients. Entrepreneurs with high emotional intelligence can comprehend, communicate, and form relationships with employees and clients better because they are more sensitive to others' emotional states. Entrepreneurs with strong emotional intelligence are more likely to provide goods or services that are specifically catered to the demands of their clients and are aware of their customers' problems. Based on their expertise and attention to detail, those that comprehend their consumers' wants may produce the best products and services (Sabharwal, 2022). As a result, the current study is founded on conclusions drawn from a review of the literature that was mostly gathered from Scopus and Web of Science. The purpose of this study is to develop a conceptual framework for examining how EI fosters creativity and innovation in order to achieve entrepreneurial success.

2. REVIEW OF LITERATURE

The present study focuses on reviewing the existing literature published to understand the opportunities and challenges posed by Emotional Intelligence (EI), Innovation(IN) and Entrepreneurial Success(ES). The study used databases from Scopus, Web of science and google scholar to search for the relevant studies. The search was carried out using the keyword combinations viz. "Emotional Intelligence and Innovation, Emotional Intelligence and Innovation, Innovation and Entrepreneurial Success.

The existence and development of organizations in today's chaotic environment, where many are prone to change, depends on the creativity and adaptability of all the society's active classes. (Shojaei&Siuki, 2014). One quality that could greatly aid in developing original ideas in the context of making decisions in emergency and unknowable scenarios is emotional intelligence. (Steiner, 2007). According to Hayashi and Ewert (2006), The performance improves and becomes more efficient the more emotional intelligence there is. Furthermore, people who are emotionally intelligent—that is, those who can identify, control, and effectively handle their own emotions as well as those of others—stand out in every aspect of life, particularly in affective and sincere encounters. Additionally, it was said that the emotional intelligence may be described in terms of our awareness of feelings and emotions and how we manage them(Dulewicz et al. (2003), influencing and affecting others, maintaining and boosting one's own motivation through sensible, moral, and diligent behavior (Samadi&Keyvan, 2013). The presentation of inventive behavior was then taken into consideration, and several original ideas were explored, including regulating procedures, problem analysis, idea discovery, concept development and combination, idea testing in theoretical terms, and ultimately the study of an idea's benefit(Mumford et al (2002). Studying the relationship between emotional intelligence and creative work practices in the Turkish banking industry, it was found that there was a strong connection between the two. (Orhan & Dinçer (2012). Additionally, it was proposed that emotional intelligence, or the importance placed on emotional competencies to explain a person's entrepreneurial conduct, is a significant component of the entrepreneurial mentality (Michellod et al. (2013). Dyke and Murphy (2006) define success in business is defined as the production of riches, fame, credibility, position in society, or dignity. In addition to this, Wach et al. (2016) using standards like generating wealth and individual pleasure, explain what it means to be an entrepreneurial success. In this respect, Kirkwood (2016) says that numerous interpretations can be made of the personal satisfaction criterion because it can be obtained from work performance, creative satisfaction, emotional control, or fulfilling goals. This highlights how various entrepreneurs can interpret the standards used to determine personal satisfaction.

2.1 Emotional Intelligence and Innovation

Emotional intelligence is a cooperative problem-solving ability that aids individuals in thriving and achieving their goals. Internal conflict is less likely to occur when behavior is consistent because the motivations that fuel it are lessened. Aqqad et al. (2019) discovered that EI behaviors were regarded as characteristics of influential leaders and crucial to future success for potential leaders in the businesses they researched by both prospective and experienced leaders. The authors also identified an attribute of seasoned leaders known as organizational altruism, which is understood to be familiarity with the organization and a dedication to its success. Positive correlations were found between transformative leadership and EI and group cohesion. Pathak and Muralidharan (2020) discussed the importance and utility of EI and asserted that interpersonal approaches to leadership are essentially dynamic, making EI a key component of the leadership process. Similarly, Zhang et al. (2018) argued that leaders' emotional intelligence (EI) enhanced the value of member-leader exchange interactions, and Rinfret et al. (2020) came to the conclusion that EI might enhance leadership in team settings.

It can be concluded that emotional intelligence leads to innovation.

2.2 Innovation and Entrepreneurial Success

A COVID 19 pandemic has witnessed a larger downfall in the enterprises. In the tightened economy, a lot of business enterprises are fighting for survival. Enterprises are constantly exploring new and creative ways to grow and advanced their selves to survive in a dynamic environment. Businesses are looking at innovative options to meet market difficulties, gain a competitive edge, and increase the market acceptance of their existing products. Most businesses will not succeed in the market if they do not alter their business practices to grow with new and innovative technology. Entrepreneurs are innovators who develop new goods, processes, and markets. They also act as creators of new items and ways of production(Schumpeter, 1949). It will not be out of place to perceive entrepreneurs as playing a crucial role in institutional and national development if they are seen as inventors, creators, and occasionally developers. Therefore, it is crucial to research how innovation affects entrepreneurship success.

Table 1. Studies reflecting the link between emotional intelligence and innovation goals and thrive

S.NO.	AUTHOR	YEAR	FINDINGS
1.	Parke et al.	2015	Employment creativity has been linked to emotional regulation, a part of emotional intelligence (EI), via preserving good emotions.
2.	Ngah and Salleh	2015	Positive emotional intelligence is associated with improved inventiveness, which can result in successful entrepreneurship.
3.	Lea et al.	2018	People with high emotional intelligence (EI) have the capacity to recognize, comprehend, regulate, and make use of their emotions. This enables them to recognize problems more effectively, gather information for problem solving in a constructive and open way, avoid unpleasant emotions, and increase their natural desire to do so. This, in turn, encourages the production of creative work.
4.	Newman et al.; Alessandri et al;	2018	Higher levels of positive emotional stability, more cognitive flexibility, and innovative methods of thinking that foster domain-specific creativity are produced by people with high levels of resilience.
5.	Buehring and Moore	2018	Interdisciplinary innovation teams will be able to find innovation opportunities by applying emotional intelligence.
6.	Wang et al;	2019	It may be possible to increase team innovation performance through the use of emotional intelligence.
7.	Andrabi and Rainayee	2020	Innovative work behavior is essential for assessing emotional intelligence and aids in effectively managing emotional dissonance. As a result of emotional dissonance at work, emotional tiredness and emotional stress are common side effects of workplace conduct that is inventive and emotional intelligent.
8.	MacCann et al.	2020	A higher level of resilience can be maintained by people with high EI since they can better control their emotions and encourage their growth in a positive manner.
9.	Pathak and Muralidharan	2020	Positive relationships between EI and group cohesion and transformative leadership were found. While discussing the significance and utility of EI, it was further mentioned that interpersonal approaches to leadership are fundamentally dynamic, making EI a crucial component of the leadership process.
10.	Al-Omoush et al	2020	Innovative people respond differently to creative ideas or practices, according to the innovation diffusion theory. Because most markets are dynamic, it is practically impossible to find an industry that is not inventive and involved in developments that are market-sensitive.
11.	Polizzi and Lynn	2021	High emotion control, which is a facet of emotional intelligence, was proven to boost resilience.
12.	Jena and Goyal	2022	Enhancing the emotional intelligence of working professionals through training will enable them to better manage the fear and anxiety brought on by COVID-19, prompt them to behave creatively, and influence a company to be more forward-thinking and creative.
13.	Jena and Goyal	2022	People that are emotionally intelligent have higher levels of self-control and self-regulation, as well as being adaptable, flexible, and positive.

Brazeal and Herbert (1999) investigated the innovation process as a crucial component that ultimately leads to the entrepreneurial event or performance. According to Hanif and Marnavi (2009), in order to be successful in the knowledge-based economy, innovative measures must be used in addition to quality initiatives. According to Henrik (2007), innovation is the successful application of a creation, and this innovation appears to promote success, growth, and profit. Innovation is the introduction of new concepts, theories, or methods that haven't been tried before or are distinctive, according to the Oxford Advanced Learner's Dictionary of Current English (2015). For the success of the business, the majority of firms nowadays are implementing fresh concepts or changing old ones. As a result, we can draw the conclusion that innovation is essential for business and entrepreneur success.

From the above discussion it can be concluded that innovation leads to entrepreneurial success.

Table 2. Studies reflecting the link between innovation and entrepreneurial success

S NO.	AUTHOR	YEAR	FINDINGS
1.	Hsieh	2016	The level of employee satisfaction influences innovation behavior favorably, and the non-financial performance of service innovation positively influences its financial performance.
2.	CegarraNavarroetal.	2016	The capacity to maintain a proper balance between economic and social goals while delivering benefits to an organization that have the potential to maintain its survival in a global economy is one way to measure the success of innovation.
3.	Crudu	2019	The concept of entrepreneurship promotes economic expansion and enhances business success. It increases job possibilities and innovation, boosting the competitiveness of the businesses.
4.	Urbano et al.	2020	Entrepreneurs are very interested in studying how new ventures succeed because it primarily focuses on how businesses may perform better, how the economy can flourish, and how to create value.
5.	Akpan et al.	2020	Businesses' proposed innovations in digitalization play a crucial role in advancing business knowledge and fostering entrepreneurship. Similar to this, the research demonstrates that technical expertise improves business operations, increasing performance effectiveness.
6.	Bresciani et al.	2021	Entrepreneurs concentrate on understanding how to build and implement innovation in products and services by utilizing the information and potential value of open data.
7.	Nouman and Cnaan	2021	Entrepreneurship can take many different shapes, but it always needs a creative approach to putting a solution into action. For example, changing the organizational structure, coming up with unique ways to pool resources, or putting action plans into action in novel ways.
8.	Bunjak et al	2022	Through individualized consideration, intellectual stimulation, inspirational motivation, and idealized influence, leaders encourage employees to participate in technical breakthroughs that can assist to shape the organization's future success.
9.	Brook and Beckley	2023	Beckley asserts that individuals that innovate the most will ultimately experience long-term entrepreneurial success.

2.3 Emotional Intelligence and Entrepreneurial Success

Due to organizational downsizing and ongoing unemployment as a result of the current economic climate, an increasing number of people are aspiring to work for themselves. Considering the economic, executive, and emotional hurdles involved with entrepreneurial professions, people are seeking out entrepreneurial employment at an ever-increasing pace (Zimmerer et al., 2007). From the viewpoint of an individual, starting a new business is frequently established as a component of the entrepreneur's personal life strategy, in order to provide for their financial needs (Littunen, 2000). Self-employment offers many people both a way out of the traditional organizational hierarchies and a chance to increase their own financial status (Walker & Webster, 2007). Opportunities for adaptability, independence, success, and self-awareness are provided by self-employment. Today's successful entrepreneurs are those who are adept at managing both their teams and their finances. Entrepreneurial activities like bargaining, gathering and managing resources, spotting and seizing chances, controlling stress, gaining and keeping clients, and exercising leadership all have an impact on emotional intelligence. In today's society, entrepreneurs are generally required to be more adaptable and flexible than employees of larger companies, who are, in some ways, shielded by the company as a whole. This is because the business environment is always changing. Entrepreneurs with strong emotional intelligence are able to handle the challenges of running a business with poise and resiliency. Self-awareness and emotional intelligence assist entrepreneurs to make wise decisions even under stressful circumstances. Empathy and emotional intelligence allow innovators to create goods and services that actually resonate with their customers' needs. Understanding emotions is only one aspect of emotional intelligence; another is efficiently controlling them in oneself and in social interactions.

Table 3. Studies reflecting link between innovation and entrepreneurial success

S NO.	AUTHOR	YEAR	FINDINGS
1.	Ahmetoglu	2014	To be successful in their new firm, entrepreneurs need to have a certain set of talents and abilities, such as the capacity to innovate, make decisions, overcome obstacles, interact, and cooperate with others.
2.	Ngah and Saleh	2015	ES has been identified as the standards used by business owners to determine the level of success of their endeavors.
3.	Kirkwood	2016	It has been argued that the personal fulfillment criterion is open to several interpretations because satisfaction can come from a variety of sources, including job performance, gaining creative satisfaction, controlling one's emotions, or accomplishing goals.
4.	Ingram et al.,	2017	Entrepreneurs who practice emotional management techniques and have a high level of emotional self-awareness are better able to make wiser judgments, resolve problems, and negotiate deals.
5.	Zhou and Bojica	2017	Entrepreneurs may be more inclined to view their performance as an entrepreneur favorably as their EI level rises, demonstrating self-awareness of entrepreneurial abilities and competencies.
6.	Nead	2022	High emotional intelligence makes you a better manager and leader as an entrepreneur. It has an effect on how you conduct oneself, but it also improves the way you interact with coworkers, business partners, and even clients.
7.	Sabharwal	2022	In the workplace and in tests, emotional intelligence is a greater indicator of success than high IQ.

From the above reviewed literature it can be summarized as emotional intelligence leads to entrepreneurial success

3. ANALYSIS

The table highlights innovation and entrepreneurial success based on an exhaustive examination of the literature on the connection between emotional intelligence and these two traits. Enhancing performance and responding to innovative competitors are two of the biggest issues that every organization faces, which calls for supporting employee innovation. In order for a firm to take advantage of opportunities and resolve problems, it is vital to unleash the creative potential of its workforce. Employee innovation may be improved when employees are given opportunities to develop their EI. According to Vasudevan (2013), EI may be learned as an adult and virtually certainly has a positive impact on career or life outcomes. Intervention strategies for employee innovation may need to concentrate on helping staff members achieve psychological well-being by raising their EI levels. The training geared at increasing EI and psychological well-being is likely to promote employee creativity, helping their organization stay ahead of the competition because EI has been proved to improve psychological wellness. As found, psychological health might mediate the relationship between EI and IN. As a result, managers can promote employee innovation by supporting their mental health. Positive emotions can create opportunities for social and personal growth, which eventually results in better job and life outcomes. According to research, emotionally intelligent business owners are more likely to evaluate their success as an entrepreneur favorably when considering the following factors: business performance, employee satisfaction, ethical behavior, personal fulfillment, and consumer satisfaction. The distinguishing feature among all criteria is that they all involve social skills of controlling one's own and other people's emotions or moods in order to reach a certain goal. This is true even when corporate performance criteria are less clear. These criteria also take into account the important social interactions that occur in the day-to-day operations of entrepreneurial organizations, such as acquiring and retaining clients and attracting, hiring, and managing employees—important resources in especially for small businesses. Managing these interactions can give entrepreneurs a competitive edge if they have a strong ability to recognize, comprehend, and control people' and their own emotional reactions (Ingram et al., 2017).

Table 4. Frequency of the analyzed studies

Relationship	Author	Frequency
EI IN	Salovey and Mayer (1989); DeJong (2006); (Sirem 2009); (Chopra & Kanji, 2010);Alguezaui and Filieri(2010);(Barczak et al., 2010);Laursen et al.(2012);Goleman(2013);Parke et al(2015); (Ngah& Salleh, 2015);Lea et al; (Newman etal. 2018; Alessandri et al. 2018) (Buehring& Moore, 2018); (Wangetal 2019); (Andrabi &Rainayee, 2020); (MacCann et al. 2020); Pathak and Muralidharan (2020); (Al-Omoush et al., 2020); (Polizzi and Lynn 2021);(Jena & Goyal, 2022);	13
IN ES	Heunk (1998);Brazeal and Herbert (1999); Trott (2005); (Riederer, Baier &Graefe, 2005); (Buganza and Verganti, 2006); Henrik (2007); Hanif and Marnavi (2009); (Tan and Nasurdin, 2011);(Oncioiu, 2013); (Lin, 2007; Wang and Wang, 2012); (Hsieh, 2016); (CegarraNavarro et al., 2016); (Crudu 2019);(Urbanoetal,2020); (Akpan et al.2020); (Bresciani et al., 2021); (Nouman and Cnaan, 2021); (Bunjak et al., 2022); (Brook and Beckley,2023).	9
EI ES	(Baron&Markman,2000);(Baron&Markman,2003); Gardner (2011); (Cardon & Shepherd, 2012); (Ahmetoglu, 2014);(Ngah and Saleh,2015); (Kirkwood, 2016); (Ingram et al., 2017);(Zhou and Bojica (2017));(Nead,2022);(Sabharwal,2022)	7

Figure 1. Proposed framework

4. DISCUSSIONS

This research adds to the corpus of knowledge about emotional intelligence, business success, and starting new ventures. It has been demonstrated that entrepreneurs' emotional quotient significantly influences the emergence of new businesses. Entrepreneurs are driven by opportunities, and they are the ones who seize those chances and turn them into existence by integrating fresh technology into tried-and-true practices. It is one of the most crucial characteristics of an entrepreneur because without it, businesspeople would only be able to connect with others who have similar communication styles to themselves, which would limit their capacity to communicate their vision and objectives (Bonnstetter, 2012). Researchers found that opportunity-driven entrepreneurs are professional and self-assured (Solymossy, 1997); as a result, these businesspeople have high levels of self-awareness and social awareness. They are growth-oriented and see obstacles as chances to start something new. They effectively rely on, develop, and use their social networks to access markets, gather knowledge, and acquire resources, which positively affects their performance (Cantzler & Svante, 2007). The impact of emotional intelligence as a predictor of business success was also examined in this study. In the early stages of entrepreneurial development, Boyd and Vozikis (2009) claimed that those with higher levels of emotional intelligence will have better entrepreneurial success.

It is clear from the aforementioned evidence that emotional intelligence directly and favorably affects an entrepreneur's success and development. Entrepreneurs that possess emotional intelligence are more self-aware and have more control over their emotions. Emotional intelligence should aid business owners in developing strong working relationships with their team members. It should also contribute to the expansion of a company. It aids in stress management and encourages the entrepreneur to think imaginatively and creatively. It helps business owners avoid emotional roadblocks like anxiety, fear, irritation, boredom, etc. that impair an entrepreneur's effectiveness. Emotional intelligence (EI) is the capacity to detect and comprehend one's own emotions. EI can encourage innovation in entrepreneurs by encouraging their curiosity and eagerness to learn and advance. The human connection continues to capture our attention even as the world adopts more and more cutting-edge technologies, such as artificial intelligence (AI). Entrepreneurs report feeling less stressed when EI rises, and they also say they have a tendency to think more positively, which helps an enterprise expand and succeed. They can choose a problem-focused coping technique with ease. Instead of ignoring a problem, an entrepreneur can readily address it and focus on finding a solution. An entrepreneur with high EI not only performs better, but also fosters an encouraging atmosphere with sensitivity and guides the team in working toward the group's primary goal.

5. CONCLUSION

This study adds to our understanding of innovation, entrepreneurial success, and emotional intelligence. According to research, emotional intelligence refers to a person's capacity to regulate their own and other people's feelings in order to guide their behaviors and thinking. Entrepreneurs should use their emotional intelligence to their advantage and enhance innovation and creativity within the company. The ability to feel would enable business owners to lead well and encourage and motivate their staff to be inventive and creative (Modassir and Singh 2008). It will make it easier for business owners to comprehend their own needs for more successful new venture formation. Entrepreneurs who can control their emotions will be able to handle difficult situations and make wise financial decisions on their own or for the firm as a whole. The likelihood of success in the workplace increases with emotional intelligence. Employees who are emotionally intelligent do better in work.

The results of this study imply that emotional intelligence is crucial to the success of new ventures and their creation. Entrepreneurs should take care to keep their emotions under control so that they do not get in the way of their business' success. People who are skilled at controlling their emotions are also much better at running their company's affairs. He is no longer under stress and is able to make judgments that are beneficial to the company. Before climbing the success stairs, highly creative entrepreneurs frequently labor hard and remove stress. They can channel their enthusiasm into the development and expansion of the company and generate the greatest concepts for its success.

6. RECOMMENDATIONS

Emotional Intelligence led to positive impact on innovation and entrepreneurial success. If the emotions are managed it leads to create new ideas that helps in the growth and success of an enterprise. Entrepreneurs need to have a specific set of talents in order to be successful in their new ventures, including the ability to innovate, make decisions, solve problems, communicate, and cooperate with people (Ahmetoglu, 2014). Business leaders who possess emotional intelligence are typically aware of their own thoughts and how their behavior can effect others. A leader can undertake duties that are directly related to attaining the objectives of the organization by establishing positive relationships and working effectively with the team. This study adds to the body of knowledge on emotional intelligence, innovation, and entrepreneurial success by describing how EI traits can affect innovation and ES examining the various connections between EI, IN, and ES. The relationships established above must be put to the test by gathering primary data. Future research can also be carried out by expanding the current model across multiple industries to include moderator and mediator. As a result, it is advised to examine the relationship between EI, IN, and ES using quantitative analysis and testing, as well as determine whether the association is present or not.

REFERENCES

Ahmetoglu, G., Leutner, F., & Chamorro-Premuzic, T. (2011). EQ-nomics: Understanding the relationship between individual differences in Trait Emotional Intelligence and entrepreneurship. *Personality and Individual Differences*, *51*(8), 1028–1033. doi:10.1016/j.paid.2011.08.016

Akpan, I. J., Soopramanien, D., & Kwak, D. H. (2021). Cutting-edge technologies for small business and innovation in the era of COVID-19 global health pandemic. *Journal of Small Business and Entrepreneurship, 33*(6), 607–617. doi:10.1080/08276331.2020.1799294

Al-Omoush, K. S., Simón-Moya, V., & Sendra-García, J. (2020). The impact of social capital and collaborative knowledge creation on e-business proactiveness and organizational agility in responding to the COVID-19 crisis. *Journal of Innovation & Knowledge, 5*(4), 279–288. doi:10.1016/j.jik.2020.10.002

Andrabi, N. F., & Rainayee, R. A. (2020). Emotional intelligence and innovative work behaviour: A review. *International Journal of Engineering and Management Research, 10*(4), 10. doi:10.31033/ijemr.10.4.26

Andries, P., & Hünermund, P. (2020). Firm-level effects of staged investments in innovation: The moderating role of resource availability. *Research Policy, 49*(7), 103994. doi:10.1016/j.respol.2020.103994

Aqqad, N., Obeidat, B., Tarhini, A., & Masa'deh, R. E. (2019). The relationship among emotional intelligence, conflict management styles, and job performance in Jordanian banks. *International Journal of Human Resources Development and Management, 19*(3), 225–265. doi:10.1504/IJHRDM.2019.100636

Avdic, S., Elsaman, H. A., & Gernal, L. (2021). COVID-19 Pandemic and Performance: Empirical Study of Integrated Remote Site Management Services in Dubai, United Arab Emirates. JPAIR Multidisciplinary Research, 46(1), 51-75.

Awan, M. I., Shamim, A., & Ahn, J. (2021). Implementing 'cleanliness is half of faith'in re-designing tourists, experiences and salvaging the hotel industry in Malaysia during COVID-19 pandemic. *Journal of Islamic Marketing, 12*(3), 543–557. doi:10.1108/JIMA-08-2020-0229

Bahadori, M. (2012). The effect of emotional intelligence on entrepreneurial behaviour: A case study in a Medical Science University. *Asian Journal of Business Management., 4*(1), 81–85.

Barczak, G., Lassk, F., & Mulki, J. (2010). Antecedents of team creativity: An examination of team emotional intelligence, team trust and collaborative culture. *Creativity and Innovation Management, 19*(4), 332–345. doi:10.1111/j.1467-8691.2010.00574.x

Baron, R. A., & Markman, G. D. (2000). Beyond social capital: How social skills can enhance entrepreneurs' success. *The Academy of Management Perspectives, 14*(1), 106–131. doi:10.5465/ame.2000.2909843

Baron, R. A., & Markman, G. D. (2003). Beyond social capital: The role of entrepreneurs' social competence in their financial success. *Journal of Business Venturing, 18*(1), 41–60. doi:10.1016/S0883-9026(00)00069-0

Bonnstetter, B. J., & Fry, C. C. (2012). Creating and Assessing a New Class of Entrepreneurially-Minded Engineers. In *VentureWell. Proceedings of Open, the Annual Conference* (p. 1). National Collegiate Inventors & Innovators Alliance.

Boyd, N. G., & Vozikis, G. S. (1994). The influence of self-efficacy on the development of entrepreneurial intentions and actions. *Entrepreneurship Theory and Practice, 18*(4), 63–77. doi:10.1177/104225879401800404

Brandstätter, H. (1997). Becoming an entrepreneur — A question of personality structure? *Journal of Economic Psychology, 18*(2-3), 157–177. doi:10.1016/S0167-4870(97)00003-2

Brandstätter, H. (2011). Personality aspects of entrepreneurship: A look at fve meta-analyses. *Personality and Individual Differences*, *51*(3), 222–2. doi:10.1016/j.paid.2010.07.007

Buehring, J. H., & Moore, P. (2018). Emotional and social intelligence as 'magic key'in innovation: A designer's call toward inclusivity for all. *Journal of Innovation Management*, *6*(2), 6–12. doi:10.24840/2183-0606_006.002_0002

Buganza, T., & Verganti, R. (2006). Life-cycle flexibility: How to measure and improve the innovative capability in turbulent environments. *Journal of Product Innovation Management*, *23*(5), 393–407. doi:10.1111/j.1540-5885.2006.00212.x

Bunjak, A., Bruch, H., & Černe, M. (2022). Context is key: The joint roles of transformational and shared leadership and management innovation in predicting employee IT innovation adoption. *International Journal of Information Management*, *66*, 102516. doi:10.1016/j.ijinfomgt.2022.102516

Byggeth Sophie, H., Henrik, N., Johan, W., Göran, B., & Karl-Henrik, R. (2007). Introductory procedure for sustainability-driven design optimization. *Guidelines for a Decision Support Method Adapted to NPD Processes.*

Cantzler, I., & Svante, L. (2007). Team-oriented women entrepreneurs: A way to modern. *Journal of Small Business and Enterprise Development*, *14*(4), 732–746. doi:10.1108/14626000710832802

Cardon, M. S., Foo, M. D., Shepherd, D., & Wiklund, J. (2012). Exploring the heart: Entrepreneurial emotion is a hot topic. *Entrepreneurship Theory and Practice*, *36*(1), 1–10. doi:10.1111/j.1540-6520.2011.00501.x

Cavazotte, F., Moreno, V., & Hickmann, M. (2012). Effects of leader intelligence, personality and emotional intelligence on transformational leadership and managerial performance. *The Leadership Quarterly*, *23*(3), 443–455. doi:10.1016/j.leaqua.2011.10.003

Cegarra-Navarro, J. G., Reverte, C., Gómez-Melero, E., & Wensley, A. K. (2016). Linking social and economic responsibilities with financial performance: The role of innovation. *European Management Journal*, *34*(5), 530–539. doi:10.1016/j.emj.2016.02.006

Chopra, P. K., & Kanji, G. K. (2010). Emotional intelligence: A catalyst for inspirational leadership and management excellence. *Total Quality Management & Business Excellence*, *21*(10), 971–1004. doi:10.1080/14783363.2010.487704

Cross & Travaglione. (2003). *The untold story: is the entrepreneur of the 21st century defined by emotional intelligence?* Academic Press.

Crudu, R. (2019). The role of innovative entrepreneurship in the economic development of EU member countries. *Journal of Entrepreneurship, Management and Innovation*, *15*(1), 35–60.

De Jong, J. P., & Den Hartog, D. N. (2008). Innovative work behavior: Measurement and validation. *EIM Business and Policy Research*, *8*(1), 1–27.

DePierro, J., Katz, C. L., Marin, D., Feder, A., Bevilacqua, L., Sharma, V., Hurtado, A., Ripp, J., Lim, S., & Charney, D. (2020). Mount Sinai's Center for Stress, Resilience and Personal Growth as a model for responding to the impact of COVID-19 on health care workers. *Psychiatry Research*, *293*, 113426. doi:10.1016/j.psychres.2020.113426 PMID:32861094

Dincer, H., & Orhan, N. (2012). *Relationship between emotional intelligence and innovative work behaviors in Turkish banking sector*. Academic Press.

Dulewicz, V., & Higgs, M. (2003). Leadership at the top: The need for emotional intelligence in organizations. *The International Journal of Organizational Analysis*, *11*(3), 193–210. doi:10.1108/eb028971

Dyke, L. S., & Murphy, S. A. (2006). How we define success: A qualitative study of what matters most to women and men. *Sex Roles*, *55*(5-6), 357–371. doi:10.100711199-006-9091-2

Extremera, N., Quintana-Orts, C., Mérida-López, S., & Rey, L. (2018). Cyberbullying victimization, self-esteem and suicidal ideation in adolescence: Does emotional intelligence play a buffering role? *Frontiers in Psychology*, *9*, 367. doi:10.3389/fpsyg.2018.00367 PMID:29623058

Gardner, W. L., Cogliser, C. C., Davis, K. M., & Dickens, M. P. (2011). Authentic leadership: A review of the literature and research agenda. *The Leadership Quarterly*, *22*(6), 1120–1145. doi:10.1016/j.leaqua.2011.09.007

Goleman, D. (2006). *Emotional intelligence*. Random House LLC.

Goleman, D., Boyatzis, R. E., & McKee, A. (2013). *Primal leadership: Unleashing the power of emotional intelligence*. Harvard Business Press.

Guerrero, M., Urbano, D., & Gajón, E. (2020). Entrepreneurial university ecosystems and graduates' career patterns: Do entrepreneurship education programmes and university business incubators matter? *Journal of Management Development*, *39*(5), 753–775. doi:10.1108/JMD-10-2019-0439

Hameed, I., Ijaz, M. U., & Sabharwal, M. (2022). The impact of human resources environment and organizational identification on employees' psychological well-being. *Public Personnel Management*, *51*(1), 71–96. doi:10.1177/00910260211001397

Hayashi, A., & Ewert, A. (2006). Outdoor leaders' emotional intelligence and transformational leadership. *Journal of Experiential Education*, *28*(3), 222–242. doi:10.1177/105382590602800305

Hoecht, A., & Trott, P. (2006). Innovation risks of strategic outsourcing. *Technovation*, *26*(5-6), 672–681. doi:10.1016/j.technovation.2005.02.004

Huang, L. C., Ahlstrom, D., Lee, A. Y. P., Chen, S. Y., & Hsieh, M. J. (2016). High performance work systems, employee well-being, and job involvement: An empirical study. *Personnel Review*, *45*(2), 296–314. doi:10.1108/PR-09-2014-0201

Hussain, M., & Khan, S. M. (2016). Leadership Qualities of Administrators in the Light of Seerat-Ul-Nabi (Saw). *Abha'th*, *1*(4), 17.

Ingram, A., Peake, W.O., Stewart, W., & Watson, W. (2017). Emotional Intelligence and Venture Performance. *Journal of Small Business Management*. doi:10.1111/jsbm.12333

Jena, L. K., & Goyal, S. (2022). Emotional intelligence and employee innovation: Sequential mediating effect of person-group fit and adaptive performance. *European Review of Applied Psychology*, *72*(1), 100729. doi:10.1016/j.erap.2021.100729

Kirkwood, J. J. (2016). How women and men business owners perceive success. *International Journal of Entrepreneurial Behaviour & Research*, *22*(5), 594–615. doi:10.1108/IJEBR-01-2016-0024

Laursen, K., Masciarelli, F., & Prencipe, A. (2012). Regions matter: How localized social capital affects innovation and external knowledge acquisition. *Organization Science*, *23*(1), 177–193. doi:10.1287/orsc.1110.0650

Lea, R. G., Qualter, P., Davis, S. K., Pérez-González, J. C., & Bangee, M. (2018). Trait emotional intelligence and attentional bias for positive emotion: An eye tracking study. *Personality and Individual Differences*, *128*, 88–93. doi:10.1016/j.paid.2018.02.017

Lee, T. K. W., Castilho, A., Cheung, V. C. H., Tang, K. H., Ma, S., & Ng, I. O. L. (2011). CD24+ liver tumor-initiating cells drive self-renewal and tumor initiation through STAT3-mediated NANOG regulation. *Cell Stem Cell*, *9*(1), 50–63. doi:10.1016/j.stem.2011.06.005 PMID:21726833

Littunen, H. (2000). Entrepreneurship and the characteristics of the entrepreneurial personality. *International Journal of Entrepreneurial Behaviour & Research*, *6*(6), 295–310. doi:10.1108/13552550010362741

Lopetcharat, K., Paredes, D., & Beckley, J. H. (2022). Future Trends and Direction. *Product Innovation Toolbox: A Field Guide to Consumer Understanding and Research*, 509-519.

MacCann, C., Erbas, Y., Dejonckheere, E., Minbashian, A., Kuppens, P., & Fayn, K. (2020). Emotional in- telligence relates to emotions, emotion dynamics, and emotion complexity: A meta-analysis and experience sampling study. *European Journal of Psychological Assessment*, *36*, 460. doi:10.1027/1015-5759/a000588

Mayer, J. D., Caruso, D. R., & Salovey, P. (2016). The ability model of emotional intelligence: Principles and updates. *Emotion Review*, *8*(4), 290–300. doi:10.1177/1754073916639667

McCann, P., & Soete, L. (2020). *Place-based innovation for sustainability.* Publications Office of the European Union.

Modassir, A., & Singh, T. (2008). *Relationship of emotional intelligence with transformational leadership and organizational citizenship*. Academic Press.

Modassir & Singh. (2008). Relationship of Emotional Intelligence with Transformational Leadership and Organizational Citizenship Behavior. *International Journal of Leadership Studies*, *4*(4), 3–21.

Nabi, G., & Khan, S. (2020). Risk of COVID-19 pneumonia in aquatic mammals. *Environmental Research*, *188*, 109732. doi:10.1016/j.envres.2020.109732 PMID:32502685

Newman, A., Herman, H. M., Schwarz, G., & Nielsen, I. (2018). The effects of employees' creative self-efficacy on innovative behavior: The role of entrepreneurial leadership. *Journal of Business Research*, *89*, 1–9. doi:10.1016/j.jbusres.2018.04.001

Ngah, R., & Salleh, Z. (2015). Emotional intelligence and entrepreneurs' innovativeness towards entrepreneurial success: A preliminary study. *American Journal of Economics*, *5*(2), 285–290.

Nouman, H., & Cnaan, R. A. (2021). Toolbox recommendations for social workers to promote successful social entrepreneurship. *Social Work*, *66*(4), 317–328. doi:10.1093wwab037 PMID:34458923

Odame, C., Pandey, M., & Pathak, P. (2020). Emotional Intelligence and Its Importance in Sustainable Development of Human Resources: A Conceptual Model. *Sustainable Human Resource Management: Transforming Organizations, Societies and Environment*, 273-287.

Oju, O. (2017). Impact of innovation on the entrepreneurial success in selected business enterprises in South-West Nigeria. In *Driving Innovation and Business Success in the Digital Economy* (pp. 16–25). IGI Global. doi:10.4018/978-1-5225-1779-5.ch002

Oncioiu, I. (Ed.). (2013). *Business innovation, development, and advancement in the digital economy*. IGI Global. doi:10.4018/978-1-4666-2934-9

Park, B., Knörzer, L., Plass, J. L., & Brünken, R. (2015). Emotional design and positive emotions in multimedia learning: An eyetracking study on the use of anthropomorphisms. *Computers & Education*, *86*, 30–42. doi:10.1016/j.compedu.2015.02.016

Pathak, S., & Muralidharan, E. (2020). Implications of culturally implicit perspective of emotional intelligence. *Cross-Cultural Research*, *54*(5), 502–533. doi:10.1177/1069397120938690

Pathak, S., & Muralidharan, E. (2020). A two-staged approach to technology entrepreneurship: Differential effects of intellectual property rights. *Technology Innovation Management Review*, *10*(6), 5–13. doi:10.22215/timreview/1364

Polizzi, C. P., & Lynn, S. J. (2021). Regulating emotionality to manage adversity: A systematic review of the relation between emotion regulation and psychological resilience. *Cognitive Therapy and Research*, *45*(4), 1–21. doi:10.100710608-020-10186-1

Polizzi, C. P., & Lynn, S. J. (2021). Regulating emotionality to manage adversity: A systematic review of the relation between emotion regulation and psychological resilience. *Cognitive Therapy and Research*, *45*(4), 577–597. doi:10.100710608-020-10186-1

Riederer, J. P., Baier, M., & Graefe, G. (2005). Innovation management–An overview and some best practices. *C-Lab Report, 4*(3), 1-58.

Rinfret, N., Laplante, J., Lagacé, M. C., Deschamps, C., & Privé, C. (2020). Impacts of leadership styles in health and social services: A case from Quebec exploring relationships between emotional intelligence and transformational leadership. *International Journal of Healthcare Management*, *13*(1), 329–339. do i:10.1080/20479700.2018.1548153

Salovey, P., & Mayer, J. (1989). Emotional Intelligence. *Imagination, Cognition and Personality*, *9*(3), 185–211. doi:10.2190/DUGG-P24E-52WK-6CDG

Samadi, A., & Keyvan, N. (2013). A study on emotional intelligence of teachers in establishing the effective communication. *Governmental Management*, *1*, 129–148.

Shojaei, M., & Siuki, M. (2014). A study of relationship between emotional intelligence and innovative work behavior of managers. *Management Science Letters*, *4*(7), 1449–1454. doi:10.5267/j.msl.2014.6.021

Shujahat, M., Sousa, M. J., Hussain, S., Nawaz, F., Wang, M., & Umer, M. (2019). Translating the impact of knowledge management processes into knowledge-based innovation: The neglected and mediating role of knowledge-worker productivity. *Journal of Business Research*, *94*, 442–450. doi:10.1016/j.jbusres.2017.11.001

Smith, R., Killgore, W. D., Alkozei, A., & Lane, R. D. (2018). A neuro-cognitive process model of emotional intelligence. *Biological Psychology*, *139*, 131–151. doi:10.1016/j.biopsycho.2018.10.012 PMID:30392827

Solymossy, E. (1997). Push/pull motivation: Does it matter in venture performance. *Frontiers of Entrepreneurship Research, 17*(5), 204-217.

Spiegel, M., & Tookes, H. (2022). All or nothing? Partial business shutdowns and COVID-19 fatality growth. *PLoS One*, *17*(2), e0262925. doi:10.1371/journal.pone.0262925 PMID:35139100

Tanphan, I., Pongsamran, S., Saounpong, R., Visitnitikija, C., Yeesoontes, W., & Mahamud, T. (2022). Lessons from Entrepreneurs Covid-19 Affecting in Resource Work in Business Digital Approach. *Journal of Positive School Psychology*, 6182–6191.

Thirumalesh Madanaguli, A., Kaur, P., Bresciani, S., & Dhir, A. (2021). Entrepreneurship in rural hospitality and tourism. A systematic literature review of past achievements and future promises. *International Journal of Contemporary Hospitality Management*, *33*(8), 2521–2558. doi:10.1108/IJCHM-09-2020-1121

Valodkienė, G., & Snieška, V. (2012). Tarptautinis konkurencingumas ir jį lemiantys veiksniai ekonomikos nuosmukio laikotarpiu. *Economics and Management, 17*(2), 602-608.

Vasudevan, H. (2013). The influence of emotional intelligence and creativity on employee's work commitment and performance. *International Journal of Management and Business Research*, *3*(3), 233–255.

Wach, D., Stephan, U., & Gorgievski, M. (2016). More than money: Developing an integrative multi-factorial measure of entrepreneurial success. *International Small Business Journal*, *34*(8), 1098–1121. doi:10.1177/0266242615608469

Walker, E. A., & Webster, B. J. (2007). Gender, age and self-employment: Some things change, some stay the same. *Women in Management Review*, *22*(2), 122–135. doi:10.1108/09649420710732088

Walmsley, A., Partington, S., Armstrong, R., & Goodwin, H. (2019). Reactions to the national living wage in hospitality. *Employee Relations*, *41*(1), 253–268. doi:10.1108/ER-02-2018-0044

Yitshaki-Hagai, R., & Rothstein, M. (2011). Does entrepreneurs' emotional intelligence impact performance? The mediating role of managerial style and social capital (interactive paper). *Frontiers of Entrepreneurship Research*, *30*(4), 15.

Zhang, L., Cao, T., & Wang, Y. (2018). The mediation role of leadership styles in integrated project collaboration: An emotional intelligence perspective. *International Journal of Project Management*, *36*(2), 317–330. doi:10.1016/j.ijproman.2017.08.014

Zhang, L., Cao, T., & Wang, Y. (2018). The mediation role of leadership styles in integrated project collaboration: An emotional intelligence perspective. *International Journal of Project Management*, *36*(2), 317–330. doi:10.1016/j.ijproman.2017.08.014

Zhang, M. J., Law, K. S., & Wang, L. (2021). The risks and benefits of initiating change at work: Social consequences for proactive employees who take charge. *Personnel Psychology*, *74*(4), 721–750. doi:10.1111/peps.12423

Zhang, X., & Bartol, K. M. (2010). Linking empowering leadership and employee creativity: The influence of psychological empowerment, intrinsic motivation, and creative process engagement. *Academy of Management Journal*, *53*(1), 107–128. doi:10.5465/amj.2010.48037118

Zhou, H., & Bojica, A. M. (2017). The role of emotional intelligence in entrepreneurs' perceptions of success: An exploratory study. *International Review of Entrepreneurship*, *15*(3), 341–360.

ZhouH.EstradaI.BojicaA. (n.d.). The role of emotional intelligence on entrepreneurs' perception of success. doi:10.2139/ssrn.2436333

Zhou, J., & George, J. M. (2003). Awakening employee creativity: The role of leader emotional intelligence. *The Leadership Quarterly*, *14*(4-5), 545–568. doi:10.1016/S1048-9843(03)00051-1

Zimmerer, T. W., Scarborough, N. M., & Wilson, D. (2007). *Essentials of entrepreneurship and small business management* (5th ed.). Pearson Prentice Hall.

Zvobgo, V., Abraham, R., & Sabharwal, M. (2022). Faking Versus Feeling Emotions: Does Personality–Job Fit Make a Difference. *Public Personnel Management*, *51*(1), 125–148. doi:10.1177/00910260211034213

Chapter 4
Emotional Intelligence for Effective Leadership:
Future Research Trends Using Bibliometric Analysis

Rachna Bhopal
https://orcid.org/0000-0003-2954-7838
Central University of Himachal Pradesh, India

Rita Devi
https://orcid.org/0000-0002-9874-8679
Central University of Himachal Pradesh, India

ABSTRACT

Emotional intelligence is the individual's ability to recognize, understand, and manage one's own emotions and to influence the emotions of others. In an organization, the leaders connect emotionally with the employees for the organization's success, growth, sustainability, and development. After the COVID-19 pandemic, effective leadership comes more into action where leaders need to understand, regulate self and others' emotions, and act accordingly for organizational change, development, growth, transformation, and sustainability. The study aims to provide insights into emotional intelligence and effective leadership using bibliometric techniques on 403 Scopus-indexed articles from 2012-2022. The study depicts performance analysis, intellectual structure, and thematic structure of emotional intelligence and leadership effectiveness. The results highlighted the publication trends, themes and derives future research trends by showcasing the role of emotional intelligence in effective leadership for shaping the future of the work.

DOI: 10.4018/979-8-3693-0418-1.ch004

1. INTRODUCTION

Emotional intelligence (EI) is equally important for both an institute and for an individual It holds a special position in the communication process for the organization and its employees (Yao et al., 2019). Salovey and Mayer (1990, p. 189) defined EI as "the subset of social intelligence that involves the ability to monitor one's own and other's feelings and emotions, to discriminate among them and to use this information to guide one's thinking and actions". Goleman (2012), defined EI as "the ability of individuals to recognize others and their own feelings and to manage these emotions". For an individual EI impacts satisfaction towards life, career development, work engagement, and an individual's relationship with peers and friends. For an organization, EI adds to job satisfaction, employee role, performance, and commitment towards the firm. Motivational EI and work-related EI (Bacon & Corr, 2017; Krishnakumar et al., 2017) help people in dealing with emotions and express feelings comfortably. Individuals noticed the emotions, differentiated them from each other, and further managed these emotions by encapsulating EI (Mayer & Salovey, 1990).

According to Mayer et al. (2001), EI is divided into four approaches "the emotional perception, emotional assimilation, emotional comprehension, and the management of the individual's own emotions. The first approach involves the correct identification, expression, and differentiation of emotions; the second approach expresses emotion-based thinking, directing attention to important information; the third approach indicates the ability to recognize feelings between words and emotions and the last approach is the management of the individual's own emotions."

Job satisfaction, career success, and healthy relationships are experienced by individuals with higher EI (Schutte et al., 2007). EI affects individual behavior and possesses a positive relationship with stress and job dissatisfaction (Lee & Ok, 2012). EI affects one's ability to cope with environmental demands and pressures (Shi et al., 2014). Employees with high EI are more satisfied with their jobs, more committed towards their workplace (D'amato and Herzfeldt, 2008) and easily adapt to the work environment (Rozell et al., 2014).

Effective term is added to the quality of the leaders only when they have the power to influence employees in achieving organizational goals (Bodinson, 2005; Vardiman et al., 2006). The emotional competency of effective leader is attained when leader possess the characteristic to handle stress, increase the job outcomes (Rajah et al., 2011). Amagoh (2009) emphasized on the contextual factors to nurture and sustain effective leadership in person.

EI is considered as one of the most important components of the effective leadership, where the strategic decisions of the organization rely on EI for the directional approach (George,2000; Miao et al., 2018). The absence of EI in leaders results in undesired results and situations for the employee and the organization (Ovans, 2015). Antonakis and Dietz (2011); Cavazotte et al. (2012) in the study recognized EI as the antecedent of effective leadership. Emotional intelligence has gained growing prominence both as an assessment tool for identifying individuals with the potential to be effective leaders and as a resource for enhancing the skills necessary for effective leadership (Batool, 2013). Emotional intelligence holds paramount importance within leadership as it enables leaders to proficiently communicate, cultivate robust interpersonal connections, adeptly handle conflicts, and motivate their teams toward the attainment of shared objectives.

Mandell and Pherwani (2003) described transformational and transactional leaders as the two prominent leadership styles comprising the characteristics of effective leadership. Transformational leadership is typically characterized by four key dimensions: idealized influence, inspirational motivation, intellectual stimulation, and individual consideration (Bass &Avolio, 1994). A transactional leader is someone who utilizes a system of rewarding or disciplining staff based on their performance. They place a strong emphasis on maintaining work standards, ensuring task completion, and enforcing employee compliance. Their primary method of influencing employee performance is through the use of organizational rewards and punishments (Bass &Avolio, 1994).These dimensions collectively define the approach and qualities associated with transformational and transactional leaders. Emotional intelligence is associated with multiple aspects of transformational leadership, indicating that it plays a significant role in effective leadership (Palmer et al., 2001). Researchers exploring the impacts of transformational and transactional leadership have discovered that transformational leadership tends to lead to higher assessments of effectiveness and satisfaction (Bass et al., 2003), improved group performance, and increased effort from subordinates (Seltzer & Bass, 1990), as compared to transactional leadership.

The descriptive framework along with bibliometric analysis is performed to identify key trends, influential studies, prominent authors, and emerging research areas. This analysis is widely operated on a large volume of scientific data (Donthu et al., 2021). The bibliometric literature review provides valuable insights for further research in the subject domain (Pattnaik et al., 2020). The following seven research questions are addressed to investigate the research issues.

RQ (1) What is the current trend of research for EI?
RQ (2) Which journals and articles contributed the most to scientific research in this field?
RQ (3) Which are the most contributing countries and authors in the area of EI?
RQ (4) Which keywords, co-occurrence networks, and clusters are the most frequent?
RQ (5) Which are prominent themes prevailing in the area of EI?
RQ (6) What is the role of EI in effective leadership?
RQ (7) What are the future research trends and challenges for EI and Leadership?

Bibliometric analysis is used to analyze the research questions RQ(1), RQ(2), RQ(3), RQ(4), RQ(5), and the secondary data review is performed to analyze questions RQ(6), RQ(7).

The bibliometric analysis identified the trends and gaps in the research on emotional intelligence and leadership. The future research directions are guided by the outcomes of the study to improve the understanding of the relationship between emotional intelligence and leadership for developing interventions in improving leadership effectiveness.

2. RESEARCH METHODS AND STUDY DESIGN

The study is an outcome of bibliometric analyses and a literature review of secondary data from Scopus and other publications. Bibliometric work analyse and classify the studies by framing graphical summaries of the previous work (Donthu et al., 2020)

2.1 Search Strategy and Data Retrieval Process

The data retrieval process from Scopus database used the search criteria as explained in given table (see "Table 1"). The search strategy involves selecting relevant keywords, applying search filters, and setting inclusion/exclusion criteria. Boolean operators are employed to construct precise search queries, while citation searching is used to identify related literature. Adopting the bibliometric review approach is critical for gaining a thorough comprehension of the scientific literature related to the field (Durieux & Gevenois, 2010).

TITLE-ABS-KEY ("emotional intelligence" AND " leadership") AND (LIMIT-TO (PUBYEAR, 2022) OR LIMIT-TO (PUBYEAR, 2021) OR LIMIT-TO (PUBYEAR, 2020) OR LIMIT-TO (PUBYEAR, 2019) OR LIMIT-TO (PUBYEAR, 2018) OR LIMIT-TO (PUBYEAR, 2017) OR LIMIT-TO (PUBYEAR, 2016) OR LIMIT-TO (PUBYEAR, 2015) OR LIMIT-TO (PUBYEAR, 2014)) AND (LIMIT-TO (SUBJAREA, "BUSI") OR LIMIT-TO (SUBJAREA, "SOCI") OR LIMIT-TO (SUBJAREA, "PSYC") OR LIMIT-TO (SUBJAREA, "ECON")) AND (LIMIT-TO (LANGUAGE, "English")) AND (LIMIT-TO (DOCTYPE, "ar") OR LIMIT-TO (DOCTYPE, "ch") OR LIMIT-TO (DOCTYPE, "re"))

Table 1. Bibliographic data retrieval process

Stage	Filtering Criteria	Eliminated	Accepted
1	Initial search result (on search term)	-	1708
2	Year filter (2012-2022)	628	1080
3	Subject filter (Economics, Econometrics, Business, Management and Accounting, Psychology, and Social Sciences)	407	673
4	Language filter (English)	28	645
5	Document Type (Article, Review, Book Chapter)	79	566
6	Scimago ranking (Q1,Q2,Q3)	163	403

Source: Authors' own findings

The data were subjected to bibliometric analysis using the R 4.0.3 package programme. "Biblioshiny," an R-based library and "Bibliometric'" web-based interface. Bibliometrics is an open-source software, has the features of flexibility, rapid upgrade and integration with other statistical R package as it is very useful in an ever-changing science discipline such as Bibliometric (Aria & Cuccurullo, 2017). Unlike other literature review, bibliometric review establishes visualization for large amount of domain specific data (Goodell et al., 2021).

3. RESULTS AND DISCUSSION

3.1 Publication Activity

Figure 1 shows an increasing line graph for research trend in publications of emotional intelligence from 2014-2022. The graph depicts that the majority of the work on emotional intelligence is on year 2022. The scientific production of articles in the field is constantly increasing with annual growth rate of 16.11%. The rising trajectory of this trend is raising growing apprehension among researchers and academics in this research domain.

Figure 1. Research trend in publication from 2014-2022
Source: Author's own findings

3.2 Most Influential Journals

The top 10 journals publishing the content on emotional intelligence, the name of publisher, h index, and SCimago ranking of the journal are presented in tabular form (see Table 2). Leadership And Organization Development Journal from Emerald Group Publishing Ltd. Publishers adds highest to the study with 15 articles. The high-impact journals, validated through bibliometrics, enhances the credibility of the research. It serves as a stamp of approval, signifying that the study has met rigorous standards of quality and significance

The majority of the journals contributing to the study are with Q1 and Q2 Scimago ranking. Personality And Individual Differences with highest h index 193 contributes to 12.40% of all the articles under review for the study. The table represents the influence and impact of the sources in the forms of h-index and Scimago ranking.

3.3 Most Cited Articles

The top 10 cited article with highest global citation are represented in the table showing the total count and year of publication (see Table 3). Among the highly cited articles, the work of (Ashkanasy N.M. & Dorris A.D., 2017) "Emotions in the Workplace "attains the topmost position with 208 total citations. Mostly the citation is above 100 or around 100 for top 10 articles. Identifying the most cited articles in the field, aids in building a solid foundation for the new study. It provides information of the latest developments, trends and the studies contributed significantly fir the advancement of knowledge within the field.

Table 2. Top 10 Journals on Emotional Intelligence (authors' own findings)

Journal	Publisher	H Index	Country	Scimago Ranking	Total Articles
Leadership And Organization Development Journal	Emerald Group Publishing Ltd.	78	United Kingdom	Q1	15
Frontiers In Psychology	Frontiers Media S.A.	157	Switzerland	Q2	12
Educational Management Administration And Leadership	SAGE Publications Ltd.	54	United Kingdom	Q1	7
Journal Of Leadership Studies	John Wiley And Sons Ltd	19	United Kingdom	Q3	7
American Journal of Pharmaceutical Education	American Association Of Colleges Of Pharmacy	74	United States	Q1	6
International Journal Of Organizational Analysis	Emerald Group Publishing Ltd.	36	United Kingdom	Q2	5
Leadership In Health Services	Emerald Group Publishing Ltd.	30	United Kingdom	Q2	5
Nurse Education Today	Churchill Livingstone	92	United Kingdom	Q1	5
Personality And Individual Differences	Elsevier BV	193	United Kingdom	Q1	5
Sa Journal Of Industrial Psychology	AOSIS (Pty) Ltd	28	South Africa	Q3	5
Sustainability	MDPI AG	136	Switzerland	Q1	5

Table 3. Top 10 documents with global total citations (TC) (authors' own findings)

Article Title	Author(s)	TC	Year
Emotions in the Workplace	Ashkanasy N.M., Dorris A.D.	208	2017
Job Demands–Resources theory and self-regulation: new explanations and remedies for job burnout	Bakker A.B., de Vries J.D.	195	2021
Emotional Intelligence in Organizations	Côté S.	166	2014
Academic Leadership in a Time of Crisis: The Coronavirus and COVID-19	Fernandez A.A., Shaw G.P.	157	2020
Leader emotional intelligence and subordinate job satisfaction: A meta-analysis of main, mediator, and moderator effects	Miao C., Humphrey R.H., Qian S.	115	2016
Beyond metrics? Utilizing 'soft intelligence' for healthcare quality and safety	Martin G.P., McKee L., Dixon-Woods M.	111	2015
The Impact of Emotional Intelligence, Project Managers' Competencies, and Transformational Leadership on Project Success: An Empirical Perspective	Maqbool R., Sudong Y., Manzoor N., Rashid Y.	107	2017
Exploring the affective impact, boundary conditions, and antecedents of leader humility	Wang L., Owens B.P., Jason Li J., Shi L.	96	2018
Emotions and salesperson propensity to leave: The effects of emotional intelligence and resilience	Bande B., Fernandez-Ferrin P., Varela j.A., Jaramillo F.	91	2015
Emotional intelligence, emotional labor, coach burnout, job satisfaction, and turnover intention in sport leadership	Lee Y.H., Chelladurai P.	83	2018

3.4 Most Cited Countries

The scientific production of articles on emotional intelligence by top 10 countries are presented in a tabular form (see Table 4). USA holds the topmost position with maximum count of 1490 publications with 12.6 article citation frequency. The highest publication by the developed nation indicates the increasing trend of research on emotional intelligence. India stands on twelfth rank with 88 total citations. The global leaders in the area of study are recognized to facilitate the international collaboration.

Table 4. The most cited countries (authors' own findings)

Country	TC	Average Article Citations
USA	1490	12.6
CHINA	530	21.2
UNITED KINGDOM	281	12.2
CANADA	260	23.6
NETHERLANDS	247	82.3
AUSTRALIA	206	17.2
SPAIN	144	11.1
KOREA	107	17.8
SOUTH AFRICA	101	5.3
MALAYSIA	100	8.3
GHANA	93	15.5
INDIA	88	4.4

3.5 Most Relevant Authors

The most relevant ten authors contributing to the study on emotional intelligence is represented in the Figure 2. Dartey-Baah K. and Humphrey RH. have published 5 articles each on the emotional intelligence. Whereas the other contributing authors Kareem OA., Kin TM., Lorber M., Martin J., Miao C., Mulmel D., and Nafukho FM. have contributed to the literature with 4 articles each on the emotional intelligence. Understanding the work of relevant authors is analogous to unraveling the intricate web of scholarly influence. It provides researchers with the skill to adeptly traverse complex citation networks, follow the lineage of ideas, and pinpoint seminal works that have exerted a profound and transformative influence on the field's evolution.

3.6 Relationship Between Keywords

Figure 3 represents the co-occurrence network showing the relationship between keywords constituting the three clusters presenting the thematic analysis of co-citation network (Xu et al., 2018). Cluster 1 (red coloured) consists 35 keywords, cluster 2 (blue coloured) consists 10 keywords, and cluster 3 (green coloured) is formed of 5 keywords. The relatedness of the items in the clusters can be explained by the distance between them (Goyal & Kumar, 2020). The keywords revealed the web of relationships among different research areas, underpins the robustness and effectiveness of scholarly investigations across various fields of study. Accurate and targeted keyword selection ensures researchers to retrieve pertinent and comprehensive sources for research leading to enhanced the quality of work

Figure 2. Most relevant authors
Source: Authors' own findings

Figure 3. Co-occurrence network
Source: Biblioshiny

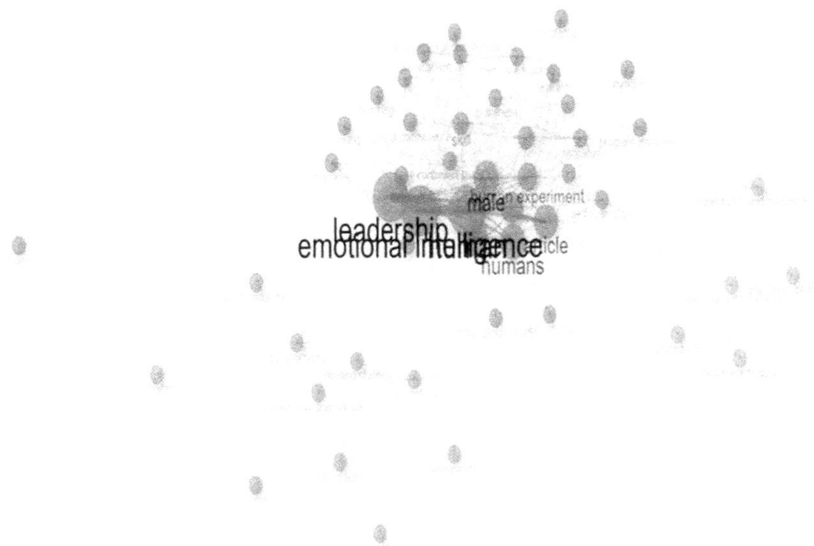

Figure 4 represents the word count depicting emotional intelligence and leadership as the most explored keywords. Co-occurrence of authors' specified keywords identifies the spatial links among the research on emotional intelligence (Baker et al., 2021). Keyword leadership constitutes to 12% and keyword emotional intelligence to 11% with 128 and 122 articles on them. The keywords contribute to conceptual clarity. A word count transforms text into tags, where the prominence and significance of words are visually represented in the resulting cloud based on their size and color.

Figure 4. Word count
Source: Biblioshiny

3.7 Prominent Themes

The thematic map in Figure 5 represents the research interest and future research direction. The map is formed with four clusters present in various themes. Emotional intelligence and leadership forms the cluster in motor theme (3rd quadrant) directing the current research trend. The dense cluster is formed in the motor theme representing the high emergence of the topic. Motor themes are regarded as both highly developed and essential for organizing the research domain. It represents the transdisciplinary research issues where ross-pollination of ideas can lead to innovative research and collaboration opportunities.

3.8 Role of Emotional Intelligence in Effective Leadership

Managing emotions and monitoring emotions were associated significantly with transformational leadership. Leaders paying special attention to the subordinate needs and achievements get more considerations from the individuals as these leaders sense the subordinate needs (Yammarino *et al.*, 1993). Transformational leaders utilize the EI, and stimulate their subordinates by presenting them with new ideas and new approaches to old issues (Bass, 1985). Creative thinking and flexible planning of EI (Avolio *et al.*, 1991) is needed by transformational leaders (Avolio *et al.*, 1991) to assimilate emotions into thoughts (Salovey and Mayer, 1990). EI used to manage emotions in oneself and others, is an essential competency for transformational leadership (Carless, 1998). Mills (2009) in a meta analysis study affirmed the positive influence of EI on leadership effectiveness. The motivated leaders inspire subordinates to work towards common goals by managing the emotion both within themselves and others (Palmer et al., 2001).

Figure 5. Thematic map
Source: Biblioshiny

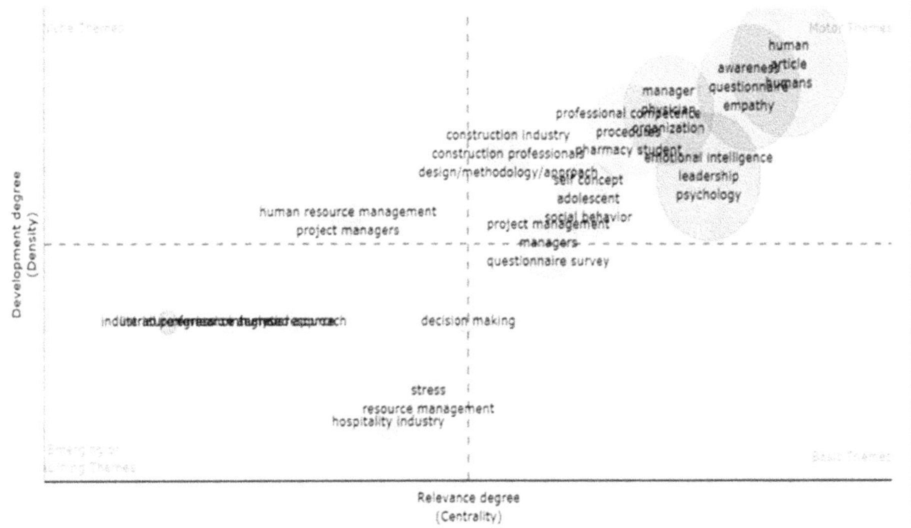

Saha et al., (2023) described the importance of EI in leadership roles, the manifestation of leadership, for human resource management by leaders, and in leadership congruence. The meta-analysis and review studies agreed that EI is the trait of an individual predicting the outcome (Harms and Cred_e, 2010; Barbuto et al., 2014; Miao et al., 2018a, b). The trait leadership competency predicts the outcome of leadership effectiveness when EI is involved by leaders.

3.9 Future Research Trends and Challenges for EI and Leadership

Future Research Trends

EI is identified as a promising attribute of leaders that may be advantageous in the selection criteria for identifying effective leaders. The knowledge driven from EI and effectiveness studies of the leaders may emerge as a powerful tool for enhancing organization's performance by using it in the selection, training, and development process of the leaders.

Future research in EI and effective leadership will identify new skills based purely on emotions that can be used for individual training, job satisfaction, and development. EI in effective leadership helps to achieve organizational growth, success, development, and sustainability (George, 2000; Wong and Law, 2002; Cavazotte et al., 2012; Madanchian et al., 2017). Leadership effectiveness is build on the clear vision, mission, perfect strategies, and conduciveness to growth to attain organizational outcomes.

Future research in the field of Emotional Intelligence (EI) and effective leadership should prioritize investigating causal relationships, refining assessment tools, and exploring the contextual and cultural nuances of EI's impact on leadership effectiveness. Longitudinal studies tracking the development of EI in leaders over time, its influence on team dynamics, and its role in ethical and sustainable leadership are crucial areas to explore. Cross-disciplinary collaboration and research that integrates psychology, organizational behavior, neuroscience, and ethics will provide a more comprehensive understanding of how EI contributes to organizational growth, success, development, and sustainability, thereby offering valuable insights for organizations aiming to enhance their leadership practices.

Challenges

Cultivating the EI in leadership role brings in array of challenges with it to manage and articulate the emotions. The leader needs to develop self awareness and regulate their emotions in way to avoid personal biasness in influencing the decisions. The leader needs to maintain the professional boundaries while balancing emotions and understanding diverse subordinates. The challenge arises in avoiding misinterpretation while resonating the emotions with active listening. The organizations lack ideas on providing comprehensive EI training and measuring its impact on effective leadership. These challenges require self reflection, learning, and practical implementation of EI to develop stronger and effective leadership.

4. LIMITATIONS

To stimulate the future research in this field, the paper is limited in several ways. The bibliometric approach is undertaken to review the papers on EI and leadership, which is only limited to the objective overview. The systematic and meta-analysis review may derive more insights of the topic under study. The paper lacks the critical review on the effect of EI and its importance for effective leadership. This study is limited to bibliometric and bibliographic data retrieved from the Scopus database. More databases like web of science, ProQuest can be included to increase the number of documents. The study is review-based analysis so the outcomes are dependent only on the secondary data. For more accurate results the study using primary data should be taken. Despite these limitations the bibliometric review identifies the pertinent gaps through objective amalgamation of the literature.

5. CONCLUSION

The study provided the bibliometric review on the literature of EI and leadership for past 10 years. The analysis represented the future increasing research trends in the number of applications and number of citations. The study highlighted the importance of EI in effective leadership to achieve organizational growth and success. The paper highlighted the performance analyis (trends in publication activity and top articles, authors, countries and journals), intellectual structure (themes and topic), and thematic structure of to reveal the information on existing research trends for EI and leadership. The paper shed light on the future research trends and challenges and showcased the role of EI in effective leadership for shaping the organizational outcomes. The study underscores the pivotal role of Emotional Intelligence in effective leadership, emphasizing its potential to shape organizational outcomes positively. This study not only served as a review of the past decade's literature but also as a beacon guiding future research efforts in the dynamic intersection of EI and leadership.

Leaders who possess crucial skill of Emotional Intelligence can cultivate workplace environments that foster innovation and open communication. They create spaces where employees feel safe to take calculated risks and freely share their ideas. Additionally, they excel in making tough decisions, adeptly resolving conflicts, and displaying adaptability in response to evolving business objectives and situations. The absence of emotional intelligence impairs a leader's capacity to engage in effective collaboration and communication with others. When a leader struggles to manage their own emotions, it can diminish employees' willingness to openly contribute their ideas and can limit their ability to achieve their highest potential.

6. CONTRIBUTION OF THE STUDY

This bibliometric study examines the relationship between emotional intelligence and effective leadership and offers a structured, data-driven approach to understanding this critical intersection of psychology and leadership. By quantifying the impact, trends, and key themes in the existing body of literature, these studies help researchers pinpoint influential authors and publications, identify research gaps, and track the evolution of this field over time. Furthermore, they assist policymakers, educators, and organizational leaders in making evidence-based decisions regarding leadership development programs and practices. In essence, bibliometric analyses contribute to evidence-based decision-making, guiding the development of leadership training programs and organizational practices that harness the power of emotional intelligence for more effective leadership. Leaders who posses crucial skill of Emotioanl Intelligence can cultivate workplace environments that foster innovation and open communication. They create spaces where employees feel safe to take calculated risks and freely share their ideas. Additionally, they excel in making tough decisions, adeptly resolving conflicts, and displaying adaptability in response to evolving business objectives and situations.

REFERENCES

Amagoh, F. (2009). Leadership development and leadership effectiveness. *Management Decision*, *47*(6), 989–999. doi:10.1108/00251740910966695

Antonakis, J., & Dietz, J. (2011). Looking for validity or testing it? The perils of stepwise regression, extreme-scores analysis, heteroscedasticity, and measurement error. *Personality and Individual Differences*, *50*(3), 409–415. doi:10.1016/j.paid.2010.09.014

Aria, M., & Cuccurullo, C. (2017). bibliometrix: An R-tool for comprehensive science mapping analysis. *Journal of Informetrics*, *11*(4), 959–975. doi:10.1016/j.joi.2017.08.007

Ashkanasy, N. M., & Dorris, A. D. (2017). Emotions in the workplace. *Annual Review of Organizational Psychology and Organizational Behavior*, *4*(1), 67–90. doi:10.1146/annurev-orgpsych-032516-113231

Bacon, A. M., & Corr, P. J. (2017). Motivating emotional intelligence: A reinforcement sensitivity theory (RST) perspective. *Motivation and Emotion*, *41*(2), 254–264. doi:10.100711031-017-9602-1

Baker, H. K., Kumar, S., & Pattnaik, D. (2021). Twenty-five years of the Journal of Corporate Finance: A scientometric analysis. *Journal of Corporate Finance, 66*, 101572.

Bakker, A. B., & de Vries, J. D. (2021). Job Demands–Resources theory and self-regulation: New explanations and remedies for job burnout. *Anxiety, Stress, and Coping*, *34*(1), 1–21. doi:10.1080/10615806.2020.1797695 PMID:32856957

Bande, B., Fernández-Ferrín, P., Varela, J. A., & Jaramillo, F. (2015). Emotions and salesperson propensity to leave: The effects of emotional intelligence and resilience. *Industrial Marketing Management*, *44*, 142–153. doi:10.1016/j.indmarman.2014.10.011

Barbuto, J. E. Jr, Gottfredson, R. K., & Searle, T. P. (2014). An examination of emotional intelligence as an antecedent of servant leadership. *Journal of Leadership & Organizational Studies*, *21*(3), 315–323. doi:10.1177/1548051814531826

Bass, B. M., & Avolio, B. J. (1994). Transformational leadership and organizational culture. *International Journal of Public Administration*, *17*(3-4), 541–554. doi:10.1080/01900699408524907

Bass, B. M., Avolio, B. J., Jung, D. I., & Berson, Y. (2003). Predicting unit performance by assessing transformational and transactional leadership. *The Journal of Applied Psychology*, *88*(2), 207–218. doi:10.1037/0021-9010.88.2.207 PMID:12731705

Batool, B. F. (2013). Emotional intelligence and effective leadership. *Journal of Business Studies Quarterly*, *4*(3), 84.

Bodinson, G. W. (2005). Change healthcare organizations from good to great. *Quality Progress*, *38*(11), 22–29.

Carless, S. (1998). Assessing the discriminant validity of transformational leader behavior as measured by the MLQ. *Journal of Occupational and Organizational Psychology*, *71*(4), 353–359. doi:10.1111/j.2044-8325.1998.tb00681.x

Cavazotte, F., Moreno, V., & Hickmann, M. (2012). Effects of leader intelligence, personality and emotional intelligence on transformational leadership and managerial performance. *The Leadership Quarterly*, *23*(3), 443–455. doi:10.1016/j.leaqua.2011.10.003

Côté, S. (2014). Emotional intelligence in organizations. *Annual Review of Organizational Psychology and Organizational Behavior*, *1*(1), 459–488. doi:10.1146/annurev-orgpsych-031413-091233

D'Amato, A., & Herzfeldt, R. (2008). Learning orientation, organizational commitment and talent retention across generations: A study of European managers. *Journal of Managerial Psychology*, *23*(8), 929–953. doi:10.1108/02683940810904402

Donthu, N., Kumar, S., Mukherjee, D., Pandey, N., & Lim, W. M. (2021). How to conduct a bibliometric analysis: An overview and guidelines. *Journal of Business Research*, *133*, 285296. doi:10.1016/j.jbusres.2021.04.070

Donthu, N., Kumar, S., & Pattnaik, D. (2020). Forty-five years of Journal of Business Research: A bibliometric analysis. *Journal of Business Research*, *109*, 1–14. doi:10.1016/j.jbusres.2019.10.039

Durieux, V., & Gevenois, P. A. (2010). Bibliometric indicators: Quality measurements of scientific publication. *Radiology*, *255*(2), 342–351. doi:10.1148/radiol.09090626 PMID:20413749

Fernandez, A. A., & Shaw, G. P. (2020). Academic leadership in a time of crisis: The Coronavirus and COVID-19. *Journal of Leadership Studies*, *14*(1), 39–45. doi:10.1002/jls.21684

George, J. M. (2000). Emotions and leadership: The role of emotional intelligence. *Human Relations*, *53*(8), 1027–1055. doi:10.1177/0018726700538001

Goleman, D. (1995). *Emotional Intelligence*. Bantam Book.

Goodell, J. W., Kumar, S., Lim, W. M., & Pattnaik, D. (2021). Artificial intelligence and machine learning in finance: Identifying foundations, themes, and research clusters from bibliometric analysis. *Journal of Behavioral and Experimental Finance*, *32*, 100577. doi:10.1016/j.jbef.2021.100577

Harms, P. D., & Credé, M. (2010). Emotional intelligence and transformational and transactional leadership: A meta-analysis. *Journal of Leadership & Organizational Studies*, *17*(1), 5–17. doi:10.1177/1548051809350894

Krishnakumar, S., Hopkins, K., & Robinson, M. D. (2017). When feeling poorly at work does not mean acting poorly at work: The moderating role of work-related emotional intelligence. *Motivation and Emotion*, *41*(1), 122–134. doi:10.100711031-016-9588-0

Lee, J. J., & Ok, C. (2012). Reducing burnout and enhancing job satisfaction: Critical role of hotel employees' emotional intelligence and emotional labor. *International Journal of Hospitality Management*, *31*(4), 1101–1112. doi:10.1016/j.ijhm.2012.01.007

Lee, Y. H., & Chelladurai, P. (2018). Emotional intelligence, emotional labor, coach burnout, job satisfaction, and turnover intention in sport leadership. *European Sport Management Quarterly*, *18*(4), 393–412. doi:10.1080/16184742.2017.1406971

Madanchian, M., Hussein, N., Noordin, F., & Taherdoost, H. (2017). Leadership effectiveness measurement and its effect on organization outcomes. *Procedia Engineering*, *181*, 1043–1048. doi:10.1016/j.proeng.2017.02.505

Mandell, B., & Pherwani, S. (2003). Relationship Between Emotional Intelligence and Transformational Leadership Style: A Gender Comparison. *Journal of Business and Psychology*, *17*(3), 387–404. doi:10.1023/A:1022816409059

Maqbool, R., Sudong, Y., Manzoor, N., & Rashid, Y. (2017). The impact of emotional intelligence, project managers' competencies, and transformational leadership on project success: An empirical perspective. *Project Management Journal*, *48*(3), 58–75. doi:10.1177/875697281704800304

Martin, G. P., McKee, L., & Dixon-Woods, M. (2015). Beyond metrics? Utilizing 'soft intelligence' for healthcare quality and safety. *Social Science & Medicine*, *142*, 19–26. doi:10.1016/j.socscimed.2015.07.027 PMID:26282705

Mayer, J. D., & Salovey, P. (1990). Perceiving affective content in ambiguous visual stimuli: A component of emotional intelligence. *Journal of Personality Assessment*, *54*(3), 772–781. doi:10.120715327752jpa5403&4_29 PMID:2348356

Miao, C., Humphrey, R. H., & Qian, S. (2016). Leader emotional intelligence and subordinate job satisfaction: A meta-analysis of main, mediator, and moderator effects. *Personality and Individual Differences*, *102*, 13–24. doi:10.1016/j.paid.2016.06.056

Miao, C., Humphrey, R. H., & Qian, S. (2018a). Emotional intelligence and authentic leadership: A meta-analysis. *Leadership and Organization Development Journal*, *39*(5), 679–690. doi:10.1108/LODJ-02-2018-0066

Miao, C., Humphrey, R. H., & Qian, S. (2018b). A cross-cultural meta-analysis of how leader emotional intelligence influences subordinate task performance and organizational citizenship behavior. *Journal of World Business*, *53*(4), 463–474. doi:10.1016/j.jwb.2018.01.003

Mills, L. B. (2009). A meta-analysis of the relationship between emotional intelligence and effective leadership. *Journal of Curriculum and Instruction*, *3*(2), 22–38. doi:10.3776/joci.2009.v3n2p22

Ovans, A. (2015). How emotional intelligence became a key leadership skill. *Harvard Business Review*, *28*, 3–6.

Palmer, B., Walls, M., Burgess, Z., & Stough, C. (2001). Emotional intelligence and effective leadership. *Leadership and Organization Development Journal*, *22*(1), 5–10. doi:10.1108/01437730110380174

Pattnaik, D., Kumar, S., & Vashishtha, A. (2020). Research on trade credit – a systematic review and bibliometric analysis. *Qualitative Research in Financial Markets*, *12*(4), 367–390. doi:10.1108/QRFM-09-2019-0103

Rajah, R., Song, Z., & Arvey, R. D. (2011). Emotionality and leadership: Taking stock of the past decade of research. *The Leadership Quarterly*, *22*(6), 1107–1119. doi:10.1016/j.leaqua.2011.09.006

Rozell, E. J., Pettijohn, C. E., & Parker, R. S. (2004). Customer-oriented selling: Exploring the roles of emotional intelligence and organizational commitment. *Psychology and Marketing*, *21*(6), 405–424. doi:10.1002/mar.20011

Saha, S., Das, R., Lim, W. M., Kumar, S., Malik, A., & Chillakuri, B. (2023). Emotional intelligence and leadership: Insights for leading by feeling in the future of work. *International Journal of Manpower*, *44*(4), 671–701. doi:10.1108/IJM-12-2021-0690

Salovey, P., & Mayer, J. D. (1990). "Emotional intelligence", imagination. *Imagination, Cognition and Personality*, *9*(3), 185–211. doi:10.2190/DUGG-P24E-52WK-6CDG

Schutte, N. S., Malouff, J. M., Thorsteinsson, E. B., Bhullar, N., & Rooke, S. E. (2007). A meta-analytic investigation of the relationship between emotional intelligence and health. *Personality and Individual Differences*, *42*(6), 921–933. doi:10.1016/j.paid.2006.09.003

Seltzer, J., & Bass, B. M. (1990). Transformational leadership: Beyond initiation and consideration. *Journal of Management*, *16*(4), 693–703. doi:10.1177/014920639001600403

Shi, Y., Prentice, C., & He, W. (2014). Linking service quality, customer satisfaction and loyalty in casinos, does membership matter? *International Journal of Hospitality Management*, *40*, 81–91. doi:10.1016/j.ijhm.2014.03.013

Vardiman, P. D., Houghton, J. D., & Jinkerson, D. L. (2006). Environmental leadership development: Toward a contextual model of leader selection and effectiveness. *Leadership and Organization Development Journal*, *27*(2), 93–105. doi:10.1108/01437730610646606

Wang, L., Owens, B. P., Li, J. J., & Shi, L. (2018). Exploring the affective impact, boundary conditions, and antecedents of leader humility. *The Journal of Applied Psychology*, *103*(9), 1019–1038. doi:10.1037/apl0000314 PMID:29781636

Wong, C. S., & Law, K. S. (2002). The effects of leader and follower emotional intelligence on performance and attitude: An exploratory study. *The Leadership Quarterly*, *13*(3), 243–274. doi:10.1016/S1048-9843(02)00099-1

Xu, X., Chen, X., Jia, F., Brown, S., Gong, Y., & Xu, Y. (2018). Supply chain finance: A systematic literature review and bibliometric analysis. *International Journal of Production Economics*, *204*, 160–173. doi:10.1016/j.ijpe.2018.08.003

Yammarino, F. J., Spangler, W. D., & Bass, B. M. (1993). Transformational leadership and performance: A longitudinal investigation. *The Leadership Quarterly*, *4*(1), 81–102. doi:10.1016/1048-9843(93)90005-E

Yao, S., Wang, X., Yu, H., & Guchait, P. (2019). Effectiveness of error management training in the hospitality industry: Impact on perceived fairness and service recovery performance. *International Journal of Hospitality Management*, *79*, 78–88. doi:10.1016/j.ijhm.2018.12.009

Chapter 5
Leveraging AI for the Reinforcement of GHRM

Anshima
https://orcid.org/0000-0001-8178-4123
Central University of Himachal Pradesh, India

Bhawana Bhardwaj
https://orcid.org/0000-0002-0564-2964
Central University of Himachal Pradesh, India

ABSTRACT

The backbone of any organization is considered its human capital and potential capabilities to lead the competitive and dynamic business environment. This research synthesizes the existing literature substantiated by documentary pieces of evidence to integrate AI and green HR practices to achieve sustainable goals. Green Human Resource Management or GHRM and Artificial Intelligence or AI have emerged to take precedence among the most crucial workplace transformation initiatives. GHRM refers to the systematic, planned alignment of typical human resource management practices with the organization's environmental goal. AI in HRM is the process of stimulating a computer's cognitive intelligence to enhance its effectiveness. This research aims to develop the conceptual framework and offer propositions as the foundation for empirical research. The research will highlight the AI augmentation to green HR practices in furthering sustainability goals. Additionally, the results of the research will be insightful for future researchers to further the literature on AI and GHRM.

1. INTRODUCTION

The corporation is experiencing several transformations at the workplace driven by the advent of Artificial Intelligence and the increased consciousness of individuals over sustainable development. Organizations shifting from conventional work environments to adopting modern business techniques are increasingly aligning with algorithm-based AI and serving sustainable development goals (Prikshat et al., 2023). This

DOI: 10.4018/979-8-3693-0418-1.ch005

trend of AI-HRM and GHRM is increasingly sparking the interest of researchers, academicians, and practitioners all over the world (Vrontis et al., 2021; Townsend et al., 1998; Akpan & Ibidunni;2021). The term "sustainability" has been popular in political leaders' speeches, conference agendas, print media, and other informational contexts. "Artificial intelligence" (AI here onwards) is the other buzzword of the present age which is pervasive at societal, organizational, and government levels all around the world. Anchored on the "Resource-based view" Collins and Clarks (2003), advocate the relevance of strategic advantage of utilizing the organizational capabilities (technology and human capital) to enable HR practices for achieving performance objectives. Renwick et al. (2013) in their seminal paper suggest activating human elements for successful implications of environmental management. The evolution of personal management to strategic human resource management and now sustainable human resource management (Kramar, 2014) covers the wide range of outcomes (financial, social, and environmental) crucial to organizations (Wagner, 2013). Proceeding along the same line of interest, it is interesting to study the role of AI-augmented green HR practices in influencing sustainable development.

The concept of GHRM stemmed from sustainable HRM which has emerged in the past few decades as instrumental for organizational environmental management. According to Deloitte (2022), the demand for green skills is substantially increasing to gain a competitive advantage. Wehrmeyer (1996) first time used the term "Green Human Resource Management" in the book titled *Greening People: Human Resources and Environmental Management.* Further defined by pioneers of the field, GHRM refers to "the systematic, planned alignment of typical human resource management practices with the organization's environmental goal" (Jabbour,2013 pp. 147-148). Renwick et al. (2013) categorize the GHRM grounded on the A-M-O theory and illustrate its role in sustainability. The central idea of the GHRM is the deployment of environmentally focused "recruitment", "selection", "appraisal" and "employees' engagement" to promote environmental management. Deployment of GHRM is instrumental in influencing the pro-environmental behaviour of employees and subsequently increases the environmental performance of organizations (Renwick et al., 2013). Furthermore, the advent of AI and its pervasive nature point to the dearth of knowledge on the benefits of AI as an enabler of GHRM toward sustainable development.

AI in simplified words is "machine-based systems which collect information and make decisions autonomously, mimicking human intelligence" (Figueroa-Armijos et al., 2022). The increasing popularity of the domain of AI-augmented HRM illustrates the effectiveness of intelligent automation in processing vast amounts of data, reducing time costs, delivering decision outcomes quickly and deploying human resources for jobs requiring more critical thinking (Basu et al., 2023). AI as a facilitating tool may help managers and employees to create engendered value for the organization to avail strategic advantages and suffice organizational sustainable goals (Di et al., 2020). To survive the globally competitive corporate world, organizational settings need to be more efficient than traditional organizational settings and work environments. AI is a great means to multi-fold the managerial efficiency to strategically redeem the vision of organizational leaders and the economic, social, and environmental goals set by organizations (Pillai & Sivathanu 2020). Technology has advanced to the point where it is now ingrained in each individual's daily existence. AI advances human resource management practices to improve employees' experience at the workplace, remain competitive in a rapidly transforming business environment, and enhance the outcomes of HR services (Guenole & Feinzig, 2018).

To address the existing lacuna about integrating AI-GHRM the research aims to build a conceptual model based on the literature on AI-enabled HRM and green Human Resource Management to engender the sustainable performance of organizations. To suffice the objective of the study, existing literature and documents are synthesized to propose the conceptual framework. The study is significant to anticipate the role of AI in reinforcing the impact of GHRM to achieve sustainability goals. Furthermore, future researchers can conduct empirical studies to generalize the model developed by the authors.

2. WORKPLACE TRANSFORMATIONS IN A GLOBAL BUSINESS ENVIRONMENT

The workforce today confronts several obstacles in adapting to workplace transformations caused by the dynamism and volatility of modern business. Among other external influences, the Industrial Revolution 4.0 is obliterating established corporate processes and demanding transformation. The induction of human-centric AI pursues to advance the quality of decision-making, making predictions, evaluating performance and other arduous jobs. This algorithmic aid facilitates employees and managers to enhance the quality of decision output produced after processing a large volume of data (Leesakul et al., 2022). AI has many advantages, but there additionally exist some drawbacks, like the potential loss of entry-level jobs, concern regarding ethical decision-making, the opaque nature of the decision-making process etc. This increases the need for academicians, organizations, and the government to pinpoint the skill gap, understand how technology interference affects lower-level workers, and upgrade the knowledge of employees and stakeholders to ensure their compatibility with intelligent automation (Rydzik & Kissoon,2022).

Furthermore, sustainability is an area addressed by additional transformational experiences in the organizational setting. Constructing organizational processes focusing on environmental management is critical to lowering energy consumption and promoting sustainability in industrial sector actions. (Bulińska-Stangrecka & Bagieńska,2021). For organizations to develop sustainable programs, human inputs are essential. Strategic planning, employee attitudes, and leadership styles are crucial components of the implications of sustainability in the industrial sector (Beloff et al., 2004).

3. ESTABLISHING GHRM TO ACHIEVE SUSTAINABLE GOALS IN ORGANIZATIONS

The concept of sustainable development initially evolved during the global environmental crises of the 1980s. Brundtland Commission (1987), in his report, stated that "development that meets the needs of the present without compromising the ability of future generations to meet their own needs" is called sustainable development. Since 1990, international organizations have been pursuing the goal of ensuring that industrial expansion is sustainable through new environmental protection possibilities, environmental legislation, and numerous international environmental management standards (UNIDO, 2010). GHRM has grown alongside sustainable development in the preceding decade to endorse the eco-friendly behaviour of employees and ultimately contribute to the environment. Renwick et al. (2013) synthesized several studies in HRM and the environmental management domain to define green HR practices that organizations might use to further their environmental objectives. GHRM, which is built on the AMO theory, aims to empower employees while also enabling employees' potential through training and development and rewarding them for their environmental actions (Luu, 2018; Paillé et al., 2014). Extent literature additionally, reports enhanced creativity among employees influenced by GHRM (Imran et al., 2021). Subsequently, GHRM enhances profitability in the longer run driven by product stewardship and induction of environment-friendly techniques (Gedam et al., 2021; O'Donohue & Torugsa, 2016).

Table 1. HR functions hired for environmental management

Green HR Function	Description	Source
Green recruitment	Studies support green recruitment to achieve sustainable goals.	Yong et al. (2020); (Karatepe et al., 2022); (Kim et al., 2019)
Green hiring	Green recruiting practices enable employees to know that an organization is committed to environmental sustainability.	Jerónimo et al. (2020); (Pham et al., 2020); (Obeidat et al., 2020)
Green training	For employees to adopt environmentally friendly values and practices to meet sustainability goals, green training is essential.	Jerónimo et al. (2020), Luu (2018), Pham et al. (2019), Yong et al. (2020), Cop et al. (2020); Cabral & Chiappetta Jabbour (2020)
Green compensation & reward	Green incentives inspire employees to act in environment-friendly conduct to subsequently affect Env P	Luu (2018); Pham et al. (2020); Ahmad et al., (2022); Ahmed et al., (2021); Wagner (2013)
Green performance management	Performance management influences organizational environmental stewardship behavior	Pham et al. (2020); Pham et al. (2019); Harvey et al. (2013)
Green employee involvement	The involvement of human capital is crucial in the line of furthering the environmental goal	Pham et al. (2019); Farooq et al. (2022); Yu et al. (2020); Aftab et al. (2022)

NOTE Env P- Environmental performance
Source: Developed by authors

4. ROLE OF AI IN HRM

Since days beyond we can recall there is only one constant process: "the process of evolution". The world is now evolving sprightly with advanced technologies permeating the personal, professional, and social lives of individuals. Advanced technology like Artificial intelligence is alluring organizations to AI-human collaborations for enhancing the effectiveness of decision-making and operational tasks (Malinowski et al., 2008). The modern era is navigating businesses to become apt to survive the dynamic and fluctuating business conditions(Varma et al., 2023). Therefore, the adoption of AI to engender the effectiveness of HR practices emerges as a strong weapon against the rising competition globally to raise strategic advantages. The intervention of AI in HRM practices enhances the effectiveness of operations and tasks performed manually and reduces the time cost in HR functions spanning from employee recruitment and selection to providing training to employees and performance management (Vrontis et al., 2021). Prikshat et al. (2023) in a study shed light on the AI intervention to strengthen the conventional HRM functions pertaining to selection, performance management, job evaluation, reward, talent management, employee engagement and retention. Furthermore, role of employees' perceptions has significant place in the successful implementation of AI at workplace. Users expectations of effective performance by AI in HR functions like recruitment and selection influence their trust for organization (Figueroa-Armijos et al., 2022). Additionally, the efficiency and quality of AI facilitate managerial functions in such a way that it ameliorates employer branding (Kot et al.,2021). Besides the advantages of AI, there are significant drawbacks to depending on AI decisions for HRM. Budhwar et al. (2022), raising ethical and legal concerns, question the transparency and dependability of AI in the administrative process and its impact on the conduct of employees. In response to ethical concerns Rodgers et al. (2022), propose a throughput model to direct the process of effective decision-making in Algorithmic HRM. The adoption of AI in HR practices is at its initial stage and deprived of the anticipated advantages of AI deployment. Chowdhury et al. (2023), build a conceptual model depicting how AI capabilities influence HR functions, employee satisfaction, cognitive development, and inventive attitudes leading to favourable outcomes spanning from data-driven decision-making to brand image.

Table 2. Examples of realistic AI applications for HR professionals

HR Functions	AI Tools Used	Advantages	Source
Attracting employees	Watson candidate assistant (WCA), Pymetrics	• Suggest the best-fit match for the job • Reduces the time to hire	(Guenole & Feinzig, 2018; ORACLE, 2019; Analytics Vidhya, 2023; Upadhyay and Khandelwal, 2018; Pereira et al., 2021)
Hiring	IBM Watson Recruitment (IWR), New hire chatbot, Omazing hiring, Oracle recruiting,	• Reduces the biases in hiring • Matches the candidate's resume to the job requirement • Predict the performance of the candidate based on the information processed • New hire chatbot answers multiple queries in seconds	(Guenole & Feinzig,2018; ORACLE, 2019; Analytics Vidhya, 2023); (Figueroa-Armijos et al., 2022)
Employee engagement	AI talent alerts, AI engagement analysis, Entelo	• Specified techniques help managers in decisions regarding promotion and retaining employees in the organization	(Guenole & Feinzig,2018; ORACLE, 2019; Analytics Vidhya, 2023; Analytics Vidhya, 2023; Malik et al., 2023).
Reward and compensation	AI-based compensation support	• Evaluation of the skill • The market rate for the skill • Appropriate reward or bonus for performance	(Guenole & Feinzig,2018; ORACLE, 2019).
Training and development	Your learning, AI- skill inference technology, Watson Career Coach (WCC), Textio	• Improve employee learning and maintain the relevance of workforce skills • Aid to reduce the skill gap • Assistance to the employee in planning their career	(Guenole & Feinzig,2018; ORACLE, 2019; Analytics Vidhya, 2023).

Source: Developed by authors

5. AUGMENTATION OF AI TO REINFORCE THE GREEN HUMAN RESOURCE MANAGEMENT

Extent literature advocates the relevance of HR practices to suffice the objective of environmental management (Singh et al., 2020). However, conventional HR practices are evolving with the digital interface and AI to enhance managerial efficiency, reduce the time cost in the globally competitive market (Pessach et al., 2020) and aid the workforce in filling the skill void in a dynamic workplace environment (Bhardwaj

& Sharma, 2022). The value of AI in HR practices can be viewed from multifarious perspectives (Pan et al., 2022). Table 2. Indicates the increased efficiency of hiring the best-fit candidates for the required job role. To achieve environmental performance, it is relevant to select the candidate fulfilling the green criteria. Therefore, we propose the following proposition.

Figure 1. Conceptual framework

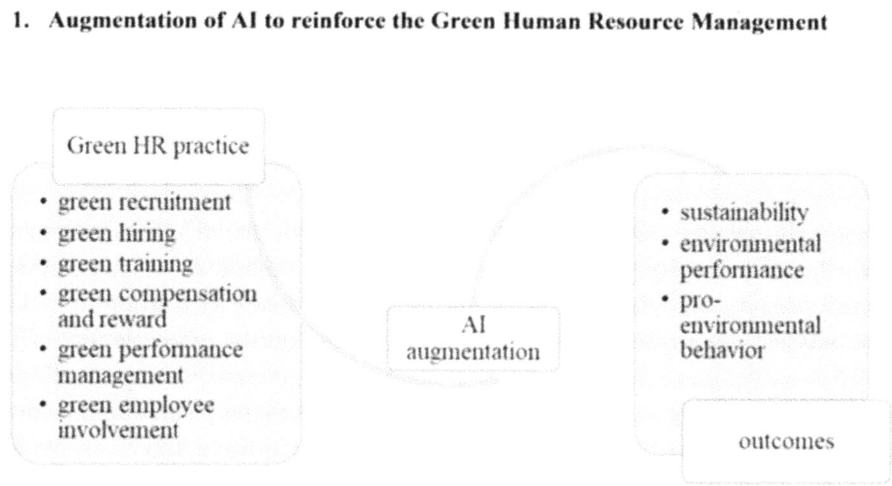

P. 1. AI assistance in green hiring magnifies its impact on environmental performance.

The complexity of managing human capital is due to the diverse attributes and shortcomings among individuals. large amount spent on training and development programs for all employees doesn't necessarily serve the purpose of learning. However, AI offers personalized learning experiences to individuals (Malik et al., 2022). In the line of GHRM, green training and development are prioritized to develop green behaviour and subsequently environmental performance (Jerónimo et al., 2020). Therefore, our second proposition follows:

P. 2. AI- assistance in training and development programs translates the green learning experience of employees into pro-environmental behaviour.

More than acquiring the talent, attention is required to manage the talent. To support employees in the direction of achieving goals determined, AI offers feedback, performance evaluation, and career planning (Tambe et al., 2019). Table 1. Corroborates the importance of performance management to prosper pro-environmental behaviour. Therefore, it may be relevant to propose:

P.3. AI-assistance advances green performance management to enhance pro-environmental behaviour.

Integration of AI and digital interface to the Human Resource Management functions is at its early stage. Despite its benefits, there continue to be many challenges to overcome. Lack of interpretation in decision-making processes by AI continues to be a problem that negatively affects employee satisfaction (Radonjić et al.,2022). Nevertheless, AI-augmented operations allow organizations to improve their knowledge bases and develop their competitive capacities (Vrontis et al., 2022). Additionally, dynamic capability argues the best use of available resources (such as human resources and technology aid) to advance organizational performance and attain a competitive gain (Trujillo-Gallego et al., 2022).

6. DISCUSSION

In the vein of organizational goals, sustainable development is illuminated as first and foremost. GHRM the mechanism to achieve the goal of sustainability is grounded on the shoulder of environmentally focused effective human resource management. Additionally, the rising popularity of adopting AI at workplaces indicates the readiness of organizations to integrate AI to augment the effectiveness of HR functions. Drawing on the DCV (dynamic capability view) Teece (2018), integrating organizations' internal resources i.e., GHRM and AI technology may render strategic advantages to the organization for a longer duration. A DCV can be defined as "the firm's ability to integrate, build, and reconfigure internal and external competencies to address rapidly changing environments". Human capital and Algorithmic-HRM are intangible resources possessed by organizations and difficult to imitate by competitors. AI-enabled GHRM will be informed by the unstructured large volume of data further processed by the algorithmic capabilities (Haenlein & Kaplan, 2019) and supported by the critical rationales of managers to gain strategic advantages. A significant gap in the existing literature remains to empirically test the role of AI in the reinforcement of GHRM. The present study serve as the foundation for empirical studies to establish the integration of AI and GHRM in the direction of sustainable development.

7. CONCLUSION

The objective of the research was to create a conceptual model to support the impacts of AI in environmentally friendly HR practices to meet organizational goals. To suffice this objective, document analysis of secondary data is used to support a synthesis of the literature that already exists in the fields of GHRM and AI-enabled HRM. The current study is consistent with the dynamic capabilities view in its explanation to leverage the existing resources and access external resources (Danneels, 2011; Collins and Clark, 2003). Resource-based view theory further supports the idea of the acquisition and implementation of resources that are complementary to the current resources, which are uncommon and difficult to replicate to ensure a competitive advantage (Barney and Arikan, 2005). The findings of the study suggest integrating AI into green human resources practices to accomplish sustainable goals. Employing AI and digital interfaces to assist with managerial responsibilities minimizes the amount of time required for completing a particular assignment, and the time saved can be put to use in strategic planning. The achievement of sustainable development, which is a crucial component of organizational operations, depends on the input of employees who are knowledgeable, productive, and environmentally conscious.

Results support the employment of AI to improve human capital's ability to serve the organization's diverse goals. The present study is limited to empirically supporting the concept model; therefore, it is advised that future researchers conduct empirical studies to generalize the findings.

REFERENCES

Aftab, J., Abid, N., Cucari, N., & Savastano, M. (2022). Green human resource management and environmental performance: The role of green innovation and environmental strategy in a developing country. *Business Strategy and the Environment*, *32*(4), 1782–1798. doi:10.1002/bse.3219

Ahmad, I., Ullah, K., & Khan, A. (2022). The impact of green HRM on green creativity: Mediating role of pro-environmental behaviors and moderating role of ethical leadership style. *International Journal of Human Resource Management*, *33*(19), 3789–3821. doi:10.1080/09585192.2021.1931938

Ahmed, M., Guo, Q., Qureshi, M. A., Raza, S. A., Khan, K. A., & Salam, J. (2021). Do green HR practices enhance green motivation and proactive environmental management maturity in hotel industry? *International Journal of Hospitality Management*, *94*, 102852. doi:10.1016/j.ijhm.2020.102852

Akpan, I. J., & Ibidunni, A. S. (2021). Digitization and technological transformation of small business for sustainable development in the less developed and emerging economies: A research note and call for papers. *Journal of Small Business and Entrepreneurship*, 1–7.

Barney, J. B., & Arikan, A. M. (2005). The resource-based view: origins and implications. The Blackwell handbook of strategic management, 123-182. doi:10.1111/b.9780631218616.2006.00006.x

Basu, S., Majumdar, B., Mukherjee, K., Munjal, S., & Palaksha, C. (2023). Artificial Intelligence–HRM Interactions and Outcomes: A Systematic Review and Causal Configurational Explanation. *Human Resource Management Review*, *33*(1), 100893. doi:10.1016/j.hrmr.2022.100893

Beloff, B., Tanzil, D., & Lines, M. (2004). Sustainable development performance assessment. *Environmental Progress*, *23*(4), 271–276. doi:10.1002/ep.10045

Bhardwaj, B., & Sharma, D. (2022). Migration of skilled professionals across the border: Brain drain or brain gain?. *European Management Journal*. https://doi.org/10.1016/j.emj.2022.12.011

Brundtland, G. H. (1987). *Report of the World Commission on Environment and Development: Our Common Future*. Retrieved from chrome-extension://bocbaocobfecmglnmeaeppambideimao/pdf/viewer.html?file=https%3A%2F%2Fsustainabledevelopment.un.org%2Fcontent%2Fdocuments%2F5987our-common-future.pdf accessed on 30/07/2023

Budhwar, P., Malik, A., De Silva, M. T., & Thevisuthan, P. (2022). Artificial intelligence–challenges and opportunities for international HRM: A review and research agenda. *International Journal of Human Resource Management*, *33*(6), 1065–1097. doi:10.1080/09585192.2022.2035161

Bulińska-Stangrecka, H., & Bagieńska, A. (2021). Culture-based green workplace practices as a means of conserving energy and other natural resources in the manufacturing sector. *Energies*, *14*(19), 6305. doi:10.3390/en14196305

Cabral, C., & Chiappetta Jabbour, C. J. (2020). Understanding the human side of green hospitality management. *International Journal of Hospitality Management*, *88*(April), 102389. doi:10.1016/j.ijhm.2019.102389

Chen, J. C., Lin, T. L., & Kuo, M. H. (2002). Artificial worlds modeling of human resource management systems. *IEEE Transactions on Evolutionary Computation*, *6*(6), 542–556. doi:10.1109/TEVC.2002.802279

Chowdhury, S., Dey, P., Joel-Edgar, S., Bhattacharya, S., Rodriguez-Espindola, O., Abadie, A., & Truong, L. (2023). Unlocking the value of artificial intelligence in human resource management through AI capability framework. *Human Resource Management Review*, *33*(1), 100899. doi:10.1016/j.hrmr.2022.100899

Collins, C. J., & Clark, K. D. (2003). Strategic human resource practices, top management team social networks, and firm performance: The role of human resource practices in creating organizational competitive advantage. *Academy of Management Journal*, *46*(6), 740–751. doi:10.2307/30040665

Cop, S., Alola, U. V., & Alola, A. A. (2020). Perceived behavioral control as a mediator of hotels' green training, environmental commitment, and organizational citizenship behavior: A sustainable environmental practice. *Business Strategy and the Environment*, *29*(8), 3495–3508. doi:10.1002/bse.2592

Danneels, E. (2011). Trying to become a different type of company: Dynamic capability at Smith Corona. *Strategic Management Journal*, *32*(1), 1–31. doi:10.1002mj.863

Deloitte. (2022). *A blueprint for green workforce transformation*. Accessed from chrome-extension://bocbaocobfecmglnmeaeppambideimao/pdf/viewer.html?file=https%3A%2F%2Fwww2.deloitte.com%2Fcontent%2Fdam%2FDeloitte%2Fuk%2FDocuments%2Fconsultancy%2Fdeloitte-uk-a-blueprint-for-green-workforce-transformation.pdf accessed on 01/06/2023

Di, A., Palladino, R., Hassan, R., & Escobar, O. (2020). Artificial intelligence and business models in the sustainable development goals perspective : A systematic literature review. *Journal of Business Research*, *121*(January), 283–314. doi:10.1016/j.jbusres.2020.08.019

Farooq, R., Zhang, Z., Talwar, S., & Dhir, A. (2022). Do green human resource management and self-efficacy facilitate green creativity? A study of luxury hotels and resorts. *Journal of Sustainable Tourism*, *30*(4), 824–845. doi:10.1080/09669582.2021.1891239

Figueroa-Armijos, M., Clark, B. B., & da Motta Veiga, S. P. (2022). Ethical Perceptions of AI in Hiring and Organizational Trust: The Role of Performance Expectancy and Social Influence. *Journal of Business Ethics*, *186*(1), 179–197. doi:10.100710551-022-05166-2 PMID:33758450

Gedam, V. V., Raut, R. D., Lopes de Sousa Jabbour, A. B., Narkhede, B. E., & Grebinevych, O. (2021). Sustainable manufacturing and green human resources: Critical success factors in the automotive sector. *Business Strategy and the Environment*, *30*(2), 1296–1313. doi:10.1002/bse.2685

Guenole, N., & Feinzig, S. (2018). *The Business Case for AI in HR. IBM Corporation. United states of America*. Retrieved from chrome-extension://bocbaocobfecmglnmeaeppambideimao/pdf/viewer.html?file=https%3A%2F%2Fwww.ibm.com%2Fdownloads%2Fcas%2FAGKXJX6M accessed on 16/04/2023

Haenlein, M., & Kaplan, A. (2019). A Brief History of Artificial Intelligence: On the past, present, and future of artificial intelligence. 1–10. doi:10.1177/0008125619864925

Harvey, G., Williams, K., & Probert, J. (2013). Greening the airline pilot: HRM and the green performance of airlines in the UK. *International Journal of Human Resource Management*, *24*(1), 152–166. doi:10.1080/09585192.2012.669783

Imran, R., Alraja, M. N., & Khashab, B. (2021). Sustainable Performance and Green Innovation: Green Human Resources Management and Big Data as Antecedents. *IEEE Transactions on Engineering Management*. Advance online publication. doi:10.1109/TEM.2021.3114256

Jabbour, C. J. C. (2013). Environmental training in organisations: From a literature review to a framework for future research. *Resources, Conservation and Recycling*, *74*, 144–155. doi:10.1016/j.resconrec.2012.12.017

Jerónimo, H. M., Henriques, P. L., de Lacerda, T. C., da Silva, F. P., & Vieira, P. R. (2020). Going green and sustainable: The influence of green HR practices on the organizational rationale for sustainability. *Journal of Business Research*, *112*, 413–421. doi:10.1016/j.jbusres.2019.11.036

Karatepe, O. M., Hsieh, H., & Aboramadan, M. (2022). The effects of green human resource management and perceived organizational support for the environment on green and non-green hotel employee outcomes. *International Journal of Hospitality Management*, *103*, 103202. doi:10.1016/j.ijhm.2022.103202

Kim, Y. J., Kim, W. G., Choi, H. M., & Phetvaroon, K. (2019). The effect of green human resource management on hotel employees' eco-friendly behavior and environmental performance. *International Journal of Hospitality Management*, *76*, 83–93. doi:10.1016/j.ijhm.2018.04.007

Kot, S., Hussain, H. I., Bilan, S., Haseeb, M., & Mihardjo, L. W. (2021). The role of artificial intelligence recruitment and quality to explain the phenomenon of employer reputation. *Journal of Business Economics and Management*, *22*(4), 867–883. doi:10.3846/jbem.2021.14606

Kramar, R. (2014). Beyond strategic human resource management: Is sustainable human resource management the next approach? *International Journal of Human Resource Management*, *25*(8), 1069–1089. doi:10.1080/09585192.2013.816863

Leesakul, N., Oostveen, A. M., Eimontaite, I., Wilson, M. L., & Hyde, R. (2022). Workplace 4.0: Exploring the implications of technology adoption in digital manufacturing on a sustainable workforce. *Sustainability (Basel)*, *14*(6), 3311. doi:10.3390u14063311

Luu, T. T. (2018). Employees' green recovery performance: The roles of green HR practices and serving culture. *Journal of Sustainable Tourism*, *26*(8), 1308–1324. doi:10.1080/09669582.2018.1443113

Malik, A., Budhwar, P., Mohan, H., & Srikanth, N. R. (2023). Employee experience –the missing link for engaging employees: Insights from an MNE's AI-based HR ecosystem. *Human Resource Management*, *62*(1), 97–115. doi:10.1002/hrm.22133

Malik, A., Budhwar, P., Patel, C., & Srikanth, N. R. (2022). May the bots be with you! Delivering HR cost-effectiveness and individualised employee experiences in an MNE. *International Journal of Human Resource Management*, *33*(6), 1148–1178. doi:10.1080/09585192.2020.1859582

Malinowski, J., Weitzel, T., & Keim, T. (2008). Decision support for team staffing: An automated relational recommendation approach. *Decision Support Systems*, *45*(3), 429–447. doi:10.1016/j.dss.2007.05.005

O'Donohue, W., & Torugsa, N. A. (2016). The moderating effect of 'Green' HRM on the association between proactive environmental management and financial performance in small firms. *International Journal of Human Resource Management*, *27*(2), 239–261. doi:10.1080/09585192.2015.1063078

Obeidat, S. M., Al Bakri, A. A., & Elbanna, S. (2020). Leveraging "Green" Human Resource Practices to Enable Environmental and Organizational Performance: Evidence from the Qatari Oil and Gas Industry. *Journal of Business Ethics*, *164*(2), 371–388. doi:10.100710551-018-4075-z

ORACLE (2019). *AI in Human Resouce: The Time is Now*. Retrieved from chrome-extension://bocbaocobfecmglnmeaeppambideimao/pdf/viewer.html?file=https%3A%2F%2Fwww.oracle.com%2Fa%2Focom%2Fdocs%2Fapplications%2Fhcm%2Foracle-ai-in-hr-wp.pdf accessed on 26/07/2023 doi:10.1016/j.tourman.2018.12.008

Pham, N. T., Tučková, Z., & Chiappetta Jabbour, C. J. (2019). Greening the hospitality industry: How do green human resource management practices influence organizational citizenship behavior in hotels? A mixed-methods study. *Tourism Management, 72*, 386–399. doi:10.1016/j.tourman.2018.12.008

Paillé, P., Chen, Y., Boiral, O., & Jin, J. (2014). The Impact of Human Resource Management on Environmental Performance: An Employee-Level Study. *Journal of Business Ethics*, *121*(3), 451–466. doi:10.100710551-013-1732-0

Pan, Y., Froese, F., Liu, N., Hu, Y., & Ye, M. (2022). The adoption of artificial intelligence in employee recruitment: The influence of contextual factors. *International Journal of Human Resource Management*, *33*(6), 1125–1147. doi:10.1080/09585192.2021.1879206

Pereira, V., Hadjielias, E., Christofi, M., & Vrontis, D. (2021). Human Resource Management Review A systematic literature review on the impact of artificial intelligence on workplace outcomes : A multi-process perspective. *Human Resource Management Review*, *100857*(July), •••. doi:10.1016/j.hrmr.2021.100857

Pessach, D., Singer, G., Avrahami, D., Chalutz Ben-Gal, H., Shmueli, E., & Ben-Gal, I. (2020). Employees recruitment: A prescriptive analytics approach via machine learning and mathematical programming. *Decision Support Systems*, *134*(March), 113290. doi:10.1016/j.dss.2020.113290 PMID:32501316

Pham, N. T., Chiappetta Jabbour, C. J., Vo-Thanh, T., Huynh, T. L. D., & Santos, C. (2020). Greening hotels: Does motivating hotel employees promote in-role green performance? The role of culture. *Journal of Sustainable Tourism*, *31*(4), 951–970. doi:10.1080/09669582.2020.1863972

Pham, N. T., Vo Thanh, T., Tučková, Z., & Thuy, V. T. N. (2020). The role of green human resource management in driving hotel's environmental performance: Interaction and mediation analysis. *International Journal of Hospitality Management*, *88*(August), 102392. Advance online publication. doi:10.1016/j.ijhm.2019.102392

Pillai, R., & Sivathanu, B. (2020). Adoption of artificial intelligence (AI) for talent acquisition in IT/ITeS organizations. *Benchmarking*, *27*(9), 2599–2629. doi:10.1108/BIJ-04-2020-0186

Prikshat, V., Islam, M., Patel, P., Malik, A., Budhwar, P., & Gupta, S. (2023). Technological Forecasting & Social Change AI-Augmented HRM : Literature review and a proposed multilevel framework for future research. *Technological Forecasting and Social Change, 193*(May), 122645. doi:10.1016/j.techfore.2023.122645

Radonjić, A., Duarte, H., & Pereira, N. (2022). Artificial intelligence and HRM: HR managers' perspective on decisiveness and challenges. *European Management Journal*. Advance online publication. doi:10.1016/j.emj.2022.07.001

Renwick, D. W., Redman, T., & Maguire, S. (2013). Green human resource management: A review and research agenda. *International Journal of Management Reviews, 15*(1), 1–14. doi:10.1111/j.1468-2370.2011.00328.x

Rodgers, W., Murray, J. M., Stefanidis, A., Degbey, W. Y., & Tarba, S. Y. (2022). An artificial intelligence algorithmic approach to ethical decision-making in human resource management processes. *Human Resource Management Review*. Advance online publication. doi:10.1016/j.hrmr.2022.100925

Rydzik, A., & Kissoon, C. S. (2022). Decent work and tourism workers in the age of intelligent automation and digital surveillance. *Journal of Sustainable Tourism, 30*(12), 2860–2877. doi:10.1080/09669582.2021.1928680

Singh, S. K., Giudice, M. Del, Chierici, R., & Graziano, D. (2020). Green innovation and environmental performance: The role of green transformational leadership and green human resource management. *Technological Forecasting and Social Change, 150*, 119762. https://doi.org/ doi:10.1016/j.techfore.2019.119762

Tambe, P., Cappelli, P., & Yakubovich, V. (2019). Artificial intelligence in human resources management: Challenges and A path forward. *California Management Review, 61*(4), 15–42. doi:10.1177/0008125619867910

Teece, D. J. (2018). Dynamic capabilities as (workable) management systems theory. *Journal of Management & Organization, 24*(3), 359–368. doi:10.1017/jmo.2017.75

Townsend, A. M., DeMarie, S. M., & Hendrickson, A. R. (1998). Virtual teams: Technology and the workplace of the future. *The Academy of Management Perspectives, 12*(3), 17–29. doi:10.5465/ame.1998.1109047

Trujillo-Gallego, M., Sarache, W., & de Sousa Jabbour, A. B. L. (2022). Digital technologies and green human resource management: Capabilities for GSCM adoption and enhanced performance. *International Journal of Production Economics, 249*, 108531. doi:10.1016/j.ijpe.2022.108531

UNIDO. (2010). *A Greener Footprint for Industry: opportunities and challenges of sustainable industrial development.* Accessed from https://www.greenpolicyplatform.org/research/greener-footprint-industry-opportunities-and-challenges-sustainable-industrial-development

Upadhyay, A. K., & Khandelwal, K. (2018, October 8). Applying arti fi cial intelligence : Implications for recruitment. *Strategic HR Review, 17*(5), 255–258. Advance online publication. doi:10.1108/SHR-07-2018-0051

Varma, A., Dawkins, C., & Chaudhuri, K. (2023). Artificial intelligence and people management: A critical assessment through the ethical lens. *Human Resource Management Review*, *33*(1), 100923. doi:10.1016/j.hrmr.2022.100923

Vidhya, A. (2023). *How to Use AI and ML Tools for HR Management in 2023?* Retrieved from https://www.analyticsvidhya.com/blog/2023/03/ai-and-ml-tools-for-hr/

Vrontis, D., Christofi, M., Pereira, V., Tarba, S., Makrides, A., & Trichina, E. (2022). Artificial intelligence, robotics, advanced technologies and human resource management: A systematic review. *International Journal of Human Resource Management*, *33*(6), 1237–1266. doi:10.1080/09585192.2020.1871398

Wagner, M. (2013). "Green" Human Resource Benefits: Do they Matter as Determinants of Environmental Management System Implementation? *Journal of Business Ethics*, *114*(3), 443–456. doi:10.100710551-012-1356-9

Wehrmeyer, W. (Ed.). (2017). *Greening people: Human resources and environmental management*. Routledge. doi:10.4324/9781351283045

Yong, J. Y., Yusliza, M. Y., Ramayah, T., Chiappetta Jabbour, C. J., Sehnem, S., & Mani, V. (2020). Pathways towards sustainability in manufacturing organizations: Empirical evidence on the role of green human resource management. *Business Strategy and the Environment*, *29*(1), 212–228. doi:10.1002/bse.2359

Yu, W., Chavez, R., Feng, M., Wong, C. Y., & Fynes, B. (2020). Green human resource management and environmental cooperation: An ability-motivation-opportunity and contingency perspective. *International Journal of Production Economics*, *219*, 224–235. doi:10.1016/j.ijpe.2019.06.013

Chapter 6
Emotional Intelligence as a Predictor of Psychological Wellbeing and Workplace Performance

Yashpal Azad
https://orcid.org/0000-0003-2957-8917
Eternal University, India

Amit Kumar
https://orcid.org/0000-0002-1686-3279
Eternal University, India

ABSTRACT

Understanding emotional well-being is crucial in today's tech-driven world for effective coping and stress management in personal and professional life. Managing emotional intelligence is vital for employee interaction, fostering a positive work environment, and enhancing performance and overall well-being. This chapter aims to conduct a systematic literature review and develop a comprehensive conceptual model illustrating the intricate relationships among emotional intelligence, overall well-being, and work performance. It guides organizations, managers, policymakers, and future research in tailoring policies and practices. The review affirms a strong association between EI, overall well-being, and work performance, impacting both well-being and work outcomes. The conceptual model illustrates how emotional intelligence significantly affects well-being and workplace performance through direct and indirect factors. These findings suggest the need for effective interventions and strategies to improve emotional intelligence, overall well-being, and work performance.

DOI: 10.4018/979-8-3693-0418-1.ch006

1. INTRODUCTION

Emotional intelligence (EI) has gained significant attention in recent years as a crucial construct that can greatly impact an individual's ability to navigate and cope with stressful situations, ultimately contributing to a healthy and stable workforce. The processing of sensitive information plays a pivotal role in this regard, as it can significantly influence various life domains, including work success and overall well-being (Salovey & Grewal, 2005). The recognition that emotional skills vary among individuals and can be quantitatively measured has sparked a surge of interest and research in this field (Segal, 2002).

1.1. Overview: Unveiling Emotional Intelligence (EI)

Emotional intelligence (EI), introduced by Salovey and Mayer in 1990, revolves around perceiving, understanding, and regulating emotions (Salovey & Mayer, 1990). It has garnered extensive research interest across psychology, education, and organizational behavior due to its potential impact on mental health, relationships, and workplace success (Ruiz-Aranda et al., 2014; Joseph et al., 2015). In leadership and organizational contexts, EI plays a vital role, in enhancing team management, conflict resolution, and goal achievement (Goleman, 1998; Boyatzis & McKee, 2005). Employees with higher EI excel in roles like sales, customer service, and leadership (Carmeli et al., 2009), making EI a pivotal concept with broad implications for well-being, professional success, and effective leadership.

1.2. Comprehending Well-Being: Multidimensional Aspects and Psychological Dimensions

Well-being is a multidimensional construct encompassing physical, psychological, and social aspects of life (Diener, 2000). It reflects an individual's overall satisfaction in life and the presence of positive sentiments, without having any negative feelings (Diener et al., 1999). A crucial component of Psychological well-being is positive Psychological functioning, which encompasses self-acceptance, personal growth,, a sense of purpose in life, positive relationship with others, autonomy, and environmental mastery (Ryff, 1989). It's closely tied to emotional intelligence, defined as the effective perception, understanding, regulation, and expression of emotions (Salovey & Mayer, 1990).

1.3. Understanding Workplace Performance: Key Dimensions and Impact on Organizational Success

In essence, workplace performance involves employee effectiveness and productivity in meeting organizational objectives, encompassing task, contextual, and adaptive performance. Task performance relates to meeting deadlines, maintaining quality, and achieving set targets. Contextual performance (organizational citizenship behavior) includes actions beyond job requirements, aiding in smooth organizational functioning. Adaptive performance pertains to an employee's ability to adapt to changes and respond effectively to new challenges, showcasing flexibility and skill acquisition (Borman & Motowidlo, 1997; Pulakos et al., 2000).

Therefore, effective workplace performance is crucial for organizational success, impacting productivity, customer satisfaction, and overall performance. It's influenced by individual attributes, organizational dynamics, and the broader work environment, representing a critical factor in achieving organizational success (Robbins & Coulter, 2005; Salanova, Agut & Peiró, 2005; Luthans & Youssef, 2007).

1.4. Emotional Intelligence (EI): A Catalyst for Psychological Well-Being and Workplace Excellence

Emotional Intelligence (EI) strongly influences career growth and well-being (Brackett & Rivers, 2011). It significantly contributes to well-being and psychological adjustment, reducing depression symptoms (Extremer & Fernández-Berrocal, 2005; Mayer et al., 2008; Balluerka et al., 2013). Moreover, EI is a robust predictor of job performance and satisfaction in the professional realm. Senior managers with high EI consistently exhibit positive work attitudes, behaviors, and outcomes (Carmeli, 2003).

Moreover, individuals with higher EI excel in tasks requiring emotional intelligence (Schutte et al., 2001; Ali et al., 2012). In the contemporary corporate landscape, organizations prioritize EI during recruitment, often valuing it more than traditional qualifications. This emphasis is due to its significant impact on communication, relationship-building, and stress management (Cherniss & Goleman, 2001; Emmerling & Boyatzis, 2012). Hence, prioritizing EI development is vital for both individuals and organizations, profoundly affecting psychological well-being and workplace performance (Jordan et al., 2002; Wong et al., 2007).

1.5. The Fundamental Role of Emotional Intelligence (EI) in Well-Being and Professional Fulfillment

Emotional intelligence (EI) profoundly affects key life areas: career progression, social dynamics, stress management, motivation, and decision-making. It intricately intertwines with social connections and guides decision-making, especially in economic contexts (Bechara & Damasio, 2005). EI shapes social interactions and boosts job performance (Cote & Miners, 2006), and proficient emotion regulation is pivotal in reducing stress and enhancing well-being (Extremera & Rey, 2015). Altogether, EI significantly influences human behavior and functioning.

Adept emotional intelligence management is crucial for workplace success, career growth, positive relationships, mental well-being, and a harmonious work environment. Strong empirical evidence supports its significant impact on workplace performance, employee happiness, organizational success, and job satisfaction (Slaski & Cartwright, 2003; Law, Wong & Song, 2004). Additionally, emotional intelligence enhances psychological well-being, positive emotions, career aspirations, work-life balance, and overall employee happiness and satisfaction (Balluerka et al., 2016).

Therefore, fostering emotional intelligence through tailored training is vital for improving work performance and overall well-being. This is crucial for individuals at all stages, impacting personal growth, success, and fulfillment in various life domains.

1.6. Significance of Present Study and Research Gap

The present study is an attempt to investigate the complex relationship between emotional intelligence's impact on overall well-being (physical and mental), and workplace performance. The outcome of this relationship will shed dynamic insights for organizations, managers, policymakers, future researchers, and the general public, highlighting the need for a well-adjusted amalgamation of emotional intelligence to improve well-being and performance levels at the workplace and in various life domains of individuals. Although the extensive literature findings strengthen the positive impact of emotional intelligence on both overall well-being and workplace performance, there is a scope for further exploration. There is a dire need for future research to emphasize varied forms of emotional intelligence, internal factors affecting it, and an in-depth understanding of the impact of these forms on well-being and work performance. This in-depth understanding will shed light on developing more effective strategies and dynamics for organizations and individuals.

1.7. Objectives of the Study

The purpose of the present study is to perform a systematic review of the literature to develop a descriptive model that explains the connections between various literature findings. The focus is on examining and outlining the intricate connections between emotional intelligence, well-being, and workplace performance. This will result in a thorough comprehension of how EI affects both general well-being and work performance. Therefore, the present study aims to specifically achieve the following objectives by synthesizing and analyzing the empirical data available in the literature:

1.7.1. To study and evaluate the outcomes of previous literature on emotional intelligence, overall well-being, and workplace performance.

1.7.2. To develop a thorough and descriptive model that explains the intricate relationship between emotional intelligence, overall well-being, and workplace performance.

1.7.3. To investigate the degree to which emotional intelligence, overall well-being, and workplace performance differ from one another.

1.7.4. To derive a thorough understanding of the significant impact of emotional intelligence on overall well-being, and workplace performance.

1.7.5. To assess the empirical findings to establish general assumptions about the impact of emotional intelligence on overall well-being, and workplace performance that organizations, managers, policymakers, and future researchers can use.

2. LITERATURE REVIEW AND CONCEPTUAL FRAMEWORK

This section of the article provides a concise overview of the literature findings, aimed at achieving the objectives of the present study by synthesizing the intricate relationship between the study variables. The literature review served as the foundation for developing propositions that conceptualize the relationship between emotional intelligence, psychological well-being, and workplace performance.

2.1. Emotional Intelligence and Psychological Well-Being

Numerous empirical studies consistently affirm that EI reliably predicts physical and mental well-being. This strong association highlights a direct link between EI and overall well-being. Effective emotional state management is shown to boost both physical and psychological health, empowering individuals to navigate and mitigate stress adeptly (Pau & Croucher, 2003; Spence, Oades & Caputi, 2004; Tsaousis & Nikolaou, 2005; Zeidner, Matthews & Roberts, 2012; Malinauskas et al., 2018; Di Fabio & Kenny, 2016; Ahmadi, 2019).

Research emphasizes a strong link between emotional intelligence (EI) and job burnout, explaining 43% of mental health variance and 13.5% of physical health variance (Mohammadyfar, Khan & Tamini, 2009). Additionally, EI impacts psychological aspects like self-esteem, life satisfaction, and self-acceptance, showcasing its diverse influence on overall well-being (Carmeli et al., 2009). Individuals with higher EI experience reduced stress and anxiety, as studies consistently highlight a negative correlation between higher EI and perceived stress, underscoring EI's crucial role in mitigating stress effects on mental well-being (Schutte et al., 2007; Schutte & Loi, 2014).

Furthermore, research consistently links higher EI to increased positive emotions, improved mental health, and greater life satisfaction (Extremera & Fernandez-Berrocal, 2005; Ghaderi & Shamsi, 2015). These findings underscore EI's positive influence on psychological adjustment and the reduction of psychopathological symptoms, ultimately boosting mental well-being.

Additionally, EI correlates with enhanced coping skills during challenging times. Individuals with elevated EI levels tend to employ adaptive coping strategies when facing stress (Mikolajczak et al., 2007; MacCann et al., 2011; Por et al., 2011). Cultivating EI equips individuals with valuable tools to navigate and cope with stressors effectively, promoting mental well-being and resilience. These studies lead to the following proposition:

Proposition 1: Emotional Intelligence (EI) has an impact on both physical and mental well-being.

Research consistently confirms that high emotional intelligence (EI) reduces stress, anxiety, and depression, enhancing mental health. High-EI individuals show increased productivity and engagement at work, positively influencing satisfaction in both work and social interactions. EI helps navigate workplace dynamics, foster positive relationships, and resolve conflicts, showcasing its significant impact (Brunetto et al., 2012; Extremera et al., 2018; Barreiro & Treglown, 2020; Alsughayir, 2021).

Furthermore, studies emphasize a direct positive link between EI and overall well-being, highlighting EI's role as a moderator in shaping this relationship. Understanding these effects is crucial to comprehend the impact of emotional intelligence on well-being (Extremera & Fernández-Berrocal, 2005; Gorgens-Ekermans & Brand, 2012; Sanchez-Álvarez, Extremera & Fernández-Berrocal, 2016).

Literature also reveals that EI influences job satisfaction, mediated by work-related stress, depression, and job satisfaction itself (Psilopanagioti et al., 2012; Devonish, 2016; Lee, 2021). A comprehensive 30-year longitudinal review showcases the impact of job insecurity on well-being and somatic health (De Witte et al., 2016). Moreover, studies exploring the interplay between emotional intelligence, work-life balance, and occupational well-being highlight well-being as a mediator, especially in the context of job insecurity (Singh, 2016; Akanni, Oladejo & Oduaran, 2018; Malik, Haider & Hussain, 2019; Akanni, Kareem & Oduaran, 2020). Consequently, this establishes a proposition:

Proposition- 1a: Emotional Intelligence (EI) has a significant impact on both well-being and the work environment.

Research emphasizes internal factors' significant influence on Emotional Intelligence (EI) and well-being, encompassing emotions, personality traits, subjective experiences, learning, and perception (Grewal, Brackett et al., 2006; Petrides, Pita, & Kokkinaki, 2007; Mikolajczak & Luminet, 2008; Petrides, 2011; Llinares-Insa, Casino-García & García-Pérez, 2020). Understanding these interconnected elements illuminates EI's complexities and its impact on well-being. Additionally, emotional regulation significantly shapes EI and overall well-being, aiding psychological well-being (Cote et al., 2011; Webb, Miles, & Sheeran, 2012).

Mindfulness closely links to heightened self-awareness and emotional intelligence, supported by studies showing its positive impact on emotional perception and understanding (Brown & Ryan, 2003; Schutte & Malouff, 2011; Taylor, Harrison & Haimovitz, 2016). Furthermore, self-awareness within EI profoundly influences various life domains, including workplace performance, leadership, relationships, mental health, and academic achievement (Robins & Pals, 2002; Boyatzis & Sala, 2004; Brackett et al., 2006). These findings underscore self-awareness as a vital skill enhancing success across various life domains. Based on these studies, the following proposition is suggested:

Proposition 2: Internal factors influence both Emotional Intelligence (EI) and well-being.

2.2. Emotional Intelligence and Work Performance

Extensive research consistently shows a positive correlation between emotional intelligence (EI) and critical workplace factors like job satisfaction, overall well-being, worker engagement, and organizational commitment (Salguero, Palomera & Fernández-Berrocal, 2012; Pérez-Fuentes et al., 2018). This underscores EI's pivotal role in fostering a positive work environment and enhancing individuals' satisfaction and dedication to their work and organizations.

Enhanced emotional intelligence has been proven to have a substantial positive impact on various aspects of professional life, encompassing job performance, interpersonal skills, workplace relationships, stress management, and communication. Extensive research, such as studies by Cherniss and Goleman (2001) as well as Joseph and Newman (2010), consistently underscores a strong connection between emotional intelligence and job performance, underscoring its vital role in achieving excellence in one's professional endeavors. Moreover, adept emotional management, as evidenced by studies by Grandey (2000) and Cote (2014), is directly linked to enhanced job performance and more harmonious workplace relationships, making a significant contribution to both individual and organizational success.

Elevated Emotional Intelligence (EI) levels are acknowledged as a pivotal factor linked to heightened performance and effectiveness in employees, demonstrating the considerable potential to impact organizational success positively. The research conducted by Rana et al. (2017) illustrates a robust and favorable correlation between EI and workplace behavior, covering critical areas like job performance, transformational leadership, organizational commitment, team cohesion, decreased workplace stress, and effective conflict resolution strategies.

Furthermore, research consistently supports that key element of EI, such as self-awareness, self-control, motivation, empathy, and social skills are also reliably linked to improved work performance. Understanding and enhancing these elements hold great potential for optimizing individual performance and fostering success within the organizational context (Carmeli, 2003; Joseph & Newman, 2010; Cote, 2014; Ismail, Nopiah & Rasul, 2020). Based on these studies, the following proposition is suggested:

Proposition 3: A high level of Emotional Intelligence was linked to enhanced work quality and performance.

2.3. Emotional intelligence, General Well-Being, and Job Satisfaction

An expanding body of research consistently underscores the profound influence of emotional intelligence on overall well-being, employee behavior, work-related aspects, career decisions, and attitudes such as job satisfaction. Cultivating emotional intelligence stands as a pivotal strategy for both individuals and organizations aiming to elevate both employee well-being and performance (Gujral, Gupta & Aneja, 2012; Vesely et al., 2013).

Moreover, research underscores the intricate relationship between emotional intelligence, self-efficacy, and job satisfaction, demonstrating a positive correlation between emotional intelligence and job satisfaction, as well as favorable employee behavior (Cote, 2014). Furthermore, studies emphasize the mediating role of emotional intelligence in the dynamics of emotional labor, job stress, burnout, and turnover intention (Wong & Law, 2002; Chew & Zain, 2018; Sokmen & Sarikaya, 2022). Recognizing and fostering emotional intelligence emerge as pivotal strategies to cultivate a positive work environment, ultimately enhancing employee well-being and fortifying organizational effectiveness. Hence, the following proposition is evident:

Proposition-3a: Emotional Intelligence (EI) and overall well-being both influence employee behavior and job satisfaction.

Life experiences play a crucial role in shaping emotional intelligence (EI) and its impact on work performance. Workplace experiences strongly influence emotional and interpersonal skills. The integration of Social and Emotional Learning (SEL) in education significantly enhances the development and competencies of EI (Mayer, Caruso & Salovey, 2000; Jordan & Troth, 2004; Durlak et al., 2011). Life experiences act as key mediators between EI development and workplace effectiveness, particularly childhood experiences involving family dynamics and early social interactions (Koubova & Buchko, 2013; Lopes et al., 2016). These studies lead to the following proposition:

Proposition-3b: Life experiences play a mediating role in developing Emotional Intelligence (EI) and significantly impact work performance.

Multiple studies consistently show that emotional intelligence (EI) significantly influences work performance and job satisfaction, utilizing diverse measurement models such as ability-based, trait-based, and mixed models (Lopes, Salovey & Straus, 2003; Van Rooy & Viswesvaran, 2004; Cote & Miners, 2006; Petrides, Pérez-González & Furnham, 2007; Mikolajczak et al., 2007; Laborde et al., 2014; Akhtar et al., 2015; Mayer, Caruso & Salovey, 2016; Miao, Humphrey & Qian, 2017; Pradhan et al., 2022). Overall, these studies emphasize EI's diverse and significant role in enhancing workplace dynamics, covering performance and job satisfaction. The following proposition can be put forward based on these findings:

Proposition 3c: All types of emotional intelligence (ability, trait, and mixed) significantly affect well-being and Work performance.

2.4. Theoretical Models and Conceptualization

In this section of the present study, our objective is to establish a robust theoretical foundation by incorporating models and theories applicable to the study variables. The valuable insights derived from the existing literature and theoretical models are essential for proposing the conceptual framework of our study.

2.4.1. Mayer, Salovey, and Caruso's EI Ability Model

The EI model propounded by Mayer, Salovey, and Caruso suggests that information from the perceived understanding of emotions is used to facilitate thought patterns and further guide our decision-making. They proposed four interlinked abilities in this model viz. perceiving emotions, utilizing emotions to facilitate thought, comprehending emotions, and regulating emotions (See Figure 1).

Figure 1.

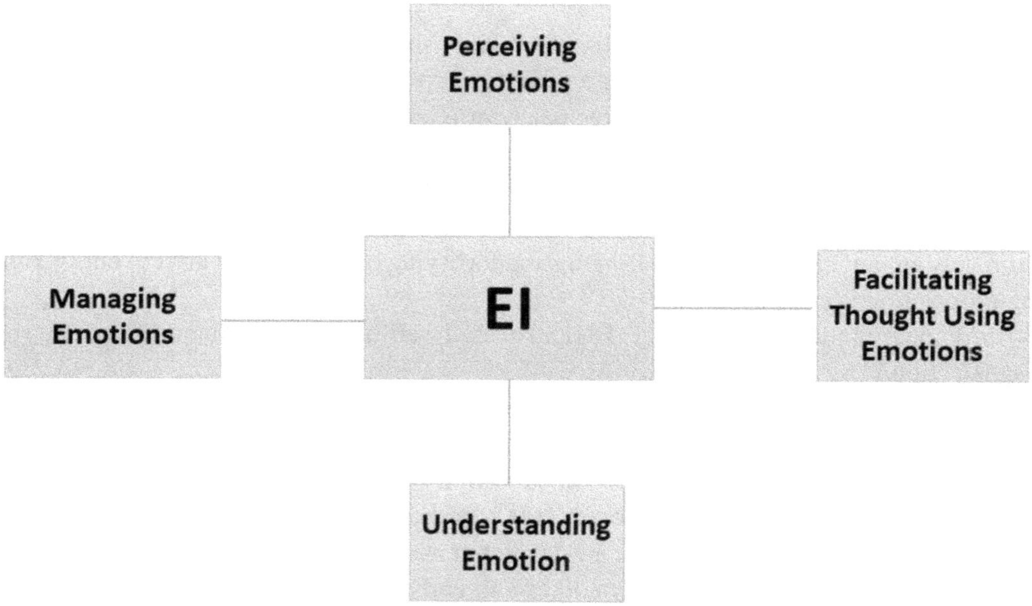

These abilities highlight the key role of EI competencies in both personal and professional domains of development, underscoring their applicability across diverse aspects of life (Salovey & Mayer, 1990; Mayer, Salovey & Caruso, 1999, 2000; Mayer, Roberts & Barsades, 2008).

2.4.2. Daniel Goleman's EI Performance Model

Daniel Goleman's model expands on Mayer and Salovey's foundation, highlighting that EI is a cluster of skills and competencies which are relied on five fundamental capabilities vital for the development of emotional intelligence viz. self-regulation of emotions, motivation aligned to personal values, empathy, and social skills, such as communication and conflict management (See Figure 2). Goleman's model has a wide application in the fields, particularly education, workplace management, and enhancement of professional relationships (Goleman, 2001).

Further, Goleman's model emphasizes essential aspects of emotional intelligence, contributing significantly to the cultivation and application of emotional intelligence in diverse aspects of life.

2.4.3. The Bar-On Social and Emotional Intelligence Model

Reuven Bar-On's model offers a comprehensive definition of Emotional Intelligence (EI) by portraying it as a fusion of emotional and social skills significantly impacting intelligent behavior. This model delineates five primary dimensions of EI, further categorized into 15 components, spanning various domains (See Figure 3).

Figure 2.

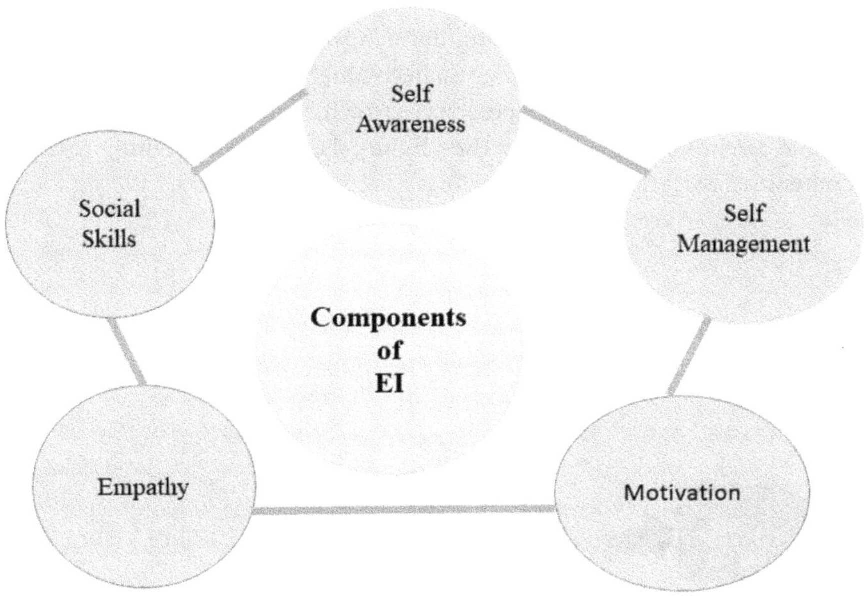

Figure 3.

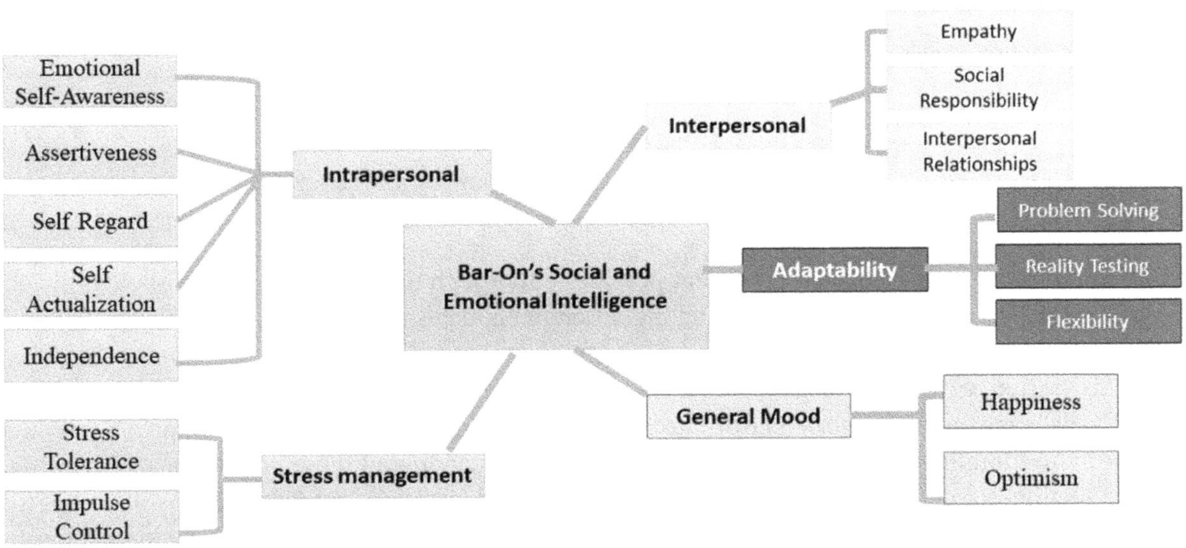

Bar-On's model provides a holistic understanding of emotional intelligence and its profound implications across diverse aspects of an individual's life such as academic achievement, career success, as well as mental and physical health and well-being (Bar-On, 1997).

2.4.4. Ryff's Six Factor Model of Psychological Well-Being

Carol Ryff's model of Psychological Well-being defines well-being through six critical dimensions, providing a multifaceted framework for assessing an individual's overall mental and emotional wellness. These dimensions include self-acceptance, personal growth, purpose in life, personal relations with others, autonomy, and environmental mastery (See Figure 4), each contributing to a person's sense of fulfillment and contentment (Ryff, 1989).

Figure 4.

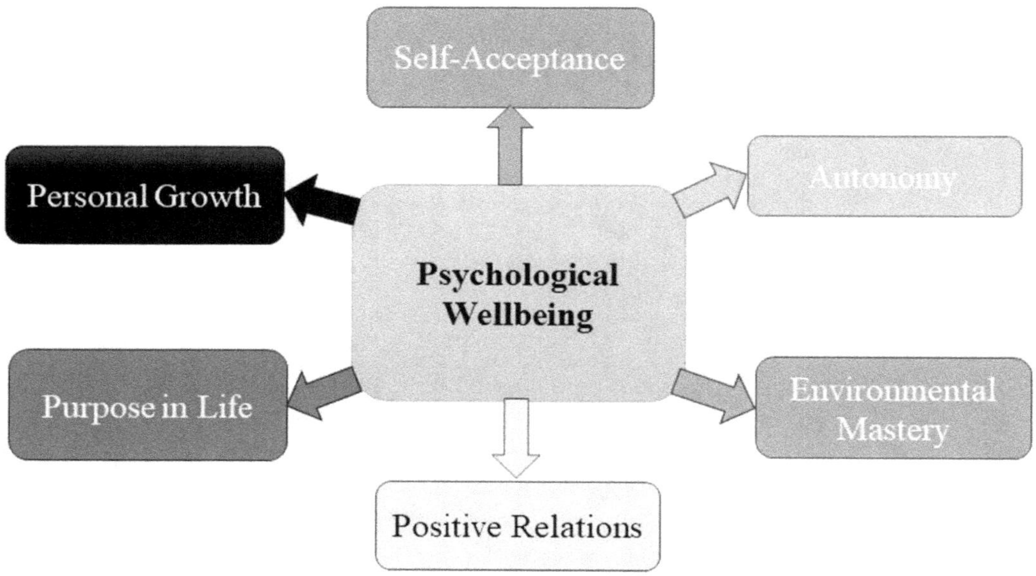

Therefore, Ryff's multifaceted viewpoint provides a thorough understanding of well-being, including more than just happiness and examining the different elements that encourage individuals to lead a fulfilling and meaningful life.

In this section, we explore the complex relationship between emotional intelligence models, psychological well-being, and workplace performance. By integrating these models, we develop a conceptual framework to illuminate the dynamics, enhancing our understanding of these interactions.

This section examines the complex connections between theories and models of EI, Well-being, and work performance that shed light on dynamics and improve our understanding of these interactions to propose conceptual framework and future implications.

2.5. Conceptual Model

The existing body of literature emphasizes the profound influence of EI on human behavior and emotions. Our rigorous analysis through a systematic literature review has revealed the complex interplay between EI, Well-being, and workplace performance. This insight has led us to assert that EI plays a substantial role in shaping an individual's overall well-being and work performance. This influence is mediated by various components of individual experiences, work environment, and mental and physical health of an individual, as depicted in Figure 5.

To enhance our understanding the model proposes to conduct future research in the direction of exploring the direct effects of EI on various dimensions of well-being and workplace outcomes, as well as its indirect effects through an individual's subjective experiences and environmental context. Our comprehensive conceptual model encapsulates these complex relationships, offering an integrative approach to managing these dynamics. By thoroughly examining both indirect and direct impacts, this model deepens our understanding of the EI's role in nurturing well-being and workplace performance. This contributes to a more profound understanding of the phenomenon.

Figure 5.

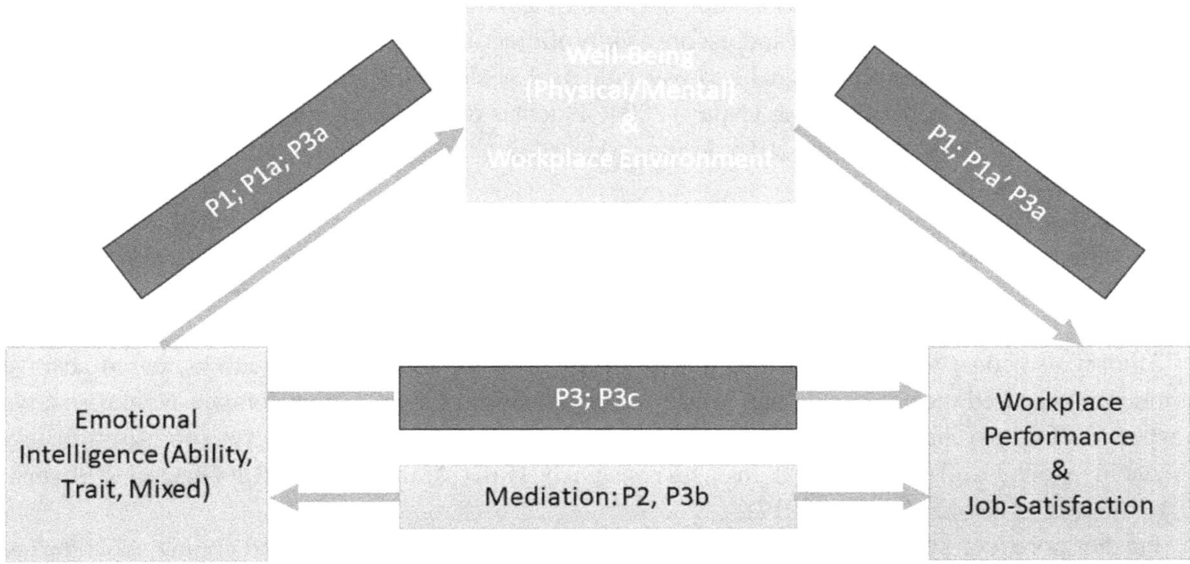

3. REVIEW METHODOLOGY

To systematically review emotional intelligence's impact on psychological well-being and workplace performance, we followed key methodologies from pivotal studies (Tranfield, Denyer, & Smart, 2003; Grant & Booth, 2009). Tranfield et al. emphasized structured systematic reviews, emphasizing critical steps like study selection and organization, while Grant and Booth provided insights into defining inclusion and exclusion criteria for effective review methodology.

Our three-step review methodology included a literature search, defining inclusion/exclusion criteria, and data extraction. For the literature search, we extensively utilized specific keywords across various databases (Google Scholar, Scopus, PubMed, Wiley online library, etc.) for studies published between 2000 and 2023. Inclusion criteria covered studies showing the relationship between emotional intelligence, psychological well-being, and work performance, focusing on aspects like physical/mental well-being, job satisfaction, work engagement, and job stress. The data extraction process began with an initial screening, resulting in 163 unique articles after refining from duplicates. A meticulous examination led to 81 articles for a thorough review, revealing the intricate interplay between emotional intelligence, well-being, and workplace performance.

This systematic review aims to establish a robust theoretical foundation by presenting propositions and arguments that emphasize emotional intelligence's substantial influence on employee well-being and workplace performance.

4. DISCUSSION AND CONCLUSION

Emotional Intelligence (EI) has emerged as a critical factor influencing both physical and mental well-being, drawing substantial attention from researchers. Our systematic review corroborates the existing literature, demonstrating a strong association between EI and overall well-being. The consistent findings across numerous empirical studies underscore that proficient management of emotional states significantly elevates levels of both physical and psychological health. This observation aligns with studies by (Pau & Croucher, 2003; Oades & Caputi, 2004; Tsaousis & Nikolaou, 2005; Zeidner, Matthews & Roberts, 2012; Di Fabio & Kenny, 2016; Malinauskas et al., 2018), highlighting the reliability of EI as a predictor of well-being.

Moreover, our review highlights a significant negative correlation between higher EI and perceived stress. Individuals with higher EI tend to experience reduced stress and anxiety, emphasizing EI's critical role in mitigating the adverse effects of stress on mental well-being. This finding is consistent with research by (Schutte et al., 2001; Schutte & Loi, 2014).

Studies also consistently demonstrate that higher levels of EI are associated with increased positive emotions, improved mental health, and greater life satisfaction. These findings emphasize the positive impact of EI on psychological adjustment and reduction of psychopathological symptoms, ultimately enhancing mental well-being. This aligns with research by (Ruiz-Aranda et al., 2014; Ghaderi & Shamsi, 2015; Szczygieł & Mikolajczak, 2017).

Furthermore, our systematic review suggests that EI correlates with enhanced coping skills during challenging times, reinforcing the idea that cultivating EI can equip individuals with valuable tools to navigate and cope with stressors, promoting mental well-being and resilience. This proposition is in line with research by (Mikolajczak et al., 2007; MacCann et al., 2014; Por et al., 2011).

The profound influence of high emotional intelligence (EI) on better mental health, higher engagement at work, increased workplace and social satisfaction, and a deeper understanding of the workplace is substantiated by various studies. The positive correlation between EI and favorable work-related outcomes highlights the instrumental role of EI in enhancing the well-being of individuals in their professional settings. This aligns with studies by (Brunetto et al., 2012; Alsughayir, 2019; Bhardwaj et al., 2023).

Our study provides a comprehensive theoretical foundation by linking various models and theories to the key variables under investigation: Emotional Intelligence (EI), Psychological Well-being (PWB), and Workplace Performance. The Mayer, Salovey, and Caruso Model of Emotional Social Intelligence, Daniel Goleman's Model of Emotional and Social Intelligence, The Bar-On Social and Emotional Intelligence Model, and Ryff's Six Factor Model of Psychological Well-being offer valuable frameworks to understand the dynamics between EI, PWB, and workplace performance.

Building upon the theoretical foundations, our conceptual model unravels the intricate interplay among emotional intelligence, psychological well-being, and workplace performance. This model posits that emotional intelligence significantly affects an individual's psychological well-being and work performance, with various mediating factors influencing this relationship. By scrutinizing both direct and indirect effects, this model contributes to a deeper understanding of how emotional intelligence fosters well-being and workplace performance.

4.1. Implications for Organizations, Managers, Policymakers, and Future Research

Our research carries significant implications for organizations, managers, policymakers, and future research.

4.1.1. Implications for Organizations and Managers

This study suggests that integrating emotional intelligence training programs can enhance employee well-being, reduce stress levels, and increase job satisfaction (Cherniss & Goleman, 2001; Zeidner, Matthews & Roberts, 2012; Di Fabio & Kenny, 2016; Malinauskas et al., 2018). Prioritizing emotional intelligence in the recruitment process can create a positive workplace environment, improve team dynamics, and boost productivity (Salovey & Mayer, 1990; Alsughayir, 2019; Bhardwaj et al., 2023). Focusing on developing emotional intelligence in leaders can foster a positive work atmosphere, effective communication, and stronger team relationships, ultimately enhancing organizational outcomes (Caruso & Salovey, 2004). Additionally, providing emotional intelligence-based conflict resolution training can enhance workplace harmony and promote better employee mental well-being (Bradberry & Greaves, 2009).

4.1.2. Implications for Policymakers

Policymakers can integrate emotional intelligence education into school curricula for long-term positive effects on individuals, contributing to a healthier and more emotionally intelligent society (Brackett et al., 2011). This research can inform policymakers in designing effective workplace policies. Encouraging or mandating emotional intelligence programs, incentives, or guidelines in organizations can create a positive work environment (Cherniss, 2010; Bhardwaj et al., 2023). Policies supporting and funding mental health initiatives focusing on enhancing emotional intelligence can help manage stress, anxiety, and mental health issues effectively, creating a healthy workforce and boosting performance (Weare, 2013; Schutte & Loi, 2014; Ghaderi & Shamsi, 2015; Szczygieł & Mikolajczak, 2017).

4.1.3. Implications for Future Research

Longitudinal studies are vital to comprehend the lasting impact of improved emotional intelligence on both well-being and work performance (Salovey & Mayer, 1990). Intervention studies are necessary to evaluate the effectiveness of emotional intelligence enhancement programs, offering practical insights for individuals and organizations aiming to boost emotional intelligence and, subsequently, enhance well-being and work performance (Brackett et al., 2011). Cross-cultural studies are important to understand how cultural differences influence the relationship between emotional intelligence, well-being, and workplace performance (Matsumoto & Hwang, 2013), aiding in tailoring strategies for diverse populations. Moreover, conducting multi-level analyses to scrutinize emotional intelligence's broader effects on well-being and workplace performance is critical for shaping organizational policies and practices, providing a holistic understanding of how emotional intelligence impacts the overall dynamics within an organization (Jordan & Troth, 2004).

5. LIMITATIONS OF THE STUDY

While offering initial insights into the complex interplay of EI, well-being, and workplace performance, this study has limitations. Firstly, relying on an extensive literature review might have missed critical studies, potentially affecting the findings' comprehensiveness and accuracy. Secondly, the study predominantly concentrates on specific work-related aspects when exploring the mediating role of psychological well-being (PWB), disregarding other dimensions of well-being that could influence employee behavior and job satisfaction. Moreover, being primarily literature-based, empirical studies are essential to directly validate the model's proposed relationships. Future research should address these constraints by conducting empirical studies, considering broader well-being dimensions, and ensuring a thorough literature review to enhance validity and the findings' applicability.

6. DECLARATION OF CONFLICTING INTERESTS

The authors affirm no conflicts of interest related to the research, writing, or publication of this article.

REFERENCES

Ahmadi, S. A. A. (2019). Relationship between emotional intelligence and psychological well-being. In *Relationship Between Emotional Intelligence and Psychological Well Being*. Academic Press.

Akanni, A. A., Kareem, D. B., & Oduaran, C. A. (2020). The relationship between emotional intelligence and employee wellbeing through perceived person-job fit among university academic staff: A Structural Equation Modelling Approach. *Cogent Psychology*, *7*(1), 1869376. doi:10.1080/23311908.2020.1869376

Akanni, A. A., Oladejo, O. E., & Oduaran, C. A. (2018). Work-life Balance, Job Insecurity and Counterproductive Work Behaviour among Brewery Workers. *North American Journal of Psychology*, *20*(2).

Akhtar, R., Boustani, L., Tsivrikos, D., & Chamorro-Premuzic, T. (2015). The engageable personality: Personality and trait as predictors of work engagement. *Personality and Individual Differences*, *73*, 44–49. doi:10.1016/j.paid.2014.08.040

Al Ali, O. E., Garner, I., & Magadley, W. (2012). An exploration of the relationship between emotional intelligence and job performance in police organizations. *Journal of Police and Criminal Psychology*, *27*(1), 1–8. doi:10.100711896-011-9088-9

Alsughayir, A. (2021). The effect of emotional intelligence on organizational commitment: Understanding the mediating role of job satisfaction. *Management Science Letters*, *11*(4), 1309–1316. doi:10.5267/j.msl.2020.11.008

Balluerka, N., Aritzeta, A., Gorostiaga, A., Gartzia, L., & Soroa, G. (2013). Emotional intelligence and depressed mood in adolescence: A multilevel approach. *International Journal of Clinical and Health Psychology*, *13*(2), 110–117. doi:10.1016/S1697-2600(13)70014-0

Balluerka, N., Gorostiaga, A., Alonso-Arbiol, I., & Aritzeta, A. (2016). Peer attachment and class emotional intelligence as predictors of adolescents' psychological well-being: A multilevel approach. *Journal of Adolescence*, *53*(1), 1–9. doi:10.1016/j.adolescence.2016.08.009 PMID:27596053

Barreiro, C. A., & Treglown, L. (2020). What makes an engaged employee? A facet-level approach to trait emotional intelligence as a predictor of employee engagement. *Personality and Individual Differences*, *159*, 109892. doi:10.1016/j.paid.2020.109892

Bechara, A., & Damasio, A. R. (2005). The somatic marker hypothesis: A neural theory of economic decision. *Games and Economic Behavior*, *52*(2), 336–372. doi:10.1016/j.geb.2004.06.010

Borman, W. C., & Motowidlo, S. J. (1997). Task performance and contextual performance: The meaning for personnel selection research. *Human Performance*, *10*(2), 99–109. doi:10.120715327043hup1002_3

Boyatzis, R. E., & McKee, A. (2005). *Resonant leadership: Renewing yourself and connecting with others through mindfulness, hope, and compassion*. Harvard Business Press.

Boyatzis, R. E., & Sala, F. (2004). Assessing emotional intelligence competencies. *The Measurement of Emotional Intelligence*, *2*, 147.

Brackett, M. A., Rivers, S. E., & Salovey, P. (2011). Emotional intelligence: Implications for personal, social, academic, and workplace success. *Social and Personality Psychology Compass*, *5*(1), 88–103. doi:10.1111/j.1751-9004.2010.00334.x

Brackett, M. A., Rivers, S. E., Shiffman, S., Lerner, N., & Salovey, P. (2006). Relating emotional abilities to social functioning: A comparison of self-report and performance measures of emotional intelligence. *Journal of Personality and Social Psychology*, *91*(4), 780–795. doi:10.1037/0022-3514.91.4.780 PMID:17014299

Brown, K. W., & Ryan, R. M. (2003). The benefits of being present: Mindfulness and its role in psychological well-being. *Journal of Personality and Social Psychology*, *84*(4), 822–848. doi:10.1037/0022-3514.84.4.822 PMID:12703651

Brunetto, Y., Teo, S. T., Shacklock, K., & Farr-Wharton, R. (2012). Emotional intelligence, job satisfaction, well-being and engagement: Explaining organisational commitment and turnover intentions in policing. *Human Resource Management Journal*, *22*(4), 428–441. doi:10.1111/j.1748-8583.2012.00198.x

Carmeli, A. (2003). The relationship between emotional intelligence and work attitudes, behavior and outcomes: An examination among senior managers. *Journal of Managerial Psychology*, *18*(8), 788–813. doi:10.1108/02683940310511881

Carmeli, A., Brueller, D., & Dutton, J. E. (2009). Learning behaviours in the workplace: The role of high-quality interpersonal relationships and psychological safety. Systems Research and Behavioral Science. *The Official Journal of the International Federation for Systems Research, 26*(1), 81–98.

Carmeli, A., Yitzhak-Halevy, M., & Weisberg, J. (2009). The relationship between emotional intelligence and psychological wellbeing. *Journal of Managerial Psychology, 24*(1), 66–78. doi:10.1108/02683940910922546

Cherniss, C. (2010). Emotional intelligence: Toward clarification of a concept. *Industrial and Organizational Psychology: Perspectives on Science and Practice, 3*(2), 110–126. doi:10.1111/j.1754-9434.2010.01231.x

Cherniss, C., & Goleman, D. (2001). *The emotionally intelligent workplace: How to select for, measure, and improve emotional intelligence in individuals, groups, and organizations*. John Wiley & Sons.

Chew, B. H., & Zain, A. M. (2018). Emotional intelligence as a mediator between emotional labor, job stress, burnout, and turnover intention among clinical nurses. *The Journal of Nursing Research, 26*(6), 348–354.

Cote, S. (2014). Emotional intelligence in organizations. *Annual Review of Organizational Psychology and Organizational Behavior, 1*(1), 459–488. doi:10.1146/annurev-orgpsych-031413-091233

Cote, S., DeCelles, K. A., McCarthy, J. M., Van Kleef, G. A., & Hideg, I. (2011). The Jekyll and Hyde of emotional intelligence: Emotion-regulation knowledge facilitates both prosocial and interpersonally deviant behavior. *Psychological Science, 22*(8), 1073–1080. doi:10.1177/0956797611416251 PMID:21775654

Cote, S., & Miners, C. T. (2006). Emotional intelligence, cognitive intelligence, and job performance. *Administrative Science Quarterly, 51*(1), 1–28. doi:10.2189/asqu.51.1.1

De Witte, H., Pienaar, J., & De Cuyper, N. (2016). Review of 30 years of longitudinal studies on the association between job insecurity and health and well-being: Is there causal evidence? *Australian Psychologist, 51*(1), 18–31. doi:10.1111/ap.12176

Diener, E. (2000). Subjective well-being: The science of happiness and a proposal for a national index. *The American Psychologist, 55*(1), 34–43. doi:10.1037/0003-066X.55.1.34 PMID:11392863

Diener, E., Suh, E. M., Lucas, R. E., & Smith, H. L. (1999). Subjective well-being: Three decades of progress. *Psychological Bulletin, 125*(2), 276–302. doi:10.1037/0033-2909.125.2.276

Durlak, J. A., Weissberg, R. P., Dymnicki, A. B., Taylor, R. D., & Schellinger, K. B. (2011). The impact of enhancing students' social and emotional learning: A meta-analysis of school-based universal interventions. *Child Development, 82*(1), 405–432. doi:10.1111/j.1467-8624.2010.01564.x PMID:21291449

Emmerling, R. J., & Boyatzis, R. E. (2012). Emotional and social intelligence competencies: Cross cultural implications. *Cross Cultural Management, 19*(1), 4–18. doi:10.1108/13527601211195592

Extremera, N., & Fernández-Berrocal, P. (2005). Perceived emotional intelligence and life satisfaction: Predictive and incremental validity using the Trait Meta-Mood Scale. *Personality and Individual Differences, 39*(5), 937–948. doi:10.1016/j.paid.2005.03.012

Extremera, N., Mérida-López, S., Sánchez-Álvarez, N., & Quintana-Orts, C. (2018). How does emotional intelligence make one feel better at work? The mediational role of work engagement. *International Journal of Environmental Research and Public Health, 15*(9), 1909. doi:10.3390/ijerph15091909 PMID:30200548

Extremera, N., & Rey, L. (2015). The moderator role of emotion regulation ability in the link between stress and well-being. *Frontiers in Psychology, 6*, 1632. doi:10.3389/fpsyg.2015.01632 PMID:26579017

Ghaderi, M., & Shamsi, A. (2015). The correlation between emotional intelligence and mental health among students of Jiroft city. *Journal of Healthcare Protection Management, 5*(1), 62–72.

Goleman, D. (1998). *Working with emotional intelligence*. Bantam Books.

Goleman, D. (2001). An EI-based theory of performance. *The emotionally intelligent workplace: How to select for, measure, and improve emotional intelligence in individuals, groups, and organizations, 1*(1), 27-44.

Goleman, D., & Intelligence, E. (1995). *Why it can matter more than IQ*. Emotional Intelligence.

Görgens-Ekermans, G., & Brand, T. (2012). Emotional intelligence as a moderator in the stress–burnout relationship: A questionnaire study on nurses. *Journal of Clinical Nursing, 21*(15-16), 2275–2285. doi:10.1111/j.1365-2702.2012.04171.x PMID:22788561

Grandey, A. A. (2000). Emotional regulation in the workplace: A new way to conceptualize emotional labor. *Journal of Occupational Health Psychology, 5*(1), 95–110. doi:10.1037/1076-8998.5.1.95 PMID:10658889

Grewal, D., Brackett, M., & Salovey, P. (2006). Emotional Intelligence and the Self-Regulation of Affect. In D. K. Snyder, J. Simpson, & J. N. Hughes (Eds.), *Emotion regulation in couples and families: Pathways to dysfunction and health* (pp. 37–55). American Psychological Association. doi:10.1037/11468-002

Ismail, K., Nopiah, Z. M., & Rasul, M. S. (2020). Emotional intelligence and work performance among vocational teachers. *Journal of Technical Education and Training, 12*(3), 106–117.

Jordan, P. J., Ashkanasy, N. M., Härtel, C. E., & Hooper, G. S. (2002). Workgroup emotional intelligence: Scale development and relationship to team process effectiveness and goal focus. *Human Resource Management Review, 12*(2), 195–214. doi:10.1016/S1053-4822(02)00046-3

Jordan, P. J., & Troth, A. C. (2004). Managing emotions during team problem solving: Emotional intelligence and conflict resolution. *Human Performance, 17*(2), 195–218. doi:10.120715327043hup1702_4

Joseph, D. L., Jin, J., Newman, D. A., & O'Boyle, E. H. (2015). Why does self-reported emotional intelligence predict job performance? A meta-analytic investigation of mixed EI. *The Journal of Applied Psychology, 100*(2), 298–342. doi:10.1037/a0037681 PMID:25243996

Joseph, D. L., & Newman, D. A. (2010). Emotional intelligence: An integrative meta-analysis and cascading model. *The Journal of Applied Psychology, 95*(1), 54–78. doi:10.1037/a0017286 PMID:20085406

Koubova, V., & Buchko, A. A. (2013). Life-work balance: Emotional intelligence as a crucial component of achieving both personal life and work performance. *Management Research Review, 36*(7), 700–719. doi:10.1108/MRR-05-2012-0115

Law, K. S., Wong, C. S., & Song, L. J. (2004). The construct and criterion validity of emotional intelligence and its potential utility for management studies. *The Journal of Applied Psychology*, *89*(3), 483–496. doi:10.1037/0021-9010.89.3.483 PMID:15161407

Lee, H. J. (2021). Relationship between emotional labor and job satisfaction: Testing mediating role of emotional intelligence on South Korean public service employees. *Public Organization Review*, *21*(2), 337–353. doi:10.100711115-020-00490-5

Llinares-Insa, L. I., Casino-García, A. M., & García-Pérez, J. (2020). Subjective well-being, emotional intelligence, and mood of parents: A model of relationships. Impact of giftedness. *Sustainability (Basel)*, *12*(21), 8810. doi:10.3390u12218810

Lopes, P. N. (2016). Emotional intelligence in organizations: Bridging research and practice. *Emotion Review*, *8*(4), 316–321. doi:10.1177/1754073916650496

Lopes, P. N., Salovey, P., & Straus, R. (2003). Emotional intelligence, personality, and the perceived quality of social relationships. *Personality and Individual Differences*, *35*(3), 641–658. doi:10.1016/S0191-8869(02)00242-8

Luthans, F., & Youssef, C. M. (2007). Emerging positive organizational behavior. *Journal of Management*, *33*(3), 321–349. doi:10.1177/0149206307300814

MacCann, C., Fogarty, G. J., Zeidner, M., & Roberts, R. D. (2011). Coping mediates the relationship between emotional intelligence (EI) and academic achievement. *Contemporary Educational Psychology*, *36*(1), 60–70. doi:10.1016/j.cedpsych.2010.11.002

Malik, M., Haider, Z., & Hussain, A. (2019). Perceived emotional intelligence, work life balance and job satisfaction among healthcare professionals in Pakistan. *International Journal of Pharmaceutical Research & Allied Sciences*, *8*(2), 80–86.

Malinauskas, R., Dumciene, A., Sipaviciene, S., & Malinauskiene, V. (2018). Relationship Between Emotional Intelligence and Health Behaviours among University Students: The Predictive and Moderating Role of Gender. *BioMed Research International*, *2018*, 1–11. doi:10.1155/2018/7058105 PMID:29967780

Mayer, J. D., Caruso, D. R., & Salovey, P. (1999). Emotional intelligence meets traditional standards for an intelligence. *Intelligence*, *27*(4), 267–298. doi:10.1016/S0160-2896(99)00016-1

Mayer, J. D., Caruso, D. R., & Salovey, P. (2016). The ability model of emotional intelligence: Principles and updates. *Emotion Review*, *8*(4), 290–300. doi:10.1177/1754073916639667

Mayer, J. D., Roberts, R. D., & Barsade, S. G. (2008). Human abilities: Emotional intelligence. *Annual Review of Psychology*, *59*(1), 507–536. doi:10.1146/annurev.psych.59.103006.093646 PMID:17937602

Mayer, J. D., Salovey, P., & Caruso, D. R. (2000). Emotional intelligence as zeitgeist, as personality, and as a mental ability. In R. Bar-On & J. D. A. Parker (Eds.), *The handbook of emotional intelligence: Theory, development, assessment, and application at home, school, and in the workplace* (pp. 92–117). Jossey-Bass/Wiley.

Miao, C., Humphrey, R. H., & Qian, S. (2017). A meta-analysis of emotional intelligence and work attitudes. *Journal of Occupational and Organizational Psychology*, *90*(2), 177–202. doi:10.1111/joop.12167

Mikolajczak, M., & Luminet, O. (2008). Trait emotional intelligence and the cognitive appraisal of stressful events: An exploratory study. *Personality and Individual Differences*, *44*(7), 1445–1453. doi:10.1016/j.paid.2007.12.012

Mikolajczak, M., Luminet, O., Leroy, C., & Roy, E. (2007). Psychometric properties of the Trait Emotional Intelligence Questionnaire: Factor structure, reliability, construct, and incremental validity in a French-speaking population. *Journal of Personality Assessment*, *88*(3), 338–353. doi:10.1080/00223890701333431 PMID:17518555

Mohammadyfar, M. A., Khan, M. S., & Tamini, B. K. (2009). The effect of emotional intelligence and job burnout on mental and physical health. *Journal of the Indian Academy of Applied Psychology*, *35*(2), 219–226.

Pau, A. K., & Croucher, R. (2003). Emotional intelligence and perceived stress in dental undergraduates. *Journal of Dental Education*, *67*(9), 1023–1028. doi:10.1002/j.0022-0337.2003.67.9.tb03685.x PMID:14518841

Pérez-Fuentes, M. D. C., Molero Jurado, M. D. M., Gázquez Linares, J. J., & Oropesa Ruiz, N. F. (2018). The role of emotional intelligence in engagement in nurses. *International Journal of Environmental Research and Public Health*, *15*(9), 1915. doi:10.3390/ijerph15091915 PMID:30177621

Petrides, K. V. (2011). Ability and trait emotional intelligence. In T. Chamorro-Premuzic, S. von Stumm, & A. Furnham (Eds.), *The Wiley-Blackwell handbook of individual differences* (pp. 656–678). Wiley Blackwell. doi:10.1002/9781444343120.ch25

Petrides, K. V., Pérez-González, J. C., & Furnham, A. (2007). On the criterion and incremental validity of trait emotional intelligence. *Cognition and Emotion*, *21*(1), 26–55. doi:10.1080/02699930601038912

Petrides, K. V., Pita, R., & Kokkinaki, F. (2007). The location of trait emotional intelligence in personality factor space. *British Journal of Psychology*, *98*(2), 273–289. doi:10.1348/000712606X120618 PMID:17456273

Por, J., Barriball, L., Fitzpatrick, J., & Roberts, J. (2011). Emotional intelligence: Its relationship to stress, coping, well-being and professional performance in nursing students. *Nurse Education Today*, *31*(8), 855–860. doi:10.1016/j.nedt.2010.12.023 PMID:21292360

Psilopanagioti, A., Anagnostopoulos, F., Mourtou, E., & Niakas, D. (2012). Emotional intelligence, emotional labor, and job satisfaction among physicians in Greece. *BMC Health Services Research*, *12*(1), 1–12. doi:10.1186/1472-6963-12-463 PMID:23244390

Pulakos, E. D., Arad, S., Donovan, M. A., & Plamondon, K. E. (2000). Adaptability in the workplace: Development of a taxonomy of adaptive performance. *The Journal of Applied Psychology*, *85*(4), 612–624. doi:10.1037/0021-9010.85.4.612 PMID:10948805

Rana, S., Mahavidyalaya, K., Rathore, D., & Chadha, N. K. (2017). Emotional intelligence in the workplace. *Indian Journal of Positive Psychology*, *8*(2), 162–165.

Robbins, S. P., & Coulter, M. (2005). *Management* (8th ed.). Pearson.

Robins, R. W., & Pals, J. L. (2002). Implicit self-theories in the academic domain: Implications for goal orientation, attributions, affect, and self-esteem change. *Self and Identity, 1*(4), 313–336. doi:10.1080/15298860290106805

Ruiz-Aranda, D., Extremera, N., & Pineda-Galan, C. (2014). Emotional intelligence, life satisfaction and subjective happiness in female student health professionals: The mediating effect of perceived stress. *Journal of Psychiatric and Mental Health Nursing, 21*(2), 106–113. doi:10.1111/jpm.12052 PMID:23578272

Ryff, C. D. (1989). Happiness is everything, or is it? Explorations on the meaning of psychological well-being. *Journal of Personality and Social Psychology, 57*(6), 1069–1081. doi:10.1037/0022-3514.57.6.1069

Salanova, M., Agut, S., & Peiró, J. M. (2005). Linking organizational resources and work engagement to employee performance and customer loyalty: The mediation of service climate. *The Journal of Applied Psychology, 90*(6), 1217–1227. doi:10.1037/0021-9010.90.6.1217 PMID:16316275

Salguero, J. M., Palomera, R., & Fernández-Berrocal, P. (2012). Perceived emotional intelligence as predictor of psychological adjustment in adolescents: A 1-year prospective study. *European Journal of Psychology of Education, 27*(1), 21–34. doi:10.100710212-011-0063-8

Salovey, P., & Grewal, D. (2005). The science of emotional intelligence. *Current Directions in Psychological Science, 14*(6), 281–285. doi:10.1111/j.0963-7214.2005.00381.x

Salovey, P., & Mayer, J. D. (1990). Emotional intelligence. *Imagination, Cognition and Personality, 9*(3), 185–211. doi:10.2190/DUGG-P24E-52WK-6CDG

Sanchez-Álvarez, N., Extremera, N., & Fernández-Berrocal, P. (2016). The relation between emotional intelligence and subjective well-being: A meta-analytic investigation. *The Journal of Positive Psychology, 11*(3), 276–285. doi:10.1080/17439760.2015.1058968

Schutte, N. S., & Loi, N. M. (2014). Connections between emotional intelligence and workplace flourishing. *Personality and Individual Differences, 66*, 134–139. doi:10.1016/j.paid.2014.03.031

Schutte, N. S., & Malouff, J. M. (2011). Emotional intelligence mediates the relationship between mindfulness and subjective well-being. *Personality and Individual Differences, 50*(7), 1116–1119. doi:10.1016/j.paid.2011.01.037

Schutte, N. S., Malouff, J. M., Thorsteinsson, E. B., Bhullar, N., & Rooke, S. E. (2007). A meta-analytic investigation of the relationship between emotional intelligence and health. *Personality and Individual Differences, 42*(6), 921–933. doi:10.1016/j.paid.2006.09.003

Schutte, N. S., Schuettpelz, E., & Malouff, J. M. (2001). Emotional intelligence and task performance. *Imagination, Cognition and Personality, 20*(4), 347–354. doi:10.2190/J0X6-BHTG-KPV6-2UXX

Segal, J. (2002). Good leaders use" emotional intelligence". Emotionally intelligent leadership is a skill that can be learned and taught throughout life. *Health Progress (Saint Louis, Mo.), 83*(3), 44–46. PMID:12038009

Singh, T. (2016). Relating emotional intelligence and organisational commitment though moderated mediation of psychological well being and work life balance: A study on teachers of NGOs. *Rupkatha Journal on Interdisciplinary Studies in Humanities, 8*(2), 28–42. doi:10.21659/rupkatha.v8n2.04

Slaski, M., & Cartwright, S. (2003). Emotional intelligence training and its implications for stress, health and performance. *Stress and Health*, *19*(4), 233–239. doi:10.1002mi.979

Sokmen, Y., & Sarikaya, İ. (2022). The mediating role of self-efficacy between emotional intelligence and job satisfaction of primary school teachers. *European Review of Applied Psychology*, *72*(4), 100779. doi:10.1016/j.erap.2022.100779

Spence, G., Oades, L. G., & Caputi, P. (2004). Trait emotional intelligence and goal self-integration: Important predictors of emotional well-being? *Personality and Individual Differences*, *37*(3), 449–461. doi:10.1016/j.paid.2003.09.001

Szczygieł, D., & Mikolajczak, M. (2017). Why are people high in emotional intelligence happier? They make the most of their positive emotions. *Personality and Individual Differences*, *117*, 177–181. doi:10.1016/j.paid.2017.05.051

Taylor, C., Harrison, J., Haimovitz, K., Oberle, E., Thomson, K., Schonert-Reichl, K., & Roeser, R. W. (2016). Examining ways that a mindfulness-based intervention reduces stress in public school teachers: A mixed-methods study. *Mindfulness*, *7*(1), 115–129. doi:10.100712671-015-0425-4

Van Rooy, D. L., & Viswesvaran, C. (2004). Emotion intelligence: A meta-analytic investigation of predictive validity and nomological net. *Journal of Vocational Behavior*, *65*(1), 71–95. doi:10.1016/S0001-8791(03)00076-9

Webb, T. L., Miles, E., & Sheeran, P. (2012). Dealing with feeling: A meta-analysis of the effectiveness of strategies derived from the process model of emotion regulation. *Psychological Bulletin*, *138*(4), 775–808. doi:10.1037/a0027600 PMID:22582737

Wong, C. S., Foo, M. D., Wang, C. W., & Wong, P. M. (2007). The feasibility of training and development of EI: An exploratory study in Singapore, Hong Kong and Taiwan. *Intelligence*, *35*(2), 141–150. doi:10.1016/j.intell.2006.04.008

Wong, C.-S., & Law, K. S. (2002). *Wong and Law Emotional Intelligence Scale (WLEIS)* [Database record]. APA PsycTests.

Zeidner, M., Matthews, G., & Roberts, R. D. (2012). The emotional intelligence, health, and well-being nexus: What have we learned and what have we missed? *Applied Psychology. Health and Well-Being*, *4*(1), 1–30. doi:10.1111/j.1758-0854.2011.01062.x PMID:26286968

Chapter 7
The Role of Emotional Intelligence in Effective Leadership and Decision-Making in Business Management

Rohan Sharma
Shoolini University, India

Rozy Dhanta
Shoolini University, India

Dahlak Daniel Solomon
Shoolini University, India & Adama Science and Technology, Ethiopia

ABSTRACT

Effective leadership and decision-making are essential in today's dynamic corporate environment. This study explores how important company management components are impacted by emotional intelligence (EI). EI entails the ability to identify, evaluate, and control one's own emotions as well as those of others. It examines the elements of EI and how it is used in decision-making and leadership. Highly empathetic leaders motivate and engage their staff, improving the workplace and performance. The study reveals how EI affects decision-making, taking into account both cognitive and emotional components for better results in difficult circumstances. The importance of training, mentoring, and feedback in the development of EI in executives is stressed. This promotes efficiency and thoughtful decision-making, which eventually leads to organizational success. It is essential to give EI top priority while developing leaders. The report also suggests prospective lines of inquiry and provides helpful advice for practitioners.

DOI: 10.4018/979-8-3693-0418-1.ch007

INTRODUCTION

Effective leadership and decision-making are key components for organizational success in the ever-changing face of corporate management. In the dynamic world of corporate management, effective leadership and decision-making are essential components for assuring organizational success. Higher productivity and employee happiness are the results of strong leadership because it guides teams, motivates them, and cultivates a positive workplace environment. Organizations may overcome obstacles, seize opportunities, and keep a competitive edge by making wise decisions. Organizations may handle complexity, spur growth, and achieve long-term success in a dynamic and competitive business environment by combining effective leadership with educated decision-making. Leaders were traditionally evaluated primarily based on their technical ability, experience, and cognitive talents. However, as businesses become more complicated and diverse, it has become clear that emotional intelligence is crucial in moulding leaders' capacities to negotiate problems, motivate teams, and make informed judgments (Kang et al., 2020; Wong, C. S., & Law, K. S. (2017)). The ability to identify, analyse, and manage one's emotions, as well as perceive and sympathize with the emotions of others, is referred to as emotional intelligence. It includes a variety of abilities such as self-awareness, self-regulation, motivation, social awareness, and relationship management. Collectively, these abilities help leaders to handle the intricacies of interpersonal interactions, inspire collaboration, and create a healthy work environment (George, 2000; Goleman et al., 2009). The notion of emotional intelligence was first developed in the early 1990s by psychologists Peter Salovey and John Mayer. Still, it achieved broad attention and popularity because to the work of Daniel Goleman. Goleman's seminal book, "Emotional Intelligence: Why It Can Matter More Than IQ," popularized the notion that emotional intelligence can be a significant predictor of success not only in personal life but also in professional domains such as leadership and decision-making (Caruso et al., 2013; James Thomas, 2004). Emotional intelligence technologies offer promising ways to enhance decision-management processes (Palmer et al., 2001; Alzoubi & Aziz, 2021). These technologies aim to integrate emotional understanding and empathy into decision-making to ensure more thoughtful and empathetic outcomes. One application involves sentiment analysis, where natural language processing is used to identify and categorize emotions expressed in text or speech (Kang et al., 2020). This allows decision-makers to gain valuable insights into stakeholders' emotional states and respond accordingly. Another essential aspect involves recognizing emotional cues through facial expressions, enabling real-time assessment of emotional states during interactions (Canedo & Neves, 2019). This can be particularly useful in customer service scenarios, helping agents respond more effectively and empathetically. Emotion-aware virtual assistants and chatbots are also developed to gauge users' emotional states through speech patterns and adjust their responses with greater empathy and understanding. Furthermore, emotional intelligence technologies provide emotional feedback in decision support systems, helping decision-makers understand the emotional impact of their choices on stakeholders. This encourages more compassionate and empathetic decision-making, considering the emotional well-being of those involved (Nelis et al., 2011). Additionally, in educational settings, emotion-driven adaptive learning is facilitated by monitoring students' emotional responses during learning activities, enabling the system to adapt its approach and content for better engagement and understanding (Mayer et al., 2009). However, the integration of emotional intelligence technologies in decision management also raises ethical concerns related to privacy, consent, and responsible data use. Extensive study has been undertaken throughout the years to investigate the relationship between emotional intelligence and leadership effectiveness. Numerous studies have found a link between emotional intelligence and beneficial outcomes such as employee happiness, performance, and organizational success (Goleman et al., 2009). Leaders with high emotional intelligence are more likely to create engaged and motivated teams, build trust and rapport, and effectively manage conflicts (Carmeli & Josman, 2006). The capacity to make wise decisions is an important part of effective leadership. In corporate management, decision-making is a multidimensional process that involves examining complex information, considering many perspectives, and weighing potential risks and advantages. Emotional intelligence is critical in this process because it equips leaders with the ability to navigate and manage emotions, both their own and those of others, which can have a substantial impact on decision outcomes (Petrides, K. V., & Furnham, A. 2000). Emotionally intelligent leaders are adept at understanding and managing their own emotions, helping them to stay calm and composed under pressure (Mayer et al., 2008). Instead of being led only by their emotions, this self-regulation allows people to think more clearly and make sensible judgments. Furthermore, leaders with high emotional intelligence are skilled at understanding the feelings of others, allowing them to gain new insights, consider alternative viewpoints, and make better informed judgments (Palmer et al., 2001). In today's international and diverse business environment, emotional intelligence plays an even more important role in leadership and decision-making. Organizations operate in a globalized environment with many cultural, social, and emotional distinctions. To handle these difficulties, leaders must demonstrate empathy, cultural sensitivity, and the capacity to create relationships across varied teams and stakeholders (Alzoubi & Aziz, 2021). Leaders may use emotional intelligence to promote inclusive work environments, successfully communicate across cultures, and bridge understanding gaps. Through this comprehensive exploration, we aim to provide a nuanced understanding of the significance of emotional intelligence in leadership and decision-making. By recognizing the multifaceted nature of effective leadership, organizations can develop strategies to identify, nurture, and leverage emotional intelligence competencies in their leaders. Ultimately, this knowledge can contribute to the development of more effective leaders who can navigate complexities, inspire teams, and make informed decisions in the dynamic world of business management, self-awareness, self-regulation, empathy, and relationship management. We hope to present a nuanced knowledge of the importance of emotional intelligence in leadership and decision-making through this comprehensive investigation. Organizations can establish ways to discover, foster, and leverage emotional intelligence competencies in their leaders by acknowledging the complex nature of good leadership. Finally, this understanding can help to produce more effective leaders who can traverse complexities, inspire teams, and make sound decisions in the fast-paced world of company management.

1 UNDERSTANDING EMOTIONAL INTELLIGENCE

1.1 Definition and Components of Emotional Intelligence

The ability to detect, understand, and control one's own emotions as well as the emotions of others is referred to as emotional intelligence (EI). It requires the capacity to recognize and comprehend how emotions affect behavior and judgment. EI is essential for building solid connections, efficient communication, and effective leadership. People with strong emotional intelligence are more adept at resolving disagreements, navigating social settings, and creating supportive and effective work environments. Self-awareness, empathy, and general emotional health can all be improved by developing emotional intelligence.

Table 1. Componets of emotional intelligence

Self-awareness:	The ability to recognize and understand one's emotions, strengths, weaknesses, and values.
Self-regulation:	The capacity to manage and control one's emotions, impulses, and reactions, especially in challenging situations.
Empathy:	The ability to comprehend and share the feelings and perspectives of others, demonstrating understanding and sensitivity.
Social skills:	Proficiency in communication, collaboration, and conflict resolution to foster positive interactions and build strong relationships with others.

1.2 Historical Background and Development of Emotional Intelligence

In the early 1990s, psychologists Peter Salovey and John Mayer pioneered the notion of emotional intelligence (Brackett & Mayer, 2003). Their research helped to provide the groundwork for understanding the role of emotions in cognition and behavior. However, it was Daniel Goleman's seminal 1995 book, "Emotional Intelligence: Why It Can Matter More Than IQ," that popularized the concept among a wider audience. Goleman's research stressed the importance of emotional intelligence in personal and professional success, emphasizing its influence on leadership and decision-making.

1.3 Importance of Emotional Intelligence in Business Management

Because of its impact on effective leadership and decision-making, emotional intelligence is critical in corporate management. Leaders with high emotional intelligence are capable of inspiring, motivating, and engaging their people, resulting in a favorable work environment (Mayer et al., 2009). Through their own emotional awareness and comprehension of others' emotions, emotionally intelligent leaders establish deep connections, improve team performance, and inspire collaboration (Jordan et al., 2002). In today's complicated and fast-paced corporate environment, emotional intelligence enables leaders to negotiate problems, create relationships, and adapt to a variety of scenarios, all of which contribute to organizational success.

2 THE IMPACT OF EMOTIONAL INTELLIGENCE ON EFFECTIVE LEADERSHIP

2.1 Emotional Intelligence and Leadership Effectiveness

The ability to effectively lead teams and organizations is a major advantage held by emotionally intelligent leaders. They are able to make wise and insightful decisions thanks to their deep comprehension and skillful emotional control (Petrides, K. V., & Furnham, A. 2000). A pleasant and effective work environment is fostered by this emotional intelligence, which encourages a sympathetic and empathetic reaction to the needs and difficulties faced by their coworkers. Highly empathetic leaders demonstrate motion intelligence. They are able to relate to and comprehend the thoughts and feelings of their team members. Because of their capacity for empathy, they can establish close relationships with their coworkers, encouraging openness and trust in the workplace. Effective emotion management is a key component of emotional intelligence in leadership. Instead of stifling feelings, these leaders manage them in a constructive manner (Sosik & Megerian, 1999). Emotionally intelligent leaders foster a good and supportive work environment, which leads to higher job satisfaction and employee engagement.

2.2 Emotional Intelligence and Team Performance

A work atmosphere that encourages trust, transparency, and collaboration among team members, ultimately resulting in improved team performance, needs to be fostered by emotionally intelligent leaders. These leaders have a deep understanding of emotions, and they make use of this knowledge to foster an environment in the workplace where workers feel valued, encouraged, and inspired to give it their all (Bhardwaj, B. 2021). Building trust is one of the key components of emotional intelligence in leadership. Integrity, consistency, and empathy are qualities that emotionally intelligent leaders exhibit when establishing trust. Their team members appreciate and trust them because they set a good example and are honest about their actions and judgments. Strong relationships and productive teamwork are built on trust (Sy et al., 2006; Côté & Miners,2006).

Figure 1. The impact of emotional intelligence on effective leadership

2.3 Emotional Intelligence and Employee Engagement

Since they place a high priority on encouraging trust, openness, and collaboration among team members, emotionally intelligent leaders have a significant impact on team dynamics, which ultimately improves team performance. Their capacity for empathy and understanding their team's feelings enables them to foster a welcoming and inclusive workplace where everyone feels respected and inspired to put out their best efforts. The ability to foster a sense of trust among the team members is one of the main attributes of emotionally intelligent leaders. Team members are more likely to feel safe and confident in their interactions when their leaders are transparent, honest, and sincere. Communication becomes more open and honest as trust increases, fostering stronger bonds and improved teamwork (Wong & Law, 2017).

2.4 Emotional Intelligence and Building Positive Work Environments

Leaders that are emotionally intelligent actively foster a healthy work environment by handling problems well, encouraging candid communication, and motivating and praising their team members. They take a proactive stance when dealing with issues and disputes, looking for group initiatives that will strengthen the team as a whole. Team members feel more connected and trusted as a result, which improves collaboration and productivity. Emotionally intelligent leaders foster an environment where ideas and opinions are openly exchanged and respected through promoting open communication. This unrestricted flow of ideas and points of view encourages creativity and problem-solving, which advances the company as a whole. Additionally, emotionally intelligent leaders understand the value of expressing gratitude to their workforce. They really applaud the efforts and accomplishments of their team members.

3 EMOTIONAL INTELLIGENCE AND DECISION-MAKING IN BUSINESS MANAGEMENT

3.1 The Role of Emotional Intelligence in Decision-Making

Decision-making is highly impacted by emotional intelligence since it allows leaders to take both cognitive and emotional factors into account. Leaders may make choices that resonate with their teams and are in line with the goals and values of the organization by being conscious of their own emotions as well as those of others. This well-rounded strategy promotes trust and understanding, leading to more sensible and well-liked decisions that contribute to the organization's overall success (Hess & Bacigalupo, 2011).

Figure 2. Role of emotional intelligence in decision-making

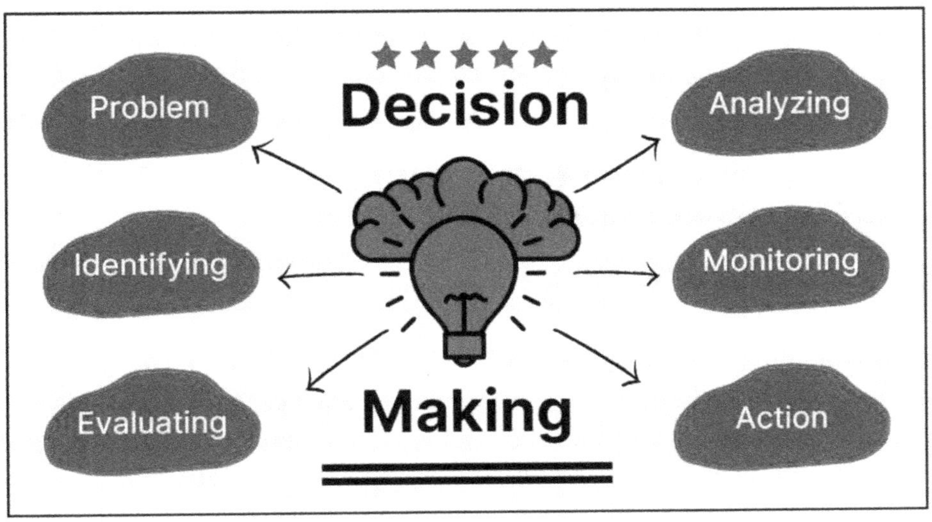

3.2 Emotional Intelligence and Rational Decision-Making

The ability to regulate one's emotions during decision-making enables emotionally savvy leaders to approach issues with critical thought and reason. These leaders make thoughtful judgments that are in the best interests of the team and the organization by avoiding impulsive choices that are entirely based on emotional reactions. This emotional self-regulation improves their ability to make decisions and leads to more productive outcomes.

3.3 Emotional Intelligence and Intuitive Decision-Making

Leaders with higher emotional intelligence have better intuition and decision-making skills. Because they have developed their capacity to recognize and comprehend emotions in both themselves and others, people with high emotional intelligence can put their trust in their gut sensations and instincts. These leaders obtain more in-depth understanding of events, which enables them to make more educated and reasonable decisions by taking into consideration emotional cues and nonverbal indications from stakeholders and team members. They are better equipped to negotiate challenging situations with more confidence and produce outcomes that are more favorable for their teams and organizations because to the integration of emotional awareness and rational judgment.

3.4 Emotional Intelligence and Navigating Complex Situations

Leaders that possess emotional intelligence have the abilities to successfully negotiate challenging situations. Leaders can better handle possible issues and conflicts by understanding the emotions of stakeholders and staff. Because of their greater understanding of emotions, they are better able to tackle issues with empathy and tact, encouraging candid dialogue and group problem-solving. Leaders are better able to develop cooperative and constructive solutions by being aware of the emotional dynamics at play, which fosters a happy and productive workplace. Leaders that are emotionally intelligent may skillfully negotiate their way through challenges, strengthening their bonds with their team members and stakeholders and succeeding in solving complex problems.

4 STRATEGIES FOR DEVELOPING EMOTIONAL INTELLIGENCE IN BUSINESS LEADERS

4.1 Emotional Intelligence Training Programs

Organizations give thorough training packages to their leaders because they understand the importance of emotional intelligence in leadership. Essential emotional intelligence competencies including self-awareness, empathy, emotional control, and social skills are the main focus of these programs. Leaders can make more informed judgments by gaining self-awareness, which gives them insights into their emotions, strengths, and flaws. Empathy enables leaders to comprehend the thoughts and feelings of their team members, improving teamwork and communication. Leaders who are able to control their emotions, especially in difficult circumstances, are better able to make wise decisions. Additionally, social skill development gives leaders the ability to create trust among their team members, forge lasting connections, and settle disputes. Overall, emotional intelligence training enables leaders to become more powerful and effective in their responsibilities, which is advantageous for the company as well as the leaders.

4.2 Coaching and Mentoring for Emotional Intelligence Development

To improve their emotional intelligence, leaders can benefit greatly from coaching and mentorship. Leaders can learn a lot about their emotional strengths and areas for development by receiving individualized one-on-one mentoring and criticism from seasoned mentors. Leaders can receive advice from mentors on how to improve critical skills like self-awareness, empathy, and emotional regulation as well as how to identify any emotional intelligence blind spots they may have (Nelis, D., Kotsou, I., Quoidbach, J., 2011) Mentors can also offer helpful guidance on implementing emotional intelligence programs within the company. They can impart best practices, real-world examples, and methods for establishing an emotional intelligence-positive society. With this assistance, leaders can foster a culture where emotional intelligence is recognized and actively used across the company. Leaders can improve their emotional intelligence by investing in coaching and mentoring, which will increase their leadership effectiveness and produce better results for their teams and companies. These connections provide invaluable knowledge and counsel that can contribute to the success of the organization as a whole as well as the personal development of the leaders (Higgs, M., & Dulewicz, V., 2016).

4.3 Feedback Mechanisms for Emotional Intelligence Enhancement

The growth of leaders' emotional intelligence can be considerably aided by establishing an open feedback culture within the firm. Leaders can learn a lot about their strengths and potential areas for improvement by allowing team members to offer constructive criticism on their emotional intelligence skills. Through this open feedback, leaders can better grasp how their actions and emotions affect other people, which promotes a higher degree of self-awareness. Leaders can spot trends in team members' emotional reactions and communication styles by soliciting regular input from the team. Armed with this knowledge, leaders can consciously work to develop their emotional intelligence abilities by engaging in activities like active listening, stress management techniques, and empathic team response A culture that welcomes criticism also emphasizes the value of emotional intelligence within the company. It sends a strong message to the rest of the team about the importance of emotional intelligence in fostering a good and productive work environment when leaders actively seek and embrace feedback on their emotional intelligence competencies. Leaders with a growth mentality and a dedication to constant improvement constantly seek out criticism and examine it. A leader's ability to manage conflicts, encourage collaboration, and motivate their employees to perform to their highest potential increases as they practice and hone their emotional intelligence skills. In the end, fostering an open feedback culture helps the organization succeed overall by supporting emotionally intelligent leadership and cultivating a culture of trust, respect and growth.

4.4 Cultivating Emotional Intelligence in Leadership Development Initiatives

Initiatives for leadership development that take emotional intelligence into account are crucial for producing well-rounded and effective leaders. Along with technical skills and knowledge, emotional intelligence should be regarded as a core competency in leadership training. Organizations may guarantee that their leaders have the skills necessary to negotiate the complexity of the contemporary workplace by include emotional intelligence in their leadership development programs. Leaders that possess emotional intelligence are able to comprehend and control their own emotions as well as those of their stakeholders and team members. Due to their increased knowledge, leaders may create more solid bonds among their employees, promote trust, and encourage cooperation. When emotional intelligence is incorporated into leadership training, leaders develop the ability to make judgments out of empathy and regard for the welfare of their team, which fosters a more positive work environment. Emotional intelligence is also essential for resolving disputes, having productive conversations, and changing with the times. Emotionally intelligent leaders can manage difficult situations with grace, which improves problem-solving and decision-making outcomes. By including emotional intelligence in leadership development programs, leaders may be sure that they are equipped to handle the interpersonal parts of their jobs, which is in addition to their technical knowledge. This strategy encourages a more all-encompassing and people-centered leadership style, which enhances employee engagement, lowers attrition, and boosts corporate effectiveness.

5 CASE STUDIES AND REAL-WORLD EXAMPLES

5.1 Successful Leaders Demonstrating High Emotional Intelligence

The case studies of outstanding leaders who displayed remarkable emotional intelligence and the profound effects it had on their teams and organizations are presented in this section. These case studies offer actual instances of how emotional intelligence may improve leadership and lead to fruitful results. Readers can learn from these leaders' experiences how using emotional intelligence enabled them to overcome obstacles, form close bonds with their team members, and promote a climate of trust and cooperation. These case studies demonstrate how emotionally intelligent leaders successfully handled disagreements, empathized with others, and inspired their teams to achieve exceptional results. Readers can comprehend the practical uses of emotional intelligence in diverse leadership scenarios through these in-the-real-world examples. The case studies provide organizations wanting to improve their leadership development programs with ideas and inspiration. In the end, they stress how crucial emotional intelligence is to effective leadership and how it may foster flourishing, high-performing teams and companies.

5.2 How Emotional Intelligence Contributed to Positive Organizational Outcomes

Real-world examples offer convincing proof of how emotional intelligence in leaders has a substantial positive impact on organizational success. Increased productivity is one of these results. High emotional intelligence leaders are adept at inspiring and involving their team members, fostering a work climate that promotes innovation, collaboration, and creativity (Sosik, J. J., & Megerian, L. E. 1999). They are skilled in appreciating and recognizing their workers' accomplishments, which promotes a feeling of gratitude and belonging, increasing productivity and commitment to achieving corporate goals. Another significant result that is influenced by a leader's emotional intelligence is employee satisfaction. Strong emotional intelligence enables leaders to empathize with their team members, comprehend their requirements, and offer the support and resources they require. Employees will feel valued and cared for in such a culture of open communication and trust.

5.3 The Consequences of Low Emotional Intelligence in Leadership and Decision Making

Case studies that highlight the negative effects of poor emotional intelligence on decision-making and leadership serve as potent reminders of how crucial it is to acquire emotional intelligence competencies. These real-world examples highlight the dangers and unfavourable effects that can occur when leaders are unable to recognize and successfully control their emotions. These case studies show that leaders with low emotional intelligence frequently have trouble communicating with empathy, which has a negative impact on relationships with team members and stakeholders. Misunderstandings, disputes, and a decline in organizational trust result from their inability to recognize and react to other people's emotions. This communication breakdown makes it difficult to collaborate and operate as a team, which lowers productivity as a whole and makes it harder to accomplish corporate objectives.

6 CHALLENGES AND LIMITATIONS OF EMOTIONAL INTELLIGENCE IN BUSINESS MANAGEMENT:

6.1 Addressing Barriers to Emotional Intelligence Development

There may be a number of obstacles that the development of emotional intelligence must overcome. Personal prejudices are a frequent barrier. People may have preconceived conceptions or stereotypes that make it difficult for them to appropriately recognize and comprehend the emotions of others. To combat this, people need to reflect on themselves, develop an open attitude, and actively work to confront and alter their prejudices through knowledge and exposure to many viewpoints (Nelis, D., Kotsou, I.,2011). The resistance to change is still another difficulty. People who want to develop their emotional intelligence frequently need to venture outside of their comfort zones and embrace unconventional ways of thinking and acting. Creating a welcoming environment that promotes development and learning is key to overcoming this reluctance. People can embrace change by being given opportunities for skill-building programs, coaching, and mentorship. The development of emotional intelligence is also hampered by time constraints and conflicting objectives. Setting aside time for emotional growth and self-reflection in hectic work environments may seem difficult. Organizations can reduce this by including emotional intelligence training into regular programs for leadership development and by offering ongoing assistance and tools for lifelong learning. Additionally, it takes dedication from both individuals and organizations to address these issues. Leaders need to emphasize the development of emotional intelligence and set an example for their people. Organizations should promote a culture that emphasizes emotional intelligence, where people feel secure to express their emotions and experiences and where feedback and open communication are encouraged.

6.2 Potential Risks of Overemphasizing Emotional Intelligence

Even though emotional intelligence is unquestionably important for effective leadership, emphasizing it over other leadership skills might result in unbalanced leadership styles. Beyond emotional intelligence, effective leadership requires a broad range of abilities, including technical know-how, strategic thinking, decision-making, and the capacity to encourage and inspire colleagues. Recognizing that emotional intelligence should enhance rather than replace other leadership skills is crucial for creating a balanced strategy. In order to fulfill the diverse requirements of their positions, leaders must concentrate on developing a wide range of talents. Achieving this balance through self-evaluation and ongoing education is one approach to do it. Leaders should evaluate their strengths and areas for improvement in terms of emotional intelligence and other leadership abilities. By identifying their weaknesses, they can focus on developing particular skills. Another beneficial tactic is to encourage feedback from coworkers, managers, and team members. Constructive criticism reveals perceptions of leaders and identifies their areas of strength and development as a leader. This criticism can help leaders make minor adjustments to their style, resulting in a comprehensive and well-balanced leadership strategy. Furthermore, by offering thorough leadership development programs, businesses can aid in the development of balanced leadership. These programs ought to cover instruction in emotional intelligence, the improvement of technical skills, communication, problem-solving, and other crucial leadership abilities.

6.3 Balancing Emotional Intelligence With Other Leadership Competencies

Effective leadership is a complex activity that calls for the seamless integration of many different skill sets. Technical expertise is necessary to comprehend the nuances of a particular sector or subject, but strategic thinking empowers executives to foresee and plan for the future of the firm. Leaders must, however, also have high emotional intelligence if they hope to effectively connect with and motivate their staff. By emphasizing the comprehension and control of emotions in oneself and others, emotional intelligence serves as a supplement to technical and strategic talents. Empathizing with their team members, anticipating their needs, and changing their leadership style to fit various personalities and circumstances are all skills that leaders with high emotional intelligence possess. This capacity for emotional connection encourages loyalty, trust, and commitment among team members, which enhances collaboration and overall team performance. Combining these abilities is necessary to effectively incorporate emotional intelligence into a bigger leadership framework. To make wise decisions and direct their teams toward accomplishing organizational objectives, leaders should make use of their technical expertise. Leaders may also recognize possibilities and potential obstacles with the help of strategic thinking, while emotional intelligence facilitates successful communication and the execution of strategic projects. Emotional intelligence is also crucial for resolving disputes and fostering employee growth. Leaders with emotional intelligence are able to resolve disputes amicably and diplomatically, fostering team cohesion in the process. Emotionally intelligent leaders may offer supportive criticism and mentoring that encourages team members to advance both personally and professionally when it comes to employee development. Positive workplace culture is fostered by the inclusion of emotional intelligence within the leadership framework. Leaders that place a high priority on emotional intelligence foster a culture where team members are supported, appreciated, and heard. This improves company success by lowering turnover rates and increasing employee morale and engagement.

7 FUTURE DIRECTIONS AND IMPLICATIONS FOR RESEARCH

7.1 Identifying New Dimensions of Emotional Intelligence in Business Management

It is crucial to investigate new degrees and dimensions of emotional intelligence in corporate management as work situations continue to change. A deeper look into the function of emotional intelligence in leadership is warranted in light of the evolving working environment, which includes the development of remote work, rising diversity, and technological advancements (Walls, M., Burgess, Z. et, 2001). Examining the effect of emotional intelligence on virtual leadership is one area of future research. Leaders must modify their emotional intelligence competencies to effectively lead and encourage their teams from a distance as the trend of remote work and geographically separated teams continues to develop. Successful leadership in the digital workplace requires an understanding of how emotional intelligence translates into the virtual world and how it affects team dynamics and performance. The study of cross-cultural emotional intelligence is another interesting area for research. Leaders must navigate complex cultural contexts and interact effectively with individuals from a variety of backgrounds as businesses become more global. Culturally competent leadership and the promotion of inclusive and harmonious work environments can be improved by researching how emotional intelligence shows itself across cultural boundaries and how cultural norms affect emotional expression and perception. Future studies should also explore the link between innovative leadership and emotional intelligence. Understanding how emotional intelligence encourages creativity, risk-taking, and the capacity for change can offer helpful insights for fostering an innovation culture as innovation becomes a crucial engine of business success.

7.2 Examining the Long-Term Impact of Emotional Intelligence on Organizational Success

Our understanding of the long-term effects of emotionally intelligent leadership will likely be much improved by future study examining the impact of emotional intelligence on organizational performance and sustainability. The importance of emotional intelligence in achieving long-term goals grows as firms work to maintain success in a constantly shifting corporate environment. Understanding how emotional intelligence impacts key performance measures like productivity, employee engagement, and customer happiness over time can help organizations perform better. Strong relationships with their staff, fostering a great work environment, and inspiring dedication to the organization's objectives are all skills that leaders with high emotional intelligence are better able to do. As a result, this long-lasting favorable effect on team relationships and performance may eventually increase organizational performance. Furthermore, understanding how leaders with high emotional intelligence may foster long-term success requires examining the relationship between emotional intelligence and organizational sustainability. Leaders who are emotionally intelligent are adept at handling change, negotiating uncertainty, and encouraging adaptability in their employees. The organization's capacity to flourish in the face of difficulties and disruptions may be influenced by its capacity to create resilient teams and encourage a culture of continuous learning. Future studies could also look into how emotional intelligence affects talent development and leadership succession planning. The organization's long-term leadership stability and effectiveness can be ensured by identifying emotionally intelligent leaders and developing emotional intelligence competencies in possible successors.

7.3 Exploring the Cultural and Contextual Influences on Emotional Intelligence in Leadership

Different cultural circumstances can have a substantial impact on how emotional intelligence is perceived and demonstrated. Investigating how cultural influences affect emotional intelligence in leadership and decision-making is crucial. Research in this field can provide important insights into how cultural norms, beliefs, and communication philosophies influence how emotions are expressed and interpreted in leadership roles. The differences in acceptable emotional expression and display behaviors are one component of how culture influences emotional intelligence. Openly expressing emotions like anger or sadness may be frowned upon in some cultures while being more socially acceptable in others. These display guidelines must be followed by leaders working within diverse cultural contexts because emotional expression has a big impact on team relationships and communication styles. Additionally, the perception of emotional intelligence may be impacted by cultural variations in communication patterns. While indirect and implicit communication may be more common, direct and clear communication may be appreciated in some cultures. In order to excite their staff and connect with them successfully, leaders with high emotional intelligence must be aware of these cultural nuances. Moreover, how emotional intelligence is viewed and used in leadership can be influenced by cultural perspectives on hierarchy and power distance. Leaders may be required to exhibit a certain level of emotional control and authority in cultures with high power gap, whereas they may be encouraged to adopt a more collaborative and sympathetic leadership style in cultures with low power distance. Emotional intelligence can also interact with cultural impacts on problem-solving and decision-making. Collectivist leaders might put more emphasis on achieving consensus within the group, whereas individualistic leaders might place more emphasis on making decisions for oneself. Effective leadership in a variety of global settings requires an understanding of how emotional intelligence is applied to decision-making in these cultural situations.

CONCLUSION AND FUTURE WORK

In conclusion, the importance of emotional intelligence in corporate management cannot be emphasized, in my opinion. Enhancing team performance, employee engagement, and leadership effectiveness are crucial for the success of an organization. Additionally, emotional intelligence influences decision-making positively, leading to well-informed and reasonable decisions. As a result, investing in the growth of emotional intelligence among leaders through training, mentoring, and feedback systems is essential for developing happy work environments and attaining long-term results. But in order to develop well-rounded and successful leaders, it is essential to recognize the difficulties and constraints of emotional intelligence and strike a balance with other leadership abilities.

Future work: There are still many areas that need to be further investigated despite the significant progress achieved in understanding the influence of emotional intelligence on leadership and decision-making. Future studies should focus further on the individual components of emotional intelligence and the complex relationships between them that affect organizational performance and leadership effectiveness. The long-term effects of emotional intelligence on leader performance and corporate culture may be revealed via long-term impact studies.

REFERENCES

Alzoubi, H. M., & Aziz, R. (2021). Does emotional intelligence contribute to quality of strategic decisions? The mediating role of open innovation. *Journal of Open Innovation*, *7*(2), 130. Advance online publication. doi:10.3390/joitmc7020130

Bhardwaj, B. (2021). *Short-term foreign trips correlates of the four factors model of cultural intelligence*. Rajagiri Management Journal. doi:10.1108/RAMJ-01-2021-0008

Bhardwaj, B., & Sharma, D. (2022). Migration of skilled professionals across the border: Brain drain or brain gain? *European Management Journal*. Advance online publication. doi:10.1016/j.emj.2022.12.011

Brackett, M. A., & Mayer, J. D. (2003). Convergent, discriminant, and incremental validity of competing measures of emotional intelligence. *Personality and Social Psychology Bulletin*, *29*(9), 1147–1158. doi:10.1177/0146167203254596 PMID:15189610

Canedo, D., & Neves, A. J. R. (2019). Facial expression recognition using computer vision: A systematic review. *Applied Sciences (Basel, Switzerland)*, *9*(21), 1–31. doi:10.3390/app9214678

Carmeli, A., & Josman, Z. E. (2006). The Effects of Cognitive Appraisal and Emotion on Social Motive and Negotiation Behavior : The Critical Role of Agency of Negotiator Emotion. *Human Performance*, *19*(4), 403–419. doi:10.120715327043hup1904_5

Caruso, D. R., Bienn, B., & Kornacki, S. A. (2013). Emotional intelligence in the workplace. *Emotional Intelligence in Everyday Life*, (January), 187–205. doi:10.4324/9780203943397-20

Côté, S., & Miners, C. T. H. (2006). Emotional intelligence, cognitive intelligence, and job performance. *Administrative Science Quarterly*, *51*(1), 1–28. doi:10.2189/asqu.51.1.1

George, J. M. (2000). Emotions and leadership: The role of emotional intelligence. *Human Relations*, *53*(8), 1027–1055. doi:10.1177/0018726700538001

Goleman, D., Boyatzis, R., & McKee, A. (2009). Primal Leadership: The Hidden Driver of Great Performance. *Discovering Leadership*, 63–72. doi:10.1007/978-1-137-24203-7_6

Hess, J. D., & Bacigalupo, A. C. (2011). Enhancing decisions and decision-making processes through the application of emotional intelligence skills. *Management Decision*, *49*(5), 710–721. doi:10.1108/00251741111130805

Higgs, M., & Dulewicz, V. (2016). Coaching and mentoring: A critical text. *Sage (Atlanta, Ga.)*.

James Thomas, K. (2004). Emotional intelligence: The new science of interpersonal effectiveness. *Human Resource Development Quarterly*, *15*(4), 489–495. doi:10.1002/hrdq.1117

Jordan, P. J., Ashkanasy, N. M., Härtel, C. E. J., & Hooper, G. S. (2002). Workgroup emotional intelligence. Scale development and relationship to team process effectiveness and goal focus. *Human Resource Management Review*, *12*(2), 195–214. doi:10.1016/S1053-4822(02)00046-3

Kang, Y., Cai, Z., Tan, C. W., Huang, Q., & Liu, H. (2020). Natural language processing (NLP) in management research: A literature review. *Journal of Management Analytics*, *7*(2), 139–172. doi:10.1080/23270012.2020.1756939

Mayer, J. D., Salovey, P., & Caruso, D. R. (2008). Emotional Intelligence: New Ability or Eclectic Traits? *The American Psychologist*, *63*(6), 503–517. doi:10.1037/0003-066X.63.6.503 PMID:18793038

Mayer, J. D., Salovey, P., & Caruso, D. R. (2009). *Psychological Inquiry An International Journal for the Advancement of Psychological Theory*. https://doi.org/ doi:10.1207/s15327965pli1503

Nelis, D., Kotsou, I., Quoidbach, J., Hansenne, M., Weytens, F., Dupuis, P., & Mikolajczak, M. (2011). Increasing emotional competence improves psychological and physical well-being, social relationships, and employability. *Emotion (Washington, D.C.)*, *11*(2), 354–366. doi:10.1037/a0021554 PMID:21500904

Palmer, B., Walls, M., Burgess, Z., & Stough, C. (2001). Emotional intelligence and effective leadership. *Leadership and Organization Development Journal*, *22*(1), 5–10. doi:10.1108/01437730110380174

Petrides, K. V., & Furnham, A. (2000). On the dimensional structure of emotional intelligence. *Personality and Individual Differences*, *29*(2), 313–320. doi:10.1016/S0191-8869(99)00195-6

Sharma, D., Chaudhary, M., Jaswal, N., & Bhardwaj, B. (2022). Hiding Behind The SWOT: Gender Equality and COVID-19. *Journal of Positive School Psychology*, 730–740.

Sosik, J. J., & Megerian, L. E. (1999). Understanding Leader Emotional Intelligence and Performance: The Role of Self-Other Agreement on Transformational Leadership Perceptions. *Group & Organization Management*, *24*(3), 367–390. doi:10.1177/1059601199243006

Sy, T., Tram, S., & O'Hara, L. A. (2006). Relation of employee and manager emotional intelligence to job satisfaction and performance. *Journal of Vocational Behavior*, *68*(3), 461–473. doi:10.1016/j.jvb.2005.10.003

Thakur, D. J., Verma, P., & Sharma, D. (2019). Influence of Leadership Style: A Review. International. *Journal of Advanced Science and Technology*, *28*(20), 945–952.

Weiss, R. P. (2000). Promoting Emotional Intelligence in Organizations: Making Training in Emotional Intelligence Effective. *Training & Development, 54*(8), 67. link.gale.com/apps/doc/A64705693/AONE?u=anon~4491e680&sid=googleScholar&xid=83fe5508

Wong, C. S., & Law, K. S. (2017). The effects of leader and follower emotional intelligence on performance and attitude: An exploratory study. In Leadership Perspectives (Vol. 13). doi:10.4324/9781315250601-10

Chapter 8

Demystifying the Relationship Between Emotional Intelligence and Leadership Effectiveness: Focusing on Mental Health and Happiness

Meena Chaudhary
https://orcid.org/0000-0001-8582-0355
Central University of Himachal Pradesh, India

Nidhi Jaswal
https://orcid.org/0000-0002-4066-7171
Central University of Himachal Pradesh, India

Anu Sohal
https://orcid.org/0000-0003-4737-0992
Central University of Himachal Pradesh, India

ABSTRACT

The disruptive VUCA environment affects both the organizations as well as the leaders. To survive in this unruly environment, and to find new solutions to this problem organizations need leaders with strong mental and emotional competencies. Prior research contends that a leader's emotional intelligence favorably promotes leadership effectiveness; however, the relationship is only studied superficially and not considering the VUCA circumstances. Furthermore, there is scant literature on the relationship between emotional intelligence and leadership effectiveness with mental health and happiness at work as mediators. Also, a thorough understanding of the influence of EI on positive psychology concepts remains elusive. From the authors' perspective, the ability of aspiring leaders and their effectiveness in handling this challenging environment will be greatly influenced by their emotional intelligence, mental health, and happiness at work. This study utilizes an integrative literature review methodology and attempts to theoretically link prior literature to fill the void.

DOI: 10.4018/979-8-3693-0418-1.ch008

"It is very important to understand that emotional intelligence is not the opposite of intelligence, it is not the triumph of heart over head- it is the unique intersection of both". - David Caruso

1. INTRODUCTION

The rapid and dynamic transformations characterize the world of today and the VUCA best describes this nature of the world. According to Rodriguez & Rodriguez, (2015), Volatility, Uncertainty, Complexity, and Ambiguity (VUCA) are the four features of the real world that are frequently depicted in contemporary literature. In the 1990s this description first appeared, following the fallout from the terrorist attacks of September 11, 2001, and the economic crisis that developed in the United States between 2007 and 2008. The whole business environment and work settings are becoming disruptive due to, drastic changes like, the VUCA business environment, the emergence of Industry 4.0, and further with the advent of technologies like virtual reality, cloud environments, machine learning, digital ecosystems, blockchain, AI, etc. In addition, Covid-19 has altered the entire nature of this dynamic milieu. New and developing technologies are contributing to bringing about a paradigm shift in the work environment and workplace culture (Bhardwaj & Sharma, 2022).

The European Agency for Safety and Health at Work (2007), asserts that a negative association between work settings and employees, results in behavioral issues, physiological changes, and emotional disturbances. Contrarily if a cordial relationship between employees and work settings is created, it can result in an increase in motivation, self-esteem, job performance, and general health (Brun & Milczarek, 2007).

The importance of Emotional Intelligence (EI) to organizational leadership was established by Daniel Goleman (1998) in his article "What Makes a Leader", published in the Harvard Business Review (HBR). Business leaders in the VUCA environment should align high-order and decision-making skills with values and vision and integrate potential outcomes for all stakeholders (P., 2015). While Intelligence Quotient (IQ) alone is insufficient, EI is essential to foster healthy interactions at work. Certainly, EI plays a significant role for leaders, since it is linked with motivation, realistic and rational perceptions, and the recognition and self-regulation of emotions. Lack of EI skills impact individuals in varied contexts such as job performance, emotional stability, interpersonal relations, and well-being (Orejarena et al., 2019).

The most crucial factor in a person's behavior that can affect his EI is his mental health. A leader's psychological well-being is crucial because it keeps him/ her happy and provides the energy needed to deal with mental health issues (Vaidya et al., 2020). Extant literature indicates that individual differences in EI reliably predict human behavior. Additionally, EI is acknowledged by the scientific community as a significant psychological factor for crucial real-life domains such as mental health, socialization, and individual well-being (Mancini et al., 2022).

EI is a leadership skill, that can be developed and utilized to boost leadership effectiveness and is moreover, crucial for Human Resource Management (HRM) (Saha et al., 2023). In today's world, effective leaders are not only recognized by their technical skills and hierarchical authority but also by their ability to understand and nurture the psychological well-being of their teams. Leaders who prioritize and promote a positive psychological atmosphere to their employees can harness the power of intrinsic motivation, job satisfaction, and life satisfaction. The traditional view of leadership has evolved into a multifaceted approach that integrates Emotional Intelligence (hereafter referred to as EI), Mental Health (hereafter referred to as MH), and employee happiness at work (hereafter referred to as HAW). This chapter considers EI as a crucial leadership competency, which can recognize how a leader's feelings and behavior affect those around them. Further, it provides a contemporary perspective on positive psychology concepts: Happiness and Mental Health as mediators in EI and Leadership effectiveness relationship.

This paper attempts to explore the following objectives:

1. To determine whether a relationship exists between Emotional Intelligence and Leadership effectiveness.
2. To establish the relationship of Mental Health, and Happiness at Work as mediators in Emotional Intelligence and Leadership Effectiveness relationship.

2. LITERATURE REVIEW

2.1 Emotional Intelligence (EI) Theory

EI, is a psychological construct, which has recently become a focus of research. It has been advocated as an individual difference variable that influences varied human behaviors and performances (Itzkovich & Dolev, 2017). The term EI first appeared as "emotional quotient" in a study by Barbara Leuner in 1966, (Leuner, B., 1966). EI was coined by Payne, (1985) in his Doctoral dissertation titled, "A study of emotion: developing emotional intelligence; self-integration; relating to fear, pain, and desire". In 1920, Edward Thorndike was the first to define social intelligence, while Gardner in 1983 put forth the notion that people have both interpersonal and intrapersonal intelligence (Gardner, H. E., 2011). Riggio et al., (2002) in his study emphasized that there was much more to the EI construct than the mental abilities. However, in 1990 Salovey and Mayer were the first to conceptualize EI as the subset of social intelligence, and in 1996, an article titled "Emotional Intelligence and Emancipation was published"(Mapuranga et al., 2022).

Intelligence and emotion are the two constituents that make up the construct of EI, and they must be defined to fully comprehend the construct (Conte, 2005; Côté, 2010; Côté, 2014). The word "emotion" refers to the affective component, and the word "intelligence" refers to the cognitive component (Kanesan & Fauzan, 2019). Emotions are defined as "brief, organized sets of responses (including physiological adjustments, expressive behaviors, action tendencies, and subjective experiences) that optimize how individuals address the challenges and exploit the opportunities that arise in the events that they encounter" (Levenson, 1994). Intelligence is defined as, "one's ability to form and grasp concepts, especially higher-level or more abstract concepts (Locke, 2005). Abilities, here refers to variations in an individual's completion of tasks in a specific domain under optimum conditions. The widely recognized definition of EI as a subset of social intelligence: EI is defined as, "the ability to monitor one's own and other's emotions, to discriminate among them, and to use the information to guide one's thinking and actions". It is comprised of three processes: emotions evaluation and expression, emotions adjustment, and emotions application (Salovey, P., & Mayer, J. D., 1990). Later, in 1997, the definition of EI was updated as, "a person's capability to perceive, express, understand, use and manage emotions in oneself, personal intelligence and in others, social intelligence, which leads to adaptive behaviors consequently resulting in effective leadership (Salovey, P., & Sluyter, D. J. (Eds.), 1997). Mayer et al.,(2016) defined EI as, "a set of abilities including the appraisal, expression, and regulation of emotions, as well as the ability to use feelings to facilitate performance and solve problems". EI refers to "a collection of personal, emotional, and social skills, and abilities that affect a person's capacity to successfully cope with environmental pressures and demands" (Bar-on, 2006). Seminal studies by Salovey and Mayer in 1990 and 1997 and the books by Goleman in 1995 and 1998 sparked interest in EI in organizations (Vaidya et al., 2020).

2.1.1 EI Models

Existent research concurs that the effectiveness of EI theory depends on how it is measured. EI is viewed by Ability models as a standard intelligence that makes use of a unique set of mental skills, while, mixed and trait models both define and quantify EI as a collection of perceived abilities, competencies, and personality traits. Ability EI and Trait EI are categories of EI, Ability EI signifies the ability to understand one's own and others' emotions and can be measured by performance assessments only while Trait EI is a component of personality and emphasizes an individual's self-efficacy, it is measured using self-reporting scales.

There are currently three main models of EI: the Ability model (Salovey, P., & Mayer, J. D., 1990) (Salovey, P., & Sluyter, D. J. (Eds.), 1997), the Trait model (Petrides & Furnham, 2003), and the Mixed model (Bar-on, 2006; Boyatzis, 2004)

a) ABILITY MODEL: (Four-Branch Model of Mayer and Salovey)

Emotions are seen in the ability-based paradigm as a valuable source of information that aids in understanding and navigating the social environment. The fundamental abilities related to emotion that comprise EI are: i) perception or expression of emotion, ii) using emotion to facilitate thinking, iii) understanding emotion, and, iv) managing emotions in oneself and others.

b) TRAIT MODEL

The trait model of EI focuses on specific personality traits beneficial in perceiving and controlling emotions. It highlights that emotional self-perceptions and emotional personality features play a crucial role in an individual's EI, and is concerned with people's perceptions of their emotional capacities. Trait EI is defined as "a constellation of emotional self-perceptions located at the lower levels of personality hierarchies". This implies that emotions are subjective and EI is an individual's perception of his abilities to manage emotions.

c) MIXED MODELS

The model developed by Daniel Goleman places a strong emphasis on EI as a broad range of talents and skills that influence leadership effectiveness. The five main EI components are illustrated in Figure 1:

i) **Self-Awareness:** It is the ability to understand one's emotions, values, aspirations, strengths, and weaknesses, and realize their influence on others. A person with high EI is aware of his emotions and can express them.

ii) **Self–Regulation:** After achieving the first component, self-regulation can be pursued. The emotions and behaviors can be better managed when an individual is aware of his own emotions. This entails restraining or channeling one's impulsive and disruptive emotions as well as adjusting to changing situations.

iii) **Motivation:** It involves encouraging and guiding someone towards accomplishing their goals. An individual who is motivated may stick with their goals and persevere even in challenging times.

iv) **Empathy:** How sensitive a person is to the feelings of others is referred to as empathy. An individual with high EI may recognize the emotions that another person is experiencing and distinguish between real and fake emotions when making judgments specifically considering other people's feelings.

v) **Social Skills:** It involves relationship management to influence others in the desired way. An individual with greater EI levels may be more adept at suitably engaging with others than a person with lower EI. EI can help in forming connections, communicating with others, and upholding friendships.

Figure 1. Daniel Goleman's emotional intelligence model (2002)

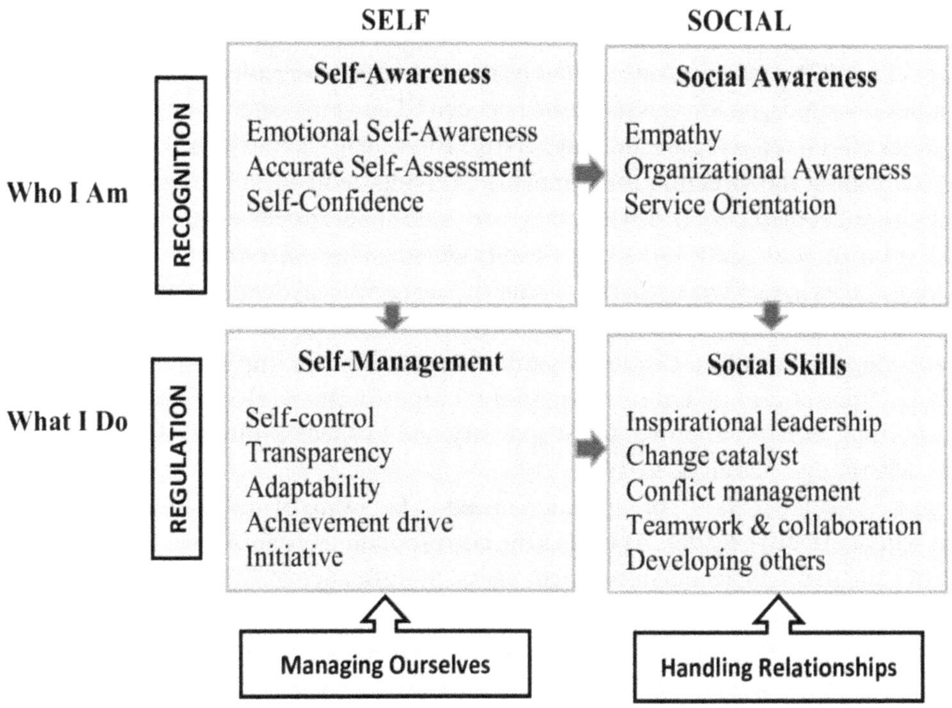

2.2. Emotional Intelligence (EI) and Leadership Effectiveness (LE)

Due to the lack of a direct relationship between a leader's emotional competency and leadership effectiveness, it becomes essential to establish a theoretical link between the two concepts, and to create a groundwork for future empirical study (Mapuranga et al., 2022; Saha et al., 2023). The significance of EI for corporate leadership was first highlighted by Daniel Goleman in 1995. Consequently, in his 1998 article titled, "What makes a Leader", published in Harvard Business Review, he postulates that a significant indicator of effective leadership is the ability to encourage others. He claims that the most effective leaders share a crucial trait in common: they possess a high level of EI. It is not that Intelligence Quotient (IQ) and technical proficiency are not important, they prove significant as entry-level requirements for executive roles. However, Daniel Goleman and contemporary researchers amply demonstrate the necessity of Emotionally Intelligent leaders. A greater emphasis is laid on the emotional states of leaders and how contagious their emotions are at work (Cherniss et al., 1998).

EI fosters trust among coworkers and encourages a positive attitude both within and among organizational members, enabling leaders to handle their emotions successfully while dealing with organizational problems. Additionally, those individuals who can manage their emotions will likely be more successful as leaders because they will be able to make faster judgments, adapt to rapidly changing events, handle team member's disputes, and build relations with their subordinates, thereby emerging as efficacious leaders (Zeidner et al., 2004; Fianko et al., 2020).

Many studies have delved into EI as a field of research with a keen interest on its influence on effective leadership (Shorey & Chaffin, 2018; Varshney & Varshney, 2020; Chigeda et al., 2022). Additionally studies have established that EI is crucial for resolving organizational issues (Day & Carroll, 2004; Saha et al., 2023). However, on account of its contradictory results, EI continues to be a debated concept. Studies revealed a positive association between EI and job performance (Vidyarthi et al., 2014), and better leader effectiveness (Kellner et al., 2018). EI is seen as an essential component of improved leadership establishing the direction for companies, relying upon EI in tactical decisions (Miao et al., 2018). Leaders are deemed effective when they persuade subordinates to work towards organizational objectives (Vardiman et al., 2006). Lack of EI in leaders can have negative outcomes on stakeholders, employees and clients (A., Ovans, 2015). Traits of successful leadership such as conscientiousness, extraversion, EI, self-efficacy, gender, self-monitoring, emotional stability and dominance influence effective leadership (Kim, 2007). Leader's emotional competencies impacted their capabilities of managing employee stress, burnout and its impact on their performance (Rajah et al., 2011). Leaders can be imparted training in EI to improve their capability and to successfully lead initiatives at workplace (Mills, 2009; Mattingly & Kraiger, 2019).

According to Amagoh, (2009), organizations need to be aware of the contextual elements that may affect the growth of effective leaders as well as the corresponding organizational conditions that must be created to foster and maintain leadership effectiveness. Significance of EI seems pervasive as it is studied in varied industries such as leaders in multinational consulting company (Boyatzis, 2006), sales leaders in marketing industry (Boyatzis et al., 2012), project managers in the construction industry (Maqbool et al., 2017), medical professionals in healthcare industry (Nightingale et al., 2018). Furthermore, existent literature in the education context also confirms the significance of Emotionally Intelligent school administrators and their effective leadership (Berkovich & Eyal, 2015; Gómez-Leal et al., 2022).

The existent literature acknowledges that empathy for oneself and others, as well as the capacity to deal with one's emotions, contribute to the development of relationships and acceptance of needed change (Côté, 2014; Sánchez-Núñez et al., 2015; Mayer et al., 2016; Lopes, 2016). Additionally, EI better equips school administrators to make the right decisions for themselves, others, and the school as well as to deal with job stress. The attitude, perspectives, and actions of the principal as a school leader gradually shape the school's culture and students' well-being (Tan, 2018; Russo-Netzer & Shoshani, 2019). Another interpersonal skill associated with EI is the leader's capacity to foster trust among stakeholders (Hackett et al., 2008). According to Carmeli, (2003), there exists a positive relationship between optimistic work attitudes, behaviors, and outcomes. Mérida-López et al., (2019), confirmed that EI might be a crucial component of effective leadership, making a significant contribution to efficacious team performance. Druskat & Wolff, (2001) confirmed, that leaders demonstrating high EI levels foster a positive attitude both within and among the members of the organization. A strong leader-subordinate relationship is facilitated by excellent emotion management in leaders. Individuals with greater EI levels are better at handling and resolving disputes successfully (Bodtker, 2001). According to Foo et al., (2004), EI is a key factor in attaining integrative outcomes while examining the association between EI and negotiations. A study by Lopes et al., (2005) claimed that people with high EI levels experience fewer conflicts in their relationships. Another study discovered that the degree of EI had a substantial impact on both cooperative and compromising conflict management strategies (Yu et al., 2006).

Additionally EI is one such antecedent that is significant in the digital and AI era but has received little attention. Higher EI levels have been linked to a wide range of psychosocial benefits, including improved physical and psychological health (Ruiz-Aranda et al., 2012; Domínguez-García & Fernández-Berrocal, 2018), better life satisfaction and well-being (Xu et al., 2021;Villanueva et al., 2022), improved academic and professional performance (Sánchez-López et al., 2022) and lower aggressiveness (Vega et al., 2022). EI helps to maintain relationships, foster trust and is beneficial to both individual and organizational performance (Wang X & Dong B, 2022).

Various theories such as Affective events theory, theory of social exchange, leader-member exchange theory, theory of EI, social cognitive theory, theory of social learning have been utilized to substantiate the significance of EI among leaders and their subordinates. The EI theory by Goleman (1995) postulates that the four components of EI i.e. self-awareness, self-management, social-awareness and relationship management significantly regulate and exhibit affective behavior. Affective events theory by Weiss and Cropanzano, 1996 contends that events at workplace have a considerable impact on employee's job performance, behavior at workplace and job satisfaction. Furthermore, the interaction of leader-member exchange and EI can augment job satisfaction and reduce employee burnout, with the social interactions between leaders and the followers (Liden et al., 1997; Huang et al., 2010).

Thus, existent literature reveals that EI is a crucial trait in a leader. Charismatic and transformational leaders frequently focus on developing positive relationship with subordinates while giving them the freedom to own tasks and carry them out independently. As confirmed by Harms & Credé, (2010) in their study on 7,145 leaders from 62 separate populations, EI differentiates transformational and charismatic leaders from transactional leaders wherein empathy is emphasized as a significant component needed for supervision by transformational and charismatic leaders (Wolff et al., 2002). Additionally, the emotional competencies outlined by Goleman (1998), are also related to corporate performance indicators like stock market performance, return on investment, and profit margins, which also act as a testimony of leadership effectiveness (Hackett et al., 2008).

Thus, the extant literature concurs that EI is both a Leadership trait or a competency and an antecedent of leadership effectiveness and its consequences (Harms & Credé, 2010; Barbuto et al., 2014; Miao et al., 2018). Building on the relationship studied in existent literature, we propose that,

Proposition 1: Emotional Intelligence relates positively to Leadership Effectiveness.

2.3. Incorporating EI in the Workplace: Examples

The positive effect of EI on business is experienced by various businesses. The following examples make a case for how EI contributes to positive outcomes.

i. When financial Advisors from American Express underwent emotional competence training, the trained advisors saw an increase in business with 18.1% as opposed to 16.2% for a control group (Bianca Cardenas, 2022).
ii. 93% of workers enhanced productivity after receiving stress management and EI training at a Motorola manufacturing facility (Bianca Cardenas, 2022).

iii. In an analysis of fifteen international companies with more than 300 executives at top level, six emotional abilities: Influence, Organizational Awareness, Team Leadership, Self Confidence, Leadership, and Achievement Drive, were found in star performers which differentiated them from the average ones (Cherniss, 1999).

iv. Deficits in emotional abilities are the main reason of derailment among executives. According to a research by the Center for Creative Leadership the three important reasons for this are being unable to handle change, performing poorly in team and having poor interpersonal relationships (Cherniss, 1999).

v. Among several hundred managers from 12 different firms, accurate self-assessment, as one of the pillars of emotional competence, was linked to higher performance (Boyatzis, R. E., 1991).

3. POSITIVE PSYCHOLOGY CONCEPTS: MENTAL HEALTH AND HAPPINESS AT WORK, AS MEDIATORS IN EMOTIONAL INTELLIGENCE AND EFFECTIVE LEADERSHIP RELATIONSHIP

According to Goleman, EI is the ability to be aware of one's emotions and use those feelings to guide their decisions, regulate distressing moods, develop high motivation, and maintain hope and an optimistic attitude during adversities (Hackett et al., 2008). In the domain of positive psychology, EI has progressively become the focus of researchers, especially because of its positive association with well-being consequences (Sánchez-Álvarez et al., 2016), where positive mental health and happiness are the key contributors to the overall well-being of an individual (Allahverdipour et al., 2021). Along the same lines, we propose that leaders with high levels of EI will demonstrate positive behavior even in difficult situations and promote happiness and better mental health of subordinates.

3.1 Happiness Theory

With the advent of positive psychology (M. E. P. Seligman, 2002), the concept of happiness, well-being at work, and numerous positive human aspects have been receiving attention in both academic as well as organizational contexts for the past 20 years (Kun & Gadanecz, 2022). Happiness is defined as a subjective state of human emotions of joy, satisfaction, and contentment that involves a feeling of well-being experienced by people when they consider their lives meaningful and rewarding (Lyubomirsky et al., 2005). Happiness is generally concerned with individuals' subjective well-being which means how they evaluate their lives and it involves both emotional and cognitive evaluations (Kesebir & Diener, 2009).

The recent growth of positive psychology has drawn researchers' attention towards the positive outlook of the organizational world; particularly the aspects like employee well-being and happiness in their work-life is gaining the supreme attention of researchers and academicians. Positive psychology is a scientific field that studies the positive strengths, traits, and other positive elements of human behavior that promote human flourishing and well-being (Salas-Vallina & Alegre, 2018; M. E. Seligman & Csikszentmihalyi, 2000).

Happiness is a multidisciplinary concept that was primarily studied in the field of psychology. Along with psychology, it has now gained the top attention of researchers in the field of management sciences and organizational behavior (Fisher, 2010; Salas-Vallina & Alegre, 2018).

Due to the paradigm shift towards the changing work culture and employee well-being, the concept of happiness in the context of work is gaining the utmost significance in contemporary organizations as it has a great influence on both individual as well as organizational well-being.

3.1.1 EI and Happiness at Work (HAW)

Happiness at Work (HAW), has been receiving due consideration in the psychology domain, the reason being a growing emphasis on the mental well-being of employees and the economic and social pressures of globalization. (Diener et al., 1999). As organizations have come to recognize the overwhelming impact of employee happiness on their performance, productivity, and overall well-being, the concept of happiness at work has been gaining attention in recent times. In this highly competitive and dynamic business world, where people spend a considerable amount of their lives at work, the pursuit of employee happiness has become a crucial element in shaping contemporary organizational structures and positive work culture. The term "happiness at work" refers to the presence of positive emotions, feeling of job satisfaction, and well-being at work (Fisher, 2010; Kun & Gadanecz, 2022). As defined by (Pryce-Jones, 2011), "Happiness at work is a mindset which allows you to maximize performance and achieve your potential. You do this by being mindful of the highs and lows when working alone or with others."

Happiness is often regarded as subjective well-being and these two terms are used interchangeably (Diener et al., 1999; Veenhoven, 2012). With regards to subjective well-being, happiness is determined by three core components: the presence of positive affect, the absence of negative affect, and cognitive evaluations of life satisfaction (Diener et al., 1997; Singh & Duggal Jha, 2008). Thus, happiness is said to have both cognitive as well as emotional aspects of well-being (Diener et al., 1999; Ghahramani et al., 2019). Further, numerous sub-factors can affect the emotional aspect of happiness, and one such factor is emotional intelligence (Ghahramani et al., 2019). Emotional intelligence plays a vital role in nurturing and maintaining employee well-being and happiness of individuals as well as teams or groups which are emotionally sound contribute to a happy, healthy, and positive work environment (Luca et al., 2001; Zeidner et al., 2004). Research has shown that a high level of emotional intelligence leads to increased happiness and satisfaction with life and on the other hand, it reduces the level of stress among employees (Mérida-López et al., 2022; Naseem, 2018). Further, a study conducted by (Mérida-López et al., 2019) revealed that higher emotional intelligence in the form of emotion-regulation ability is positively related to a higher amount of happiness and job satisfaction. A recent study done in the education sector disclosed that happiness at work was positively influenced by emotional intelligence through the mediating role of affective organizational commitment and job satisfaction (Elayan et al., 2023). Additionally, studies have demonstrated that happy individuals perform superior to unhappy individuals (McKee, 2017). This study seeks to clarify that a leader's EI may affect employees' HAW. As emotions are fundamental to every organization, they ought to be at the center of the organizational theory. Effective and supportive leadership is a key factor in fostering employee happiness (Zietsma, et al., 2019).

Based on the literature, we propose that:

Proposition 2: Emotional Intelligence relates positively to Happiness At Work.

3.1.2. Happiness at Work (HAW) and Leadership Effectiveness

In today's dynamic business environment, positive human aspects such as happiness at work and employee well-being have become the top priorities of almost every business organization. Employees who are happy at their work tend to complete their job tasks efficiently, seek better co-workers' as well as supervisor's support, and always come up with innovative and creative ideas for their organizational growth (El-Sharkawy et al., 2023; Gulyani & Sharma, 2018). Happy employees are more enthusiastic, productive, and motivated towards their individual as well as organizational goals (Oswald et al., 2015; Yang & Hung, 2017), which can further stimulate their level of self-confidence and develop effective leadership skills among them. In order to strengthen the productivity and leadership effectiveness of workers, workplace happiness is what most organizations see as their prior concern (Alameeri et al., 2021). About leadership, happiness in the form of a positive effect has a positive impact on leadership, and at the same time, the negative effect or the absence of happiness is adversely related to effective leadership (Joseph et al., 2015). Sufficient research has been conducted to examine the relationship between leadership and happiness at work (Ghadi & Almanaga'h, 2020; Salas-Vallina, 2020; Semedo et al., 2019). Studies have found the significant impact of various types of leadership in escalating a level of happiness in organizational settings. For instance, a study found that transformational leadership style, through the mediation of organizational learning affects workplace happiness significantly (Salas-Vallina et al., 2017). Inspirational leadership, which is said to have special attention towards their followers, has a positive impact on the happiness of followers (Salas-Vallina et al., 2020). Although there is plenty of literature available examining the influence of leadership on happiness, studies on their reciprocal relationship are very rare. Hence, we propose that,

Proposition 3: Happiness At Work leads to Leadership effectiveness.

3.2 Mental Health Theory

The term "Mental Health" sprang to prominence as social science and medical practitioners began to recognize the importance of addressing psychological well-being along with physical and social well-being. It's important to note that the idea of mental health is still evolving as a result of continuous research, changes in societal attitudes, and initiatives to lessen the stigma associated with mental health problems.

Mental Health constitutes a vital facet of holistic well-being, encompassing emotional, psychological, and social dimensions. The WHO defines mental health as "a state of well-being in which an individual realizes his or her abilities, can cope with the normal stresses of life, can work productively, and can contribute to his or her community" (WHO, 2014). One in every four individuals suffers from some mental health problems at a certain point in time in their lives which makes it a global concern (WHO, 2021). Therefore, it became a top priority for all the nations to understand the value of funding MH services and developing settings that support people with MH issues. Prior studies confirm that high levels of EI predict improved physical and psychological health (Schutte et al., 2007; Martins et al., 2010; Kotsou et al., 2019). EI also contributes to individual well-being (Walter et al., 2021). Studies have suggested that leaders with higher levels of EI can promote better mental health of employees which further leads to organizational productivity and performance. Therefore, we also propose that, Mental Health acts as a mediator in Emotional Intelligence and Leadership Effectiveness relationship.

3.2.1 Emotional Intelligence and Mental Health

The association between emotional intelligence and mental health has received much attention from researchers and other professionals. EI provides valuable insight into the study of emotions and acts as a protective factor for MH by encouraging resilience, coping mechanisms, and positive relationships in the workplace. The studies have found a positive and significant association between EI dimensions (Attention, Clarity, and Repair) and Mental Health (Schutte et al., 2007). In terms of clarity, the researchers concur that an ability to differentiate between moods and emotions is positively associated with better mental health and it also results in minimizing the level of anxiety and depression (Extremera & Fernández-Berrocal, 2006). Whereas considering the repair element, individuals who believe they can endure their pleasant moods are less likely to report mental illness in comparison to those individuals who demonstrate no sign of trying to improve their mood (Goldman et al., 1996). Furthermore, a negative and significant relationship was found between attention and MH which indicates that people who concentrate on themselves are likely to experience more adverse emotions (Costa et al., 2013).

Scholars have also used the AI measure as a moderator when analyzing the association between mental well-being and its predictors. A study exploring the relationship between AI, stress, and MH revealed that EI moderates the relationship between stress and MH (Ciarrochi et al., 2002). Another research conducted on Australian adult workers proposed that EI operates as a moderator in the relationship between workplace incivility and mental health. This suggests that individuals with high EI tend to experience less psychological distress when confronted with workplace incivility, owing to their adeptness in positively regulating negative emotions. (Carter and Loh, 2017). Along with the other determinants of MH, EI also plays a significant role in encouraging good mental health. EI possesses the capability to recognize and regulate negative emotions, enabling individuals to effectively cope with workplace stress and thereby help in managing mental health (Extremera & Fernández-Berrocal, 2006). Leaders with higher levels of EI can promote the better mental health of employees. Along the same lines, we propose that,

Proposition 4: Emotional Intelligence is positively associated with Mental Health.

3.2.2. Mental Health and Leadership Effectiveness

A number of studies and theories in the field of organizational behavior, psychology, and leadership have investigated the relationship between mental health and leadership effectiveness. Regardless of its practical utility, leadership is most likely a significant occupational health factor in and of itself. Mentally healthy leaders are more likely to be productive in their positions, be able to handle stress, make sound decisions, and continue to inspire their teams. The existing literature also shows that the levels of mental health may have a big impact on effective leadership as well as help in enhancing productivity and organizational performance (Montano et al, 2017).

Leaders who emphasize more on their mental health tend to display more successful and positive leadership styles because they have the emotional ability to create meaningful connections and navigate challenges with resilience. The relationship between employee well-being, leadership style, and organizational outcomes has repeatedly demonstrated that employee overall well-being has consequences for organizational outcomes (Samad et al., 2015). Leadership intervention also plays a significant role in promoting mental health needs and developing an environment where employees feel supported and well-cared (Stuber et al., 2021). Such interventions acknowledge the role of mental health in effective leadership and work to provide a supportive environment for leaders to thrive. Thus, we propose that:

Proposition 5: Mental Health is positively associated with Leadership Effectiveness

4. LEADERSHIP EFFECTIVENESS THROUGH THE LENS OF VUCA ENVIRONMENT

Leaders possess the power to persuade, inspire and enable others to contribute to the success of an organization and have a significant impact on the workplace through regular interpersonal encounters (Drucker, 1999). A source of long-lasting competitive advantage in the vibrant milieu is competent management. Motivating employees, effective communication, and fostering cultures where teams thrive are all positively and significantly connected with effective leadership (Gilley et al., 2009; Thakur et al., 2019). However, in the face of a disruptive business environment, even the most capable and successful leaders possibly might discover that their skills are becoming obsolescent before they even realized it. Consequently, to flourish in this environment leaders must continuously upgrade their technologies, procedures, personnel, and organizational structures (Vaidya et al., 2020).

Figure 2. VUCA prime approach

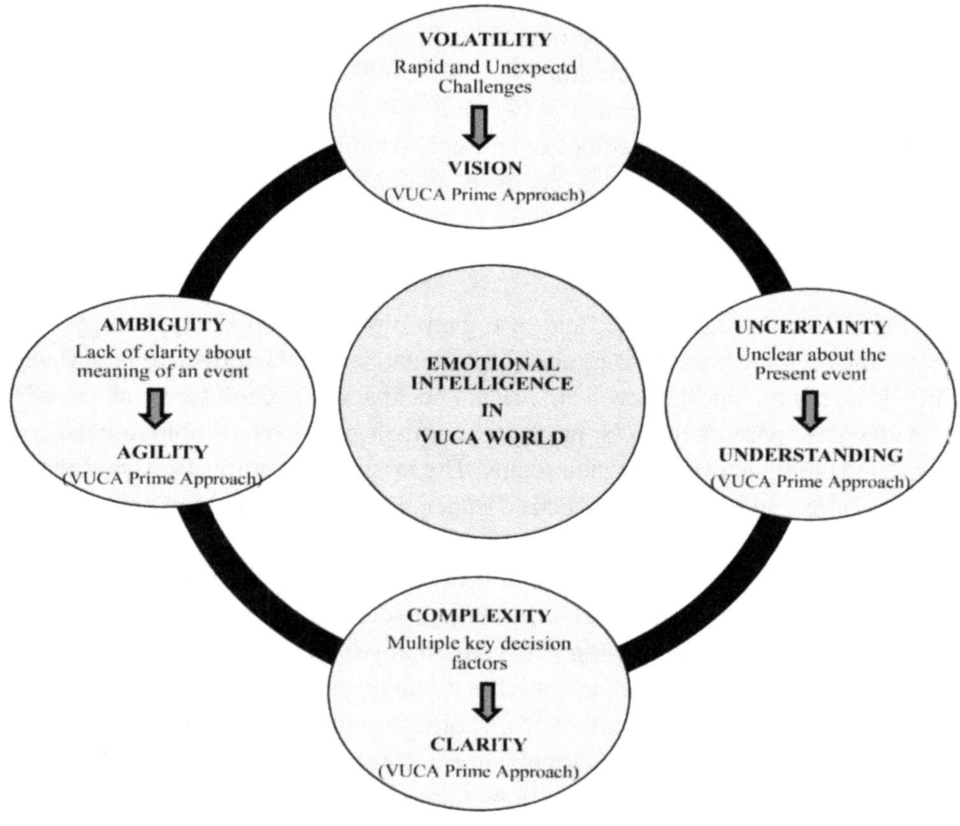

The book, “Leaders Make the Future: Ten New Leadership Skills for an Uncertain World”, by Bob Johansen, presents a behavioral leadership model which aims to counterbalance each of the four VUCA concepts with unique responses beginning with the same letters. Figure 2 demonstrates the model, known as VUCA prime, developed in 2007 by Bob Johansen. It provides four elements of VUCA with a positive response as Vision over Volatility, Understanding over Uncertainty, Clarity over Complexity, and Agility over Ambiguity. These are the four pillars of the model that describe the best future leaders (Bob Johansen, 2013). Thus, success in VUCA conditions can be attained through VUCA Prime by developing a mentality and skill set that enables one to be VUCA-ready and steer the dynamic environment.

Visionary leaders would make business decisions to address the turbulence while keeping the organization's vision in mind. Leaders must be visionary, multi-functional, and see beyond their functional areas. Additionally, uncertainties may be overcome by clarity in thinking and a thorough understanding of disruptive conditions. The leader should be able to handle unpredictability with agility. The ambiguous corporate environment presents adversities that need to be turned into an advantage (Johansen, 2012). It becomes essential for everyone to be adaptable and resilient, change their approaches to problems, and respond positively to new challenges of the VUCA world (Folan L., 2022). New projects, discoveries, and problem-solving approaches are necessary for enterprises to thrive in this VUCA environment, and as a result, organizations need leaders to propel them forward. According to Abbas et al., (2022), workplace stress has significantly grown in the VUCA world, thereby affecting the physical and mental health of workers. An individual's EI skills and healthy working environment would be useful in minimizing the effects of VUCA.

5. CONCEPTUAL FRAMEWORK

This study proposes a conceptual framework based on the review of literature on EI, MH, HAW, and Leadership effectiveness. The suggested framework emphasizes that leaders who prioritize EI not only create a conducive environment for mental health and happiness at work but also lay the groundwork for high-performing teams and successful leadership outcomes.

EI serves as the foundational component of this framework. Leaders with high EI have characteristics like self-awareness, compassion, and impactful communication, which allows them to maintain and promote a healthy and positive environment within the workplace. It helps the team members to experience improved mental well-being and greater happiness at work which directly translates into high leadership effectiveness. This conceptual framework proposes a positive relationship between Emotional Intelligence and Leadership Effectiveness and ascertains the mediating role of Happiness at Work, and Mental Health in Emotional Intelligence and Leadership Effectiveness relationship.

6. PRACTICAL IMPLICATIONS

Since the conceptualization of EI in 1990, organizations have utilized EI in hiring, assessments, training, development of team or leadership, and performance to attain competitive advantage. EI can also be developed by coaching, training, assessments, awareness, and practice (Fierro L., 2021). This implies that leaders may be able to improve their competencies and grow into better leaders through EI awareness and development programs timely organized by organizations. The EI competencies reviewed in the above sections echo the traits essential in leaders. Our findings suggest that organizations should focus on developing EI competencies in leaders with the goal to enhance employees' subjective well-being and organizing intervention programs that seek to improve happiness at work and build better mental health. According to (Schutte Nicola S. et al., (2001) higher EI scores were positively related to better interpersonal relationships and can improve social skills, empathy, relationship ties, cooperation, life satisfaction, and self-monitoring. Thus, there is the possibility to increase EI, and emotional self-efficacy by providing intensive training and effectively utilizing emotional regulation strategies like Response Modulation, Cognitive re-appraisal, attentional deployment, etc. (Xu et al., 2021). A variety of instruments and tests including the Mayer-Salovey-Caruso Emotional Intelligence Test (MSCEIT), the Emotional and Social Competence Inventory (ESCI), and the Emotional Quotient Inventory (EQ-i), can be used by leaders to measure their EI. These assessments can help them in identifying their strengths and weaknesses, additionally, they can compare their perceptions with those of their peers, staff, and managers for feedback. EI, teamwork skills, and situational awareness could be developed through simulation coaching. The technique of simulation-based coaching mirrors real-life scenarios, it views the teacher as a coach, whose prime responsibility is to support and encourage professionals, in their ongoing professional development, improve collaboration, collegial sharing, interpersonal communications, and reflection. (Salminen-Tuomaala, 2020). Leaders can improve their physical, emotional, and mental well-being by practicing mindfulness, which can be practiced through yoga, breathing exercises, and meditation.

Figure 3. Proposed conceptual framework

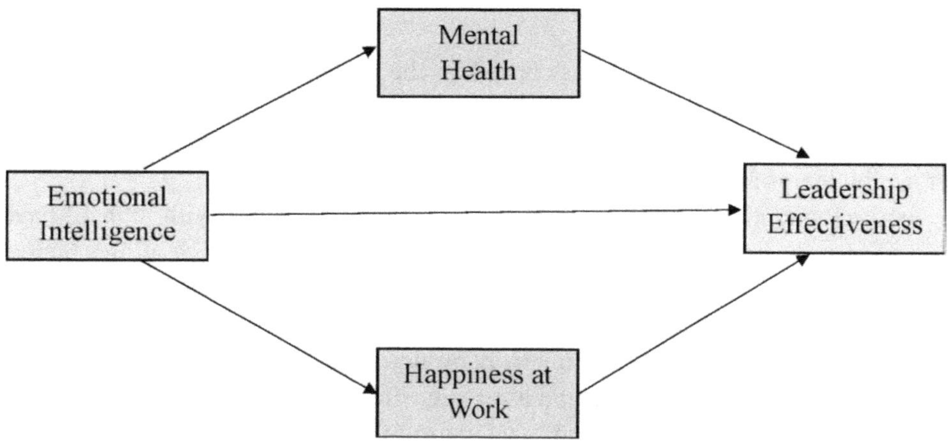

7. CONCLUSION

The uncertainties in business environment influence individual's behavior, leading to elevation in organizational culture, utilizing advanced technology, employing high performance equipment and encourages the employees to think creatively. The extreme global crisis has forced leaders all over the world to lead remotely, utilizing virtual platforms to interact with their teams. Emotionally intelligent leaders communicate effectively, develop trust, engage, and support even when leading remotely. Employing EI assessments to profile top performers depicts an increase in retention rates and saves $ 2.7 million yearly (Bianca Cardenas, 2022). This is due to the fact that employing Emotionally Intelligent employees is associated with high-performing businesses and improved performance, retention of talent, increase in job satisfaction, and results in leadership effectiveness. Despite the cause for concern and dread caused by VUCA, there are certain opportunities also for the growth and development of organizations and employees. Flexible and creative leaders can consider it as an opportunity and change the whole business model. This can be achieved when leaders employ their cognitive, behavioral, and emotional well-being (Vaidya et al., 2020). According to Nadler R, (2020), EI is, “being smart about your emotions”. To ensure that an organization’s operations run smoothly, it is crucial that employees develop strong leadership abilities (Neong et al., 2022). This study demonstrates that utilizing EI in creating VUCA–ready leadership is important for ensuring better mental health of employees and fostering happiness at work. It ensures survival of changing organizational structures, procedures, and systems. VUCA is a world of conundrums without universal solutions, but it calls for each organization’s employee to have the perseverance to eliminate uncertainties, and consider the capacity to learn incessantly, and the flexibility to adapt in every situation.

According to the studies cited above, it appears that people with greater levels of EI seem to control their emotions when dealing with workplace issues. Additionally, those who can manage their emotions will likely be more successful as leaders because they will be able to adapt and make quick decisions, manage conflicts and build relations with subordinates. Thus, the leader may transform volatility into vision, uncertainty into understanding, complexity into clarity, and ambiguity into adaptability by being agile and robust to turn adverse VUCA into opportunistic VUCA. The increased agility and flexibility that organizations expected to provide has an impact on the demands placed on leaders and workforce.

REFERENCES

Abbas, S., AL-Abrrow, H., Abdullah, H. O., Alnoor, A., Khattak, Z. Z., & Khaw, K. W. (2022). Encountering Covid-19 and perceived stress and the role of a health climate among medical workers. *Current Psychology (New Brunswick, N.J.)*, *41*(12), 9109–9122. doi:10.100712144-021-01381-8 PMID:33519147

Amagoh, F. (2009). Leadership development and leadership effectiveness. *Management Decision*, *47*(6), 989–999. doi:10.1108/00251740910966695

Bar-on, R. M. (2006). The Bar-On model of emotional-social intelligence (ESI). *Psicothema*, *18*(1), 13–25. https://dialnet.unirioja.es/servlet/articulo?codigo=4679040&info=resumen&idioma=SPA PMID:17295953

Barbuto, J. E. Jr, Gottfredson, R. K., & Searle, T. P. (2014). An Examination of Emotional Intelligence as an Antecedent of Servant Leadership. *Journal of Leadership & Organizational Studies*, *21*(3), 315–323. doi:10.1177/1548051814531826

Berkovich, I., & Eyal, O. (2015). Educational Leaders and Emotions. *Review of Educational Research*, *85*(1), 129–167. doi:10.3102/0034654314550046

Bhardwaj, B., & Sharma, D. (2022). Migration of skilled professionals across the border: Brain drain or brain gain? *European Management Journal*. Advance online publication. doi:10.1016/j.emj.2022.12.011

Bob Johansen. (2013). Leaders make the future: ten new leadership skills for an uncertain world. Berrett-Koehler Publishers. doi:10.5860/CHOICE.50-2757

Bodtker, A. M., & Katz Jameson, J. (2001). Emotion in conflict formation and its transformation: Application to organizational conflict management. *International Journal of Conflict Management*, *12*(3), 259–275. doi:10.1108/eb022858

Boyatzis, R. E. (2006). Using tipping points of emotional intelligence and cognitive competencies to predict financial performance of leaders. *Psicothema*, *18*(SUPPL.1), 124–131. PMID:17295969

Boyatzis, R. E., Good, D., & Massa, R. (2012). Emotional, Social, and Cognitive Intelligence and Personality as Predictors of Sales Leadership Performance. *Journal of Leadership & Organizational Studies*, *19*(2), 191–201. doi:10.1177/1548051811435793

Brun, E., & Milczarek, M. (2007). Expert forecast on emerging psychosocial risks related to occupational safety and heath - European Risk Observatory Report. European Agency for Safety and Health at Work.

Carmeli, A. (2003). The relationship between emotional intelligence and work attitudes, behavior and outcomes: An examination among senior managers. *Journal of Managerial Psychology*, *18*(7–8), 788–813. doi:10.1108/02683940310511881

Cherniss, C. (1999). The Business Case for Emotional Intelligence Prepared. *Consortium for Research on Emotional Intelligence in Organizations*. www.econsortium.org

Cherniss, C., Goleman, D., Emmerling, R., Cowan, K., & Adler, M. (1998). *Bringing emotional intelligence to the workplace*. Consortium for Research on Emotional Intelligence in Organizations, Rutgers University.

Chigeda, F., Ndofirepi, T. M., & Steyn, R. (2022). Continuance in organizational commitment : The role of emotional intelligence, work-life balance support, and work-related stress. *Global Business and Organizational Excellence*, *42*(1), 22–38. doi:10.1002/joe.22172

Conte, J. M. (2005). A review and critique of emotional intelligence measures. *Journal of Organizational Behavior*, *26*(4), 433–440. doi:10.1002/job.319

Côté, S. (2010). Taking the "Intelligence" in Emotional Intelligence Seriously. *Industrial and Organizational Psychology: Perspectives on Science and Practice*, *3*(2), 127–130. doi:10.1111/j.1754-9434.2010.01211.x

Côté, S. (2014). Emotional Intelligence in Organizations. *Annual Review of Organizational Psychology and Organizational Behavior*, *1*(1), 459–488. doi:10.1146/annurev-orgpsych-031413-091233

Day, A. L., & Carroll, S. A. (2004). Using an ability-based measure of emotional intelligence to predict individual performance, group performance, and group citizenship behaviours. *Personality and Individual Differences*, *36*(6), 1443–1458. doi:10.1016/S0191-8869(03)00240-X

Der Foo, M., Elfenbein, H. A., Tan, H. H., & Aik, V. C. (2004). Emotional intelligence and negotiation: The tension between creating and claiming value. *International Journal of Conflict Management*, *15*(4), 411–429. doi:10.1108/eb022920

Diener, E., Suh, E. M., Lucas, R. E., & Smith, H. L. (1999). Subjective Well-Being: Three Decades of Progress. *Psychological Bulletin*, *125*(2), 276–302. doi:10.1037/0033-2909.125.2.276

Domínguez-García, E., & Fernández-Berrocal, P. (2018). The Association Between Emotional Intelligence and Suicidal Behavior: A Systematic Review. *Frontiers in Psychology*, *9*(NOV), 1–12. doi:10.3389/fpsyg.2018.02380 PMID:30555393

Drucker, P. F. (1999). Knowledge-worker productivity: The biggest challenge. *California Management Review*, *41*(2), 79–94. doi:10.2307/41165987

Druskat, V. U., & Wolff, S. B. (2001). Building the emotional intelligence of groups. *Harvard Business Review*, *79*(3). PMID:11246926

Fianko, S. K. Jnr, Jnr, S. A., & Dzogbewu, T. C. (2020). Does the interpersonal dimension of Goleman's emotional intelligence model predict effective leadership? *African Journal of Business and Economic Research*, *15*(4), 221–245. doi:10.31920/1750-4562/2020/v15n4a10

Gilley, A., McMillan, H. S., & Gilley, J. W. (2009). Organizational change and characteristics of leadership effectiveness. *Journal of Leadership & Organizational Studies*, *16*(1), 38–47. doi:10.1177/1548051809334191

Gómez-Leal, R., Holzer, A. A., Bradley, C., Fernández-Berrocal, P., & Patti, J. (2022). The relationship between emotional intelligence and leadership in school leaders: A systematic review. *Cambridge Journal of Education*, *52*(1), 1–21. doi:10.1080/0305764X.2021.1927987

Hackett, P. P. T., Hortman, J., Hortman, W. J., & Hortman, J. (2008). The Relationship of Emotional Competencies to Transformational Leadership: Using a Corporate Model to Assess the Dispositions of Educational Leaders. *Journal of Educational Research & Policy Studies*, *8*(1), 92–111. http://www.eric.ed.gov/ERICWebPortal/recordDetail?accno=EJ809444%5Cnhttp://search.proquest.com/docview/61945952?accountid=17215

Harms, P. D., & Credé, M. (2010). Emotional Intelligence and Transformational and Transactional Leadership: A Meta-Analysis. *Journal of Leadership & Organizational Studies*, *17*(1), 5–17. doi:10.1177/1548051809350894

Huang, X., Chan, S. C. H., Lam, W., & Nan, X. (2010). The joint effect of leader–member exchange and emotional intelligence on burnout and work performance in call centers in China. *International Journal of Human Resource Management*, *21*(7), 1124–1144. doi:10.1080/09585191003783553

Itzkovich, Y., & Dolev, N. (2017). The Relationships between Emotional Intelligence and Perceptions of Faculty Incivility in Higher Education. Do Men and Women Differ? *Current Psychology (New Brunswick, N.J.)*, *36*(4), 905–918. doi:10.100712144-016-9479-2

Kanesan, P., & Fauzan, N. (2019). Models of Emotional Intelligence: A Review. *Journal of Social Sciences and Humanities*, *16*(7), 1823–1884.

Kellner, F., Chew, E., & Turner, J. (2018). Understanding the Relationship Eff ectiveness through Emotional Intelligence : An Integrative. *Performance Improvement Quarterly*, *31*(1), 35–56. doi:10.1002/piq.21254

Kim, S. (2007). Learning goal orientation, formal mentoring, and leadership competence in HRD A conceptual model. *Journal of European Industrial Training*, *31*(3), 181–194. doi:10.1108/03090590710739269

Kotsou, I., Mikolajczak, M., Heeren, A., Grégoire, J., & Leys, C. (2019). Improving Emotional Intelligence: A Systematic Review of Existing Work and Future Challenges. *Emotion Review*, *11*(2), 151–165. doi:10.1177/1754073917735902

Liden, R. C., Sparrowe, R. T., & Wayne, S. J. (1997). Leader-member exchange theory: The past and potential for the future. *Research in Personnel and Human Resources Management*, *15*, 47–119.

Lopes, P. N. (2016). Emotional Intelligence in Organizations: Bridging Research and Practice. *Emotion Review*, *8*(4), 316–321. doi:10.1177/1754073916650496

Lopes, P. N., Salovey, P., Côté, S., & Beers, M. (2005). Emotion regulation abilities and the quality of social interaction. *Emotion (Washington, D.C.)*, *5*(1), 113–118. doi:10.1037/1528-3542.5.1.113 PMID:15755224

Mancini, G., Biolcati, R., Joseph, D., Trombini, E., & Andrei, F. (2022). Editorial: Emotional intelligence: Current research and future perspectives on mental health and individual differences. *Frontiers in Psychology*, *13*, 1049431. Advance online publication. doi:10.3389/fpsyg.2022.1049431 PMID:36312187

Mapuranga, R., Sharon, C., & Manhimanzi, G. (2022). Emotional intelligence as a conduit for effective business leadership in a volatile, uncertain, complex and ambiguous (VUCA) environment. *Journal of Leadership, Governance and Development, 1*(1&2).

Maqbool, R., Sudong, Y., Manzoor, N., & Rashid, Y. (2017). The Impact of Emotional Intelligence, Project Managers' Competencies, and Transformational Leadership on Project Success: An Empirical Perspective. *Project Management Journal*, *48*(3), 58–75. doi:10.1177/875697281704800304

Martins, A., Ramalho, N., & Morin, E. (2010). A comprehensive meta-analysis of the relationship between Emotional Intelligence and health. *Personality and Individual Differences*, *49*(6), 554–564. doi:10.1016/j.paid.2010.05.029

Mattingly, V., & Kraiger, K. (2019). Can emotional intelligence be trained? A meta-analytical. *Human Resource Management Review*, *29*(2), 140–155. doi:10.1016/j.hrmr.2018.03.002

Mayer, J. D., Caruso, D. R., & Salovey, P. (2016). The Ability Model of Emotional Intelligence: Principles and Updates. *Emotion Review*, *8*(4), 290–300. doi:10.1177/1754073916639667

McKee, A. (2017). How to be happy at work. *Leader to Leader*, *2017*(86), 47–52. doi:10.1002/ltl.20321

Mérida-López, S., Extremera, N., Quintana-Orts, C., & Rey, L. (2019). In pursuit of job satisfaction and happiness: Testing the interactive contribution of emotion-regulation ability and workplace social support. *Scandinavian Journal of Psychology*, *60*(1), 59–66. doi:10.1111jop.12483 PMID:30240014

Miao, C., Humphrey, R. H., & Qian, S. (2018). Emotional intelligence and authentic leadership: A meta-analysis. *Leadership and Organization Development Journal*, *39*(5), 679–690. doi:10.1108/LODJ-02-2018-0066

Mills, L. B. (2009). A Meta-Analysis of the Relationship Between Emotional Intelligence and Effective Leadership. *Journal of Curriculum and Instruction*, *3*(2), 22–38. doi:10.3776/joci.2009.v3n2p22

Neong, S. C., Isa, Z. M., & Abdul Manaf, M. R. B. H. (2022). Emotional Intelligence And Organisational Culture: A Systematic Literature Review. *Journal of Pharmaceutical Negative Results*, *13*(5), 1582–1592. doi:10.47750/pnr.2022.13.S05.249

Nightingale, S., Spiby, H., Sheen, K., & Slade, P. (2018). The impact of emotional intelligence in health care professionals on caring behaviour towards patients in clinical and long-term care settings: Findings from an integrative review. *International Journal of Nursing Studies, 80*, 106–117. doi:10.1016/j.ijnurstu.2018.01.006

Orejarena, H., Zambrano, O., & Carvajal, M. (2019). Emotional intelligence and its influence on organizational leadership in the VUCA world. *Proceedings of the 4th International Conference on Social, Business, and Academic Leadership (ICSBAL 2019), 359*, 185–188. 10.2991/icsbal-19.2019.32

P., A. (2015). KESHAVA- Holistic Employee Selection Framework in the VUCA World. *SCMS Journal of Indian Management, 12*(4), 5–18. https://search.ebscohost.com/login.aspx?direct=true&db=buh&AN=112038228&site=ehost-live

Payne, W. L. (1985). *A Study of Emotion: Developing Emotional Intelligence; Self-Integration; Relating to Fear, Pain and Desire.* Union for Experimenting Colleges and Universities. https://www.scirp.org/(S(351jmbntvnsjt1aadkozje))/reference/referencespapers.aspx?referenceid=2979927%0Ahttps://books.google.com.eg/books/about/A_Study_of_Emotion.html?id=9EhKAQAACAAJ&redir_esc=y

Petrides, K. V., & Furnham, A. (2003). Trait emotional intelligence: Behavioural validation in two studies of emotion recognition and reactivity to mood induction. *European Journal of Personality*, *17*(1), 39–57. doi:10.1002/per.466

Rajah, R., Song, Z., & Arvey, R. D. (2011). Emotionality and leadership : Taking stock of the past decade of research. *The Leadership Quarterly*, *22*(6), 1107–1119. doi:10.1016/j.leaqua.2011.09.006

Riggio, E. R., Murphy, S., & Pirozzolo, F. (2002). Multiple Intelligences and Leadership. Lawrence Erlbaum Associates. doi:10.4324/9781410606495-8

Rodriguez, A., & Rodriguez, Y. (2015). Metaphors for today's leadership: VUCA world, millennial and "Cloud Leaders.". *Journal of Management Development*, *34*(7), 854–866. doi:10.1108/JMD-09-2013-0110

Ruiz-Aranda, D., Salguero, J. M., Cabello, R., Palomera, R., & -Berrocal, P. F. (2012). Can an Emotional Intelligence Program Improve Adolescents' Psychosocial Adjustment? Results from the Intemo Project. *Social Behavior and Personality*, *40*(8), 1373–1379. doi:10.2224bp.2012.40.8.1373

Russo-Netzer, P., & Shoshani, A. (2019). Becoming teacher leaders in Israel: A meaning-making model. *Cambridge Journal of Education*, *49*(3), 369–389. doi:10.1080/0305764X.2018.1533524

Saha, S., Das, R., Lim, W. M., Kumar, S., Malik, A., & Chillakuri, B. (2023). Emotional intelligence and leadership: Insights for leading by feeling in the future of work. *International Journal of Manpower*, *44*(4), 671–701. doi:10.1108/IJM-12-2021-0690

Salminen-Tuomaala, M. H. (2020). Developing emotional intelligence and situational awareness through simulation coaching. *Clinical Nursing Studies*, *8*(2), 13. doi:10.5430/cns.v8n2p13

Sánchez-López, M. T., Fernández-Berrocal, P., Gómez-Leal, R., & Megías-Robles, A. (2022). Emotional Intelligence and Risk Behaviour: A Risk Domain-Dependent Relationship. *Psicothema*, *34*(3), 402–409. doi:10.7334/psicothema2021.527 PMID:35861002

Sánchez-Núñez, M. T., Patti, J., & Holzer, A. (2015). Effectiveness of a Leadership Development Program that Incorporates Social and Emotional Intelligence for Aspiring School Leaders. *Journal of Educational Issues*, *1*(1), 65. doi:10.5296/jei.v1i1.7443

Schutte, N. S., Malouff, J. M., Thorsteinsson, E. B., Bhullar, N., & Rooke, S. E. (2007). A meta-analytic investigation of the relationship between emotional intelligence and health. *Personality and Individual Differences*, *42*(6), 921–933. doi:10.1016/j.paid.2006.09.003

Schutte Nicola, S., & John, M. (2001). Emotional Intelligence and Interpersonal Relations. *The Journal of Social Psychology*, *141*(4), 523–536. doi:10.1080/00224540109600569 PMID:11577850

Shorey, H. S., & Chaffin, J. S. (2018). Leader – Follower Attachment : Implications for Personality Assessment in Organizational Contexts Leader – Follower Attachment : Implications for Personality Assessment. *Journal of Personality Assessment*, *100*(5), 1–11. doi:10.1080/00223891.2018.1472100 PMID:29897260

Tan, C. Y. (2018). Examining school leadership effects on student achievement: The role of contextual challenges and constraints. *Cambridge Journal of Education*, *48*(1), 21–45. doi:10.1080/0305764X.2016.1221885

Thakur, D. J., Verma, P., & Sharma, D. (2019). Influence of leadership style: A review. *International Journal of Advanced Science and Technology*, *28*(20), 945–952.

Vaidya, R. W., Prasad, K., & Mangipudi, M. R. (2020). Mental and emotional competencies of leader's dealing with disruptive business environment - A conceptual review. *International Journal of Management*, *11*(5), 366–375. doi:10.34218/IJM.11.5.2020.036

Vardiman, P. D., Houghton, J. D., & Jinkerson, D. L. (2006). Environmental leadership development : Toward a contextual model of leader selection and effectiveness Environmental leadership development : Toward a contextual model of leader sel .... *Leadership and Organization Development Journal*, *27*(2), 93–105. doi:10.1108/01437730610646606

Varshney, D., & Varshney, N. K. (2020). Workforce agility and its links to emotional intelligence and workforce performance : A study of small entrepreneurial firms in India. *Global Business and Organizational Excellence*, *39*(5), 1–11. doi:10.1002/joe.22012

Vega, A., Cabello, R., Megías-Robles, A., Gómez-Leal, R., & Fernández-Berrocal, P. (2022). Emotional Intelligence and Aggressive Behaviors in Adolescents: A Systematic Review and Meta-Analysis. *Trauma, Violence & Abuse*, *23*(4), 1173–1183. doi:10.1177/1524838021991296 PMID:33568015

Vidyarthi, P. R., Anand, S., & Liden, R. C. (2014). Do emotionally perceptive leaders motivate higher employee performance? The moderating role of task interdependence and power distance. *The Leadership Quarterly*, *25*(2), 232–244. doi:10.1016/j.leaqua.2013.08.003

Villanueva, L., Prado-Gascó, V., & Montoya-Castilla, I. (2022). Longitudinal analysis of subjective well-being in preadolescents: The role of emotional intelligence, self-esteem and perceived stress. *Journal of Health Psychology*, *27*(2), 278–291. doi:10.1177/1359105320951605 PMID:32830558

Walter, O., Shenaar-Golan, V., & Routray, S. (2021). Cross-Cultural Comparison of How Mind-Body Practice Affects Emotional Intelligence, Cognitive Well-Being, and Mental Well-Being. *Frontiers in Psychology*, *12*(July), 1–8. doi:10.3389/fpsyg.2021.588597 PMID:34335347

Wang, X., & Dong, B. (2022). Emotional Intelligence and Knowledge Hiding Behaviors: The Mediating Role of Job Stress. *Frontiers in Psychology*, *13*(May), 845782. Advance online publication. doi:10.3389/fpsyg.2022.845782 PMID:35645869

Wolff, S. B., Pescosolido, A. T., & Druskat, V. U. (2002). Emotional intelligence as the basis of leadership emergence in self-managing teams. *The Leadership Quarterly*, *13*(5), 505–522. doi:10.1016/S1048-9843(02)00141-8

Xu, X., Pang, W., & Xia, M. (2021). Are emotionally intelligent people happier? A meta-analysis of the relationship between emotional intelligence and subjective well-being using Chinese samples. *Asian Journal of Social Psychology*, *24*(4), 477–498. doi:10.1111/ajsp.12445

Yu, C. S., Sardessai, R. M., Lu, J., & Zhao, J. H. (2006). Relationship of emotional intelligence with conflict management styles: An empirical study in China. *International Journal of Management and Enterprise Development*, *3*(1–2), 19–29. doi:10.1504/IJMED.2006.008240

Zeidner, M., Matthews, G., & Roberts, R. D. (2004). Emotional Intelligence in the Workplace: A Critical Review. *Applied Psychology*, *53*(3), 371–399. doi:10.1111/j.1464-0597.2004.00176.x

Chapter 9
The Correlation Between Emotional Intelligence and Job Satisfaction Among Hospital Nurses

Dimpal Roy
The ICFAI University, Jaipur, India

ABSTRACT

This study aimed to investigate the association between the job satisfaction experienced by hospital nurses in Jaipur and their level of emotional intelligence. The triumphs and accomplishments of a person are directly proportional to their level of intelligence. In Jaipur, a correlational research study was carried out. For the study, one hundred registered general nurses were recruited from three private hospitals in Jaipur (50 females and 50 males). Both emotional intelligence and work contentment were evaluated using the Schutte self-report emotional intelligence inventory and the job contentment survey. Both of these surveys were administered online. The research showed a significant positive association between nurses' emotional intelligence and job satisfaction. In addition, the findings did not point to any substantial gender disparities in terms of emotional intelligence or happiness with one's place of employment.

1. INTRODUCTION

Employees are an integral part of the organization and their satisfaction along with engagement helps in organizational performance (Amir et al; 2011; Anarfi et al., 2010; Adeyemo et al, 2011; Adeyemo, 2007;Bhardwaj and Kalia,2021; Bhardwaj et al., 2023). Various forms of intelligence such as General intelligence, Social intelligence, cultural intelligence (Bhardwaj, 2022) and emotional intelligence play a role in Employee's job performance (Bradberry and Greaves, 2005; Cekmecelioglu et al., 2012; Cekmecelioglu, 2014). It is just as essential to recognize, evaluate, and react appropriately to other people's feelings as it is to be able to regulate and communicate one's feelings. For example, imagine living in a

DOI: 10.4018/979-8-3693-0418-1.ch009

community where you cannot understand your close friend's anguish or frustration your colleague felt. This skill is referred to as emotional intelligence by psychologists, and others believe that having high levels of emotional intelligence is more crucial.

Several key emotional intelligence indications and examples include:

i. The ability to detect and express others' feelings.
ii. Realizing one's capabilities and limitations
iii. Confidence in oneself and acceptance of oneself
iv. The ability to overlook mistakes
v. The ability to tolerate and welcome change
vi. great interest, particularly about other individuals; and
vii. compassion and empathetic concern for others
viii. Sensitivity to the feelings of others
ix. Accepting responsibility for mistakes

1.1 Emotional Intelligence Components

Studies have shown that emotional intelligence may be broken down into four distinct subdomains: the capacity to perceive emotions, the ability to use emotions as a tool for thinking, the ability to comprehend emotions, and the ability to manage emotions.

i. Perception of emotional states: Accurate emotion perception is the initial step in comprehending feelings. The ability to read nonverbal cues such as body language and facial expressions is often required for this task.
ii. Emotional reasoning: The next step involves using feelings to boost one's intellect and cognitive function. What we prioritize regarding what we concentrate on and how we react is greatly influenced by our emotional responses to things that catch our attention.

There is a wide range of possible interpretations associated with the feelings that we go through. The observer is responsible for determining the cause of the person's anger and what it may signify if the individual is exhibiting angry feelings. For example, if your boss is acting angry, it may be a sign that they are dissatisfied with your performance, that they received a speeding ticket on their way to work that morning, or that they have been arguing with their partner. On the other hand, your boss's anger may indicate their dissatisfaction with your performance.

The capacity to keep one's emotions under control is considered to be the hallmark of the most highly developed levels of emotional intelligence. Emotional management includes regulating one's feelings, acting acceptably whenever those feelings emerge and reacting appropriately to the feelings of others.

The limbs of this model are structured hierarchically, with the less complicated operations located at, the lower levels and the more intricate ones found at the upper levels. At the lowest levels, for instance, feeling and expressing emotions is a part of the process, but at higher levels, when a more conscious effort is required, managing emotions is a part of the process.

1.2 Job Satisfaction

A non-quantifiable statistic known as job satisfaction is a positive emotional reaction one experiences when completing duties or being present at work. This definition describes job satisfaction as a feeling of fulfilment. In the wake of the widespread adoption of employee satisfaction surveys as a standard practice in most workplaces, notable businesses are looking for ways to measure this experience more often. It is important to remember that people experience work satisfaction in various ways. It's possible that the things that make one worker happy at their job won't make another worker happy doing the same work in the same environment and with the same set of circumstances. As a consequence of this, it is essential to take a multifaceted approach to the happiness of workers, which addresses the following areas:

I. The demanding nature of the work encourages workers to push themselves to new limits and accomplish more incredible things.
II. A certain amount of comfort (short commutes, access to the right digital tools, and flexible hours)
III. The immediate management, as well as the rest of the organization, consistently show gratitude.
IV. Pay that is competitive and provides workers with the means to maintain a satisfactory standard of living
V. The assurance is given to workers that their professional advancement would be in line with their personal development goals

1.3 Nursing Job Contentment

In nursing, much research has been done on job satisfaction. A wide range of factors, including job satisfaction, have been investigated by researchers to understand this connection better. Job satisfaction among nurses has been linked to several factors, including relationships between nurses and doctors, the size of the unit, the severity of a patient's sickness, workload, and the degree to which the nurse is given autonomy in their function (Collins et al., 2000; McNeese-Smith, 1999). Research on job happiness in nursing has generally been motivated by the objective of determining the extrinsic motivational or hygienic variables that impact levels of job satisfaction. There was no evidence of any particular study about the status of work satisfaction experienced by newly licensed nurses.

2. OPERATIONALIZATION OF JOB SATISFACTION

Work fulfilment is notoriously tricky to pin down, even at its most fundamental level. It is not a stable condition and may be influenced or changed by the environment of the job as well as other influences (Fraser, 1983). According to Fraser (p. 24), a worker is said to experience job satisfaction when "the perceived benefits of the activity surpass the perceived costs by a margin considered reasonable by the worker given the circumstances." For this study, "work satisfaction" was defined as an individual's favourable attitude toward their employment or the aspects of their job they enjoyed (Adams & Bond, 2000; Weiss, 2002).

In the context of the two-factor theory of work satisfaction, contentment and dissatisfaction are not antonyms but independent concepts that should be considered separately. The two-factor approach establishes a connection between motivation (such as success, recognition, development, growth, and responsibility) and works satisfaction, as opposed to job unhappiness. According to Bickhard's definition, motivation and emotion are interacting processes (n.d.). He advanced the hypothesis that feelings are the product of evaluative processes dependent on individual motivators and affect behaviour. Consequently, it is projected that emotional intelligence and work satisfaction would have a closer association than emotional intelligence and job unhappiness. In this particular research, only occupational contentment was analyzed and scored.

2.1Potential Implications for Nursing

According to Knoop (1995), an individual who is content with their professional life is more likely to be engaged and loyal to that vocation. Knoop found a correlation between overall job satisfaction and job commitment that was relatively strong (r = 0.64), based on his research with 171 registered nurses. He concluded that if nurses have happiness in their jobs, they are more likely to stay in their current roles. Emotional intelligence refers to a person's capacity to generate emotions to influence a situation (facilitate), understand emotions in terms of their relationships, and manage them without exaggerating or underestimating the significance of their feelings. Therefore, their level of emotional intelligence may influence an individual's level of job satisfaction. Researchers may find it helpful to determine the association between nurses' dedication to their professions and their retention if they better understand the degree to which new nurses are satisfied with their jobs.

2.2 Early Practice Nursing

The present nursing crisis requires an emphasis on new nurses, notwithstanding the potential relevance of all nurses' relationships between emotional intelligence, burnout, and work satisfaction. According to Wieck, Prydun, and Walsh (2002), the nursing profession's attempts to attract new members and engage in educational pursuits will impact nursing practice and leadership for the next forty years. At the beginning of a nurse's career, there is very little focused research on nurses themselves. The National Council of State Boards of Nursing is in charge of providing oversight for newly licensed nurses. A survey is administered once every three years to evaluate the entry-level nursing skills of registered nurses who have worked for a minimum of six months. Data on nurses engaged in early nursing practice was obtained from the National Council of State Boards of Nursing (Smith & Crawford, 2002) and then used to design and update the National Council Licensure Examination for Registered Nurses (NCLEX-RN). The National League of Nursing also surveyed recently certified nurses to get information that can be relied upon in the nursing labour force. The National League of Nursing is responsible for collecting the vast bulk of the demographic information on newly licensed nurses (Louden, Crawford, & Trotman, 1996). Even though demographic data and evaluations of entry-level nursing competence are very important, this does not mean that they can provide a framework for understanding the experiences and views of nurses when they are still in their first few years of practice.

2.3 Implementation of Early Nursing Practice

According to McNeese-Smith (2000), most first-year nurses self-identified as being in the first stage of professional growth when asked where they were in their careers. The phases of a nurse's career may be broken down into three categories: entry, mastery, and disengagement. Few registered nurses still believed themselves at the entrylevel after working in the field for two years. In addition, just 4% (n = 412) of nurses said they felt disengaged with their job within the first six months of their professional careers. The disengagement stage from one's place of employment, characterized by depersonalization and emotional tiredness for the individual, has many characteristics of the burnout phase. After one year on the job, according to Gardner (1992), role conflict in the workplace may become more apparent. McNeese-Smith and Gardner (1992) investigated the first six months of a nurse's career and found no statistically significant differences between the nurses. Finkelstein (1996) suggests that the first year of a nurse's job is the most formative of their career. During this period, nurses can improve their feeling of self-assurance, further develop their abilities, and create a sense of devotion to the nursing profession. "The first year of nursing may have been challenging, if not discouraging, but it also enhanced these nurses' resolve to become nurses," says Finkelstein (p. xvii). It would seem that a period greater than six months but less than two years would be able to distinguish between a nurse who is just beginning her career and an experienced one. In the context of this research, "newly-qualified" registered nurses were defined as those with less than six years of professional experience.

3. REVIEW OF LITERATURE

Several studies have tried to measure job expectation and satisfaction of employees in various organizations. Various research scholars have tried to study determinants of job contentment and Engagement (Kalia and Bhardwaj, 2019; Emdady &Bagheri, 2013; Thakur at al, 2019). It has been proved that EI play a role in job satisfaction (Lee,& Ok, 2012; Laschinger, 1996; Mabekoje, 2009; Kwansah et al, 2012;Kumar et al., 2013; Hosseinian, 2008). We conducted a study to determine the level of job satisfaction experienced by nursing staff working in a tertiary care hospital in northern India. The degree of management and working conditions at an institution may be accurately predicted by the amount of job satisfaction experienced by registered nurses. The gender also play a role in job satisfaction (Mason, 2005; Moradi et al., 2013). Therefore, the field of nursing might profit economically, humanitarianally, and professionally from more investigation into the factors that contribute to job satisfaction. This study aimed to understand better the degree to which nursing officers (NOs) working in tertiary care hospitals are satisfied with their professions. The majority of nurses, according to the poll, were pleased. However, numerous characteristics were typically connected to unhappiness.

Theophilus Tagoe and Emmanuel Nii-Boye Quarshie (2017) Conducted a study in Accra on the relationship between nurses' emotional intelligence and their level of job satisfaction. This research aimed to evaluate the relationship between emotional intelligence and the level of job satisfaction experienced by nurses working in Accra, Ghana. In Ghana, a correlational study was done the following year, in 2015. For the study, the researchers chose a suitable sample of 120 registered general nurses working in private hospitals around Accra (83 females and 37 men). The Schutte Self-Report Emotional Intelligence Inventory and the Job Satisfaction Survey were used to gauge respondents' emotional intelligence and job satisfaction levels, respectively. The findings indicated a significant and favourable connection between emotional quotient and the level of job satisfaction experienced by nurses. On the other hand, the studies failed to reveal substantial gender differences in emotional intelligence or levels of pleasure at work.

Tara Chand Sahu (2020) and Kumar et al. (2013) An Investigation Into The Relationship Between Job Satisfaction And Emotional Intelligence Among Secondary School Teachers In The Jaipur District The primary objective of this study was to investigate the emotional intelligence of secondary school teachers as well as the level of job satisfaction they experienced about their gender, location, and the kind of school they worked in. This study takes the form of a descriptive survey in its methodology. As the overall sample for this study, 240 different teachers were selected randomly to participate. According to the results, secondary school teachers' emotional well-being and job satisfaction were not significantly influenced by their gender, location, or the kind of institution where they worked.

4. METHODOLOGY

Objective:

1. To explore the Emotional Intelligence and Job Performance
2. To compare the Job performance and motional intelligence of male and female nurses
   a) Hypothesis:

H_1 There will be a significant relationship between emotional intelligence and Job satisfaction among male nurses.

H_2There will be a significant relationship between emotional intelligence and job satisfaction among female nurses.

b) Sample Design:

This sample used simple methods of random selection throughout the selection process. Using methods of stratified random selection, Selected one hundred male and female nurses worked at Jaipur's Metro mass hospital, Manus hospital, and Sanjivani hospital. The hospitals were Metro mass hospital, Manus hospital, and Sanjivani hospital. One hundred registered nurses are working at the district hospitals of Jaipur, of whom 50 are male, and 50 are female. Two different methods are used here to assemble the necessary materials for the research project. Depending on the requirements, the data was collected from the three hospitals at other times during the process.

c) Data collections:

The use of questionnaires was a component of the data collecting process. Three components make up the questionnaires. Section A collected data on the demographic characteristics of the respondents, such as sex, age, and educational attainment. Sections B and C included tests of emotional intelligence and work happiness, respectively. Section A collected data on the demographic characteristics of the respondents.

1. Schutte et al. (1998) developed the Schutte Self-Report Emotional Intelligence Inventory to evaluate a person's emotional intelligence. There are 33 components to this scale. One component that makes up the scale is "I know when to share personal issues with others." According to Ciarrochi, Forgas, and Mayer, the internal and test-retest reliabilities of the SSRI total score are quite high. The values for these reliabilities are s = 0.93 and 0.73, respectively (2006). (p. 38). The responses

were given a score between one and five, with one representing "strongly disagree" and five representing "strongly agree." The scale ran from one to five. The total scores on the scale range from 33 to 165, and a higher score indicates greater emotional intelligence—the range of possible scores on the scale.

2. The concept of contentment in one's employment was evaluated using Spector's (1997) Job Satisfaction Survey (JSS). There are a total of 36 questions that assess various facets of work. The JSS scale has an overall internal consistency of 0.91 on a scale from 0 to 10. In addition, it was determined that there was test-retest reliability of 0.71. The responses are graded using a scale of six points, where a score of one indicates a strong disagreement and a score of six indicates a firm agreement. The scale has a theoretical total score range of 36 to 216, with the ranges 36–108 suggesting discontent, 144–216 representing contentment, and 108–144 denoting ambivalence. Field 36–108 means unhappiness.

d) Statistical analysis: Descriptive statistics (mean, standard deviation, etc.) were employed for each variable in the current research, and correlation was also used.

5. RESULT AND DISCUSSION

Table 1 reveals that the mean, standard deviation and standard error of 'emotional intelligence" among male and female nurses, i.e., the male nurses group was 41.26,3.390 and .334, respectively,and the female nurse's group was 38.42,2.870, and .432 .mean difference in male and female nurses are .420. So, this is significant at a .05 level of confidence.

Table 1. Statistical comparison of emotional intelligence among male nurses and female nurses

Group	N	Mean	Standard Deviation	St. Error Mean	Mean Differences	Result
Male nurses	50	41.26	3.390	.334	.420	Significant
Female nurses	50	38.42	2.870	.432		

* Significant at .05 level of significance ₋ .05(98)= .97
** Significant at .0 level of significance ₋ .05(98)= .60

Table 2 reveals that the mean, standard deviation and standard error of 'emotional intelligence" among male nurses and female nurses, i.e., the male nurses group was 40.11,2.120 and .220, respectively, and the female nurse's group was 32.21,1.820, and .180 .mean difference in male and female nurses are .380. So, this is significant at a .05 level of confidence.

Table 2. Statistical comparison of 'job satisfaction' among male nurses and female nurses

Group	N	Mean	Standard Deviation	St. Error Mean	Mean Differences	Result
Male Nurses	50	40.11	2.120	.220	.380	Significant
Female Nurses	50	32.21	1.820	.180		

* Significant at .05 level of significance _t' at .05(98)= .97
** Significant at .0 level of significance _t' at .05(98)= .60

Table 3. Job satisfaction with emotional intelligence relation among male nurses and female nurses

		Emotional Intelligence (Total Group)	Emotional Intelligence (Male Nurses)	Emotional Intelligence (Female Nurses)
Job Satisfaction	Pearson correlation	-.220**	-.168**	-.126**
	Sign.(2-tailed)	.000	.000	.000
	N	100	50	50

* d.f. 200 at .05=.14 d.f. 100 at .05=.19
**d.f. 200 at .01=.18 d.f. 100 at .01 =.25

6. DISCUSSION

This study aims to investigate whether or not emotional intelligence is related to the level of job satisfaction experienced by nurses in their respective roles and whether or not such a connection exists. Examining the data using statistical methodology yields three significant findings about the nursing profession in Jaipur, Rajasthan. First, no statistically significant gender differences are seen in either the survey's conclusions measuring job happiness or the results of the test measuring emotional intelligence.

The first conclusion is consistent with previous research done in this area. It demonstrates a substantial positive connection between emotional intelligence and contentment with one's place of employment (Manus hospital, global hospital, and metro mass hospital). The nurse-patient relationship has the potential to be stressful, complex, or even traumatic; nonetheless, nurses are often educated and trained to participate in cooperative and helpful interactions with their patients. This is the case even if such partnerships may be complex. Nursing practitioners with high emotional intelligence can build the social and interpersonal skills that are the foundation of emotional intelligence. Emotional intelligence is a measure of how well one can read and respond to the emotions of others. To give adequate and timely treatment, one may argue that a nurse practitioner has to be able to identify and assess their feelings, keep those emotions under control and channel them appropriately. It would seem that emotional intelligence and satisfaction with one's work have nothing to do with one another. Therefore, if a nurse's work performance demonstrates a high degree of emotional intelligence, then they are more likely to report feeling content with their positions. This is because emotional intelligence is directly related to job satisfaction.

The second noteworthy conclusion, which is that judgments of emotional intelligence did not substantially differ by gender, is consistent with the findings of previous research that have been conducted on the subject (Manus hospital, global hospital, and metro mass hospital). These results may also be ascribed to the professional socialization and training that nurses get, which helps them acquire values such as self-respect, ethical confidence, and the significance of empathizing with their patients.

Because nurses place some significance on their professional nursing values within the context of nursing practice, they are skilled at appropriately assessing and expressing their emotions through verbal and nonverbal abilities. Nurses emphasize professional matters related to emotion regulation, self-esteem, and emotional intelligence. It is conceivable that any evident gender differences would go undetected because they apply professional nursing values to their nursing obligations. One such ideal is emotional intelligence.

7. CONCLUSION AND LIMITATION

Post covid era has posed various challenges for organizations in contemporary era (Sharma et al., 2022). Even though this study does not give conclusive evidence owing to various constraints, it does provide the groundwork for more research on the emotional intelligence of nurses. This study did not look at the significant components of the participants' jobs that may have contributed to a rise in their overall work satisfaction and a decrease in their degree of discontentment with their jobs. The study also did not evaluate the participant's performance on the various subtests of emotional intelligence, nor did it consider any other potential variables that may have influenced or mediated the discovered relationships. As a result, it is recommended that future studies investigate the numerous facets of emotional intelligence and occupational qualities and the variables that moderate and mediate the relationship between these two factors. In addition, the sample size might be increased in further research to enhance the research's external validity. Future studies can also be untaken related to various job dimensions like job engagement (Bhardwaj et al., 2023), intensions to move abroad for job contentment (Dovlo, 2007; Anarfi et al, 2010;Bhardwaj and Sharma, 2022; Akhund et al., 2011; Bhardwaj, 2017), AI and various such dimensions.

Based on the findings presented in this study, it is plausible to conclude that the emotional intelligence scores of nurses have a positive and direct relationship to the levels of job satisfaction they report experiencing in their careers. However, there is no correlation between gender and work happiness, and the relationship between gender and emotional intelligence is very weakly significant. There is growing knowledge on the connection between emotional intelligence and other psychological characteristics important to the nursing profession in Jaipur; however, more study is required to add to this body of information.

REFERENCES

Adeyemo, D. A. (2007). Emotional Intelligence and The Relationship Between Job Satisfaction & Organizational Commitment of the employee in public parastatals in Oyo state, Nigeria, Pakistan. *Journal of Social Sciences*, *4*(2), 324–330.

Akhund Lotfali, P., Khanneh, H. R., Fallahi Khoshknab, M., & Hosseinzadeh, S. (2011). The Effect of Emotional Intelligence Education on Nurses' JobInteraction. *Health Promotion Management*, *1*(1), 7–16.

Amir Kabiri, A., Hejazi Farz, N., & Ziaei, Z. (2011). Evaluation of the Relationship between Emotional Excitement and Job Satisfaction among Overseer Deputy Officers of IRIB. *Journal of State Administration Mission*, *2*(1), 123–130.

Anarfi, J., Quartey, P., & Agyei, J. (2010). *Key determinants of migration among health professionals in Ghana*. Development Research Centre on Migration, Globalisation and Poverty. Research report. Available from: https://www.gov.uk/dfid-research-outputs/key-determinants-of-migration-among-health-professionals-in-ghana#citation

Bhardwaj, B. (2017). Migration vulnerability: Role of digital media and internet in stimulating and inhibiting brain drain. *International Journal of Advances in Management and Economics*, *6*(6), 24–32.

Bhardwaj, B. (2021). *Short-term foreign trips correlates of the four factors model of cultural intelligence*. Rajagiri Management Journal. doi:10.1108/RAMJ-01-2021-0008

Bhardwaj, B., & Kalia, N. (2021). *Contextual and task performance: role of employee engagement and organizational culture in hospitality industry*. Vilakshan-XIMB Journal of Management. doi:10.1108/XJM-08-2020-0089

Bhardwaj, B., Kalia, N., Chand, M., & Sharma, D. (2023). Engaged Organizational Culture as a precursor to job performance: An evidence from the hospitality industry of Himachal Pradesh. *International Journal of Hospitality and Tourism Systems*, *16*(4), 48–57.

Bhardwaj, B., & Sharma, D. (2022). Migration of skilled professionals across the border: Brain drain or brain gain? *European Management Journal*. Advance online publication. doi:10.1016/j.emj.2022.12.011

Bradberry, T., & Greaves, J. (2005). *The Emotional Intelligence Quick Book*. Simon & Schuster.

Butts, J. B., & Rich, K. L. (2012). *Nursing ethics*. Jones & Bartlett.

Cekmecelioglu, H. G., Gunsel, A., & Ulutas, T. (2012). Effects of emotional intelligence on job satisfaction: An empirical study on call center employees. *Procedia: Social and Behavioral Sciences*, *58*, 363–369. doi:10.1016/j.sbspro.2012.09.1012

Ciarrochi, J. V., Forgas, J. P., & Mayer, J. D. (Eds.). (2006). *Emotional intelligence in everyday life* (2nd ed.). Psychology Press.

Danquah, E. (2014). Analysis of the impact of emotional intelligence on organizational performance: A banking perspective. *British Journal of Marketing Studies*, *2*, 34–50.

Dovlo, D. (2007). Migration of nurses from sub-Saharan Africa: A review of issues and challenges. *Health Services Research*, *42*(3p2), 1373–1388. doi:10.1111/j.1475-6773.2007.00712.x PMID:17489920

Emdady, M., & Bagheri, N. (2013). The relation between emotional intelligence and job satisfaction. *European Journal of Experimental Biology*, *3*, 554–558.

Gay, L. R., Mills, G. E., & Airasian, P. W. (2011). *Educational research: Competencies for analysis and application* (10th ed.). Pearson Education.

Ghoniem, A., Elkhouly, S., Mohsen, G., & Ibrahim, M. (2011). Impact of Emotional Intelligence and Gender on Job Satisfaction among Egyptian Government Sector Employees. *J Soc Sci.*, *3*(1), 7–22.

Gutek, B. A. (1988). Sex segregation and women at work: A selective review. *Applied Psychology*, *37*(2), 103–120. doi:10.1111/j.1464-0597.1988.tb01130.x

Haghighatjoo Z, Shafigh Pour, M. R, & Anari, H. (2008). The relationship between emotional intelligence and job satisfaction among men and women working for Iran medical sciences universities. *Journal of Nursing and Midwifery Urmia University of Medical Sciences, 6*(4), 159-169.

Hosseinian, S., Yazdi, S. M., Zahraie, S., & Fathi-Ashtiani, A. (2008). Emotional intelligence and job satisfaction. *Journal of Applied Sciences (Faisalabad), 8*(5), 903–906. doi:10.3923/jas.2008.903.906

Iacobucci, T. A., Daly, B. J., Lindell, D., & Griffin, M. Q. (2013). Professional values, self-esteem and ethical confidence of baccalaureate nursing students. *Nursing Ethics, 20*(4), 479–490. doi:10.1177/0969733012458608 PMID:23166146

Kalia, N., & Bhardwaj, B. (2019). Contextual and Task Performance: Do Demographic and Organizational variables matter? *Rajagiri Management Journal, 13*(2), 30–42. doi:10.1108/RAMJ-09-2019-0017

Kalia, N., & Bhardwaj, B. (2019). Contextual and Task Performance: Do Demographic and Organizational variables matter? *Rajagiri Management Journal, 13*(2), 30–42. doi:10.1108/RAMJ-09-2019-0017

Kumar, P., Khan, A. M., Inder, D., & Sharma, N. (2013). Primary Health Care Providers (Public Sector) job satisfaction in an urban setting. *Journal of Family Medicine and Primary Care, 2*, 227–233. doi:10.4103/2249-4863.120718 PMID:24479088

Kwansah, J., Dzodzomenyo, M., Mutumba, M., Asabir, K., Koomson, E., Gyakobo, M., & Snow, R. C. (2012). Policy talk: Incentives for rural service among nurses in Ghana. *Health Policy and Planning, 27*(8), 669–676. doi:10.1093/heapol/czs016 PMID:22349086

Laschinger, H. K. S. (1996). A theoretical approach to studying work empowerment in nursing: A review of studies testing Kanter's theory of structural power in organizations. *Nursing Administration Quarterly, 20*(2), 25–41. doi:10.1097/00006216-199602020-00006 PMID:8700383

Lee, J., & Ok, C. (2012). Reducing burnout and enhancing job satisfaction: Critical role of hotel employees' emotional intelligence and emotional labor. *International Journal of Hospitality Management, 31*(4), 1101–1112. doi:10.1016/j.ijhm.2012.01.007

Mabekoje, S. O. (2009). Gender differences in job satisfaction among secondary school teachers. *African Journal of Research in Personnel and Counselling Psychology, 1*, 99–108.

Mason, E. S. (1995). Gender differences in job satisfaction. *The Journal of Social Psychology, 135*(2), 143–151. doi:10.1080/00224545.1995.9711417 PMID:7776638

Mayer, J. D., Salovey, P., & Caruso, D. R. (2004). Emotional intelligence: Theory, findings, and implications. *Psychological Inquiry, 1*(3), 197–215. doi:10.120715327965pli1503_02

Mehrizi, M. Z. Z. (2014). Evaluation of emotional intelligence and job satisfaction in employees of Kashan Hospitals. *Nursing and Midwifery Studies, 3*, e11977. PMID:25414889

Moradi, M., Khatouni, M., Zeighami, R., Hashemi Global, H., & Sheikhi, M. R. (2013). *The Relationship between Professional Engagement and Job Satisfaction among Nurses in Governmental Hospitals Affiliated to Qazvin University of Medical Sciences*. Academic Press.

Sharma, D., Chaudhary, M., Jaswal, N., & Bhardwaj, B. (2022). Hiding Behind The SWOT: Gender Equality and COVID-19. *Journal of Positive School Psychology*, 730–740.

Thakur, D. J., Verma, P., & Sharma, D. (2019). Influence of Leadership Style: A Review. *International Journal of Advanced Science and Technology*, *28*(20), 945–952.

ADDITIONAL READING

Rezaei, A., Bahreini, M., Sarvghad, S., & Shahamat, S. (2013). Prediction of Nurses' Job Satisfaction Based on Emotional Intelligence and Competency, Bushehr University of Medical Sciences. *South of The Year*, *16*(2), 128–137.

Salovey, P., & Grewal, D. (2005). The science of emotional intelligence. *Current Directions in Psychological Science*, *14*(6), 281–285. doi:10.1111/j.0963-7214.2005.00381.x

Chapter 10
Role of Emotions and Spirituality at Modern Day Efficient Work Spaces

Mayura Kemkar
https://orcid.org/0000-0001-9756-1020
Shri Govindram Seksaria Institute of Technology and Science, India

Mohit Lohani
Lal Bahadur Shastri Institute of Management, India

Vaniki Joshi Lohani
https://orcid.org/0009-0006-6097-2137
Jawaharlal Nehru University, India

ABSTRACT

Conventionally, intelligence has typically been associated solely with cognitive and logical abilities. Nevertheless, this conventional perspective on intelligence overlooks the wide range of other inherent faculties within the human mind. Human behavior emerges from an individual's inherent qualities, encompassing a diverse spectrum of actions and behaviors, especially in their interactions with others. Emotional quotient (EQ) delves into a person's capacity to effectively respond and react within diverse situations involving people. Meanwhile, spiritual quotient (SQ) forms the foundational basis not only for intelligence quotient (IQ) but also for emotional quotient (EQ). The present narrative study delves into how the fusion of emotional and spiritual quotients can empower a leader to make informed and empathetic decisions, consequently propelling the organization towards elevated levels of success. The study delves into various facets encompassing both dimensions.

DOI: 10.4018/979-8-3693-0418-1.ch010

1. INTRODUCTION

Modern day work places depend on team work where human interaction is at its core. Technology has enabled us to work-from-anywhere but still, person-to-person interactions are at the foundation of all organizational activities.

Our interactions with our peers, family, friends etc. are guided by our personality.

Human personality is defined as sum total of ways in which a person interacts with and reacts to the environment. Gestalt theory “Whole is greater than the sum of its parts” provides us the perfect explanation of how different intelligences or capacities come together and lead to the formation of personality.

Traditionally intelligence has been associated with cognitive and logical abilities only. Ability that leads one to perform well on some standardized problem solving tests. However, this definition of intelligence did not take into account the various other faculties available with the human mind. Personal intelligence is no longer taken as the true and only indicator of human performance. Human behaviors stems from the innate qualities of an individual. Behavior encompasses a whole range of actions and human conducts, specially towards others.

By taking a very confined view of intelligence, and limiting oneself to cognitive intelligence or intelligence quotient (IQ) only one cannot define the wide variations or ranges in human behavior. Continued research in this area has provided us with a new definition of human intelligence, one which takes into account other forms of intelligences as well.

Gardner (1983) has described nine types of intelligences.

Table 1. Nine types of Intelligences by Gardner (1983)

S.No	Intelligence	Manifestation
1.	Naturalist	Sensitive towards nature
2.	Musical	Being aware of rhythm and sound
3.	Logical-Mathematical	Inclination towards number-reasoning
4.	Existential	Aware about practical life
5.	Interpersonal	Perceptive about people
6.	Bodily-Kinesthetic	Mind-body co-ordination
7.	Linguistic	Responsive towards languages
8.	Intra-personal	Perceptive towards relationships
9.	Spatial	Responsive towards mental imagery

This chapter aims to discuss the interconnection between different intelligences and their contribution towards shaping the modern day work spaces.

Goleman (1998) concluded that intelligence quotient (IQ) or cognitive intelligence can explain only about 20 percent of professional success. Sternberg (2001) said that by broadening the scope of intelligence beyond the cognitive intelligence or intelligence quotient (IQ), better prediction of leadership performance can be achieved. Morris & Feldman (1997) have concluded that a relationship exists between intelligence and emotions, which effects the performance of an employee. Therefore, it is required to delve into the area of multiple intelligences to explain the construct of managerial effectiveness. Hence an emotionally intelligent workspace can lead to self sustained environment devoid of any mutual enmity or comparison and an equal growing space is given to all the people.

Since as early as eighteen century researchers started to think about a three part division of the mind. Mendelssohn is credited with the origins of this three part system. This system consists of the following parts:-

1. Cognition (or thought)
2. Affect (or emotion)
3. Motivation (Conation)

Functions such as judgment, reasoning, human memory and abstract thought were believed to originate from the cognitive sphere. It is this cognitive sphere that the term intelligence as used by the psychologists is associated with how well this cognitive sphere works. Walsh and Betz (1995) defined intelligence as the "power to combine and separate". Spearman (1927) advocated the importance of abstract reasoning while defining intelligence. Sattler (1982) defined intelligence as the power to reason and judge.

2. EMOTIONAL INTELLIGENCE

Emotional quotient (EQ) is a score that gives an idea about the person's ability to act and react in situations and with people. People who are emotionally stable are most likely to score high on an EQ scale and exhibit corresponding behaviour when dealing with stressful, unexpected and demanding situations or people in professional or personal front. To harvest the true potential of a human being the mere knowledge of facts and figures is not sufficient. To be able to become a good leader requires an understanding of self, ones emotions and feelings, how this affects our behaviour towards and then armed with this knowledge one can truly be a leader.

Wechsler (1943) proposed that the "non-intellective abilities are essential for predicting one's ability to succeed in life". The term emotional quotient was first used by Salovey and Mayer (1990), which referred to intelligence in how people recognize feelings and manage emotions in life.To gain a comprehensive comprehension of Emotional Intelligence, it becomes essential to delve into its foundational components: Emotions and Intelligence.

Beginning as early as the 1930s, scholars commenced their exploration of intelligence. Initially, their focus was predominantly on the cognitive realm, encompassing problem-solving and memory capabilities. Nonetheless, even in these formative years, a select few individuals recognized and comprehended that intelligence extended beyond the cognitive aspects. Another facet, the non-cognitive dimension, held equal significance. Wechsler (1943) put forward the notion that "non-intellectual abilities play a crucial role in predicting an individual's potential for achieving success in life."The phrase "emotional quotient" was initially coined by Salovey and Mayer (1990), referring to a form of intelligence that involves recognizing emotions and effectively managing them in various life situations.

Emotional quotient (EQ) is a metric that provides insight into an individual's capacity to respond appropriately in different scenarios and when interacting with others. Those who possess emotional stability are more likely to obtain high scores on an EQ assessment and demonstrate corresponding behaviours when confronted with stress, unforeseen challenges, or demanding individuals, both personally and professionally. According to Goleman (1995), someone with a high IQ might excel as a finance educator, yet a combination of high IQ and high EQ is what truly befits a capable financial leader. To tap into a person's true potential, mere factual and numerical knowledge falls short. Becoming an effective leader necessitates a profound understanding of oneself, one's emotions, and their impact on behaviour. Armed with this awareness, one can genuinely assume a leadership role. Tischler, Biberman, and McKeage (2002) have documented a positive correlation between workplace success and emotional intelligence. The skill of managing a diverse group, fostering their motivation toward shared objectives, springs from a foundation of heightened EQ.

Stein, Papadogiannis, Yip, and Sitarenios (2009) have illustrated through their research that managers who possess high scores in empathy, self-regard, and problem-solving capability are more likely to contribute to the growth of high-performing companies. As observed, companies are placing significant emphasis on EQ as a vital skill in the era of globalization, recognizing that cognitive intelligence alone is insufficient. Training initiatives geared toward introducing managers and leaders to the concept of EQ have gained traction over time. Mojtaba Rafiei (2017) showcases that all dimensions of EQ directly and significantly influence the Organizational Citizenship Behaviour of hospital staff in Zahedan. The ability to align personal aspirations with organizational objectives and foster a sense of unity with the company holds paramount importance.

3. SPIRITUAL INTELLIGENCE

The term "spiritual" originates from the Latin word 'spiritus,' which translates to 'breath,' symbolizing the essence of life. It encompasses the pursuit of comprehending the genuine purpose and significance of life and experiencing the presence of a higher energy.

Spiritual Intelligence (SQ), also referred to as spiritual quotient, forms the foundation for both Intelligence Quotient (IQ) and Emotional Quotient (EQ). It facilitates the harmonious utilization of cognitive intelligence and emotional understanding to attain higher life purposes. Spiritual intelligence involves the capacity to access deeper meanings, enduring values, profound purposes, and the unconscious facets of the self. These aspects are then woven into one's life, resulting in a more enriched and creative existence. Indicators of a heightened SQ include unconventional thinking, humility, and the ability to tap into energies beyond ego-centric concerns, extending into realms beyond personal daily matters.Spiritual quotient aids in comprehending individual lives within a broader context, infusing life with genuine significance and direction. It unlocks latent potential within individuals, fostering creativity and self-expression. Zohar and Marshall (1999), alongside Sisk and Torrance (2001), emphasize the interconnectedness of theories surrounding intellectual, emotional, and spiritual intelligences.

Numerous studies have shown that spirituality at work improves employee performance, enhances organizational citizenship behaviour, increases motivation as well as reduces workplace stress.

Hyson Peter (2013) highlights the pivotal role of a high spiritual quotient in addressing common leadership challenges such as waning motivation and a lack of purpose in one's work. SQ plays a crucial role in developing effective leaders, spurring enhanced staff motivation, improved follower performance, and ultimately yielding better outcomes. The dimensions of Spiritual Quotient include:

- **The Inner Self:** Reflecting an individual's authentic self.
- **The Inter Self:** Pertaining to one's capacity to influence others.

- **Biostoria**: Representing life's journey, comprising diverse experiences that offer profound insights.
- **Life Perspectives**: Shaping one's outlook on life, providing insights into life's meaning and one's purpose.
- **Spiritual Actualization**: Achieving the highest level of spirituality by realizing life's true meaning and purpose.
- **Value Orientation**: Guiding one's pursuit of virtuous goals, distinguishing right from wrong.

Mike George (2006) underscores the significance of a high spiritual quotient in enhancing a leader's efficiency, nurturing relationships, overcoming obstacles, and facilitating smooth change management. A spiritual foundation begins with self-understanding, which extends outward to foster harmonious interactions, building trust and respect, thus facilitating mutually beneficial relationships. Robert Burke (2006) illustrates how Spiritual Intelligence influences a leader's interactions with subordinates and those beyond their immediate circle, extending to the wider impact of their leadership. Leadership, as an amalgamation of art, science, and spirituality, encompasses not only business acumen but also sociology, psychology, technology, and self-awareness. Spirituality aids in understanding one's inner self, thereby enhancing interactions with others. Dan Butts (1999) posits that integrating spirituality into daily professional life can lead to substantial success. By incorporating spirituality into existing skill sets, decision-making, creativity, innovation, and organizational health can all be improved, ultimately contributing to long-term success. Abdullah, Alzaidiyeen, & Aldarabah (2009) emphasize the significance of workplace spirituality for effective leadership. A comprehensive understanding of workplace spirituality can illuminate its substantial impact, prompting psychologists and researchers to recognize its subtle yet substantial influence. Yukl (2002) notes that companies with highly satisfied and committed employees tend to be led by individuals who exhibit strong spiritual competencies. Profound self-awareness translates into effective leadership practices, culminating in a motivated workforce and organizational success. In essence, a high spiritual quotient transcends cognitive and emotional capabilities, enabling a deeper understanding of oneself and the world, fostering unity with the universe. Spirituality encourages acceptance of the cyclical nature of life and death and emphasizes contributing positively to humanity. It advocates for a life of humility, peace, and love. A robust comprehension of Spiritual Quotient assists in motivating individuals to strike a balance between work, family time, and personal growth.

4. MANAGERIAL EFFECTIVENESS

Managerial effectiveness pertains to a manager's capability to achieve desired outcomes. The extent to which a manager utilizes their skills and competencies to motivate and guide others is the determining factor for their effectiveness.

According to Likert (1961), displaying a high level of effectiveness in accomplishing personal and work-related objectives necessitates a manager's adaptability to diverse situations and the needs of their followers. Reddin (1970) characterized managerial effectiveness as the output generated, contingent on one's position within the organizational structure. Campbell (1970) defined managerial effectiveness within the context of complexity and ambiguity. An effective manager, in his view, optimizes resources to enhance organizational performance. There are many challenges linked to managerial effectiveness and we need to find out qualifications aimed at addressing these issues.

It has been often observed that Emotional Quotient (EQ), and Spiritual Quotient (SQ) has competencies influencing Managerial Effectiveness (ME). Fisher, Clark, and Fourastie (1940) introduced the three-sector model of economics, upon which the Indian economy is structured. This model classifies economies into three sectors: Primary (raw material extraction), Secondary (manufacturing), and Tertiary (services). The service industry falls under the tertiary sector. The service sector constitutes a significant portion of the Indian Economy, contributing around 60% of the country's Gross Domestic Product (GDP). This sector has emerged as a prominent and rapidly growing segment on both national and global scales. It plays a pivotal role in economic output and offers substantial employment opportunities. Given that the service industry hinges on relationships, including interpersonal, intergroup, and interdepartmental, adept team-building skills are indispensable for sustaining these workplace connections. Certain core competencies are pivotal in bolstering workplace teams, including:

- Proficient communication encompassing attentive and uninterrupted listening, coupled with the ability to convey accurate responses.
- Skillful conflict management involving negotiation and problem-solving prowess.
- Motivation and guidance provision for team members.
- Readiness to adapt to change and future requirements.
- Collaborative and cooperative orientation toward shared objectives.

Therefore, understanding the roles of Intelligence, Emotions, and Spirituality is crucial in shaping a manager's effectiveness. An emotionally and spiritually grounded manager can navigate adverse circumstances and emergent situations within the organization.

Imagine an office setup with a team working on a critical project with fast approaching deadline and there is Alex, a project manager with a remarkable blend of Emotional Quotient (EQ) and Spiritual Quotient (SQ) that sets him apart as a transformative leader. Alex's unique approach to managing his team and projects is a testament to the power of combining emotional awareness and spiritual insight.

One day, Alex's team faces a critical deadline. The pressure is mounting, and tension is palpable among team members. Instead of simply focusing on the tasks at hand, Alex starts the morning with a brief mindfulness exercise, allowing everyone to centre themselves and acknowledge their emotions. This simple practice helps alleviate anxiety and cultivates a sense of unity among the team. During a team meeting, Alex notices that one of his team members, Lily, seems unusually distant and withdrawn. Drawing from his high EQ, he approaches Lily privately and asks if everything is alright. With genuine concern in his voice, he creates a safe space for her to express her feelings. Alex's empathetic approach helps Lily open up about a personal struggle she's been facing, allowing him to offer support and flexibility in her work tasks.

As the project progresses, unexpected challenges arise that could potentially derail the team's progress. Alex, drawing on his Spiritual Quotient, remains grounded and resilient. Instead of viewing these challenges as setbacks, he encourages his team to see them as opportunities for growth and learning. He shares an inspiring story from his own life that aligns with the team's current predicament, providing a spiritual perspective that uplifts their morale. During a particularly heated team discussion, emotions run high as differing opinions clash. Alex's EQ comes to the forefront as he skilfully navigates the conversation. He ensures that each team member feels heard and understood, promoting open dialogue while preventing conflicts from escalating. By fostering an environment of emotional safety and respect, Alex guides the team to a consensus that incorporates diverse viewpoints. Alex's leadership style, combining

Emotional Quotient and Spiritual Quotient, fosters a sense of purpose and camaraderie within his team. He encourages them to take breaks and practice mindfulness when stress levels rise, recognizing the connection between emotional well-being and overall effectiveness. His consistent display of compassion and spiritual insight fosters a workplace culture characterized by trust, mutual support, and a shared sense of meaning.

The day and hour of the meeting dawns, people are filling in the meeting room, all sceptical about the outcome. The team is tensed as to what would be the result of this meeting. The boss enters, presentations are given and later everybody awaits with forced calm the boss's feedback. However, in an unexpected turn of events, the boss empathizes with everybody, tells them that he understands that they are giving their best and that together they can deliver the project on time and of exceptional quality that will surpass the client's expectations. The team is happily surprised In the end, Alex's holistic approach not only helps the team successfully meet their project goals but also contributes to their personal growth and well-being. By embracing emotions, fostering empathy, and infusing spirituality into his leadership,

So, what just happened here?

Emotional and spiritual awareness on the part of the Alex and boss helped change course of the whole meeting. During the complete process of project working Alex tried to reduce the pressure by applying his Spiritual quotient he exemplifies how a balanced blend of EQ and SQ can create a transformative and harmonious work environment. Also in case of the boss to whom the presentation was given he was full of Emotional Quotient and Instead of being harsh and accusing towards his team the boss practiced understanding and compassion which increased individual motivation and team cohesiveness. Hence, emotionally and spiritually intelligent bosses and co-workers help in creating supportive and happier work places which in turn help in increasing work efficiency.

Every one of us would want to have a high level of emotional and spiritual intelligence. Practice Self-Regulation. Self-regulation makes adaptation to changing situations easier. People who practice self-regulation are adept at finding out the most appropriate time and way to express their feelings rather than being impulsive.

Practice mindful listening. Listen to colleagues with full concentration and provide real and constructive feedback. Don't give in to the urge to comment immediately. Even if you don't agree with the way the team mate is working, give them the space and freedom to pursue their own idea. Use techniques like Johari window and Transactional Analysis to understand relationship with self and team in a better and structured manner. Be more empathetic. This can be difficult to practice when you feel that the other person is not right. To avoid disagreements and confrontations building up to major conflicts, try to see things from other's point of view. Agree to disagree. This can be a good starting point towards finding a middle ground and totally bypassing any conflict. Encourage employees to identify and understand the emotions they feel at the workplace. As understanding emotions is the first step towards managing emotions. Do they feel anger, anxiety, frustration, impatience often?

Help employees to find out the triggers that lead to such emotional outburst and ways in which these trigger situations can be handled so that toxic or negative emotions can be controlled in pre-emptive manner. Focus on motivators. Intrinsic motivation is the cornerstone of emotional intelligence. Money, status, fame are all great but highly successful people at workplace are motivated by something more than these external motivators. People who are high on emotional intelligence are very passionate about what they do; they love new challenges and continuously update themselves. Finding things you love to do and focusing on these is a very good way of being motivated.

This positive attitude goes a long way in increasing emotional intelligence and people with high level of emotional intelligence have more positive attitudes towards work and life. Emotional intelligence plays a vital role in not only self well-being and personal success at work but also helps in creating a more inclusive, productive and efficient workplace. It opens up new opportunities and helps people connect better with others. The increased levels of positivity and work satisfaction that accompany high emotional intelligence are a bonus!!

5. IMPACT OF IQ, EQ, AND SQ ON ME

5.1 Intelligence as the Gate-Way for Managerial Effectiveness

From time immemorial, people have always focused on improving their Intelligence Quotient (IQ) in order to be more successful at work. IQ represents the intellectual raw material required for success, be it at home, at work or in the societal settings. It represents the potential that a person has. However, IQ is limited more to performance on some specific type of tests rather than conversion of this theoretical performance to the various tests or challenges that life presents, day in and day out, at home or at workplace.

Possessing very high intelligence can help in making someone an effective manager, but only up to a certain point. After this point other variables like personality, environment and culture play a critical role in improving the effectiveness of the managers. It is said that the brightest brains are not always the best managers. With an increase in the intelligence quotient scores the managerial effectiveness of managers also increases, Dean Keith Simonton (2006) has explored the idea of relationship between leader intelligence and individual leader performance. The author has used correlation analysis to establish the relationship between IQ and leader performance. The data analysis proves that individual differences in intelligence are consistently associated with leader performance. Rockstuhl, Seiler, Ang, Dyne, Annen (2011) have studied intelligence quotient, emotional quotient and cultural intelligence as a critical leadership competency for effective management in culturally diverse settings. The data analysis showed that general intelligence (IQ) predicted both domestic and cross border leadership effectiveness.

5.2 Emotions as facilitator for Managerial Effectiveness

If Intelligence Quotient is the raw material for success, then Emotional Quotient is the process/machinery that converts this raw material into the finished product which is performance or accomplishment in real life. Organizations today believe that emotional intelligence is a critical component required for effective leadership. High emotional intelligence translates into the ability of being in tune with oneself and one's emotions. This leads to a sound awareness of the surrounding situation and becomes an important factor when managing a team of diverse people.

An employee may be highly qualified in all the required areas, but if the employee is not able to work along with peers, subordinates, bosses and clients then that employee may not be a good fit for the organization. Emotional quotient is an art of being aware of, accepting, and responding to emotions, withstanding stress, being stable even in difficult situations, and always being conscious of how our words and actions affect others. The attributes of emotional intelligence also have a positive association with managerial effectiveness.

Emotional quotient consists of ten attributes; these are Self-Awareness, Empathy, Self-Motivation, Emotional Stability, Managing Relations, Integrity, Self-Development, Value-Orientation, Commitment and Altruistic Behaviour.

Each attribute impacts the managerial effectiveness in a unique way.

1. Self-Awareness – This factor defines how aware a person is of oneself.

It defines the degree to which a person has a clear understanding of his/her emotional states and the reason behind these emotions. This ability makes people aware of their strengths and weaknesses and helps in improving their strengths and overcoming their weaknesses. Being aware of one's potential as well as limits is extremely crucial for behaviormodeling and requires a realistic self assessment.

2. Management of Relations – Self awareness leads to better management of relations. This ability leads to an improved management of impulses and disruptive emotions. Self management trains people to be focused on goals even in the face of difficult situations.
3. Empathy – The ability to understand and experience, what the other person is feeling, especially by keeping oneself in other's position is empathy. This leads to building of better relationships and leads to improved communication with peer and subordinates, thus improving effectiveness.
4. Self Motivation – Being motivated not just by immediate results but working towards long term success is self motivation. High self motivation leads to increased productivity and effectiveness.
5. Emotional Stability – It is an internal coping ability of a person. The quality of a person to manage the day-to-day stresses of personal and work life and face the challenges and crisis that arise with a calm and cool frame of mind. Emotionally stable people are less disheartened by failures and recover more quickly afterwards. This ability enhances the effectiveness of a person and makes them better at team handling as well.
6. Integrity – Integrity means the quality of being honest and having strong moral principles. This leads to being righteous and fair in all manners of work, ultimately leading to higher performance.
7. Self-Development – A person, who is aware of one's emotions, motivated from within and stable in the face of a crisis, paves the way for one's development in professional as well as personal settings. This discovery of self leads to an increase in the work potential and improvement in performance.
8. Value Orientation – Value Orientation reflects the notion of what is right and what is wrong, as accepted by an individual. This quality leads to high standards in working, fairness in dealing with peers and subordinates and maintaining an ethical culture in the organization. This quality leads to development of high moral standards and paves the path for current and future success.
9. Commitment – Commitment denotes the quality of being dedicated to a cause or activity. It also signifies the level of enthusiasm that one has towards the assigned task. This translates into an involvement of a person towards the goal. High commitment also leads to an alignment of personal goals with the mission and vision of the organization. This ensures long term loyalty and success.
10. Altruistic Behavior – Altruism is the principle and practice which concerns with the happiness of other human beings. The aim of altruistic behaviour is to enhance the welfare of another person, without the expectation of any external rewards. Altruism becomes a critical competency, especially for managers as they are responsible for the development of a diverse team of people or unit.

Therefore, all the above stated attributes of emotional quotient play a significant role in improving the effectiveness of a manager.

A manager's ability to relate behaviours and emotions with workplace performance is a critical advantage for building an outstanding team. A manager with low emotional quotient is often not able to judge the needs, wants and expectations of the subordinates and peers. Reacting from raw emotions, without understanding and sorting them out, creates mistrust and confusion in co-workers. This can lead to strained working relationships hampering the team and individual performances. Improper emotional handling on the part of manager's is damaging to the organizational culture and can lead to negative feelings toward the company. The mark of a great manager is the ability to understand the impact of verbal and non verbal communications on his/her subordinates and peers. Langhorn (2004) has explored the relationship between emotional competencies of managers and their performance outputs. The author has used correlation analysis to determine the relationship between emotional competencies of managers and their performance. The results indicate a high degree of correlation between profit performances connected to the emotional intelligence pattern of the manager.

Hsi, An Shih, Ely Susanto (2010) have investigated the relationships between emotional intelligence (EI), conflict management styles and job performance. The data analysis results indicate that emotional intelligence is a precursor of conflict management styles. The authors also confirm that integrating style of conflict management acts as a mediating variable for the relationship between emotional intelligence and job performance.

Edelman, Knippenberg (2018) have explored the relationship between emotional intelligence (EI) and leadership effectiveness. The results indicate that emotional intelligence (EI) can quite accurately forecast the correctness of leader responses to their subordinate's emotions. The results also show that there exists a strong relationship between emotional intelligence (EI) and leadership effectiveness, where the leader's responses act as a mediating variable.

Hence, we can say that emotional quotient makes people work better with each other. It lies at the core of how people work in their relationships and with themselves. Thus high emotional quotient brings with it multiple advantages and thus forms a key competency that improves the managerial effectiveness.

5.3 Spirituality as an Enhancer for Managerial Effectiveness

In a room full of hundreds of people, if a question is posed to each person as to what do they mean by spirituality, then the answers will be varied. The responses will start to get blurry and unclear. Hence, for each one of us, spirituality might mean something completely different from the other person. For some it may mean the quality of being connected with the human spirit as opposed to material things. For some, spirituality might mean practicing yoga or meditation, praying together in a group or being close to nature and getting the felling of being one with the universe. Spiritual intelligence forms a higher element of intelligence. We can understand spirituality as being able to think and act with an understanding of the inner self. This dimension activates the qualities and potential of the self or soul. Higher spiritual intelligence in human beings manifests itself in the form of wisdom, creativity, compassion, integrity, joy, love and peace. Spiritual intelligence leads to a feeling of deeper understanding and purpose of life. This wisdom translates into improvements in a wide variety of critical skills, at personal life and work as well.

In today's workplaces, spirituality is seen as a highly appropriate topic for healthy discussions. If we want to describe the meaning and essence of spirituality in one word, it would be "interconnectedness". Spiritual quotient as a key competency in the workplaces refines the actions as well as the purpose behind these actions. Spiritual quotient has a strong positive association with managerial effectiveness. Spiritual quotient consists of six attributes. These are The Inner self, The Inter Self, Biostoria, Life Perspectives, Spiritual Actualization and Value orientation. Furthermore, all the attributes of Spiritual Quotient also have a positive association with managerial effectiveness, except for the attribute of spiritual actualization. Each attribute is unique in its contribution towards managerial effectiveness. The individual attributes are defined as follows:

1. The Inner self – This refers to the real or internal or true nature or soul of a person. By being in realization of one's true nature, one's uniqueness, a person becomes aware of one's internal identity. This identity is separate from the ones defined by the external social forces or relationships. This inner self depends on the persons own values, goals and motivations. This knowledge promotes greater self awareness and increases the working efficiency.
2. The Inter Self – This attribute indicates as to how well a person influences others. People with high degree of inter self act as great leaders or managers by providing guidance and motivation, to their subordinates, in the direction of task completion.
3. Biostoria – The varied experiences that a person has over a period of time defines Biostoria. These experiences that a person accumulates over the life time can be negative as well as positive. All this contributes towards the building of spiritual quotient of a person.
4. Life Perspectives – Perspective defines the way of looking at things. The perspective of a person towards the various challenges of life defines the probable success or failure to a great extent. A positive outlook towards life significantly improves the chances of success and also makes one more effective. This dimension also measures the awareness about the purpose of life.
5. Spiritual Actualization – Spiritual development is a mental exercise, achieved by contemplation. By retrospection and introspection of one's life, the path towards spiritual actualization can be envisaged. In today's fast paced and highly competitive world, spiritual actualization can mean different things to different people. Thus, spiritual actualization can come to people in different ways. For some it could mean being close to nature, for some it could mean relishing an exotic dish, further still for some it could mean listening to a favorite soulful song. This implies that people are able to achieve their own standards of spiritual actualization, but they are not able to reach up to the norms for spiritual actualization as defined by the society.

Thus, as the ultimate level spiritual actualization is difficult to attain, people are always in the pursuit or quest of spiritual actualization.

6. Value Orientation – The attribute of Value Orientation refers to the value system of an individual. This pertains to the ideas of what is right and what is wrong for an individual in the day to day conduct, be at home or at work.

By creating a connection between the outer and inner self one is able to view the surroundings with a profound sense of calmness. This leads to a better thought and emotional control, better communication with team members and a sense of community while taking decisions. The accumulated life experiences of a person and his / her journey in life so far help in sharpening this understanding of self. These past experiences form the building blocks for improvement in the future performance. However, in today's fast paced life of cut-throat competition, where each one wants to overtake the other person, the value of spiritual actualization is missing. Karakas (2010) has researched to find out the ways in which spirituality impacts and improves employees' performances and thus leads to organizational effectiveness. The author concludes that spirituality augments an employee's feeling of well-being. Spirituality also improves the quality of life. It gives a better understanding of the self and provides meaning to all our actions, be it at work or in the personal front, the impact of employee's individual spirituality and organizational spirituality on the employee's experience of meaning in work. The results indicate that workplace spirituality has a strong relationship with the employee's understanding of meaning of work.

6. CONCLUSION

In conclusion the authors want to state that human intelligence is a complex concept that is all-encompassing in its nature. However with time the capabilities that matter most in business and management continue to change. The role that Intelligence Quotient, Emotional Intelligence and Spiritual Intelligence play in overall effectiveness of managers is tested and proven. The skills needed to navigate through the testing waters of modern day business organizations require a solid foundation of both intelligence and expertise.

Management is both an art and science and thus, efficient managers of today need the hard skills of focus, strategic thinking and the capacity to unlearn-relearn as well as softer skills of relationship management, communication, self-awareness, and awareness of others, a sense of purpose and strong values and ethics.

A good blend of these qualities will go a long way in ensuring that our modern day workplaces are resilient, sustainable and innovative. This will ensure that we continue to grow and thrive even in the uncertain and turbulent times of economy. Resilient workplaces will thus pave a way for a stronger economic environment and a stable, growth oriented and happy society.

REFERENCES

Abdullah, A.G.K., Alzaidiyeen, N., & Aldarabah, I. (2009). Workplace Spirituality and Leadership Effectiveness Among Educational Managers in Malaysia. *European Journal of Soil Science*, *10*, 307–319.

Andrew Morris, J., & Daniel, C. (1996). The Dimensions, Antecedents, and Consequences of Emotional Labor. Academy of Management Review, 21(4). doi:10.5465/amr.1996.9704071861

Burke, R. (2006). Leadership and spirituality. *Foresight*, *8*(6), 14–25. doi:10.1108/14636680610712504

Butts, D. (1999). Spirituality at work: An overview. *Journal of Organizational Change Management*, *12*(4), 328–332. doi:10.1108/09534819910282162

Campbell, J. J., Dunnette, M. D., Lawler, E. E., & Weick, K. E. (1970). *Managerial behavior, performance, and effectiveness*. McGraw-Hill.

Edelman, P., & van Knippenberg, D. (2018). Emotional intelligence, management of subordinate's emotions, and leadership effectiveness. *Leadership and Organization Development Journal, 39*(5), 592–607. doi:10.1108/LODJ-04-2018-0154

Gardner, H. (1983). *Frames of mind: The theory of multiple intelligences*. Basic Books.

George, M. (2006). Practical application of spiritual intelligence in the workplace. *Human Resource Management International Digest, 14*(5), 3–5. doi:10.1108/09670730610678181

Goleman, D. (1995). *Emotional intelligence*. Bantam Books, Inc.

Hyson, P. (2013). The spirited leader: The potential of spiritual intelligence to improve leadership. *The International Journal of Leadership in Public Services, 9*(3/4), 109–115. doi:10.1108/IJLPS-10-2013-0028

John, D. (1999, December). Emotional intelligence meets traditional standards for an intelligence. *Intelligence, 27*(4), 267–298. doi:10.1016/S0160-2896(99)00016-1

Langhorn, S. (2004). How emotional intelligence can improve management performance. *International Journal of Contemporary Hospitality Management, 16*(4), 220–230. doi:10.1108/09596110410537379

Likert, R. (1961). *New Patterns of Management*. McGraw-Hill.

Rafiei, M. (2017). The effect of emotional quotient on organizational citizenship behavior in some Iranian hospitals. *Kybernetes, 46*(7), 1189–1203. doi:10.1108/K-01-2017-0001

Reddin, W. J. (1970). *Managerial Effectiveness*. McGraw-Hill.

Rockstuhl, T., Seiler, S., Ang, S., Van Dyne, L., & Annen, H. (2011). Beyond general intelligence (IQ) and emotional intelligence (EQ): The role of cultural intelligence (CQ) on cross-border leadership effectiveness in a globalized world. *The Journal of Social Issues, 67*(4), 825–840. doi:10.1111/j.1540-4560.2011.01730.x

Shih, H.-A., & Susanto, E. (2010). Conflict management styles, emotional intelligence, and job performance in public organizations. *International Journal of Conflict Management, 21*(2), 147–168. doi:10.1108/10444061011037387

Spearman, C. (1927). *The abilities of man*. Macmillan.

Stein, S. J., Papadogiannis, P., Yip, J. A., & Sitarenios, G. (2009). Emotional intelligence of leaders: A profile of top executives. *Leadership and Organization Development Journal, 30*(1), 87–101. doi:10.1108/01437730910927115

Sternberg, R. J., & Zhang, L.-f. (Eds.). (2001). *Perspectives on thinking, learning, and cognitive styles*. Lawrence Erlbaum Associates Publishers.

Tischler, L., Biberman, J., & McKeage, R. (2002). Linking emotional intelligence, spirituality and workplace performance: Definitions, models and ideas for research. *Journal of Managerial Psychology, 17*(3), 203–218. doi:10.1108/02683940210423114

Walsh, W. B., & Betz, N. E. (1995). *Tests and assessment* (3rd ed.). Prentice-Hall, Inc.

Wechsler, D. (1943). Non-intellective factors in general intelligence. *Journal of Abnormal and Social Psychology*, *38*(1), 101–103. doi:10.1037/h0060613

Yukl, G. A. (2002). *Leadership in Organizations* (5th ed.). Prentice Hall.

Zohar, D., & Marshall, I. (2000). *Spiritual Intelligence: The Ultimate Intelligence*. Bloomsburry.

Chapter 11
Models of Emotional Intelligence and Its Impact on Employee Engagement and Productivity

Monica Negi
Dr. Y.S.P. University of Horticulture and Forestry, India

Kapil Kathuria
Dr. Y.S.P. University of Horticulture and Forestry, India

Nidhi Sharma
Dr. Y.S.P. University of Horticulture and Forestry, India

Shabnam Pangtu
Dr. Y.S.P. University of Horticulture and Forestry, India

ABSTRACT

The chapter will comprise show how EI and employment engagement go hand in hand. Moreover, it's important to understand the impact of emotional intelligence on employee engagement. When employees possess strong emotional intelligence skills, they are better equipped to navigate interpersonal dynamics, manage their emotions effectively, and contribute positively to the workplace. The authors have made an effort to explain how emotional productivity is influenced by emotional intelligence.

1. INTRODUCTION

Emotional Intelligence is an important part of the competence of an employee/manager. It can be learned and applied to meet goals and targets to create happy and healthier working culture. Adamska and Minarova (2014) defined competence as employees' ability (consisting of three components of general

DOI: 10.4018/979-8-3693-0418-1.ch011

ability with technical sense, scientific and practical knowledge and individual and social maturity) with competence i.e., duty, power and responsibility).

Another author Goleman (2000) defines emotional intelligence as the ability to manage and control the emotions. He felt that level of emotional intelligence cannot be determined by genetics but these qualities have to learned and can only increase in long term.

Emotional intelligence has increasingly become a topic of interest in research on employee engagement. Previous research has demonstrated that both intellectual intelligence and emotional intelligence can impact an individual's ability to achieve success, with the level of competence being measured by awareness and management of emotional and related cognitive intelligence. Furthermore, studies have shown that employees with higher levels of emotional intelligence, psychological capital, and proactivity are more likely to exhibit better job performance. Moreover, research has indicated that emotional intelligence can directly affect employee job satisfaction. Gulyani and Sharma in 2018, conducted a study that concluded that emotional intelligence positively correlates with employee job performance, as well as organizational citizenship behavior which is defined as discretionary behavior that contributes to organizational effectiveness but is not part of an employee's formal job requirements (Zapata, 2015).

Bansibihari and Surwade (2006), research supports this finding, indicating that employees who display higher levels of emotional intelligence are generally more responsible toward the organization and tend to have higher levels of job satisfaction, which leads to greater engagement and lower turnover intentions. In addition, the interaction between emotional intelligence and role ambiguity has been found to play an important role in explaining employee engagement. It has been suggested that emotional intelligence can be developed through training programs, such as mindfulness training, and it is possible to improve employee engagement by developing employees.

The chapter will comprise of importance to understand how the two EI and employment engagement go hand in hand. Moreover, it's important to understand the impact of Emotional intelligence on employee engagement. According to a study by Boyatzis (2000), there is a positive and significant correlation between employees' performance levels and the five characteristics of emotional intelligence (EI), including self-awareness, self-regulation, motivation, empathy, and social skills. A study by Yarmohammadi Monfared et al. (2010) found that meeting teachers' basic needs and providing them with amenities could increase their job satisfaction. The study discovered a connection between improved emotional intelligence and emotional intelligence training. A study by Shooshtarian et al. (2013) found a positive and substantial correlation between emotional intelligence and job performance and job satisfaction. Additionally, it promotes self-management, social awareness, self-awareness, and job adaption. Furthermore, the findings of a study by Golparvar et al. (2010) revealed a strong and favorable link between the emotional intelligence components and both self-evaluation and job performance. Additionally confirming the link between emotional intelligence and job success was a 2018 study by Divandari et al.

There are two scientific approaches to emotional intelligence. Further they are characterized as ability and mixed models (Mayer, Caruso & Salovey,2000). The ability model shows views emotional intelligence as a standard and then argues to construct traditional criteria for intelligence (Altbach, 1970).

Mixed models are called mix because of the ability to conception with personality traits and competencies such as optimism, self-esteem and emotional self-efficacy (Cherniss, 2010).

Mayer and Salovey Model of Emotional Intelligence (1977) described by Green in 2018 defines as four discrete mental abilities. (i) perception of emotion, (ii) use of emotion to facilitate thought, (iii) understanding of emotions, (iv) management of emotions. These were written in hierarchical order to understand the psychological process that tackles place (Mayer and Salovey,1977; Mayer et al., 2008 a, b). A strategy was developed by Dr. Brackett and Dr. Rivers known as RULER approach to Social and Emotional learning, which has put forward skills for teaching such as recognizing, understanding, labelling, expressing and regulating emotion contributes to positive development.

Impact on Employee engagement: The absorption studied with respect to gender and work engagement, Anju (2000) said, it was significantly higher among males than females. It was speculated that males' greater job engagement scores might be explained by the gendered idea that men find it easier to express their work involvement than women do. Gulyani and Sharma (2018), said that research show that people who are more educated or have higher levels of education will be able to anticipate better work engagement. It is anticipated that highly educated workers will learn more in their coursework and become more invested in their jobs as a result.

Relationship between EI and Employee Engagement: Total work engagement and emotional intelligence scores were shown to be strongly correlated, as were absorption and emotional intelligence overall, work engagement total and self-awareness, and absorption and self-awareness. a reasonable. There was a correlation between vigor and self-awareness, social skills, emotional receptivity, and overall emotional intelligence. There was also a correlation between commitment and emotional intelligence overall, absorption and emotion regulation, self-motivation, and work engagement overall and emotion regulation, self-motivation, social skills, and emotional receptivity. Only the emotion control aspect of emotional intelligence has been linked to work engagement and life and work satisfaction, according to research (Arya, 1977; Merida-Lopez and Extremera, 2020).

Even though the result did not reach statistical significance, a different study found a positive correlation between engagement and emotional intelligence, with the exception of the well-being component (Shukla et al., 2013). Additionally, it was discovered that perceived job-person fit and emotional intelligence had a significant favorable impact on employees' wellbeing (Akanni et al., 2020). A creative personality and emotional intelligence have been linked, with emotional intelligence even being able to predict an employee's level of work engagement (Bastian et al., 2005; Bataineh, 2013).

The correlation between emotional intelligence and management implications for the organization's sustainability through its engaged workforce is greater (Berndt, 2002; Brown, 2004). The chapter will comprise of further more investigations that may even theories about the self-emotional patterns of the employee, engagement at work and their separate dimensions painted a picture of their connection, as did their emotional intelligence (Anna, 2016).

1.1. Emotional Intelligence

Emotional acuity similar to Like IQ, emotional intelligence develops as a result of a combination of genetics and upbringing I.Q., or intelligence quotient, has long been held up as the best indicator of future achievement in school, work, and life in general. However, recent research has cast doubt on this long-held belief. As a result, IQ tests are frequently used to sort applicants, place them in jobs, and determine advancement opportunities. It is generally agreed that the last decade of the 20th century saw the greatest advancement in the study of emotional intelligence. Research on the topic of EQ has grown rapidly in recent years, in part due to the claims that EQ is as powerful a predictor of work performance as IQ (Goleman, 1995and Campbell et al, 2007). It was previously believed that intelligence is the sum of a set of abilities that lead to successful outcomes. Emotions, in addition to intelligence, are increasingly understood to have a significant role in success. Some individuals with the same IQ do better than others. These points to a mechanism at work that is independent of IQ. The majority of that something is emotional intelligence. Emotions are a performance booster when they are recognized and channelled positively. Contrary to intelligence, which is fixed at birth, emotional intelligence (EQ) can be cultivated and improved upon throughout one's life? EI can be taught and improved through time, while IQ is fixed beyond a certain age. EI can only be honed with time and practice. People become more adept at managing their emotions, swaying the opinions of others, and navigating social situations as they gain experience.

Social cognizance is worked with by the ability to appreciate anyone on a deeper level. As per studies, "social and profound capacities were for times more significant than level of intelligence in deciding proficient achievement renown" (Carlson, 2010).

Successful people have been found to have high levels of emotional intelligence, which includes skills like emotion regulation and stress tolerance. The term "emotional intelligence" was coined by psychologist Daniel Goleman in 1998 to describe a set of traits that contribute to success in the business world (Anju, 2000).

Goleman defines empathetic intelligence as "the capacity to remember one's own sentiments and those of others; the ability to spur oneself; and the capacity to deal with feelings in oneself and in connections." Abilities that go beyond common knowledge are exemplified by this. The capacity to appreciate others on a deeper level depends on five pillars: introspection, self-control, altruism, compassion, and social skills.

- **Self-awareness**: Self-awareness is the capacity to recognize and take responsibility for one's own thoughts, feelings, and behaviors.
- **Self-regulation**: Be joyful and bring joy to others; be in charge of your emotions; be self-assured and angry; channel your emotions; let your anger out in a healthy way.
- **Self-motivation**: Observant, diligent, honest, proactive, confident, capable, goal-oriented, and inspiring of more success.
- **Empathy**: Sympathy is the ability to perceive and sympathize with the encounters and feelings of someone else.
- **Social skills**: Adjectives: popular, outgoing, friendly, helpful, democratic in dealing, humorous, playful, and socially competent.

One's capacity for in-depth interpersonal comprehension is a function of his or her general capacity for:

a) Recognize and understand his own feelings and emotions;
b) Perceive and grasp the sentiments and feelings of others (by means of facial perusing, non-verbal communication, voice tone, and so forth). To achieve harmony, prosperity, and peace, one must be able to:
c) Integrate his obvious emotions into his thinking (using his emotional sentiments in analysis, critical thinking, leadership, etc.);
d) Possess an accurate understanding of the nature, power, and outcomes of his emotions;
e) Exert appropriate control and guidance over the expression and use of emotions in managing oneself and others.

Processing emotions is a focus of the ability approach to emotional intelligence, which has consequences for educational approaches (Gyanani and Kushwaha, 2001)

Emotional intelligence is a crucial psychosocial skill in the diagnosis of clinical and social illnesses that are common in teenagers. Salovey and Mayer (1990) argue that emotional intelligence is a key determinant of practical competence. Numerous prosocial and behavioural traits, including greater empathy, (Davies et al, 1998) improved peer interaction, and less hostility with friends, have been linked in studies to emotional intelligence.

There are numerous distinct and overlapping conceptual models for emotional intelligence, but almost all of them include the dimensions of self-awareness of emotion, other-awareness of emotion, expressing emotion, emotion regulation, and emotion use. All approaches used to measure emotional intelligence can be divided into two types. Among the first set of skills is emotional intelligence, as measured by the Mayer-Salovey-Caruso Emotional Intelligence Test (MSCEIT), developed by Mayer et al. in 2004. The second kind is emotional intelligence traits. Bar-On proposed an emotional intelligence model based on a feature he named EQ-i. Emotional intelligence is often broken down into the following five categories:

(i) Understanding how one feels and being able to identify and understand the feelings of others;
(ii) The ability to regulate one's emotions in the moment;
(iii) Motivation: the capacity to channel feelings toward a goal.
(iv) Empathy, often known as compassion or sensitivity to the feelings of others
(v) Managing relationships - social skills and the capacity to control other people's emotions are included.

Trait emotional intelligence is measured by self-report instruments and takes into account all facets of a person's character (Chotai et al, 2003), including their awareness of and control over their emotions. From these studies' findings and evidence, we may infer the following four criteria (Franky and Chamundeswari, 2014):

(i) Emotional Intelligence
(ii) Motivational Insight
(iii) Empathic Maturity
(iv) Social Competence

Emotional Intelligence (EI) refers to the ability to perceive, understand, manage, and use emotions effectively in oneself and others. It encompasses a range of skills and competencies that play a crucial role in personal and social functioning. EI is essential for building and maintaining healthy relationships, making informed decisions, managing stress, and achieving personal and professional success. Here are some key details about emotional intelligence:

Components of Emotional Intelligence: Different models of emotional intelligence propose various components. Common components include:

Self-Awareness: Recognizing and understanding one's own emotions, strengths, weaknesses, and values.

Self-Regulation: Managing and controlling one's emotions, impulses, and reactions in various situations.

Empathy: Sensing and understanding the emotions of others, and showing compassion and understanding.

Social Skills: Building and maintaining healthy relationships, effective communication, conflict resolution, and collaboration.

Motivation: Being driven to achieve personal and professional goals, even in the face of challenges.

Importance of Emotional Intelligence

Relationships: High EI is linked to better interpersonal relationships, as individuals with strong EI can understand and respond to the emotions of others in a more empathetic and supportive manner.

Communication: Effective communication often requires understanding and managing emotions, which is a key aspect of EI.

Leadership: Leaders with high EI can create positive work environments, understand and motivate their teams, and manage conflicts more effectively.

Decision-Making: Emotional intelligence helps in making rational decisions by considering both emotions and facts.

Stress Management: Individuals with high EI tend to cope better with stress and adversity, as they can regulate their emotions and maintain a positive outlook.

Development of Emotional Intelligence

Self-Reflection: Taking time to understand your emotions, triggers, and responses.

Self-Management: Practicing techniques to regulate emotions, such as mindfulness, deep breathing, and positive self-talk.

Empathy: Actively listening to others, seeking to understand their perspectives, and showing genuine concern.

Social Skills: Engaging in active communication, practicing empathy, and working on building rapport with others.

Assessment of Emotional Intelligence: There are various tools and assessments available to measure emotional intelligence. These assessments often involve self-report questionnaires or performance-based tasks that evaluate different aspects of EI.

Cultural and Contextual Differences: The expression and perception of emotions can vary across cultures. Therefore, emotional intelligence may manifest differently in different cultural contexts.

Lifelong Learning: Developing emotional intelligence is an ongoing process. It involves continuous self-awareness, learning from experiences, and adapting to different situations.

Emotional intelligence is not only about recognizing emotions but also about managing them effectively to achieve positive outcomes. It's an essential skill that can be learned and enhanced over time, leading to improved personal and professional well-being.

The research model was expanded to incorporate the four aforementioned aspects in order to examine emotional intelligence as a predictor of personality traits and life skills in teenagers and how it differs with demographic factors.

For what it's worth, Salovey and Mayer's (1990) definition of emotional intelligence as "the ability to monitor one's own and others' feelings and emotions, to discriminate among them and to use this information to guide one's thinking and actions" is possibly the first explicit use of the term with a well-validated conception. Mayer and Salovey (1999) added to their original notion with the capacity to perceive later on. David W. Chan is able to recognize and manage his emotions because he has learned to recognize and integrate the sentiments that accompany them. These days, we don't just mean one particular talent when we talk about "emotional intelligence," but rather a wide range of competencies that work together to make a person successful in social and professional settings.

Goleman (1995) popularized the concept of emotional intelligence by describing it as the ability to understand and control one's own emotions as well as those of others, as well as the ability to read and respond appropriately to those of others. The original notion of emotional intelligence was developed by Salovey and Mayer (1990), although this definition departs somewhat from that. Bellack (1999) explained Goleman had expanded the concept to include a wide variety of skills and traits like the ability to accurately assess one's own emotions, confidence in one's own abilities, self-control, trustworthiness, conscientiousness, flexibility, innovation, accomplishment drive, dedication, etc. Goleman's (1995, 1998) concept stands for the mixed model, in opposition to the ability model of Mayer and Salovey (1997). The ability model is more focused and precise in its explanation of the aspects of emotional intelligence and their relationship to traditional intelligence. In contrast, the mixed models include not just the core ability components but also a wide range of personality qualities such as empathy, optimism, and impulsivity, as well as possible correlates such as motivation, self-awareness, and happiness (Bharsakhale, 2013).

Given that personality qualities may be difficult, if not impossible, to modify due to genetic, biochemical, and early learning impacts, the claim that emotional intelligence may be learnt is puzzling. If these characteristics are included in the definition of emotional intelligence, then I consider myself emotionally intelligent. However, the truth of the different constructions that go by the label of Emotional Intelligence, as well as assertions that Emotional Intelligence "out predicts IQ" or is "twice as important as IQ," should be approached with caution. In contrast to the other conceptualizations, Mayer and Salovey's (1997) ability model places significant emphasis on Emotional Intelligence as a genuine intelligence inside personality.

- **Perceiving Emotion**

The first and most essential issue is the nonverbal communication of emotions. Emotional expressiveness evolved in animals as a means of social communication, which has been recognized by psychologists and evolutionary biologists. One might potentially tell what a person is feeling just by glancing at their face. Emotions scholars, evolutionary biologists, specialists on nonverbal behavior, and others have made considerable strides in their knowledge of how humans experience and communicate emotions. Recognizing emotions in other people's faces or voices is a crucial initial step toward developing a deeper understanding of emotions.

- **How Emotions Can Promote Thought**

It seemed like the second area was as easy as the first. This was the emotional faculty of stimulating the mind to think. Cognitive scientists, for instance, have shown that emotional responses consistently outweigh logical ones. In other words, when we pay attention to anything, we have some kind of emotional response. Having a robust emotional input system should, then, help direct attention to the matters that really matter. Some types of creativity, for instance, may only emerge in the presence of particular feelings. For instance, both ups and downs in mood have been associated with more creative problem solving.

- **Recognizing Emotions**

When someone is happy, it's usually because they want to hang out with friends and family, when they're angry, it's because they want to hurt or attack others, when they're afraid, they want to run away, and so on. There is a distinct set of signals that may be sent by each emotion, and corresponding behaviors. For instance, if the sender expresses anger, it may be because they feel they have been treated unjustly. Actions like making peace, fighting, seeking vengeance and revenge, or retiring to find tranquillity may be associated with the rage. Understanding emotional cues and the behaviors that accompany them is a key component of this skill (Martin et al., 2005).

Once a person has developed the capacity to detect these emotional signals and behaviors, the ability to reason with and about them becomes crucial. To completely understand feelings, one has to know what they signify and be able to analyze them critically. It is crucial to this set of emotional intelligence skills.

- **Controlling Emotions**

One more thing: it's usually possible to rein in one's emotions. Recognizing the informative potential of one's feelings is critical. To the degree that it is within their power to do so, a person may choose to maintain an openness to emotional signals so long as they are not too painful, while blocking out those that are too intense. Within a person's emotional safety zone, it becomes possible to regulate and manage one's own and other people's feelings until more permanent solutions can be found. advance one's own and others' social and personal objectives. More studies on how to control your emotions have been conducted in this decade than any other.

While there are a number of different conceptualizations of emotional intelligence based on ability and mixed models, both approaches highlight the fundamental role that emotional intelligence plays in human relationships. There has been much consideration devoted to the topic of how to enhance emotional intelligence, as it is likely to be used in settings such as the family, job, school, and others. Although the home is often seen as the primary environment in which a person learns to manage their emotions, the educational institution is often seen as the most crucial place where these abilities may be fostered and further developed. Schools need to step up to the challenge of fostering learning environments that support the development and application of emotional skills and Emotional Intelligence by incorporating emotional literacy into the core curriculum, as this is the term some educators use to refer to the teachable skills of emotional intelligence. Despite the importance of encouraging students' emotional intelligence, schools have been slow to include emotional literacy into their framework.

Finally, it is believed that evaluating and improving such programs would lead to the establishment of classroom settings that foster children' all-around growth. The goals of education reform should extend beyond the smooth functioning of schools and the establishment of clear benchmarks for student performance. In order to understand how emotional intelligence affects intermediate students' academic performance, it has been added as a significant variable (Chan, 2002).

1.2. Elements and Substances of Emotional Intelligence

According to Dr. S.K. Mangal and Shubhra Mangal (2013), emotional intelligence has four components.

1. **Intra-Personal Awareness:** This refers to understanding one's own feelings. The parts of intrapersonal awareness are as follows.
    a. **Emotional Self-Awareness:** Emotional self-awareness (ESA) is a kind of emotional intelligence (EI) that helps a person understand their own emotions and how those emotions affect them and others around them.

b. **Accurate Self-Assessment:** Accurate self-assessment is a skill or competency of an individual's EI that falls under the category of inter-personal awareness and is intended to give him a clear understanding of his strengths and limitations through the use of techniques for self-assessment and the analysis of other people's points of view in order to improve his performance and thereby contribute to his success in life.
c. **Self-Confidence:** An ability or skill in emotional intelligence that enables a person to have complete faith and confidence in his or her own abilities for improved performance and success in life.

2. **Intra-Personal Management:** It's about controlling one's own emotions. The parts of intrapersonal management are as follows.
   a. **Emotional Self-Control:** A talent that helps people with emotional intelligence (EI) get along with themselves and others by exerting desired control over their emotions.
   b. **Stress Tolerance:** Instead of crumbling under strain or displaying indications of pessimism and helplessness, an EI skill is helpful in handling stressful situations.
   c. **Independence:** Making oneself independent in one's thinking, feeling, and behaviours can be achieved with the use of an EI skill or talent.
   d. **Self-Regard:** Self-respect and honest self-awareness are essential elements of emotional intelligence.
   e. **Assertiveness:** An EI talent or ability that enables a person to effectively control his emotions in order to assert himself in a given circumstance and say or do what he wants to without offending or upsetting others.
   f. **Self-Actualization:** An EI talent that aids a person in realizing their potential and achieving their life goals.
   g. **Optimism:** Having the resilience and self-assurance to face life's challenges while firmly believing that there is a sunrise after every dark night is a valuable EI trait or ability.
3. **Inter-Personal Awareness:** It entails being aware of others' feelings. The elements of interpersonal awareness are as follows.
   a. **Awareness About Others:** Getting aware of and identifying the feelings and emotions of others is an EI talent or ability important in interacting and dealing with others.
   b. **Empathy:** An EI skill or ability that helps one think and feel like others do in a given circumstance and communicate those thoughts and feelings in a way that makes others feel understood.
   c. **Reality Testing:** An EI trait or talent that aids in acting in a way that is most desired by observing and evaluating things and situations from their true perspectives.
4. **Inter-Personal Management:** It entails controlling people' feelings. The elements of interpersonal management are as follows.
   a. **Managing Interpersonal Relationships:** An EI trait or ability that aids in fostering appropriate, mutually rewarding relationships with others that foster wholesome friendships, personal partnerships, and social interactions.
   b. **Flexibility:** With the aid of effective emotion management in accordance with the demands of the altered situation, a human can adapt his conduct as necessary.
   c. **Problem Solving:** An EI talent or skill is beneficial for both tackling a challenge with confidence and solving it in a methodical and scientific approach.

d. **Conflict Management:** It refers to a methodical and well-thought-out procedure used to manage and regulate disputes of any kind that might arise between and among people or groups who are living and working in a certain situation at a specific moment.
e. **Cooperation and Collaboration:** A capability or skill in emotional intelligence (EI) that is useful in collaborating and cooperating with others to uphold healthy interpersonal relationships and attain individual or collective goals.
f. **Inspirational Leadership:** An EI trait or ability that makes it easier for one to lead effectively and motivate a group of people to work together toward a common objective.

Some Notable Models of Emotional Intelligence

Mayer and Salovey's Model

Developed by Peter Salovey and John Mayer, this model defines emotional intelligence as the ability to perceive, understand, manage, and use emotions effectively. It consists of four branches: perceiving emotions, using emotions, understanding emotions, and managing emotions.

Goleman's Mixed Model

Proposed by Daniel Goleman, this model highlights five components of emotional intelligence: self-awareness, self-regulation, motivation, empathy, and social skills. Goleman's model emphasizes the practical application of emotional intelligence in various life situations.

Bar-On Model

Developed by Reuven Bar-On, this model suggests that emotional intelligence involves a set of emotional and social skills that influence the way individuals perceive, understand, express, and manage emotions. Bar-On's model includes five main areas: intrapersonal, interpersonal, adaptability, stress management, and general mood.

Emotional Competence

Framework: Richard Boyatzis introduced this model, which emphasizes the development of emotional competencies over time. It highlights emotional self-awareness, emotional self-regulation, empathy, adaptability, and emotional mastery as key components of emotional intelligence.

Petrides and Furnham's Trait Model

Developed by K. V. Petrides and Adrian Furnham, this model focuses on trait-based emotional intelligence. It identifies individual differences in emotional intelligence based on traits such as emotion perception, emotion understanding, emotion management, and emotion utilization.

Genos Model

The Genos model, created by Dr. Ben Palmer, emphasizes emotionally intelligent behaviors in the workplace. It highlights six core emotional intelligence competencies: emotional self-awareness, emotional expression, emotional awareness of others, emotional reasoning, emotional self-management, and emotional management of others.

Schutte's Trait Model

Developed by Nicola Schutte and John Mayer, this model considers emotional intelligence as a trait. It focuses on emotional self-awareness, emotional expression, emotional reasoning, and emotional regulation.

Emotional Competence Framework

Create a diagram with a timeline representing personal growth and development. Along the timeline, depict key stages or milestones such as "Emotional Self-Awareness," "Emotional Self-Regulation," "Empathy," "Adaptability," and "Emotional Mastery." Use arrows or pathways to connect these stages, indicating the progression of emotional competencies over time.

Each of these models offers a unique perspective on emotional intelligence and provides insights into understanding and enhancing emotional awareness, understanding, and management.

Elements in The Emotional Maturity Scale

The five major elements in the Emotional Maturity Scale (EMS) are used to evaluate various facets of emotional maturity in people. Researchers may acquire a thorough grasp of a person's emotional development by using each element to reflect a certain aspect of emotional development. Let's investigate each of the five elements in more depth:

Figure 1.

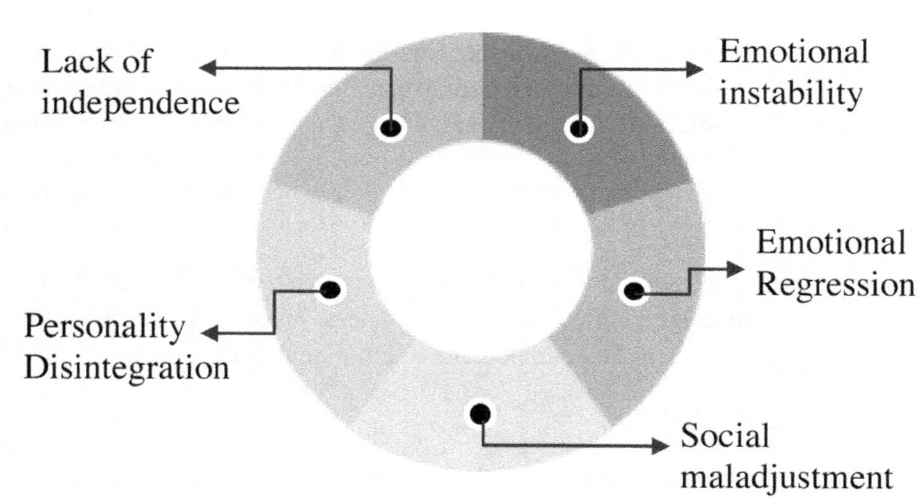

1. Emotional Instability: Emotional instability refers to a person's inability to maintain emotional composure, resilience, and equilibrium even in the face of trying or stressful circumstances. The ups and downs of life may be more easily handled by those with stronger emotional stability without succumbing to their emotions. They are able to keep composure and control, which improves their coping skills and general emotional health.

2. Emotional Regression: Emotional regression measures a person's propensity to return to less emotional maturity, especially under stressful or challenging conditions. It entails acting in ways that may be more characteristic of younger age groups or those with less emotional maturity. Higher scores in this category indicate a stronger predisposition to behave emotionally immaturely when faced with difficulties.
3. Social maladjustment: The capacity of a person to adapt and perform successfully in social circumstances and relationships is the focus of social maladjustment. Higher scores in this aspect may be a sign of trouble establishing and keeping good social connections, interpersonal conflict, or difficulty navigating social norms.
4. Personality Disintegration: Personality disintegration measures alterations or contradictions in a person's behaviour and personality features. Higher ratings for this category might indicate problems maintaining a constant and stable sense of self. Lower emotional maturity may cause individuals' emotions, behaviours, and self-concept to fluctuate.
5. Lack of Independence: Lack of independence describes a person's amount of independence and self-reliance in making decisions and controlling their emotions. A greater reliance on others for emotional support, decision-making, or overcoming obstacles in life may be indicated by higher scores in this aspect.

The researchers may get a thorough evaluation of the emotional maturity of college-bound teenagers in the Barabanki District by incorporating these five broad elements in the Emotional Maturity Scale. The precise questions on the scale under each element provide a sophisticated knowledge of emotional development, assisting in the identification of areas for strength and growth in each dimension. The EMS is a useful instrument for assessing emotional development and may bring important insights to the investigation of emotional maturity and emotional intelligence in this particular group.

Employee Engagement

Employee engagement refers to the emotional and psychological connection that employees have with their work, their colleagues, and their organization as a whole. Engaged employees are deeply committed, enthusiastic, and motivated to contribute their best efforts to achieve the organization's goals and objectives. This level of commitment goes beyond mere job satisfaction, as engaged employees actively invest their time, energy, and creativity to enhance their own performance and contribute positively to the overall success of the company.

Key Aspects of Employee Engagement Include

1. Commitment: Engaged employees are committed to their organization's mission and values. They understand how their individual roles contribute to the larger objectives and are dedicated to fulfilling their responsibilities.
2. Enthusiasm: Engaged employees exhibit genuine enthusiasm and passion for their work. They take pride in their accomplishments and consistently strive for excellence.
3. Motivation: Engaged employees are self-motivated. They are driven by a sense of purpose, achievement, and personal growth, which leads to increased productivity and innovation.

4. Initiative: Engaged employees proactively seek opportunities to contribute beyond their job descriptions. They take ownership of their tasks, propose ideas, and contribute to a culture of continuous improvement.
5. Collaboration: Engaged employees willingly collaborate with their colleagues, recognizing the value of teamwork and synergy. They are open to sharing knowledge, ideas, and expertise.
6. Positive Attitude: Engaged employees maintain a positive attitude even in challenging situations. Their optimism and resilience help maintain a constructive work environment.
7. Alignment with Values: Engaged employees feel a sense of alignment between their personal values and the values of the organization. This alignment enhances their sense of belonging and loyalty.
8. Career Development: Engaged employees are invested in their own career development. They seek opportunities for learning and growth, and they appreciate organizations that support their professional advancement.
9. Feedback and Recognition: Engaged employees value feedback and recognition. Regular feedback sessions and acknowledgment of their contributions reinforce their commitment and motivation.
10. Well-Being: Engaged employees often experience higher levels of well-being. They find satisfaction in their work, which can lead to reduced stress and improved overall quality of life.

Organizations benefit significantly from fostering employee engagement. Engaged employees tend to be more productive, innovative, and customer-focused. They contribute to a positive workplace culture that attracts and retains top talent. Organizations with high employee engagement levels often experience lower turnover rates and higher levels of customer satisfaction, leading to improved business performance and competitive advantage.

To cultivate employee engagement, organizations should focus on creating a supportive work environment, offering opportunities for growth and development, recognizing and rewarding contributions, and promoting open communication and collaboration.

Employee Productivity

Employee productivity refers to the efficiency and effectiveness with which employees complete their tasks and contribute to the organization's goals. It is a key factor in determining the overall performance and success of a company. High levels of employee productivity result in increased output, improved efficiency, and ultimately, enhanced organizational growth and competitiveness.

Here are some key aspects and factors that influence employee productivity:

1. Effective Time Management: Employees who manage their time well can prioritize tasks, set goals, and allocate sufficient time to different activities, leading to higher productivity.
2. Clear Expectations: When employees have a clear understanding of their roles, responsibilities, and performance expectations, they are better equipped to focus on relevant tasks and achieve desired outcomes.
3. Skill Development: Continuous learning and skill development contribute to improved competency and efficiency, enabling employees to complete tasks more quickly and with higher quality.
4. Workplace Environment: A comfortable and well-equipped workspace can positively impact productivity by reducing distractions, enhancing focus, and promoting a conducive atmosphere for concentration.

5. Effective Tools and Technology: Providing employees with the right tools, software, and technology helps streamline processes, automate repetitive tasks, and increase overall efficiency.
6. Employee Engagement: Engaged employees tend to be more motivated and committed, resulting in increased effort, creativity, and a willingness to go the extra mile to achieve goals.
7. Feedback and Recognition: Regular feedback on performance and recognition of achievements can boost morale and drive employees to maintain or improve their productivity levels.
8. Work-Life Balance: Striking a healthy work-life balance is crucial for preventing burnout and ensuring sustained productivity. Well-rested and rejuvenated employees are more likely to perform effectively.
9. Effective Communication: Clear communication channels and open dialogue among team members and management help prevent misunderstandings, reduce errors, and enhance productivity.
10. Task Delegation: Efficient delegation of tasks ensures that each team member is assigned responsibilities aligned with their strengths, leading to optimized outcomes.
11. Goal Setting: Setting specific, measurable, achievable, relevant, and time-bound (SMART) goals provides employees with a clear direction and motivation to work towards accomplishments.
12. Recognition and Rewards: A fair system of recognizing and rewarding productivity incentivizes employees to consistently perform at their best.
13. Collaboration and Teamwork: Effective collaboration fosters the exchange of ideas, skills, and knowledge among team members, resulting in improved problem-solving and overall productivity.
14. Health and Well-Being: Employee well-being, including physical and mental health, directly impacts productivity. Organizations that prioritize wellness initiatives tend to have more productive and engaged employees.

Organizations can enhance employee productivity through a combination of effective management practices, employee development programs, a positive work culture, and a focus on employee well-being. By creating an environment that supports and empowers employees, organizations can maximize their productivity and achieve their goals more efficiently.

CONCLUSION

Emotional intelligence (EI) has a profound impact on employee engagement and productivity within an organization. When employees possess strong emotional intelligence skills, they are better equipped to navigate interpersonal dynamics, manage their emotions effectively, and contribute positively to the workplace. Here's how emotional intelligence influences both employee engagement and productivity:

Emotional Intelligence and Employee Engagement:

1. Effective Communication: High emotional intelligence fosters better communication, as employees can understand and convey their emotions and thoughts more clearly. This leads to fewer misunderstandings, stronger relationships, and increased engagement.
2. Empathy and Collaboration: Employees with strong EI are more empathetic, allowing them to understand and support their colleagues. This empathy fosters collaboration, teamwork, and a sense of unity, enhancing employee engagement.

3. Conflict Resolution: EI enables employees to manage conflicts and disagreements more constructively. They can approach conflicts with empathy and find solutions that maintain positive relationships, reducing tension and enhancing engagement.
4. Positive Work Environment: Emotionally intelligent individuals contribute to a positive and inclusive work environment. When employees feel valued, respected, and understood, their engagement levels rise, leading to improved morale and job satisfaction.
5. Leadership Impact: Leaders with high EI can inspire and motivate their teams, creating a work atmosphere where employees are more engaged and committed. EI-equipped leaders can recognize and appreciate employee contributions effectively.

Emotional Intelligence and Productivity:

1. Stress Management: Employees with strong EI can manage stress and pressure more effectively. They remain composed, make rational decisions, and maintain productivity even during challenging situations.
2. Time Management: Emotional intelligence helps individuals prioritize tasks and manage their time efficiently. They can focus on high-priority tasks, avoid procrastination, and meet deadlines.
3. Adaptability: EI enhances adaptability, allowing employees to embrace change more readily. They can adjust to new circumstances, technologies, and strategies, maintaining productivity during transitions.
4. Decision-Making: Emotionally intelligent individuals consider both rationality and emotions when making decisions. This balanced approach often leads to well-informed decisions that positively impact productivity.
5. Innovation: EI encourages creativity and innovative thinking. Emotionally intelligent employees can think outside the box, propose new ideas, and contribute to problem-solving, fostering a culture of innovation.
6. Focus and Concentration: EI supports self-regulation, helping employees maintain focus and concentration on tasks. This ability minimizes distractions and enhances overall productivity.
7. Motivation and Goal Achievement: Employees with high EI are often intrinsically motivated. They set meaningful goals, remain persistent, and achieve their objectives with determination, driving productivity.
8. Interpersonal Effectiveness: Emotionally intelligent individuals build strong interpersonal relationships. Positive interactions create a supportive atmosphere, reducing conflicts and promoting a productive work environment.

In summary, emotional intelligence significantly influences both employee engagement and productivity. Organizations that recognize the importance of developing emotional intelligence skills in their employees can create a more positive, collaborative, and efficient workplace. By fostering emotional intelligence, organizations can enhance employee satisfaction, boost team performance, and ultimately achieve higher levels of productivity and success.

REFERENCES

Adamska, M., & Minárová, M. (2014). *Role of learning organization in building consumer confidence.* Economics and Management. doi:10.15240/tul/001/2014-1-005

Akanni, A. A., Kareem, D. B., & Oduaran, C. A. (2020). The relationship between emotional intelligence and employee wellbeing through perceived person-job fit among university academic staff: A Structural Equation Modelling Approach. *Cogent Psychology*, *7*(1), 1869376. doi:10.1080/23311908.2020.1869376

Altbach, P. G. (1970, December). Commitment and Powerlessness on the American Campus: The Case of the Graduate Student. *Liberal Education*, *56*, 562–582.

Anju. (2000). *A comparative study of Emotional maturity in relation to Intelligence and Sex* [Unpublished M.Ed. dissertation]. Punjab University, Chandigarh.

Anna, S. (2016, November). Measuring the Effects of Self-Awareness: Construction of the Self-Awareness Outcomes Questionnaire. *The Journal of Psychology*, *12*(4), 645–658.

Arya, A. (1997). *Emotional Maturity and values of superior children in family. Fourth survey of research in Education* (Vol. 11). NCERT.

Bansibihari, P., & Surwade, L. (2006). The Effect of Emotional Maturity in Teacher Effectiveness. Educational Tracks, 6(1).

Bartlett, S. (2015). *The relationship between emotional intelligence, work engagement, creativity and demographic variables* [Unpublished Master's thesis]. University of South Africa.

Bastian, V. A., Burns, N. R., & Nettlebeck, T. (2005). Emotional intelligence predicts life skills, but not as well as personality and cognitive abilities. *Personality and Individual Differences*, *39*(6), 1135–1145. doi:10.1016/j.paid.2005.04.006

Bataineh, M. Z. (2013, January). Academic stress among undergraduate students: The case of education faculty at King Saud University. *International Interdisciplinary Journal of Education*, *2*(1), 82–88. doi:10.12816/0002919

Bellack, J. P. (1999). Emotional Intelligence: A Missing Ingrethent? *The Journal of Nursing Education*, *38*(1), 3–4. doi:10.3928/0148-4834-19990101-03 PMID:9921779

Berndt, T. J. (2002). Friendship quality and social development. *Current Directions in Psychological Science*, *11*(1), 7–10. doi:10.1111/1467-8721.00157

Bharsakhale, R. L. (2013). A Study of Emotional Intelligence among Marathi and English Medium Students in Aurangabad City. *Indian Streams Research Journal*, *3*(5), 1–5. doi:10.9780/22307850

Boyatzis, R. E., Goleman, D., & Rhee, K. (2000). Clustering competence in emotional intelligence: Insights from the Emotional Competence Inventory (ECI). Handbook of Emotional Intelligence, 99(6), 343-362.

Brown, B. (2004). Adolescents' relationships with peers. In R. Lerner & L. Steinberg (Eds.). Handbook of adolescent psychology. Wiley. doi:10.1002/9780471726746.ch12

Campbell, A., & Ntobedzi, A. (2007). Emotional intelligence, coping and psychological distress: A partial least squares approach to developing a predictive model. Electronic Journal of Applied Psychology: Emotional Intelligence. *Coping and Psychological Distress*, *3*(1), 39–54.

Carlson, N. R. (2010). *Psychology: The science of behaviour*. Pearson Education Canada.

Chan, D. W. (2002). Emotional Intelligence: Implications for Educational Practice in Schools. *Educational Research Journal*, *17*(2), 183–196.

Cherniss, C. (2010). Emotional intelligence: Toward clarification of a concept. *Industrial and Organizational Psychology: Perspectives on Science and Practice*, *3*(2), 110–126. doi:10.1111/j.1754-9434.2010.01231.x

Cherniss, C., & Goleman, D. (2000). Emotional intelligence. *Annual meeting of the society for industrial and organizational psychology*. www. eiconsortium. org

Chotai, J., Lundberg, M., & Adolfsson, R. (2003). Variations in personality traits among adolescents and adults according to their season of birth in the general population: Further evidence. *Personality and Individual Differences*, *35*(4), 897–908. doi:10.1016/S0191-8869(02)00306-9

Davies, M., Stankov, L., & Roberts, R. D. (1998). Emotional intelligence: In search of an elusive construct. *Journal of Personality and Social Psychology*, *75*(4), 989–1015. doi:10.1037/0022-3514.75.4.989 PMID:9825531

Divandari, A., Nazari, M., Seyed Javadin, S. R., Haji Karimi, A., & Rayej, H. (2018). Investigating the Effect of Compensation on Individual Performance: A Study on the Mediating Role of Internal Motivation and the Moderating Role of Self-efficacy and Reward Expectancy. *Journal of Business and Management*, *10*(3), 673–694.

Goleman, D., & Intelligence, E. (1995). Why it can matter more than IQ. *Emotional Intelligence*.

Green, R. (2018). Mayer and Salovey model of emotional intelligence. The Emotional Intelligence Institute, 1-6.

Gulyani, G., & Sharma, T. (2018, October). Total rewards components and work happiness in new ventures: The mediating role of work engagement. In Evidence-based HRM: A global forum for empirical scholarship (Vol. 6, No. 3, pp. 255-271). Emerald Publishing Limited.

Gyanani, T. C., & Kushwaha, S. S. (2001). Emotional Intelligence and Its Development. *Journal of Indian Education, NCERT*, *25*(2), 66–75.

Mangal, S. K., & Mangal, S. (2013). *Research methodology in behavioural sciences*. PHI Learning Pvt. Ltd.

Mayer, J. D., Caruso, D. R., & Salovey, P. (1999). Emotional intelligence meets traditional standards for an intelligence. *Intelligence*, *27*(4), 267–298. doi:10.1016/S0160-2896(99)00016-1

Mayer, J. D., Caruso, D. R., & Salovey, P. (2000). Emotional intelligence meets traditional standards for an intelligence. *Intelligence*, *27*(4), 267–298. doi:10.1016/S0160-2896(99)00016-1

Mayer, J. D., Salovey, P., & Caruso, D. R. (2004). Emotional intelligence: Theory, findings and implications. *Psychological Inquiry*, *60*(3), 197–215. doi:10.120715327965pli1503_02

Mérida-López, S., Sánchez-Gómez, M., & Extremera, N. (2020). Leaving the teaching profession: Examining the role of social support, engagement and emotional intelligence in teachers' intentions to quit. *Intervención Psicosocial*, *29*(3), 141–151. doi:10.5093/pi2020a10

Salovey, P., & Mayer, J. D. (1990). Emotional intelligence. *Imagination, Cognition and Personality*, *9*(3), 185–211. doi:10.2190/DUGG-P24E-52WK-6CDG

Shooshtarian, Z., Ameli, F., & Amini Lari, M. (2013). The effect of labor's emotional intelligence on their job satisfaction, job performance and commitment. *Iranian Journal of management studies, 6*(1), 27-43. Golparvar, M., & Nadi, M. (2010). Cultural values and overall fairness. *Journal of Iranian Cultural Research*, *3*(1), 207–228.

Shukla, R., & Nagar, D. (2013). Impact of gender and managerial levels on emotional intelligence and job performance of Indian revenue service officers. *Indian Journal of Health and Wellbeing, 4*(1), 83.

Yarmohammadi Monfared, S., Hemmati NezhadTouli, M., & Ramazani, R. (2010). The relationship between emotional intelligence and job satisfaction in physical education teachers. *Sport Management Journal*, *2*(6), 47–111.

Zapata, A. (2015). The Emotional Stability and Emotional Maturity of Fourth Year Teacher Education Students of the Bulacan State University. *Journal of Social Sciences & Humanities Research.*, *1*(2), 1–5.

Chapter 12
Artificial Intelligence Applications in Human Resource Management:
A Bibliometric Content Analysis and Future Research Agenda

Chandni Rani
Department of Commerce, Baba Farid College, Bathinda, India

Tanveer Kajla
https://orcid.org/0000-0002-5528-9804
Department of Management Studies, NALSAR University of Law, Hyderabad, India

ABSTRACT

Human resource is facing a transformation challenge with artificial intelligence(AI). AI's position is larger in various human resource (HR) functions where robotics companies are able to handle recruiting, employing, analyzing data, collecting data, reducing workplace workload, and improving workplace performance. To report this gap, the current study purposes to head to the digital revolution by means of various methods to streamline resources through usage of big data analytics, AI, and cloud computing. The prime role of this research is to address the ensuing research on significant journals, keywords, and affiliations, authors, countries, elevating the literature on AI in human resource management (HRM) using bibliometric content analysis approach. Four prominent themes emerged in the literature which give directions on the role of information systems in building the framework for AI, machine learning applications, decision making, and handling the recruitment process with neural networks. Further, the current research recommends several suggestions for the part of future direction AI in HRM.

DOI: 10.4018/979-8-3693-0418-1.ch012

1. INTRODUCTION

Artificial Intelligence (AI) mimics the intelligence of human brain. In other words, it is the technique to make machines work and behave like humans (Tayarani N., 2021). It is the primary source of innovation and efficient working in organizations. AI is the umbrella term comprising of machine learning and deep learning (Di Vaio et al., 2020). Therefore, it can be apprehended that AI is the constellation of different technologies working in synergy to produce human-like output for complex problems with multiple inputs. There is a misconception that robots solely use AI; however, AI technology has been embedded in our daily lives.

AI is being extensively used by the social media platforms like Facebook to give customized feed to their users. Google used AI to optimize the query results on their search engine. AI combined with information systems, analytics, and intelligence helps business organizations in achieving solutions to complex tasks such as understanding the perceptions of the customers or automating monotonous tasks requiring less human intervention (Berezina et al., 2019). Currently, artificial intelligence has accelerated an organization's overall structure and in the human resource department where human beings are replaced by AI.

Human resources (HR) research with artificial intelligence, such as recruitment inferences, performance assessments, preparation and orientation procedures, career management, and coaching is handled in an effective manner both financially and in terms of time (Votto et al., 2021). AI technologies provide extensive opportunities for enhancing HR processes such as self-service transactions, recruitment and talent creation, payroll, tracking, policies, and procedures regarding access (Johnson et al., 2021). A company's performance depends on how well it intelligently integrates assets, processes, and technology to deliver the benefit of change at an optimized cost. AI will help to automate various back-office activities in a better way for productive HR transactions. The application for several different HRM activities has developed including compensation, financial advantages, job recruitment, and human resource planning (Ahmed O., 2018). It is presenting new opportunities and at the same time bringing new challenges never encountered before. On one hand, Artificial Intelligence can help the HR manager in helping and retaining their employees by employing work related flexibility, job enrichment, etc. It can help in finding the candidates for skill shortage areas and also help in bringing positive changes in the way they work.

Artificial Intelligence is a novel and revolutionizing technology that is modifying every facet of the system we work. A report by Alsop Thomas (2022) depicted that corporate and HR leaders graphed wide-reaching use AI to support employees in their organizations, fifty percent of these appealed that the fundamental use of AI in this framework was to improve consistency and quality. Furthermore, twenty six percent stated that AI is used to support employees by improving efficiency up to sixteen percent to expand insights.

Management of human resources is a strategic practice within organizations. HRM cultivated by cultural, political, economic, legal, social, and mainly technological change as well as demand for competitiveness and operational excellence.

Previous researchers highlighted the importance of conducting bibliometric analysis (Alsharif et al., 2021; Kumar et al., 2023). Recently, researchers have explored the literature on AI applications in the HRM process (Liu & Duffy, 2008; Votto & Liu, 2023; Qamar et al., 2021; Votto et al., 2021). However, we could find some prominent gaps that need to be addressed to have a profound understanding of the topic. For instance, recently, Liu & Duffy (2023) did research typically on the role of chatbots in HRM by taking the articles from WoS database and ignoring the Scopus database. The Scopus database is the biggest database for the literature, and ignoring Scopus creates a vacuum in analysis of the existing literature on AI and HRM. This gap is covered in our research using the Scopus database. Although, Kaushal et al. (2023) took the data from Scopus database but the search string used in the research does not cover the whole list of topics, not considering the synonyms for Artificial Intelligence and its other application areas in management.

Therefore, our research will provide a holistic understanding of AI applications considering wider aspects and exhaustive literature related to AI and HRM. Our research is not specific to processes in HRM, but rather expanding a broader scope to assist future researchers in understanding the overall integration of AI and HRM. Hence, the aim of this research is to address the subsequent research questions:

RQ1. What are the influential journals, authors, countries, keywords, and affiliations, elevating the literature on AI in HRM?
RQ2. What are the emerging themes in the research of AI and HRM?
RQ3. What are the prominent topics for future research?

The present study explained the works concerning AI in HRM with bibliometric analysis to have a systematic assessment of AI in HRM and identify the lacunae in the current literature.

2. RELATED WORK

The past literature on AI can be outlined back to Shenkar (1990) who address the impact of industrial robots on organizations and their employees. Subsequent this influential article, the new study in the successive decade Impact of AI on workplace outcomes (Pereira et al., 2023). Further, research from (1990-2019) expanded the literature on AI and HRM practices (Di Vaio et al., 2020). The growing research on AI and HRM, previous researchers have similarly endeavoured to evaluation the existing works in the field. Nevertheless, in furthermost occurrences, such evaluations were inadequate to a definite facet of AI and HRM. Further, chatbots with AI-driven recruitment assistants that allow personal and up to date opportunities to communicate with candidates via text messages, emails (Majumder & Mondal, 2021).

AI is changing the way things are done in every area of the business. Moreover, continuous advancement of developments in machine learning technology, the imminent perspective of HR industry lies in the rare combination of digital AI and human services (Dhamija & Bag, 2020). AI is very useful in automating the interview procedure by observing the candidates' conversation choices, voice patterns and facial expressions of candidates. AI can transform a 15-minute video interview to a list of 20,000 facial expressions, imagination and word selection data points for entrant assessment. Companies use resources like Amy and Clara Labs to schedule interviews, work quickly, seamlessly and without taking any time to interfere (Claralabs, 2021). AI human resource manager can able to trace exact applicant in less time of duration and technology will assist out to classify the most suitable candidates as per essential skills sets (Johnson et al., 2021). In addition, companies will be able to leverage AI technologies and e-learning stages to improve employee skills (Maity, 2019). This will develop a customized training system for individuals depends on their skills and needs of the concern. The Online learning tool will help workers learn new strategies, refine existing features, and find it more comfortable at workplace.

Through AI, the effectiveness and performance of resources and team can be measured and controlled by simply allowing individual to accurately report the tasks performed, time taken to complete them and their achievement, etc. (DiClaudio, 2019). Companies will test candidates against personalized baseline score and rate them in order of weighting and priority order.

3. METHODOLOGY

This research gathered bibliometric data on AI and HRM envisioned for its evaluation. The Biblioshiny and VOS viewer software was utilized to comport the deepness and reckonable investigation of the AI in HRM to conduct bibliometric analysis (BA). The current research was done on 467 articles. The Scopus database was selected for searching the articles from 1982 to 2023. The steps involved in the process has been illustrated in the Figure 1.

Figure 1. Bibliometric analysis process

Assembling

- **Search keywords:** ("chatbot* " OR "Conversation* Agent*" OR "Machine Learn*" OR "Natural Language Processing" OR "NLP" OR "Artificial Intelligen*" OR "Neural Net*" OR "Virtual Assistant*" OR "Deep Learning" OR "Robotic*" AND human AND resource*)
- **Search Database:** Scopus
- **Search Results:** 459

Arranging

- **Organizing Filters:** Year, Subject area, document type, publication stage, source , type and language
- **Filtered Year for inclusion:** 1982-2023
- **Filtered subject area for inclusion:** Business, Management
- **Filtered Document type for inclusion:** "Article"
- **Filtered publication stage for inclusion:** "Journal"
- **Filtered language for inclusion:** "English"
- **Filtered Search Results:** 173 Articles

Assessing

- **Analysis Method:** Bibliometric analysis technique namely "performance analysis (Publication trend, influential articles, Top contributing journals, authors, institutions, countries, and Scientific analysis (thematic analysis)
- **Agenda Proposal Method:** Reading of articles and reflection of extant gaps for each major theme.
- **Reporting Convention:** figure, tables, and words
- **Limitation:** Accuracy and completeness of bibliometric data from Scopus
- **Support:** No funding received

3.1. Assembling

Towards gathering the articles on AI in HR, the current study recognized its search keywords connecting to AI in HR from the primary review of related literature in the preceding segment and checked with 7 specialists to determine the appropriateness of those keywords to signify AI in HR. This directed us to select 12 keywords, which were used to form a search string:

("chatbot*" OR "Conversation* Agent*" OR "Machine Learn*" OR "Natural Language Processing" OR "NLP" OR "Artificial Intelligen*" OR "Neural Net*" OR "Virtual Assistant*" OR "Deep Learning" OR "Robotic*" AND human AND resource*)

The search string formed with the selected keywords were used in the "article title, abstract, and keywords" on Scopus database, which is a very extensive database of scholarly articles. In total, 459 documents were returned.

3.2. Arranging

To assemble 459 articles returned from the previous stage, the current research used the shortlisting criteria used were subject, document and source type, language, year, publication stage, and "business management, and accounting", "article", "final", "Journal", and "English". Filteration process was aligned with the study by Paul et al. (2021), because AI exists within business, management, and accounting; only article included and peer-reviewed articles not included and in-press articles were also discarded; conference proceeding; Book and book chapter, and proceedings of conference were not included; and non-English articles were also extracted. Further, this reduced to 301 articles. Moreover, 128 articles also eliminated after downloaded and read all articles. This last corpus of 173 article kept for review.

3.3. Assessing

To measure the concluding expanse of 173 articles on artificial intelligence in HRM, this current study implements a BA method for its evaluation (Donthu et al., 2021). Current research executes a BA by a performance analysis(PA) trend of publication, the highest cited articles and most contributed authors, institutions, countries and journals. The subsequent segments explained the findings of the review, where descriptions are augmented by tables and figures.

4. BIBLIOMETRIC RESULTS

Table 1 gives the overview of the composed data from the associated review of literature. The timespan of the data is from 1990 to 2023. There are 111 journals in which 173 articles were published during these years.

4.1. Performance Analysis

PA defines the performance of a research domain (Donthu et al., 2021), in the field of AI and HRM. In current work, a PA is directed to discose the publication trend, significant articles, countries, institutions, authors, journals, authors, and countries in the context of AI in HRM research.

4.1.1. Trend of Publication

Table 2 provides detail of the years having maximum number of publications. Table 2 depicted year 2022 as the year with the uppermost number of publications. Table 2 also portrayed a sudden rise in publications from three publications in 2017 to 16 publications in 2020.

Table 1. Data description.

Description	Results
Timespan	1990:2023
Sources (Journals, Books, etc)	111
Documents	173
Annual Growth Rate %	10.74
Document Average Age	3.29
Average citations per doc	18.95
References	9862
Keywords Plus (ID)	568
Author's Keywords (DE)	644
Authors	487
Authors of single-authored docs	18
Single-authored docs	19
Co-Authors per Doc	3.1
International co-authorships %	36.69

Table 2. Year-wise publications

Year	Articles
2022	46
2021	32
2023	29
2020	25
2019	16
2017	3
2018	3
2004	2
2008	2
2010	2

The year-wise publication inclination of artificial intelligence in HRM research is presented in Figure 2. Publications have grown up over the past 30 years (1990 –2022). Moreover, only one article published in 1990 and single-digit number continued till 2017, however, it has multiplied substantially in the next 6 years, with 46 publications in 2022.

Figure 2. Yearly publication for AI in HRM research between 1990-2022

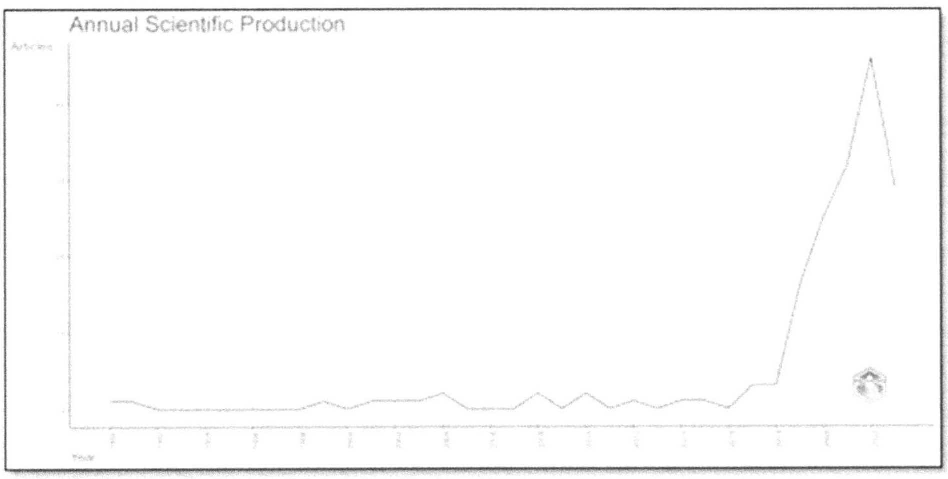

4.1.2. Most Influential Articles for Artificial Intelligence in HRM

The highly cited articles for artificial intelligence in HRM research were shown in Table 3. This tabular depicts that Huang & Rust (2018) article is the greatest cited article on this, by an average of 150 citation per year a total of 900 citations since it is published in 2018. It is also shadowed by Tambe (2019) and Todd & Benbasat (1991) articles in California Management Review and Information Systems Research, which have been cited for 233 and 190 times. Noteworthy, the topmost 10 cited article in the field have total 1861 citations, which reproduces the noteworthy influence on AI in HRM.

Table 3. Globally most cited documents

S.No.	Paper	DOI	Total Citations	TC per Year	Normalized TC
1	Artificial intelligence in service	10.1177/1094670517752459	900	150.00	2.97
2	Artificial intelligence in human resources management: Challenges and a path forward	10.1177/0008125619867910	233	46.60	9.66
3	An Experimental Investigation of the Impact of Computer Based Decision Aids on Decision Making Strategies	10.1287/isre.2.2.87	190	5.76	1.00
4	Artificial intelligence for sustainability: Challenges, opportunities, and a research agenda	10.1016/j.ijinfomgt.2020.102104	146	36.50	6.10
5	Artificial intelligence, robotics, advanced technologies and human resource management: a systematic review	10.1080/09585192.2020.1871398	104	52.00	13.75
6	AI-enabled recruiting: What is it and how should a manager use it?	10.1016/j.bushor.2019.12.001	80	20.00	3.34
7	Adoption of artificial intelligence (AI) for talent acquisition in IT/ITeS organizations	10.1108/BIJ-04-2020-0186	54	13.50	2.26
8	How will service robots redefine leadership in hotel management? A Delphi approach	10.1108/IJCHM-05-2019-0505	54	13.50	2.26
9	Training for Crisis Decision-Making: Psychological Issues and Computer-Based Solutions	10.1080/07421222.2002.11045704	51	2.32	1.00
10	Employees recruitment: A prescriptive analytics approach via machine learning and mathematical programming	10.1016/j.dss.2020.113290	49	12.25	2.05

*TC = Total Citations

4.1.3. Top Contributing Journals for Artificial Intelligence in HRM

The corpus of 173 articles on artificial intelligence in HRM were published across 111 journals. After removing two discontinued Scopus listed journal, table 4 provides the list of the eight top journals; namely decision support systems have highest H-index of 170. Specifically, followed by international journal of human resource management, industrial management and data systems, international journal of contemporary hospitality management, human resource management review, business horizons with 130, 117, 113, 111, and 106 citations respectively. These top indexed journals were categorised in first quartile (Q1).

Table 4. Top contributing journals.

S.No.	Sources	Articles	H Index	Quartile
1.	HUMAN RESOURCE MANAGEMENT REVIEW	10	111	Q1
2.	INTERNATIONAL JOURNAL OF MANPOWER	5	67	Q2
3.	DECISION SUPPORT SYSTEMS	4	170	Q1
4.	INTERNATIONAL JOURNAL OF HUMAN RESOURCE MANAGEMENT	4	130	Q1
5.	BUSINESS HORIZONS	3	106	Q1
6.	IEEE ENGINEERING MANAGEMENT REVIEW	3	32	Q2
7.	INDUSTRIAL MANAGEMENT AND DATA SYSTEMS	3	117	Q1
8.	INTERNATIONAL JOURNAL OF CONTEMPORARY HOSPITALITY MANAGEMENT	3	113	Q1

4.1.4. Topmost Contributing Authors

The topmost contributing authors for AI in HRM research are depicted in table 5. Table 5 specifies 'VARMA A' as the author with 27 citations from two articles having the highest contribution in the local citations. In the top 10 list of authors, 'BUDHWAR P' and 'MALIK A' has the highest number of publications with three articles published and each having 7 citations.

Table 5. Top contributing authors.

S. No.	Author	Local Citations	No. of Articles
1.	VARMA A	27	2
2.	CHAUDHURI K	26	1
3.	DAWKINS C	26	1
4.	COGGBURN JD	11	1
5.	JOHNSON BAM	11	1
6.	LLORENS JJ	11	1
7.	AGGARWAL V	7	1
8.	BUDHWAR P	7	3
9.	MALIK A	7	3
10.	STANLEY DS	7	1

4.1.5. Top Contributing Institutions

The highest contributing institutions for AI in HRM research are depicted in table 6. The most contributing institutions are Aston University and Poznan University of Technology with 6 articles respectively. Then followed by Ben-gurion University of the Negev, Universidad Tecnológica Equinoccial, Universidad Ute, University of Goettingen, with 5 articles each respectively.

Table 6. Top contributing institutions

S. No.	Affiliation	Articles Published
1.	ASTON UNIVERSITY	6
2.	POZNAN UNIVERSITY OF TECHNOLOGY	6
3.	BEN-GURION UNIVERSITY OF THE NEGEV	5
4.	UNIVERSIDAD TECNOLÓGICA EQUINOCCIAL	5
5.	UNIVERSIDAD UTE	5
6.	UNIVERSITY OF GOETTINGEN	5
7.	ABU DHABI SCHOOL OF MANAGEMENT	4
8.	HONG KONG POLYTECHNIC UNIVERSITY	4
9.	HUAZHONG UNIVERSITY OF SCIENCE AND TECHNOLOGY	4
10.	INDIAN INSTITUTE OF TECHNOLOGY DELHI	4

4.1.6. Top Contributing Countries

The highest contributing countries for AI in HRM research are depicted in table 7. This table specifies that utmost creative country is the USA with 73 articles, shadowed by India, China, Germany, and UK with 59, 55, 33, 29 citations respectively.

Table 7. Top contributing countries

S. No.	Country	Freq
1.	USA	73
2.	INDIA	59
3.	CHINA	55
4.	GERMANY	33
5.	UK	29
6.	ISRAEL	18
7.	FRANCE	14
8.	AUSTRALIA	12
9.	CANADA	12
10.	ITALY	11

Figure 3 also characterizes the top countries in standings of publications on the world map. The regions with blue colour are the countries with maximum publications, and the countries having lighter shade on the gradient were the countries having less publications.

Figure 3. Top contributing countries on the world map

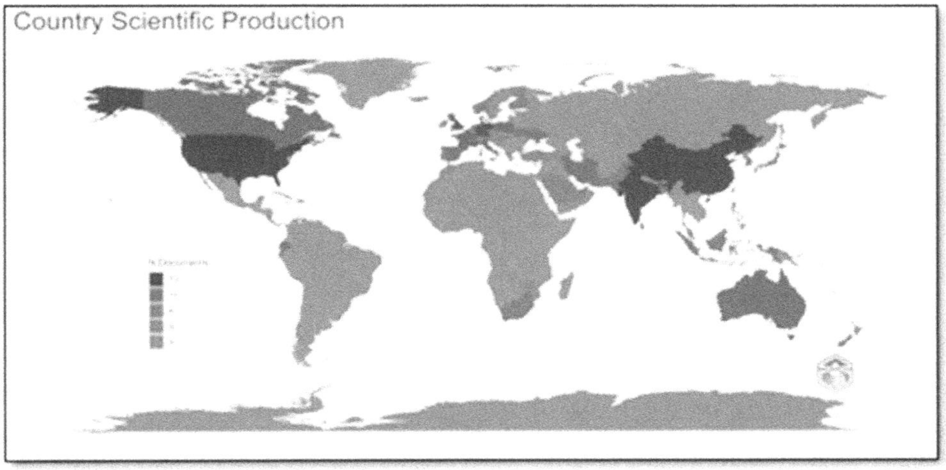

4.2. Thematic Analysis

The results of thematic analysis discovered four clusters from the literature work associated to the role of AI in the HRM sector. The four clusters were discovered with the help of Vos Viewer Software. This software helps in exploring the themes or underlying structure in the related literature. In our study, four major themes emerged, such as universal role of AI in HRM, machine learning (ML) algorithms, decision-making with AI and ML, and the application of neural networks in recruitment process. These themes were developed in the form of clusters.

In Figure 4, cluster 1 is in blue colour and it is named as "Role of AI and its associated concepts in the HRM". Cluster 2 is in red colour and is named as "Applications of Machine Learning algorithms". Cluster 3 is named as "Decision-making with AI and ML" and is given in green colour. Cluster 4 is provided in yellow colour and this cluster is named as "Neural Networks in recruitment process".

4.2.1. Cluster 1: AI in HR Information Systems

This cluster reflects the part of information management in the field of HRM. The cluster also described Industry 4.0 and its relevance in the field of HRM. Information systems are used to form a platform for implementing AI technologies in the organizations. The implementation of data-driven decision making cannot be done without setting up the information systems. Industry 4.0 came as an important terminology in this cluster. Since Industry 4.0 encompasses the applications of advanced information technologies such as IoTs (Internet of Things), robotics, and role of big data in the field of AI. Industry 4.0 leads to the creation of intelligent systems which optimises the business operations and other processes related to human resources. However, the researchers raised concerns on privacy issues, integrity and integration of data sources, scalable systems to handle big data, and user interaction with the analytics-based information systems.

Figure 4. Thematic analysis

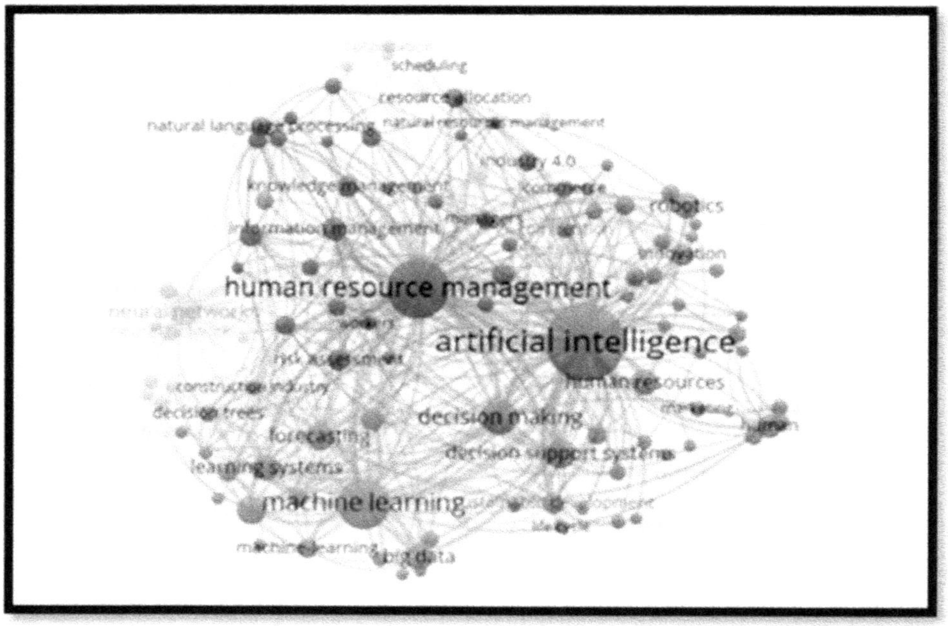

4.2.2. Cluster 2: Applications of Machine Learning Algorithms

The machine learning is the subset of AI. The machine learning algorithms developed intelligent systems which have the human like thinking capabilities. The cluster reflects on decision trees as the most widely used machine learning algorithms. Decisions trees creates a hierarchical tree of various decisions which enables managers to takes efficient decisions based on different scenarios. Decision trees are widely used in automating the screening of candidates applying for various job roles based on their educational qualifications and various other significant parameters considered by HR recruiters. They also help in the forecasting the attrition rate in the organizations, and performance of the employees in various organizational tasks. Hence, machine learning algorithms such as decision trees assists the HR department in making data-driven decisions. Big data also evolved as significant concept in the machine learning since there is a use of unstructured data such as audio files, videos, and text data generated from surveys, open-ended interviews, and other machine data source involved in analysing the employee data.

4.2.3. Cluster 3: Decision-Making With AI and ML

Since the machine learning has a very significant role in the AI, this cluster typically emphasized on the role of AI and ML in decision making capabilities. The technology and algorithms used in making data driven decisions were discussed. The widely used algorithm in the making decisions by using machine learning algorithms is the decision trees. The word 'robotics' also appeared in this cluster, signifying the importance of task automation. The most important application of robotic process automation is the chatbots. Chatbots are the conversational agents that interacts with humans by using natural language processing. These conversational bots help the HR department in automating the tasks. Contextual awareness is the main reason of popularity among organizations. It is benefiting lot of organizations, since chatbots are very efficient in handling very monotonous tasks such as salary details, leave requests, bonus received, appointment status, hence giving time to employees for having a high value customer engagement.

The researchers also highlighted some trust-based issues in the conversational bots, suspicions in delivering very reliable services, establishing their competency among customers. Hence there is also a downside of robotic technology, which paves the way for new researchers in analysing the trust-based issues while interacting with conversational agents.

4.2.4. Cluster 4: Neural Networks in Recruitment Process

Neural networks are subset of machine learning models. Neural networks mimic human brain, in which they learn from the patterns and perform predictive analytics on the data. Neural networks are mostly used, where the data is very large and complex. The data has increased in the volume and variety giving rise to big data; hence the neural networks are used in the recruitment process. Mostly, the researchers were using the deep neural networks with the structured equation modelling to increase the knowledge-based view theory. The researchers were also exploring the employee turnover behaviour with Artificial Neural Networks, to identify the internal variables contributing to the employee turnover intentions. The studies in this cluster also proposed infrastructure for decision support systems, which is capable of efficiently allocating the resources in an organization.

Hence the neural networks are recently been used over traditional machine learning approaches, due to the complexity of the data sources. Nowadays, it is used in building up the complex human resource information systems to assist managers in handling and understanding the complex personnel data.

5. FUTURE DIRECTIONS

The analysis of the literature intersecting the field of AI and HR reveals gaps leading scholars to the future research. The future research directions provide the new avenues for the researchers. Firstly, the researchers were identifying the role of information systems in building AI framework, however very few researchers highlighted the need for ethical systems which comply with the organizational data. There is a non-existence of trust on the AI based structure, and future researchers may discover the factors affecting the trustworthiness of the AI based systems. This will build the trust on AI based systems from the customer side, and even helps managers in creating algorithms that are accurate and helps managers in data driven decision making.

There are lacunae in cross-cultural and multicultural communications with the AI based systems. The current AI tools are not considering the diversity in the workplaces and how the decisions need to be made considering the cultural factors. The future research may showed the role of culture in decision-making, and create intelligent systems capable of handling the cross-cultural problems while making decisions. The machine learning models were used in HR to classify the data and make decisions based on those classifications. However, there is a lack of interpretable machine learning models, which are not giving classifications, but also prescribe the possible solutions so that HR professional can understand the variables impacting the decisions.

AI based systems emphasize on identifying the factors that can impact turnover intention or the important factors in the recruitment process. The current research lacks in the AI systems that can identify the skill gaps for the employees. By identifying the skill gaps, the new training programs can be customised for the employees. In the long run, AI based platform may be developed, which also handles the well-being, safety and health of the employees.

The present research is not emphasizing on the use of using immersive technologies with AI in the HR domain. The role of immersive technologies like virtual reality and augmented reality integrated with AI can also be applied to create a personalised training environment for the employees in an organization. The effectiveness of AI based virtual environment can be checked by the future researchers by having the feedback from the employee and the organizations. Furthermore, in the immersive environments, personalised AI tutors may be developed for the training the employees. The efficiency of personalised AI based tutors in improving the productivity of the employees should be checked by the future researchers.

Since the AI based systems cannot give benefits to the organizations in the short run, therefore, proper evaluation plan should be developed in the long run. The future studies should may explore the framework needed in the longer run for evaluating the effectiveness of the AI based intelligent systems. The present research assists the managerial positions and organisations to understand the role of AI in HR information systems, how the systems are developed using machine learning algorithms and the use of advance techniques like neural networks in building advanced recruitment process that scrutinises the candidates in the organizations.

The current studies does not focus on workforce collaboration with AI by using big data in HR domain. Workforce collaboration can be enhanced using big data with AI based technologies. AI is mainly applied in enhancing the efficiency of the employees, however future researchers may also investigate the use of AI technologies using big data in improving the communication among employees, managing the employees and sharing the knowledge among the peers. The routine communications related to repetitive queries can be automated through virtual assistants like chatbots. Moreover, the human touch in the chatbots while handling queries could be analysed in the future research. The effectiveness of language translation based chatbots in removing employee communication barrier in the cross-national organizations is also a prominent future research area in the field of virtual assistants.

6. CONCLUSION

The current research shadows a systematic review approach using BA to shed light usage of AI In HRM. The current research pave in a new way on the influence of AI with HRM and it provide bigger visibility to discover the utmost significant articles, topmost contributing journals, institutions, authors, and countries. To this end, we summarize the review of 173 articles on AI and HRM over the last 33 years (1990-2023).

AI-enabled HR applicants have the ability to evaluate, anticipate, diagnose and improve stronger and more capable instruments. Staffs will be influenced by the AI features in several ways, so it is vital to concentrate on employees requirements and potential consequences.

The present study is limited to Scopus database and further multiple databases can be included to have robust analysis. The study is scrutinised on the basis of articles published in management and business field. Further studies can include articles from the domain of computer science or engineering to understand the role of new technologies, their efficiency of new machine learning models. Extending the study based on these limitations will advance the research in the part of AI and HRM.

REFERENCES

Ahmed, O. (2018). Artificial intelligence in HR. *International Journal of Research and Analytical Reviews*, *5*(4), 971–978.

Alsharif, A. H., Salleh, N. Z., Baharun, R., Rami, A., Hashem, E., Alsharif, A. H., Salleh, N. Z., & Baharun, R. (2021). Neuromarketing research in the last five years : A bibliometric analysis. *Cogent Business & Management*, *8*(1), 1978620. Advance online publication. doi:10.1080/23311975.2021.1978620

Berezina, K., Ciftci, O., & Cobanoglu, C. (2019). Robots, artificial intelligence, and service automation in restaurants. In *Robots*. Artificial Intelligence and Service Automation in Travel, Tourism and Hospitality. doi:10.1108/978-1-78756-687-320191010

Black, J. S., & van Esch, P. (2020). AI-enabled recruiting: What is it and how should a manager use it? *Business Horizons*, *63*(2), 215–226. doi:10.1016/j.bushor.2019.12.001

Claralabs. (2021). *Clara, can you find a time for us to meet next week?* Clara Labs. https://claralabs.com/

Dhamija, P., & Bag, S. (2020). Role of artificial intelligence in operations environment: A review and bibliometric analysis. *The TQM Journal*, *32*(4), 869–896. doi:10.1108/TQM-10-2019-0243

Di Vaio, A., Palladino, R., Hassan, R., & Escobar, O. (2020). Artificial intelligence and business models in the sustainable development goals perspective: A systematic literature review. *Journal of Business Research*, *121*, 283–314. doi:10.1016/j.jbusres.2020.08.019

DiClaudio, M. (2019). People analytics and the rise of HR: How data, analytics and emerging technology can transform human resources (HR) into a profit center. *Strategic HR Review*, *18*(2), 42–46. doi:10.1108/SHR-11-2018-0096

Donthu, N., Kumar, S., Mukherjee, D., Pandey, N., & Lim, W. M. (2021). How to conduct a bibliometric analysis: An overview and guidelines. *Journal of Business Research*, *133*, 285–296. doi:10.1016/j.jbusres.2021.04.070

Huang, M. H., & Rust, R. T. (2018). Artificial intelligence in service. *Journal of Service Research*, *21*(2), 155–172. doi:10.1177/1094670517752459

Johnson, R. D., Stone, D. L., & Lukaszewski, K. M. (2021). The benefits of eHRM and AI for talent acquisition. *Journal of Tourism Futures*, *7*(1), 40–52. doi:10.1108/JTF-02-2020-0013

Kaushal, N., Kaurav, R. P. S., Sivathanu, B., & Kaushik, N. (2023). Artificial intelligence and HRM: Identifying future research Agenda using systematic literature review and bibliometric analysis. *Management Review Quarterly*, *73*(2), 455–493. doi:10.100711301-021-00249-2

Kumar, S., Lim, W. M., Sivarajah, U., & Kaur, J. (2023). Artificial Intelligence and Blockchain Integration in Business: Trends from a Bibliometric-Content Analysis. *Information Systems Frontiers*, *25*(2), 871–896. doi:10.100710796-022-10279-0 PMID:35431617

Liu, L., & Duffy, V. G. (2023). Exploring the Future Development of Artificial Intelligence (AI) Applications in Chatbots: A Bibliometric Analysis. *International Journal of Social Robotics*, *15*(5), 703–716. doi:10.100712369-022-00956-0

Maity, S. (2019). Identifying opportunities for artificial intelligence in the evolution of training and development practices. *Journal of Management Development*, *38*(8), 651–663. doi:10.1108/JMD-03-2019-0069

Majumder, S., & Mondal, A. (2021). Are chatbots really useful for human resource management? *International Journal of Speech Technology*, *24*(4), 969–977. doi:10.100710772-021-09834-y

Nishant, R., Kennedy, M., & Corbett, J. (2020). Artificial intelligence for sustainability: Challenges, opportunities, and a research agenda. *International Journal of Information Management*, *53*, 102104. doi:10.1016/j.ijinfomgt.2020.102104

Pereira, V., Hadjielias, E., Christofi, M., & Vrontis, D. (2023). A systematic literature review on the impact of artificial intelligence on workplace outcomes: A multi-process perspective. *Human Resource Management Review*, *33*(1), 100857. doi:10.1016/j.hrmr.2021.100857

Pessach, D., Singer, G., Avrahami, D., Ben-Gal, H. C., Shmueli, E., & Ben-Gal, I. (2020). Employees recruitment: A prescriptive analytics approach via machine learning and mathematical programming. *Decision Support Systems*, *134*, 113290. doi:10.1016/j.dss.2020.113290 PMID:32501316

Pillai, R., & Sivathanu, B. (2020). Adoption of artificial intelligence (AI) for talent acquisition in IT/ITeS organizations. *Benchmarking*, *27*(9), 2599–2629. doi:10.1108/BIJ-04-2020-0186

Qamar, Y., Agrawal, R. K., Samad, T. A., & Jabbour, C. J. C. (2021). When technology meets people: The interplay of artificial intelligence and human resource management. *Journal of Enterprise Information Management*, *34*(5), 1339–1370. doi:10.1108/JEIM-11-2020-0436

Shenkar, O. (1990). Managing in a Robotic Age. *Human Systems Management*, *9*(2), 107–114. doi:10.3233/HSM-1990-9206

Sniezek, J. A., Wilkins, D. C., Wadlington, P. L., & Baumann, M. R. (2002). Training for crisis decision-making: Psychological issues and computer-based solutions. *Journal of Management Information Systems*, *18*(4), 147–168. doi:10.1080/07421222.2002.11045704

Tambe, P., Cappelli, P., & Yakubovich, V. (2019). Artificial intelligence in human resources management: Challenges and a path forward. *California Management Review*, *61*(4), 15–42. doi:10.1177/0008125619867910

Tayarani, N. M. H. (2021). Applications of artificial intelligence in battling against covid-19: A literature review. *Chaos, Solitons, and Fractals*, *142*, 110338. doi:10.1016/j.chaos.2020.110338 PMID:33041533

Todd, P., & Benbasat, I. (1991). An experimental investigation of the impact of computer based decision aids on decision making strategies. *Information Systems Research*, *2*(2), 87–115. doi:10.1287/isre.2.2.87

Votto, A., & Liu, C. Z. (2023). *Transparent Artificial Intelligence and Human Resource Management: A Systematic Literature Review*. Academic Press.

Votto, A. M., Valecha, R., Najafirad, P., & Rao, H. R. (2021). Artificial Intelligence in Tactical Human Resource Management: A Systematic Literature Review. *International Journal of Information Management Data Insights*, *1*(2), 100047. doi:10.1016/j.jjimei.2021.100047

Vrontis, D., Christofi, M., Pereira, V., Tarba, S., Makrides, A., & Trichina, E. (2022). Artificial intelligence, robotics, advanced technologies and human resource management: A systematic review. *International Journal of Human Resource Management*, *33*(6), 1237–1266. doi:10.1080/09585192.2020.1871398

Xu, S., Stienmetz, J., & Ashton, M. (2020). How will service robots redefine leadership in hotel management? A Delphi approach. *International Journal of Contemporary Hospitality Management*, *32*(6), 2217–2237. doi:10.1108/IJCHM-05-2019-0505

Chapter 13
Artificial Intelligence in Behavioral Finance for Investment Decision-making

Asheetu Bhatia Sarin
VIPS, Guru Gobind Singh Indraprastha University, India

Shivangi Sharma
Delhi University, India

ABSTRACT

This chapter talks about how artificial intelligence has evolved into the minds of investors. Owing to the transformation in technology, machines have become increasingly capable. This will help to predict market movements using the behavioral aspect of the investors. There are also challenges in using AI in behavioral finance, such as the need for high-quality data, the potential for bias in AI algorithms themselves, and ethical considerations around using AI to make investment decisions. How these challenges will have an impact on investment decision-making is also discussed in this chapter. Further, the chapter talks about the interaction of behavioral finance and artificial intelligence and in turn enabling investors to be future-ready with fewer biases and efficient decision-making.

1. INTRODUCTION

In the late 1980s, Professors Richard Thaler, Robert Shiller, Daniel Kahneman, Amos Tversky, Vernon Smith, Meir Statman, and Hersh Shefrin began to publish relevant pieces of research that gave light to the Behavioral Finance field. In a nutshell, the growing interest in Behavioral Finance has resulted from an accretion of empirical anomalies. It has been established that human cognitive intuitions have taken away investors' rationality when it comes to stock investment decision-making (Sarin & Chowdhury, 2018). Investors think of themselves as rational and logical. But at the time of decisions related to investment, they tend to be emotionally prone and make mistakes (Sarin, 2023). The main point during investment decisions is the consideration of the investor's decision-making process. Proper evaluation

DOI: 10.4018/979-8-3693-0418-1.ch013

of the alternatives that are available to investors is the key to any investment decisions (Sarin, 2023). Time and consideration of cognitive psychology play an important role in the behavioral impact of investment decisions. Therefore, for effective decision-making, the investors need to develop a positive vision, emotional stability, perseverance, and foresight (Sarin& Chowdhury, 2018; Sarin, 2023).

Avoiding any mistakes requires a more authentic approach and reduces human errors. This requires the need for Artificial Intelligence (AI) which is an upcoming technology to map the human thinking process. Machine learning (ML) and Artificial Intelligence have opened the world of finance to the new world of technology. A large data can be collected with just a click of a button to predict future trends to make maximum returns and incomes. The business world is coming out of the paper era to the digital world and it will be exciting to see how technology would bring about this change.

However, there are also challenges in using AI in behavioral finance, which can be the high-quality data needs, the biases in AI algorithms themselves, and ethical considerations around using AI to make investment decisions. As such, the use of AI in behavioral finance should be approached with caution and care and should be balanced with human judgment and oversight.

It can be seen that AI algorithms can help in improving investment decision-making algorithms analyse large quantities of data and recognize trends and patterns that may be hard for humans to spot. This can help investors make more informed decisions based on objective data (Hilovska & Koncz, 2012). AI algorithms can use predictive analysis to forecast future market trends and help investors make more accurate investment decisions. It can be used to manage risks associated with investments by analyzing data and providing alerts when certain risk thresholds are exceeded. It can optimize investment portfolios by analyzing historical data and recommending the best portfolio based on an investor's objectives and risk nature (Pietikäinen & Silven, 2022). Overall, the use of AI algorithms can help investors make more informed and objective investment decisions, while also improving risk management and portfolio optimization. However, it is important to note that AI algorithms should be used in conjunction with human judgment and oversight, as there are limitations and potential biases associated with relying solely on AI for investment decision-making.

2. ARTIFICIAL INTELLIGENCE IN FINANCE

To understand artificial intelligence, there are a few prerequisites like discussing human intelligence, though the same is itself debatable in psychology (Conway & Kovacs, 2015). Despite the difficulty of describing and measuring human intelligence, the main thing is that AI seeks to mimic some features of social intellect like emotions, learning, inventiveness, self-awareness, language, problem-solving, cognitive thinking, or tactics (Russell & Norvig, 2010).

AI can be defined as "the capability of a machine to imitate aspects of human intelligence". Alan Turing's (1950) revolutionary paper came with many thoughts that ultimately became the base for AI, including ML, DL, and others (Russell & Norvig, 2010). AI intelligence encompasses the capacity to think, problem-solve, acquire knowledge, and combine various human abilities such as perception, thinking, memory, communication, and planning (Kopka &Grashof, 2022); Kar et al., 2022). However, disparities started in the field of computer science (Russell & Norvig, 2020, pp. 19–23), where this term was invented in the year 1955(Russell & Norvig, 2020, pp. 19–23). The timeline of AI is as below:

Figure 1. Timeline of artificial intelligence (AI)
Source: Russell and Norvig (2023)

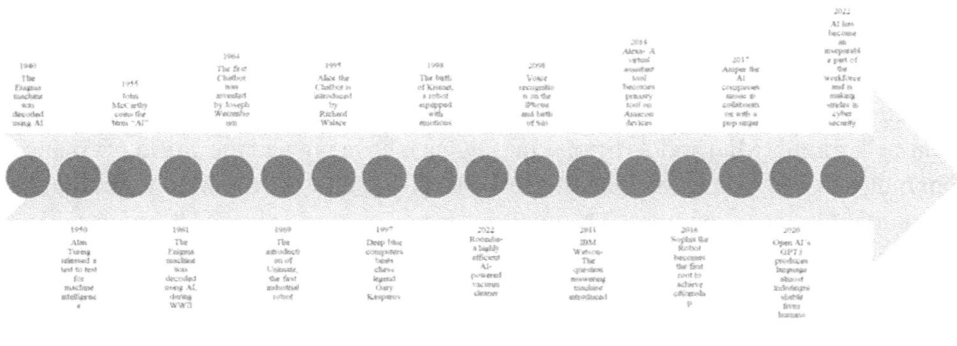

Thereby, by looking at the timeline, it can be said that in the history of AI, there has been a series of successes, optimism, and cutbacks in enthusiasm and funding. There have also been a series of introducing new, creative approaches and systematically refining the best ones as we can observe in today's world (Russell & Norvig, 2023, p.45). Artificial Intelligence (AI), a phrase coined by the respected Stanford Professor John McCarthy in 1955, was described by him as "the discipline and art of creating smart machines." While much effort has been invested in programming machines to act intelligently, like in chess, today's focus is on machines that can learn in a manner somewhat like humans (Russell & Norvig, 2023, p.45).AI are intelligence systems with different autonomy levels that for set of objectives, make forecasts, decisions or can even do various recommendations basis models to cater to the needs of human requirements.AI techniques are gradually leveraging large volumes of alternative data sources and data analytics, commonly referred to as 'big data.' This data is used to fuel machine learning (ML) models, allowing them to autonomously enhance predictability and performance through experience and data analysis, without requiring explicit programming by humans. AI can be described as a convergence of various technologies or models (Tredinnick, 2017; Kar et al. 2022), which can take on analytical and symbolic forms (Hoehndorf & Queralt-Rosinach, 2017). Its primary objective is to replicate human cognitive functions (Jiang et al., 2017) or simulate aspects of human intelligence when performing various decision-making tasks (Kushwaha et al., 2022; Kar et al. 2022). These applications are predominantly found in domains that involve analytics, intuition, and empathy, mirroring human capabilities (Jiang et al., 2017).

AI has evolved in the process, during COVID-19 AI was strengthened towards a digitalization trend like it played an essential role in any nation's growth (Sharma et al., 2022;pwc, 2018). According to the IDC report, the global spending on AI is expected to double in 2020-24 and will be reaching to more than$110 billion in 2024 (IDC, 2020). AI adoption is growing in various areas like asset management, algorithmic trading, credit underwriting, and blockchain-based financial services (IDC, 2020). AI in finance is expected to have a strategic advantage from the point of financial firms through the following ways. Firstly, this will help in improving efficiencies via a reduction in cost and at the same time increasing the production capacities. Secondly, financial services' quality will be improved and offered to the ultimate consumers.

Jain (2019) conducted a research study encompassing 50 decision-makers and employees from Indian corporate entities. Subsequently, a comprehensive data analysis was performed, utilizing a range of frequency tables and employing the one-way ANOVA statistical technique. The outcomes of this analysis indicated that artificial intelligence (AI) offers multiple opportunities and exerts a significant, favorable influence on the growth of businesses. Furthermore, AI enjoys widespread acceptance within corporate sectors. Moreover, it is anticipated that AI will play a pivotal role in aiding businesses to adapt to forthcoming technological advancements that will affect both human lifestyles and the business landscape. Finally, AI has demonstrated a positive impact across all facets of business processes (Jain, 2019).

Berdiyeva and her colleagues (2021) conducted an exhaustive examination of 150 research papers spanning from 1989 to 2020. Their objective was to assess the influence of AI systems on the realms of accounting and finance, ultimately revealing a favorable impact. The dynamic evolution and progress within the industry have led to a narrowing of the traditional scope of accounting and finance. The integration of AI applications has notably enhanced efficiency within these domains, primarily through the implementation of AI techniques such as expert systems for auditing and tax-related tasks, machine learning for decision-making processes, and intelligent agents for customer service. These advancements have the potential to minimize errors and augment overall effectiveness (Berdiyeva et al., 2021).

Aziz and his colleagues (2021) conducted a paper that undertook a comprehensive review of academic articles about the intersection of AI and finance. Utilizing a probabilistic topic modeling approach, the research extracted 14 distinct and logically interconnected research topics from the pool of papers. This study represented an innovative application of topic modeling within the context of a diverse body of literature encompassing machine learning (ML) and its various applications in the financial domain. The outcomes of the study demonstrated how this approach can effectively organize and structure a vast collection of research into coherent and discernible themes and issues (Aziz et al., 2021).

AI has significantly transformed the way the stock market operates, bringing several changes to various aspects of stock market trading and investment. Firstly Automated trading i.e. AI algorithms has revolutionized trading by enabling automated and high-frequency trading. AI-powered trading systems can analyze vast amounts of data, including market prices, news, and social media sentiment, to identify trading opportunities and execute trades with speed and precision. This has led to increased efficiency and liquidity in the market. By analyzing large volumes of transaction data, AI systems can flag suspicious activities and enhance regulatory compliance in the stock market. Moreover, AI-powered robo-advisors leverage machine learning algorithms help to provide personalized investment advice to individual investors (Russell & Norvig, 2023, p.906). These platforms analyze user preferences, risk profiles, and market data to offer tailored investment strategies. AI-based robo-advisors aim to democratize access to professional investment advice and cater to individual investor needs.

In a study conducted by Lui et al. (2022), the focus was on examining the impact of AI investments on firm value through an analysis of company announcements and their corresponding market responses. The primary objective of their research was to assess the value associated with investing in AI. The study encompassed an evaluation of announcements made between 2015 and 2019, which resulted in the collection of 119 observations from 62 different firms. The results of their analysis revealed that AI implementation hurt a firm's market value (Lui et al., 2022).

Therefore it can be said that Algorithmic trading and reliance on AI systems can introduce new sources of market volatility and potential systemic risks. Ethical considerations, transparency, and regulatory oversight are crucial to ensure the responsible and fair use of AI in the stock market. It's imperative to understand that while AI can provide valuable insights and support decision-making, it should be used as a tool to assist human decision-makers rather than replacing human judgment entirely. Ethical considerations, transparency, and human oversight are crucial when incorporating AI into decision-making processes.

3. ROLE OF BEHAVIORAL FINANCE IN INVESTMENT DECISION MAKING

As predicted in the process, behavioral finance has evolved into a critical component of decision-making, especially when integrated with AI modeling (Sarin, 2023). Behavioral finance revolves around understanding the cognitive psychology of investors and individuals engaged in investment activities. To excel in making investment decisions, investors must emphasize positivity, and forward-thinking behavior, and exhibit unwavering perseverance (Sarin & Chowdhury, 2018). The emotional aspect of human nature significantly influences investment decisions, resulting in the fluctuations observed in investment outcomes (Cristofaro, 2019). Consequently, identifying behavioral predispositions and judgment errors can enhance investment performance (Huang, 2022). In all these scenarios, recognizing the aspects of behavioral finance is crucial, as it enables individuals to make better investment choices and avoid costly errors (Sarin, 2019, pp.1-3; Sarin,2023).

Daniel Kahneman and Amos Tversky" were pioneers in introducing and defining various concepts related to anomalies. Their research indicated that the prospect is inherently indeterminate, and results made under such situations do not conform to the principles of standard finance (Sarin, 2023). The human mind often takes cognitive shortcuts that deviate from the assumptions of standard finance. In 1979, Kahneman & Tversky proposed the Prospect Theory, which posited that decisions are typically influenced more by "perceived gains" than "losses", and that "gains and losses" are evaluated differently (Kahneman & Tversky, 1979). Loss aversion is another phenomenon wherein individuals tend to prioritize potential gains as their ultimate financial outcome, as represented in the value function diagram in Figure 2, which illustrates a greater aversion to losses than an attraction to gains (Chandra, 2016).

As the field of Behavioral Finance gained prominence, Eugene Fama, often regarded as the father of the Efficient Market Hypothesis (EMH), expressed the view that financial markets were generally efficient but acknowledged that they could deviate from efficiency when investors made irrational decisions driven by their cognitive biases (Fama, 1970). This recognition marked a departure from the earlier EMH perspective, which asserted that markets were consistently efficient and that prices always reflected all available information. Fama's acknowledgment of the impact of behavioral biases on market deviations was a significant contribution to the development of behavioral finance. Various types of anomalies affect the investor's decision-making:

1. Market Anomalies

The primary definition of an "Anomaly" refers to a deviation from the norm, resulting in errors and a departure from the intended process. Drawing from Tversky & Kahneman's paper in 1986, market anomalies are described as deviations from the currently accepted paradigms that are too widespread to be ignored, too systematic to be dismissed as random errors, and too fundamental to be accommodated by relaxing normative systems. In this context, market inefficiencies exhibit a logical and rational behavior that contradicts the Efficient Market Hypothesis (EMH). This discrepancy helps explain the variations observed in stock market prices and returns within the realm of Behavioral Finance.

Figure 2. Prospect theory value function
Source: Prasanna Chandra (2016)

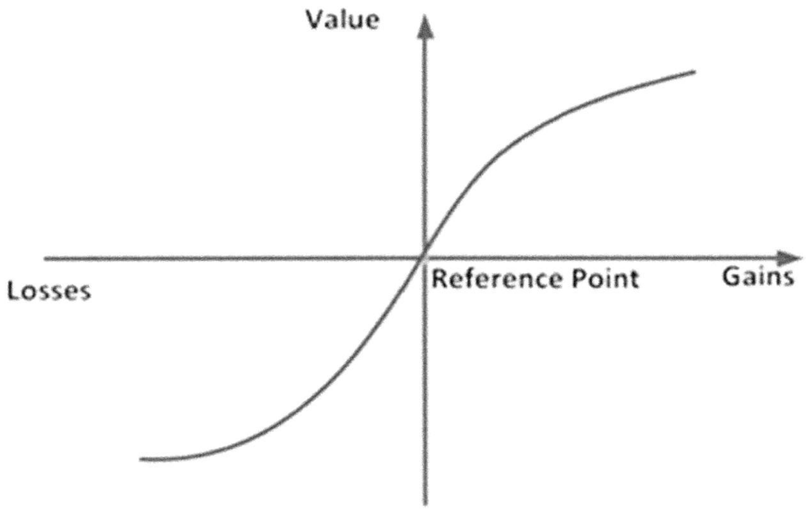

2. Fundamental Anomaly

This type of anomaly helps to outrun the basis irregularities in stock performance which is contradictory to the Efficient Market Hypothesis. It helps the investors to earn an abnormal return in due course of time. These phenomena have their origins in various layers of value anomalies and effects, including the small-cap effect, price-to-book value, high-dividend, price-to-sales, price-to-earnings, and more (Iqbal et al., 2013).

3. Calendar Anomaly

This type of anomaly is specific to the time and calendar events related to the stock market. There are various periods in the market like weekends, specific days in the month or specific times in a day say the January effect which has an impact on this kind of anomaly. The expanded framework encompasses the disclosure of information related to stock splits, dividend pay-outs, financial results, earnings per shares, and mergers & acquisitions (Iqbal et al., 2013).

4. Technical Anomaly

This is a process to analyze the stock prices based on their history and historical performance in the market. There are various techniques to measure such kinds of anomalies like trend analysis, historical charts, and figures like moving averages, the relative strength of the stock in the market, and various resistances in the time which the stock has handled. In short, this tends to identify the basic loophole in the EMH model. Such anomalies have always raised questions about the existence of effective and robust market conditions that are 'efficient' and 'stable' in turn. The 'irrational behavior of investors' tends to raise and give birth to the notion of biases, enabling the investors to raise questions on the reaction to certain events in the environment.

The investors who are active in the market have a specific behavior that can be identified using various time-specific data points as pointed out in the textbook by Thaler (2005). Behavioral finance employs a range of empirical data, often derived from surveys and experiments, to explore how specific events can influence an investor's decision-making process. Additionally, it seeks to elucidate the impact of these outcomes on the collective behavior of financial markets. The core objective is to gain insights into the reasons behind individuals' financial choices and how these decisions can diverge from rational expectations and conventional financial models (Sarin, 2023).

For Economists, understanding collapses in financial markets has been tough. The theoretical underpinnings of financial economics are fundamentally built upon the premise of market efficiency (Kalsie and Kalra, 2015). In contrast, behavioral economics reveals consistent departures from rational decision-making among investors. These departures stem from cognitive biases that individuals are prone to, giving rise to the existence of financial market inefficiencies, vulnerabilities, and anomalies. Behavioral finance studies seek to provide insights into the decision-making behaviors of investors in stock market settings (Alsabban & Alarfaj, 2020). This research aims to propose that the enigma of cryptocurrency market prices can be understood through the lens of behavioral finance, where cognitive biases and emotional biases of investors play a significant role in explaining market volatility. "Emotional biases" (EB) put forward that the decisions of investors are not anticipated and are prejudiced by various reasons that differ among individuals (Akinkoye & Bankole, 2020). In the context of investors in Nigeria, EB indicates that their investment decisions are susceptible to individual feelings, often leading to irrational choices and resulting in market inefficiencies (Akinkoye & Bankole, 2020; Sarin, 2023).

According to Shah et al. (2018), heuristics has a direct influence on the investor's decision-making abilities, in PSX. The paper strongly advises investors against relying on heuristics or their emotions when making investment decisions. It emphasizes the importance of being aware of and understanding heuristic biases in investment management. This knowledge can prove invaluable for decision-makers and professionals in financial institutions, including portfolio managers, brokers, traders in commercial and investment banks, and mutual funds, among others. The author of the paper assists investors in selecting better investment tools and avoiding costly errors stemming from heuristic biases. By helping individuals recognize their biases and errors in judgment, which we are all susceptible to, the paper contributes to making the market more efficient. It underscores the need to adopt specific investment strategies to mitigate "mental mistakes" driven by heuristic biases. The Heuristics theory underscores that human reasoning is consistently skewed and prone to errors (Parikh, 2017, p. 254).

Under Ritter (2003), heuristics are clearly defined guidelines that assist in simplifying decision-making, particularly in intricate and unstable environments. However, these rules of thumb can occasionally introduce biases, especially when circumstances change abruptly and prompt decisions are required. These biases can result in less-than-optimal investment choices. For instance, when an individual, post-retirement, is confronted with multiple investment options for their retirement funds, many opt to employ the 1/N rule. In this scenario, if there are three investment options, an equal 33.33% or one-third is allocated to each. This approach allows for diversification, meaning that if two of the options are stock funds, two-thirds of the investment is placed in equities and one-third in equities if only one of the three is a stock fund. Benartzi and Thaler (2001) noted that a substantial number of individuals adhere to the

1/N rule or this rule of thumb. On the whole, heuristics prove to be quite valuable, particularly when time is limited, but occasionally, they can introduce biases, as observed by Kahneman and Tversky (1979).

Kathpal et al. (2021) examined the link between investors' perceptions of the severity of Covid-19 and their reliance on heuristic biases. This analysis is based on the responses of 290 stock investors located in the National Capital Region (NCR) of India. The data undergo validation through Cronbach's alpha, and the model is assessed using Exploratory Factor Analysis (EFA). Confirmatory Factor Analysis (CFA) is then employed to explore the connection between Covid-19 and heuristic biases. The research findings indicated that COVID-19 does not exert any influence on investors' overconfidence. However, a significant positive relationship was observed between COVID-19 and the other three heuristics, specifically availability, anchoring, and representativeness (Kathpal et al., 2021).

Baber and Odean (2001) considered in their study the overconfidence bias in gender and its impact on trading activities by taking data 35000 household data from 1991 to 1996. The result indicates men are more confident than women so their trading is greater, it also showed that their returns will decrease to 2.45 percent for men and 1.75 percent for women. Biais et al. (2005) studied the impact of judgmental overconfidence and self-mongering bias in the investment decision by observing the behavior of 215 participants. The results showed that under calibration reduces and self-monitoring enhances trading performance. Park et al. (2010) investigated the impact of overconfidence bias and confirmation bias on investment performance by getting data from 502 investors in South Korea. The results showed that the confirmation makes the investor overconfident and it adversely affects the performance of the investor trading.

Humans tend to rely on heuristics, which are rules of thumb when making decisions. However, these biases are automatic and unconscious, making them difficult to detect. It would be inaccurate to claim that bias plays a minor role in human decision-making. Despite ongoing advancements in filtering methods, there is currently no single solution for improving AI. Both AI and human minds remain prone to errors. Consequently, no AI system will ever fully replace a person in any of its computations, regardless of how proficient neural networks become at predicting future actions. The availability heuristic, which suggests that people often favor information that confirms their existing beliefs, is a notable cognitive bias in AI decision-making. In most cases, we rely on a logical interpretation of available evidence when faced with a dilemma. While these strategies are generally effective, they can sometimes lead to failures. For instance, memory leaks occur when algorithms heavily rely on heuristics for decision-making and end up incorporating irrelevant information (Pietikäinen & Silven, 2022).

Emotions play a vital role in humans' investment decisions (Chandra, 2016, pp.9.9-9.10). There are various proven concepts wherein we as humans either follow others (known as herding) or research and make our investment decisions (Chandra, 2016, pp.9.9-9.10). It's the emotional quotient in all scenarios that makes us either align or misalign with the path. Research has indicated that the results of soccer/football games can impact investors' moods. In cases where a country experiences a loss in the World Cup, it has been observed that the financial market tends to decline on the following day (Edmans, Garcia, and Norli, 2007).

Nobel Laureate Daniel Kahneman, in his book "Thinking, Fast, and Slow," has described the role of emotions in investment decisions. Based on various research, he very precisely concluded that we are controlled by two forces that, for simplicity, are termed as "System 1" and "System 2". As Kahneman explained,

In the context of attitudes, however, System 2 is more of an apologist for the emotions of System 1 than a critic of those emotions-an endorser rather than an enforcer. (Kahneman, 2011, p. 103)

As per him, System 1 operates automatically and quickly, with little or no effort and no sense of voluntary control (something automatic and present in our subconscious mind) (Kahneman, 2011, pp.20-21). As an example, a trained driver will drive using his System 1 on a non-busy highway wherein his mind subconsciously controls the steering and drives the car at a controlled level of speed. System 2 gives attention to the effortful mental activities that demand it, including complex computations (Kahneman, 2011, pp.20-21). System 2 is associated with the subjective experience of agency, choice, and concentration (Kahneman, 2011, pp.20-21). For example, if someone asks us to multiply 22 X 23, our System 2 comes into play. Similarly, everything in and around us is controlled by our emotional behavior controlled through Systems 1 or System 2 to achieve desired results. System 2 primary function is to monitor and control thoughts and actions "suggested" by System 1, allowing some to be expressed directly in behavior and suppressing or modifying others (Kahneman, 2011, p.44).

The emotions associated with investment can be visualized along an emotional timeline, as depicted in Figure 3. Investment decisions are positioned at the left end of the timeline, while investment goals are at the right end. According to psychologists, investors undergo a range of emotions, including both positive and negative ones (Chandra, 2016, pp. 7.8-7.9). Positive emotions are represented above the timeline and include feelings such as hope, which can evolve into anticipation, ultimately leading to pride. On the negative side, emotions like fear can transition into anxiety and, in the end, transform into regret (Sarin and Chowdhury, 2018, pp. 320-330).

Investors undergo a spectrum of emotions throughout their investment journey. These emotions come into play when they contemplate their choices, determine their risk tolerance, observe the outcomes of their decisions, evaluate whether adjustments to their initial strategy are necessary, and ultimately assess their progress in achieving their financial goals. Based on emotional involvement, investors form beliefs and attitudes (Chandra, 2016, p.7.8). They can have happy or sad feelings, optimistic or pessimistic attitudes, and overreactions that encourage or discourage them from the investing process (Sarin and Chowdhury 2018, p.326). Emotions are considered a controlling factor in an investment person's lifetime (career, experience, savings, etc.), so they are not left out. Opposing EMH proponents' belief that emotions should not be considered in analytical decision-making processes, behavioral finance emphasizes emotional reactions to market events. It asserts that emotions are the pillar of its theoretical framework (Sarin and Chowdhury 2018, p.326).

Figure 3. Emotional timeline
Source: Prasanna Chandra (2016)

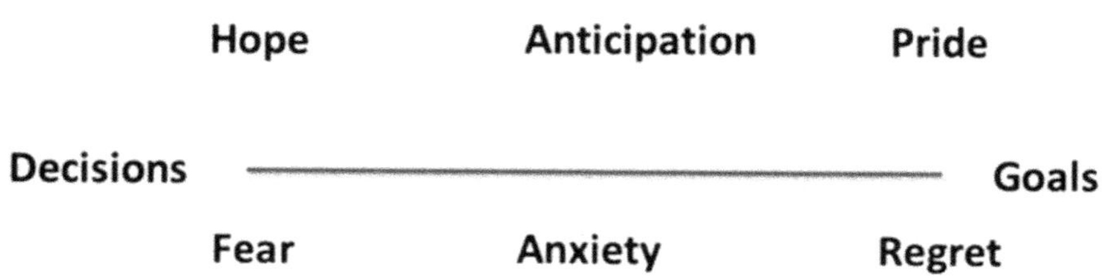

EB is affected by individual dispositions affecting how they make a decision (Sarin, 2021). EB is how an individual will frame information and make decisions (Sarin, 2021). Therefore for investors to be wise, they need to recognize their individual EB and learn to adjust or adapt to it rather than eliminate it. Behavioral biases are categorized under EB: endowment bias, self-control bias, optimism bias, loss-aversion bias, regret aversion bias, and status-quo Bias (Pompian 2006, 49-50). AI and emotional bias are closely related, as AI systems can both be influenced by and help mitigate emotional biases. Emotional biases refer to the tendency of individuals to make decisions based on their emotions rather than objective reasoning. To overcome bias in responses, scientists have created complex algorithms with the help of artificial intelligence and machine learning using computer vision to capture human emotions. The captured human emotions are further quantified for researchers to analyze and gather insights into the stimuli. The base of all is, that no matter how much humans try to hide their biases; they cannot hide their emotions towards a stimulus.

In accordance with Gensler's perspective, artificial intelligence has the potential to increase financial instability. This is because it might encourage a herding behavior among individual actors, leading them to make similar decisions based on signals derived from a common model or data aggregator. This tendency could foster uniformity or monocultures in financial decision-making. Additionally, AI could worsen the existing interconnectedness within the global financial system due to these shared decision patterns.

4. ROLE OF AI IN BEHAVIORAL FINANCE

The dawn of artificial intelligence (AI) has had a significant impact on various fields, including behavioral finance. Behavioral finance is a branch of finance that studies how psychological and cognitive biases influence investors' decision-making and market outcomes. Over recent years, the emergence of artificial intelligence (AI) has revolutionized information processing, enabling speeds and accuracy that surpass what human capabilities alone could accomplish (Hastie et al., 2009; Jordan & Mitchell, 2015)

AI and Behavioral Finance are two distinct fields that can complement each other in understanding and improving decision-making in financial contexts. AI and behavioral finance intersect in the following ways. Firstly through Data analysis i.e. AI can analyze vast amounts of financial data, including market prices, economic indicators, news articles, and social media sentiment. By processing this data, AI can identify patterns and relationships that contribute to behavioral biases observed in financial decision-making. This analysis can provide insights into the impact of human behavior on markets. Secondly, as Behavioral finance studies how cognitive biases and heuristics influence investor decision-making, AI can help identify and quantify these biases by analyzing historical data and comparing actual decisions with rational decision-making models. By considering these prejudices, AI can help investors and financial professionals to make conscious choices. Thirdly through personalized recommendations i.e., AI algorithms can leverage behavioral finance principles to provide personalized investment recommendations tailored to individual investors. By considering factors such as risk tolerance, investment goals, and biases, AI systems can suggest investment strategies that align with an investor's unique profile. Fourthly, AI can analyze social media, news articles, and other textual data to gauge market sentiment. By understanding the emotions and sentiments expressed by market participants, AI algorithms can provide insights into market trends and sentiment-driven price movements. This information can be valuable for making investment decisions (Sarin, 2021). Fifthly, AI-powered trading systems can leverage behavioral finance insights to design trading strategies that exploit behavioral biases in the market.

For example, AI algorithms can identify patterns associated with investor herding behavior or irrational market reactions and capitalize on these inefficiencies. Lastly, AI-powered robo-advisors combine behavioral finance principles with automated investment advice to help in efficient investment decision–making. These platforms use AI algorithms to analyze user preferences, risk profiles, and market data to offer customized investment recommendations. By considering behavioral biases, robo-advisors can help investors avoid common pitfalls and make better-informed investment decisions. Recent strides in machine learning (ML) have empowered individuals to handle vast quantities of swiftly evolving and unstructured data from an almost limitless array of origins. These technologies facilitate the generation of impartial forecasts concerning forthcoming occurrences (Agarwal & Dhar, 2014) and are currently being utilized to augment decision-making processes in financial markets (Sarin, 2023).

The role of AI in behavioral finance is to improve investment decision-making by identifying and analyzing human biases and heuristics that can lead to suboptimal investment decisions. AI algorithms can analyze large amounts of data and identify patterns, without being influenced by emotions or cognitive biases. For example, AI can help investors avoid the sunk cost fallacy by analyzing market trends and recommending when to sell an asset based on objective data, rather than holding onto it because of a previous investment. AI can also help investors avoid the disposition effect by analyzing historical data and recommending when to sell an asset based on its true value, rather than holding onto it because of emotional attachment.

Emotion AI also named "Affective Computing" is a subset of "Artificial Intelligence" where machines study and capture non-verbal cues like facial expressions, and the voice tonality of a person to detect their emotional state (Russell & Norvig, 2023, p.45).AI systems can analyze textual, visual, and auditory data to detect emotional signals. This capability can be useful in understanding users' emotions and sentiments, which can impact their decision-making and interactions with AI systems. Chabot and virtual assistants equipped with emotion analysis can adapt their responses based on users' emotional cues. This can enhance the user experience and tailor interactions to individuals' emotional states. AI can provide decision support by considering objective data and reducing the influence of emotions on choices. This is particularly important in investment decisions, where emotional biases can lead to poor outcomes. AI can design user interfaces that consider emotional states, adapting the presentation of information to match users' emotions (Russell & Norvig, 2023, p.45). For instance, a calming interface might be presented to a user expressing frustration. AI-driven sentiment analysis can gauge public sentiment and investor emotions by analyzing social media posts, news articles, and other sources. This information can be used to make more informed decisions in finance and other domains. AI-driven sentiment analysis can gauge public sentiment and investor emotions by analyzing social media posts, news articles, and other sources. This information can be used to make more informed decisions in finance and other domains. AI can help identify and mitigate emotional biases in decision-making processes. By analyzing patterns in decision data, AI can alert decision-makers when emotions might be unduly influencing choices. AI-powered systems can offer emotional support to individuals in various contexts, such as mental health apps or customer service interactions. These systems can provide empathetic responses; potentially alleviating emotional biases. AI should be developed and deployed ethically to avoid exploiting users' emotions or creating emotionally manipulative experiences. Responsible AI development aims to enhance emotional well-being and decision-making rather than exacerbating emotional biases. AI-driven educational tools can help individuals recognize their emotional biases and learn strategies to manage them. This can lead to more rational and effective decision-making systems that can provide feedback on emotional biases and trends over time, helping individuals become more aware of their emotional tendencies and make conscious efforts to mitigate them. It's important to note that AI systems themselves can inherit biases from their training data and algorithms, which could potentially exacerbate emotional biases. Responsible AI development includes thorough testing, monitoring, and addressing of biases to ensure that AI systems contribute positively to decision-making and emotional well-being.

As emotional and cognitive biases are inherent to human nature and are not likely to vanish, AI systems must take them into account. It's important to recognize that achieving a perfectly unbiased AI system is not feasible. Even though AI can assist in mitigating behavioral biases, it's essential to remain cautious and ensure that AI systems are well-designed, regularly monitored, and aligned with ethical standards (Al-Dahan et al., 2019). Human judgment and oversight should still play a vital role in financial decision-making to ensure that the recommendations provided by AI align with individual goals and preferences. The existing methods can be improved, optimized, and fine-tuned, all the while imbuing other aspects of the system with human-like qualities. Greater awareness of cognitive biases enables more effective utilization of machine learning (ML) and artificial intelligence (AI) (Al-Dahan et al., 2019).

5. CHALLENGES IN USING AI IN BEHAVIORAL FINANCE

The financial industry, spearheaded by Fintech companies, has been experiencing a rapid surge in the integration of AI/ML systems. The recent adoption of technological advancements like big data and cloud computing, along with the expansion of the digital economy, has paved the way for the effective utilization of AI/ML systems. According to a recent survey conducted by the World Economic Forum (WEF) in 2020, 77 percent of the surveyed financial institutions anticipate that AI will hold significant importance, rating it as high or very high within the next two years (WEF, 2020). In a study by McKinsey in 2020, the potential value of AI in the banking sector is projected to reach a substantial $1 trillion. The capabilities of AI/ML are revolutionizing the financial domain. These systems are reshaping client experiences across various fronts, including interactions with financial service providers (such as chatbots), investment strategies (as seen with robo-advisors), lending processes (as exemplified by automated mortgage underwriting), and even identity verification (as demonstrated by image recognition technologies). The adoption of AI/ML systems is revolutionizing the financial sector, yielding significant cost savings through process automation, predictive analytics for enhanced product offerings, and improved risk management and regulatory compliance. Additionally, these systems provide central banks and prudential oversight authorities with advanced tools to strengthen systemic risk surveillance.

1. **Data Quality**: The accuracy of algorithms heavily relies on high-quality input data. Even from reputable sources, data may conceal biases, necessitating meticulous efforts to gather and prepare suitable datasets. This challenge is exemplified in nascent industries like self-driving automotive, where extensive video labeling efforts have created an offshore industry dedicated to this task. In the financial domain, data reconciliation and quality issues are already prevalent, making a data-quality program essential for any large-scale AI implementation. Sun & Medaglia (2019) shaded many challenges related to the analysis of data and data integrity.
2. **Black-Box Effect**: Intelligent algorithms often yield opaque and unverifiable results, providing statistical truths that may be incorrect in specific cases, and hidden biases may be challenging to identify. This lack of explanation can be disconcerting for rational decision-makers, posing a hindrance to AI adoption in trading.

3. **Constricted Focus**: Intelligent algorithms are designed for specific tasks and cannot address other problems. For instance, an algorithm trained to detect suspicious payments may not recognize other suspicious activities related to trading. Additionally, algorithms lack human qualities such as emotional intelligence and contextual understanding, leading to instances where banking chatbots, while smart, may disappoint due to their lack of empathy. Mitchell (2019) emphasized that AI systems currently lack the fundamental aspects of human intelligence. These systems are incapable of comprehending the situations that humans encounter and extracting the correct contextual meaning from them (Dwivedi et al., 2021).
4. **Responsibility:** The use of intelligent machines raises concerns about liability in case of errors or failures. Financial institutions often prefer to retain human supervisors to validate critical decisions made by machines, as their behavior remains unpredictable. This approach partly defeats the purpose of using AI. Present AI systems necessitate the incorporation of advanced technologies to enhance human-computer interaction and seamlessly integrate with the information flow (Dwivedi et al., 2021). Research has underscored that organizations encounter substantial challenges when they lack a strategy addressing the implications of AI, potentially impacting crucial business aspects, and failing to address the concerns of their human workforce (Sun & Medaglia, 2019).
5. **Ethical Challenges**- Scholars and policymakers have engaged in discussions regarding the ethical dimensions of AI and the potential consequences of its increased utilization (Dwivedi et al., 2021). Concerns have emerged from both individuals and organizations, stemming from a lack of trust and apprehensions regarding the ethical aspects of AI systems and their utilization of shared data (Sun & Medaglia 2019). The swift pace of transformation and advancement in AI technologies raises concerns that ethical issues are not being adequately addressed formally. Questions persist about how to resolve ethical and legal concerns, especially those pertaining to responsibility and the analysis of decisions made by AI-based systems (Dwivedi et al., 2021). To mitigate these issues, regulators should establish and enforce comprehensive policies, regulations, ethical guidelines, and a legal framework to prevent the misuse of AI (Duan et al., 2019). Gupta & Kumari (2017) support these assertions, emphasizing the ethical challenges associated with increased AI usage, data sharing dilemmas, and system incompatibilities. Even though AI-based systems make decisions without human intervention, there is a risk of discrimination, highlighting the importance of transparency in AI algorithms (Bostrom & Yudkowsky 2011).

AI and human minds can work together synergistically to mitigate behavioral biases and enhance decision-making processes. AI can examine large data and find patterns that humans might overlook. By incorporating AI-generated insights, humans can make decisions based on comprehensive data analysis rather than relying solely on intuition or cognitive biases. AI can detect behavioral biases in decision-making patterns by analyzing historical data. Humans can then use this information to recognize their own biases and adjust their decision-making accordingly. AI can provide real-time feedback on decisions, alerting individuals when they might be influenced by behavioral biases. This feedback loop helps users become more aware of their biases and encourages them to reconsider their choices. AI can present alternative viewpoints and data-driven insights, encouraging individuals to consider a broader range of information before making decisions. This can counteract biases like confirmation bias and anchoring can simulate different scenarios and outcomes, helping individuals understand the potential consequences of their decisions. Humans can then factor these insights into their choices, reducing the impact of overconfidence bias. AI can offer personalized recommendations based on individual preferences, goals, and risk tolerance. Humans can use these recommendations as a reference while also considering their insights. Also, AI can help individuals recognize and address ethical biases by analyzing decisions for potential ethical implications. This prompts users to consider broader societal impacts beyond their immediate biases. Moreover, AI-powered tools can provide cognitive training to help individuals become more aware of their biases and develop strategies to manage them effectively.

Human intuition, experience, and critical thinking are valuable in assessing the context and nuances that AI might miss. Humans can provide ethical and contextual judgment that AI lacks. Both AI systems and human minds can learn from each other's strengths. AI can learn from human corrections and refine its algorithms, while humans can adopt data-driven insights from AI. The machine can learn more about the preferences of humans but it will never achieve absolute certainty (Russell, 2019, p.7). These machines will be motivated to ask questions, permission, or feedback before undertaking any potentially risky course of action (Russell, 2019, p. 7).

While AI can reduce the impact of biases, humans should play a role in determining the final decisions, especially in complex and morally nuanced situations. Ultimately, a successful collaboration between AI and human minds requires mutual understanding, open communication, and a willingness to acknowledge and address biases. Combining AI's data-driven capabilities with human critical thinking can lead to more informed, rational, and ethical decision-making processes that actively work against the influence of behavioral biases.

6. CONCLUSION

This chapter focuses on how behavioral finance has evolved over the years. Since behavioral finance involves human minds which can lead to Cognitive Biases and Emotional Biases (EB) and can affect investment decision-making, it requires AI and Machine Learning. As research on AI bias is still in its infancy across management domains, opportunities for innovation and policies to minimize bias abound. The integration of AI in the financial sector has the potential to accentuate existing risks in financial markets. This is primarily due to AI's capacity to learn and adapt autonomously to evolving conditions, which can lead to new, overarching challenges and risks. Current vulnerabilities are linked to the improper utilization of data or the use of low-quality data, which can introduce biases and discriminatory outcomes, ultimately negatively affecting financial consumers. It's essential to view AI in finance as a tool that enhances human capabilities rather than replacing them, as suggested by Zheng et al. (2017).

A "human and machine" approach, where AI aids human judgment instead of taking over decision-making entirely (acting as a decision-aid rather than a decision-maker), can harness the advantages of AI while upholding accountability and control measures in the final decision-making process, as advocated by Chui et al. (2016).

Collaboration across diverse domains is indispensable for advancing technical innovations, refining operational methods, and establishing ethical standards to mitigate bias in business operations. While AI can enhance human decision-making, it's equally crucial for humans to play an active role in enhancing AI capabilities (Dwivedi et al., 2021). Human intelligence possesses a distinctive strength in its capacity to learn and adapt to new situations and challenges. The continuous improvement of AI through ongoing learning has historically presented a formidable challenge, only recently addressed by advancements in deep learning and Big Data (Dwivedi et al., 2021).

It's important to recognize the prominence of human decision-making, particularly in high-value scenarios like lending decisions, financial decisions, etc. (Singh et al., 2019). In such cases, human involvement should be emphasized to maintain control and ensure responsible decision-making This chapter will help researchers, investors, and academicians in understanding the behavioral factors affecting investment decisions with the use of automation.

7. RECOMMENDATIONS, IMPLICATIONS, AND LIMITATIONS

Our research findings offer valuable insights for practical applications. The study, which draws upon a comprehensive analysis of existing literature, confirms that managerial and business experts, investors, and researchers have two distinct prospects to detect and address prejudices within establishments. Firstly, AI can be employed to detect and address human biases. Secondly, improving AI systems to avoid perpetuating societal prejudices or introducing biases of their own while leveraging data for model development and deployment is crucial. The cooperation and collaboration between various domains are vital for the creation and adoption of technical innovations, operational strategies, and ethical guidelines with the goal of minimizing bias within businesses. Professionals and leaders in business strategy can effectively reduce the risks associated with AI by implementing the following strategies: comprehending the contexts in which AI can rectify biases and those in which it might exacerbate biases within organizations; formulating guidelines and methodologies for identifying and alleviating prejudice in AI and ML systems; thereby actively participating in evidence-driven conversations regarding cognitive and emotional decision making biases (Silberg & Manyika, 2019; Varsha, 2023). Subsequently, leaders and staff can spend additional time in multidisciplinary study to address ethical concerns, or migration intentions (Bhardwaj and Sharma, 2022), cultural intelligence(Bhardwaj, 2022) and data privacy issues related to bias. Motivating employees to engage in study for advancement necessitates inter-department disciplinary contribution (de Almeida et al., 2021; Varsha, 2023). Encouraging Artificial intelligence in the education-sector and providing access to various prospects can foster the development of an AI community within firms, working towards the elimination of unfair biases and promoting overall well-being.

For example, Accenture (2020) report, which surveyed wealth managers in the United States, found that over 80% of the participants foresaw a substantial overhaul of the industry within the next five years because of artificial intelligence (AI) integration. This optimistic outlook grounded in the belief that AI can optimize the tasks of financial advisors by autonomously overseeing investment portfolios while circumventing the biases previously identified as potential impediments to achieving long-term success. Consequently, advisors can allocate their time nurturing client relationships and pursuing new prospects. In addition to its role in time management, AI also holds promise in minimizing potential downside risks. Furthermore, by eliminating emotional influences, it has the potential to facilitate more rational decision-making, devoid of personal beliefs or convictions. Through machine learning capabilities, AI can process and analyze extensive datasets in manners that surpass human capacities (Accenture, 2020).

Despite being in the early stages, AI bias research presents exciting opportunities for future investigations. This study has certain limitations, notably the methodology, which restricted articles to those related to corporate, and business-organization, for the review of literature. Exploring these limitations can pave the way for further advancements in the field.

REFERENCES

Accenture. (2020). Retrieved from https://www.accenture.com/us-en/insights/capital-markets/wealth-management-artificial-intelligence

Agarwal, R., & Dhar, V. (2014). Editorial—Big data, data science, and analytics: The opportunity and challenge for IS research. *Information Systems Research*, *25*(3), 443–448. doi:10.1287/isre.2014.0546

Akinkoye, E. Y., & Bankole, O. E. (2020). Effect of Emotional Biases on Investor's Decision Making in Nigeria. *International Journal of Business and Management Future*, *4*(1), 33–39. doi:10.46281/ijbmf.v4i1.548

Al-Dahan, N. S. H., Hasan, M. F., & Jadah, H. M. (2019). Effect of cognitive and emotional biases on investor decisions: An analytical study of the iraq stock exchange. *International Journal of Innovation. Creativity and Change*, *9*(10), 30–47.

Alsabban, S., & Alarfaj, O. (2020). An Empirical Analysis of Behavioral Finance in the Saudi Stock Market:Evidence of Overconfidence Behavior. *International Journal of Economics and Financial Issues*, *10*(1), 73–86. doi:10.32479/ijefi.8920

Aziz, S., Dowling, M., Hammami, H., & Piepenbrink, A. (2022). Machine learning in Finance: A topic modelling approach. *European Financial Management*, *28*(3), 744–770. doi:10.1111/eufm.12326

Bailey, W., Kumar, A., & Ng, D. (2011). Behavioral biases of mutual fund investors. *Journal of Financial Economics*, *102*(1), 1–27. doi:10.1016/j.jfineco.2011.05.002

Barber, B. M., & Odean, T. (2001). Boys will be boys: Gender, overconfidence, and common stock investment. *The Quarterly Journal of Economics*, *116*(1), 261–292. doi:10.1162/003355301556400

Benartzi, S., & Thaler, R. H. (2001). Naive Diversification Strategies in Defined Contribution Saving Plans, The American Economic Review. *American Economic Association*, *91*(1), 79–98.

Berdiyeva, O., Islam, M. U., & Saeedi, M. (2021). Artificial Intelligence in Accounting and Finance: Meta-Analysis. *International Business Review*, *3*(1), 56–79.

Bhardwaj, B. (2021). *Short-term foreign trips correlates of the four factors model of cultural intelligence*. Rajagiri Management Journal., doi:10.1108/RAMJ-01-2021-0008

Bhardwaj, B., & Sharma, D. (2022). Migration of skilled professionals across the border: Brain drain or brain gain? *European Management Journal*. Advance online publication. doi:10.1016/j.emj.2022.12.011

Bostrom, N., & Yudkowsky, E. (2011). The ethics of Artificial Intelligence. In K. Frankish (Ed.), *Cambridge Handbook of Artificial Intelligence*. Cambridge University Press.

Boukherouaa, E. B., AlAjmi, K., Deodoro, J., Farias, A., & Ravikumar, R. (2021). Powering the DigitalEconomy: Opportunities and Risks of Artificial Intelligence in Finance, *Departmental Papers*, (24), A001. https://doi.org/ doi:10.5089/9781589063952.087.A001

Broussard, M. (2019). *Artificial Unintelligence: How computers misunderstand the world*. MIT Press.

Chandra, P. (2016). *Behavioral Finance*. McGraw Hill Education.

Chui, M., Manyika, J., & Miremadi, M. (2016). *Where machines could replace humans—And where they can't (yet).* https://www.mckinsey.com/business-functions/digital-mckinsey/our-insights/where-machines-couldreplace-humans-and-where-they-can't-yet

Conway, R. A., & Kovacs, K. (2015). New and emerging models of human intelligence. *Wiley Interdisciplinary Reviews: Cognitive Science*, *6*(5), 419–426. doi:10.1002/wcs.1356 PMID:26267702

Cristofaro, M. (2019). The role of affect in management decisions: A systematic review. *European Management Journal*, *37*(1), 6–17. doi:10.1016/j.emj.2018.12.002

Duan, Y., Edwards, J. S., & Dwivedi, Y. K. (2019). Artificial intelligence for decision making in the era of bigdata – evolution, challenges and research agenda. *International Journal of Information Management*, *48*, 63–71. doi:10.1016/j.ijinfomgt.2019.01.021

Dwivedi, Y. K., Hughes, L., Ismagilova, E., Aarts, G., Coombs, C., Crick, T., Duan, Y., Dwivedi, R., Edwards, J., Eirug, A., Galanos, V., Ilavarasan, P. V., Janssen, M., Jones, P., Kar, A. K., Kizgin, H., Kronemann, B., Lal, B., Lucini, B., ... Williams, M. D. (2021). Artificial Intelligence (AI): Multidisciplinary Perspectives on Emerging Challenges, Opportunities, and Agenda for Research, Practice and Policy. *International Journal of Information Management*, *57*, 101994. doi:10.1016/j.ijinfomgt.2019.08.002

Edmans, A., Garcia, D., & Norli, Ø. (2007). Sports sentiment and stock returns. *The Journal of Finance*, *62*(4), 1967–1998. doi:10.1111/j.1540-6261.2007.01262.x

Fama, E. F. (1970). Efficient capital markets: A review of theory and empirical work. *The Journal of Finance*, *25*(2), 383–417. doi:10.2307/2325486

Gupta, R. K., & Kumari, R. (2017). Artificial intelligence in public health: Opportunities and challenges. *JK Science*, *19*(4), 191–192.

Hastie, T., Tibshirani, R., & Friedman, J. (2009). Unsupervised learning. In *The elements of statistical learning* (pp. 485–585). Springer. doi:10.1007/978-0-387-84858-7_14

Hilovska, K., & Koncz, P. (2012). Application of Artificial Intelligence and Data Mining Techniques to Financial Markets. *Economic Studies & Analyses / Acta VSFS*, *6*(1), 62-76.

Hoehndorf, R., & Queralt-Rosinach, N. (2017). Data Science and Symbolic AI: Synergies, Challenges and Opportunities. Data Science, 1(1-2), 27-38. doi:10.3233/DS-170004

IDC. (2020). Retrieved from https://www.idc.com/getdoc.jsp?containerId=US45569118

Iqbal, S., Hussain, N., Latif, M., & Aslam, S. (2013). Investor Type and Financial Market Anomalies: A Comparison of Individual, Institutional and Foreign Investors and Role of Their Behaviors in Investing Decisions. *Middle East Journal of Scientific Research*, *17*, 1591–1596. doi:10.5829/idosi.mejsr.2013.17.11.11787

Jain, V. (2019). An impact of artificial intelligence on business. *International Journal of Research and Analytical Reviews*, *6*(2), 302–308.

Jordan, M., & Mitchell, T. (2015). Machine learning: Trends, perspectives, and prospects. *Science*, *349*(6245), 255–260. doi:10.1126cience.aaa8415 PMID:26185243

Kahneman, D. (2011). *Thinking, Fast and Slow*. Macmillan.

Kahneman, D., & Tversky, A. (1979). Prospect Theory: An Analysis of Decision under Risk. *Econometrica*, *47*(2), 263–292. doi:10.2307/1914185

Kalsie, A., & Kalra, J. K. (2015). An empirical study on efficient market hypothesis of Indian capital markets. *Journal of Management Research and Analysis*, *2*(2), 108–114.

Kar, A. K., Kar, A. K., Choudhary, S. K., Choudhary, S. K., Singh, V. K., & Singh, V. K. (2022). How can artificial intelligence impact sustainability: A systematic literature review. *Journal of Cleaner Production*, *376*, 134120. doi:10.1016/j.jclepro.2022.134120

Kathpal, S., Akhtar, A., Zaheer, A., & Khan, M. N. (2021). Covid-19 and heuristic biases: Evidence from India. *Journal of Financial Services Marketing*, *26*(4), 305–316. doi:10.105741264-021-00116-x

Kopka, A., & Grashof, N. (2022). Artificial intelligence: Catalyst or barrier on the path to sustainability? *Technological Forecasting and Social Change*, *175*, 121318. Advance online publication. doi:10.1016/j.techfore.2021.121318

Kushwaha, A. K., Pharswan, R., Kumar, P., & Kar, K. A. (2022). How do users feel when they use artificial intelligence for decision making? A Framework for Assessing Users' Perception. *Information Systems Frontiers*. Advance online publication. doi:10.100710796-022-

Lui, A. K., Lee, M., & Ngai, E. W. (2022). Impact of artificial intelligence investment on firm value. *Annals of Operations Research*, *308*(1), 373–388. doi:10.100710479-020-03862-8

Mitchell, M. (2019). Artificial Intelligence: A Guide for Thinking Humans. *Picador*.

Parikh, P. (2017). *Value Investing and Behavioral Finance*. McGraw Hill Education.

Park, J., Konana, P., Gu, B., Kumar, A., & Raghunathan, R. (2010). *Confirmation bias, overconfidence, and investment performance: Evidence from stock message boards*. McCombs Research Paper Series No. IROM-07-10.

Pietikäinen, M., & Silven, O. (2022). *Challenges of Artificial Intelligence-From Machine Learning and Computer Vision to Emotional Intelligence*. arXiv preprint arXiv:2201.01466.

Pompian, M. M. (2006). *Behavioral Finance and Wealth Management – How to Build Optimal Portfolios That Account for Investor Biases*. John Wiley and Sons Inc. Retrieved from http://library.perbanas.ac.id/images/book/behavioralfinance.pdf

PwC. (2018). https://www.pwc.com/m1/en/publications/potential-impact-artificial-intelligence-middle-east.html

Ritter, J. (2003). Behavioral finance. *Pacific-Basin Finance Journal*, *11*(4), 429–437. doi:10.1016/S0927-538X(03)00048-9

Russell, S. (2019). *Human compatible: Artificial Intelligence and the problem of control*. Penguin.

Russell, S., & Norvig, P. (2023). *Artificial Intelligence: A modern approach* (4th ed.). Pearson.

Russell, S. J., & Norvig, P. (2010). *Artificial intelligence: A modern approach* (3rd ed.). Prentice Hall.

Sarin, A. B. (2019). *Behavioral Factors affecting Investment Decisions and Performance: An Empirical Study of Investors in Delhi*. Ph.D., Lingayas Vidhyapeeth.

Sarin, A. B. (2021). Emotional Bias in Investment Decision Making. In M. Cristofaro (Ed.), *Emotion, Cognition, and Their Marvellous Interplay in Managerial Decision-Making. Cambridge Scholars Publishing*.

Sarin, A. B. (2023). Behavioral Finance and Cryptocurrency Market. In K. Mehta, R. Sharma, & P. Yu (Eds.), *Revolutionizing Financial Services and Markets Through FinTech and Blockchain* (pp. 217–236). IGI Global. doi:10.4018/978-1-6684-8624-5.ch014

Sarin, A. B., & Chowdhury, J. K. (2018). Understanding behavioral biases influencing investment decisions: An exploratory study. *International Research Journal of Management and Commerce*, *1*, 584–596.

Shah, S. Z. A., Ahmad, M., & Mahmood, F. (2018). Heuristic biases in investment decision-making and perceived market efficiency: A survey at the Pakistan stock exchange. *Qualitative Research in Financial Markets*, *10*(1), 85–110. doi:10.1108/QRFM-04-2017-0033

Sharma, D., Chaudhary, M., Jaswal, N., & Bhardwaj, B. (2022). Hiding Behind The SWOT: Gender Equality and COVID-19. *Journal of Positive School Psychology*, 730–740.

Singh, G., Garg, V., & Tiwari, P. (2019). Application of Artificial Intelligence on Behavioral Finance. *International Conference on Information Technology and Applied Mathematics*.

Singh, V., Chen, S. S., Singhania, M., Nanavati, B., Kar, A. K., & Gupta, A. (2022). How are reinforcement learning and deep learning algorithms used for big data based decision making in financial industries–A review and research agenda. *International Journal of Information Management Data Insights*, *2*(2), 100094. doi:10.1016/j.jjimei.2022.100094

Sun, T. Q., & Medaglia, R. (2019). Mapping the challenges of artificial intelligence in the public sector:Evidence from public healthcare. *Government Information Quarterly*, *36*(2), 368–383. doi:10.1016/j.giq.2018.09.008

Thaler, R. (2005). Advances in Behavioral Finance II. Princeton University Press.

Turing, A. M. (1950). Computing machinery and intelligence. *Mind*, *59*(236), 433–460. doi:10.1093/mind/LIX.236.433

Varsha, P. S. (2023). How can we manage biases in artificial intelligence systems – A systematic literature review. *International Journal of Information Management Data Insights*, *3*(1). Advance online publication. doi:10.1016/j.jjimei.2023.100165

Zheng, N., Liu, Z., Ren, P., Ma, Y., Chen, S., Yu, S., Xue, J., Chen, B., & Wang, F. (2017). Hybrid-augmented intelligence: Collaboration and cognition. *Frontiers of Information Technology and Electronic Engineering*, *18*(2), 153–179. doi:10.1631/FITEE.1700053

Chapter 14
Artificial Intelligence and Employment: Issues and Challenges

Pyare Lal
Rajiv Gandhi Government College, Shimla, India

ABSTRACT

Technological progress in the form of information technology has helped industries immensely by operating efficiently and competitively. In the past decade, the pace of progress in information technology, especially in the area of artificial intelligence, has transformed the way these industries function. Today, almost every aspect of production and business activity is influenced by artificial intelligence. While such transformation has greatly benefited production activities, its impact on social constructs, especially employment, is a matter of debate. This chapter studied the potential impact of artificial intelligence on employment. Based upon the review of the research studies from across the globe, the study concludes that adoption of artificial intelligence will have a positive impact on economic growth, whereas its impact on employment to a great extent depends upon the technology absorption capacity of the economies and the government's ability to incorporate the existence of artificial intelligence while preparing policies meant to mitigate the concerns of society.

1. INTRODUCTION

The advent and advancement of information technology paved the way for the transformation of societies in various ways (Rehman Khan SA et al., 2022; Rodríguez et al., 2015). The intervention of technology in every sphere of life continues to be a matter of debate due to the positive and negative externalities associated with its use. In the last almost two decades, the pace with which information technology has made progress has made the world witness many wonders. In today's competitive world, almost all business entities are dependent upon information technology for almost all tasks, ranging from simple routine tasks to much more complex production processes. The use of information technology has re-

DOI: 10.4018/979-8-3693-0418-1.ch014

sulted in many advantages, including a reduction in production costs, improvements in the quality of products, new business opportunities, and a more competitive work environment (Nikoloski, 2014). The dependence of business firms, societies, and economies on information technology has grown to the extent that today, life without technology is an impossible idea.

In the past decade, the advancements made by information technology, especially in the areas of artificial intelligence, have posed an altogether different situation in front of societies, corporations, and economies. The impact of artificial intelligence is so deep that, in a short span of time, almost every individual is aware of the technology and usage associated with it. Artificial intelligence techniques has changed the way societies deal with information and how corporations function (Dwivedi et al., 2021; Makridakis, 2017). Given the intensity of usefulness associated with the use of artificial intelligence, there are certain issues that have also creeped up in the academic community due to the advancement of the technique of artificial intelligence. The issue of employment is one such big issue that has caused concerns for the economies. Before moving ahead with the possible issues and challenges associated with the use of artificial intelligence, an overview and understanding of artificial intelligence and its evolution are required.

2. ARTIFICIAL INTELLIGENCE

In a simple sense, artificial intelligence is the process by which machines, particularly computers, imitate human intelligence processes. OECD (2006) and UNCTAD (2017) defines artificial intelligence as "the ability of machines and systems to acquire and apply knowledge and to carry out intelligent behaviour". Under artificial intelligence, machines are designed to learn from experience, think, work, make decisions, and perform tasks like humans.

The concept of innovation in technology is as old as the invention of technology itself. As far as the idea of artificial intelligence goes, it came into existence even before the invention of computers. Ancient thinkers developed this idea of mechanizing non-human machines with human thinking (Gerber & Hiernaux, 2022). Their idea got a boost with the invention of programable digital computers in the 1940s. The invention of computers encouraged scientists to visualize and materialize the development of the electronic brain, which today is known as artificial intelligence (Copeland, 1993). This idea of including human intelligence in machines in the form of artificial intelligence can be traced back to the 1940s, when Warren Ms. Culloch and Walter Pits proposed a model of artificial neurons. This was followed by demonstration of a rule called Hebbian Learning. Hebbian learning is Donald Hebb's rule for changing the strength of connections between neurons. In 1950, Alan Turing, a mathematician by profession, published an article titled 'Computing Machinery and Intelligence," in which he proposed a test to measure machines ability to replicate human behaviour (Turing, 1950). During the same decade, Johan McCarthy coined the term artificial intelligence (Kim, 2022).

In 1955, Allen Newel and Herbert A. Simons developed the first AI program in an article called "The Logic Theory Machine: a Complex Information Processing System" which was able to solve a bunch of mathematical problems (Newell & Simon, 1956). This was followed by decades of ups and downs in the development of artificial intelligence with little tangible success. It was only in 2006 that artificial intelligence was used for the first time in business activities, especially in the social media sector. Today, artificial intelligence has developed in many dimensions. The use of concepts like deep learning, big data, data science, etc. is becoming the order of the day. Many multinational technology-centric companies, such as Google, Meta, IBM, Amazon, etc., are investing heavily in artificial intelligence. While the growth of artificial intelligence is phenomenal, there are certain issues and challenges that the evolution of artificial intelligence has given birth to. The section ahead deals with all such issues and challenges, especially in the area of employment. Prior to that, a review of the industries and fields that are progressively using artificial intelligence is carried out.

3. TYPES OF ARTIFICIAL INTELLIGENCE

Artificial Intelligence has been classified by various authors in various ways [see, for example, Mughal et al. (2022), Al-Imam et al. (2020), Quach (2022)]. Each classification of artificial intelligence is based on the domain and functions performed by the artificial intelligence. In its simplest form, artificial intelligence designed to perform only some specific domain-specific tasks, such as image recognition and virtual assistants like Siri and Alexa, is referred to as narrow or weak artificial intelligence. Similarly, the artificial intelligence that performs human-kind activities such as understanding, learning, and creative thinking is termed as general or strong artificial intelligence. This form of artificial intelligence is still not fully realized by the developers. There is a more advanced level of artificial intelligence that includes emotional intelligence along with all aspects that are covered by general or strong artificial intelligence. This type of artificial intelligence is termed as artificial superintelligence.

Another type of artificial intelligence is known as reactive artificial intelligence, which does not have any memory and is task-specific (Kar et al., 2020). They can respond to specific inputs, such as consumer data with regards to purchase and search history, and use this data to deliver the output of the consumer's choice. Another type of artificial intelligence is known as limited memory artificial intelligence. The difference between reactive artificial intelligence and limited memory artificial intelligence is that limited memory artificial intelligence possesses memory and can learn from historical data and past experiences to make better decisions. There is another more advanced form of artificial intelligence that is yet to be accomplished, which is known as theory of mind artificial intelligence. This form of artificial intelligence would be able to understand human emotions, beliefs, intentions, and thoughts. It would also be able to communicate with humans. Similar to mind-based artificial intelligence, another type of artificial intelligence, namely, self-aware artificial intelligence, is also in its concept stage. This form of artificial intelligence is a matter of controversy due to various ethical issues associated with it. Such artificial intelligence would have awareness of its existence, consciousness, and subjective experience of the world.

The visualisation of artificial intelligence's future and how it will affect human life for future generations are undoubtedly astounding. However, artificial intelligence in its present form, can be divided into two broad categories: a) software-based artificial intelligence and b) embodied artificial intelligence. Software-based artificial intelligence is in use to assist users in performing tasks like analysing images and recognizing faces and voices. Majority of e-commerce sites, search engines use this form of artificial intelligence to assist users in getting better results. On the other hand, embodied artificial intelligence is used in machines such as robots, drones, vehicles, and machines as sensors, electronic systems, etc. Both of these forms of artificial intelligence are being used by various entities in various ways, depending on the utility they provide. The section ahead will deal with the uses of artificial intelligence, followed by the issues associated with the use of artificial intelligence.

4. USES OF ARTIFICIAL INTELLIGENCE

The evolution of artificial intelligence may have taken more than half a century to materialize, but the pace with which it is growing in its dimensions of usage is remarkable. Today, almost every area of our lives, ranging from the ordinary business of life to complex works related to business activities such as medicine, accounting, computer science, telecommunication, manufacturing, and business organizations, is touched directly or indirectly by artificial intelligence. In our day-to-day lives, everything from online shopping and advertising to web-based search, digital personal assistants, translators, etc., is based on the use of artificial intelligence. Major social media feeds in the meta (Twitter, Instagram, chatbots, etc.) are based on the use of artificial intelligence by the media houses. In the area of healthcare, artificial intelligence is used for increasing the speed of imaging and diagnosis, decreasing healthcare costs, performing risk analysis, lifestyle management, and monitoring (Racine et al., 2019). Along with these common uses, artificial intelligence has also helped with complex life tasks and has helped technology immensely. Today, many multinational corporations and industries prefer artificial intelligence to make them more productive and cost-effective in their business activities. Be it robotics, healthcare, computer vision, machine learning, finance, gaming, education, or virtual assistants, in every area of corporate functioning, the use of artificial intelligence is increasing. In healthcare, the way artificial intelligence is used for image analysis, discovery of new drugs, diagnosis of disease, and management of patient databases is remarkable (Racine et al., 2019). Similarly, in the area of finance, artificial intelligence is used for activities such as fraud detection, algorithm trading, chatbots used for customer care services, credit risk assessment, and providing personalized financial assistance (Ahmed et al., 2022; Fernandez, 2019).

Apart from healthcare and finance, in the field of gaming, artificial intelligence is predominantly used to create intelligent character opponents and a dynamic game environment to give a challenging experience to the player. The robotic form of artificial intelligence is widely used in activities like manufacturing, logistics, healthcare, etc. In self-driving cars, artificial intelligence is used for navigation and for making real-time decisions.

In the field of education, artificial intelligence is used to provide a personalized learning experience, access student performance, and provide targeted feedback. Artificial intelligence is also used in the area of cybersecurity to detect cyber threats and identify anomalous behavior and potential security breaches. Along with these areas and activities, there are numerous other fields in which the use of artificial intelligence is increasing. With the advancements in technology, it is expected that in the years to come, hardly any area of human life or industrial activity will be left untouched by artificial intelligence.

Acknowledging the fact that the usage of artificial intelligence is increasing day by day, its impact on different aspects of human life is inevitable. The usage of artificial intelligence has led to a situation where there is a need to carry out studies to consider and analyse the issues associated with the utilization of artificial intelligence. The section below discusses the development of Artificial Intelligence in India and the following section discusses the identification of issues related to the utilization of Artificial Intelligence.

5. ARTIFICIAL INTELLIGENCE AND INDIA

Most of the research studies mentioned in the previous section are focused on the increased use of artificial intelligence tools in the day-to-day lives of common individuals and corporations. However, to what extent the adoption of artificial intelligence has impacted a country like India needs to be highlighted. Like the rest of the globe, in India as well, artificial intelligence is transforming the functioning of economic activities at the industry level. The data on the number of patents in artificial intelligence applied for by different countries and universities located there reveals that India has relatively low exposure to research in artificial intelligence. The World Intellectual Property Organization (WIPO) data for the year 2019 shows that there has been a phenomenal increase in the number of artificial intelligence patents since 2013, with the majority of these patent applications received from countries like America, China, Japan, etc. Among the top patent-filling nations, India stands way down in ranking, reflecting relatively less exposure to research in the field of artificial intelligence.

However, keeping in view the size of the Indian market and the extent of diversity prevalent in India, the future of artificial intelligence is also brightest in India. As per the estimates of the Artificial Intelligence Index Report 2023 published by Stanford University, India comes in fifth place in terms of funds received in artificial intelligence-based goods and services start-ups. The same report estimated India as the sixth largest recipient of artificial intelligence investments during the period 2013–2022. In terms of research publications, measured in terms of the number of artificial intelligence publications, journals, journal citations, conferences, and conference publications, India's position is significantly improving.

As per the estimates of the NASSCOM AI Adoption Index 2022, a unit increase in the intensity of artificial intelligence can increase total factor productivity growth by 0.05 percent (NASSCOM, 2022). The report highlighted artificial intelligence as one of the most important factors responsible for India's achievement of its 5-trillion-dollar gross domestic product target by 2026–2027). The report further highlighted BFSI, CPG and Retail, healthcare, and Industrial and Automotive as the highest contributors (approximately 60 percent) to the achievement of the 5 trillion dollar economy target.

On the part of the government's attitude towards artificial intelligence, the Government Artificial Intelligence Readiness Index published by Oxford Insights (2022) placed India at 32nd globally in the list of 181 countries (Oxford Insights, 2022). There is growing consciousness on the part of the government to promote digital India in the fields of artificial intelligence, big data, machine learning, and robotics (Dhanabalan & Sathish, 2018). Foreseeing the growth of artificial intelligence at the international level, the Indian national policy think tank NITI Aayog has already started to work on the opportunities and risks associated with artificial intelligence. The first such initiative came in the year 2018 with the release of the National Strategy for Artificial Intelligence' under the theme AI for All' (NITI Aayog, 2018). This paper examines in detail the system-related challenges and societal considerations associated with artificial intelligence. The paper highlighted the employment aspect of artificial intelligence as the top societal consideration associated with the use of artificial intelligence. Given such readiness on the part of the government to attract and promote artificial intelligence, its implications for the functioning of industries and societies are bound to happen. The section ahead explains in brief all the issues that the adoption of artificial intelligence is bound to give birth to.

6. ISSUES IN THE USE OF ARTIFICIAL INTELLIGENCE

The pace with which artificial intelligence is used in human lives and the industrial world has also raised concerns related to challenges and issues associated with its usage. The biggest challenge posed by artificial intelligence is in the form of ethical dilemmas. The use of artificial intelligence gives rise to debate on ethical issues such as privacy, data protection, transparency, discrimination, surveillance, loss of empathy, kindness, and moral thinking. The issue becomes a more serious cause of concern when the areas in which artificial intelligence gives rise to such ethical issues are healthcare and the media.

Similarly, the use of artificial intelligence can also address both the issue of transparency and the lack of prejudice in decision-making. Since the majority of decisions taken under the use of artificial intelligence will be based on the data it is trained on, this may lead to discriminatory outcomes that may be harmful and reiterate and promote already existing social inequalities and prejudices. Lack of transparency, trust, and validation of the decisions taken under the influence of artificial intelligence is another issue associated with artificial intelligence.

Figure 1. Major issues with artificial intelligence
Source: Author's Compilation

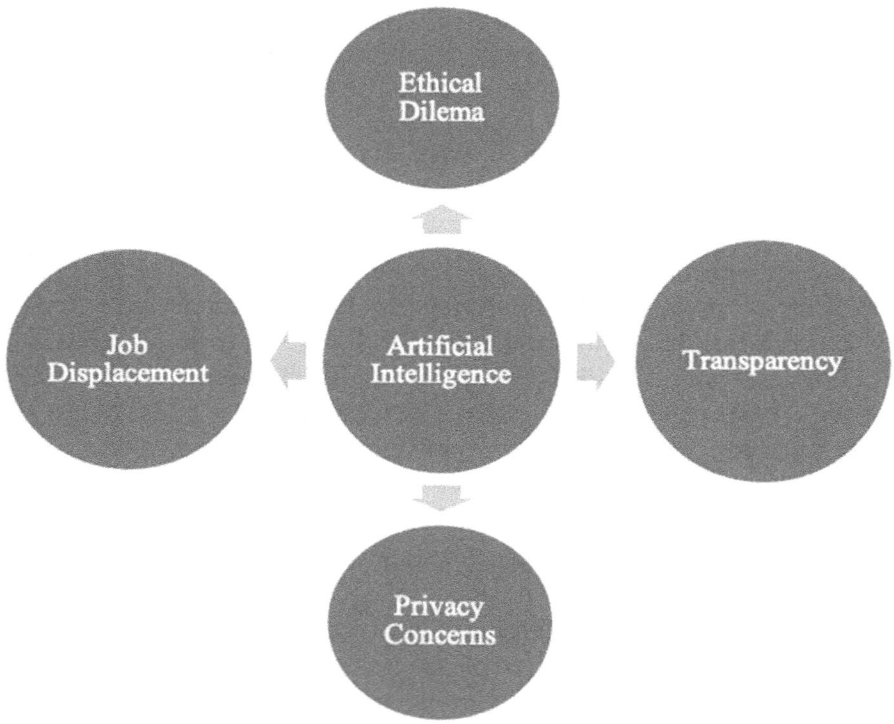

Similarly, there are issues such as data privacy, security concerns, and regulatory and legal challenges that are major causes of concern for societies. These issues require effective redress by way of creating rules, laws, technical standards, and best practices for ethical artificial intelligence (Floridi & Cowls, 2022). Failure to provide such a mechanism could lead to catastrophic consequences, especially in areas where human judgment and ethical considerations are required.

Along with these ethical and privacy-related concerns, another big challenge that the artificial intelligence revolution is feared to generate is the problem of job displacement and unemployment. The section ahead explains in detail why employment is a major issue associated with the use of artificial intelligence.

7. ARTIFICIAL INTELLIGENCE AND EMPLOYMENT

From the above description, it has been established that during the past two decades, the use of artificial intelligence has increased rapidly, both in day-to-day tasks and also in the industrial world. With the pace at which artificial intelligence is evolving, it undoubtedly has the potential to transform the way industries and sectors of any economy function. This transformation certainly has many issues and challenges that policymakers need to incorporate over time. Among all such challenges, the one on the employment front is of utmost concern. There is limited research to study the implication of advancements in artificial intelligence on employment in the economy. Any work on this issue has been done either as an implication of any technological advancement or of machine intelligence, such as artificial intelligence and robotics, on employment. The debate on the impact of technology on the labour market, especially employment, is old. There is a general, established hypothesis that any technological change is labour-saving in nature, resulting in an increase in unemployment. During the Great Depression of the 1930s, J.M. Keynes raised concern about the effects of technological changes on job losses. According to him, any technological innovation can influence employment status either by displacing labour from existing works or by increasing the labour requirement in newly evolved techniques of production. According to him, a balance is required to be maintained between the pace of technological innovations and the search for new uses of labour (Floridi, 2014). To what extent the displacement effect and productivity effect come into play depends on the extent to which technological advancement is adopted by the economy.

With regards to research studies on the impact of technological progress such as artificial intelligence and the use of robotics at the workplace on employment, it is only in recent times that growing interest among the academic world has crept up. The academic work is further concentrated around the change in the nature of employment, the reorganization of the nature of labour demanded, its social implications, and the polarization of jobs and wages (De Acypreste & Paraná, 2022).

Brambilla et al. (2023) did a study on the effects of technology change adoption on employment. Their research concentrated on how the usage of robots affected the labour markets in Argentina, Brazil, and Mexico. The survey found that formal salaried employment have been supplanted by machines, with young and semi-skilled workers suffering the most. The study also comes to the conclusion that the informal economy served as a safeguard against joblessness. The study concluded that although the employment of technical innovations like artificial intelligence and robots at the workplace has an impact on formal jobs, it has no impact on jobs in the informal sector.

Arntz et al. (2017) challenged the economic debate by stating that in the next 10 to 20 years, adoption of artificial intelligence and robotics will substantially substitute human labour in industrialized countries. According to the researchers, any estimate or forecast on the effect of technological change on employment should only be made after considering the diversity of tasks within jobs and the flexibility of jobs in digital transformation. The study, which was based on task data, found that the estimated risk of automation of jobs decreased from thirty eight percent to nine percent.

In another research study, Aghion (2021) surveyed the literature on the impacts of automation on employment. The study highlighted that automation will have both positive and negative effects on employment. According to them, adoption of automation at the firm level will lead to a reduction in wage rates and, hence, the creation of new jobs. However, it will not be able to compensate for job losses. The study further highlighted that automation would make firms more productive, making them reduce prices and hence increase demand for their products. This would lead to more employment in automated firms. Based upon their empirical work on French firm-level data, the study concludes that at firm level, the automation has a positive and direct effect on employment.

Ting-Ting Gu et al. (2022), using data for the period 2007–2020, examine the effect of artificial intelligence development on employment in the service sector of the Chinese economy. Their findings reveal that artificial intelligence influences service sector employment directly via creation and substitution effect and indirectly through competition effect). The results of the study indicate that the utilization of AI in the service industry leads to an increase in employment opportunities, workers' incomes, cross-sectoral labour flows, and competition for mid-skilled labour; however, the distribution of this positive effect on employment is heterogeneous.

A study conducted by Tyson & Zysman (2022) concludes that, whereas the use of artificial intelligence in the manufacturing and services sectors displaces humans from existing tasks, it further provides opportunities for new tasks. They further conclude that artificial intelligence-enabled digital platforms will adversely affect the labour sector by polarising employment, stagnating wage growth in middle- and low-skilled jobs, increasing inequalities, and reducing good-quality jobs. The study argues that the productivity and growth benefits of artificial intelligence will not be good enough to mitigate the increase in inequality. The study further highlights the importance of intelligent policy interventions to mitigate or offset the adverse effect of artificial intelligence on labour.

Aghion et al. (2020) study the effects of robotization on employment in France for a time period ranging from 1994 to 2014. Their study shows that robotization reduces employment, with non-educated workers being more affected compared to educated workers. They suggest the adoption of appropriate labour market and education policies to mitigate the adverse effects of robotization.

Many international research institutions have also looked into the effects of automation, robotics, and artificial intelligence on employment. Goldman Sachs has conducted in-depth research to examine how artificial intelligence would affect employment. According to one study by Jan Hatzius et al. (2023) looking at how artificial intelligence affects economic growth, generative AI will aid sectors in increasing output and reducing expenses. However, there may be substantial disruptions to the labour economy. The researchers discovered that two-thirds of jobs are subject to the risk associated with the deployment of automation in the form of artificial intelligence using data from the United States and Europe on occupational tasks. They also predicted that the deployment of generative artificial intelligence may influence 300 million full-time employment globally. This extensive investigation to study the potential effects of artificial intelligence reveals that as compared to manufacturing and construction industries, it is legal and administrative industries that are more exposed to employment risk. The nature of risk on employment due to artificial intelligence ranges from full to partial substitution of jobs. The study however also established that adoption of artificial intelligence will help industries achieve better productivity which further leads to growth of annual global gross domestic product by seven percent.

World Economic Forum (2023) conducted a research to capture the opinions of more than 800 businesses from 27 industries and 45 economies about the potential effects of technological adoption on employment. The report concludes that whereas approximately 75 percent of surveyed companies have adopted artificial intelligence in their functioning, only 50 percent of organizations expect that adoption of artificial intelligence will create new jobs, and 25 percent expect that this will result in job loss. Erin Winick (2020) compiled the opinions of international organizations and global experts on the possible impact of automation, robots, and artificial intelligence on employment. The conclusion of this review paper fails to provide any quantitative estimate of the job loss due to the varied estimates given by each estimating firm or researcher.

McKinsey Global Institute (2017) did a study and discovered that one-fifth of the world's workforce will be impacted by automation. The study used data from 800 industries spanning across 46 nations. The survey also found that those most impacted by this automation will be food and machine operators. According to the paper, automation would have the least impact on poor countries because there is less investment in that sector.

In order to forecast the effects of artificial intelligence on global economic development and unemployment, The CFM Surveys (2023) conducted a survey titled Artificial Intelligence and the Economy. Members of the European panel from high-income nations participated in the poll. Most panellists agreed that artificial intelligence would accelerate global economic development by more than 4 percent annually. The majority of the panellists were either of the opinion that artificial intelligence would not alter employment rates in high-income nations or were unsure of the effect of artificial intelligence on employment when it came to this subject.

Academics and organisations that have conducted research on the employment implications of artificial intelligence and are included in the section are summarised in the table below.

Table 1. Impact of artificial intelligence on employment

Author	Country/Geographic Region	Findings
Brambilla et al. (2023) De Acypreste & Paraná, (2022)	Argentina, Brazil, and Mexico	Technical innovations like artificial intelligence and robots at the workplace has an impact on formal jobs, it has no impact on jobs in the informal sector.
Arntz et al. (2017)	Industrialized countries	Adaptability of jobs will reduce the automation risk of jobs from 38 percent to 9 percent
Aghion (2021)	France	Adoption of automation at the firm level will lead to a reduction in wage rates, fall in prices, increase in demand and, hence, the creation of new jobs
Ting-Ting Gu et al. (2022)	China	Artificial intelligence in the service sector results in an increase in the number of jobs, the income of the workers
Tyson & Zysman (2022)		Artificial intelligence-enabled digital platforms will adversely affect the labour sector by polarising employment, stagnating wage growth in middle- and low-skilled jobs, increasing inequalities, and reducing good-quality jobs
(Jan Hatzius et al., 2023)	United States and European Data	two-thirds of jobs are subject to the risk associated with the deployment of automation in the form of artificial intelligence
(World Economic Forum, 2023)	800 businesses from 27 industries and 45 economies	50 percent of organizations expect that adoption of artificial intelligence will create new jobs, and 25 percent expect that this will result in job loss
(Erin Winick, 2020)		Fails to provide any quantitative estimate of the job loss
(McKinsey Global Institute, 2017)	800 industries spanning across 46 nations	One-fifth of the world's workforce will be impacted by automation
(The CFM Surveys, 2023)	Members of the European panel	The majority of the panellists believes that artificial intelligence would not alter employment rates in high-income nations or were unsure of the effect of artificial intelligence on employment.

Based on reviews of research studies conducted by renowned institutions and academicians, it can be concluded that the majority of industry experts and academicians are divided over the impact of artificial intelligence on employment. The use of artificial intelligence in the production process will certainly have a positive impact on labour productivity, the cost of production, and economic growth. However, its impact on employment depends to a great extent on the intensity of technology absorption and the government's ability to address the issues of employment associated with the use of artificial intelligence.

8. SCOPE FOR FURTHER STUDIES

The brain drain has adversely impacted the growth trajectory of many developing countries (Bhardwaj & Sharma, 2022). India being no exception, the impact of artificial intelligence on brain drain is required. Therefore, a comprehensive study to see the implication of the development of artificial intelligence on brain drain can be performed to supplement the research findings. Along with this, the issues and concerns highlighted in the previous section have pointed towards the various concerns that emerged after the evolution of artificial intelligence. To what extent such concerns are safeguarded by the existing policies and practices requires a detailed analysis, and that can be of great help for the policymakers in identifying the shortcomings in the existing laws and practices.

9. CONCLUSION

The employment implications of artificial intelligence is one of the highly debatable topic among academia. However, due to infancy state of development of the artificial intelligence, the availability of data on effect of artificial intelligence on employment is a major challenge. Therefore, majority of the academic studies made use of historical evidences to justify their arguments on employment implications of artificial intelligence. Based on the global experiences and research findings of researchers and international research organizations, it can be established that the influence of artificial intelligence in industries, the workplace, and societies is bound to grow with time. Due to the complexities involved with the availability of quantitative data on the influence of artificial intelligence on various aspects of our lives, the synthesis of global academic research findings on the issue of the impact of artificial intelligence on economic growth and employment was used. The synthesis of existing literature established that for artificial intelligence to yield a sustainable positive impact on economic growth and employment, an integrated effort of policymakers, artificial intelligence developers, academicians, and conscious society is required. All participants in this ecosystem need to give importance to the valid concerns of society. Issues and concerns in the form of transparency, privacy, ethical considerations, and employment shall be considered before going ahead with any major intervention in the existing eco-system.

REFERENCES

Aayog, N. I. T. I. (2018). *National Strategy for Artificial Intelligence.* NITI Aayog. https://niti.gov.in/sites/default/files/2019-01/NationalStrategy-for-AI-Discussion-Paper.pdf

Aghion, P. (2021). *The Direct and Indirect Effects of Automation on Employment: A Survey of the Recent Literature*. https://www.semanticscholar.org/paper/The-Direct-and-Indirect-Effects-of-Automation-on-%3A-Aghion/006a9a1c0c0784d617b5b946115f9f1c7d884102

Aghion, P., Antonin, C., & Bunel, S. (2020). Artificial Intelligence, Growth and Employment: The Role of Policy. *Economie et Statistique / Economics and Statistics, 510-511-512*, 149–164. doi:10.24187/ecostat.2019.510t.1994

Ahmed, S., Alshater, M. M., Ammari, A. E., & Hammami, H. (2022). Artificial intelligence and machine learning in finance: A bibliometric review. *Research in International Business and Finance*, *61*(C), 101646. doi:10.1016/j.ribaf.2022.101646

Al-Imam, A., Motyka, M. A., & Jędrzejko, M. Z. (2020). Conflicting opinions in connection with digital superintelligence. *IAES International Journal of Artificial Intelligence (IJ-AI), 9*(2), 336. doi:10.11591/ijai.v9.i2.pp336-348

Arntz, M., Gregory, T., & Zierahn-Weilage, U. (2017). Revisiting the risk of automation. *Economics Letters*, *159*(C), 157–160. doi:10.1016/j.econlet.2017.07.001

Bhardwaj, B., & Sharma, D. (2022). Migration of skilled professionals across the border: Brain drain or brain gain? *European Management Journal*. Advance online publication. doi:10.1016/j.emj.2022.12.011

Brambilla, I., César, A., Falcone, G., & Gasparini, L. (2023). The impact of robots in Latin America: Evidence from local labor markets. *World Development, 170*. doi:10.1016/j.worlddev.2023.106271

Copeland, J. (1993). *Artificial Intelligence: A Philosophical Introduction*. John Wiley & Sons.

De Acypreste, R., & Paraná, E. (2022). Artificial Intelligence and employment: A systematic review: Inteligência Artificial e emprego: uma revisão sistemática. *Brazilian Journal of Political Economy. Revista de Economia Política*, *42*(4), 1014–1032. doi:10.1590/0101-31572022-3320

Dhanabalan, T., & Sathish, A. (2018). Transforming Indian Industries Through Artificial Intelligence and Robotics in Industry 4.0. *Editor@iaeme.Com International Journal of Mechanical Engineering and Technology, 9*(10), 835–845.

Dwivedi, Y. K., Hughes, L., Ismagilova, E., Aarts, G., Coombs, C., Crick, T., Duan, Y., Dwivedi, R., Edwards, J., Eirug, A., Galanos, V., Ilavarasan, P. V., Janssen, M., Jones, P., Kar, A. K., Kizgin, H., Kronemann, B., Lal, B., Lucini, B., ... Williams, M. D. (2021). Artificial Intelligence (AI): Multidisciplinary perspectives on emerging challenges, opportunities, and agenda for research, practice and policy. *International Journal of Information Management*, *57*, 101994. doi:10.1016/j.ijinfomgt.2019.08.002

Fernandez, A. (2019). *Artificial Intelligence in Financial Services* (*SSRN* Scholarly Paper 3366846). doi:10.2139/ssrn.3366846

Floridi, L. (2014). Technological Unemployment, Leisure Occupation, and the Human Project. *Philosophy & Technology*, *27*(2), 143–150. doi:10.100713347-014-0166-7

Floridi, L., & Cowls, J. (2022). A Unified Framework of Five Principles for AI in Society. In *Machine Learning and the City* (pp. 535–545). John Wiley & Sons, Ltd. doi:10.1002/9781119815075.ch45

Gerber, S., & Hiernaux, Q. (2022). Plants as Machines: History, Philosophy and Practical Consequences of an Idea. *Journal of Agricultural & Environmental Ethics*, *35*(1), 4. doi:10.100710806-021-09877-w

Gu, T.-T., Zhang, S.-F., & Cai, R. (2022). Can Artificial Intelligence Boost Employment in Service Industries? Empirical Analysis Based on China. *Applied Artificial Intelligence*, *36*(1), 1–18. doi:10.1080/08839514.2022.2080336

Hatzius, J., Briggs, J., Kodnani, D., & Pierdomenico, G. (2023). *The Potentially Large Effects of Artificial Intelligence on Economic Growth* (Global Economics Analyst). Goldman Sachs. https://www.gspublishing.com/content/research/en/reports/2023/03/27/d64e052b-0f6e-45d7-967b-d7be35fabd16.html# doi:10.1001/jamasurg.2020.0839

Insights, O. (2022). *Government AI Readiness Index 2022*. Oxford Insights.

Kim, H. (2022). Historical Sketch of Artificial Intelligence. In H. Kim (Ed.), *Artificial Intelligence for 6G* (pp. 3–14). Springer International Publishing. doi:10.1007/978-3-030-95041-5_1

Makridakis, S. (2017). The forthcoming Artificial Intelligence (AI) revolution: Its impact on society and firms. *Futures*, *90*, 46–60. doi:10.1016/j.futures.2017.03.006

McKinsey Global Institute. (2017). *A Future that Works: Automation, Employment, and Productivity*. McKinsey & Company.

Mughal, F., Wahid, A., & Khattak, M. A. K. (2022). Artificial Intelligence: Evolution, Benefits, and Challenges. In S. Garg, G. S. Aujla, K. Kaur, & S. Hassan Ahmed Shah (Eds.), *Intelligent Cyber-Physical Systems for Autonomous Transportation* (pp. 59–69). Springer International Publishing. doi:10.1007/978-3-030-92054-8_4

NASSCOM. (2022). *NASSCOM AI Adoption Index 2022*. https://nasscom.in/system/files/publication/nasscom-ai-adoption-index-2022-upload.pdf

Newell, A., & Simon, H. (1956). The logic theory machine–A complex information processing system. *IEEE Transactions on Information Theory*, *2*(3), 61–79. doi:10.1109/TIT.1956.1056797

Nikoloski, K. (2014). The Role of Information Technology in the Business Sector. *International Journal of Scientific Research*, *3*(12), 12. http://www.ijsr.net/v3i12.php#sthash.x82xSS6g.JbQkpxXM.dpbs

OECD. (2006). *OECD Science, Technology and Industry Outlook 2006*. Organisation for Economic Co-operation and Development. https://www.oecd-ilibrary.org/science-and-technology/oecd-science-technology-and-industry-outlook-2006_sti_outlook-2006-en

Quach, K. C. (2022). Types of artificial intelligence (AI) in marketing management. In Artificial Intelligence for Marketing Management. Routledge.

Racine, E., Boehlen, W., & Sample, M. (2019). Healthcare uses of artificial intelligence: Challenges and opportunities for growth. *Healthcare Management Forum*, *32*(5), 272–275. doi:10.1177/0840470419843831 PMID:31234654

Rehman Khan, S. A., Ahmad, Z., Sheikh, A. A., & Yu, Z. (2022). Digital transformation, smart technologies, and eco-innovation are paving the way toward sustainable supply chain performance. *Science Progress*, *105*(4). Advance online publication. doi:10.1177/00368504221145648 PMID:36573795

Rodríguez, D., Busco, C., & Flores, R. (2015). Information technology within society's evolution. *Technology in Society*, *40*, 64–72. doi:10.1016/j.techsoc.2014.08.006

The CFM Surveys. (2023). *Artificial Intelligence and the Economy*. https://cfmsurvey.org/surveys/artificial-intelligence-and-economy

Turing, A. M. (1950). Computing Machinery and Intelligence. *Mind*, *59*(October), 433–460. doi:10.1093/mind/LIX.236.433

Tyson, L. D., & Zysman, J. (2022). Automation, AI & Work. *Daedalus*, *151*(2), 256–271. doi:10.1162/daed_a_01914

UNCTAD. (Ed.). (2017). *Digitalization, trade and development*. United Nations.

Winick, E. (2020, April 2). *Every Study We Could Find on What Automation Will Do to Jobs, in One Chart*. MIT Technology Review. www.technologyreview.com/2018/01/25/146020/every-study-we-could-find-on-what-automation-will-do-to-jobs-in-one-chart/

World Economic Forum. (2023). *Future of Jobs Report, 2023* [Insight Report]. https://www3.weforum.org/docs/WEF_Future_of_Jobs_2023.pdf

Chapter 15
Artificial Intelligence: Next Level Customer Service

Vinod Negi
HPUBS, Himachal Pradesh University, Shimla, India

ABSTRACT

Artificial intelligence's (AI) importance in customer service has significantly expanded in our daily lives. Businesses and customers are already swiftly adjusting to the new reality thanks to AI's simplicity of use. Artificial intelligence is useful in many areas and corrects common mistakes in conventional customer service. The three most prevalent problems customers have with customer service involve delays in responses, a lack of contact control, and the difficulty to receive help outside of typical business hours. The good news is that AI can handle these problems with ease, especially when it comes to customer service. Since AI is ultimately dependent on the data provided, and today data is available in abundance and an effective analysis of that data is required in order to gain competitive advantage over rivals and only with the help of AI can this be achieved, it may be essential for businesses to employ AI-enabled customer experience solutions that capture and model data in order to improve both customer satisfaction and the overall health of the company.

1. INTRODUCTION

In the era of digital world, customer service (CS), whether business-to-business or business-to-consumer, must offer procedures and modifications that should result in improved customer service. Covid- 19 era has changed the thinking pattern and behaviour of individual (Sharma et al, 2022). The IT department initially has the only organizational responsibility for steering customer service through the technology process; this is a business issue that has an impact on all levels of management and personnel (Nobles, 2018).

According to McLean and Osei-Frimpong (2019), artificial intelligence (AI) has power to primarily alter the marketplace and how businesses interact with their clients. By providing businesses with a greater understanding of customers' preferences and purchase patterns, AI advances can improve the

DOI: 10.4018/979-8-3693-0418-1.ch015

purchaser experience in particular (Evans, 2019). As a result, strategically integrating enhancing artificial intelligence technology at various pivotal consumer interaction points holds significant potential for organizations, potentially leading to improved customer satisfaction, employee engagement(Bhardwaj and Kalia, 2021) and overall organizational benefits (Ameen et al., 2021).Artificial intelligence technologies are omnipresent in our daily lives and improve our quality of life. Artificial intelligence's inevitable advancement has already begun to show up in marketing tactics, brand management, and long-term client relationship management. In a world where 4 billion people use the internet, artificial intelligence is practically impossible to ignore.

The term "artificial intelligence," originating from the Turing machines of the 1940s, was coined by Minsky and McCarthy during a 1956 conference on machine intelligence held in the United States. Since then, it has found extensive applications in various domains, including computer hardware and software, computer vision, image and speech recognition in robotics, machine learning, cognitive modeling, information retrieval, search technologies, and game theory. These applications have been widely explored in numerous academic publications, research initiatives, and practical implementations (Gere 2019).

2. ARTIFICIAL INTELLIGENCE AND BIG DATA

Artificial intelligence, which can be termed as both a robot and a phone, automate mundane human tasks, recall things that are elapsed, intelligently summarize complex information, learn from you, and even make suggestions (Gilbert, 1997). Since AI ultimately depends on the data that is provided, it may be crucial for organizations to increase both customer satisfaction and the general health of the company, AI-enabled customer experience solutions that record and model data should be implemented.Big data, machine learning, and potent solutions form the foundation of artificial intelligence's strength. This is where the idea of "big data" comes into play. By making it easier for businesses to gather and organise huge, complicated volumes of data, big data gives organisations the chance to employ more assimilated data. Based on this client self-data, it makes sure that consumers receive the products that correspond to their demands and needs at the appropriate time and location via the appropriate distribution methods.

The 3V model explains big data (Laney, 2001). The *volume* that describes the size, the *variety* of unstructured and semi-structured data unfolding, complicated data, the amount of time it takes to analyse big data and today's most significant aspect is speed or *velocity*.

Machine learning (deep learning) it is a very important aspect which lets the marketers to obtain an advantage over rivals in the market by understanding the logical conclusions from their big data collections and having the authority toentice customers to buy their products. Most crucially, because of this idea of artificial intelligence, firms who use it in their marketing strategies can forecast customer inclinations, track and analyse consumer purchasing behaviour, and forecast the consumer's subsequent purchase behaviour.

Strong solution is the third basic states that in the twenty-first century, when machines and people both understand the world similarly, computers can easily interpret emotions and human communication, find concepts and themes utilizing a multitude of data, and reply to clients in the best way possible.. They can also predict customers' behaviour and decisions and use this information to solve future issues (Dimitrieska, Stankovska, and Efremova, 2018).

2.1 AI and Big Data

Getting as much information about customer behaviors, likes and dislikes, interests, and personal preferences as is currently feasible owing to the internet was not possible ten years ago. Through social network profiles, product reviews, tagged interests, "liked" and shared content, loyalty/rewards apps, and CRM (customer relationship management) software management) systems, and product reviews, insightful data may be contributed to the big data pool.

2.1.1 Collection of Customer Data

The ability of AI to learn is one of its biggest capabilities, regardless of the industry. Its capacity to identify data patterns is only handy if it can acclimate to them as they alter and shift. By identifying outliers in the data, AI can determine if user input is important and make the appropriate corrections.

Big data and AI are seen as being inseparable due to AI's capacity to expertly blend data analytics with AI. Every data input is used by AI machine learning and deep learning, and these inputs are used to create new rules for potential business analytics..

2.1.2 Business Analytics

Big data and AI can mechanize up to 80% of all physical work, 70% of data processing jobs, and 64% of data gathering chores, according to the most recent research, which Forbes reported. This suggests that the two ideas might have a significant influence on the workplace in addition to their contributions to marketing and commercial operations.

For instance, as supply chain and fulfillment operations rely on data substantially, businesses are looking to AI developments to provide them with real-time insights on customer feedback. Businesses can do this by relying on the flow of new information when making marketing, financial, and strategic choices.

In essence, a set procedure for data collecting (mining) and data structure must exist before the data is sent via a machine learning or deep learning algorithm. Corporate data analytics graduates can be of assistance in this case. Analytics derived from data will be highly valued by businesses who are committed to maximizing their worth

2.2 Combining AI and Big Data

AI and big data can work together to deliver better outcomes. The AI engine is initially fed with data to make it smarter. In addition, less human interaction is needed for the AI to work correctly. The less reliant society is on people to manage this ongoing AI/big data cycle, the closer it will be to realizing its full potential.The ultimate objectives of AI, according to software provider XenonStack, are as follows:

- Reasoning
- Automated scheduling and learning
- Computer learning
- Natural language processing, or the capacity to comprehend spoken English,
- Computer vision (the capacity to accurately extract data from a single or a collection of image)

- Robotics
- General Intelligence

These AI disciplines will need colossal volumes of data in order for their AI algorithms to develop. Natural language processing, for instance, would not be thinkable without millions of human voice samples which have been recorded and dissected into a arrangement that AI engines can more readily handle.As more occupations can be automated with AI, big data will endure to grow, and AI as a discipline will grow as extra data is available for learning and analysis.

3. ARTIFICIAL INTELLIGENCE AND CUSTOMER SERVICE

In our daily lives, artificial intelligence's (AI) significance in customer service has greatly increased. Due to AI's ease of use, businesses and customers are already quickly adjusting to the new reality. Artificial intelligence is beneficial in many fields and corrects frequent errors in traditional customer care. Delays in responses, a lack of contact control, and the inability to get assistance outside of regular business hours are the three most frequent issues customers encounter while interacting with customer support. The good news is that AI can easily solve these issues, particularly in the area of customer service. Customers who interact with chatbots are aware that a machine is speaking to them, but they are grateful when the chatbots increase customer service.AI has been used in customer service and it is supposed to improve client satisfaction and result in more engaging client encounters.

According to research published in a paper titled "The CX Journey: Understanding Corporate Strategies and Best Practices," businesses have significantly raised their budgets since 2017 for the use of customer service solutions that are powered by artificial intelligence (AI). According to the data, the proportion of businesses utilising such technology climbed from 17% in 2017 to more than 30% at the end of last year.

However, a separate Gartner survey reveals even more deployment of AI in customer service. As per Gartner research findings following advantages can occur when businesses implement bots and VCAs in their contact centres:

Greater capability and scale: AI bots are better suited to handle the straightforward problems that prompt customers to use self-help in the first place, freeing up support representatives to work on tasks and concerns that are more complicated.

Faster chat speeds: AI chatbots can significantly cut down on customer wait times. For instance, a company's chatbots can answer to customer inquiries in five seconds after the consumer contacts them; compared to the 51 seconds it typically takes for support representatives to respond.

Better gatekeeping: AI bots can be trained to identify other bots attempting to access systems, leaving customer care representatives to concentrate solely on actual consumers.

4. CUSTOMER SERVICE TO NEXT LEVEL

Have you ever wondered what occurs when a client is asked, "On a scale of 0-to-10, how satisfied were you with your customer service experience?" The number that customers select in response to a text or email prompt gives statistics, but that data could not provide decision-makers with any framework to what made the practice wonderful or awful. Was a "0" given because the call centre representative was disappointing, or was it merely because the person had too many unpleasant administrative tasks to complete? A "10" was given as a reflexive show of courtesy, or did exceptional customer service actually take place?

Employing predictive and prescriptive data—what customers need before they even know it themselves—is made possible by artificial intelligence (AI) learning. Furthermore, these pivots can happen instantly across all interactions, not just a sample of them. There are various ways by which business set up AI for customer service like chatbots, augmented messaging, and sentiment analysis, voice Analysis etc.These various(AI) applications are explained in following section.

4.1 Expectation Transfer

Consumers anticipate excellent customer service across firms, a phenomenon called as expectation transfer, based on standard set by leaders across industries. When one important business raises the bar and customers expect that everywhere, expectation transfer occurs.

The three things that customers want most are customization, convenience, and a smooth, trouble-free engagement. No matter what sector a company is in, being able to alter customer perception of an engagement in the moment can be essential for enhancing customer satisfaction and distinguishing service.

Services, however, do not come in a single size. Data may be instantaneously analysed by AI and machine learning, this allows stakeholders to swiftly change their direction and make precise decisions depending on the requirements and services of their organization.

4.2 Amplification in Customer Satisfaction

AI supports customer service in a number of ways, including real-time conversation monitoring, agent feedback, and the use of intelligence to display language, speech patterns, and psychographic profiles to foresee future customer needs. However, automation and AI's capacity for independent learning are at the core of machine learning's true strength.A customer's specific wants can be used by AI to match them with representatives. In order to find the ideal match and the best prospects for downstream automation, AI can expand this power to predict emotion and purpose. And even for those consumers who never speak to a customer care professional directly, this learning may be extended to provide a wonderful experience. AI capabilities enhance customer satisfaction rates by 3.5 times claimed by an Aberdeen Research 2020.

Since AI ultimately depends on the data that is provided, it may be crucial for businesses to execute AI-enabled customer friendly solutions that capture and model data in order to not only improve customer satisfaction but also the overall state of the business.

5. ARTIFICIAL INTELLIGENCE APPLICATIONS IN CUSTOMER SERVICE

Organisations are turning to AI because it bridges the gap as demand for a improved, more personalised consumer experience rises. Increased efficiency throughout the organisation, especially in customer service, is made possible by advances in AI. Although chatbots are still at the vanguard of this transformation, other technologies like interactive voice response systems and machine learning are creating a new paradigm for what customers and customer service employees should anticipate. AI will be crucial to the future of customer service, but not every piece of technology is appropriate for every company. There are various types of technologies which AI uses in the field of customer service like:

Figure 1.
Source: Author's compilation

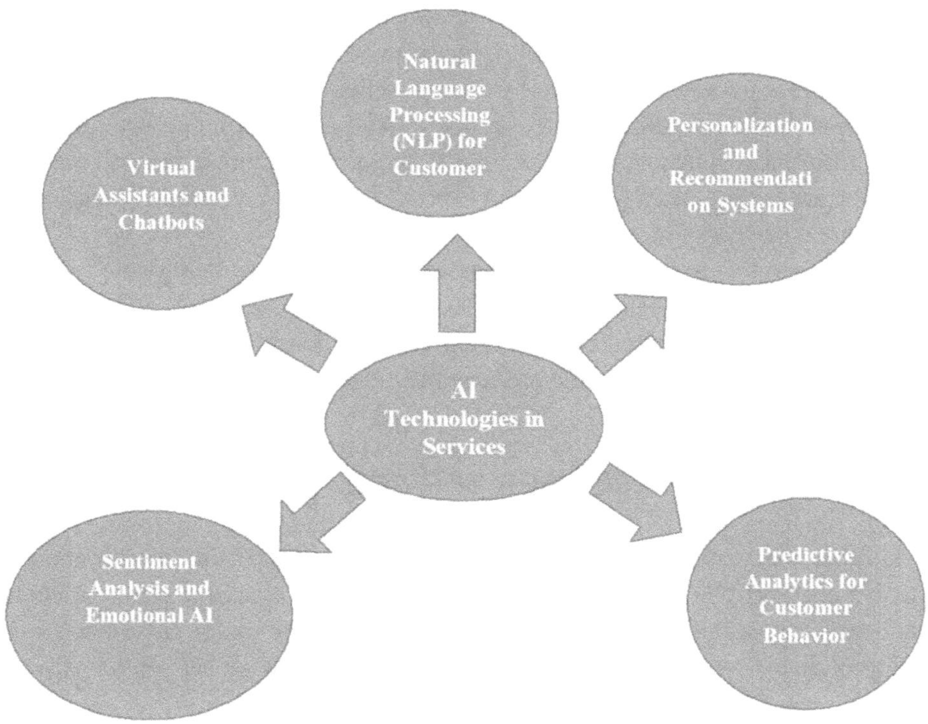

5.1 Virtual Assistants and Chatbots: A virtual assistant chatbot combines a chatbot and a virtual assistant, two different programmes. The fact that both of these programmes are designed to facilitate human communication is the only thing they have in common. Let's examine the fundamental distinctions between chatbots and virtual personal assistants.

Programmes called chatbots are created with the intention of conversing with clients in a manner akin to that of a human. As a result, companies use chatbots to engage with clients (or potential clients) and provide support as needed e.g. "MyGov Corona Helpdesk" In 2020, the MyGov Corona Helpdesk chatbot was launched on WhatsApp to help users dispute misleading information and spread accurate information on COVID-19. Users can use it to find the COVID-19 vaccination facility closest to them, retrieve immunisation records, and get alerts about COVID-19 issues.

5.2 Natural Language Processing (NLP) for Customer Interactions: When talking about artificial intelligence in customer service, we frequently refer to natural language processing (NLP), a subset of machine learning. The goal of NLP, or natural language processing, a segment of artificial intelligence, is to enable robots to read, understand, and infer from human language. For instance, NLP is used by chatbots and personal assistants like Siri and Alexa to understand what users say and respond accordingly.

5.3 Personalization and Recommendation Systems: Personalised suggestions are given to each user by AI-based reference systems, which employ a range of data sources to find patterns and trends. Following that, recommendations for comparable goods or services that the consumer might find interesting are created using this information.AI-based recommendation systems frequently employ the following data sources: Information about the user, such as past shopping habits, click patterns, search terms, and browsing patterns. Item information: This can include things like pricing, reviews, ratings, and product descriptions.

5.4 Sentiment Analysis and Emotional AI: Sentiment analysis is a system that assesses the overall sentiment of text data, including social network posts, reviews, and customer feedback. This can help businesses identify areas for development and learn what clients think about their products and services.

Affective computing—often abbreviated as emotion AI—allows computers to decipher and analyze nonverbal signs from individuals, such as their body language, gestures, and voice tones—in order to ascertain how they are feeling. As a result, visual Emotion AI analyzes facial expressions in images and videos to determine a person's emotional state.

5.5 Predictive Analytics for Customer Behavior: For marketers, being able to accurately foresee customer demands is invaluable. Perhaps in the past, assumptions were effective, but today's world is dominated by data-driven insight obtained by AI and machine learning algorithms. They are capable of doing it much more accurately than people are, and they can even make long-term predictions.

6. AI'S ADVANTAGES IN CUSTOMER SERVICE

The use of AI in customer service has enormous advantages; First and foremost, it's about simplicity and effectiveness. No need for paperwork, a bothersome callback, or a waiting period. Second, AI enables more personalised interactions, which are crucial for dealing with major customer service issues like recovering a forgotten password or cancelling an order. In the following section lets discuss the benefits of AI in customer service.

6.1 Improved Response Time and Availability: Tasks may be quickly automated with the use of AI-driven solutions, which helps organisations cut labour costs while boosting productivity and efficiency. People don't have to wait for an agent to handle their problems because chatbots can respond to simple questions and requests right away. Instead, users can merely request assistance from the chatbot. Employing AI in customer service enables companies to offer clients 24/7 assistance, which is important because it gives customers the flexibility and convenience of receiving support day or night.

6.2 Enhanced Customer Experience and Satisfaction: Machine learning and artificial intelligence work together to collect and analyse social, historical, and behavioural data, giving brands a much better understanding of their clients.AI can analyse client behaviour and data, and it continuously learns and gets improved over time, contrasting conventional data analytics tools. Using such data, it may then project future client behavior. Brands can offer highly relevant information, increase sales, and enhance customer satisfaction with the use of this technology.

6.3 Cost Efficiency and Resource Optimization: There is no restriction on how many virtual agents you can use; it depends on your company's requirements and server power. AI virtual agents can give your consumers all the information they require, from answering simple questions to delivering product insights, freeing up your service representatives to focus on more complicated problems. Due to their improved ability to divert voice volume to other channels, faster average response times, and higher aptitude for resolution rates, AI virtual agents reduce customer support expenses.

6.4 Scalability and Handling Increased Workloads: Scalability is the capacity of the system to expand and manage a growing dataset, workload, or new operations. The scalability of an AI solution determines how reliable it is in producing the results that decide whether a transaction is successful or unsuccessful.

Scalability has a direct impact on your customer service in addition to giving your organisation the security it needs. Transactions do not complete if the system is slow. Fraudulent transactions may need to be manually approved if the system can't handle real-time processing. Additionally, a default may occur if credit risk cannot be accurately detected. Increased transaction speed and quick growth are made possible through scalability.

7. AI CHALLENGES IN CUSTOMER SERVICE

AI-enhanced customer service has benefits and drawbacks of its own. The cost of a human customer care crew may be reduced, and the company may be able to provide customers extra benefits like a quick response time, round-the-clock accessibility, etc. Additionally, if done incorrectly, it might result in a poor user experience and harm your clients. Therefore, it's vital to make a decision about whether to even invest in automation. Fellow challenges of AI are customer services are listed below.

7.1 Trust and Acceptance by Customers: The trust that our consumers have placed in us must be protected and honored as we decide how to deploy AI in customer service. Humans do have flaws, yeah. We make errors because we are biased. But recognising mistakes, clearly communicating why they occurred, and expressing regret are all important components of developing trust. To do it, someone inside the company must be aware of how a bad choice was made.

Trust must be earned over a long period of time, yet it can be lost in an instant. Customer-focused companies that wish to succeed in the age of AI will need to establish their own usage guidelines and be ready to implement only those AI-based technologies that result in reliable, dependable, and consistent customer experiences.

7.2 Maintaining Human Touch and Empathy: Customer experience is vital, especially in a digital call centre. It is definitely possible to use automation and digital platforms while still providing excellent customer care. Chatbots and other artificial intelligence tools just cannot match the personalised experience that human interaction offers. Humans are empathetic communicators who can accurately gauge the emotions of a client to provide the best course of action. In contrast to a chatbot that just responds to a sentence at face value, humans in a digital call centre recognise voice tone, inflection, and emotions.

Humans are also capable of thinking outside the box and coming up with original solutions to a particular customer's issue. For instance, a customer service professional might be aware of a unique offer that would be available shortly and realise they might provide it to the dissatisfied customer to make things right. A person might be familiar with a particular manager who would be extremely sympathetic to this customer's particular circumstance and, as a result of their friendship, refer the consumer directly to senior leadership.

7.3 Data Privacy and Security Concerns: AI systems frequently employ heftyamount of data to train their procedures and improve performance. Sensitive personal information like names, addresses, and financial information might also be included in this information, along with sensitive information like social security numbers and medical records. The gathering and processing of the data may lead to concerns regarding its use and accessibility. The likelihood of data breaches and unauthorized access to personal information are the key privacy worries with AI. There is a chance that the volume of data being collected and processed may be misused due to security flaws or hacking.

7.4 Dealing With Biases in AI Systems: The output of the system is likely to be biased if the data input is biased (Huang & Rust, 2021). For illustration, Amazon discriminates against female job applicants by using the AI tool to assess and rate applicants (Weissman, 2018). Additionally, when premiums are automatically calculated centered around religion rather than gender, AI mistakes happen in insurance firms (Villasenor, 2019). As a result, dynamic pricing and targeted discounts are biased by automated systems (Miler & Hosanagar, 2020; Brit, 2021).As a result, bias can sneak into algorithms, which is only good for systems' preparing data sets (Brit, 2020). Hence dealing with such biases is a huge challenge.

8. ETHICAL CONSIDERATIONS IN AI-POWERED CUSTOMER SERVICE

Despite being the dominant topic of conversation in the media adjacent field, the influence that artificial intelligence can have on employment loss is frequently misunderstood. Change has always accompanied disruption and evolution, and in this case, it is manifesting as a change in the types of occupations that are in demand in the market. More people will be working in these industries to replace the older ones as a result of the daily growth and adaptability requirements of AI.Similar to that, one of the greatest fears in this field has been privacy issues including data protection, privacy, and security.Following are some essential ideas to aid with AI ethics in customer service.

8.1 Transparency: AI systems must be used in customer service in a transparent manner, with explicit justifications provided for any judgments or suggestions they make. Customers should remainalert that they are dealing with artificial intelligence (AI)-enabled systems, and companies ought to be able to properly clarify how AI said technology functions, what data it consumes, and how it affects client experience.

8.2 Fairness in AI Algorithms: These systems should be constructed with evenhandedness in mind, which means that biases that can result in discrimination or unequal treatment of customers must be avoided. Both with regard to the data used for the purpose of training and the results produced, it is critical to constantly examine AI models or algorithms for potential biases. Mitigation methods, such as varied and representative training datasets and continual monitoring, can assist resolve biases and maintain fairness.

8.3 Privacy and Data Protection: Businesses must prioritise protecting consumer privacy and adhere to applicable data protection laws. It is crucial to handle client data securely when integrating AI in customer service and to have their explicit agreement before collecting, storing, or using their data in any form. This means that in order to prevent unlawful access to or misuse of user data, privacy measures should be considered while designing AI systems.

8.4 Responsibility and Accountability: The continual monitoring and appraisal of the AI systems installed is necessary to ensure adherence to ethical standards when adopting AI ethics in customer service. Excluding AI algorithms and processes from routine audits, testing, and reviews can aid in identifying and resolving any potential ethical issues or unintended repercussions.

9. A FEW REAL-WORLD EXAMPLES OF AI-DRIVEN CUSTOMER SERVICE

Additional examples of how businesses are coming up with inventive uses for AI to improve customer service and the complete customer experience are shown below:

Airline Delta

In 2018, Delta Air Lines and U.S. Customs and Border Protection (CBP) collaborated to offer customers traveling straight to an overseas destination out of particular U.S. airports with a distinctive biometrics boarding service.

This is how it functions:

- CBP receives a customer manifest from Delta for every flight and uses that manifest to produce a photo gallery.
- Customers who choose to participate in the programme have their pictures captured at airport checkpoints, and then the encrypted, de-identified pictures are sent via a secure CBP channel to be compared to the flight manifest gallery.
- After CBP has confirmed the customer's identity, it transmits confirmation and a boarding signal back to Delta.
- Customers are free to go to their final destination after CBP updates its records of who has left the country.

Domino's Pizza

The chatbot among chatbots, Domino's Dom is distinctive. In addition to providing answers to frequently asked questions, this voice-activated pizza ordering assistant streamlines the process by keeping track of previous client orders and leveraging data integration to precisely determine delivery timeframes. The greatest part is that Dom monitors each pizza's development both during preparation and after it is distributed for delivery, providing clients with real-time updates so they are never anxious about when their order will arrive.

The Muse

To enhance its marketing plan, The Muse, a well-known employment and recruitingonline portal for Millennials, teamed with Blueshift, a provider of a CDP+ marketing automation platform. The two companies work together to leverage AI and predictive analytics to create highly personalized email messages based on user past behaviors and features. The Muse's website had a 200% increase in traffic to selected pages as a result of these complex, multi-triggered campaigns that targeted different user engagements throughout multiple catalogues and sections.

India's First-ever WhatsApp Commerce Solution by JioMart

JioMart, a major player in Indian e-commerce, used WhatsApp mostly for customer service. However, it aimed to take a giant step forward by offering the "most exceptional shopping experience" on the platform, catering to more than 10 million people each month and increasing conversion rates. After all, the business is providing the first WhatsApp commerce solution ever offered in India! JioMart's goals included enhancing customer experience throughout the purchase process and maximising WhatsApp chatbot usage.In order to do this, the business introduced chat-based search, which enables customers to look up things by speaking with WhatsApp's AI assistant. The function personalizes the suggestions based on the user's pincode in addition to displaying products based on user inquiries.

MyGov Corona Helpdesk Chatbot

The COVID-19 epidemic trembled the world. During the calamity, people needed to have access to reliable and accurate information on the coronavirus. The same objective inspired the development of MyGov Corona Helpdesk, the official chatbot of the Government of Indian. The WhatsApp chatbot gives advise, proposes safety measures, and distributes the most recent Ministry of Health apprises and recommends in addition to responding to COVID-19 queries. The WhatsApp chatbot was accessible in Hindi too to increase its audience. As the statewide vaccination drive got begun, the chatbot was improved to assist millions of Indians to schedule vaccination slots and get their immunization certificates.

Railway Food Order and Delivery by Zoop India

On their train journeys, travellers often struggle to find high-quality food. That is no longer necessary thanks to Zoop India's WhatsApp chatbot service, which enables passengers on Indian trains to have their food deliveries made right to their seats. Passengers can text Zoop's WhatsApp chatbot and submit their 10-digit PNR number to have the chatbot recognise their seat or berth immediately.

Then, the passengers will be asked to choose the station where they want their food to be ordered and delivered. They can select a restaurant, place their order, and finish the payment procedure all using the app. Passengers can monitor the progress of their orders after confirmation.

Borosil Virtual Assistant

Although buying cookware can appear simple, it's actually rather complicated. The fact that there are multiple variants is sometimes a surprise to people. Borosil has set up an Intelligent Virtual Assistant to speed up the laborious process of surfing through various web sites and assist users in finding what they're searching for in the fewest number of steps. The assistant also helps with warranty registration and post-sale support.

Dr. Lal PathLabs Virtual Assistant

Health has assumed a prominent role since the beginning of a global pandemic three years ago. Additionally, a growing percentage of consumers nowadays favor online medical care over in-person treatment. The Dr.Lal PathLabs intelligent chatbot may assist customers with identifying the nearest center, tracking reports, and other COVID-related information. Additionally, it offers guidance on the various tests and their prices.

EVA by HDFCs

To explore a financial website with all of its features requires effort. Getting even the most fundamental it appears like a big job that will take a while to finish the specifics. Since the advent of EVA (Electronic Virtual Assistant), India's first and largest AI-backed banking chatbot, HDFC has freed its customers from pointless browsing, repetitive clicks, and lengthy hold times.

Customers can contact EVA anytime they need information about their accounts, cards, or any other service they have enrolled in or are interested in. It provides assistance with submitting grievances, paying bills, and much more. It can be accessed on Google Assistant and Amazon Echo devices.

To Sum Up

As ChatGPT demonstrates how potent new generative AI capabilities are, AI is almost certain to become an even more effective tool in customer support in the future. Businesses are naturally motivated to implement AI in customer service since it offers customers quicker and occasionally better service. In addition, it avoids the additional costs and inconveniences associated with having to find, hire, and manage human workers. There are also challenges and ethical issues related to AI in customer service which needs to dealt with utmost care. Future researchers can empirically investigate the role of AI in Customer Experience and can also link it with other dimensions of intelligence such as emotional intelligence, social intelligence and cultural intelligence (Bhardwaj, 2022) in national and cross-national contexts. Thus, we can conclude that AI can definitely bring customer satisfaction and delight to next level.

REFERENCES

Aguiar-Costa, L. M., Cunha, C. A., Silva, W. K., & Abreu, N. R. (2022). Customer satisfaction in service delivery with artificial intelligence: A meta-analytic study. *RAM. Revista de Administração Mackenzie*, *23*(6), 23. doi:10.1590/1678-6971/eramd220003.en

Ameen, N., Tarhini, A., Reppel, A., & Anand, A. (2021). Customer experiences in the age of artificial intelligence. *Computers in Human Behavior*, *114*, 106548. doi:10.1016/j.chb.2020.106548 PMID:32905175

Bhardwaj, B. (2021). *Short-term foreign trips correlates of the four factors model of cultural intelligence*. Rajagiri Management Journal. doi:10.1108/RAMJ-01-2021-0008

Bhardwaj, B., & Kalia, N. (2021). *Contextual and task performance: role of employee engagement and organizational culture in hospitality industry*. Vilakshan-XIMB Journal of Management. doi:10.1108/XJM-08-2020-0089

Brit, P. (2020). Overcoming Bias Requires an AI Reboot. Speech Technology, 25(2), 14–17.

Brit, P. (2021). *Tips for battling bias in ai-based personalization*. https://www.destinationcrm.com/Articles/Editorial/Magazine-Features/Tips-for-Battling-Bias-in-AI-Based-Personalization-147143.aspx

Dimitrieska, S., Stankovska, A., & Efremova, T. (2018). Artificial intelligence and marketing. *Entrepreneurship*, *6*(2), 298–304.

Evans, M. (2019). Build A 5-Star Customer Experience with Artificial Intelligence. *Forbes*.

Gilbert, N. (1997). A simulation of the structure of academic science. *Sociological Research Online*, *2*(2), 91–105. doi:10.5153ro.85

Huang, M. H., & Rust, R. T. (2021). A strategic framework for artificial intelligence in marketing. *Journal of the Academy of Marketing Science*, *49*(1), 30–50. doi:10.100711747-020-00749-9

Laney, D. (2001). 3D Data management: Controlling data volume, velocity and variety. Meta Group. *Lakshen, Guma Abdulkhader*, 1-4.

McLean, G., & Osei-Frimpong, K. (2019). Hey Alexa… examine the variables influencing the use of artificial intelligent in-home voice assistants. *Computers in Human Behavior*, *99*, 28–37. doi:10.1016/j.chb.2019.05.009

Miller, A., & Hosanagar, K. (2020). *Personalized discount targeting with causal machine learning*. Academic Press.

Sharma, D., Chaudhary, M., Jaswal, N., & Bhardwaj, B. (2022). Hiding Behind The SWOT: Gender Equality and COVID-19. *Journal of Positive School Psychology*, 730–740.

Varsha, P. S. (2023). How can we manage biases in artificial intelligence systems–A systematic literature review. *International Journal of Information Management Data Insights*, *3*(1), 100165.

Villasenor, J. (2019). *Artificial intelligence and bias: Four key challenges*. Academic Press.

Yeğin, T. (2020). The place and future of artificial intelligence in marketing strategies. *Ekev Akademi Dergisi*, (81), 489–506.

APPENDIX

Webliography

https://aisel.aisnet.org/icis2020/digital_commerce/digital_commerce/7

https://brighterion.com/why-scalable-ai-matters-for-your-growth-and-decision-speed/

https://economictimes.indiatimes.com/news/how-to/ai-and-privacy-the-privacy-concerns-surrounding-ai-its-potential-impact-on-personal-data/articleshow/99738234.cms?from=mdr

https://global.hitachi-solutions.com/blog/ai-customer-service-trends/#:~:text=The%20truth%20is%20AI%2Denabled,priority%20and%20more%20complex%20issues.

https://hirehoratio.com/horatio-insights/the-ethics-of-ai-in-customer-experience-balancing-automation-with-human-touch/

https://levity.ai/blog/ai-for-customer-support

https://livevox.com/how-do-ai-virtual-agents-lower-customer-service-costs/#gref

https://maxicus.com/importance-of-artificial-intelligence-in-customer-service/

https://online.maryville.edu/blog/big-data-is-too-big-without-ai/

https://pathmonk.com/artificial-intelligence-improve-customer-experience/#:~:text=AI%2Dpowered%20chatbots%20can%20provide,increased%20customer%20satisfaction%20and%20retention.

https://spd.group/artificial-intelligence/ai-for-customer-behavior-analysis/

https://techcrunch.com/sponsor/nice/how-ai-brings-customer-service-to-the-next-level/

https://viso.ai/deep-learning/visual-emotion-ai-recognition/

https://www.analyticsinsight.net/top-5-government-apps-that-use-ai-chatbots-to-help-users/#:~:text=%E2%80%9CAadhaar%20Mitra%2C%E2%80%9D%20an%20AI,on%20the%20official%20UIDAI%20website.

https://www.cmswire.com/customer-experience/4-ways-that-ai-is-improving-the-customer-experience/

https://www.computer-talk.com/blogs/how-to-maintain-a-human-touch-while-embracing-customer-service-automation

https://www.freshworks.com/freshdesk/customer-engagement/virtual-assistant-chatbot-blog/

https://www.haptik.ai/blog/10-best-ai-chatbots-in-india

https://www.helpscout.com/blog/trust-ai-and-customer-service
/

https://www.linkedin.com/pulse/look-how-ai-based-recommendat
ion-systems-changing-e-commerce--1f#:~:text=AI%2Dbased%20rec
ommendation%20systems%20use,user%20might%20be%20interested%2
0in.

https://www.morphcast.com/sentiment-analysis-vs-emotion-ai-u
nderstanding-the-differences/

https://www.phonexia.com/blog/benefits-of-artificial-intelli
gence-in-customer-service/

https://www.techtarget.com/searchcustomerexperience/feature/
10-examples-of-AI-in-customer-service

Chapter 16
Exploring the Efficacy of Artificial Intelligence Techniques in Predicting Stock Market Trends

Shantnu Sood
Himachal Pradesh University, India

Yashwant Kumar Gupta
Himachal Pradesh University, India

Puneet Bhushan
https://orcid.org/0009-0006-9114-8781
Himachal Pradesh University, India

ABSTRACT

Stock price prediction is a challenging task, traditionally relying on fundamental, technical, and time series analysis. However, AI and ML techniques offer new opportunities for enhancing predictions in equity markets. In recent years, considerable efforts have been made to identify these patterns in stock markets, with the aim of facilitating profitable trading and investment decisions. Consequently, a wealth of studies and research endeavors have emerged in this field. This chapter explores diverse techniques used for stock market prediction, analyzing their effectiveness. The techniques examined in this study are categorized into three groups: traditional ML, deep learning, and sentiment analysis. Results show naive Bayesian and random forests as promising conventional ML models, while LSTM neural network provides accurate predictions among deep learning models. This chapter sheds light on the employed and researched ML models, offering insights into their strengths in forecasting market trends.

DOI: 10.4018/979-8-3693-0418-1.ch016

1. INTRODUCTION

The stock market has captivated the interest of investors, academicians and other market participants for a long time due to its dynamic and unpredictable nature coupled with rapid price movements. These characteristics lead to considerable challenges to those that are trying to make informed investment decisions. The fascinating yet complex dynamics of the stock market result from its multifaceted ecosystem, which includes a wide range of actors, information sources, emotional factors, and external factors. This ecosystem creates a constantly changing and unpredictable landscape, characterised by a low signal-to-noise ratio, which frequently takes the form of nonlinear phenomena.

As a result, academics, researchers, and practitioners have shown an increasing interest in employing machine learning (ML) techniques for research in the field of finance in recent years. Due to the use of non-linear activation functions, which are good at capturing complicated data correlations that the linear models might not be able to perceive successfully, ML models have the potential to extract signals from data laden with noise. Additionally, unlike linear models, ml models do not have multicollinearity problems, a significant problem in the analysis of financial data.

This paper's goal is to give a thorough overview of ML methods used in stock market forecasting. This research examines the approaches employed by scholars and industry experts to discuss the advantages and disadvantages of stock market forecasting using ML algorithms.

The main objective of this research is to gain an understanding of this field. The study examines algorithms with the intention of offering insights, to investors and financial institutions.

In order to predict stock market trends numerous machine learning methods have been utilized. For instance in a study by Li et al. (2018) they employed a network model to estimate changes, in stock prices using historical trading data. Their approach yielded short term price predictions. In another study (Goh et al., 2020) looked at how well Long Short Term Memory (LSTM) networks predicted stock market volatility, LSTM networks outperformed traditional econometric models.

As a result, the objective of this review paper is to provide a thorough study of the state of machine learning (ML) algorithms for stock market prediction. Through a critical examination of methodologies, challenges, and opportunities, the study hopes to contribute to the advancement of this field and facilitate the development of more accurate and robust models for stock market prediction.

The proposed paper is structured in the following way Section 1 - Introduction, Section 2 -Methodology discusses some of the most prominent machine learning techniques as well as metrics used to evaluate them, Section 3 - Literature Review provides an overview of the various research works done in this field, Section - 4 is about results and discussion, and Section - 5 concludes the paper and outlines the future scope of work.

2. METHODOLOGY

I. Traditional Machine Learning Techniques

Predictive modelling and pattern identification in many domains have long been built on the foundation of traditional machine learning approaches. The following is a discussion of some of the methods used in this area:

i. **Linear regression** is a supervised learning approach that establishes a linear relationship between input characteristics and a continuous target variable. By fitting a line to the data, it captures the underlying trend and enables predictions of the target variable for new instances. The coefficients of the linear regression equation can be calculated using ordinary least squares or gradient descent algorithm. Linear regression is widely employed in fields like economics, finance, and social sciences to forecast outcomes based on historical data.
ii. Another supervised learning technique is **logistic regression**, which is usually utilised for binary classification issues. Based on a logistic function, it evaluates the likelihood of a sample belonging to a specific class. The algorithm fits a decision boundary that separates the two classes in the feature space. By calculating the odds ratio, logistic regression quantifies the influence of input features on the outcome. Logistic regression finds extensive applications in areas such as medical diagnosis, fraud detection, and sentiment analysis.
iii. **Decision Trees** are versatile and interpretable models used for classification as well as regression problems. They hierarchically split the feature space based on conditions or features, enabling the construction of a tree-like structure. Every internal node represents a decision based on specific factors, leading to further splits until reaching the leaf nodes, which correspond to the predicted class or value. Decision trees are widely employed in various domains due to their simplicity and interpretability.
iv. The probabilistic method **Naive Bayes** is centred on the Bayes theorem. It presumes feature independence and computes the posterior likelihood of a class given the input features using prior probabilities and conditional probabilities. Naive Bayes is useful in a variety of tasks such as tasks related to classification of text, filtering spam mails, and sentiment analysis, where the assumption of independence holds true.
v. **Support Vector Machines (SVM)** are supervised learning models that are used for classification and regression problems. SVMs try to find an ideal hyperplane that separates various classes with the greatest possible margin. SVMs can handle difficult decision boundaries by mapping data points into a high-dimensional feature space. They are well-known for their capacity to deal with high-dimensional data and nonlinear interactions using kernel functions.
vi. **K-Nearest Neighbors (KNN)** is a straightforward yet powerful non-parametric technique for classification and regression tasks. It classifies new instances in the feature space based on the majority class of their K nearest neighbours. KNN identifies the nearest neighbours using proximity measurements such as Euclidean distance or cosine similarity. It is frequently employed in pattern recognition and recommendation systems.

II. Deep Learning

Deep learning, a field within machine learning, trains neural networks with multiple layers unlike a single layer neural network, to learn complex patterns hidden deep within data. Neural networks, are made of a network of nodes (neurons) organized in layers.

Deep learning has garnered a tremendous amount of attention and has attained extraordinary success in fields such as computer vision, NLP, and speech recognition. The key characteristics of deep learning include its ability to automatically learn hierarchical representations from raw data and its capacity to handle large-scale datasets.

Table 1. Comparison of traditional machine learning techniques

Model Type	Linear Regression	Logistic Regression	Decision Trees	Naïve Bayes	SVM	k-Nearest Neighbors
Type of Learning	Supervised (Regression)	Supervised (Classification)	Supervised (Classification/ Regression)	Supervised (Classification)	Supervised (Classification/ Regression)	Supervised (Classification)
Model Type	Linear	Linear	Non-linear (Tree)	Probabilistic (Generative)	Non-linear (Hyperplane)/Linear	Non-linear (Instance-based)
Use Cases	Predict numeric values	Binary classification, probability estimation	Classification, Regression	Classification	Classification	Classification, Regression
Scalability	Generally scales well	Scales well	Scales well	Scales well	Scales well	Scales well
Handling Categorical Variables	Requires encoding categorical variables	Requires encoding categorical variables	Can handle categorical variables directly	Requires encoding categorical variables	Can handle categorical variables directly	Requires one-hot encoding or other techniques
Complexity and Overfitting	Prone to underfitting and simple models	Less prone to overfitting	Prone to overfitting	Prone to overfitting	Prone to overfitting	Prone to overfitting
Hyperparameter Tuning	Few hyperparameters to tune	Few hyperparameters to tune	Hyperparameters include tree depth, criterion, etc.	Hyperparameter: Smoothing parameter (Laplace or other)	Hyperparameters include kernel type, C, gamma, etc.	Hyperparameter: Number of neighbors (k)
Data Requirements	Works with both small and large datasets	Works with both small and large datasets	Works with both small and large datasets	Works with both small and large datasets	Works well with small datasets	Works with both small and large datasets
Performance on High-Dimensional Data	May not perform well on high-dimensional data	May not perform well on high-dimensional data	May suffer from curse of dimensionality	May require feature selection or dimensionality reduction	Works well with high-dimensional data when using kernel methods	Suffers from curse of dimensionality

Source: Authors' Compilation

i. The classification of images and the detection of objects are two computer vision tasks that frequently employ **convolutional neural networks (CNNs)**. CNNs employ convolutional layers that convolve input images with learnable filters, enabling them to capture local spatial patterns and invariant features.
ii. **Recurrent neural networks (RNNs)** are built to handle sequential data and have memory that allows them to retain information over time. They have been found useful in processes including time series analysis, speech recognition, and natural language processing. The vanishing gradient problem is addressed with the Long Short-Term Memory (LSTM) and Gated Recurrent Units (GRUs) versions of RNNs, which make it easier to capture long-term dependencies.

Table 2. Comparison of deep learning techniques

Model Type	Convolutional Neural Networks (CNNs)	Recurrent Neural Networks (RNNs)	Generative Adversarial Networks (GANs)
Architecture Type	Specialized for grid-like data (images)	Specialized for sequential data	Comprised of a generator and discriminator
Use Cases	Image and video analysis, computer vision	Natural language processing, time series	Image generation, style transfer, data augmentation
Handling High-Dimensional Data	Handles high-dimensional data efficiently	Handles sequential data naturally	Handles high-dimensional data efficiently
Interpretability	Features can be visualized in convolutional layers	Sequential patterns can be visualized	Interpretability is challenging
Complexity and Overfitting	Complex, may require regularization	Complex, may require regularization	Complex, may require regularization
Training Time	Long training times	Long training times	Long training times
Scalability	Scales with increased model size	Scales with sequence length	Scales with increased model complexity
Hyperparameter Tuning	Hyperparameters include architecture, kernel size, etc.	Hyperparameters include architecture, dropout, etc.	Hyperparameters include network structure, learning rates, etc.
Data Requirements	Requires labeled image data	Requires sequential data with labeled sequences	Requires large amounts of data
Performance on High-Dimensional Data	Well-suited for grid-like data such as images	Well-suited for sequential data such as text and time series	Well-suited for high-dimensional data such as images
Handling Long Sequences	Limited ability to handle very long sequences	Suitable for long sequences with gated units (LSTM, GRU)	Limited ability to handle very long sequences
Generative Capabilities	Mainly used for feature extraction and classification	Used for sequence generation and prediction	Specifically designed for data generation and manipulation
Applications	Image classification, object detection, style transfer	Language modeling, sentiment analysis, speech recognition	Image generation, super-resolution, anomaly detection
Training Challenges	Requires large labeled datasets	Suffers from vanishing/ exploding gradients	GAN training stability and mode collapse
Interactions Between Data Points	Typically independent (convolutions)	Sequential interactions between data points	Generates data by modeling probability distributions

Source: Authors' Compilation

iii. A generator and a discriminator are the two parts of the neural network architecture known as **generative adversarial networks (GANs)**. GANs acquire the ability to create fresh data samples that resemble training data.

III. Error Metrics

i. **MAPE** stands for mean absolute percentage error, which is a relative measure that scales MAD to be in percentage units rather than the variable's units. MAPE is a measure of relative error that makes use absolute values to block positive and negative errors from cancelling each other out to evaluate forecast accuracy across time-series models.

MAPE = Σ|(Actual - Forecast)/Actual| / n

ii. **Accuracy** is a measure of how well a machine learning model predicts the correct result for a given input. The accuracy is determined by dividing the number of correct predictions by the total number of predictions made. For example if a model makes 100 predictions and 80 of them turn out to be true then the accuracy would be 80%.

Accuracy = (TP + TN) / (TP + TN + FP + FN)

iii. **The F score** represents a measure of how a model performs by combining precision and recall. It is calculated as the harmonic mean of precision and recall.

F-Score = 2 * (precision * recall) / (precision + recall)

where:

Precision refers to the proportion of predicted instances that're actually positive.

Recall represents the proportion of actual positive instances that are correctly predicted as positive.

The F score is a metric for assessing the effectiveness of a model as it considers both precision and recall. Precision measures the accuracy of the model while recall gauges its comprehensiveness. A high F score signifies that the model is not only accurate but also complete. The F score finds application, in evaluating classification models, which are designed to predict whether an instance belongs to a specific class or not.

iv. **Recall** is the fraction of actual positive instances that are predicted positive.

Recall = TP / (TP + FN)

where:

TP = True Positives

FN = False Negatives

True Positives refer to values that the model accurately predicted as positive. On the hand False Negatives are values that were mistakenly identified as negative. Recall is a metric used to evaluate the performance of a model by assessing how effectively it identifies instances. It is determined as the proportion of correctly detected positive instances to total positive instances.

For example, if a model makes 100 predictions and correctly identifies 90 of the positive instances, the recall would be 90%. Recall is a helpful measure of model performance since it accounts for the number of positive cases missed by the model. A high recall value shows that the model is effective at detecting positive events. Recall is often used to evaluate the performance of binary classification models. Binary classification models are models that are used to predict whether an instance belongs to a particular class or not.

3. REVIEW OF LITERATURE

Traditional Machine Learning Models

Support vector machines (SVM's) were employed by (Marković et al., 2014) to forecast the Belex15 index's trend. As input features, six variables - closing price, % change in index value from previous trading day, open price, high price, low price, and trading volume—were used. In contrast to the random walk model's hit rate of 0.500, the SVM model's hit rate was .5516.

These were also utilised by (Tripathy, n.d.) to forecast the S&P BSE TECK index closing price. The study's findings showed that after the 2008 financial crisis, the average prediction accuracy was 60.2%. According to the study, SVM models perform better at making predictions in the short- and medium-term than they do in the long-term.

In order to anticipate stock market behaviour, the writers of (Kumar et al., 2018) researched the behaviour of the share market and selected the model of best fit from a variety of traditional ml methods, including RF, SVM, Naive Bayes, KNN, and Softmax. The data was collected from many different data sources, including Yahoo, NSE-India, and several technical analysis indicators were applied to the data as the authors concluded their comparative examination of these methodologies. The study found that Naive Bayesian has the highest accuracy for small datasets while RF provided the most adequate results for comparatively larger datasets.

The stock price trend prediction technique put forward by (Zhang et al., 2018) is capable of foreseeing changes in the stock price as well as its interval of growth (or drop) rate within predetermined prediction durations. In order to categorise several scrips into the four primary classifications (up, down, flat, and unknown) based on the shapes of their close prices, they trained a random forest model using historical data from the Shenzhen Growth Enterprise Market (China). Their analysis reveals that the suggested approach is resilient to market volatility and beats several current prediction techniques in terms of accuracy and return per trade.

Deep Learning Models

Deep learning models have drawn a lot of interest and demonstrated promising results in a number of industries, including banking. Deep learning models are highly suited for applications such as financial time series forecasting, risk assessment, portfolio management, fraud detection, and sentiment analysis due to their capacity to automatically learn and extract complex patterns from large-scale financial data.

For learning feed-forward neural networks, Asadi et al. (2016) suggested a model that combines data pre-processing techniques, genetic algorithms, and the Levenberg-Marquardt (LM) algorithm. By using it to forecast stock prices for several stock exchanges, including Taiwan Stock Exchange, Tehran Stock Exchange index, and other indices of Tehran Stock Exchange, such as top 50 Companies index, Industry index, and Financial Group index, the suggested method's potential is tested. According to the study's findings, the model is consistently superior to the Random Walk (RW) model.

Fathali et al. (2022) developed a model utilising three distinct deep learning algorithms—RNN, LSTM, and CNN to predict the stock returns of the Nifty 50 index, and found that the LSTM model performs the best.

Dey et al. (2016) investigated a distinctive approach called Extreme Gradient Boosting (XGBoost) and made the comparison of its results to SVM and ANN, finding that it outperformed both. This method has only been tested on two stocks, and given that Yahoo's stock prediction accuracy is 99%, the model seems to be overfitting.

Bao et al. (2017) for the purpose of identifying and taking advantage of the underlying patterns in financial time series data, the research suggests an architecture that combines stacked autoencoders and LSTM. In order to learn high-level representations of the input data, reduce dimensionality, and extract pertinent features, stacked autoencoders are used as a pre-training phase. An LSTM network is then fed the encoded representations derived from the autoencoders for sequential modelling and prediction. The researchers compare the performance of their proposed framework to more established machine learning models like Support Vector Regression (SVR) and Multi-Layer Perceptron (MLP) using tests on various financial datasets, including stock price data.

The outcomes show that, in terms of prediction accuracy, the deep learning framework including stacked autoencoders and LSTM surpasses the conventional machine learning models.

In order to anticipate stock prices, Kim & Han (2000) proposed combining an ANN technique with a genetic algorithm (GA). Here, the GA was used to discretize the feature space in addition to optimising the model parameters. Additionally, Qiu & Song (2016) improved an ANN for predicting the direction of the price of the Japanese stock index using GA. In the area of stock market forecasting, Ebadati E. & Mortazavi T. (2018) additionally laid out a similar strategy (GA + ANN).

Sentiment Analysis

In the context of the stock market, sentiment analysis entails the use of natural language processing (NLP) methods to examine textual data, such as financial news, social media posts, and company reports, in order to extract sentiment-related information that could influence stock prices or investor behaviour.

Sentiment analysis in the stock market is to evaluate the general attitude or mood of market participants towards a specific stock, business, or market. Researchers and investors use sentiment analysis to learn more about market sentiment trends, market responses to breaking news, and prospective adjustments in investor sentiment that could affect stock prices.

Researchers and investors can learn more about market sentiment, market patterns, and possible market responses to news or events by combining sentiment analysis into stock market study. Making more educated investment decisions is possible with the help of this information, which may be used to supplement conventional financial analyses.

Bollen et al. (2011) tried to correlate the DJIA prices with collective mood states derived from large scale twitter feeds and concluded that among the 7 observed mood dimensions only some are granger causative of the DJIA. They achieved an accuracy of 86.7%.

Mizumoto et al. (2012) focuses on using semi-supervised learning algorithms to conduct sentiment analysis on news related to the stock market. The challenge of sentiment analysis, which entails identifying the sentiment expressed in textual data, is discussed in the study. The authors suggest using semi-supervised learning to analyse the tone of stock market-related news stories. In semi-supervised learning, classification performance is enhanced by combining a smaller labelled dataset with a larger unlabelled dataset. The researchers combine semi-supervised methods with well-known machine learning algorithms like Naive Bayes and Support Vector Machines.

They make use of the substantial volume of unlabelled news data to discover new features that can improve the precision of sentiment classification. Real-world stock market news stories were used in the experiments, with each article's sentiment being categorised as positive, negative, or neutral. The performance of the semi-supervised strategy is contrasted with that of a supervised approach that only uses labelled data. The results demonstrate that the semi-supervised learning approach outperforms the supervised approach in terms of sentiment analysis accuracy. By leveraging the unlabelled data to augment the feature representation, the model gains a better understanding of sentiment patterns, leading to improved sentiment classification performance.

Based on Bollen et al. (2011) research, Mittal et al. (2012) offered their strategy. Their study differs from that of Velay & Daniel (2018) in that they used a larger dataset and discovered that even "happiness" is a reliable predictor of DJIA prices. In addition, they devised a straightforward portfolio approach that works well and used K-fold sequential cross-validation, which is appropriate for financial data. But compared to the accuracy Bollen et al. (2011) had achieved, the accuracy was less.

A sentiment analysis model was proposed by Kalyanaraman et al. (2014) that would analyse news stories for sentiments and output the results to two independent machine learning algorithms. The authors obtained news for a variety of companies by utilising the Bing API. The words in the article were evaluated against the dictionary for positive and negative meanings, as well as frequency. If a poor word appeared three times in the piece, it would receive a -3 score. The model's output was then fed into a linear regression model. The ML model predicted actual stock prices with an accuracy of 81.82%.

Carosia et al. (2019) conducted numerous experiments using various machine learning approaches to investigate the influence of social media attitudes (in tweets) on the Brazilian stock market.

Huang & Liu (2019) employed chip indications, social media reviews and responses as study data to construct a sentiment-based stock forecasting model. According to the data, there is a link between mood ratings and stock price changes.

Table 3. A comparison of algorithms and their performance in predicting stock prices

Category	Algorithm	Metrics Used
Traditional Machine Learning	Support Vector Machines vs Random Walk Model (Markovic et al. 2014)	Hit Ratio - 0.5516 vs 0.5
	Support Vector Machines (Tripathy, n.d.)	Accuracy - 60.2%
	Support Vector Machines (Kumar et al., 2018)	Accuracy/F-Score - 67.16%/75.98%
	Naive Bayes (Kumar et al., 2018)	Accuracy/F-Score - 70.80%/60.42%
	K-Nearest Neighbour (KNN) (Kumar et al., 2018)	Accuracy/F-Score - 65.56%/77.00%
	Softmax (Kumar et al., 2018)	Accuracy/F-Score - 57.80%/64.74%
	Random Forest (RF) (Kumar et al., 2018)	Accuracy/F-Score - 72.36%/80.55%
	XG Boost (Dey et al., 2016)	Accuracy - 85% to 99% (Overfitting)
Deep Learning	PELMNN (Taiwan Stock Exchange) (Asadi et al., 2016)	MAPE - 0.51
	WSAEs - LSTM (Bao et al., 2017)	MAPE - 0.011
	WLSTM (Bao et al., 2017)	MAPE - 0.014
	LSTM (Bao et al., 2017)	MAPE - 0.020
	RNN (Bao et al., 2017)	MAPE - 0.033
	LSTM (Velay & Daniel, 2018)	Recall - 0.97
	2D CNN (Velay & Daniel, 2018)	Recall - 0.73
	1D CNN (Velay & Daniel, 2018)	Recall - 0.64
Sentiment Analysis	Self-Organizing Fuzzy Neural Network (Bollen et al., 2011)	Accuracy - 87.6%
	Self-Organizing Fuzzy Neural Network (Bollen et al., 2011)	Accuracy - 75%
	Linear Regression Model (Kalyanaraman et al., 2014)	Accuracy - 81.82%

Source: Authors' Compilation

4. RESULTS AND DISCUSSION

Although machine learning techniques, both traditional and deep learning, show promise in making stock market predictions, there remain certain challenges that can affect the predictive power of these techniques. To begin, the quality of data is critical to the effectiveness of any ML algorithm. Financial data can be noisy, incomplete, and prone to errors, which can impact the accuracy of predictions (López de Prado, 2018). Additionally, the quantity of data also plays a significant role in the effectiveness of ML algorithms. Unfortunately, financial data is often limited in comparison to other types of data, posing a challenge for stock market prediction tasks.

In the research studies discussed in this paper, an important challenge that emerges is related to the accuracy scores achieved by machine learning models. While several studies have reported relatively high accuracy scores, typically ranging from 60% to 80% (as seen in works of Tripathy, n.d.; Kumar et al., 2018; Bollen et al., 2011; Kalyanaraman et al., 2014), it's crucial to recognize that these scores may not necessarily translate into profitable investing or trading strategies.

Furthermore, some of the studies that attained these high accuracy scores faced a critical issue: severe overfitting, as demonstrated by Dey et al. (2016). When models perform extraordinarily well on training data yet struggle to generalise to new, previously unseen data, this is referred to as overfitting.

To address this issue and enhance the robustness of future research studies, it is advisable to consider various regularization techniques. These techniques, such as L1 regularization, L2 regularization, and dropout, can effectively mitigate overfitting (Coqueret & Guida, 2023). By incorporating these regularization methods into machine learning models, researchers can not only ensure strong performance on historical data but also enhance their models' ability to make accurate predictions on unseen data. This method emphasises the importance of not just obtaining high accuracy in the past but also being well-prepared for future financial modelling and prediction difficulties.

Another critical issue that must be carefully considered in machine learning models for stock market prediction is feature selection (Coqueret & Guida, 2023). The model's performance can be considerably impacted by selecting the most relevant characteristics that capture critical market indications and patterns. To select the most relevant features for the prediction models, it is critical to investigate various feature engineering strategies such as technical indicators, market sentiment indicators, and macroeconomic aspects.

Naive Bayesian and Random Forests (Kumar et al., 2018) have shown promising performance in stock market prediction tasks among classic machine learning models. To categorise data, Naive Bayesian models use probabilistic principles, whereas Random Forests use an ensemble of decision trees to make predictions. These models have proven to be successful at capturing nonlinear relationships.

Long Short-Term Memory (LSTM) (Bao et al., 2017) models outperform other architectures in the field of DL models. Because LSTM models are especially built to handle sequential data, they are highly suited for financial time series analysis. They excel at capturing long-term dependencies and patterns, enabling accurate predictions in stock market forecasting tasks.

5. CONCLUSION

While machine learning techniques offer promising avenues for stock market prediction, challenges related to data quality, data quantity, model accuracy, overfitting, and feature selection need to be addressed. Future research should focus on developing robust models that can generalize well to unseen data and incorporating additional data sources and advanced feature engineering techniques to improve prediction accuracy. By addressing these challenges and capitalizing on the strengths of both traditional and deep learning models, the potential for accurate and reliable stock market predictions can be realized.

REFERENCES

Asadi, S., Hadavandi, E., Mehmanpazir, F., & Nakhostin, M. M. (2016). *Hybridization of evolutionary Levenberg-Marquardt neural networks and data pre-processing for stock market prediction*. Academic Press.

Bao, W., Yue, J., & Rao, Y. (2017, July 14). A deep learning framework for financial time series using stacked autoencoders and long-short term memory. *PLoS One*, *12*(7), e0180944. doi:10.1371/journal.pone.0180944 PMID:28708865

Bollen, J., Mao, H., & Zeng, X. (2011, March). Twitter mood predicts the stock market. *Journal of Computational Science*, *2*(1), 1–8. doi:10.1016/j.jocs.2010.12.007

Carosia, A. E. O., Coelho, G. P., & Silva, A. E. A. (2019, October 31). Analyzing the Brazilian Financial Market through Portuguese Sentiment Analysis in Social Media. *Applied Artificial Intelligence*, *34*(1), 1–19. doi:10.1080/08839514.2019.1673037

Carta, S. M., Consoli, S., Piras, L., Podda, A. S., & Recupero, D. R. (2021). Explainable Machine Learning Exploiting News and Domain-Specific Lexicon for Stock Market Forecasting. *IEEE Access : Practical Innovations, Open Solutions*, *9*, 30193–30205. doi:10.1109/ACCESS.2021.3059960

Chen, Q., Li, S., & Wu, X. (2021). An ensemble method based on random forest and gradient boosting for stock price prediction. *Applied Soft Computing*, *107*, 107476.

Coqueret, G., & Guida, T. (2023). *Machine Learning for Factor Investing*. CRC Press. doi:10.1201/9781003121596

Dey, S., Kumar, Y., Saha, S., & Basak, S. (2016). *Forecasting to Classification: Predicting the Direction of Stock Market Price Using Xtreme Gradient Boosting*. Working Paper.

Ebadati, E. O. M., & Mortazavi, T. M. (2018). An efficient hybrid machine learning method for time series stock market forecasting. *Neural Network World*, *28*(1), 41–55. doi:10.14311/NNW.2018.28.003

Fathali, Z., Kodia, Z., & Ben Said, L. (2022, September 16). Stock Market Prediction of NIFTY 50 Index Applying Machine Learning Techniques. *Applied Artificial Intelligence*, *36*(1), 2111134. Advance online publication. doi:10.1080/08839514.2022.2111134

Goh, S. H., Lee, Y. C., & Chai, S. T. (2020). A deep learning framework for stock market volatility prediction using long short-term memory networks. *Expert Systems with Applications*, *152*, 113392.

Huang, J., & Liu, J. (2019, June 27). Using social media mining technology to improve stock price forecast accuracy. *Journal of Forecasting*, *39*(1), 104–116. doi:10.1002/for.2616

Kalyanaraman, V., Kazi, S., Tondulkar, R., & Oswal, S. (2014). *Sentiment analysis on news articles for stocks*. Paper presented at the 2014 8th Asia Modelling Symposium (AMS), Taipei, Taiwan. 10.1109/AMS.2014.14

Kim, K. J., & Han, I. (2000, August). Genetic algorithms approach to feature discretization in artificial neural networks for the prediction of stock price index. *Expert Systems with Applications*, *19*(2), 125–132. doi:10.1016/S0957-4174(00)00027-0

Kumar, I., Dogra, K., Utreja, C., & Yadav, P. (2018, April). A comparative study of supervised machine learning algorithms for stock market trend prediction. In *2018 Second International Conference on Inventive Communication and Computational Technologies (ICICCT)* (pp. 1003-1007). IEEE. 10.1109/ICICCT.2018.8473214

Li, L., Wu, X., & Yin, X. (2018). Stock price movement prediction using a deep neural network model. In *Proceedings of the 2018 International Conference on Data Mining (DMIN)* (pp. 47-53). Academic Press.

López de Prado, M. (2018). *Advances in Financial Machine Learning*. Academic Press.

Marković, I. P. (2014). *Stock market trend prediction using support vector machines*. Academic Press.

Mittal, A., & Goel, A. (2012). *Stock prediction using Twitter sentiment analysis*. Stanford University, CS229.

Mizumoto, K., Yanagimoto, H., & Yoshioka, M. (2012). Sentiment Analysis of Stock Market News with Semi-Supervised Learning. In *2012 IEEE/ACIS 11th International Conference on Computer and Information Science (ICIS)* (pp. 325-328). May. 10.1109/ICIS.2012.97

Qiu, M., & Song, Y. (2016, May 19). Predicting the Direction of Stock Market Index Movement Using an Optimized Artificial Neural Network Model. *PLoS One*, *11*(5), e0155133. doi:10.1371/journal.pone.0155133 PMID:27196055

Qiu, M., Song, Y., & Akagi, F. (2016, April). Application of artificial neural network for the prediction of stock market returns: The case of the Japanese stock market. *Chaos, Solitons, and Fractals*, *85*, 1–7. doi:10.1016/j.chaos.2016.01.004

Tripathy, N. T. (n.d.). *Stock price prediction using support vector machine approach*. Academic Press.

Velay, M., & Daniel, F. (2018). *Stock chart pattern recognition with deep learning*. Academic Press.

Xingzhou, L., Hong, R., & Yujun, Z. (2019, July). Predictive modeling of stock indexes using machine learning and information theory. In *Proceedings of the 2019 10th International Conference on E-business, Management and Economics* (pp. 175-179). 10.1145/3345035.3345087

Yadav, A., & Vishwakarma, D. K. (2020). Sentiment analysis using deep learning architectures: A review. *Artificial Intelligence Review*, *53*(6), 4335–4385. doi:10.100710462-019-09794-5

Zhang, J., Cui, S., Xu, Y., Li, Q., & Li, T. (2018). A novel data-driven stock price trend prediction system. *Expert Systems with Applications*, *97*, 60–69. doi:10.1016/j.eswa.2017.12.026

Chapter 17
Virtual Experiences, Real Consequences:
How Virtual Reality Transforms Consumer Behavior in E-Commerce

Anil Kumar Kashyap
Central University of Himachal Pradesh, India

Ity Sahu
Dr. H.S. Gour Vishwavidyalaya, India

ABSTRACT

According to Business Wire, the e-commerce market in India is expected to reach US$107.3 billion in 2023 and attract more players in online retailing. E-commerce is essentially backed by technology, and it can be assumed that e-commerce users are tech savvy, seek solutions in technology. VR is one of the important components of artificial intelligence transforming online retail experience to a large extent. The chapter explores the transformative effects of VR on consumer behavior. The chapter begins with the introduction and rise of VR in mitigating the limitations of online shopping and explains how VR is substituting physically examining of products, and how it empowers consumers to make more informed purchasing decisions. Later, the role of AI in virtual e-commerce is discussed followed by shopping convenience for e-commerce users and the future of VR in e-commerce. The findings of this chapter reveal that VR significantly impacts consumer behavior by fostering a sense of presence, interactivity, and immersion. At last, a conclusion is presented.

1. INTRODUCTION

In a digital age, businesses are constantly seeking innovative strategies to enhance customer experiences, streamline operations, and outpace the competition. One such transformative technology that has radically reshaped the shopping landscape is Virtual Reality (VR). This chapter aims to delve into the

DOI: 10.4018/979-8-3693-0418-1.ch017

burgeoning application of VR in the field of electronic commerce (e-commerce), examining its potential and shedding light on its implications for consumers.

The concept of VR involves creating an immersive, interactive 3D environment that mimics the real world. It aims at creating an entirely novel surrounding based on artificial intelligence technology. VR's realistic simulations has led to its application across diverse fields, from entertainment and gaming to education, healthcare, retailing and e- commerce. E-commerce which is the practice of buying and selling goods or services via the internet has revolutionized the traditional retail industry. It has led to provide an unparalleled shopping convenience and personalization to its customers. The interventions of AI make online shopping more promising and convenient for the shoppers. With VR, e-commerce promises to redefine the online shopping experience by bridging the gap between the physical and digital retail worlds.

This chapter will explore how VR technology is being harnessed in e-commerce, from enabling virtual storefronts that consumers can 'walk' through from the comfort of their homes. Also, highlighting the importance of immersive product demos that can help customers in taking more informed purchasing decisions. Furthermore, we will investigate the benefits and challenges of implementing VR in e-commerce and evaluate its future prospects in transforming online retailing.

The rapidly advancing VR technology is blurring the lines between reality and the virtual world, same as that of traditional retailing and e-commerce. The immersive and interactive shopping experiences often surpass those of brick-and-mortar stores; VR is gradually redefining what it means to shop online. This chapter sets the stage for understanding and exploring this exciting convergence of technologies and its potential to change the world of e-commerce.

2. RISE OF VR IN E-COMMERCE

The rise of Virtual Reality (VR) in e-commerce has been an exciting and transformative development in the online shopping landscape. As VR technology has advanced and become more accessible, e-commerce businesses have recognized its potential to redefine the consumer shopping experience and boost sales. Numerous studies have explored how VR can enhance user experience in e-commerce by creating immersive shopping environments (Jiang & Benbasat, 2004; Suh & Lee 2005; Martínez-Navarro et al., 2019; Tawira & Ivanov, 2023). VR allows customers to visualize and interact with products virtually, leading to increased engagement and satisfaction (Park and Kim, 2023). In their study (Barta et al., 2023) found that immersive technologies in online retail led to reduced cognitive effort, and increased purchase intention of consumers. This ultimately leads to improved overall shopping experience.

VR allows consumers to experience products in a more immersive and interactive way (Kim et al., 2021). Instead of relying solely on static images and text descriptions, shoppers can virtually interact with product. They can view them from different angles, and get a more realistic sense of size, scale, and features. This improved visualization leads to better and informed purchase decisions. In e- commerce set-up where the shopping is undertaken in an individual level i.e., without any human assistance, the scrutiny of every element is of utmost importance for avoiding the decision regret. Unlike in traditional retail setup, where a consumer is accompanied by different sales assistants that act as decision support to them, here the purchase decision are individual and hence bit difficult. VR, hence even helps in overcoming some of the limitations of traditional e-commerce. For example, VR experiences in the fashion industry enables customers to virtually try products on them (Chen et al., 2023), reducing the need for returns and exchanges.

Similarly, VR-powered visualization tools have been employed in the online home furnishings industry. It helps customers in visualizing how furniture and décor would look in their living spaces before buying (Oh et al., 2008), reducing both physical and financial efforts. Moreover, it enables businesses to create virtual showrooms or digital retail spaces, where consumers can explore a wide range of products in a single virtual location. This expands the reach of businesses beyond physical store locations and allows them to showcase their entire product catalog in an engaging way. VR facilitates social interactions and community engagement in virtual shopping environments (Pai & Tsai, 2011). Users can shop together; seek advice from friends, and share opinions, replicating the social aspect of traditional shopping. This fosters a sense of belonging and enhances the overall shopping experience. As VR devices become more affordable and accessible, a growing number of consumers can experience VR shopping from the comfort of their homes. This increased accessibility broadens the potential customer base for e-commerce businesses that adopt VR technology.

E-commerce businesses that embrace VR early on can gain a competitive advantage by offering a unique and cutting-edge shopping experience. VR sets them apart from traditional online stores, attracting tech-savvy consumers and fostering brand loyalty. Overall, the rise of VR in e-commerce is transforming the way consumers shop online. It enhances product exploration, reduces uncertainty, fosters social interactions, and provides a more personalized and engaging shopping experience. As VR technology continues to evolve, it is likely to play an increasingly significant role in shaping the future of e-commerce.

3. ROLE OF AI IN VIRTUAL E-COMMERCE

The relationship between Artificial Intelligence (AI) and Virtual Reality (VR) is a symbiotic one, where each technology complements and enhances the capabilities of the other. This relationship can be described in the following ways:

3.1. AI Enhances VR Interactivity

AI brings a higher level of interactivity to virtual reality experiences. By integrating AI algorithms into VR environments, virtual worlds can become more dynamic, responsive, and personalized (Taywade, 2023). AI can process user inputs, track movements, and understand natural language, enabling more sophisticated interactions within the virtual space.

3.2. AI Enables Real-Time Adaptation

VR experiences often require real-time adaptation to user behavior and preferences. AI algorithms can continuously analyze user data (Bharadiya, 2023). It includes gaze tracking, interactions, and choices to make immediate adjustments to the VR environment. This enables a more immersive experience for each user (Meißner et al., 2019).

Figure 1.

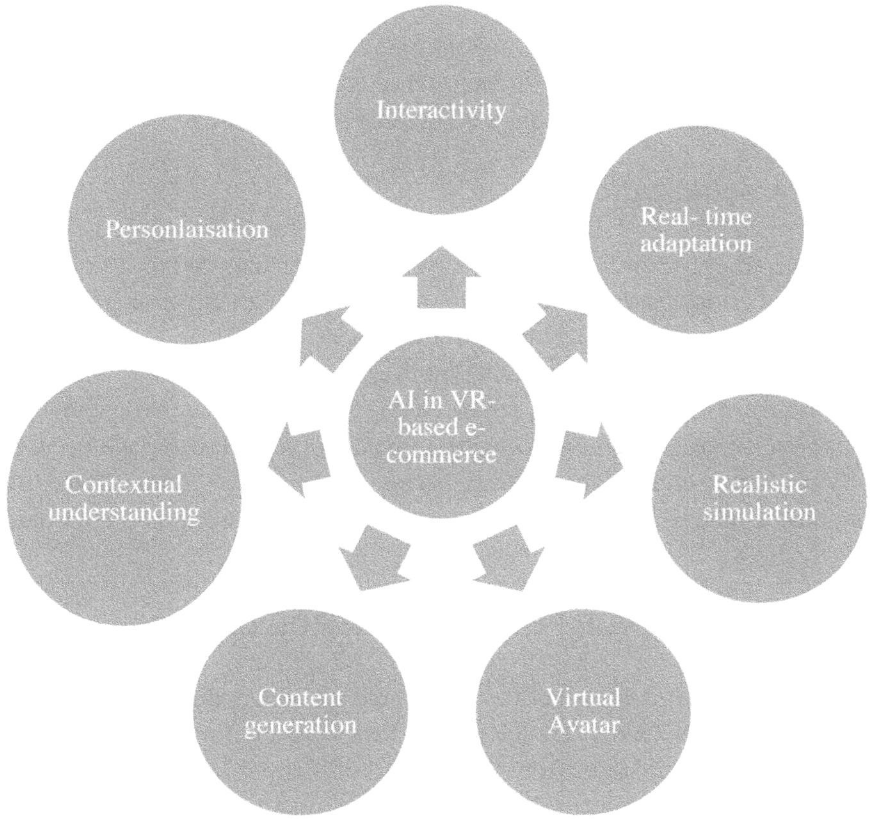

3.3. AI for Realistic Simulation

AI plays a critical role in creating realistic simulations within VR environments (Grech et al., 2023). Computer vision and machine learning techniques are used to render lifelike objects, characters, and environments. This provides users with a sense of presence and immersion.

3.4. AI-Powered Virtual Characters and Avatars

AI is used to create and control virtual characters and avatars with human-like behaviors and responses (Seymour et al., 2020). These virtual entities can engage in natural conversations with users and adapt to user preferences. They can even exhibit emotions, leading to more engaging and realistic interactions.

3.5. AI-Driven Content Generation

AI can automate and optimize content generation for VR experiences (Gravina et al., 2019). For instance, AI algorithms can create procedurally generated landscapes, textures, and objects, reducing the need for manual content creation and accelerating the development process (Kulagin et al., 2021).

3.6. AI for Contextual Understanding

AI can understand the context of VR interactions and adapt accordingly (Umbrico et al., 2020). For instance, AI can interpret voice commands, natural language queries, and contextual information to provide more relevant responses and actions within the VR environment.

3.7. AI-Driven Personalization

AI enables personalized experiences in VR by leveraging user data to tailor content, product recommendations, and interactions based on individual preferences. This level of personalization enhances user satisfaction and engagement in virtual environments.

AI and VR complement each other to create more immersive, interactive, and personalized experiences. AI's capabilities in data processing, pattern recognition, and adaptation enhance the realism and responsiveness of VR environments. VR provides a platform for AI to engage users in novel, lifelike, and contextually rich interactions. The synergy between AI and VR continues to drive innovation in various domains, from entertainment and gaming to education, healthcare, e- commerce and beyond.

4. SHOPPING CONVENIENCE FOR E-COMMERCE USERS

Shopping convenience is a critical aspect of e- commerce carrying a direct impact on consumer's satisfactions. Technological advancements are the way of achieving comfort in purchasing. VR allows users to explore virtual showrooms or stores from the comfort of their own homes. They can browse through a wide range of products without physically traveling to different locations, saving time and effort.

It helps users to see products in a more realistic and immersive way. They can inspect products from various angles, zoom in to examine details, and even interact with the products as if they were physically present. This level of product visualization helps users make more informed purchase decisions. In industries like fashion and beauty, VR enables users to virtually try on clothes, accessories, and makeup. This feature eliminates the need for physical fitting rooms, reducing the time and inconvenience associated with trying on multiple items in a physical store. Virtual try-ons and immersive product experiences can lead to more accurate product choices. As users gain a better understanding of how products fit and look, they are less likely to purchase items that don't meet their expectations, ultimately reducing the number of returns.

In a virtual environment, users from any corner of the world can shop round the globe and compare different products side by side. This convenience allows users to make comparisons efficiently, leading to faster decision-making. It can cater to users with mobility challenges or those living in remote areas with limited access to physical stores. It offers a more inclusive shopping experience, ensuring that a broader range of users can participate in e-commerce.

VR allows users to research products more efficiently. Instead of reading text descriptions or looking at static images, they can experience products in a more engaging and interactive way, leading to quicker and more thorough research. It facilitate community based social shopping experiences where users can shop together virtually, discuss products, and seek advice from friends and family. This creates a more enjoyable and communal shopping experience, despite being conducted online. VR enhances e-commerce shopping convenience by providing an immersive, interactive, and personalized experience. It reduces barriers to access, enhances product exploration, and simplifies the decision-making process, ultimately making the online shopping experience more enjoyable and efficient for users.

5. FUTURE OF VR IN E-COMMERCE

The future of VR in e-commerce is promising, with various potential advancements and applications that will reshape the way consumers shop and interact with products. Here are some key aspects of the future of VR in e-commerce:

5.1. Potential Advancements in VR Technology and Applications

5.1.1. Improved Hardware

VR headset technology is expected to become more sophisticated, offering higher resolutions, wider field-of-view, and better tracking capabilities. This will result in more immersive and realistic experiences for consumers.

5.1.2. Haptic Feedback

Advancements in haptic feedback technology will allow users to feel tactile sensations, enhancing the realism of virtual interactions. This could enable users to "touch" and "feel" virtual products, making the shopping experience even more engaging.

5.1.3. Mixed Reality (MR)

The integration of augmented reality (AR) and VR (MR) will enable users to blend virtual and real-world elements seamlessly. This will open up new possibilities for interactive product demonstrations and virtual showrooms within physical retail spaces.

5.1.4. VR on Mobile Devices

As VR technology becomes more accessible, it is likely to extend to mobile devices. This will enable users to access VR shopping experiences without the need for dedicated VR headsets, increasing user adoption and accessibility.

5.1.5. Social VR Shopping

Social VR platforms will allow users to shop together, virtually interact with friends, and seek real-time recommendations. This collaborative shopping experience will simulate the social aspect of traditional retail and foster a sense of community.

5.2. Predictions for the Integration of VR in E-Commerce Platforms

5.2.1. Mainstream Adoption

As VR technology becomes more affordable and user-friendly, e-commerce platforms will widely adopt VR to offer more engaging and personalized shopping experiences.

5.2.2. Virtual Shopping Malls

E-commerce platforms may create virtual shopping malls where multiple brands can showcase their products in shared virtual environments, offering consumers a one-stop shopping destination.

5.2.3. Customizable Avatars

Users may be able to create personalized avatars to represent themselves in virtual shopping environments, adding a sense of identity and self-expression to the VR shopping experience.

5.2.4. VR Product Demonstrations

Brands will utilize VR for interactive product demonstrations, allowing consumers to explore products in detail before making a purchase decision.

5.2.5. Virtual Product Launches

Companies may host virtual product launch events, allowing customers to be the first to experience and purchase new products in a virtual setting.

The future of VR in e-commerce holds great potential for revolutionizing the shopping experience. With advancements in technology and increased adoption by e-commerce platforms, VR will continue to redefine how consumers shop and interact with products, offering more immersive, personalized, and enjoyable shopping experiences.

6. CONCLUSION

Throughout this chapter, authors have explored how Virtual Reality (VR) significantly impacted consumer behavior in the e-commerce. Immersive and interactive encounters within virtual reality (VR) have elevated product visualization, mitigated ambiguity, and amplified engagement for online shoppers. Virtual try-ons and personalized recommendations strengthen the confident during online purchase, resulting in reduced returns and increase in customer satisfaction. Moreover, VR's social shopping features have replicated the social aspect of traditional retail, fostering a sense of community and connection among online shoppers.

The integration of VR in e-commerce has only scratched the surface of its potential. As technology advances and becomes more accessible, VR will continue to redefine the way consumers shop online. It has the power to transform the e-commerce landscape by providing users with seamless and convenient shopping experiences that bridge the gap between physical and virtual retail. VR has the potential to revolutionize product visualization, personalization, and social engagement, setting a new standard for online shopping.

For businesses in the e-commerce industry, embracing VR technology is not just a trend but a strategic necessity to remain competitive and thrive in the ever-evolving market. By incorporating VR experiences into their platforms, businesses can differentiate themselves, attract tech-savvy consumers, and foster brand loyalty. It is essential for e-commerce businesses to invest in VR content creation, optimize user interfaces for VR devices, and leverage VR analytics to offer personalized shopping experiences. Staying ahead in the market requires embracing VR's potential and adapting to the changing expectations of consumers in the digital era.

In conclusion, VR is redefining the consumer's experience in e-commerce by providing more immersive, interactive, and convenient shopping journeys. Its impact on consumer behavior has been significant, and its potential to revolutionize the e-commerce industry is vast. By adopting VR technology, businesses can unlock new opportunities for growth, engagement, and customer satisfaction, paving the way for a more dynamic and innovative future in e-commerce. The time to embrace VR and create a cutting-edge shopping experience is now.

REFERENCES

Barta, S., Gurrea, R., & Flavi, C. (2023). *Using augmented reality to reduce cognitive dissonance and increase purchase intention.* doi:10.1016/j.chb.2022.107564

Bharadiya, J. P. (2023, January 1). The role of machine learning in transforming business intelligence. *International Journal of Computing and Artificial Intelligence*, *4*(1), 16–24. doi:10.33545/27076571.2023.v4.i1a.60

Chen, H.-J., Shuai, H.-H., & Cheng, W.-H. (2023, May). A Survey of Artificial Intelligence in Fashion. *IEEE Signal Processing Magazine*, *40*(3), 64–73. doi:10.1109/MSP.2022.3233449

Gravina, D., Khalifa, A., Liapis, A., Togelius, J., & Yannakakis, G. N. (2019, August). Procedural content generation through quality diversity. In *2019 IEEE Conference on Games (CoG)* (pp. 1-8). IEEE.

Grech, A., Mehnen, J., & Wodehouse, A. (2023). An extended AI-experience: Industry 5.0 in creative product innovation. *Sensors (Basel)*, *23*(6), 3009. doi:10.339023063009 PMID:36991718

India B2C ecommerce market opportunities report 2023: A $149 billion ... (n.d.). https://www.businesswire.com/news/home/20230321005608/en/India-B2C-Ecommerce-Market-Opportunities-Report-2023-A-149-Billion-Market-by-2028---Social-Commerce-Firms-are-Refocusing-their-Efforts-on-Direct-Sales-Amid-Growing-Competition---ResearchAndMarkets.com

Jain, C. (2022). Virtual Fitting Rooms: "A Review of Underlying Artificial Intelligence Technologies, Current Developments, and the Biometric Privacy Laws in the US, EU and India." *Current Developments, and the Biometric Privacy Laws in the US, EU and India.*

Jiang, Z., & Benbasat, I. (2004). Virtual product experience: Effects of visual and functional control of products on perceived diagnosticity and flow in electronic shopping. *Journal of Management Information Systems, 21*(3), 111–147. doi:10.1080/07421222.2004.11045817

Kashyap, A. K., Sahu, I., & Kumar, A. (2022). Artificial Intelligence and Its Applications in E-Commerce – a Review Analysis and Research Agenda. *Journal of Theoretical and Applied Information Technology, 100*(24), 7347–7365.

Kulagin, K., Leksashov, A., Bolsunovskaya, M., & Shirokova, S. (2021). Development of a human flow generation module for testing machine learning algorithms. *Transportation Research Procedia, 54*, 783–792. doi:10.1016/j.trpro.2021.02.134

Martínez-Navarro, J., Bigné, E., Guixeres, J., Alcañiz, M., & Torrecilla, C. (2019). The influence of virtual reality in e-commerce. *Journal of Business Research, 100*, 475–482. doi:10.1016/j.jbusres.2018.10.054

Meißner, M., Pfeiffer, J., Pfeiffer, T., & Oppewal, H. (2019). Combining virtual reality and mobile eye tracking to provide a naturalistic experimental environment for shopper research. *Journal of Business Research, 100*, 445–458. doi:10.1016/j.jbusres.2017.09.028

Oh, H., Yoon, S. Y., & Shyu, C. R. (2008). How can Virtual Reality reshape furniture retailing? *Clothing & Textiles Research Journal, 26*(2), 143–163. doi:10.1177/0887302X08314789

Pai, P. Y., & Tsai, H. T. (2011). How virtual community participation influences consumer loyalty intentions in online shopping contexts: An investigation of mediating factors. *Behaviour & Information Technology, 30*(5), 603–615. doi:10.1080/0144929X.2011.553742

Park, H., & Kim, S. (2023). Do augmented and virtual reality technologies increase consumers' purchase intentions? The role of cognitive elaboration and shopping goals. *Clothing & Textiles Research Journal, 41*(2), 91–106. doi:10.1177/0887302X21994287

Seymour, M., Yuan, L., Dennis, A., & Riemer, K. (2020). *Facing the artificial: Understanding affinity, trustworthiness, and preference for more realistic digital humans*. Academic Press.

Suh, K. S., & Lee, Y. E. (2005). The effects of virtual reality on consumer learning: An empirical investigation. *Management Information Systems Quarterly, 29*(4), 673–697. doi:10.2307/25148705

Tawira, L., & Ivanov, A. (2023). Leveraging personalization and customization affordances of virtual try-on apps for a new model in apparel m-shopping. *Asia Pacific Journal of Marketing and Logistics, 35*(2), 451–471. doi:10.1108/APJML-09-2021-0652

Taywade. (2023, July 29). *AI-powered VR: How machine learning is enhancing the virtual reality experience*. https://community.nasscom.in/

Umbrico, A., Cesta, A., Cortellessa, G., & Orlandini, A. (2020). A holistic approach to behavior adaptation for socially assistive robots. *International Journal of Social Robotics, 12*(3), 617–637. doi:10.100712369-019-00617-9

Werdayani, D., & Widiaty, I. (2021). Virtual fitting room technology in fashion design. *IOP Conference Series. Materials Science and Engineering, 1098*(2), 022110. doi:10.1088/1757-899X/1098/2/022110

Chapter 18
How Human Resource Managers Can Utilize AI to Promote Employee Well-Being

Meena Chaudhary
https://orcid.org/0000-0001-8582-0355
Central University of Himachal Pradesh, India

Dipanker Sharma
https://orcid.org/0000-0003-0501-1473
Central University of Himachal Pradesh, India

Mohinder Chand Dhiman
https://orcid.org/0000-0002-8174-0013
Central University of Himachal Pradesh, India

Ankita Chaudhary
Central University of Himachal Pradesh, India

ABSTRACT

Artificial intelligence (AI) offers both opportunities and difficulties. In addition to significantly enhancing industrial efficiency, these technologies also have mixed or adverse influences on employee well-being. Understanding the influence of AI on employee well-being is essential given the increasing use of these technologies across HRM domains. This study raises a crucial question: Does artificial intelligence influence employee well-being? Job satisfaction, stress, overall health, and job security are considered essential dimensions of well-being. This study suggests that, even though AI can improve employee well-being, caution can be taken to address concerns and ensure a positive work atmosphere in organizations. Managers and leaders can utilize their agency significantly by influencing working conditions, technological adoptions, and AI in the interest of employee welfare. Organizational support and training programs can be relevant in reducing the negative effects of AI on employee well-being.

DOI: 10.4018/979-8-3693-0418-1.ch018

1. INTRODUCTION

Since the advent of the Internet of Things and Big data accessibility, commercial organizations have given Artificial Intelligence (AI) enabled technologies major attention. The dramatic emergence of AI has sparked a revolution that will likely continue into the future. Seventy-seven percent of consumers use AI technology, and recent estimates indicate that the entire global revenue for AI software is anticipated to increase from $9.5 billion in 2019 to as much as $ 118.6 billion in 2025, a phenomenal growth rate of more than 1,100 percent (Nazareno & Schiff, 2021; Qamar et al., 2021). The advent of the Industrial Revolution is anticipated to have a significant impact on industries all over the world (Soh & Connolly, 2021). Consequently, it will lead to integrating the digital and physical world, improving human-machine interactions, and advancing automation by incorporating smart machines and intelligent software (Xu et al., 2018; Pereira et al., 2023). According to Müller et al., (2021), AI is advancing into the 'new normal' in manufacturing and service sectors. The aim of AI is to create machines that operate better than humans while thinking like them. Additionally giving the machines the ability to autonomously receive and analyze the data to make decisions, address issues, and carry out tasks that call for human reasoning (Von Krogh, 2018). While many social, legal, ethical, and policy implications exist, related to AI, widespread labor substitution or displacement has attracted greater attention.

Several significant studies have predicted that a sizable portion of the workforce will either lose their jobs or require a significant career change in the near future owing to the adoption of AI (Peters, 2017; Korinek & Stiglitz, 2019). Around 51-52 percent of U.S. jobs are at high or moderate risk of automation, similarly Lazzerini and Pistolesi (2017) and Osborne (2017) project the risk of automation at 47 percent of U.S. employment.

Existent research also reveals that, many organizations have not realized the expected benefits of AI (Fountaine et al., 2019). According to a report by Boston Consulting Group and MIT, the percentage of companies deploying AI fell from 20 percent in 2019 to 4 percent in 2020 (The Economist: Businesses are finding AI hard to adopt., 2020). Furthermore, studies claim that organizations frequently find it challenging to integrate AI into their business processes which hinders the adoption of AI (T. H. Davenport & Ronanki, 2018). While early adopters revealed that investments in AI are not yielding economic value, recent literature has emphasized the potential for AI to enhance businesses (Ransbotham, S., Gerbert, P., Reeves, M., Kiron, D., & Spira, M., 2018)

Artificial intelligence (AI) has revolutionized several sectors in the past few years thereby enhancing production, efficiency, and consumer experiences. While, using AI has many advantages for businesses, it is crucial to consider how it will affect workers' well-being.

Diverse disciplines, organizational roles, and levels of research have been used to examine the link between artificial intelligence and workplace outcomes, leading to a range of findings concerning the effects of artificial intelligence in the workplace. It is important to have more understanding of how AI affects individuals, groups, companies, and the greater institutional landscape for those who practice attempting to incorporate intelligent machines and intelligent computerized systems at work. At the same time, by continuously charting the impact of AI at work, a roadmap for future study at the nexus of AI and workplace outcomes may be constructed. This study postulates that implementing new technologies responsibly and sustainably requires concurrent awareness of social, technical, and even biological processes (Pereira et al., 2023).

2. LITERATURE REVIEW

2.1. Artificial Intelligence

Since the latter part of the 1970's, AI has shown enormous potential for enhancing human decision-making processes and the resulting efficiency in a variety of corporate settings (Min, 2010; Jia et al., 2018). As a result of growing acceptance of AI as a decision-making tool, it is expected to become a crucial component of almost all areas of the company (Lawler & Elliot, 1993; Fountaine et al., 2019). The usage of AI techniques in varied functional areas has increased recently. Some examples include fuzzy sets, genetic algorithms, and artificial neural networks (Arrieta et al., 2019).

In organizations adopting a digital culture, AI has emerged as a primary driver of innovative business models, process transformation, and attaining a competitive edge. The use of AI has surged by 70% during the past five years (Ghosh et al., 2019). According to International Data Corporation, global investment in AI will rise from $85.3 billion in 2021 to more than $204 billion in 2025, with a compound annual growth rate of 24.5% over that period (Chowdhury et al., 2023). Forecasts made by the World Economic Forum 2022, assert that, AI adoption would eliminate 75 million jobs globally while creating 133 million new ones (Cann, O, 2018).

The workforce dynamics, nature of jobs, the relationship between employer and employee, the people and technology relationship, the experience of customers, will be significantly altered by the use of AI-based systems within the dynamic environments (James Wilson & Daugherty, 2018).

A study that involved 8,370 employees, HR leaders, and managers, from ten different countries reported that; i) In 2019, 50% of the workforce using AI in some capacity has increased from 32% in 2018. ii) It is challenging for 76% of employees and 81% HR leaders to cope up with the technological changes in the workplace. iii) 64% individuals will more likely trust a robot than their manager. iv) The majority of workers (34%) desire a simplified and better user interface, best practice training (30%), and an experience tailored to an employee's behavior (30%). v) Men (32%) are more optimistic about AI as compared to women (23%). vi) The primary issues limiting employees from using AI at work are security (31%) and privacy (30%) (Oracle., 2019).

The extant literature on AI, provides many classifications based on its types and related applications in businesses:

i. Automated Intelligence: It can carry out automated rule-based routines such as minor repetitive tasks, that free up time for human workers, in order to put efforts into significant and creative tasks. For instance; using chatbots and digital smart assistants.

ii. Assisted Intelligence: It analyses and derives insightful knowledge from several sources of heterogeneous big data and can enhance data-driven decision making. For instance; recommendation systems.

iii. Augmented Intelligence: It is derived from machine learning capacities and can support and enhance decision making in any circumstances. For instance; Visual image processing and speech recognition systems.

iv. Autonomous Intelligence: From an operational standpoint, it can acclimatize to the work environment by utilizing machine learning, and eliminating the need of human intervention. However, will necessitate the use of humans to create, administer and maintain such systems. For instance; robotic waiters, and self-driving vehicles (Haenlein & Kaplan, 2019).

The majority of definitions of artificial intelligence centre on how robots can replicate human intellect or how it is a computer science subfield. John McCarthy initially used the phrase "artificial intelligence" in the 1950s, defining it as "the science and engineering of making intelligent machines, especially intelligent computer programmes" (McCarthy, 2007). Artificial intelligence is "the ability of a digital computer or computer-controlled robot to perform tasks commonly associated with intelligent beings" (Encyclopedia Britannica). The definitions of artificial intelligence, depend on two aspects: human performance-rationality and thought-process-behavior. As a result, a system is said to be artificially intelligent if it thinks, behaves, or thinks and behaves rationally. "When it comes to the subfields of artificial intelligence, there are six requirements for machines to behave humanly: natural language processing (to communicate), knowledge representation (to store information), automated reasoning (to draw conclusions from stored data), machine learning (to extrapolate patterns), computer vision (to perceive objects), and robotics (to manipulate objects and move about)" (Russell & Norvig, 2010). AI is a system's capacity to learn from and make sense of digital data. "Artificial intelligence mimics the ability of the human brain to learn, analyze, and make decisions". (Mikalef & Gupta, 2021). Artificial intelligence imitates how the human brain learns, processes information, and makes decisions. Special artificial intelligence techniques can manage a large set of data and help professionals with creative tasks such as engineering by improving their input and making suggestions that would otherwise be difficult to develop" (Bag et al., 2020).

Figure 1. Human workforce using AI
Source: Oracle and Future Workplace (2019)

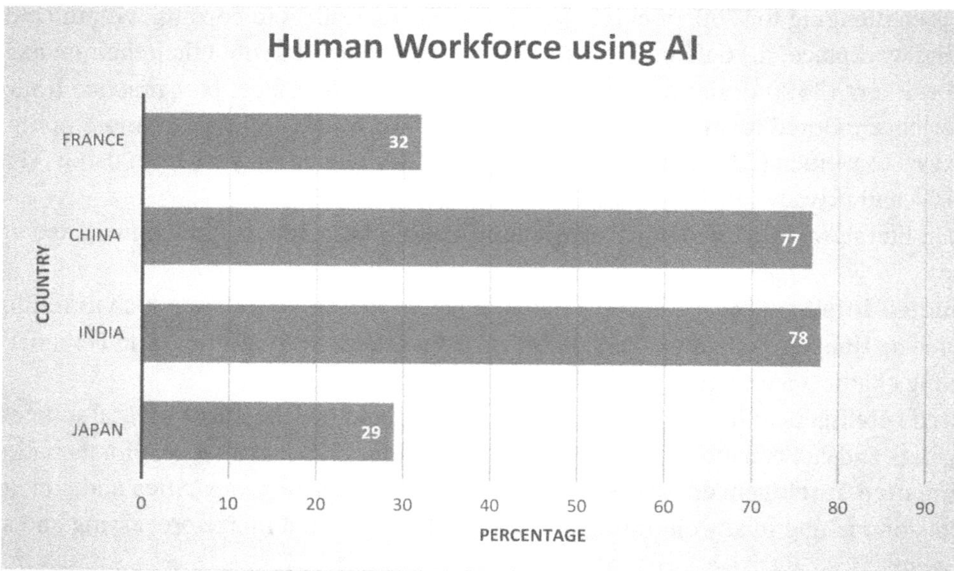

"The internet of things, also known as intranet of (digital) physical items, between machines connections, or things that are wirelessly connected via smart sensors, is another technology system related to intelligent automation (Li et al., 2015). The fundamental idea behind the internet of things is that "regular objects can be equipped with identifying, sensing, networking, and processing capabilities that will allow them to communicate with one another and with other devices and services over the internet to achieve some useful objective"(Whitmore et al., 2015). "But as new ideas and supporting technologies like cloud computing, big data, and information-centric networking have emerged, this paradigm has changed over time and is still changing today"(Atzori et al., 2017). "Pervasive robotics, where robots are present everywhere (in surroundings with linked smart objects), is the result of the fusion of artificial intelligence, robots, and the internet of things. These robots are capable of carrying out a range of activities without the need for human interaction. An illustration would be a robotic supermarket managed by cooperative robots (cobots) operating independently of human control". The implementation of an integrated system of cutting-edge technologies, such as artificial intelligence, robotics, and the internet of things, to autonomously operate service tasks within business environments without human intervention can thus be understood as applying intelligent automation in industry(Özdemir & Hekim, 2018).

While there may be some benefits for workers from AI, research on socio-technical systems and the history of technology adoption in the workplace suggests that the impacts of technology on well-being are more complex and variable, particularly in areas like worker stress, job satisfaction, and overall health (Baldry, 2012).

2.2. Employee Well-Being

Employee well-being is a multifaceted idea that includes social, psychological, and physical components. It includes elements like job satisfaction, work-life balance, stress levels, job stability, and possibilities for professional growth. While, increasing worker autonomy, creativity, and independence will lead to better work, AI may harm employees by creating a sense of purposelessness or employment insecurity. According to Chari et al., (2018), worker well-being is measured using a wide range of concepts including employee engagement, job satisfaction, good mental or physical health, positive emotions, social relationships and their associations with improved work performance and reduced mortality as an outcome.

Well – being is defined as "an integrative concept that characterizes quality of life with respect to an individual's health and work-related environmental, organizational, and psychosocial factors"

The effects of poor mental and physical health can be felt at home and affect families, communities, and society as a whole. The adoption of new technology in the workplace has the potential to have a large negative influence on employee well-being through changing tasks, processes, and organizational structures. For instance, during periods of technological change, studies have seen elevated levels of job stress, job insecurity, and worker loss of autonomy (Gallie et al., 2017; Chari et al., 2018 ; Bhardwaj & Sharma, 2022)

Recent research on the adoption of AI technology, has demonstrated that management discretion and employee agency may encourage greater acceptance of new technologies in addition to other advantageous outcomes (Nazareno & Schiff, 2021).

However, according to Cooper (1984), workplace AI adoption and people's interactions with their changing work environments could lead to an increase in occupational stress. He revealed six key elements affecting employees: job-specific characteristics, employee roles within the organization, career development, interpersonal connections with employees and employer, organizational environment and tradition, as well as the connection between the home and the office. These characteristics have the potential to cause both undesirable individual symptoms (particularly detrimental short- and long-term health consequences) and specific organizational "diseases" such as absenteeism, turnover, apathy, and problematic labour relations (Cooper, 1984).

Even when one's career is not in danger, AI could lead to worry about the loss of desired job characteristics like "opportunities for initiative or task discretion" (Gallie et al., 2017).

The well-being of the worker is a subject of significant social importance that is overlooked occasionally in discussions on artificial intelligence and the prospects of employment. Despite research suggesting that AI may reduce stress, the findings on job satisfaction and worker health contradict the most pessimistic view of technological complementarity. Organizational stress research frequently examines employee well-being, focusing on how workplace variables like technology affect employee learning (Djourova et al., 2020).

Additionally, emotional exhaustion and job satisfaction are recognized as key indicators of employee well-being and are considered significant factors in burnout (Sabri et al., 2020). Numerous elements, such as emotional exhaustion and job satisfaction, have an impact on employee withdrawal from the workplace (Singh et al., 2019).The adoption of new technology has an "enhancement effect," enabling workers to do their tasks more effectively and produce more work. Contrarily, new technology replaces the human workers who were previously performing repetitive tasks thanks to the replacement effect.

The notoriously inclusive and frequently quoted description of health, which states that it is "a state of total physical, mental, and social wellbeing and not merely the absence of disease or infirmity," was introduced with the foundation of the World Health Organisation (WHO) in 1948 (WHO,1948). This prominent usage of the word "wellbeing" attempted to redefine health and medical practise by shifting the emphasis from the person and the absence of certain disorders to health as a positive quality. However, it has taken some time for the phrase to really gain more policy traction and start to influence how people think about health and human flourishing. "As a result, despite the WHO's early use of the term in the field of health, its use in relation to health has only significantly increased in the last 20 years, primarily in the area of psycho-social health, which was developed by the positive psychology movement in the United States" (Alex Linley et al., 2006).

The concept of well-being as a gauge of general life satisfaction encompasses much more than just the concerns of corporate members. Digital technology has the potential to improve quality of people' work and life (Bravi et al., 2018). "According to studies, a company's performance depends greatly on the happiness of its employees". While Singh et al., (2019) postulated that, "employees' psychological and physical well-being is significantly impacted, which increases healthcare costs and lowers productivity" (Brynjolfsson et al., 2019a).

2.3. AI and Well-Being

The link to employee well-being may be especially significant when the use of AI aligns with workers' psychological concerns"(Havrda & Rakova, 2020). A study confirmed the potential for increased occupational stress caused by use of AI in the organization and people's interactions with their changing work environments. "Artificial intelligence's entry to the workplace and people's interactions with their changing work environments could lead to an increase in occupational stress". The characteristics inherent to the job, such as workers positions within the organization, professional advancement, relationship at work, organizational climate and culture and the link between workplace and home are few examples (Chaudhary et al., 2022). These elements could lead to detrimental short-term and long-term health effects as well as organizational issues such as turnover, absenteeism, laziness and problematic industrial relations (Cooper, 1984).

"Technology is adopted at workplace to boost output and enhance organisational outcomes, with little thought given to the impact on workers. For instance, the extensive use of technology might result in a "norm of responsiveness" that has been associated with heightened perceptions of pressures, exaggerated expectations for performance and productivity, and feelings of increased mental fatigue" (Perlow, 2012). "According to studies, technology may speed up work processes to the point that it causes more stress, overload, weariness, and burnout among employees". For instance, a recent study found that multitasking, increased work tempo, and interruptions contributed to greater feelings of workplace stress and anxiety among US employees who participated in a nationally representative survey. (Barley et al., 2011; Chesley, 2014). Barley et al., (2011) discovered another link between increased email use and employee stress brought on by rising workloads. The poll found that employees felt under pressure to respond to emails, even if doing so required working on weekend days or after hours.

Overall, technology is having a detrimental influence on mental health at work in a number of ways, including by raising demands, cutting down on resources, and altering how workers perceive the future, all of which have direct and indirect consequences for both employers and employees. "Common mental health issues are linked to a higher risk of development when work characteristics such poor job design, excessive job demand, limited job control, and high effort-reward imbalances are present"(Harvey et al., 2017).

Control, support, good feedback, and learning opportunities are all resources that are favourably correlated with work-related well-being. Fortunately, technology can and has been effectively applied in a variety of ways to create work that helps protect employees' mental health. We now examine the ways in which increase in technology and AI have benefited employee and workplace mental health. "AI has enhanced job security and decreased the likelihood of physical workplace injuries". Numerous physically demanding and time-consuming manual operations, such as repetitive heavy lifting, have been replaced by automation in the majority of nations, including Australia. "It should be less likely for employees to have psychological issues as a result of physical workplace injuries, such as mental health consequences of injuries, low motivation to return to work, loneliness, frustration, and rage (Horton et al., 2018). Technology may also support healthy mental practises, eHealth and proactive workplace mental health treatments are two of the main advantages of current technological advancements. Research reveals that people with common mental health disorders like depression and anxiety can benefit from and make substantial changes utilizing eHealth therapies that use evidence-based therapy strategies. For instance, according to meta-analytic research, mindfulness-based eHealth therapies may help employees with common mental health disorders feel better"(Stratton et al., 2017). In the same lines another study and a meta-analysis discovered that workplace delivery of digital mental health therapies might enhance employees' psychological well-being and productivity"(Carolan et al., 2017).

Privacy and surveillance, discrimination or bias and the philosophical challenges in human judgement are some of the ethical and legal issues brought to the society by AI implementation in organizations. Consequently, the use of AI in clinical settings has the potential to improve healthcare, however it also raises ethical concerns given that AI is increasingly becoming a critical component of contemporary digital systems rather than just a "nice-to-have" technology. It becomes crucial to ensure that judgements are made ethically and without unjust biases when using AI for decision-making. Thus there is a need for transparent, explicable and accountable AI systems (Naik et al., 2022). The extensive use of automated technology changes the sort of work that human employees conduct and makes people fearful that they may be replaced and lose their jobs (Fiaidhi et al., 2018). However, creative ability gives employees an advantage over artificial intelligence. This implies that even while the employees cannot be easily replaced by technology, they might not become disheartened when faced with the threat of replacement and instead search for new opportunities to develop and maintain their competitiveness. Younger individuals are more mobile, digitally savvy, and adaptable to changing conditions than previous generations (Kolnhofer-Derecskei et al., 2017).

How AI is affecting employee well-being is our main concern (Figure 2). Several theories contend that work will improve as worker autonomy, creativity, and independence increase. Other theories contend that AI may have detrimental effects on workers, such as causing a sense of purposelessness or job instability. The findings of this study will offer valuable insights for policymakers, industry professionals, and organizations in developing strategies and policies that promote a harmonious integration of AI while prioritizing the well-being of their employees. It illuminates the significance of creating a collaborative workplace wherein AI and human intelligence may co-exist within organizations. Furthermore, the study encompasses the role of HRM in AI adoption-related issues impacting employee well-being.

What would happen if modern technology eliminates millions of jobs, or what if most businesses did not require as many human workers? Bill Gates and many politicians think that in order to make up for the jobs that will be lost and to pay for retraining, governments should tax businesses instead of people. The idea that a worker's skill can suddenly become outdated actually brings to light a heated discussion over how quickly and to what extent technology will transform the workplace. Many ideas have started to circulate, some of which are still debatable, such as universal basic income, negative income tax, and the government job guarantee. Finding a balance between our concerns and the advantages of such sophisticated technology, can improve our quality of life (Fiaidhi et al., 2018).

Figure 2. Impact of AI
Source: Created by author

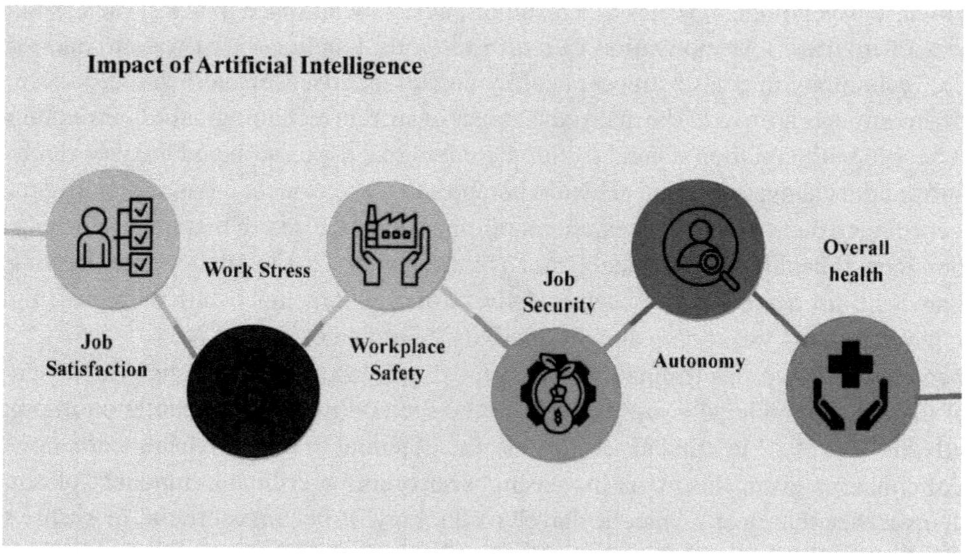

2.4. AI and Human Resource Management (HRM)

In 1994, the first AI subfield introduced in HRM literature is the expert system, fuzzy logic appeared in 2000, while artificial neural network appeared in 2001. Consequently, Data mining in 2006, Genetic algorithm in 2008, and machine learning in 2011 were introduced. The four key HRM functions are staffing, remuneration, training and development, and performance management. Staffing can either be done focussing on time and cost reduction (Maree et al., 2019; Karam et al., 2020), utilizing automation in staffing (Richter & Naveh, 2008; Gupta et al., 2018). In addition to prediction of employee performance, promotion screening of candidates based on comparative ranking was also the focus of investigation in previous research (Moon et al., 2010; Manafi & Devi Subramaniam, 2015; Noughabi et al., 2016). For training and development purposes studies have examined competency assessment focussing on prior data (Zhang & Deng, 2011) or the visualization of competency gaps (Bohlouli et al., 2017), and the need of assessing psychological capital for hiring and promotion (Alola & Atsa'am, 2020).

The impact of AI adoption has been extensively researched including the capacity of AI as an indispensable approach (Abdeldayem & Aldulaimi, 2020), its pervasive influence on HRM (Chakraborty et al., 2020), to enhance decision making (Masum et al., 2018; Oswald et al., 2020), creating an employee suggestion system (Marksberry et al., 2014).

Human Resource Management is one field of management that has started utilizing AI applications and has demonstrated a varied range of AI adoption implications (Strohmeier & Piazza, 2015). AI has been productively utilized in varied HRM functions, including employee selection (Shahhosseini & Sebt, 2011; Oswald et al., 2020), performance evaluation (Huang et al., 2001; Moon et al., 2010), turnover of employees (Sexton et al., 2005), employee assignment (Karatop et al., 2015), and level of emotional involvement of employees (Lucia-Casademunt et al., 2013). However previous research indicates that compared to other sectors, AI domain is less researched in HRM and still is in its infancy (Strohmeier & Piazza, 2013; Tambe et al., 2018; Qamar et al., 2021)

According to Chowdhury et al., (2023), AI is defined as, "the ability of a manmade system comprising of algorithms and software programs, to identify, interpret, generate insights, and learn from the data sources to achieve specific predetermined goals and tasks."

This definition focuses on the two fundamental characteristics of the developing technology: i. it is created (artificial), ii. It possesses some form of intelligence (such as the ability to infer meaning from the data, similar to how people learn from their experiences in life).

The extant literature claims and outlines the benefits of AI, such as increasing job satisfaction, customer service, and employee experience and decreasing labor costs (Bughin J.; et al., 2018), re-engineering business models (Duan et al., 2019), use of AI in decision making (Paschen et al., 2020). These benefits have caused the adoption of AI-enabled systems in HRM areas such as performance assessments and talent identification (Upadhyay & Khandelwal, 2018), training and development of employees, video interviews, and talent acquisition (Maity, S., 2019), and employee engagement (Banking & Formosa, 2020). Recent studies have described the function of AI in facilitating HR analytics (Margherita, 2022; Vrontis et al., 2022; Chowdhury et al., 2023).

To compile and interpret employee data, organizations are capitalizing on AI-enabled HR software solutions such as utilizing data stored in HR Information Systems. For instance; amassing demographic information of employees, performance appraisal reviews, and job evaluations (Angrave et al., 2016; Margherita, 2021). To comprehend human behavior, Tesco uses analytics tools to understand its customers and workforce, similarly, Mc Donald's identified employee attitudes, and management behaviors to improve the performance of employees (Sparrow, P., Cooper, C., & Hird, M., 2016). AI enables various tasks such as recruitment, selection, appointment, training, performance appraisals, employee benefits, and remuneration (Tambe et al., 2018). According to Kot et al., (2021), effective recruitment and retention of employees through AI implementation can be crucial in improving an employer's reputation.

However, a symbiotic partnership between Artificial Intelligence (AI) and Human Intelligence (HI) would result in collective intelligence. It is anticipated that AI understanding, role clarity and trust will enable creation of valued outcomes for both employees and organizations. However, this viewpoint is being expanded and considers AI more comparable to a colleague and teammate rather than a tool promoting productivity and organizational performance (Malone, T. W., 2018). AI-enabled technologies will enhance and automate HRM decision-making in firms, which has been the focus of discussion, consideration and fear in the society. Issues concerning negative effects of AI such as poor decision–making, bias and discrimination are raised by the existent literature (T. Davenport et al., 2020). According to Rampersad, (2020) there have been conflicting reports on fear that AI will replace human jobs, lack of trust in AI systems, negative perceptions that may affect decision making and bias, little agreement regarding generation of new jobs as a result of AI adoption and skepticism about governance, morality and ethics in AI decision making. In spite of enthusiasm and interest of workers for a new technology, they disregard it if it negatively impacts their psychological and financial well-being (Elkins et al., 2013).

HRM must take into account the impact of AI on employee well-being, in light of its expanding applications and usage in organizations and routine life. Employee's well-being, as well as their emotions of privacy, security and trust may be negatively impacted by issues such as bias (Chouldechova et al., 2018), intrusion, ignorance, inequality and labour displacement (Buolamwini & Gebru, 2018), and misinformation (Chesney & Citron, 2019). This resulted in the development of a standard of recommended practice for evaluating the impact of AI on well-being. Its purpose is to provide guidance for AI creators trying to comprehend and measure direct, indirect, unforeseen and intended implications to societal and human well-being. AI can bring a variety of advantages if handled aptly such as creating awareness of wellbeing, assessing the impact of interventions and changes on well-being, managing risk AI poses on well-being, promoting positive well-being initiatives, and giving information to employers into work-life balance of employees (Schiff et al., 2020).

Due to the growing breath of AI-HRM research, a comprehensive discussion is necessary to summarize existing knowledge and comprehend the scope of application of AI in HRM and gauge its potential impact on HRM activities in present and the future.

3. CONCLUSION

Many organizations develop policies, values, and code of ethics that are intended to foster an ethical culture. In order to operate in accordance with these norms, the firm must confront the moral issues that the deployment of AI would bring up for HR practices. (Qamar et al., 2021; Ferrell & Ferrell, 2021). Several procedures can be developed to manage and reduce ethical issues at various levels. Managers must consider moral implications while making decisions since they are aware of the probable repercussions that their decisions may have. For instance; the management should have the authority to override a decision if the AI output shows undue bias. The expert system, which bases judgements on the expert's knowledge, must constantly revise its orders in accordance with the moral precepts. Many organizations have undergone a fundamental transformation as a result of AI. The key function of AI in the workplace is to enable sophisticated HR management. More research is needed to get feedback from the people impacted by the AI adoption in HRM and on AI application in HRM that can be easily deployed in areas of practical implications. Additionally understanding how willing workers are to use robots is necessary (Xu et al., 2020). AI implementation may also be hampered by employee concerns about losing their employment or their inability to learn the necessary skills. Researchers have also been concerned about the potential misuse of AI applications (Strohmeier & Piazza, 2013). Additionally, concerns such as the possibility of an employee sabotaging AI devices by refusing to schedule maintenance during their shift or by falsifying the results of others work are still unanswered. To sustain AI–enabled solutions leader's perspectives on developing efficient AI solutions and how might be implemented are crucial. According to Jerman et al., (2020) leaders can help their organizations accept robotics.

This study examined the influence of artificial intelligence (AI) on employee wellbeing. Our comprehensive analysis reveals that using AI has both beneficial and detrimental consequences on employee wellbeing. The use of AI technology has the potential to improve employee work-life balance and job satisfaction. AI systems' simplicity of use, effectiveness, and accuracy help employees manage their professional and personal responsibilities more successfully, which raises their level of job satisfaction.

4. PRACTICAL IMPLICATIONS

Using AI raises issues with job stress and uncertainty. Employee job stress may grow as a result of worries about job security, technology disruptions, and the need for ongoing skill development. To reduce the detrimental effects of AI on employee well-being, organisations must prioritise employee assistance, training programmes, and open lines of communication.

To improve employee wellbeing and fully utilise the benefits of AI, organisations should create a supportive organisational culture that prioritises work-life balance, provides opportunities for professional advancement, and underlines the collaborative nature of human-AI interaction. It is also crucial to address ethical problems and ensure algorithmic transparency in order to maintain employee confidence and enforce ethical norms in the usage of AI technology.

This chapter provides an overview of the moral concerns raised due to AI applications in HRM. This could aid researchers in avoiding applying AI in sensitive functions of HRM, that deal with people and people data which could have unforeseen repercussions. Also posing a substantial problem for HR managers are ethical and privacy concerns. This study will assist HR managers in developing a comprehensive understanding of privacy threats and moral concerns in the use of AI. It will also be easier for managers to think of organizational and technology setups to better handle these challenges if they have a broader perspective on ethical issues and their management. The ultimate guardians of privacy are organizations, and ethical considerations and academic research indicate that it is often the case that personal data is misused on the organizational side.

5. RECOMMENDATION FOR FUTURE RESEARCH

A number of mediating and moderating factors, which can be further explored, can affect the link between AI and employee well-being. Employee well-being results may be influenced by the interaction of factors including organisational culture, leadership style, employee traits, and support systems with

AI adoption (Thakur et al., 2019). The complicated dynamics at work can be better understood by looking into these variables. The psychological effects of AI on employee well-being may be studied by looking at things like work satisfaction, job engagement, organisational commitment, and psychological resilience. Insights into the methods through which AI impacts employee well-being may be gained by analysing how AI technologies affect employees' emotional experiences, motivation, and general psychological well-being. Examining how employees interact with AI systems can provide insight into how these interactions affect employees' well-being. Future studies might examine how workers perceive their level of competence, autonomy, and control while interacting with AI systems. It might be easier to spot elements that improve or impair employees' well-being if we have a better understanding of how they perceive and experience their interactions with AI technology.

A thorough knowledge of the wider effects of AI deployment on employee well-being may be gained by looking into how AI affects team dynamics, collaboration, and general organizational culture. Future studies might examine the social responsibility and ethical implications of implementing AI in the tourism sector. Insights into the larger social implications of AI in the tourist industry may be gained by examining the ethical issues involved with AI decision-making, privacy issues, and the possible influence on local populations. Research is still needed to fully grasp how human-AI collaboration might be optimized to improve employee wellbeing. The creation of best practices that encourage employee engagement, job satisfaction, and general well-being can result from investigating the most efficient methods to incorporate AI technology into workers' work processes. Our findings can guide the development of research-supported policies and actions that promote employee well-being while maximising the advantages of AI technology.

In the past, "AI compute's" environmental impacts have frequently gone unnoticed. Unquestionably, the infrastructure of "AI compute" has a carbon footprint because it relates to the computational power and resources needed to train and deploy AI models. During training a typical AI model uses between 100-200 MWh of energy. Thus, it's critical to consider the sustainability of AI systems while drafting laws and regulations for the technology to reduce its negative environmental effects before creating models. Standards and tools will be required by businesses to implement sustainability regulations (Appelle, 2023). In response to high energy needs and detrimental economic and environmental effects, certain nations and towns have passed regulations governing data centers. Committing to be carbon-negative by 2030, Google, Amazon, and Microsoft pledged to tackle sustainability. According to Google's 2023 Environmental Report, its data centres might have produced up to 2.5 million tonnes of CO_2 equivalents. Thus it promised to run its operations on carbon-free energy round-the-clock (*Google Environmental Report*, 2023). On the same lines, future studies can investigate further on AI and Environmental Sustainability.

REFERENCES

Abdeldayem, M. M., & Aldulaimi, S. H. (2020). Trends and opportunities of artificial intelligence in human resource management: Aspirations for the public sector in Bahrain. *International Journal of Scientific and Technology Research*, *9*(1), 3867–3871.

Alex Linley, P., Joseph, S., Harrington, S., & Wood, A. M. (2006). Positive psychology: Past, present, and (possible) future. *The Journal of Positive Psychology*, *1*(1), 3–16. doi:10.1080/17439760500372796

Alola, U. V., & Atsa'am, D. D. (2020). Measuring employees' psychological capital using a data mining approach. *Journal of Public Affairs*, *20*(2), 1–10. doi:10.1002/pa.2050

Angrave, D., Charlwood, A., Kirkpatrick, I., Lawrence, M., & Stuart, M. (2016). HR and analytics: Why HR is set to fail the big data challenge. *Human Resource Management Journal*, *26*(1), 1–11. doi:10.1111/1748-8583.12090

Arrieta, A. B., Del Ser, J., Bennetot, A., Tabik, S., Barbado, A., Garcia, S., Gil-lopez, S., Molina, D., Benjamins, R., Chatila, R., & Herrera, F. (2019). Explainable Artificial Intelligence (XAI): Concepts, Taxonomies, Opportunities and Challenges toward Responsible AI. *Information Fusion*, *58*, 82–115. doi:10.1016/j.inffus.2019.12.012

Atzori, L., Iera, A., & Morabito, G. (2017, October). Understanding the Internet of Things: Definition, potentials, and societal role of a fast evolving paradigm. *Ad Hoc Networks*, *56*, 122–140. doi:10.1016/j.adhoc.2016.12.004

Bag, S., Wood, L. C., Xu, L., Dhamija, P., & Kayikci, Y. (2020). Big data analytics as an operational excellence approach to enhance sustainable supply chain performance. *Resources, Conservation and Recycling, 153*, 104559. doi:10.1016/j.resconrec.2019.104559

Bankins, S., & Formosa, P. (2020). When AI meets PC: Exploring the implications of workplace social robots and a human-robot psychological contract. *European Journal of Work and Organizational Psychology*, *29*(2), 215–229. doi:10.1080/1359432X.2019.1620328

Barley, S. R., Meyerson, D. E., & Grodal, S. (2011). E-mail as a source and symbol of stress. *Organization Science*, *22*(4), 887–906. doi:10.1287/orsc.1100.0573

Bhardwaj, B., & Sharma, D. (2022). Migration of skilled professionals across the border: Brain drain or brain gain? *European Management Journal*. Advance online publication. doi:10.1016/j.emj.2022.12.011

Bohlouli, M., Mittas, N., Kakarontzas, G., Theodosiou, T., Angelis, L., & Fathi, M. (2017). Competence assessment as an expert system for human resource management: A mathematical approach. *Expert Systems with Applications*, *70*, 83–102. doi:10.1016/j.eswa.2016.10.046

Bravi, L., Murmura, F., & Santos, G. (2018). Manufacturing labs: Where new digital technologies help improve life quality. *International Journal of Qualitative Research*, *12*(4), 957–974. doi:10.18421/IJQR12.04-11

Bughin J., Eric, H., Susan, L., Peter, D., Anna, W., & Armesh, S. (2018). Skill shift: Automation and the future of the workforce. *McKinsey Global Institute, 3*(84).

Buolamwini, J., & Gebru, T. (2018). Gender Shades: Intersectional Accuracy Disparities in Commercial Gender Classification. *Proceedings of Machine Learning Research*, *81*, 77–91.

Carolan, S., Harris, P. R., & Cavanagh, K. (2017). Improving Employee Well-Being and Effectiveness: Systematic Review and Meta-Analysis of Web-Based Psychological Interventions Delivered in the Workplace. *Journal of Medical Internet Research*, *19*(7), e271. doi:10.2196/jmir.7583 PMID:28747293

Chakraborty, S., Giri, A., Aich, A., & Biswas, S. (2020). Evaluating influence of artificial intelligence on human resource management using PLS-SEM (Partial least squares-structural equation modeling). *International Journal of Scientific and Technology Research*, *9*(3), 5876–5880.

Chari, R., Chang, C. C., Sauter, S. L., Petrun Sayers, E. L., Cerully, J. L., Schulte, P., Schill, A. L., & Uscher-Pines, L. (2018). Expanding the Paradigm of Occupational Safety and Health: A New Framework for Worker Well-Being. *Journal of Occupational and Environmental Medicine*, *60*(7), 589–593. doi:10.1097/JOM.0000000000001330 PMID:29608542

Chaudhary, M., Jaswal, N., & Bhardwaj, B. (2022). Hiding Behind The SWOT : Gender Equality and COVID-19. *Journal of Positive School Psychology*, *6*(6), 730–740.

Chesley, N. (2014). Information and communication technology use, work intensification and employee strain and distress. *Work, Employment and Society*, *28*(4), 589–610. doi:10.1177/0950017013500112

Chesney, R., & Citron, D. (2019). Deepfakes and the new disinformation war. *Foreign Affairs*, *98*(1), 147–155.

Chouldechova, A., Putnam-Hornstein, E., Benavides-Prado, D., Fialko, O., & Vaithianathan, R. (2018). A case study of algorithm-assisted decision making in child maltreatment hotline screening decisions. *Proceedings of Machine Learning Research*, *81*, 134–148.

Chowdhury, S., Dey, P., Joel-Edgar, S., Bhattacharya, S., Rodriguez-Espindola, O., Abadie, A., & Truong, L. (2023). Unlocking the value of artificial intelligence in human resource management through AI capability framework. *Human Resource Management Review*, *33*(1), 100899. doi:10.1016/j.hrmr.2022.100899

Davenport, T., Guha, A., Grewal, D., & Bressgott, T. (2020). How artificial intelligence will change the future of marketing. *Journal of the Academy of Marketing Science*, *48*(1), 24–42. doi:10.100711747-019-00696-0

Davenport, T. H., & Ronanki, R. (2018). Intelligence for the Real World. *Harvard Business Review*, *96*(1), 108–116.

Djourova, N. P., Rodríguez Molina, I., Tordera Santamatilde, N., & Abate, G. (2020). Self-Efficacy and Resilience: Mediating Mechanisms in the Relationship Between the Transformational Leadership Dimensions and Well-Being. *Journal of Leadership & Organizational Studies*, *27*(3), 256–270. doi:10.1177/1548051819849002

Duan, Y., Edwards, J. S., & Dwivedi, Y. K. (2019). Artificial intelligence for decision making in the era of Big Data – evolution, challenges and research agenda. *International Journal of Information Management*, *48*, 63–71. doi:10.1016/j.ijinfomgt.2019.01.021

Elkins, A. C., Dunbar, N. E., Adame, B., & Nunamaker, J. F. (2013). Are Users Threatened by Credibility Assessment Systems? *Journal of Management Information Systems*, *29*(4), 249–262. doi:10.2753/MIS0742-1222290409

Ferrell, O. C., & Ferrell, L. (2021). Applying the Hunt Vitell ethics model to artificial intelligence ethics. *Journal of Global Scholars of Marketing Science*, *31*(2), 178–188. doi:10.1080/21639159.2020.1785918

Fiaidhi, J., Mohammed, S., & Mohammed, S. (2018). The Robotization of Extreme Automation: The Balance Between Fear and Courage. *IT Professional*, *20*(6), 87–93. doi:10.1109/MITP.2018.2876979

Fountaine, T., McCarthy, B., & Saleh, T. (2019). Building the AI-Powered Organization. *Harvard Business Review*, *97*(4), 62–73.

Frey, C. B., & Osborne, M. A. (2017). The future of employment: How susceptible are jobs to computerisation? *Technological Forecasting and Social Change*, *114*, 254–280. doi:10.1016/j.techfore.2016.08.019

Gallie, D., Felstead, A., Green, F., & Inanc, H. (2017). The hidden face of job insecurity. *Work, Employment and Society*, *31*(1), 36–53. doi:10.1177/0950017015624399

Ghosh, B., Daugherty, P. R., Wilson, H. J., & Burden, A. (2019). Taking a Systems Approach To Workplace Learning. *Harvard Business Review*.

(2023). Google. *Environment Reporter*.

Gupta, P., Fernandes, S. F., & Jain, M. (2018). Automation in Recruitment: A New Frontier. *Journal of Information Technology Teaching Cases*, *8*(2), 118–125. doi:10.105741266-018-0042-x

Haenlein, M., & Kaplan, A. (2019). A Brief History of Artificial Intelligence: On the Past, Present, and Future of Artificial Intelligence. *California Management Review*, *61*(4), 5–14. doi:10.1177/0008125619864925

Harvey, S. B., Modini, M., Joyce, S., Milligan-Saville, J. S., Tan, L., Mykletun, A., Bryant, R. A., Christensen, H., & Mitchell, P. B. (2017). Can work make you mentally ill? A systematic meta-review of work-related risk factors for common mental health problems. *Occupational and Environmental Medicine*, *74*(4), 301–310. doi:10.1136/oemed-2016-104015 PMID:28108676

Havrda, M., & Rakova, B. (2020). Enhanced well-being assessment as basis for the practical implementation of ethical and rights-based normative principles for AI. *2020 IEEE International Conference on Systems, Man, and Cybernetics (SMC)*, 2754–2761. 10.1109/SMC42975.2020.9283137

Horton, J., Cameron, A., Devaraj, D., Hanson, R., & Hajkowicz, S. (2018). *Workplace Safety Futures: The impact of emerging technologies and platforms on work health and safety and workers' compensation over the next 20 years*. https://www.data61.csiro.au/en/Our-Work/Future-Cities/Planning-sustainable-infrastructure/WorkplaceSafety

Huang, L. C., Wu, P., & Kuo, R. J. (2001). A neural network modelling on human resource talent selection. *Int. J. Human Resources Development and Management*, *1*(2/3/4), 206–219.

James Wilson, H., & Daugherty, P. R. (2018). Collaborative intelligence: Humans and AI are joining forces. *Harvard Business Review*.

Jerman, A., Pejić Bach, M., & Aleksić, A. (2020). Transformation towards smart factory system: Examining new job profiles and competencies. *Systems Research and Behavioral Science*, *37*(2), 388–402. doi:10.1002res.2657

Jia, Q., Guo, Y., Li, R., Li, Y., & Chen, Y. (2018). A Conceptual Artificial Intelligence Application Framework in Human Resource Management. *International Conference on Electronic Business*, 106–114.

Karam, S., & Nagahi, M., Dayarathna, V. L., Ma, J., Jaradat, R., & Hamilton, M. (2020). Integrating systems thinking skills with multi-criteria decision-making technology to recruit employee candidates. *Expert Systems with Applications*, *160*(June), 113585. doi:10.1016/j.eswa.2020.113585

Karatop, B., Kubat, C., & Uygun, Ö. (2015). Talent management in manufacturing system using fuzzy logic approach. *Computers & Industrial Engineering*, *86*, 127–136. doi:10.1016/j.cie.2014.09.015

Kolnhofer-Derecskei, A., Reicher, R. Z., & Szeghegyi, A. (2017). The X and Y Generations' Characteristics Comparison. *Acta Polytechnica Hungarica*, *14*(8), 107–125. doi:10.12700/APH.14.8.2017.8.6

Korinek, A., & Stiglitz, J. E. (2019). Artificial Intelligence and Its Implications for Income Distribution and Unemployment. In The Economics of Artificial Intelligence (Issue May, pp. 349–390). University of Chicago Press. doi:10.7208/chicago/9780226613475.003.0014

Kot, S., Hussain, H. I., Bilan, S., Haseeb, M., & Mihardjo, L. W. W. (2021). The role of artificial intelligence recruitment and quality to explain the phenomenon of employer reputation. *Journal of Business Economics and Management*, *22*(4), 867–883. doi:10.3846/jbem.2021.14606

Lawler, J. J., & Elliot, R. (1993). Artificial intelligence in HRM: An experimental study of an expert system. *Proceedings of the 1993 Conference on Computer Personnel Research*, 473–480. 10.1145/158011.158264

Li, S., Da Xu, L., & Zhao, S. (2015). The internet of things: A survey. *Information Systems Frontiers*, *17*(2), 243–259. doi:10.100710796-014-9492-7

Lucia-Casademunt, A. M., Ariza-Montes, A., & Becerra-Alonso, D. (2013). Exploring emotional involvement in workplace by applying artificial neural networks: European study. *Actual Problems of Economics*, *143*(5), 376–385.

Manafi, M., & Devi Subramaniam, I. (2015). Balancing Performance by Human Resource Management Practices. *Asian Social Science*, *11*(10), 386–400. doi:10.5539/ass.v11n10p386

Maree, M., Kmail, A. B., & Belkhatir, M. (2019). Analysis and shortcomings of e-recruitment systems: Towards a semantics-based approach addressing knowledge incompleteness and limited domain coverage. *Journal of Information Science*, *45*(6), 713–735. doi:10.1177/0165551518811449

Margherita, A. (2021). Human resources analytics: A systematization of research topics and directions for future research. *Human Resource Management Review*, *32*(2), 100795. doi:10.1016/j.hrmr.2020.100795

Margherita, A. (2022). Human resources analytics: A systematization of research topics and directions for future research. *Human Resource Management Review*, *32*(2), 100795. doi:10.1016/j.hrmr.2020.100795

Marksberry, P., Church, J., & Schmidt, M. (2014). The Employee Suggestion System: A New Approach Using Latent Semantic Analysis. *Human Factors and Ergonomics in Manufacturing*, *24*(1), 29–39. doi:10.1002/hfm.20351

Masum, A. K., Beh, L. S., Azad, A. K., & Hoque, K. (2018). Intelligent human resource information system (i-HRIS): A holistic decision support framework for HR excellence. *The International Arab Journal of Information Technology*, *15*(1), 121–130.

McCarthy, J. (2007). *What Is Artificial Intelligence Anyway*. Academic Press.

Mikalef, P., & Gupta, M. (2021). Artificial intelligence capability: Conceptualization, measurement calibration, and empirical study on its impact on organizational creativity and firm performance. *Information & Management*, *58*(3), 103434. doi:10.1016/j.im.2021.103434

Min, H. (2010). Artificial intelligence in supply chain management: theory and applications. *International Journal of Logistics: Research and Applications, 13*(1), 13–39. https://doi.org/http://dx.doi.org/10.1080/13675560902736537

Moon, C., Lee, J., & Lim, S. (2010). A performance appraisal and promotion ranking system based on fuzzy logic: An implementation case in military organizations. *Applied Soft Computing*, *10*(2), 512–519. doi:10.1016/j.asoc.2009.08.035

Müller, J. M., Buliga, O., & Voigt, K.-I. (2021). The role of absorptive capacity and innovation strategy in the design of industry 4.0 business Models - A comparison between SMEs and large enterprises. *European Management Journal*, *39*(3), 333–343. doi:10.1016/j.emj.2020.01.002

Naik, N., Hameed, B. M. Z., Shetty, D. K., Swain, D., Shah, M., Paul, R., Aggarwal, K., Ibrahim, S., Patil, V., Smriti, K., Shetty, S., Rai, B. P., Chlosta, P., & Somani, B. K. (2022). Legal and Ethical Consideration in Artificial Intelligence in Healthcare: Who Takes Responsibility? *Frontiers in Surgery*, *9*(March), 1–6. doi:10.3389/fsurg.2022.862322 PMID:35360424

Nazareno, L., & Schiff, D. S. (2021). The impact of automation and artificial intelligence on worker well-being. *Technology in Society*, *67*(July), 101679. doi:10.1016/j.techsoc.2021.101679

Noughabi, E. A., Naseri, M. R. A., Albadvi, A., & Saeedi, M. (2016). Human resource performance evaluation from CRM perspective: A two-step association rule analysis. *International Journal of Business Performance Management*, *17*(1), 89. doi:10.1504/IJBPM.2016.073340

Oswald, F. L., Behrend, T. S., Putka, D. J., & Sinar, E. (2020). Big Data in Industrial-Organizational Psychology and Human Resource Management: Forward Progress for Organizational Research and Practice. *Annual Review of Organizational Psychology and Organizational Behavior*, *7*(1), 505–533. doi:10.1146/annurev-orgpsych-032117-104553

Özdemir, V., & Hekim, N. (2018). Birth of Industry 5.0: Making Sense of Big Data with Artificial Intelligence, "The Internet of Things" and Next-Generation Technology Policy. *OMICS: A Journal of Integrative Biology*, *22*(1), 65–76. doi:10.1089/omi.2017.0194 PMID:29293405

Paschen, J., Wilson, M., & Ferreira, J. J. (2020). Collaborative intelligence: How human and artificial intelligence create value along the B2B sales funnel. *Business Horizons*, *63*(3), 403–414. doi:10.1016/j.bushor.2020.01.003

Pereira, V., Hadjielias, E., Christofi, M., & Vrontis, D. (2023). A systematic literature review on the impact of artificial intelligence on workplace outcomes: A multi-process perspective. *Human Resource Management Review*, *33*(1), 100857. doi:10.1016/j.hrmr.2021.100857

Peters, M. A. (2017). Technological unemployment: Educating for the fourth industrial revolution. *Educational Philosophy and Theory*, *49*(1), 1–6. doi:10.1080/00131857.2016.1177412

Qamar, Y., Agrawal, R. K., Samad, T. A., & Chiappetta Jabbour, C. J. (2021). When technology meets people: The interplay of artificial intelligence and human resource management. *Journal of Enterprise Information Management*, *34*(5), 1339–1370. doi:10.1108/JEIM-11-2020-0436

Rampersad, G. (2020). Robot will take your job: Innovation for an era of artificial intelligence. *Journal of Business Research*, *116*, 68–74. doi:10.1016/j.jbusres.2020.05.019

Richter, Y., Naveh, Y., Gresh, D. L., & Connors, D. P. (2008). Optimatch : Applying constraint programming to workforce management of highly skilled employees. *Int. J. Services Operations and Informatics*, *3*(3/4), 258–270. doi:10.1504/IJSOI.2008.021338

Russell, S. J., & Norvig, P. (2010). *Artificial Intelligence A Modern Approach.* Pearson Education Inc. https://pubs.aip.org/ajp/article/56/1/18/1053122/E-mc2

Sabri, M. F., Wijekoon, R., & Rahim, H. A. (2020). The influence of money attitude, financial practices, self-efficacy and emotion coping on employees' financial well-being. *Management Science Letters*, *10*(4), 889–900. doi:10.5267/j.msl.2019.10.007

Schiff, D., Ayesh, A., Musikanski, L., & Havens, J. C. (2020). IEEE 7010: A New Standard for Assessing the Well-being Implications of Artificial Intelligence. *Conference Proceedings - IEEE International Conference on Systems, Man and Cybernetics,* 2746–2753. 10.1109/SMC42975.2020.9283454

Sexton, R. S., McMurtrey, S., Michalopoulos, J. O., & Smith, A. M. (2005). Employee turnover: A neural network solution. *Computers & Operations Research*, *32*(10), 2635–2651. doi:10.1016/j.cor.2004.06.022

Shahhosseini, V., & Sebt, M. H. (2011). Competency-based selection and assignment of human resources to construction projects. *Scientia Iranica*, *18*(2), 163–180. doi:10.1016/j.scient.2011.03.026

Singh, S. K., Pradhan, R. K., Panigrahy, N. P., & Jena, L. K. (2019). Self-efficacy and workplace well-being: Moderating role of sustainability practices. *Benchmarking*, *26*(6), 1692–1708. doi:10.1108/BIJ-07-2018-0219

Soh, C., & Connolly, D. (2021). New Frontiers of Profit and Risk: The Fourth Industrial Revolution's Impact on Business and Human Rights. *New Political Economy*, *26*(1), 168–185. doi:10.1080/13563467.2020.1723514

Stratton, E., Lampit, A., Choi, I., Calvo, R. A., Harvey, S. B., & Glozier, N. (2017). Effectiveness of eHealth interventions for reducing mental health conditions in employees: A systematic review and meta-analysis. *PLoS One*, *12*(12), 1–23. doi:10.1371/journal.pone.0189904 PMID:29267334

Strohmeier, S., & Piazza, F. (2013). Domain driven data mining in human resource management: A review of current research. *Expert Systems with Applications*, *40*(7), 2410–2420. doi:10.1016/j.eswa.2012.10.059

Strohmeier, S., & Piazza, F. (2015). Artificial Intelligence Techniques in Human Resource Management — A Conceptual Exploration. *Intelligent Techniques in Engineering Management: Theory and Applications*, 149–172. doi:10.1007/978-3-319-17906-3_7

Tambe, P., Cappelli, P., & Yakubovich, V. (2018). Artificial intelligence in human resources management: Challenges and a path forward. *California Management Review*, *61*(4), 15–42. doi:10.1177/0008125619867910

Thakur, D. J., Verma, P., & Sharma, D. (2019). Influence of leadership style: A review. *International Journal of Advanced Science and Technology*, *28*(20), 945–952.

Upadhyay, A. K., & Khandelwal, K. (2018). Applying artificial intelligence: Implications for recruitment. *Strategic HR Review*, *17*(5), 255–258. doi:10.1108/SHR-07-2018-0051

Von Krogh, G. (2018). Artificial Intelligence in Organizations: New Opportunities for Phenomenon-Based Theorizing. *Academy of Management Discoveries*, *4*(4), 404–409. doi:10.5465/amd.2018.0084

Vrontis, D., Christofi, M., Pereira, V., Tarba, S., Makrides, A., & Trichina, E. (2022). Artificial intelligence, robotics, advanced technologies and human resource management: A systematic review. *International Journal of Human Resource Management*, *33*(6), 1237–1266. doi:10.1080/09585192.2020.1871398

Whitmore, A., Agarwal, A., & Da Xu, L. (2015). The Internet of Things—A survey of topics and trends. *Information Systems Frontiers*, *17*(2), 261–274. doi:10.100710796-014-9489-2

Xu, M., David, J. M., & Kim, S. H. (2018). The Fourth Industrial Revolution: Opportunities and Challenges. *International Journal of Financial Research*, *9*(2), 90. doi:10.5430/ijfr.v9n2p90

Xu, S., Stienmetz, J., & Ashton, M. (2020). How will service robots redefine leadership in hotel management? A Delphi approach. *International Journal of Contemporary Hospitality Management*, *32*(6), 2217–2237. doi:10.1108/IJCHM-05-2019-0505

Zhang, D., & Deng, J. (2011). The Data Mining of the Human Resources Data Warehouse in University Based on Association Rule. *Journal of Computers*, *6*(1), 139–146. doi:10.4304/jcp.6.1.139-146

Chapter 19
Leveraging Artificial Intelligence for Enhancing Customer Experience and Efficiency in the Banking Industry

Pooja Verma
https://orcid.org/0000-0001-8070-6609
Shoolini University, India

Shallu Sehgal
Shoolini Institute of Life Sciences and Business Management, India

ABSTRACT

AI is a revolutionary force that could disrupt several sectors. This chapter addresses key questions about AI's impact on banking. It examines natural language processing, machine learning, and predictive analytics in finance. The study aims to elucidate how AI can enhance the banking experience for customers by exploring its role in personalized services, customer support, and fraud prevention. Further, it offers a comprehensive analysis of the pros and cons of utilizing AI in banking operations, illuminating the potential ethical and societal difficulties that may arise as a result. The research examines how AI can improve banking efficiency, transforming the business. The study's main objective is to inform industry stakeholders, policymakers, and researchers on the pros and downsides of AI adoption in this vital sector by addressing the significant AI in banking issues. This study sets the stage for a comprehensive exploration of AI's transformative potential in the banking landscape.

1. INTRODUCTION

Artificial intelligence (AI) has become a game-changing field in recent years, with the potential to alter many industries, including the financial sector (Adams, 2019). As AI continues to gain momentum across diverse industries, it is making significant inroads in the realm of banking, redefining the way financial

DOI: 10.4018/979-8-3693-0418-1.ch019

institutions operate. This study intends to delve into the application of AI in banking, illuminating its potential to better serve customers and streamline internal processes. The purpose of this research is to examine the significant effects that AI has had on the banking and finance industries.

Banks now possess a potent tool in the form of artificial intelligence (AI) that can significantly augment their ability to cater to their clientele (Kumar & Nayyar, 2019). This study undertakes a comprehensive survey of the myriad AI-driven tools that have found application within the banking sector. Notable among these are Natural Language Processing, Predictive Analytics, and Machine Learning, which have gained prominence for their transformative contributions (Jakkani & Kodali, 2020). The multifaceted potential of AI is dissected in this research, highlighting its capacity to bolster operational efficiency, curtail costs, and fortify security measures. Incorporating AI in the banking sector has benefits and drawbacks, both of which are thoroughly explored in this paper. (Deloitte, 2018).

Of particular interest is the investigation into the specific domains where AI is effecting substantial change within the banking industry. This includes its pivotal role in fraud prevention, elevating client support services, and providing bespoke financial guidance (Jakkani & Kodali, 2020). The study underscores how AI is being harnessed to proactively thwart fraudulent activities, enhance customer interactions, and deliver personalized financial advice, all of which collectively contribute to an enriched banking experience.

The paper culminates by casting a forward-looking gaze towards the future of AI in banking, uncovering the latent opportunities for novel developments and innovations in this evolving landscape (Gartner, 2019). The study sets the way for a better comprehension of how the banking sector may continue to harness the power of AI to navigate the dynamic challenges and possibilities of the digital era by examining the potential pathways for further integration of AI technologies.

2. METHODOLOGY

A comprehensive review of scholarly and industry publications is conducted to gather information on artificial intelligence's application to banking (Brynjolfsson & Mitchell, 2017; Mikhalkina & Cabantous, 2015). The literature review is structured around primary applications of AI in banking, such as fraud detection, customer service, and personalized financial advice (Gupta & Jayaraman, 2021; Guo et al., 2021; Lipton et al., 2018). The review examines the different types of AI technologies currently being utilized in banking, including natural language processing, machine learning, and predictive analytics (Li & Zhang, 2021; Panigrahi et al., 2021). And, this research seeks to answer several important questions about artificial intelligence (AI) in the banking business, including what role AI plays, what benefits and obstacles are connected with its use, and how AI may be applied to improve customer experience and operational efficiency (Geetha and Uma, 2021). The idea sheds light on sensitive topics like data privacy (Kshetri and Voas, 2021; Yang, Liu, and Guo, 2020), increased efficiency, reduced costs, and enhanced security (Li & Zhang, 2021; Mikhalkina & Cabantous, 2015) and bias that arise when using AI to the banking industry.

By performing a thorough investigation of the impact and integration of AI technologies in the banking sector, this paper attempts to respond to the following research topics:

- What are the different kinds of AI technologies that are currently being used in the banking industry?

- How can AI be used to make banks better for customers?
- What are the pros and cons of implementing AI in the financial sector?
- What are the social issues that come up when AI is used in banking?
- How can AI be used to make banking operations more efficient?

3. TYPES OF AI TECHNOLOGIES

As various forms of AI have been implemented, the banking industry has seen a dramatic change. These innovative AI solutions have proven to be instrumental in addressing a wide array of challenges and opportunities. In this discussion, we will explore the myriad types of AI technologies that have found application in the banking industry, reshaping customer experiences, operational efficiency, fraud detection, and personalized services.

Table 1. Types of AI technologies used in the banking sector

Sr. No. 3	Types of AI Technologies	References
3.1	**Natural Language Processing (NLP)**	Agrawal & Rath, 2014; Quarteroni, 2018; Kalyanathaya, Akila & Rajesh, 2019; Gerling & Lessmann, 2023; Rayson, Garside & Sawyer, 2000; Nopp & Hanbury, 2015
3.2	**Machine Learning (ML)**	Donepudi, 2017; Hashemi, Mirtaheri & Greco, 2022; Leo, Sharma & Maddulety, 2019; Dauda & Lee, 2015; Siadati & Memon, 2017; Powell, 2020
3.3	**Predictive Analytics**	Budale & Mane, 2013; Etaiwi, Biltawi & Naymat (2017); Blattberg, et. al., 2008; Ravi & Kamaruddin, 2017
3.4	**Robotic Process Automation (RPA)**	Villar & Khan, 2021
3.5	**Algorithmic Trading**	Cartea, et. al., 2022; Sheth, et. al., 2022
3.6	**Virtual Reality (VR) and Augmented Reality (AR)**	Safadel & White,2019; Kołodziej, 2017
3.7	**Image and Speech Recognition**	Sethi & Paliwal, 2015; Singh, & Pathak, 2020
3.8	**RegTech (Regulatory Technology):**	Utami & Septivani, 2022; Von Solms, 2021
3.9	**Predictive Maintenance**	Wang, et. al., 2017; Ramalingam & Venkatesan, 2019
3.10	**Automated Customer Onboarding**	Somani, et.al, 2022; Power, 2022
3.11	**Behavioral Analytics**	Agarwal, Singhal and Thomas (2021)
3.12	**Language Translation Services**	Vieira and Sehgal (2017)
3.13	**Credit and Loan Approval Automation**	Mehndiratta, Arora & Bathla, 2023; Agarwal, Singhal, and Thomas, 2021; Patel, 2023

Source: Created by the authors

3.1. Natural Language Processing (NLP)

The field of NLP focuses on the intersection of CS and linguistics. Natural language processing (NLP) focuses on the mutually beneficial relationship between computers and humans through the medium of language. (Tripathy, Agrawal & Rath, 2014)

i. *Chatbots and Virtual Assistants:* Chatbots and virtual assistants powered by AI are being used in customer service to answer questions, share account details, and do other routine banking-related operations via text-based or voice-activated conversations (Kulkarni et.al., 2017). Voice recognizers and conversational agents (or "chatbots"), commonly known as virtual assistants are used to supplement the live agent experience by providing users with an AI that can help them complete a task (Quarteroni, 2018; Kalyanathaya, Akila & Rajesh, 2019).
ii. *Document Analysis:* Information is extracted and analysed from many unstructured data sources using NLP like contracts, financial reports, and customer communications, streamlining document processing and compliance procedures (Gerling & Lessmann, 2023). NLP approaches can aid in retrieval from various sources, especially semantic analysis. (Rayson, Garside & Sawyer, 2000).
iii. *Sentiment Analysis:* NLP techniques are applied to gauge public sentiment towards the bank, helping institutions understand customer feedback and brand perception from sources like social media, reviews, and surveys. (Hasbullah, Maynard, Chik, Mohd, & Noor, 2016). The ability of sentiment analysis to gauge a bank's perspective on risk through the examination of text data has been the subject of numerous surveys. (Nopp & Hanbury, 2015).

3.2. Machine Learning (ML)

Machine Learning have been harnessed to its full potential by providing business solutions for both front- and back-end operations to boost productivity and quality of service for customers (Donepudi, 2017).

i. *Fraud Detection and Prevention:* Amidst rise in the amount of financial transactions as the use of credit cards became widespread alongside the rise of e-commerce. The high cost of banking transactions is another consequence of the dramatic rise in fraud (Hashemi, Mirtaheri & Greco, 2022). Financial institutions may now detect and prevent financial fraud in real time by using machine learning models to analyse massive volumes of transactional data for patterns suggestive of fraudulent behaviour (Priya and Saradha, 2021; Papadakis, et.al., 2020)
ii. *Credit Scoring and Risk Assessment:* ML algorithms are used to assess credit risk more accurately by considering various data points, improving loan approval processes and risk management. Machine learning has been studied for its potential use in mitigating financial institution risks such credit risk, market risk, operational risk, and liquidity risk. (Leo, Sharma and Maddulety,2019).
iii. *Customer Segmentation and Personalization:* Using ML, we can combine structured and unstructured user and content data to provide customers with content that is more likely to be helpful and interesting to them (Guni, et.al. 2021). Banks can better cater to their customers' individual needs by using ML to categorise them based on their past transactions and other preferences (Dauda & Lee, 2015).
iv. *Anomaly Detection:* ML techniques detect abnormal patterns in transactions, enabling banks to identify potential security breaches or unusual activities (Siadati & Memon, 2017; Powell, 2020). For example, Dumitrescu, Băltoiu & Budulan, 2022 designed a financial transaction anomaly detection tool to detect out money laundering.

3.3. Predictive Analytics

Many financial institutions are turning to predictive analytics in order to meet the demands from their clientele and cut down on customer churn. Financial institutions are making use of predictive analytics to work on customer service, client retention, and new marketing strategies (Budale & Mane, 2013).

i. *Customer Behavior Prediction:* By analyzing historical customer data, predictive analytics enables banks to anticipate customer behavior, such as churn prediction, allowing them to take proactive measures to retain customers. There is a wide variety of classification algorithms available for use in data analysis, categorization, and prediction (Etaiwi, Biltawi & Naymat (2017).
ii. *Cross-Selling and Upselling:* Customers' prior actions and preferences are used in predictive models to uncover product and service upsell and cross-sell opportunities (Li, Sun, & Wilcox, 2005). Database marketing models can be used for upselling and cross-selling; using hazard models and next-product-to-buy models, it is possible to anticipate a customer's next purchase (Blattberg, et. al., 2008).
iii. *Market Trends and Investment Prediction:* Banks utilize predictive analytics to forecast market trends and predict investment opportunities, aiding decision-making for their investment and wealth management services (Ravi & Kamaruddin, 2017).

3.4. Robotic Process Automation (RPA)

Data input, form processing, and reconciliation are just some examples of the kinds of mundane jobs that can be automated by robotic process automation (RPA). Banking procedures are simplified, errors are reduced, and efficiency is increased thanks to RPA (Villar & Khan, 2021).

3.5. Algorithmic Trading

Algorithms powered by artificial intelligence are employed in the financial markets to rapidly analyse market data, spot trading opportunities, and carry out deals (Cartea, et. al., 2022). Algorithmic trading can help banks optimize their trading strategies and generate profits (Sheth, et. al., 2022).

3.6. Virtual Reality (VR) and Augmented Reality (AR)

Some banks are exploring the use of VR and AR technologies to enhance customer experiences where augmented reality can aid in providing personalized financial advice and product demonstrations. (Safadel, & White, 2019). Advantages to business are gained when virtual reality is used in banking as it details a wide range of potential uses, current market tendencies, and future projections, also creating immersive virtual branches (Kołodziej, 2017).

3.7. Image and Speech Recognition

Check deposit processing, voice-based banking, and identification verification are just some of the areas where artificial intelligence image and speech recognition technologies are being used to make life easier and safer for customers (Sethi & Paliwal, 2015). For the purposes of data collection, cleaning, analysis, and dissemination, cutting-edge technologies in the field of artificial intelligence (AI) such as Machine Learning, IVR, NLP (Natural Language Processing), Deep Learning, Speech Recognition, Image Analysis, and others are readily available. (Singh, & Pathak, 2020).

3.8. RegTech (Regulatory Technology)

RegTech, short for "regulatory technology," is a growing field of study with the potential to aid financial institutions with regulatory compliance and anti-money-laundering activities (Utami & Septivani, 2022). AI-powered RegTech solutions assist banks in managing compliance and regulatory requirements more efficiently. These technologies can automatically monitor and adapt to changing regulations, reducing compliance costs and risks (Von Solms, 2021).

3.9. Predictive Maintenance

Techniques for Predictive Maintenance By anticipating when equipment may break down and scheduling necessary repairs accordingly, preventative maintenance strategies can help keep businesses running smoothly, satisfy customers, and save money (Wang, et. al., 2017). Artificial intelligence can be implemented in the financial sector for predictive maintenance, where sensors and machine learning algorithms monitor the health of critical equipment, such as ATMs and servers, to detect potential issues before they lead to failures or downtime (Ramalingam & Venkatesan, 2019).

3.10. Automated Customer Onboarding

In the future, artificial intelligence (AI) may be able to improve the efficiency of customer onboarding procedures through the automation of data validation, document verification, and risk assessment. This enables financial institutions to expedite the account opening process and improve the promptness of service provision (Somani, et.al, 2022; Power, 2022).

3.11. Behavioral Analytics

According to Vieira and Sehgal (2017), behavioural analytics powered by There is the option of using artificial intelligence (AI) to examine client interactions and trends, with the aim of identifying atypical behaviour or probable instances of fraudulent activity. This enables banks to enhance their security measures, as highlighted by Agarwal, Singhal, and Thomas (2021).

3.12. Language Translation Services

According to Vieira and Sehgal (2017), the AI technology adoption by the banking industry enables effective communication between banks and consumers, transcending language barriers and geographical boundaries. This is achieved through the provision of instantaneous language translation services.

3.13. Credit and Loan Approval Automation

The utilisation of AI-powered credit decision systems has the potential to streamline the assessment of loan applications, resulting in expedited and more precise loan approval procedures (Mehndiratta, Arora, & Bathla, 2023; Agarwal, Singhal, and Thomas, 2021). Future credit and risk management is anticipated to be profoundly affected by the convergence of robotic process automation and artificial intelligence, leading to an expansion of the client base, improved examination processes, and the capacity to make quick assessments with reduced risk (Patel, 2023).

4. APPLICATIONS OF AI IN BANKING

Artificial intelligence (AI), machine learning, and robotics are all being put to good use in India's burgeoning financial services sector, although it has only scratched the surface of their capabilities. Collaboration between established financial institutions and fintech startups is driving proof-of-concept initiatives focused on workflow automation, including chatbots for improved customer service, personalised financial planning through robot advisors and improved fraud prevention through algorithmic analysis. These innovations align with government initiatives aimed at promoting financial inclusion and transparency. AI's pivotal role in data analysis, transparency, efficiency, and compliance is especially significant in risk assessment and lending to microbusinesses and SMEs. However, persistent concerns related to data privacy and security must be addressed. Leveraging AI can lead to substantial transformations in business models and customer experiences, helping financial institutions stay competitive amid emerging tech-savvy fintech competitors (Sources: Economic Times, 2017; PWC, 2018; PTI, 2017; Gupta, 2021).

Figure 1. Applications of AI in banking
Source: Designed by authors

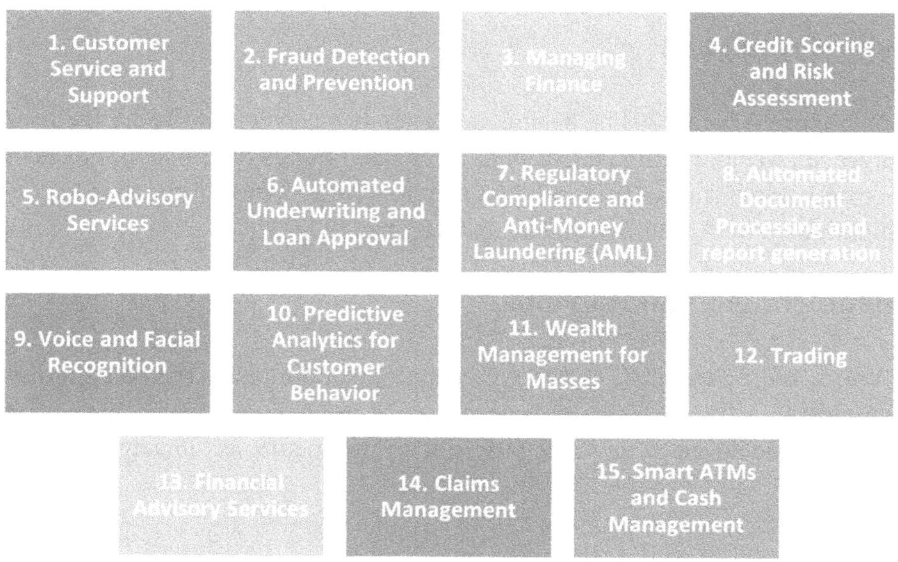

4.1. Customer Service and Support

Chatbots, voice-enabled systems, and text-based discussions are just some of the AI-enabled technologies that have supplanted more conventional means of customer support. Companies can get help from subject-matter experts at a fraction of the usual cost because to these innovations (Zainurin, et al. 2023). They use AI to address customer inquiries, offer self-learning for intelligent conversations, and provide 24/7 support for routine tasks (Lee, S.M. and Lee, D. 2020; Umamaheswari, S., & Valarmathi, A. 2023). This shift improves customer service efficiency and accessibility, transforming the industry.

4.2. Fraud Detection and Prevention

In 2016, global cybercrime costs amounted to $450 billion, disproportionately affecting Asian businesses with over $81 billion in losses. Prominent cyberattacks involve data breaches, denial-of-service attacks, and infrastructure vulnerabilities (Vieira and Sehgal 2018). Artificial intelligence plays a crucial role in identifying fraud and related financial crimes. Fraud encompasses internal (employee-driven) and external (attacks on customers or financial institutions) categories. To counter this, Fraud Detection Systems leverage techniques like feature engineering, adaptive, supervised, and unsupervised learning, utilizing traditional data for analysis and learning (Soni, V. D. 2019).

4.3. Managing Finance

In today's consumerist culture, the management of one's personal or business finances presents unique obstacles. However, a solution appears to be on the horizon with the growing adoption of AI and similar technologies in the world of fund management. The concept of Personal Financial Management (PFM) has emerged within this AI-driven financial landscape (Rajamohan & Dhanabalan, 2014). Notably, a San Francisco-based firm has developed an AI-powered wallet that aids users in making judicious spending decisions. By aggregating online data, this innovation creates visual spending patterns (Maruti Labs, 2019). This approach raises privacy concerns and legal considerations but merits consideration as a potential PFM tool. Ashish Anantharaman (2019) emphasizes AI's role as a regulatory force, shaping financial management at both micro and macro scales.

4.4. Credit Scoring and Risk Assessment

Sadok et al. (2022) assert that credit scoring models powered by artificial intelligence (AI) use a diverse array of data points, including transaction history and alternative data, in order to more precisely evaluate credit risk. This enhanced assessment capability facilitates improved lending judgements. The utilisation of artificial intelligence algorithms facilitates the detection of potential hazards and the provision of significant insights pertaining to financial transactions. This objective can be achieved by the examination of enormous amounts of data. As a consequence of this phenomenon, financial institutions possess the potential to mitigate their risk exposure and thereby enhance the quality of their decision-making processes (Dzhaparov, P. 2020).

4.5. Robo-Advisory Services

Robo-advisors use artificial intelligence (AI) algorithms to create and manage financial portfolios, aligning with clients' financial objectives, risk preferences, and market dynamics. This yields automated and cost-efficient investment guidance. AI-powered financial experts enhance users' ability to make astute decisions in financial matters, factoring in market trends vis-à-vis investment capacity and existing portfolios, aiding in informed choices concerning stock and bond transactions. Commonly dubbed "Robo-Advisors," this technology's adoption has surged with notable financial institutions and Fintech collaboration (Malali, A. B., & Gopalakrishnan, S. 2020).

4.6. Automated Underwriting and Loan Approval

Agarwal, Singhal, and Thomas (2021) advocate leveraging AI/ML models to tailor decisions, expanding deployment, bolstering edge capabilities, and creating a comprehensive digital marketing mechanism for synchronized messaging across diverse channels. Chatbots, employing algorithms, constitute a technology service engaging customers through text or voice naturally, akin to human interaction (Shawar and Atwell, 2007). This strategic application of chatbots facilitates efficient customer care, enabling users to access transactional insights and supplementary services. By comprehending individual needs, banks utilize chatbots to present fitting offers and potential rewards, enhancing customer engagement and satisfaction.

4.7. Regulatory Compliance and Anti-Money Laundering (AML)

Regulatory compliance and anti-money laundering (AML) encompass a range of rules and regulations that address many aspects, such as data privacy, data security, and equitable treatment of consumers, among other potential subjects. Noncompliance with regulations can lead to significant financial penalties and reputational damage for banks (Butler & O'Brien, 2019).

4.8. Automated Document Processing and Report Generation

Natural language generation software suppliers prioritize structured data reports and synopses for concise analyses. Prose summaries are favored for ease and efficiency over figures and graphs. Data, machine learning, and AI are interconnected, with data-driven decisions impacting higher systems. AI applications use machine learning to convert data into actionable predictions, driving real-world actions (Shambira, L. 2020).

4.9. Voice and Facial Recognition

Biometric authentication in banking apps utilises artificial intelligence-powered facial and speech recognition technologies (Goode, 2018). Customers have the ability to access their accounts, validate transactions, and provide authorization for sensitive procedures through the utilisation of facial or vocal recognition. This approach enhances security by reducing dependence on traditional personal identification numbers (PINs) and passwords, which are vulnerable to social engineering tactics or hacking attempts (Malini & Menon, 2017).

4.10. Predictive Analytics for Customer Behavior

Business planning, sales, revenue creation, and resource optimisation are all heavily impacted by prognostic analytics' use in the financial services industry (Malali & Gopalakrishnan, 2020). It revolutionizes predictive analysis by leveraging extensive data to identify patterns and forecast insights accurately, revealing future consumer behaviors, purchases, and employee tenure. This method is instrumental in calculating consumer credit scores and mitigating risky loans for banks and financial institutions (Dhanabalan et al., 2018).Predictive analysis thus draws its real conclusion from data mining's smart statistics.

4.11. Wealth Management for Masses

Computerised advisory services are increasingly available to people with lower net worth, leading to reduced fees. AI-powered smart wallets monitor spending and advise users to cut back, promoting cost-saving habits. The financial sector increasingly uses automation, integrating AI and ML into daily operations (Django Stars, 2019; LEE, 2022). This benefits low-net-worth customers by offering better advice and personalized recommendations.

4.12. Trading

Technology and data analysts are becoming increasingly important to the performance of investment organisations in making correct market position predictions. Systems process vast data quickly, trained to study historical data forms for future predictions. Despite anomalies like the 2008 financial crisis, systems learn to uncover reasons and devise strategies for avoiding such anomalies in future forecasts (Dhanabalan et al., 2018). AI offers personalized solutions based on individual risk tolerance. High-risk individuals use AI for timing stock transactions, while risk-averse ones receive alerts on market fluctuations, aiding decisions on investments and market exit (Donepudi, 2017).

4.13. Financial Advisory Services

The 2017 PWC Report explores the utilization of robot advisors to handle down payments, aiming to alleviate pressure on banks and financial institutions to lower commissions. A new concept called bionic advice, which merges mechanical and human insights, presents a more powerful solution than their individual contributions.

4.14. Claims Management

AI-enabled tools collect and intelligently analyze evidence to ensure reliable outcomes. They grasp user behavior for anomaly detection, issuing alerts on unusual transactions. In claims administration, AI, particularly machine learning, expedites settlement via streamlined steps (Park & Dhanabalan, 2019). These tools adeptly manage data, accelerating electronic claims payment. Automated settlement processes decrease processing time, cutting costs and enhancing customer satisfaction (Malali & Gopalakrishnan, 2020).

4.15. Smart ATMs and Cash Management

AI-powered intelligent automated teller machines (ATMs) employ advanced algorithms to optimise the management of cash resources. These ATMs utilise predictive models to forecast cash demand and effectively allocate cash flow, resulting in reduced expenses and improved availability of ATMs. In the context of automated teller machines (ATMs), it is possible to use a combination of real-time camera images with cutting-edge AI methods, in particular deep learning to identify and deter fraudulent activities and criminal behaviour (Vijai, 2019).

5. BENEFITS OF AI IN BANKING

Banks that use artificial intelligence offers benefits such as improved customer service through chatbots, personalized financial planning with robo-advisors, enhanced fraud detection, streamlined operations, and data-driven insights for better risk assessment and decision-making.

Figure 2. Benefits of AI in the banking industry
Source: Designed by authors

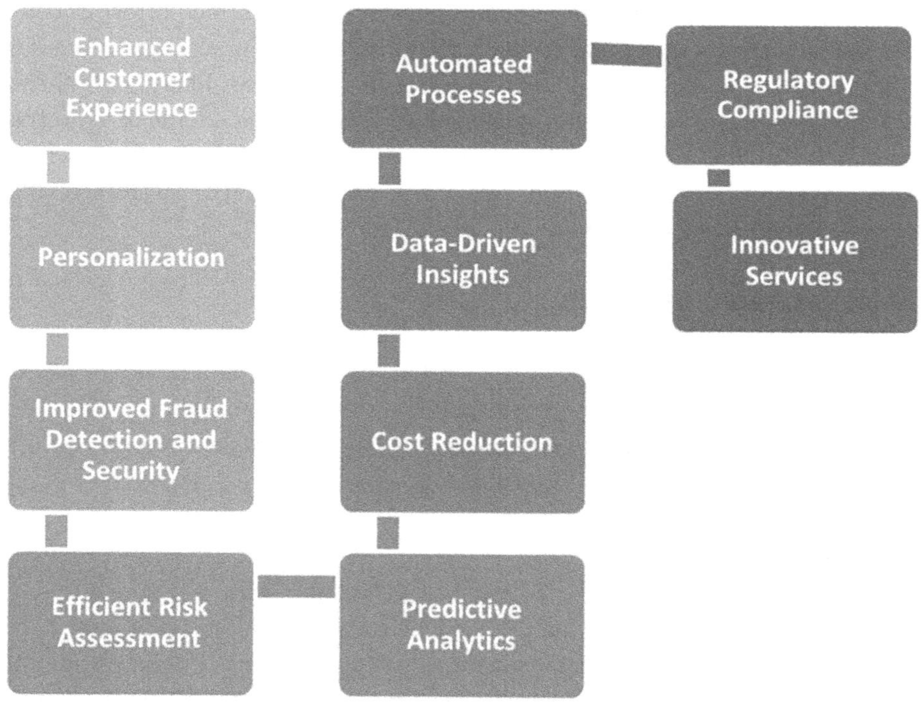

5.1. Enhanced Customer Experience

Chatbots and virtual assistants powered by AI can be used to provide assistance to customers at any time (24/7), resulting in enhanced service quality and quicker query resolution (Noreen et al., 2023). This availability ensures timely assistance, contributing to heightened customer satisfaction and more efficient interactions.

5.2. Personalization

AI empowers banks to provide tailored product suggestions, services, and financial guidance aligned with individual customer preferences and behaviors (Vijai, 2018; Mhlanga, 2020). This personalized approach enhances customer engagement, fosters loyalty, and optimizes the overall banking experience by delivering relevant solutions and insights.

5.3. Improved Fraud Detection and Security

AI algorithms possess the capability to swiftly analyze extensive real-time transaction data, effectively identifying and thwarting fraudulent activities, thereby bolstering the security of banking operations (Vieira & Sehgal, 2017). This proactive approach aids in safeguarding customer assets and maintaining the integrity of financial systems.

5.4. Efficient Risk Assessment

AI-powered credit scoring models and risk assessment algorithms empower banks to evaluate credit-worthiness with heightened precision, culminating in improved lending choices and diminished credit risks (Digalaki, 2020). By leveraging advanced data analysis, these AI-driven tools enhance the decision-making process, allowing for more informed and responsible lending practices.

5.5. Automated Processes

AI automation effectively handles mundane and repetitive tasks, including document processing and customer onboarding, optimizing operations and boosting efficiency (Malali and Gopalakrishnan, 2020). By relieving employees of routine duties, AI allows them to focus on higher-value activities, thereby enhancing productivity and overall organizational effectiveness.

5.6. Data-Driven Insights

AI-driven analytics equip banks with valuable insights extracted from extensive datasets, facilitating informed business decisions and the identification of market trends (Kaur, et al., 2020). This data-driven approach enhances strategic planning and enables financial institutions to stay responsive to evolving market dynamics, thus maintaining a competitive edge.

5.7. Cost Reduction

The implementation of AI-driven automation and process optimization can result in cost savings for banks by reducing manual tasks and streamlining operations (Tarafdar et al., 2010). This efficiency-driven approach allows financial institutions to allocate resources more effectively and achieve financial benefits while maintaining operational effectiveness.

5.8. Predictive Analytics

AI enables predictive analytics, empowering banks to anticipate customer behavior, detect potential churn, and enhance cross-selling possibilities (Königstorfer, et al., 2020; Soni, 2019). By leveraging historical data and patterns, these AI-driven insights guide targeted strategies, fostering stronger customer relationships and maximizing revenue generation.

5.9. Regulatory Compliance

AI assists banks in navigating intricate regulatory mandates and anti-money laundering (AML) regulations, thereby mitigating compliance risks (Butler & O'Brien, 2019). Through advanced data analysis and pattern recognition, AI enhances the effectiveness of monitoring and reporting processes, ensuring adherence to legal requirements and reinforcing the integrity of financial systems.

5.10. Innovative Services

AI creates avenues for banks to introduce innovative offerings like robo-advisory services and virtual banking experiences, unlocking new opportunities for customer engagement and satisfaction (Kumar, et al., 2020). These novel solutions cater to evolving consumer preferences and provide convenient, tech-driven solutions that enhance accessibility and convenience in financial interactions.

6. CHALLENGES OF AI IN BANKING

Artificial intelligence (AI) adoption by the banking industry presents immense potential for innovation and efficiency, but it also brings forth a host of formidable challenges that must be addressed for the industry to harness its full capabilities.

6.1. Data Privacy and Security

The application of AI entails handling significant volumes of sensitive customer data, sparking concerns over data privacy and security breaches (Ghandour, 2021). Ensuring robust protective measures is crucial for financial institutions as they leverage AI's potential, striking a balance between innovation and data security. Maintaining customer trust requires stringent protocols and encryption mechanisms in this evolving landscape.

Figure 3. Benefits of AI in the banking industry
Source: Designed by authors

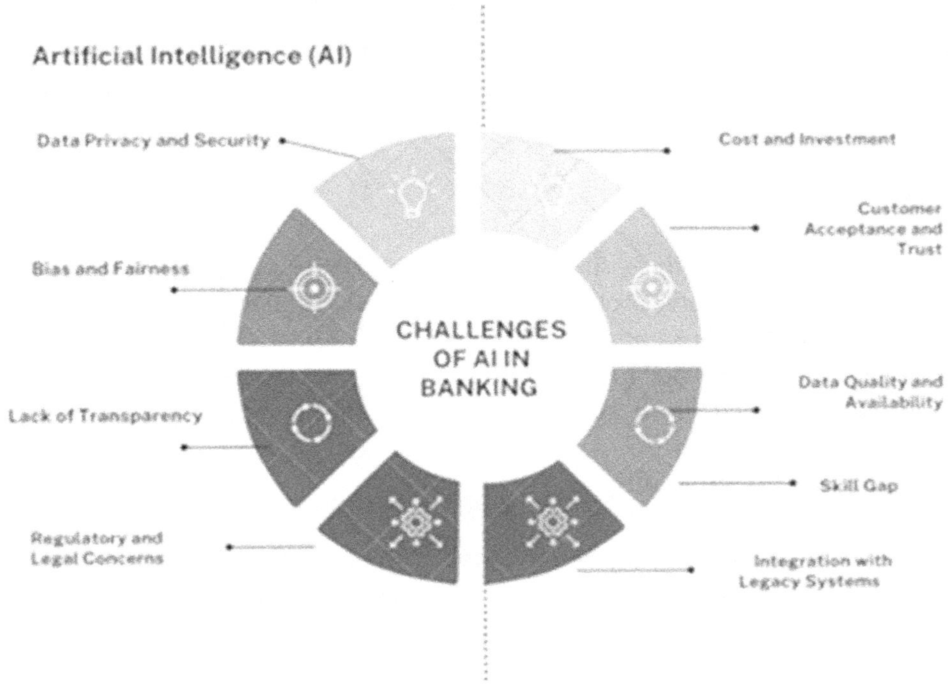

6.2. Bias and Fairness

There is a risk that discriminatory or unfair treatment of certain clientele will come from AI models adopting biases existing in their training data (Zhou, et.al., 2022; Zhou, et.al., 2021; Castelnovo, 2020). Mitigating these biases is essential to ensure equitable outcomes and prevent unintended harm, necessitating ongoing research and rigorous bias detection methods in AI development.

6.3. Lack of Transparency

AI algorithms' complexity can hinder comprehension of their decision-making, raising concerns about transparency and explainability (Balasubramaniam, 2020; Dwivedi, 2023). Addressing these challenges is crucial for building trust, necessitating efforts to develop interpretable AI models and frameworks that facilitate clearer insights into their actions.

6.4. Regulatory and Legal Concerns

The integration of AI in banking prompts legal and regulatory inquiries, particularly surrounding liability and accountability regarding AI-driven choices (Ghandour, 2021; Caron, 2019). Navigating these complex issues requires a comprehensive legal framework to define roles, responsibilities, and potential consequences in the context of AI-powered decision-making within the financial sector.

6.5. Integration with Legacy Systems

Incorporating AI technologies into existing legacy systems can present challenges, often requiring intricate and time-consuming integration processes (AL-Dosari, et. al., 2022). Adapting these advanced technologies to coexist with established infrastructures necessitates careful planning and execution to ensure seamless functionality and efficiency.

6.6. Skill Gap

Skill gap is one of the most challenging issues all over the world (Bhardwaj & Sharma, 2022). Deploying AI necessitates a proficient workforce to oversee and sustain the technology, potentially facing a shortage of AI expertise within the banking sector (Rahman, 2021; Pradhan, 2023). Addressing this talent gap becomes crucial for successful AI integration, requiring investment in training and recruitment strategies to secure the requisite skills and knowledge for effective implementation and management.

6.7. Data Quality and Availability

The quality and availability of data is crucial to the success of artificial intelligence models, with inconsistent or incomplete data exerting a noticeable influence on their performance (Thowfeek, 2020). Ensuring a robust and comprehensive dataset is imperative to maximize the accuracy and reliability of AI-driven outcomes.

6.8. Customer Acceptance and Trust

Certain customers may exhibit reluctance to engage with AI-powered services, favoring human interactions and expressing reservations regarding data privacy (Rahman, et. al., 2021; Lockey, et. al., 2021). Overcoming this hesitancy entails addressing privacy concerns and effectively communicating the benefits of AI, while maintaining options for personalized human assistance to cater to diverse customer preferences.

6.9. Cost and Investment

The integration of AI technologies demands substantial upfront investment in infrastructure, software, and staff training (Biswas, et. al., 2020; Malali, et. al., 2020). While this initial financial commitment can be substantial, the long-term benefits of enhanced efficiency and improved customer experiences often outweigh the costs, making it a strategic decision for progressive banks and financial institutions.

7. SOCIAL ISSUES THAT COME UP WHEN AI IS USED IN BANKING

As Artificial Intelligence (AI) continues to reshape the banking industry, it brings with it a host of social issues that warrant careful consideration. From concerns about job displacement and the digital divide to questions of data privacy and bias, the integration of AI in banking raises important societal and ethical questions that demand thoughtful examination and solutions.

Figure 4. Social implications of AI in banking
Source: Designed by authors

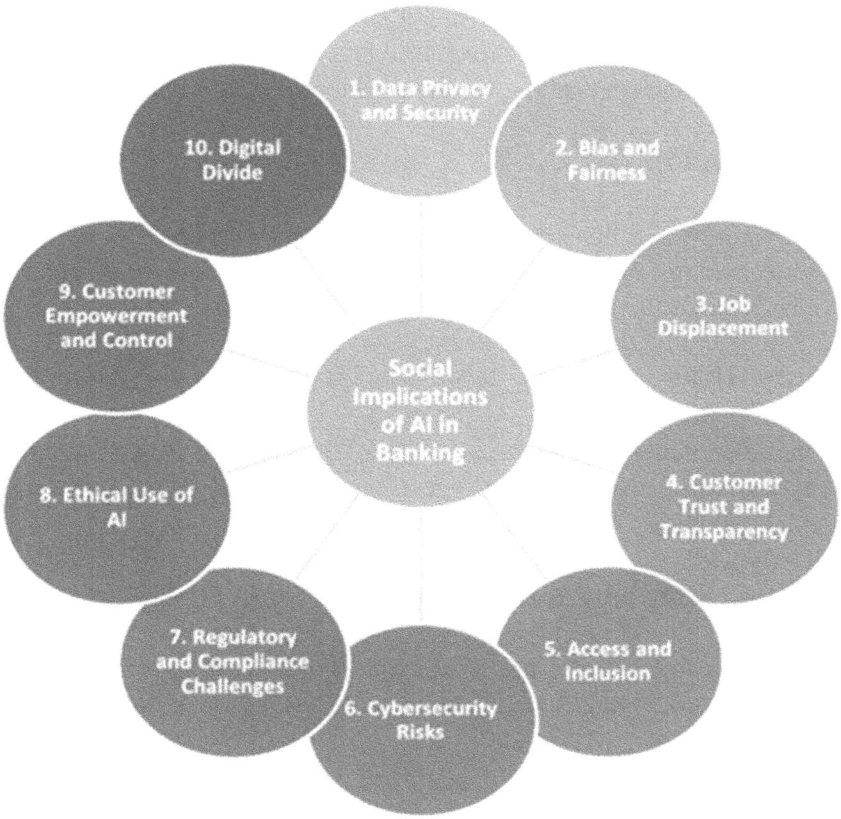

7.1. Data Privacy and Security

Using AI in the banking industry entails sifting through mountains of consumer information. It is critical to protect sensitive consumer information from theft and misuse by ensuring the privacy and security of this data (Mohammed, 2021)

7.2. Bias and Fairness

The data used to train AI systems may have inherent biases that could lead to discrimination or unfair treatment of some sectors of the population. Addressing algorithmic bias is essential to ensure equitable outcomes for all customers (Mehrotra, 2019).

7.3. Job Displacement

Employees in the banking industry may be at risk of losing their jobs as a result of the increased use of artificial intelligence to automate formerly human-only processes. This calls for reskilling and upskilling programmes to alleviate fears about job loss (Athey & Luca, 2019).

7.4. Customer Trust and Transparency

Artificial intelligence (AI) in decision-making might be seen as a black box, making it difficult for customers to grasp the reasoning behind decisions. Building customer trust requires transparency in AI algorithms and their implications on banking services (Aldboush & Ferdous, 2023).

7.5. Access and Inclusion

AI-based services may not be equally accessible to all customers, especially those with limited digital literacy or access to technology. Banks must ensure that AI-driven services are inclusive and do not leave certain customer segments behind (Swapna, 2018).

7.6. Cybersecurity Risks

As AI adoption increases, so does the risk of cyberattacks targeting AI systems and data. Banks must implement robust cybersecurity measures to safeguard against potential breaches and system vulnerabilities (Simoes, et. al., 2023).

7.7. Regulatory and Compliance Challenges

Regulations and regulatory criteria for the use of AI in banking are still being developed. Legal compliance for AI systems is a complex and resource-intensive issue (Ghandour, 2021; Caron, 2019).

7.8. Ethical Use of AI

AI technologies have the potential to impact individuals and communities significantly. Ethical AI usage in banking is essential to avoid any unintended negative consequences and maintain public trust (Aitken, et. al., 2020).

7.9. Customer Empowerment and Control

As AI-driven decision-making becomes more prevalent, customers may desire more control over the data used and the decisions made about their financial affairs. Providing customers with greater transparency and control over their data is essential (Ludwig, 2018).

7.10. Digital Divide

AI adoption may exacerbate the digital divide between individuals with access to advanced AI-powered services and those without. Bridging this divide and ensuring equitable access to banking services is vital (Van Dijk, 2006).

8. CONCLUSION: ENHANCING CUSTOMER BANKING EXPERIENCE WITH AI

Understanding how AI may help banks improve their services, increase efficiency, and enhance customer experience is why the proposed research on why Artificial Intelligence (AI) in Banking Is Crucial. According to Zhang and Liu (2021), AI technologies such as machine learning and natural language processing can help banks improve customer service by providing personalized recommendations and faster response times. Additionally, AI can assist banks in detecting fraudulent activities and making better investment decisions (Kumar & Kumar, 2021).

Figure 5. Enhancing customer banking experience with AI
Source: Designed by authors

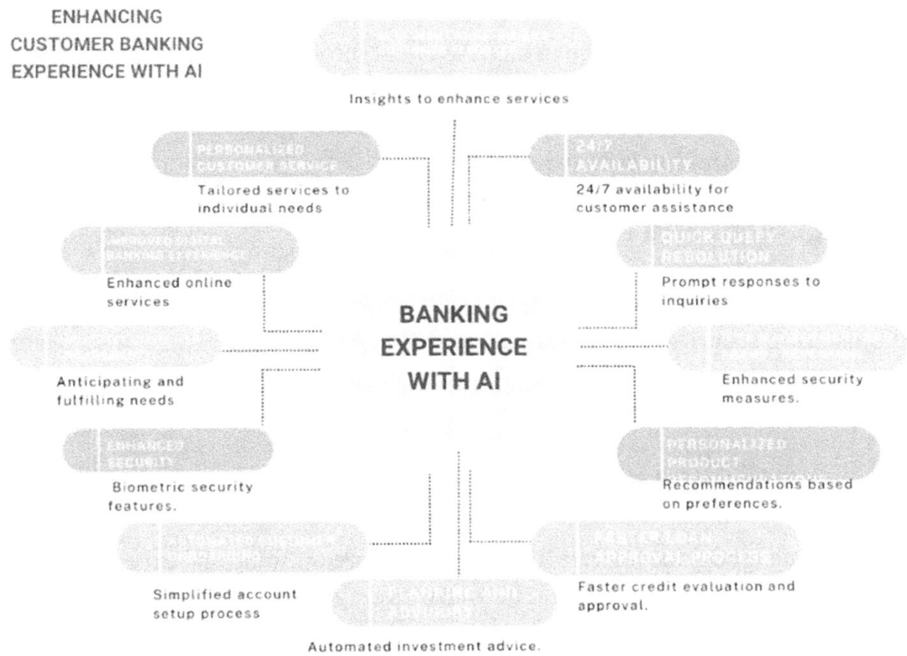

8.1. Personalized Customer Service

With the use of artificial intelligence, chatbots and virtual assistants may provide one-on-one assistance to customers and delivering customized information according to individual preferences (Vijai, 2018; Mhlanga, 2020). These technologies enhance user experiences, streamline interactions, and offer efficient solutions. By leveraging AI's capabilities, businesses can offer real-time assistance, improving customer satisfaction and engagement.

8.2. 24/7 Availability

AI-powered chatbots ensure 24/7 availability, granting customers access to support and banking services anytime, enhancing convenience and accessibility (GarimaKaneria, 2022). This continuous assistance improves user experience, enabling efficient interactions and meeting customer needs around the clock.

8.3. Quick Query Resolution

AI chatbots efficiently manage routine customer inquiries, minimizing wait times and offering swift responses to frequently asked questions (Suhel, et al., 2020). This accelerates query resolution, enhances customer satisfaction, and optimizes resource utilization for banks.

8.4. Personalized Product Recommendations

Algorithms that use artificial intelligence to analyse client information and make relevant recommendations, aiding customers in discovering banking services that match their financial objectives (Hernandez-Nieves, et al., 2021). This tailored approach enhances customer engagement, promotes relevant offerings, and fosters a more meaningful banking experience.

8.5. Risk Management and Fraud Prevention

AI-powered fraud detection systems swiftly detect and thwart fraudulent activities, safeguarding customer accounts and bolstering security (Aziz & Dowling, 2019; Alhaddad, 2018). These systems employ advanced algorithms to analyze patterns, swiftly flagging suspicious transactions and minimizing potential risks, thereby fortifying the integrity of banking operations.

8.6. Faster Loan Approval Process

AI-driven credit scoring models accelerate loan approvals, streamlining and expediting the credit acquisition process for customers (Purificato, et al., 2023). By leveraging sophisticated algorithms, these models analyze vast data sets efficiently, providing accurate assessments of creditworthiness. This enhances customer experiences, reduces processing times, and facilitates faster access to essential financial resources.

8.7. Automated Customer Onboarding

AI optimizes the onboarding process, allowing customers to swiftly open accounts and access banking services, minimizing paperwork and wait times (Villar & Khan, 2021). By automating identity verification, data entry, and compliance checks, AI expedites customer enrollment, enhancing convenience and improving the overall sign-up experience.

8.8. Financial Planning and Advisory Services

AI-driven robo-advisors provide automated investment guidance and portfolio management, assisting customers in making well-informed financial choices aligned with their objectives and risk preferences

(Northey, et al., 2022). These platforms analyze data to offer personalized recommendations, enhancing accessibility to professional investment services and facilitating prudent decision-making.

8.9. Improved Digital Banking Experience

AI technologies elevate the user interface and experience of banking apps and websites, creating more intuitive and user-friendly digital banking platforms (Bhattacharya & Sinha, 2022). Through predictive analytics, personalized recommendations, and natural language processing, AI enriches interactions, simplifies navigation, and tailors offerings, ultimately enhancing customer satisfaction and engagement.

8.10. Sentiment Analysis and Customer Feedback

AI analyzes customer feedback and sentiment across diverse channels, empowering banks to pinpoint areas for enhancement and address customer concerns with greater effectiveness (Ahmed, 2022). By extracting valuable insights from large volumes of data, AI-driven sentiment analysis enables banks to enhance their services, refine customer engagement strategies, and foster stronger relationships based on a deeper understanding of customer needs and preferences.

8.11. Proactive Customer Engagement

AI-powered analytics forecast customer behavior and needs, enabling banks to engage customers proactively through tailored offers and services (Carpenter, 2020). By analyzing historical data and patterns, AI algorithms anticipate preferences and trends, enabling banks to deliver timely and personalized solutions that enhance customer satisfaction and drive deeper loyalty.

8.12. Enhanced Security

AI-driven biometric authentication, like voice and facial recognition, offers enhanced security, permitting only authorized customers to access their accounts (Soni, 2019). By leveraging unique physiological characteristics, AI verifies identity with heightened accuracy, fortifying account protection and thwarting unauthorized access attempts, thereby ensuring a robust and trustworthy banking experience.

8.13. Seamless Omni-Channel Experience

AI facilitates smooth integration across diverse channels, guaranteeing a unified and connected customer experience across in-branch, online, and mobile app interactions (Misra & Bohra, 2020; Hamouda, 2019). By harmonizing data and interactions, AI ensures consistency, allowing customers to seamlessly transition between different touchpoints while enjoying a cohesive and personalized journey with their bank.

In summary, comprehending the profound potential of artificial intelligence (AI) within the banking sector is crucial not only for academic researchers but also for industry professionals. AI, with its remarkable capabilities, stands poised to revolutionize the very foundations of banking operations, ushering in a new era of innovation and customer-centric services. Its multifaceted contributions encompass elevating customer experiences, streamlining operational efficiencies, fortifying fraud detection mechanisms, and facilitating the delivery of personalized financial services. Beyond the immediate applications, the fusion of academic research and practical implementation carries the promise of driving strategic decisions that can significantly enhance the competitive edge of financial institutions.

This synergy between academia and industry is the crucible in which AI-powered innovations are forged, reshaping the landscape of banking as we know it. By harnessing the power of AI, banks can not only bolster their operational prowess but also fundamentally transform their relationships with customers. Future researchers can also focus on the Role of AI in affecting employee engagement which in turn can affect customer experience (Bhardwaj et al, 2023;Thakur et al, 2019). This transformation is driven by the twin engines of data-driven insights and automated decision-making, which enable banks to tailor services to individual needs with unprecedented precision. In doing so, they lay the foundation for a technologically empowered future in the financial sector, where banking isn't just a service but an integral part of customers' lives, seamlessly adapting to their evolving needs and preferences.

In conclusion, AI's influence on banking is far-reaching and transformative, offering institutions the opportunity not only to thrive in the digital age but also to set new standards of excellence. As AI continues to evolve, so too will its impact on banking, pushing the boundaries of what is possible and inspiring a future where financial services are smarter, more efficient, and deeply attuned to the desires of their customers. This symbiotic relationship between AI and banking holds the potential to redefine the industry, making it more accessible, responsive, and agile than ever before, ultimately shaping a brighter, technologically driven future for the financial world.

REFERENCES

Anantharaman, A. (2019). *How artificial intelligence is enabling financial inclusion in India*. Retrieved from: https://yourstory.com/2019/05/artificial-intelligence-enabling-financial-inclusion

Athey, S., & Luca, M. (2019). Economists (And Economics) in Tech Companies. *The Journal of Economic Perspectives*, *33*(1), 209–230. doi:10.1257/jep.33.1.209

Atwell, E., & Shawar, B. (2003). Machine learning from dialogue corpora to generate chatbots. *Expert Update Journal*, *6*(3), 25–29.

Aziz, S., & Dowling, M. (2019). Machine learning and AI for risk management. *Disrupting finance: FinTech and strategy in the 21st century*, 33-50.

Balasubramaniam, N., Kauppinen, M., Kujala, S., & Hiekkanen, K. (2020). Ethical guidelines for solving ethical issues and developing AI systems. *Product-Focused Software Process Improvement: 21st International Conference, PROFES 2020, Turin, Italy, November 25–27, 2020 Proceedings*, *21*, 331–346.

Bhardwaj, B., Kalia, N., Chand, M., & Sharma, D. (2023). Engaged Organizational Culture as a precursor to job performance: An evidence from the hospitality industry of Himachal Pradesh. *International Journal of Hospitality and Tourism Systems*, *16*(4), 48–57.

Bhardwaj, B., & Sharma, D. (2022). Migration of skilled professionals across the border: Brain drain or brain gain? *European Management Journal*. Advance online publication. doi:10.1016/j.emj.2022.12.011

Bhattacharya, C., & Sinha, M. (2022). The Role of Artificial Intelligence in Banking for Leveraging Customer Experience. *Australasian Accounting. Business and Finance Journal*, *16*(5), 89–105.

Biswas, S., Carson, B., Chung, V., Singh, S., & Thomas, R. (2020). *AI-bank of the future: Can banks meet the AI challenge*. McKinsey & Company.

Blattberg, R. C., Kim, B. D., Neslin, S. A., Blattberg, R. C., Kim, B. D., & Neslin, S. A. (2008). Cross-Selling and Up-Selling. *Database Marketing: Analyzing and Managing Customers*, 515-547.

Božić, V. (n.d.). *Risks of digital divide in using artificial intelligence (AI).* researchgate.net

Brynjolfsson, E., & Mitchell, T. (2017). What can machine learning do? Workforce implications. *Science, 358*(6370), 1530–1534. doi:10.1126cience.aap8062 PMID:29269459

Budale, D., & Mane, D. (2013). Predictive analytics in retail banking. *International Journal of Engineering and Advanced Technology, 2*(5), 508–510.

Bughin, J., Hazan, E., Ramaswamy, S., Chui, M., Allas, T., Dahlström, P., & Henke, N. (2018). *Artificial intelligence: The next digital frontier?* McKinsey Global Institute.

Butler, T., & O'Brien, L. (2019). Artificial intelligence for regulatory compliance: Are we there yet? *Journal of Financial Compliance, 3*(1), 44–59.

Caron, M. S. (2019). The transformative effect of AI on the banking industry. *Banking & Finance Law Review, 34*(2), 169–214.

Carpenter, T. (2020). Revolutionising the consumer banking experience with artificial intelligence. *Journal of Digital Banking, 4*(4), 291–300.

Cartea, Á., Chang, P., Mroczka, M., & Oomen, R. (2022). AI-driven liquidity provision in OTC financial markets. *Quantitative Finance, 22*(12), 2171–2204. doi:10.1080/14697688.2022.2130087

Castelnovo, A., Crupi, R., Del Gamba, G., Greco, G., Naseer, A., Regoli, D., & Gonzalez, B. S. M. (2020, December). Befair: Addressing fairness in the banking sector. In *2020 IEEE International Conference on Big Data (Big Data)* (pp. 3652-3661). IEEE. 10.1109/BigData50022.2020.9377894

Chlesinger, A., O'Hara, K. P., & Taylor, A. S. (2018). Let's talk about race: identity, chatbots, and AI. *Proceedings of the 2018 CHI ConferenceonHuman Factors in Computing Systems, CHI'18*, 1-14.

Dauda, S. Y., & Lee, J. (2015). Technology adoption: A conjoint analysis of consumers' preference on future online banking services. *Information Systems, 53*, 1–15. doi:10.1016/j.is.2015.04.006

Deloitte. (2018). *The rise of cognitive intelligence in banking.* Retrieved from https://www2.deloitte.com/content/dam/Deloitte/nl/Documents/financial-services/deloitte-nl-fsi-cognitive-intelligence-in-banking.pdf

Dhanabalan, T., Subha, K., Shanthi, R., & Sathish, A. (2018). Factors influencing consumers car purchasing decision in Indian automobile industry. *International Journal of Mechanical Engineering and Technology, 9*(10), 53–63.

Digalaki, E. (2020). *The impact of artificial intelligence in the banking sector & how AI isbeing used in 2020.* https://www.businessinsider.in/finance/news/the-impact-of-artificial-intelligence in-the-banking-sector-how-ai-is-being-used-in-2020/article show/728608

Donepudi, P. K. (2017). Machine Learning and Artificial Intelligence in Banking. *Engineering International*, *5*(2), 83–86. doi:10.18034/ei.v5i2.490

Dumitrescu, B., Băltoiu, A., & Budulan, Ş. (2022). Anomaly detection in graphs of bank transactions for anti money laundering applications. *IEEE Access : Practical Innovations, Open Solutions*, *10*, 47699–47714. doi:10.1109/ACCESS.2022.3170467

Dwivedi, Y. K., Kshetri, N., Hughes, L., Slade, E. L., Jeyaraj, A., Kar, A. K., Baabdullah, A. M., Koohang, A., Raghavan, V., Ahuja, M., Albanna, H., Albashrawi, M. A., Al-Busaidi, A. S., Balakrishnan, J., Barlette, Y., Basu, S., Bose, I., Brooks, L., Buhalis, D., ... Wright, R. (2023). “So what if ChatGPT wrote it?” Multidisciplinary perspectives on opportunities, challenges and implications of generative conversational AI for research, practice and policy. *International Journal of Information Management*, *71*, 102642. doi:10.1016/j.ijinfomgt.2023.102642

Dzhaparov, P. (2020). Application of blockchain and artificial intelligence in bank risk management. *Икономика иуправление*, *17*(1), 43-57.

Etaiwi, W., Biltawi, M., & Naymat, G. (2017). Evaluation of classification algorithms for banking customer’s behavior under Apache Spark Data Processing System. *Procedia Computer Science*, *113*, 559–564. doi:10.1016/j.procs.2017.08.280

Fuchs, D. J. (2018). The dangers of human-like bias in machine-learning algorithms. *MissouriS&T’sPeerPeer.*, *2*(1), 1.

GarimaKaneria. (2022). Artificial Intelligence in Banking Industry. *Impact of Artificial Intelligence on Organizational Transformation*, 327-348.

Gartner. (2019). *How AI is transforming the banking industry.* Retrieved from https://www.gartner.com/smarterwithgartner/how-ai-is-transforming-the-banking-industry/

Geetha, R., & Uma, G. (2021). Role of artificial intelligence in banking. *Journal of Computer Science and Technology, 3*(1), 1-7.

Gerling, C., & Lessmann, S. (2023). *Multimodal Document Analytics for Banking Process Automation.* arXiv preprint arXiv:2307.11845

Ghandour, A. (2021). Opportunities and challenges of artificial intelligence in banking: Systematic literature review. *TEM Journal*, *10*(4), 1581–1587. doi:10.18421/TEM104-12

Goode, A. (2018). Biometrics for banking: Best practices and barriers to adoption. *Biometric Technology Today*, *2018*(10), 5–7. doi:10.1016/S0969-4765(18)30156-5

Guni, A., Normahani, P., Davies, A., & Jaffer, U. (2021). Harnessing machine learning to personalize web-based health care content. *Journal of Medical Internet Research*, *23*(10), e25497. doi:10.2196/25497 PMID:34665146

Guo, X., Zhang, X., Li, C., & Xiong, Y. (2021). A review of applications and challenges of artificial intelligence in finance. *Journal of Industrial Information Integration*, *22*, 100168.

Gupta, M. (2021). *Financial institutions using AI.* Academic Press.

Gupta, R., & Jayaraman, R. (2021). Impact of artificial intelligence in banking sector: A systematic review. *Journal of Applied Accounting Research.*

Hamouda, M. (2019). Omni-channel banking integration quality and perceived value as drivers of consumers' satisfaction and loyalty. *Journal of Enterprise Information Management*, *32*(4), 608–625. doi:10.1108/JEIM-12-2018-0279

Hasbullah, S. S., Maynard, D., Chik, R. Z. W., Mohd, F., & Noor, M. (2016, January). Automated content analysis: A sentiment analysis on Malaysian government social media. In *Proceedings of the 10th International Conference on Ubiquitous Information Management and Communication* (pp. 1-6). 10.1145/2857546.2857577

Hashemi, S. K., Mirtaheri, S. L., & Greco, S. (2022). Fraud Detection in Banking Data by Machine Learning Techniques. *IEEE Access : Practical Innovations, Open Solutions*, *11*, 3034–3043. doi:10.1109/ACCESS.2022.3232287

Hernandez-Nieves, E., Hernández, G., Gil-Gonzalez, A. B., Rodríguez-González, S., & Corchado, J. M. (2021). CEBRA: A CasE-Based Reasoning Application to recommend banking products. *Engineering Applications of Artificial Intelligence, 104*, 104327. https://djangostars.com/blog/6-examples-ai-financial-services/

Jakkani, N., & Kodali, R. (2020). A systematic review of artificial intelligence applications in banking. *Journal of Artificial Intelligence and Data Science*, *2*(1), 29–40. doi:10.32628/JAIDS.V2I1.454

Kalyanathaya, K. P., Akila, D., & Rajesh, P. (2019). Advances in natural language processing–a survey of current research trends, development tools and industry applications. *International Journal of Recent Technology and Engineering*, *7*(5C), 199–202.

Kaur, D., Sahdev, S. L., Sharma, D., & Siddiqui, L. (2020). Banking 4.0:'The Influence of Artificial Intelligence on the Banking Industry & How AI Is Changing the Face of Modern Day Banks'. *International Journal of Management*, *11*(6). Advance online publication. doi:10.34218/IJM.11.6.2020.049

Kołodziej, M. (2017). Virtual reality as the indicator of the modern banking. *Financial Sciences. Nauki o finansach*, *2*(31).

Königstorfer, F., & Thalmann, S. (2020). Applications of Artificial Intelligence in commercial banks–A research agenda for behavioral finance. *Journal of Behavioral and Experimental Finance*, *27*, 100352. doi:10.1016/j.jbef.2020.100352

Kshetri, N., & Voas, J. (2021). AI in Banking: A Research Agenda. *IEEE Software*, *38*(3), 39–46.

Kulkarni, C. S., Bhavsar, A. U., Pingale, S. R., & Kumbhar, S. S. (2017). BANK CHAT BOT–an intelligent assistant system using NLP and machine learning. *International Research Journal of Engineering and Technology*, *4*(5), 2374–2377.

Kumar, N., & Kumar, A. (2021). Applications of artificial intelligence in banking sector: A review of literature. *International Journal of Applied Engineering Research: IJAER*, *16*(2), 276–284.

Kumar, S., Aishwaryalakshmi, S., & Akalya, A. (2020). Impact and Challenges of Artificial Intelligence in Banking. *Journal of Information and Computational Science*, *10*(2), 1101–1109.

Kumar, S., & Nayyar, P. (2019). Artificial intelligence in banking sector: Transforming the way banking is done. *International Journal of Management, Technology, and Social Sciences*, *4*(1), 1–11. doi:10.5281/zenodo.2592248

Lee, G. L. (2022). *Pivoting to robo-advisor services in wealth management.* Academic Press.

Lee, S. M., & Lee, D. (2020). "Untact": A new customer service strategy in the digital age. *Service Business*, *14*(1), 1–22. doi:10.100711628-019-00408-2

Leo, M., Sharma, S., & Maddulety, K. (2019). Machine learning in banking risk management: A literature review. *Risks*, *7*(1), 29. doi:10.3390/risks7010029

Li, L., & Zhang, H. (2021). Applications of artificial intelligence in finance: A review. *Journal of Financial Economics*, *42*(3), 49–60.

Li, S., Sun, B., & Wilcox, R. T. (2005). Cross-selling sequentially ordered products: An application to consumer banking services. *JMR, Journal of Marketing Research*, *42*(2), 233–239. doi:10.1509/jmkr.42.2.233.62288

Lipton, Z. C., Kale, D. C., & Wetzel, R. (2018). *Learning to diagnose with LSTM recurrent neural networks*. arXiv preprint arXiv:1511.03677.

Lockey, S., Gillespie, N., Holm, D., & Someh, I. A. (2021). *A review of trust in artificial intelligence: Challenges, vulnerabilities and future directions.* Academic Press.

Ludwig, E. (2018). Regulators have their eye on AI. *American Banker*, *183*(130), 1.

Malali, A. B., & Gopalakrishnan, S. (2020). Application of artificial intelligence and its powered technologies in the indian banking and financial industry: An overview. *IOSR Journal Of Humanities And Social Science*, *25*(4), 55–60.

Malini, A., & Menon, D. G. (2017, December). Technological innovations in the banking sector in India: An analysis. In *2017 International Conference on Technological Advancements in Power and Energy (TAP Energy)* (pp. 1-5). IEEE. 10.1109/TAPENERGY.2017.8397342

Maruti Techlabs. (2019). *5 Ways ai is transforming the finance industry*. Retrieved from: https://marutitech.com/ways-ai-transforming-finance/

Mehndiratta, N., Arora, G., & Bathla, R. (2023, May). The use of Artificial Intelligence in the Banking Industry. In *2023 International Conference on Recent Advances in Electrical, Electronics & Digital Healthcare Technologies (REEDCON)* (pp. 588-591). IEEE. 10.1109/REEDCON57544.2023.10150681

Mehrotra, A. (2019, April). Artificial intelligence in financial services–need to blend automation with human touch. In *2019 International Conference on Automation, Computational and Technology Management (ICACTM)* (pp. 342-347). IEEE. 10.1109/ICACTM.2019.8776741

Mhlanga, D. (2020). Industry 4.0 in finance: The impact of artificial intelligence (ai) on digital financial inclusion. *International Journal of Financial Studies*, *8*(3), 45. doi:10.3390/ijfs8030045

Mikhalkina, T., & Cabantous, L. (2015). How to identify the types of risks that "really matter"? *Journal of Risk Research*, *18*(3), 298–320.

Misra, A., & Bohra, N. S. (2020). Examining enablers of omni-channel banking in developing countries: An Indian perspective. *International Journal of Management, 11*(4).

Mohammed, I. A. (2021). The interaction between artificial intelligence and identity and access management: An empirical study. *International Journal of Creative Research Thoughts, 2320*(2882), 668–671.

Nopp, C., & Hanbury, A. (2015, September). Detecting risks in the banking system by sentiment analysis. In *Proceedings of the 2015 conference on empirical methods in natural language processing* (pp. 591-600). 10.18653/v1/D15-1071

Noreen, U., Shafique, A., Ahmed, Z., & Ashfaq, M. (2023). Banking 4.0: Artificial Intelligence (AI) in Banking Industry & Consumer's Perspective. *Sustainability (Basel), 2023*(15), 3682. doi:10.3390u15043682

Northey, G., Hunter, V., Mulcahy, R., Choong, K., & Mehmet, M. (2022). Man vs machine: How artificial intelligence in banking influences consumer belief in financial advice. *International Journal of Bank Marketing, 40*(6), 1182–1199. doi:10.1108/IJBM-09-2021-0439

Panigrahi, S., Sahoo, M., & Jena, L. K. (2021). A review on artificial intelligence and machine learning applications in banking sector. *Journal of Financial Crime, 28*(2), 299–310.

Papadakis, S., Garefalakis, A., Lemonakis, C., Chimonaki, C., & Zopounidis, C. (Eds.). (2020). *Machine Learning Applications for Accounting Disclosure and Fraud Detection*. IGI Global.

Park, J. Y., & Dhanabalan, T. (2019). What Makes Customers Repurchase Grocery Products from Online Stores in Korea. *International Journal of E-Business Research, 15*(4), 24–39. doi:10.4018/IJEBR.2019100102

Patel, R. (2023). Artificial intelligence: A tool for enhancement of lending facilities in banking institutions. *EPRA International Journal of Multidisciplinary Research, 9*(3), 214–217.

Powell, B. A. (2020). Detecting malicious logins as graph anomalies. *Journal of Information Security and Applications, 54*, 102557. doi:10.1016/j.jisa.2020.102557

Power, B. A. S. (2022). *Intelligent Automation*. Author.

Pradhan, I. P., & Saxena, P. (2023). Reskilling workforce for the Artificial Intelligence age: Challenges and the way forward. In The Adoption and Effect of Artificial Intelligence on Human Resources Management, Part B (pp. 181-197). Emerald Publishing Limited.

Priya, G. J., & Saradha, S. (2021). Fraud Detection and Prevention Using Machine Learning Algorithms: A Review. *7th International Conference on Electrical Energy Systems (ICEES),* 564-568. 10.1109/ICEES51510.2021.9383631

PTI. (2017). *Indian robot made in China steals the show at IT event*. IBEF. Retrieved from: https://www.ibef.org/news/indianrobot-made-in-china-steals-the-show-at-it-event

Purificato, E., Lorenzo, F., Fallucchi, F., & De Luca, E. W. (2023). The use of responsible artificial intelligence techniques in the context of loan approval processes. *International Journal of Human-Computer Interaction, 39*(7), 1543–1562. doi:10.1080/10447318.2022.2081284

PwC. (2017). *Artificial Intelligence and Robotics 2017: Leveraging artificial intelligence and robotics for sustainable growth*. Retrieved from:https://www.pwc.in/publications/2017/artifcial-intelligence-and-robotics-2017.html

Quarteroni, S. (2018). Natural Language Processing for Industry. *Informatik Spektrum, 41*(2), 105–112. doi:10.100700287-018-1094-1

Rahman, M., Ming, T. H., Baigh, T. A., & Sarker, M. (2021). Adoption of artificial intelligence in banking services: an empirical analysis. *International Journal of Emerging Markets*.

Rajamohan, S., & Dhanabalan, T. (2014). Beneficiaries" opinion towards the mahatma Gandhi national rural employment guarantee scheme. *International Journal of Retailing & Rural Business Perspectives, 3*(4), 1256.

Ramalingam, H., & Venkatesan, V. P. (2019, October). Conceptual analysis of Internet of Things use cases in Banking domain. In TENCON 2019-2019 IEEE Region 10 Conference (TENCON) (pp. 2034-2039). IEEE. doi:10.1109/TENCON.2019.8929473

Ravi, V., & Kamaruddin, S. (2017). Big data analytics enabled smart financial services: opportunities and challenges. *Big Data Analytics: 5th International Conference, BDA 2017, Hyderabad, India, December 12-15, 2017 Proceedings, 5*, 15–39.

Rayson, P., Garside, R., & Sawyer, P. (2000). Assisting requirements engineering with semantic document analysis. In *Content-based multimedia information access RIAO 2000 (Recherche d'Informations Assistie par Ordinateur, Computer-Assisted Information Retrieval) International Conference* (pp. 1363-1371). Academic Press.

Sadok, H., Sakka, F., & El Maknouzi, M. E. H. (2022). Artificial intelligence and bank creditanalysis: A review. *Cogent Economics & Finance, 10*(1), 2023262. doi:10.1080/23322039.2021.2023262

Safadel, P., & White, D. (2019). Facilitating molecular biology teaching by using Augmented Reality (AR) and Protein Data Bank (PDB). *TechTrends, 63*(2), 188–193. doi:10.100711528-018-0343-0

Sarkar. (2017). *Robotic process automation in insurance industry*. Nalashaa. Retrieved from: https://www.nalashaa.com/robotic-processautomation-insurance-industry/

Sethi, N., & Paliwal, M. S. Moblie Banking Security. *International Journal of Engineering Research & Technology, 4*(9).

Shambira, L. (2020). Exploring the adoption of artificial intelligence in the Zimbabwe banking sector. *European Journal of Social Sciences Studies, 5*(6). Advance online publication. doi:10.46827/ejsss.v5i6.942

Sheth, J. N., Jain, V., Roy, G., & Chakraborty, A. (2022). AI-driven banking services: The next frontier for a personalised experience in the emerging market. *International Journal of Bank Marketing, 40*(6), 1248–1271. doi:10.1108/IJBM-09-2021-0449

Siadati, H., & Memon, N. (2017, October). Detecting structurally anomalous logins within enterprise networks. In *Proceedings of the 2017 ACM SIGSAC Conference on Computer and Communications Security* (pp. 1273-1284). 10.1145/3133956.3134003

Simoes, M., Elmusrati, M., Vartiainen, T., Mekkanen, M., Karimi, M., Diaba, S., . . . Lopes, W. (2023). *Enhancing data security against cyberattacks in artificial intelligence based smartgrid systems with crypto agility.* arXiv preprint arXiv:2305.11652.

Singh, T., & Pathak, N. (2020). Emerging role of artificial intelligence in Indian banking sector. *Journal of Critical Reviews*, *7*(16), 1370–1373.

Somani, B., Tyagi, G., Mukul, M., Gaurav, M., & Preetham, A. (2022). Automation in Onboarding of Customer in Banking. *International Journal of Research in Engineering and Science, 10*(6), 1424-1428.

Soni, V. D. (2019). Role of artificial intelligence in combating cyber threats in banking. *International Engineering Journal For Research & Development*, *4*(1), 7–7.

Stars, D. (2019). *6 examples of ai in financial services*. Retrieved from: https://djangostars.com/blog/6-examples-ai-financial-services/

Suhel, S. F., Shukla, V. K., Vyas, S., & Mishra, V. P. (2020, June). Conversation to automation in banking through chatbot using artificial machine intelligence language. In *2020 8th international conference on reliability, infocom technologies and optimization (trends and future directions)(ICRITO)* (pp. 611-618). IEEE. 10.1109/ICRITO48877.2020.9197825

Swapna, M. (2018). *Ethics of Using Artificial Intelligence in Financial Banking Industry.* Available at https://medium.com/datadriveninvestor/ethics-of-using-ai-in-thefinancial-banking-industry-fa93203f6f25

Tarafdar, M., Tu, Q., & Ragu-Nathan, T. S. (2010). Impact of Technostress on End-User Satisfaction and Performance. *Journal of Management Information Systems, 27*(3), 303–334.

Thakur, D. J., Verma, P., & Sharma, D. (2019). Influence of Leadership Style: A Review. *International Journal of Advanced Science and Technology*, *28*(20), 945–952.

Thowfeek, M. H., Samsudeen, S. N., & Sanjeetha, M. B. F. (2020). Drivers of artificial intelligence in banking service sectors. *Solid State Technology*, *63*(5), 6400–6411.

Tripathy, A., Agrawal, A., & Rath, S. K. (2014, December). Requirement analysis using natural language processing. In *Fifth International Conference on Advances in Computer Engineering* (*Vol. 26*, p. 27). Academic Press.

Umamaheswari, S., & Valarmathi, A. (2023). Role of Artificial Intelligence in The Banking Sector. *Journal of Survey in Fisheries Sciences*, *10*(4S), 2841–2849.

Utami, A. M., & Septivani, M. D. (2022). Regulatory Technology (RegTech): The Solution to Prevent Money Laundering in Indonesia. *Telaah Bisnis*, *23*(1), 86–98. doi:10.35917/tb.v23i1.288

Van Dijk, J. A. (2006). Digital divide research, achievements and shortcomings. *Poetics, 34*(4-5), 221-235.

Vieira, A., & Sehgal, A. (2017). How banks can better serve their customers through artificial techniques. In *Digital marketplaces unleashed* (pp. 311–326). Springer Berlin Heidelberg.

Vijai, C. (2019). Artificial intelligence in Indian banking sector: challenges and opportunities. *International Journal of Advanced Research, 7*, 1581-1587. . doi:10.21474/IJAR01/8987

Villar, A. S., & Khan, N. (2021). Robotic process automation in banking industry: A case study on Deutsche Bank. *Journal of Banking and Financial Technology*, *5*(1), 71–86. doi:10.100742786-021-00030-9

Von Solms, J. (2021). Integrating Regulatory Technology (RegTech) into the digital transformation of a bank Treasury. *Journal of Banking Regulation*, *22*(2), 152–168. doi:10.105741261-020-00134-0

Wang, J., Li, C., Han, S., Sarkar, S., & Zhou, X. (2017). Predictive maintenance based on event-log analysis: A case study. *IBM Journal of Research and Development*, *61*(1), 11–121. doi:10.1147/JRD.2017.2648298

Yang, Y., Liu, K., & Guo, H. (2020). Ethical considerations of artificial intelligence in banking. *Journal of Financial Services Marketing*, *25*(2), 61–71.

Zainurin, M. Z. L., Haji Masri, M., Besar, M. H. A., & Anshari, M. (2023). Towards an understanding of metaverse banking: A conceptual paper. *Journal of Financial Reporting and Accounting*, *21*(1), 178–190. doi:10.1108/JFRA-12-2021-0487

Zhang, Y., & Liu, Q. (2021). Customer Relationship Management in the Banking Industry: A Literature Review and Future Directions. *International Journal of Financial Research*, *12*(4), 188–199.

Zhou, N., Zhang, Z., Nair, V. N., Singhal, H., & Chen, J. (2022). Bias, fairness and accountability with artificial intelligence and machine learning algorithms. *International Statistical Review*, *90*(3), 468–480. doi:10.1111/insr.12492

Zhou, N., Zhang, Z., Nair, V. N., Singhal, H., Chen, J., & Sudjianto, A. (2021). *Bias, Fairness, and Accountability with AI and ML Algorithms.* arXiv preprint arXiv:2105.06558.

Chapter 20
The Use of Artificial Intelligence in Data Analysis and Business Intelligence

Devesh Kumar
School of Commerce and Management Studies, Central University of Himachal Pradesh, Dharamshala, India

ABSTRACT

This chapter provides a comprehensive exploration of the integration of artificial intelligence (AI) in data analysis and business intelligence. It begins by elucidating fundamental AI techniques such as machine learning, natural language processing, and deep learning, showcasing their applicability in deciphering complex datasets. Real-world case studies spanning various industries underscore AI's capacity to unveil patterns, predict trends, and optimize operations. The chapter further delves into AI's role in enhancing business intelligence platforms, facilitating informed decision-making through timely and accurate insights. Ethical considerations and challenges inherent in AI-driven analysis are addressed, emphasizing responsible implementation. Ultimately, the chapter offers a glimpse into future advancements while highlighting AI's pivotal role in reshaping data-driven decision-making processes and fostering innovation in the business realm.

1. INTRODUCTION

In the rapidly evolving landscape of modern business, the effective utilization of data has emerged as a critical factor in driving competitive advantage and informed decision-making. The convergence of Artificial Intelligence (AI) and data analysis has catalyzed a transformative shift in the realm of business intelligence, redefining how organizations extract insights, predict trends, and optimize operations. This chapter delves into the pervasive impact of AI on data analysis and business intelligence, exploring its multifaceted applications and examining real-world instances where AI-driven approaches have reshaped conventional practices.

DOI: 10.4018/979-8-3693-0418-1.ch020

AI, encompassing machine learning, natural language processing, and neural networks, has revolutionized data analysis by empowering organizations to gather deeper insights from complex datasets. Traditional analysis methods often faltered when confronted with unstructured data sources like social media content and text documents. However, AI-driven algorithms excel in comprehending and interpreting such data, unlocking valuable insights that were previously elusive (Chen et al., 2012). This capability to analyze unstructured data expands the scope of analysis and equips decision-makers with a holistic perspective on market dynamics and consumer sentiment.

One of the paramount contributions of AI in business intelligence lies in its ability to process massive volumes of data at unparalleled speeds. The contemporary business landscape is characterized by an overwhelming influx of data from diverse sources, including IoT devices and online transactions. AI-driven data analysis not only addresses the challenge of data volume but also ensures real-time insights, facilitating agile and responsive decision-making (Davenport & Ronanki, 2018). Additionally, AI augments traditional business intelligence by enabling predictive and prescriptive analytics. This forward-looking approach enables organizations to anticipate future trends, forecast consumer behaviours, and mitigate potential risks. Through advanced machine learning models, businesses can optimize inventory management, personalize customer experiences, and enhance resource allocation, thereby gaining a competitive edge (Marr, 2021).

This chapter embark on an exploratory journey into the diverse applications of AI in data analysis and business intelligence. Real-world case studies covered in this chapter illuminate how AI-driven insights have empowered organizations across sectors such as finance, marketing, and supply chain management. Furthermore, the chapter explore the ethical considerations inherent in AI-driven data analysis, emphasizing the importance of responsible AI practices that safeguard data privacy and uphold transparency (Kudyba & Hoptroff, 2019).

As one navigates the intricate interplay between AI, data analysis, and business intelligence, it becomes evident that this symbiotic relationship is reshaping the future of decision-making. By harnessing AI's capabilities to extract profound insights from data, organizations stand poised to navigate the complexities of the modern business landscape with strategic acumen.

2. LITERATURE REVIEW

Artificial Intelligence (AI) has emerged as a transformative technology in various industries, and its applications in data analysis and business intelligence have garnered significant attention. This literature review provides an in-depth analysis of the role of AI in data analysis and business intelligence, highlighting key developments, challenges, and future prospects. The review explores the evolution of AI technologies in these domains, the impact on decision-making processes, and the potential for improving business strategies.

The integration of AI into data analysis and business intelligence represents a significant paradigm shift in how organizations extract insights from data. Historically, data analysis primarily relied on statistical techniques and manual data processing. However, with the advent of AI, particularly machine learning (ML) and deep learning (DL), data analysis has become more sophisticated and efficient (Kapoor et al., 2019). AI-based algorithms are capable of processing vast amounts of structured and unstructured data, identifying patterns, and generating actionable insights. In the realm of business intelligence, AI-driven tools and platforms have revolutionized data visualization, dashboard creation, and predictive analytics

(Sivarajah et al., 2017). These advancements have empowered organizations to make data-driven decisions, gain a competitive edge, and enhance their strategic planning. AI's impact on decision-making processes in data analysis and business intelligence is substantial. AI-driven systems enable real-time data analysis, providing decision-makers with up-to-date information for more informed choices (Wang et al., 2020). AI can identify trends, anomalies, and correlations that human analysts might overlook, facilitating proactive decision-making. Moreover, AI can automate routine tasks, such as data cleansing, ETL (Extract, Transform, Load) processes, and report generation. This automation frees up human analysts to focus on more complex and value-added tasks, leading to greater efficiency and productivity (Sheng et al., 2018).

While AI holds immense promise in data analysis and business intelligence, it is not without challenges. One of the foremost challenges is the need for high-quality, clean, and well-structured data. AI algorithms heavily depend on data quality, and poor data can lead to inaccurate insights (Chen et al., 2018). Data privacy and security concerns also arise when handling sensitive business information, necessitating robust safeguards and compliance with data protection regulations (Hassan et al., 2019). Another challenge is the interpretability of AI-driven models. Complex ML and DL models can be challenging to understand, making it difficult for decision-makers to trust their recommendations. Efforts are being made to develop explainable AI techniques to address this issue (Carvalho et al., 2020).

The future of AI in data analysis and business intelligence is promising. AI technologies will continue to evolve, enabling organizations to extract more value from their data. Advancements in natural language processing (NLP) will improve the ability to analyze unstructured text data, such as customer reviews and social media comments (Fayyad et al., 2019). Furthermore, AI will play a crucial role in the democratization of data analysis. User-friendly AI-powered tools will make data analysis and visualization accessible to non-technical users, empowering them to make data-driven decisions without extensive training (Wang et al., 2021).

The integration of AI into data analysis and business intelligence represents a transformative shift in how organizations leverage data for decision-making. AI technologies enable more efficient data processing, real-time insights, and automation of routine tasks. However, challenges related to data quality, interpretability, and data privacy must be addressed. The future holds great promise, with AI continuing to evolve and democratize data analysis, making it a vital asset for businesses seeking a competitive edge in the data-driven world.

3. THE ROLE OF ARTIFICIAL INTELLIGENCE IN DATA ANALYSIS

Artificial Intelligence (AI) has emerged as a transformative force in the realm of data analysis, revolutionizing how organizations extract insights and meaning from vast and complex datasets. The integration of AI techniques, such as machine learning and deep learning, has empowered businesses to uncover patterns, trends, and correlations that were previously hidden within the depths of data. This section explores the pivotal role of AI in data analysis and highlights its various applications in deciphering the intricacies of modern data-driven environments.

Automating Data Processing and Cleaning

One of the fundamental contributions of AI in data analysis is its ability to automate and streamline data processing tasks. AI-powered algorithms can efficiently clean and preprocess raw data, removing inconsistencies, errors, and outliers that might skew analysis results. This automation accelerates the data preparation phase, allowing analysts to focus their efforts on extracting meaningful insights rather than getting bogged down in data cleaning tasks (Provost & Fawcett, 2013).

Uncovering Complex Patterns

AI algorithms are adept at identifying complex patterns and relationships within data that might be challenging for traditional analysis methods to discern. Machine learning models, for instance, can uncover nonlinear correlations and dependencies, enabling organizations to make informed decisions based on comprehensive and accurate insights. This capability is particularly valuable in scenarios where traditional techniques fall short, such as image recognition, natural language understanding, and fraud detection (Chen et al., 2012).

Predictive Analytics

AI-driven data analysis plays a crucial role in predictive analytics, enabling organizations to forecast future trends and outcomes. By training machine learning models on historical data, businesses can make accurate predictions about customer behaviour, market trends, and other critical variables. These predictions empower companies to proactively adjust strategies, allocate resources effectively, and capitalize on emerging opportunities (Marr, 2021).

Personalization and Recommendation Systems

AI-powered data analysis facilitates personalized customer experiences by enabling the creation of recommendation systems. By analyzing user preferences and behavior, AI algorithms can suggest products, services, or content that align with individual interests. These recommendation systems not only enhance customer satisfaction but also drive sales and engagement, contributing to the overall success of businesses (Davenport & Ronanki, 2018).

Challenges and Considerations

While AI holds immense promise in data analysis, it also presents challenges and considerations that must be addressed. Ethical concerns related to bias in AI models, data privacy, and transparency are of paramount importance. Striking a balance between leveraging AI's capabilities and ensuring responsible and ethical data analysis practices is crucial to building trust and maintaining the integrity of insights derived from AI-driven analyses (Kudyba & Hoptroff, 2019).

To summarise, AI's function in data analysis is revolutionary, allowing organisations to handle, analyse, and understand data in previously unthinkable ways. AI enables businesses to make educated decisions and stay ahead in today's data-driven world by automating data processing, revealing intricate patterns, enabling predictive analytics, and improving personalisation.

4. BENEFITS OF AI IN BUSINESS INTELLIGENCE

The integration of Artificial Intelligence (AI) into business intelligence has ushered in a new era of data-driven decision-making, offering a numerous benefits that empower organizations to optimize operations, enhance customer experiences, and gain a competitive edge. This section explores the multifaceted advantages of AI in business intelligence, drawing insights from both real-world examples and scholarly research.

Enhanced Data Processing and Analysis

AI-driven business intelligence significantly accelerates data processing and analysis, enabling organizations to handle vast volumes of data more efficiently and effectively. Machine learning algorithms automate data cleansing, transformation, and aggregation, reducing the manual effort required for these tasks. This efficiency not only saves time but also ensures that analysts can focus their expertise on higher-value tasks, such as deriving actionable insights from the data (Chen et al., 2012).

Real-Time Insights

One of the distinctive advantages of AI in business intelligence is its capacity to provide real-time insights. Traditional methods of data analysis often lag behind real-world events, limiting an organization's ability to respond promptly. AI-driven analytics systems, on the other hand, process data in near real-time, allowing businesses to make informed decisions rapidly. This agility is particularly valuable in dynamic environments where timely responses can make a substantial difference (Davenport & Ronanki, 2018).

Predictive and Prescriptive Analytics

AI-powered business intelligence goes beyond retrospective analysis to offer predictive and prescriptive capabilities. Machine learning models can forecast future trends and outcomes based on historical data, enabling organizations to proactively adjust strategies and allocate resources. Additionally, prescriptive analytics suggests optimal actions to achieve desired outcomes. These capabilities empower businesses to anticipate market shifts, mitigate risks, and seize opportunities ahead of competitors (Marr, 2021).

Personalized Customer Experiences

AI-driven business intelligence plays a pivotal role in delivering personalized customer experiences. By analyzing vast amounts of customer data, AI algorithms can segment audiences and tailor offerings to individual preferences. This personalization enhances customer satisfaction, fosters brand loyalty, and drives revenue growth. Moreover, recommendation systems powered by AI algorithms provide customers with relevant product suggestions, thereby influencing purchasing decisions (Provost & Fawcett, 2013).

Efficient Resource Allocation

AI's ability to analyze data holistically enables more efficient resource allocation. Businesses can optimize inventory management, supply chain logistics, and workforce allocation based on predictive models and real-time insights. This optimization reduces costs, enhances operational efficiency, and minimizes waste. AI-powered insights ensure that resources are utilized optimally to meet changing market demands (Chen et al., 2012).

Ethical Considerations and Challenges

While the benefits of AI in business intelligence are substantial, it is important to address ethical considerations and challenges. AI models must be carefully designed to mitigate bias and ensure fairness, especially in applications such as lending and hiring. Additionally, data privacy concerns necessitate robust security measures to safeguard sensitive information. Organizations must strike a balance between harnessing AI's potential and upholding ethical and legal standards (Kudyba & Hoptroff, 2019).

To conclude, AI-driven business intelligence provides a slew of advantages that enable organisations to make educated decisions, optimise operations, and innovate in a quickly changing environment. AI's transformative influence is transforming the way businesses operate and compete in the digital age, from increased data processing and real-time insights to predictive analytics and personalised consumer experiences.

5. CHALLENGES AND RISKS OF AI IN DATA ANALYSIS AND BUSINESS INTELLIGENCE

While the integration of Artificial Intelligence (AI) into data analysis and business intelligence offers a plethora of benefits, it also presents a range of challenges and risks that organizations must navigate. As AI technologies continue to evolve and permeate various sectors, it is imperative to address these concerns to ensure responsible and effective utilization. This section examines the key challenges and risks associated with AI in data analysis and business intelligence, drawing insights from both scholarly research and real-world examples.

Data Quality and Bias

A significant challenge in AI-driven data analysis is ensuring the quality and accuracy of the underlying data. AI algorithms heavily rely on data to make informed decisions and predictions. However, if the data used is incomplete, inaccurate, or biased, the insights generated by AI can be misleading or erroneous. Biased training data can perpetuate and amplify existing biases, resulting in biased outcomes and decisions (Kudyba & Hoptroff, 2019). For instance, biased algorithms used in hiring or lending processes can lead to discriminatory practices.

Ethical Considerations and Privacy Concerns

The proliferation of AI in data analysis raises ethical concerns related to privacy and data protection. Organizations must grapple with the ethical implications of collecting and analyzing personal data, particularly when it comes to sensitive information. The improper handling of personal data can erode customer trust and result in legal repercussions. Striking a balance between leveraging AI for insights and safeguarding individual privacy is a critical challenge that requires thoughtful implementation (Davenport & Ronanki, 2018).

Lack of Transparency and Interpretability

AI algorithms, particularly deep learning models, are often considered "black boxes" due to their complex and intricate nature. This lack of transparency can make it challenging to understand how AI arrives at specific decisions or recommendations. Lack of interpretability can hinder the adoption of AI-driven insights, as stakeholders may be skeptical of relying on recommendations they cannot comprehend or validate (Provost & Fawcett, 2013).

Resource Intensiveness and Complexity

Implementing AI solutions for data analysis and business intelligence can be resource-intensive and complex. Developing and training AI models require specialized expertise, substantial computational power, and significant financial investment. Small and medium-sized businesses may face barriers to entry due to these resource requirements, limiting their ability to leverage the benefits of AI-driven insights (Chen et al., 2012).

Dependency on Data Availability and Quality

AI models heavily rely on data for training and continuous learning. In scenarios where data is scarce or of poor quality, AI performance can be compromised. Organizations must ensure access to relevant and high-quality data to drive accurate and meaningful insights. Additionally, AI models might struggle with adapting to new or unforeseen scenarios if they were not adequately trained on diverse data (Marr, 2021).

As organizations embrace AI in data analysis and business intelligence, it is crucial to be cognizant of the challenges and risks that accompany this transformation. By proactively addressing issues related to data quality, bias, ethics, transparency, and resource constraints, businesses can mitigate potential risks and harness the full potential of AI-driven insights responsibly. Striking a balance between innovation and ethical considerations is essential to building a sustainable and successful AI-powered business intelligence ecosystem.

6. REAL-WORLD EXAMPLES OF AI IN DATA ANALYSIS AND BUSINESS INTELLIGENCE

Real-world case studies provide compelling insights into the transformative impact of Artificial Intelligence (AI) on data analysis and business intelligence. These examples showcase how AI technologies are leveraged across diverse industries to enhance decision-making, streamline processes, and drive innovation.

Netflix: Personalized Content Recommendations

Netflix, a leading streaming platform, employs AI algorithms to analyze user viewing patterns and preferences. By harnessing this data, Netflix's recommendation system suggests tailored content to users, improving engagement and satisfaction. AI-driven insights have contributed significantly to Netflix's success by enhancing content discovery and viewer retention.

Starbucks: Data-Driven Customer Experience

Starbucks, a renowned coffeehouse chain, utilizes AI-powered analytics to enhance customer experiences. Through the analysis of customer preferences, purchase history, and location data, Starbucks customizes marketing campaigns and promotions. This data-driven approach allows Starbucks to offer personalized offers and recommendations, fostering loyalty and boosting sales.

Google: Natural Language Processing for Search

Google employs AI-powered natural language processing (NLP) algorithms to enhance its search engine. These algorithms enable Google to understand user queries and provide more relevant search results. By analyzing the context and intent behind search queries, Google's AI augments the accuracy and effectiveness of search results, elevating the user experience.

Amazon Go: AI-Powered Retail Shopping

Amazon Go, an innovative retail concept, relies on AI and computer vision to redefine shopping. Cameras and sensors track customer movements and interactions with products, enabling shoppers to pick items and exit the store without traditional checkout. AI-driven analysis processes the collected data to accurately bill customers and optimize store layout based on behavior.

Healthcare Diagnostics: IBM Watson

IBM Watson, a prominent AI platform, plays a significant role in healthcare diagnostics. It excels in analyzing medical records, research papers, and patient data to aid medical professionals in diagnosing complex diseases. Watson's AI-generated insights provide doctors with additional information and treatment recommendations, potentially leading to faster and more accurate diagnoses.

These real-world examples highlight the tangible benefits of AI in data analysis and business intelligence. From entertainment and retail to search engines and healthcare, AI-driven insights reshape industries by facilitating data-driven decision-making, enhancing customer experiences, and fostering innovation. These real-world examples underscore the potential of AI to unlock valuable insights from data and drive the evolution of business strategies.

7. CONCLUSION

The dynamic interplay between AI and data analysis has transformed the landscape of business intelligence, moving organisations towards an era defined by data-driven decision-making and strategic foresight. In this in-depth examination of "The Use of Artificial Intelligence in Data Analysis and Business Intelligence," the author delves into the revolutionary potential, benefits, obstacles, and real-world applications that highlight the relevance of this confluence.

AI's ability to process, analyze, and interpret massive volumes of data with remarkable speed and precision has redefined the way businesses glean insights. Traditional barriers of data complexity and unstructured formats are now manageable, enabling organizations to uncover intricate patterns, anticipate trends, and make informed choices that resonate with the demands of the modern market. The case studies presented in this chapter serve as vivid illustrations of AI's tangible impact, underscoring its role in shaping diverse sectors, from retail and entertainment to healthcare and beyond.

While the benefits of AI in business intelligence are undeniable, it is equally crucial to navigate the challenges that accompany this transformative journey. Ensuring data quality, addressing bias, upholding ethical standards, and enhancing transparency are critical endeavours that organizations must embrace to fully harness AI's potential. By treading this path responsibly, businesses can cultivate trust, foster innovation, and navigate the complexities of an AI-powered data landscape.

As we conclude this exploration, it becomes evident that AI is not merely a tool but a catalyst for innovation, redefining traditional paradigms and pushing the boundaries of what is achievable. The intertwining of AI with data analysis and business intelligence paves the way for a future where data becomes the cornerstone of strategy, empowering organizations to navigate uncertainty, capitalize on emerging opportunities, and remain agile in an ever-evolving global marketplace.

The journey into the realm of AI in data analysis and business intelligence is ongoing, marked by continuous advancements, discoveries, and paradigm shifts. This chapter serves as a testament to the transformative potential of AI, and as we stand at the intersection of technology and business, we are poised to embrace a new era of possibilities, where AI-driven insights propel us toward unprecedented heights of success and innovation.

REFERENCES

Carvalho, V. R., Ribeiro, A., & Santos, M. Y. (2020). Explainable artificial intelligence: A review of machine learning interpretability methods. *Journal of Ambient Intelligence and Humanized Computing*, *11*(2), 441–471.

Chen, H., Chiang, R. H., & Storey, V. C. (2012). Business intelligence and analytics: From big data to big impact. *Management Information Systems Quarterly*, *36*(4), 1165–1188. doi:10.2307/41703503

Chen, M., Mao, S., & Liu, Y. (2018). Big data: A survey. *Mobile Networks and Applications*, *19*(2), 171–209. doi:10.100711036-013-0489-0

Davenport, T. H., & Ronanki, R. (2018). Artificial Intelligence for the Real World. *Harvard Business Review*. Retrieved from https://hbr.org/2018/01/artificial-intelligence-for-the-real-world

Fayyad, U., Piatetsky-Shapiro, G., & Smyth, P. (2019). From data mining to knowledge discovery in databases. *AI Magazine*, *17*(3), 37–54.

Hassan, M. M., Hossain, M. S., Alelaiwi, A., & Alamri, A. (2019). Real-time and secure IoT-based smart transportation systems: A review. *IEEE Access : Practical Innovations, Open Solutions*, *7*, 6647–6665.

Kapoor, R., & Arora, A. (2019). Role of artificial intelligence in business analytics. *Procedia Computer Science*, *165*, 44–51.

Kudyba, S., & Hoptroff, R. (2019). Ethical considerations of artificial intelligence in business analytics: A synthesis and research agenda. *Journal of Business Analytics, 2*(2), 69-83.

Marr, B. (2021). How Is AI Used In Business – 5 Powerful Real-World Examples. *Forbes*. Retrieved from https://www.forbes.com/sites/bernardmarr/2021/01/25/how-is-ai-used-in-business-5-powerful-real-world-examples/?sh=1901b54f44e0

Provost, F., & Fawcett, T. (2013). Data science and its relationship to big data and data-driven decision making. *Big Data*, *1*(1), 51–59. doi:10.1089/big.2013.1508 PMID:27447038

Sheng, Q. Z., Zeadally, S., & Kumar, S. (2018). Edge computing in the big data era: From the Internet of Things to genuine intelligence. *IEEE Communications Magazine*, *56*(2), 21–27.

Sivarajah, U., Kamal, M. M., Irani, Z., & Weerakkody, V. (2017). Critical analysis of Big Data challenges and analytical methods. *Journal of Business Research*, *70*, 263–286. doi:10.1016/j.jbusres.2016.08.001

Wang, D., Zhang, Z., Zhang, L., & Li, P. (2021). Data intelligence for decision support in business: A bibliometric analysis and research agenda. *Information Processing & Management*, *58*(2), 102408.

Wang, L., Wang, W., & Zhou, L. (2020). Artificial intelligence in business intelligence: A bibliometric analysis. *Information Systems Frontiers*, *22*(2), 389–404.

Chapter 21
A Review on Marketing Tourism in the Era of AI:
Future Scope for Sustainable Tourism in India

R. J. Reejo
https://orcid.org/0000-0003-1320-7169
University College, Thiruvananthapuram, India

ABSTRACT

The chapter aims to review the extant literature of AI and AR in marketing tourism using bibliometric methods to understand the research's status, development, and growth from 2012 to 2023. The methods adopted include keyword occurrence analysis, factorial analysis using multi correspondence analysis (MCA), thematic map, and multiple collaboration networks. The use of location-based AR technology in various fields of sustainable tourism have been examined in this chapter. It also aims to review the policy initiatives of Government of India in the pandemic phase towards the attainment of sustainable tourism development in the country. It reveals that academicians in countries such as China, Spain, USA, and India have conducted substantial studies on the technical side of artificial intelligence and augmented reality in tourism. It is found that tourism sector is far behind in the use of AI and AR technology in India. Therefore, the author proposes a novel strategy based on artificial intelligence to explore the opportunities of marketing techniques in the tourism sector.

1 INTRODUCTION

One of the industries in India that is expanding the fastest is tourism, which also provides employment for locals and significantly boosts the country's GDP (Bhardwaj et al., 2023). India ranked sixth in terms of the GDP contribution of travel and tourism in 2021, according to the World Travel and Tourism Council (2022). It reports that travel and tourism contribute 5.8 percent of share in GDP. Tourism industry in the country has marked an annual growth rate of 9.4 percent in 2019 and is expected to support for about

DOI: 10.4018/979-8-3693-0418-1.ch021

46 million employment opportunities by 2025. According to India Tourism Statistics (2022), India's share in international tourist arrivals was, 1.64% in 2021. India's ranking in terms of international tourist arrivals was 19th rank in 2020. Therefore, it is understood that the tourist industry has a tremendous potential to create a sizable number of career possibilities for both qualified and untrained individuals (Bhardwaj and Kalia, 2021).

The Indian government identified tourism as a priority industry in its National Tourism Policy of 2002 because it can sustainably increase the productivity of India's natural, human, cultural, and technological resources. Additionally, it has been noted that the level of tourism development has a cap above which the environment deteriorates and people's enjoyment is reduced. As a result, the nation has started a number of sustainable tourism-related initiatives that can be used as a tool to achieve high-quality tourism that causes little harm to the ecological, social, and cultural environment. Along with ensuring that the socioeconomic advantages of tourism are fairly distributed to the local population at the destination, it also attempts to maintain the environment continuously. The idea of sustainable tourism has arisen as a framework for making the most efficient utilisation of environmental resources while taking into account the long-term viability of economic activity.

Since 2020, the COVID-19 pandemic has had an undesirable effect on the various industries (Sharma et al, 2022) and tourism industry one of the most affected. Due to the lockdown effect, earnings from travel and tourism industry fell sharply. Huge employment loss coupled with income loss had been reported during this period. According to the Economic Survey 2022, as many as 14.5 million jobs were taken away as a result of the pandemic and subsequent government shutdown in the initial three months of 2020-21, consisting of a calculated 34.8 million productive positions in the pre-pandemic phase of 2019. It not only highlighted the vulnerabilities of tourism sector but also reminded to think about the capacity to respond to such a crisis with the adaption of technological advancement in the long term. It is viewed that a continuous innovation strategy in structured tourism products and rich experiences are required to revive the sector in the post-pandemic phase. Therefore, the Draft National Tourism Policy for 2022 has been created to modernise the nation's tourism industry. Furthermore, the Draft National Tourism Policy emphasizes that marketing and promotion are critical components in increasing earnings from tourism products. Promotion, internet marketing, focusing on foreign tour operators, and media management are some of the main strategies for marketing tourism that have been considered. The goal of the policy is to increase the assistance given to the tourist sector in the digital transformation of its business models and operational procedures, which in turn results in the electronic transformation of activities connected to the growth of the tourism market.

As is well known, the global corporate landscape has been altered by the digital age. Studies show that information systems and technologies are essential to the tourism sector (Law & Buhalis, 2014). The development of the tourism sector is regarded to have been greatly influenced by both artificial intelligence and augmented reality (Liang, L., & Elliot, S., 2021; Stroumpoulis, Kopanaki, & Varelas, 2022). AI is associated with innovations and is significant to the tourism sector (Tou, 2021; Xiang, 2022). Personal travel assistants, robots, prediction and forecasting systems, language translation software, voice recognition, and natural language processing systems are just a few of the artificial intelligence (AI) applications currently being developed and tested in all facets of the travel and tourism industry (Gidumal, 2020). However, scholars and industry leaders began to acknowledge the expanding body of academic literature on the potential application of Augmented Reality (AR) in tourism as early as 2000 (Liang, L., & Elliot, S. 2021). Augmented reality (AR), according to Azuma and associates (1997), is a system that combines real and virtual components and enables users to make contact with both the actual and virtual spaces. It is a programme that enhances the physical environment with artificially made virtual objects that appear to occupy exactly the exact same space as real-life objects (Azuma R, Baillot Y, Behringer R, 2001). However, the general population still does not know much about or use AR applications (Liang, L., & Elliot, S. 2021).

In this context, it is observed that in India, even though the Draft National Tourism Policy of 2022 envisages importance of technological adaptation in tourism sector, it lacks clarity in adapting new innovative technologies. According to a preliminary finding, the methods created to promote sustainable tourism in India need to be improved more with technology advancement in the age of artificial intelligence. Additionally, it is crucial to revitalise the tourism industry by achieving sustainable development goals in order to maximise the socioeconomic benefits of the industry while minimising any potential drawbacks. The current paper seeks to investigate studies on the use of Artificial Intelligence (AI) in marketing the tourism industry globally in order to obtain a grasp of the research components in this area of study. The study also intends to evaluate the usefulness of applying Augmented Reality (AR) technology, a new type of artificial intelligence (AI) in tourism that enables experiencing real-world entities that are improved by computer-generated virtual interfaces linked to locales or activities. The use of Location based AR technology in various fields of sustainable tourism such as spatial location, description and detailing of tourist destination, transportation, and travel booking has been examined in this study. Government policy initiatives in adapting technological innovations like AI and AR in sustainable tourism activities in the post pandemic phase have also been reviewed in this chapter.

In order to examine these crucial issues, the author attempts to: 1) What is the current state, development, and expansion of global studies on the application of artificial intelligence (AI) and augmented reality (AR) in tourist industry marketing in this respect? 2) What are the real-world effects of augmented reality technology in many aspects of sustainable tourism? 3) What are the policy initiatives of the Government of India in the post-pandemic phase towards the attainment of sustainable tourism development? These research questions are relevant in the academic field and the tourism sector as well. Thus, the present paper aims to review the scope of these questions by using different literature review methods.

2 REVIEW OF LITERATURE

Business model innovation in the creative industries is facilitated by digital technologies. By encouraging the development of innovative business models, it can give visitors a fresh experience and draw attention to the tourism sector (Li F, 2020). For several decades, researchers have been interested in the applications of artificial intelligence (Gretzel 2011; Tussyadiah and Miller 2019) and augmented reality (Moro 2019; Wei 2019; Yung and Khoo Lattimore 2019) in the tourism industry. The field of artificial intelligence has gained popularity since it was first recognised in 1956. As a computer science subfield, it is now accepted on a global scale. It is a set of technological innovations capable of imitate human cognition in the exercise of figuring out solutions and aspires to think similarly to humans, according to Singh et al. (2020) and Lai and Hung (2018). In artificial intelligence, computers are designed to think, learn, infer, and behave in ways that are comparable to those of the mind of humans. As a result, machines are capable of performing activities without the need for the cognitive abilities of humans (Singh et al., 2020). Furthermore, artificial intelligence has advanced computational capabilities, allowing it to handle complicated relationships and issues (Pannu, 2015). According to Inanc-Demir and Kozak (2019), AI can quickly process large amounts of data. Hadavandi claims that due to their greater flexibility, AI models are being used more and more in tourist studies. They therefore provide a way to assess non-linear connections despite being restricted by current methodologies (Hadavandi et al., 2011). being constrained by conventional techniques (Hadavandi et al., 2011). According to the literature that is currently available, AI studies have been used in tourism research for a number of purposes, including making predictions on the occupancy of hotels and demand for tourism, handling resources in the tourism sector, evaluating social network information and online feedback (Kirilenko et al., 2018), determining the total number of travellers and the volume of tourists, as well as gauging visitor satisfaction (Casteleiro-Roca et al., 2018; González-Rodrguez et al., 2020; Law, 1998). According to Inanc-Demir and Kozak (2019), AI is considered as transforming operational and marketing tasks for tourist places and organisations.

The similarities between AI and AR have been noted to exist despite their differences. When it comes to merging virtual objects with the actual environment, the application of augmented reality is a sixth-generation technological advances that provides a realistic interface of virtual objects. Artificial intelligence is a subfield of computer science that works with making machines behave like humans (Jain, 2017). Applied augmented reality (AR) technology is a beneficial innovation that has produced multimedia materials for users. (Ronaghi, Hossein & Ronaghi, Marzieh., 2022) and can be applied to the travel and tourist sector (Lau C., Chui C.F., Au N., 2019; Loureiro S.M., Guerreiro J., Ali F., 2020). Through the use of smartphones and digital cameras, augmented reality enables tourists to interact with virtual objects (Olsson T.et al., 2012). Five value aspects for AR technology have been established, including promotional activities, commercial, visitors, epistemological, and organisational (Cranmer, Dieck, Fountoulaki, 2020). This research focused on the application of augmented reality technologies in the tourist business. According to Ronaghi, Hossein & Ronaghi, Marzieh., 2022, the COVID-19 pandemic is also seen as a key driver of the use of Virtual Reality technologies like augmented reality within the travel and tourism industry worldwide, including India. According to a study by Cranmer et al. (2020), the marketing potential of augmented reality in the tourist business is one of the study's top value elements. These studies all illustrate the importance of incorporating cutting-edge technology into the tourist industry and the potential for marketing travel-related activities in the phase of artificial intelligence. The aim of this chapter is to evaluate the studies on the application of artificial intelligence and augmented reality in tourism marketing.

3 METHODOLOGY

The current search makes use of bibliometric techniques as well as other techniques for literature reviews. Understanding the state, development, and growth of the research is made easier with the help of a thorough bibliometric study of AI and AR in tourism marketing. It helped to build a firm foundation on AI and AR based marketing tourism studies to gain an overview on the topic in one hand and to identify knowledge gap in the other. The techniques used include thematic map, multiple cooperation networks, factorial analysis employing Multi Correspondence Analysis (MCA), keyword occurrence analysis, and the analysis of keyword occurrence. Bibliometric analysis has been used in business marketing, since 2011 (Backhaus, Lügger, & Koch, 2011; Donthu, Kumar, Pattnaik, Samiee & Chabowski, 2012). In order to understand the National policy initiatives to attain Sustainable Development Goals (SDGs), government reports have been reviewed. Data regarding the sustainable development goals and initiatives of government policies have been obtained from various published and unpublished secondary sources. The basic information about the tourism destinations in the country have been collected from the tourism department of different States. Various government reports, publications, journals, newspapers, and books were also referred for the purpose of this research.

3.1 The Rationale for Bibliometric Analysis in AI, AR, and Tourism Marketing

To identify the studies on AI and AR in marketing tourism activities across the world, the author has processed 3324 research publications retrieved from Scopus database from 2012 to 2023. The principal advantage of bibliometric analysis is that it offers quantitative analysis of papers that have been came out in a specific field of scholarly research (Baker et al., 2020). They also offer helpful information on the type of document, its distribution of orgnisations, geographical spread of authors and their academic interests, details about active writers, co-authorship networks, and international and local collaborative efforts (Donthu et al., 2020). For the purpose of achieving a fair representation of the research conclusion on the studies on the application of AI and AR in tourism marketing, performance analysis based on bibliometric methodologies employing cutting-edge software and packages is beneficial.

3.2 Software and Visualisation Tools

Network visualisation tools such as VOSviewer and software based on commands such as the R package for Bibliometrics open software are commonly used bibliometric analysis softwares (Aria & Cuccurullo, 2017; Van Eck & Waltman, 2010). UCINET, Bibexcel, Gephi, Pajek, SciMat, and Sci2 are other softwares used in a similar context. All these softwares have its own advantages and disadvantages regarding the features, speed, flexibility of the generated network and the like. Several research (Baker, 2020; Donthu et al., 2021; Xu et al., 2018;) employ a mix of bibliometric tools in order to analyse and visualisation to address these software problems. Bibliometrix using Biblioshiny, an R-tool, and the software VOSviewer were used by the author in this instance to visualise the data. Based on bibliometric data, networks can be constructed and visualised using these software tools. Numerous collaboration networks, co-occurrence analysis, factorial investigation utilising Multi Correspondence Analysis (MCA), bibliographic pairing or keyword occurring analysis, and the co-occurrence analysis are some of the techniques used. Various connections between the ideas of AI, AR, and marketing tourism were discovered thanks to these tools.

3.3 Retrieval of Data and Search Tactics

Scopus, one of the most popular academic bibliographic databases, is the source of the dataset utilised in this study. Scopus provides convenient access to a vast array of multidisciplinary scientific studies that provide the data necessary to achieve the goals of this paper. Using the 'topic' search option, the research documents were gathered by experimenting with various queries. The search encompassed all Scopus-indexed publications from 2012 to 2023. After manually refining studies from engineering field, the author has retrieved 3324 publications on AI and AR in marketing tourism by using with two primary and three contextual keywords. The primary keywords are "Artificial Intelligence" AND " Tourism" while the contextual keywords used are "Artificial Intelligence" AND "Marketing Tourism", "Augmented reality" AND "marketing tourism", and "Augmented reality" AND "Tourism". These keywords are used to ensure the identification of all relevant documents in this field. The publications include articles, books, book chapters, conference papers and conference review papers. Figure 1 shows a graph showing the number of research publications that were published each year throughout the relevant sample period.

Figure 1. Annual scientific production of articles

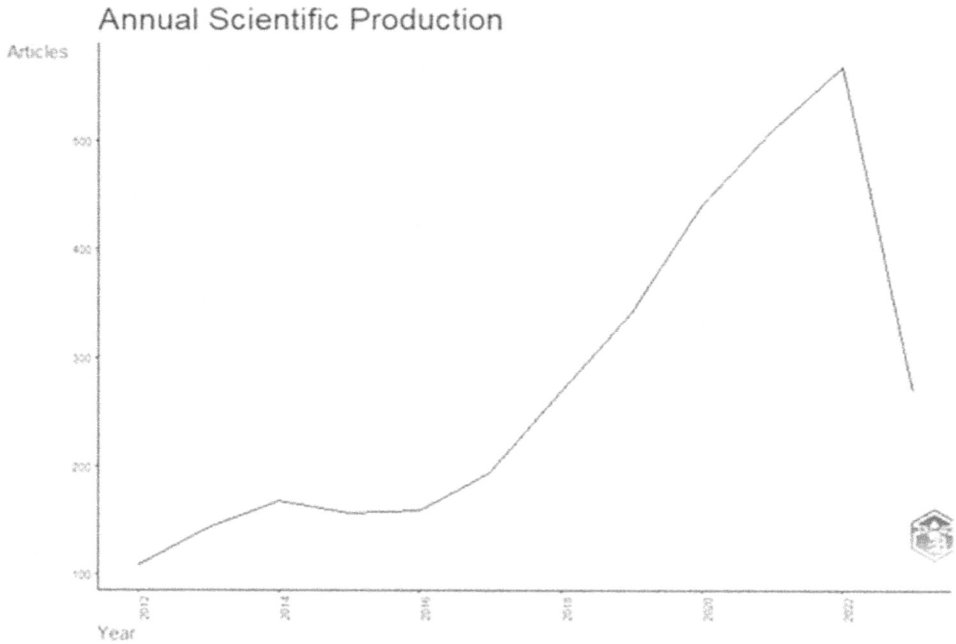

Except for a few exceptions, there is a considerable rising trend in the total number of papers during the course of the study. There has been a noticeable spike in the overall quantity of papers, with a steep increase beginning in 2017 and scaling to its maximum level in 2022, showing significantly increased interest from academicians in the prior year.

4 RESULTS: PERFORMANCE ANALYSIS

4.1 Document Distribution

Table 1 provides a complete overview of the scholarly works found in the Scopus database, organised by the number of publications on tourism-related AI and AR research. Out of 3324 documents, 1700 are articles in journals, 54 books, 317 are book chapters, 988 are conference papers and 112 are conference reviews. Average citation per document is calculated as 8.28 percent. Considering the importance of AI and AR in marketing tourism, the study has taken all the documents published in books, journals, and conferences reviews between 2012 and 2023.

Figure 2 displays the most widely cited works on the implementation of AI and AR in marketing for tourism. With the most citations (385), the paper by Martin-Gutierrez J, (2017) can be regarded as having a significant impact. Yung R, 2019, came in second with 361 citations.

Table 1. Details of scholarly works

Description	Results
Timespan	2012:2023
Sources (Journals, Books, etc)	1522
Documents	3324
Annual Growth Rate %	8.69
Document Average Age	3.99
Average citations per doc	8.284
References	116944
Keywords Plus (ID)	8544
Author's Keywords (DE)	7717
Authors	7904
Authors of single-authored docs	609
Single-authored docs	668
Co-Authors per Doc	2.93
International co-authorships %	17
Article	1700
Book	54
Book chapter	317
Conference paper	988
Conference review	112

Source: - Results from bibliometric analysis, 2023

Table 2. Most relevant sources of documents

Sources	Articles
Lecture Notes in Computer Science	115
ACM International Conference Proceeding Series	82
Journal of Physics: Conference Series	56
Geojournal of Tourism and Geosites	50
Communications in Computer and Information Science	44
Lecture Notes in Networks and Systems	43
Anatolia	41
Sustainability (Switzerland)	40
Advances in Intelligent Systems and Computing	37
CEUR Workshop Proceedings	35
IOP Conference Series: Earth and Environmental Science	33
Springer Proceedings in Business and Economics	28
Risti - Revista Iberica De Sistemas E Tecnologias De Informacao	23
Tourism Management	22

Source: - Results from bibliometric analysis, 2023

Figure 2. Top globally cited documents

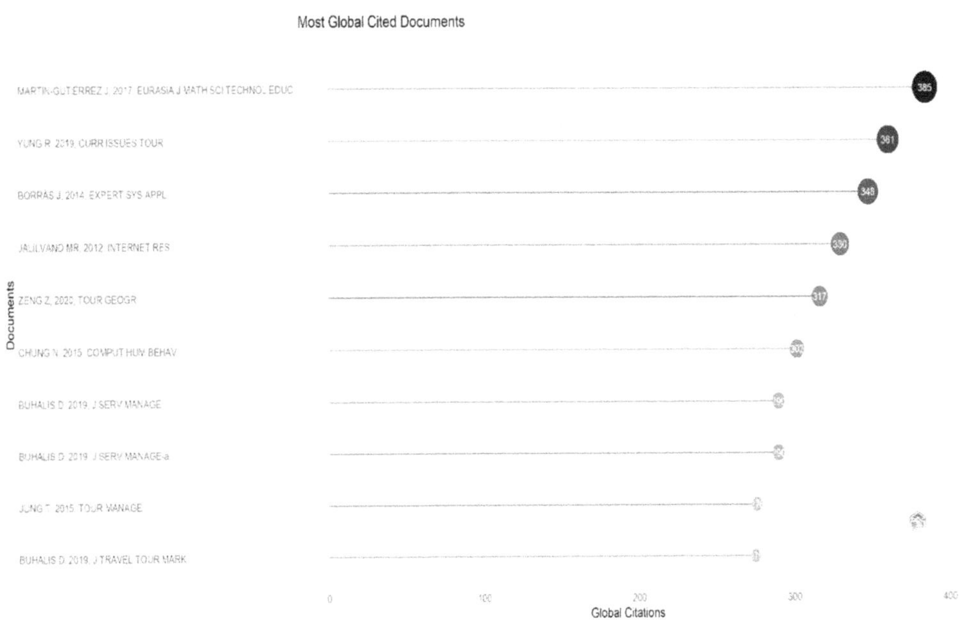

Figure 3. Density visualisation of countries citation

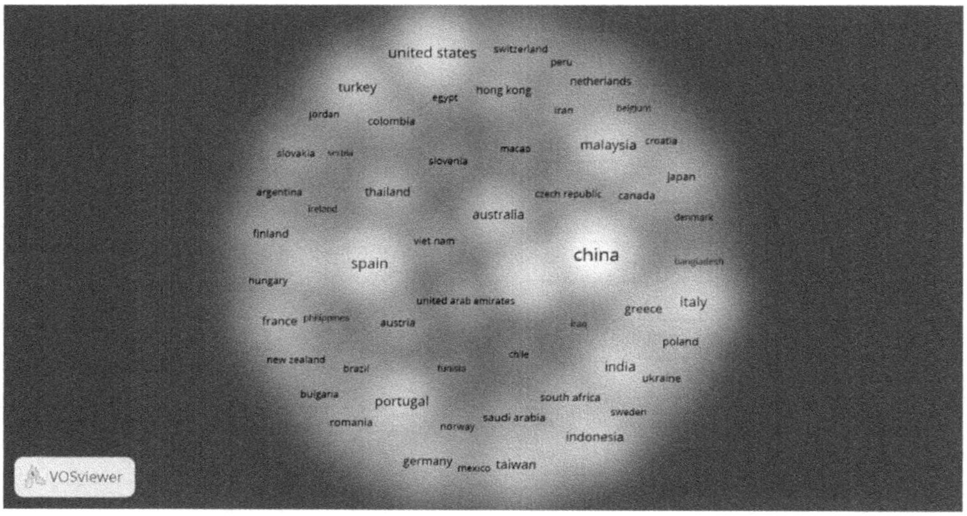

Figure 3 displays a representation of country densities. In terms of the total number of citations obtained, it shows that China is in the lead, followed by Spain and the United States of America (USA). From these, it is evident that these countries have not only published good number of works but also envisaging their quality which had earned them a significant citation count from all over the world. Table 2 shows the most relevant sources of documents related to AI and AR in marketing tourism. It is determined that the computer science lecture notes, in which 115 papers have been published, are the most significant source. The ACM international conference proceedings, which contain 82 articles, are presented after it.

4.2 Country Contribution and Relevant Research Affiliations

Table 3 shows the country-specific magnitude of documents with respect to the frequency of publication number. It is found that China is at the top with a highest amount of output of 1351 papers, thereafter by Spain with 615 publications and Italy with 564 documents. India came in fourth place, with 477 published documents. Various countries such as Malaysia, Indonesia and USA have also made a remarkable contribution to the literature on AI and AR in tourism sector.

Country-wise scientific production in the publications is shown in figure 4. If the frequency of publication is larger, the dark colour is attributed to that particular region and if the lesser the contribution, lighter shade is assigned to that specific region. The grey colour indicates that there has been no scientific production from that region. It is clear from the figure that China has contributed the highest share in publications depicting the dark blue colour and the other countries show the light shade. No scientific production has been recorded in most of the parts of African region and Russia.

Table 3. Country share in publications

Sl No.	Countries	Frequency
1	CHINA	1351
2	SPAIN	615
3	ITALY	564
4	INDIA	477
5	MALAYSIA	467
6	INDONESIA	419
7	USA	416
8	PORTUGAL	395
9	GREECE	381
10	UK	354
11	AUSTRALIA	214
12	TURKEY	193
13	SOUTH KOREA	177
14	GERMANY	143
15	JAPAN	140

Source: - Results from bibliometric analysis, 2023

Figure 4. Scientific production of publications around the world

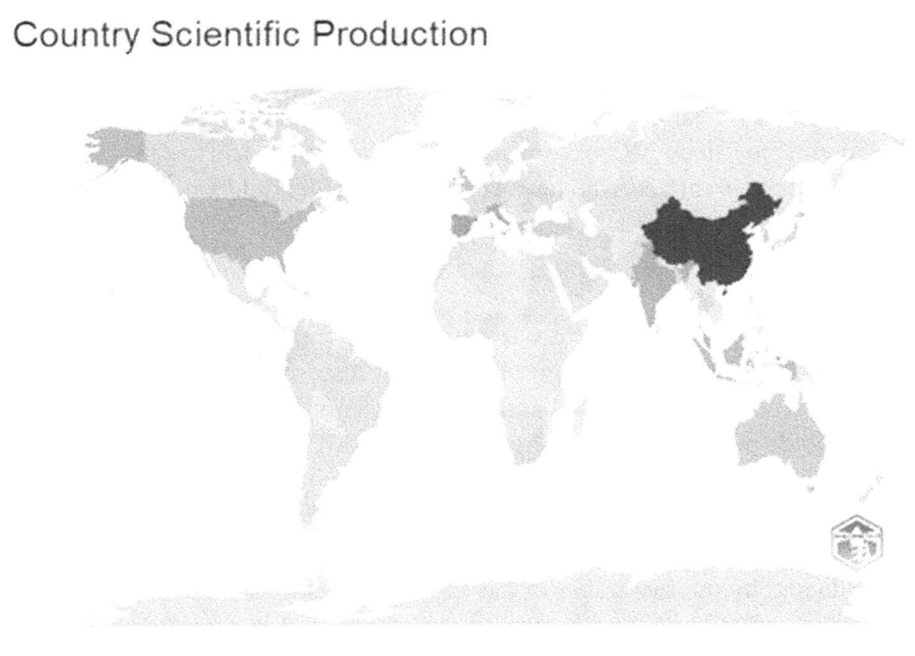

Figure 5. The most relevant authors

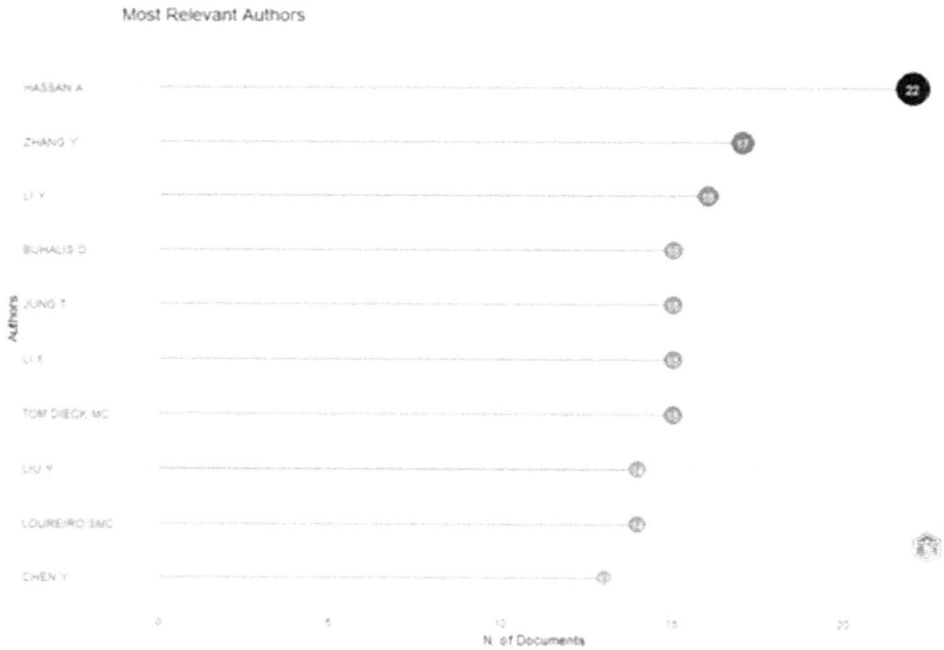

4.3 Leading Authors

The ten best writers in the particular study field are shown in Figure 5 as the most productive authors. The top 10 authors in the field have each contributed at least 10 documents. Hassan A. tops the list with 22 contributions, followed by Zhang Y. with 17 and Li Y. with 16 publications. Several other authors Buhalis D., Li X., and Tom Dieck MC have made 15 publications each to the respective literature. However, there are many other authors who have contributed in this field are given in The Figure 5.

4.4 Analysis of Keywords

Chen and Xiao (2016) states that keywords are regarded as the most fundamental components for the representation of concepts and aid in identifying the areas of research that are still under development. It offers quick access to scholarly publications and is a crucial component in bibliometric analysis when examining particular fields of knowledge (Zhang and Trubey, 2019). The most popular search terms in the dataset's research articles are shown in Figure 6. Tourism, augmented reality, artificial intelligence, virtual reality and marketing are the main research concerns within the selected documents. Figure 7 shows the result of the word cloud analysis in R studio. It provides insights to what kind of research work that has already conducted by the researcher in the field. Word cloud analysis is based on title words of publications in each cluster. The figure represents the word cloud in each cluster, based on the title words of documents contained in them. It also reveals that tourism is the most prominent word used in the documents, followed by augmented reality and then artificial intelligence.

Figure 6. Most relevant words used in research work

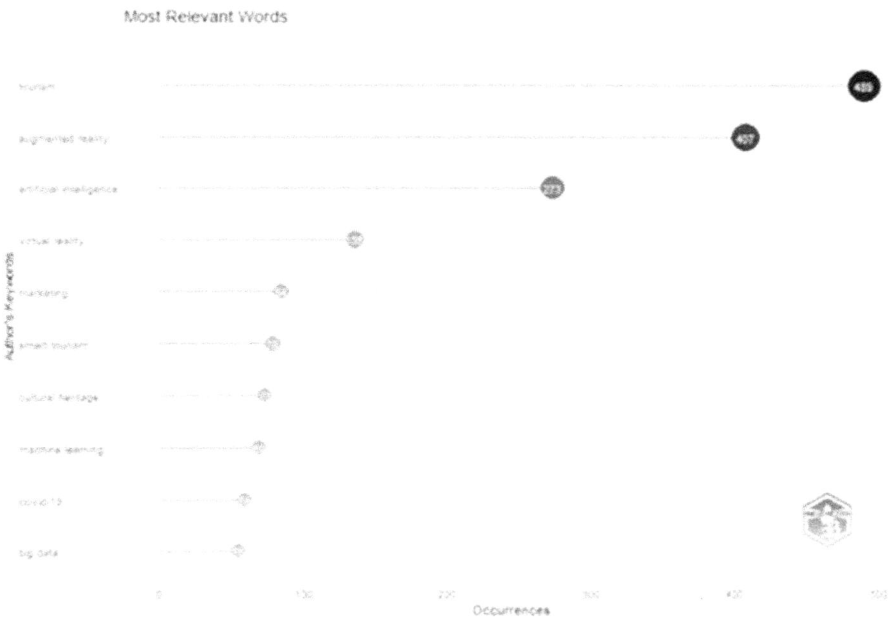

Figure 7. Word cloud

Figure 8 displays the conceptual mapping from 2012 to 2023 with the overlay visualisation of the author's keywords. A colour serves as the representation for each cluster. The dimension of the node varies with the usage of a keyword. The space between nodes is related to the frequency with which phrases co-occur. The authors keyword in the data frame can aid in understanding the document collection's themes. The tone of yellow represents the authors' most recent scholarly contributions. The overlay visualisation aids in better understanding the research trends of the documents. Earlier, the publications were focused on rural tourism, brand, promotion and destination marketing. Since 2018 focus of studies changed to tourism industry, robots, human robot interaction, augmented reality, and artificial intelligence.

Figure 8. Authors keyword

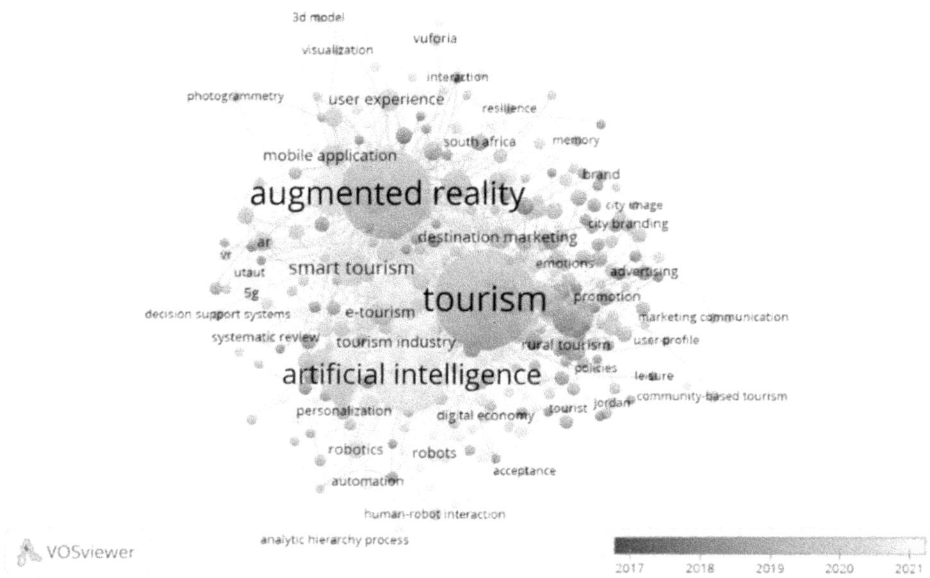

Figure 9. Co word network

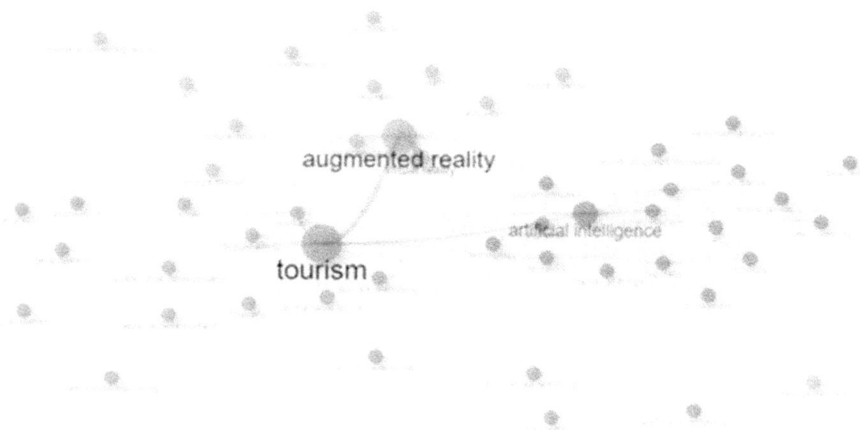

It is evident that the study frontiers have expanded to include a variety of aspects of augmented reality, the tourist business, artificial intelligence, mobile applications, marketing communication, destination marketing, the digital economy, and robots. The authors keyword reveals that the inclusion of artificial intelligence and augmented reality techniques into various aspect of tourism industry transformed the fabric of studies on tourism sector in recent years. While analysing the Co word network, there are three main circles visible for augmented reality, artificial intelligence, and tourism in Figure 9. These major words are related to other words in the documents selected. Tourism is the main word which relates to other words like marketing, eco – tourism, sustainability, and sustainable tourism. Augmented reality at the same time is used with other words like tourism, eco-tourism, cultural tourism, and user experience. Another major circle is Artificial Intelligence and it is used with other words like tourism industry, smart tourism, covid-19, data mining, deep learning, and robots.

Figure 10. Word tree map

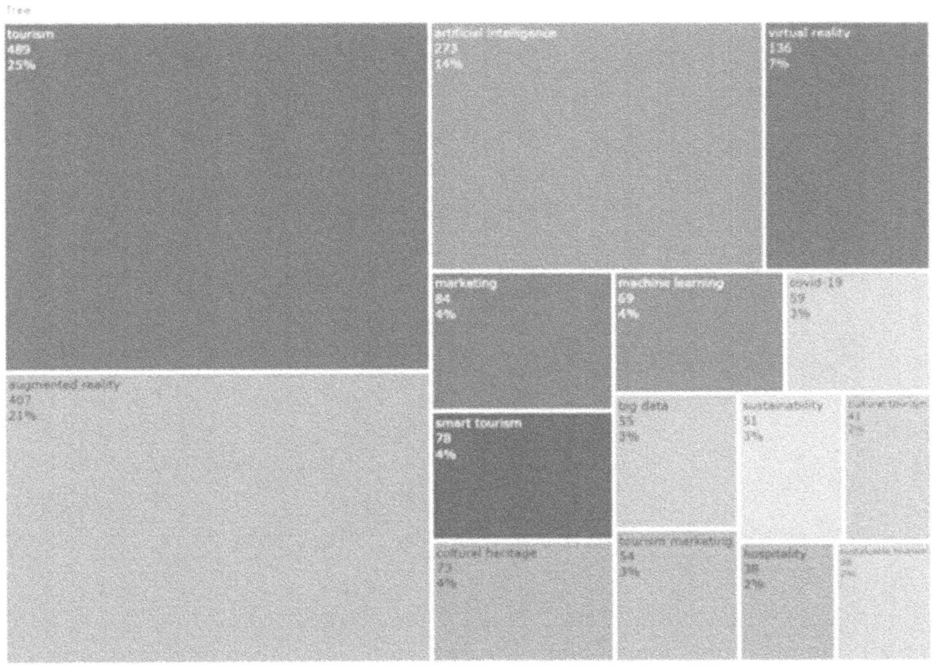

The Figure 10 reveals the Word Tree map developed from the bibliometric analysis. The most common words used in the studies are tourism, augmented reality, artificial intelligence and virtual reality. Moreover, the word tree map in Figure 10 reveals the leading 15 keywords that are often employed in the documents. In short, there has been a big publication in the tourism business on artificial intelligence and augmented reality. However, a few studies in the field of tourism marketing have been conducted.

4.4.1 Factorial Analysis-Based Conceptual Structure Map

Figure 11 displays a conceptual structure mapping of keywords using factorial analysis. The authors' keyword has been presented in the dataset in a compressed manner using the Multi-Correspondence Analysis (MCA) methodology. It looks at the relationships between words in the bibliometric database with the purpose of (i) organising the knowledge into research domains or topics and (ii) highlighting the most popular subjects and identifying patterns that may allow prediction of potential future research lines (Benomar, L., Elferjani, R., Hamilton, 2022). According to Abdi and Valentine (2007) and Xie et al. (2020), it creates a two-dimensional map that describes the variation and similarity in the keywords used in the papers.

Figure 11. Factorial investigation

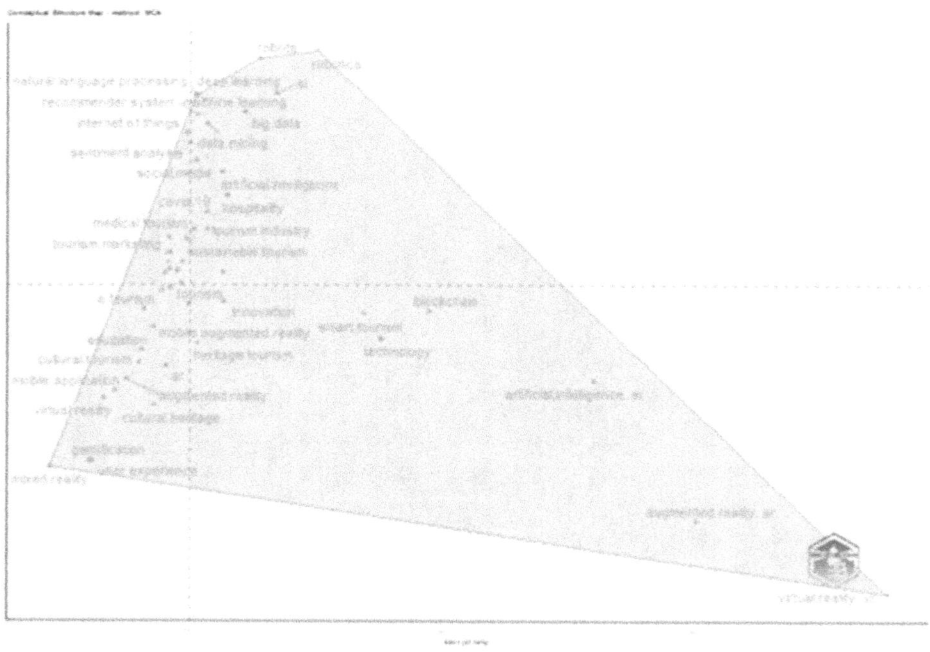

Based on the locations of the points relative to one another and their distribution along the dimensions, the factorial analysis's findings can be understood. Arai and Cuccurullo (2017) found that the closer words are displayed on the map, the more similar their distribution patterns are. The homogeneity of the dataset's word collection serves as the basis for the cluster's formation. The lone cluster in this area is red, and it has a sizable group of 50 terms related to publications on travel, augmented reality, artificial intelligence, medical tourism, smart travel, and travel marketing. Keywords like "augmented reality," "sustainable tourism," "tourism marketing," "medical tourism," "artificial intelligence," and "innovation" are getting closer to the centre of the conversation, which suggests that they have attracted a lot of attention recently and that more research is emerging in the pertinent area of concern.

4.5 Thematic Map

A scientific discipline's topic areas can be identified and their historical development can be examined using a thematic map. Additionally, it aids in identifying scientific gaps that need to be filled by additional study in the future and forecasts future trends in the advancement of the relevant scientific subject. The science map is analysed lexically using thematic maps, which are constructed from key word clusters that are regarded as topics (Tayebia, Manesha, Khalilia, and Nezhada, 2019). The Figure 12 provides the thematic map of the present study which easily assimilates the various fields of focus into one image.

Figure 12. Thematic map

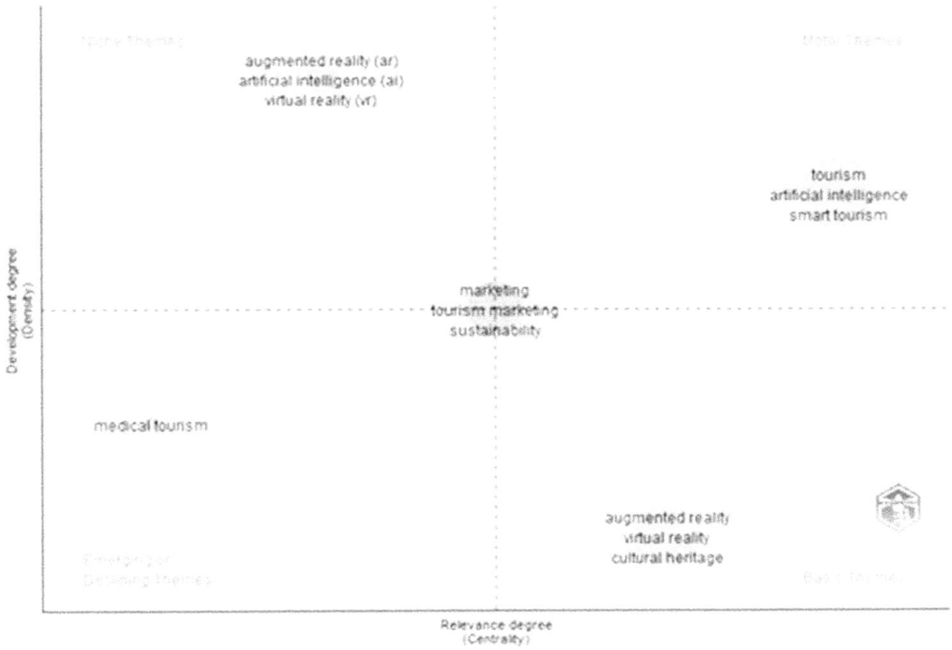

The themes can be examined according to whatever quadrant they are positioned due to the powerful visual design. Top right, in the first quadrant, are the Motor Themes, which are crucial to the research structure. Here it is tourism, artificial intelligence, and smart tourism. Quadrant two is the top left, which is identified as niche themes. They are specific emerging themes and poorly developed and marginal. The bottom left quadrant, or quadrant three, contains topics that are emerging or declining. Here it is medical tourism. Quadrant four is considered as the basic themes and it is AR, virtual reality and cultural heritage. The central position is marketing, tourism marketing and sustainability, which obtain a key focus in all the four quadrants equally.

4.6 Collaboration Network Within the Social Structure

A visual depiction of the collaborative network is created with the aid of the biblioshiny package of R studio in order to comprehend the social structure of collaboration across the countries and relationships between the authors. The country collaboration map is depicted in Figure 13. Collaborative world map is considered as a measure of social structure. The release of research papers in the area of AI and AR in tourism marketing has resulted in 1120 cooperation across nations worldwide, according to study. A collaborative partnership between two countries is indicated by the lines between them. The broadness of the line symbolises the extent of cooperation between the nations. It is found that countries like China, Spain and USA have a strong collaboration.

Figure 13. Country collaboration map

4.6.1 Authors' Collaborative Network

Figure 14 displays the network of author collaborations. The volume of co-authored articles is indicated by the connection between the circles, which represent individual authors as each circle or node. There are five colours indicating five major clusters of different authors. As the collaborative researches increases, the network shall be widened and is likely to be focused into various other authors and thereby creating a new cluster or enlarging an existing cluster. It is found that in the red cluster there is collaboration between authors such as Hassan A, Jung T, Tom Dieck and Buhalis D. Likewise other four colours represent the network of different authors working in the same area of study.

4.6.2 Co-Authorship Network by Country

The nation's involvement in the field of research and their network of collaboration are shown in Figure 15. A nation state is symbolises by a circle in each network, and the dimension of the circle denotes the percentage of each unit determined by the quantity of publications in the relevant topic. The relationship between two circles is represented by a line, and the width of the line shows the degree of cooperation between the two different nations. One cluster of circles of the same colour. The circle's diameter reflects the nation's output or the number of publications it has produced jointly with other nations. Based on co-authored articles, the narrower the space between two circles, the closer the countries are. Figure 16 reveals the time span of a country's contribution to the research area and their collaboration network. India's contribution to the specific research started after 2020. Saudi Arabia is considered to be the most recent contributor to the selected research constituents.

Figure 14. Author's collaboration network

Figure 15. Country's co-authorship network in publications

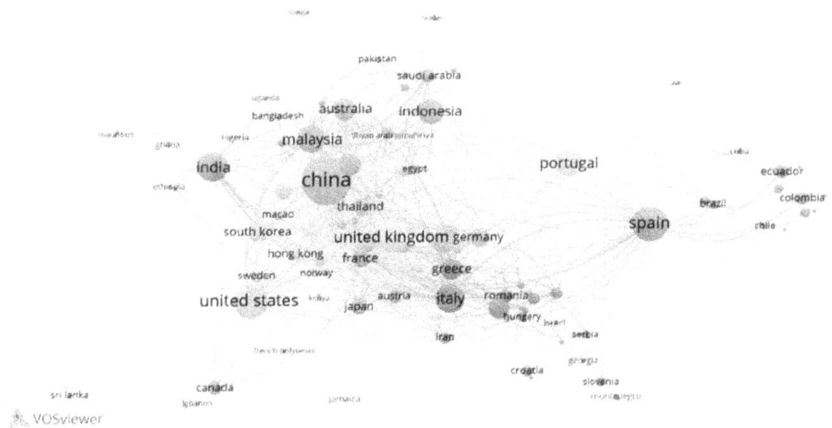

4.6.3 Academic Collaboration Network

The partnership of institutions in the scientific field is shown in Figure 17. Each node in this diagram stands for an institution, and the dimension of the node is determined by the quantity of works produced. It is seen that Hong Kong Polytechnique university and Manchester Metropolitan university have conducted large number of studies. Furthermore, the broadness of the straight line linking these circles reflects the number of collaborative articles produced by the universities. According to the analysis, Hong Kong Polytechnic University has the most publications (40), followed by Manchester Metropolitan University (37). Various distinguished institutions from China, Spain and USA have made a number of studies in the research area of AI and AR in tourism.

Figure 16. Overlay visualisation of countries co-authorship network

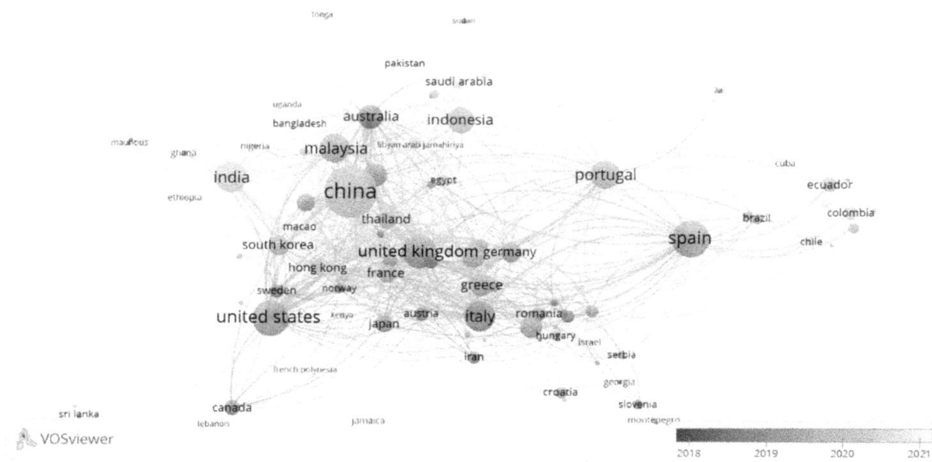

Figure 17. Institutional collaboration network

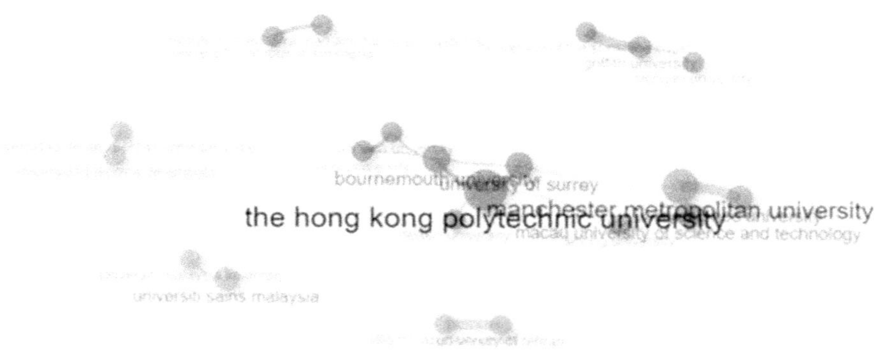

4.7 Future Research Scope

The current investigation demonstrates that academicians in nations like China, Spain, the United States, and India have carried out extensive research on the technical aspects of artificial intelligence and augmented reality in tourism. It is necessary to concentrate on the connections between these strategies and how they affect the promotion of tourism. According to keyword analytics, the tourist industry is heavily utilising artificial intelligence and augmented reality to promote medical tourism activities, rural tourism, eco-tourism, and heritage tourism in order to sustainably grow the sector. In several nations, the methods of virtual reality (VR) and augmented reality (AR) are used to promote travel. However, there are presently no empirical studies in the body of work on the use of AI and AR for marketing travel-related activities. Thematic mapping of the body of literature's insights also point out the paucity of material on the use of AI and AR in marketing travel-related activities. In order to examine the prospects in marketing strategies in the travel and tourist sector for achieving the sustainable development goals of UN 2030, the current research presents a novel strategy based on artificial intelligence.

5 USE OF AR TECHNOLOGY IN SUSTAINABLE TOURISM ACTIVITIES

India is renowned for its legislative measures to optimise the prospects of the travel and tourism sector. However, because to low foreign remittances and widespread job losses, the industry has been the hardest damaged by the Covid-19 Pandemic. It is believed that in order to recover the industry in the pandemic phase, a continual innovation strategy in organised tourist products and experiences is needed. It is suggested to incorporate the technologies employed in the industry, especially the Augmented Reality (AR) which would create a pleasant and secure experience and give visitors a very participatory medium in addition to speaking to a large audience (Attila and Edit, 2012; Kounavis et al., 2012; Vlahakis et al., 2002). The "real world" component of augmented reality (AR), which distinguishes it from virtual reality, is defined as the true time integration of data presented as text, visuals, audio, and other virtual upgrades with real-world items. AR can be used as an interactive technology to assimilate virtual world information to the real world. It can provide maximum knowledge about a specific location, real-world entities such as rivers, trees, exotic plants, animal species, buildings and other built-ups, historical and archaeological sites and many more aspects related to a tourism destination. Instead of providing a pamphlet, brochure, tour information books, tourist guides, or not even a way sign given in native language, a person can self-navigate and can get on to an enchanting self-paced, self-guided tour (Hannam, Butler, and Paris, 2014; Kounavis, Kasimati, and Zamani, 2012; Mekni and Lemieux, 2014; Sanna and Manuri 2016). There are two different kinds of augmented reality applications for tourism: marker-based AR and marker-less AR. The user can mark and share a point of interest (POI) in the marker-based augmented reality (AR) Augmented guides. Additionally, manual notes and comments can be added to audiovisual content to complete it. Location-based augmented reality, projection-based augmented reality, overlay augmented reality, and contour enhanced reality are the four subtypes of marker-less augmented reality. All of these types can include visual augmentations into physical objects.

Marker less AR uses present data to put 3D virtual items in reality. Geo-location-based augmented reality refers to augmented reality aspects that are grounded in current location. Electronically stored information is virtually retained in the physical world, allowing users to access it using AR-compatible devices such as smartphones. The smartphone game Pokémon Go, Blippar's Indoor Visual Positioning are examples of popular location-based AR. It is observed that Location based Augmented Reality would be an effective and efficient tool in Sustainable tourism methods, viz; eco-tourism, medical tourism, heritage tourism, responsible tourism, village tourism, and farm tourism of the country.

An AR-enabled mobile application, technological hardware, a smart phone and seamless internet connectivity can ensure a visual treat and enhance a tourist's perception about the place. Using AR-enabled applications, a person or a group can self-navigate to reach their place of choice, they can rent on a hotel of their taste and even find a cab using the same. The AR-based application visualized here should be highly user-friendly and simple to operate. For example, World Around Me (Germany), Smartify Museum and Art Guide, and AR City by Blippar. While considering Indian scenario, there should be a free basic version and an advanced version with paid services for the more information savvy tourists. The basic version can be made available to local tourists and paid version can be provided to the needy and tourists from outside India. The information in the AR-enabled app must be fed to the AR-cloud of the Indian Tourism website or a local server, verified by the concerned experts from all fields, accumulate all the valid information in one place prior to starting the self-guided tour.

The interactive interface shall be thoroughly improved with all the rich and pleasureful experiences as envisaged by the tourists. AR-based technological circuits have to be introduced in every tourist spot or destination in the country, that is a stakeholder of sustainable tourism initiatives. Every eco-tourism initiative must have to have an AR based application providing a self-guided tour, as there exists a restriction with reference to the entry and resource availability. A bunch of these AR- enabled tourism destinations can be coupled to make an AR-Tourism Circuit even. This will accrue the revenue of the State exchequer in multiple means. AR technology assimilation will enhance the country's tourism potential of all the selected destinations and people from all over the world could watch the AR-enabled site-seeing or tour-walks of these tourist destinations online in the respective tourism department website itself. For example, Muziris Virtual Tour Guide of Kerala Tourism Department. The service can be enabled after providing a reasonable fee, remitted by the tourist themselves. In this way, the tourism could be improved skilfully and technologically without harming the natural environment and its stability. Thus, AR-based technological initiatives have to be introduced in the near future and development of the same shall guide the country, into the status of achieving sustainable tourism by reducing the ecological footprint.

According to a recent report 'Digital 2022' performed by Data portal (2022), in a post-Covid-19 future, internet usage is now accessed by 5.03 billion people globally, which is 63.1 percent of the entire world's population. It illustrates that in July 2022, the connected population of the world rose by around 180 million people, and internet users continue to expand at a rate close to 4% each year. Furthermore, 92.1 percent of the world's internet users utilise a mobile phone to access the internet. With the adaptation of AR technology in tourism, a person with a smart phone can easily experience a welcoming and safe atmosphere through an interactive medium. Augmented Reality technology allows users to interact with real-world elements that are augmented by a computer-generated virtual interface related to certain locations or activities on a wide scale, which is adjustable by each user. The AR in tourism sector is a key to the world of tourism richness and incorporation of technology into an everlasting industry, thereby providing new experiences and unlimited knowledge

6. RECENT POLICY INITIATIVES BY THE GOVERNMENT OF INDIA TOWARDS SUSTAINABLE TOURISM

According to the Ministry of Tourism's National Strategy for Sustainable Tourism (2022), the goal is to achieve mainstream sustainability in the Indian tourism sector and assure less volatile, open and inclusive, zero carbon, and economical with resources in tourism. while protecting natural and cultural resources. The UNWTO's fundamental criterion for sustainable tourism is environmental sustainability, which is acknowledged by the ministry of tourism. It will mean maximising the best use of environmental assts, that are crucial for the growth and development of tourism activities, as well as maintaining essential ecological processes and making a contribution to the preservation of biodiversity and the natural world.

The proposed national tourism policy for 2022 highlighted issues like energy use, emissions of greenhouse gases, water use, waste management, the loss of species diversity, the efficient management of built and artistic assets, planning, and administration, in addition to the primary issues posed by climate change and Covid-19. As a result, by incorporating sustainability into the tourism industry, the Policy seeks to encourage green tourism. Through green tourism initiatives, energy efficiency and sound climate condition, reduced water consumption, waste minimisation and conservation of biodiversity can be attained. A National Green Tourism Mission must be established in order to produce local income and integrate local communities in order to enhance livelihoods and eliminate poverty. Moreover, the policy initiatives designed to promote digitalisation of tourism industry. In order to achieve the objective of maximising the potential of digitization in the tourism sector, the Ministry of Tourism will establish the National Digital Tourism Mission to facilitate information and service exchange among national and state tourism organisations, providers of tourist services, tourist attractions, items, and encounters. and visitors. The national digital tourism mission will enable travellers to access digital information and services at every stage of their trip, according to the draught national tourist policy for 2022.

According to the policy, the Mission would promote a smart tourist destination that makes it easier for people to access tourism and hospitality-related goods, services, locations, and experiences through ICT-based solutions. With the use of enormous amounts of data, Artificial Intelligence (AI), cloud-based computing, augmented and virtual reality, Augmented Reality, and the Internet of Things, it aims to encourage the innovative integration of cutting-edge digital technologies into the tourism system, giving the location competitive advantages. These technologies connect the various tourism components in a dynamic neural network.

It has been noted that all of these policy initiatives are linked to achieving the objectives in the Sustainable Development Goals (SDG) 8 (inclusive and sustainable economic growth), 9 (build resilient infrastructure, promote inclusive and sustainable industrialization, and foster innovation), 12 (sustainable consumption and production), and 14 (the sustainable use of oceans and marine resources) of the 2030 Agenda for Sustainable Development, which was approved by the UN General Assembly. It depends on sound public and private infrastructure, as well as an inventive atmosphere. To attract visitors and other types of foreign capital, the sector may also persuade national governments to update infrastructure and redesign firms to make them environmentally friendly, energy-efficient, and ethical. Furthermore, this should stimulate more sustainable industry, which is critical for encouraging creativity, expansion, and economic development. As a result, tourism businesses can boost their market share, growth, operational effectiveness, and competitive edge. Additionally, it will aid in the creation and customization of product offers, enhance connectivity within the destination, produce data to monitor performance, and aid in improving destination management (Daft National Tourism Policy, 2022).

7. CONCLUSION

The research used in this study allows us to draw the conclusion that, starting in 2017, the performance of research connected to AI and augmented reality in the tourism field is growing dramatically. According to the bibliometric analysis, academics have extensively studied the use of artificial intelligence and augmented reality in the travel industry in China, Spain, Italy, the United States, and India. The authors like Hassan A., Zhang Y., and then Li Y. have made remarkable contribution to this research field. Several other authors like Buhalis D., Li X., and Tom Dieck M C have made a number of publications to the respective literature. The keyword occurrence asserts that tourism industry is widely using artificial intelligence and augmented reality for the sustainable development of tourism activities by promoting medical tourism, rural tourism, eco-tourism and heritage tourism. The evident lack of empirical research on the use of AI and AR in marketing travel-related activities is however made clear by this. Insights from the factorial analysis and thematic mapping of extent literature also reflects a clear absence of literature on the application of AI and AR in marketing tourism activities. Employees can also play an important role in the effectiveness of tourism industry (Kalia and Bhardwaj, 2019). Therefore, future research can also be undertaken to understand the role of various human relation dimensions such as skilled migration (Bhardwaj and Sharma, 2022), cultural intelligence(Bhardwaj, 2022),Leadership styles(Thakur et al.,2019).It is also required to encourage the scholars to conduct studies on artificial intelligence to explore the opportunities in marketing techniques in travel and tourism sector. The study also reveals that the AI based AR technology could create a safe environment with a very interactive medium and thus can be a powerful tool in increasing sustainable tourism activities in the country. Moreover, it can provide fascinating experience to the visitors from all around the globe even without visiting a destination with a handheld devise such as smartphones and AR based applications.

A review on recent policy initiatives of government is focused on green tourism initiatives to attain sustainable tourism development. It also reveals that even though the country initiated technological inclusion in its tourism marketing strategy, the efforts are inadequate to attract the tourists worldwide. In India, the tourism industry is lagging far behind in the adoption of augmented reality technologies. The country can implement specific policies to implement the use of Augmented Reality technology in tourism, which can provide information on spatial location, description and detailing of tourist destination, transportation, travel booking, and accommodation at visitors' fingertips, resulting in massive earnings. The study clearly identifies a research deficit in the field of using artificial intelligence to investigate opportunities in marketing tactics in the travel and tourist industry. It necessitates the use of innovative technologies such as artificial intelligence and augmented reality in marketing tourism strategies in the country in order to meet the UN 2030 Sustainable Development Goals.

REFERENCES

Abdi, H., & Valentin, D. (2007). Multiple Correspondence Analysis. *Encyclopedia of Measurement and Statistics*. https:// perso nal. utdal las. edu/ ~Herve/ Abdi- MCA20 07- pretty.

Aria, M., & Cuccurullo, C. (2017). bibliometrix: An R-tool for comprehensive science mapping analysis. *Journal of Informetrics*, *11*(4), 959–975. doi:10.1016/j.joi.2017.08.007

Attila, K., & Edit, B. (2012). Beyond reality: The possibilities of augmented reality in cultural and heritage tourism. *2nd International Tourism and Sport Management Conference*, 5(6).

Azuma, R., Baillot, Y., Behringer, R., Feiner, S., Julier, S., & MacIntyre, B. (2001). Recent advances in augmented reality. *IEEE Computer Graphics and Applications*, *21*(6), 34–47. doi:10.1109/38.963459

Azuma, R. T. (1997). A survey of augmented reality. *Presence (Cambridge, Mass.)*, *6*(4), 355–385. doi:10.1162/pres.1997.6.4.355

Backhaus, K., Lügger, K., & Koch, M. (2011). The structure and evolution of business-to-business marketing: A citation and co-citation analysis. *Industrial Marketing Management*, *40*(6), 940–951. doi:10.1016/j.indmarman.2011.06.024

Baker, H. K., Pandey, N., Kumar, S., & Haldar, A. (2020). A bibliometric analysis of board diversity: Current status, development, and future research directions. *Journal of Business Research, 108*, 232–246. doi:10.1016/j.jbusres.2019.11.025

Benomar, L., Elferjani, R., Hamilton, J., O'Neill, G. A., Echchakoui, S., Bergeron, Y., & Lamara, M. (2022). Bibliometric analysis of the structure and evolution of research on assisted migration. *Current Forestry Reports*, *8*(2), 199–213. doi:10.100740725-022-00165-y

Bhardwaj, B. (2021). *Short-term foreign trips correlates of the four factors model of cultural intelligence.* Rajagiri Management Journal., doi:10.1108/RAMJ-01-2021-0008

Bhardwaj, B., & Kalia, N. (2021). *Contextual and task performance: role of employee engagement and organizational culture in hospitality industry.* Vilakshan-XIMB Journal of Management. doi:10.1108/XJM-08-2020-0089

Bhardwaj, B., Kalia, N., Chand, M., & Sharma, D. (2023). Engaged Organizational Culture as a precursor to job performance: An evidence from the hospitality industry of Himachal Pradesh. *International Journal of Hospitality and Tourism Systems*, *16*(4), 48–57.

Bhardwaj, B., & Sharma, D. (2022). Migration of skilled professionals across the border: Brain drain or brain gain? *European Management Journal*. Advance online publication. doi:10.1016/j.emj.2022.12.011

Casteleiro-Roca, J. L., Gómez-González, J. F., Calvo-Rolle, J. L., Jove, E., Quintián, H., Martín, J. F. A., ... Méndez-Perez, J. A. (2018). Prediction of the energy demand of a hotel using an artificial intelligence-based model. *Hybrid Artificial Intelligent Systems: 13th International Conference, HAIS 2018, Oviedo, Spain, June 20-22, 2018 Proceedings*, *13*, 586–596.

Chen, G., & Xiao, L. (2016). Selecting publication keywords for domain analysis in bibliometrics: A comparison of three methods. *Journal of Informetrics*, *10*(1), 212–223. doi:10.1016/j.joi.2016.01.006

Cranmer, E., Dieck, M., & Fountoulaki, P. (2020). Exploring the value of augmented reality for tourism. *Tourism Management Perspectives, 35*. https://www.sciencedirect.com/science/article/pii/S2211973620300398 doi:10.1016/j.tmp.2020.100672

Domínguez-Quintero, A. M., González-Rodríguez, M. R., & Paddison, B. (2020). The mediating role of experience quality on authenticity and satisfaction in the context of cultural-heritage tourism. *Current Issues in Tourism*, *23*(2), 248–260. doi:10.1080/13683500.2018.1502261

Donthu, N., Kumar, S., Mukherjee, D., Pandey, N., & Lim, W. M. (2021). How to conduct a bibliometric analysis: An overview and guidelines. *Journal of Business Research*, *133*, 285–296. doi:10.1016/j.jbusres.2021.04.070

Donthu, N., Kumar, S., Pandey, N., & Gupta, P. (2021). Forty years of the International Journal of Information Management: A bibliometric analysis. *International Journal of Information Management*, *57*, 102307. doi:10.1016/j.ijinfomgt.2020.102307

Donthu, N., Kumar, S., & Pattnaik, D. (2020). Forty-five years of Journal of Business Research: A bibliometric analysis. *Journal of Business Research, 109*, 1–14. doi:10.1016/j.jbusres.2019.10.039

Draft National Tourism Policy. (2022). *Ministry of Tourism, Government of India Economic Survey 2022- 23 (2023)*. Finance Ministry, Government of India.

Ezzaouia, I., & Bulchand-Gidumal, J. (2020). Factors influencing the adoption of information technology in the hotel industry. An analysis in a developing country. *Tourism Management Perspectives, 34*, 100675. doi:10.1016/j.tmp.2020.100675

Government of India. (2021). *India's climate vision – Success Story*. Author.

Gretzel, U. (2011). Intelligent systems in tourism: A social science perspective. *Annals of Tourism Research, 38*(3), 757–779. doi:10.1016/j.annals.2011.04.014

Hadavandi, E., Ghanbari, A., Shahanaghi, K., & Abbasian-Naghneh, S. (2011). Tourist arrival forecasting by evolutionary fuzzy systems. *Tourism Management, 32*(5), 1196–1203. doi:10.1016/j.tourman.2010.09.015

Hannam, K., Butler, G., & Paris, C. M. (2014). Developments and key issues in tourism mobilities. *Annals of Tourism Research, 44*, 171–185. doi:10.1016/j.annals.2013.09.010

Himanshu and Roshan A. (2021). *Ecotourism Market*. Retrieved from Allied Market Research: https://www.allied marketresearch.com/eco-tourism-market-A06364

Inanc–Demir, M., & Kozak, M. (2019). Big data and its supporting elements: Implications for tourism and hospitality marketing. *Big data and innovation in tourism, travel, and hospitality: Managerial approaches, techniques, and applications*, 213-223.

India Tourism Statistics 2022. (2022). Ministry of Tourism, Government of India.

Infante-Moro, A., Infante-Moro, J. C., & Gallardo-Pérez, J. (2019). The importance of ICTs for students as a competence for their future professional performance: The case of the faculty of business studies and tourism of the University of Huelva. *Journal of New Approaches in Educational Research, 8*(2), 201–213. doi:10.7821/naer.2019.7.434

Jain, A. (2017). *Study of Artificial Intelligence (AI) with Augmented Reality(AR)*. www.ijcst.com

Jingen Liang, L., & Elliot, S. (2021). A systematic review of augmented reality tourism research: What is now and what is next? *Tourism and Hospitality Research, 21*(1), 15–30. doi:10.1177/1467358420941913

Kalia, N., & Bhardwaj, B. (2019). Contextual and Task Performance: Do Demographic and Organizational variables matter? *Rajagiri Management Journal, 13*(2), 30–42. doi:10.1108/RAMJ-09-2019-0017

Kirilenko, A. P., Stepchenkova, S. O., Kim, H., & Li, X. (2018). Automated sentiment analysis in tourism: Comparison of approaches. *Journal of Travel Research, 57*(8), 1012–1025. doi:10.1177/0047287517729757

Kounavis, C. D., Kasimati, A. E., & Zamani, E. D. (2012). Enhancing the tourism experience through mobile augmented reality: Challenges and prospects. *International Journal of Engineering Business Management, 4*, 10. doi:10.5772/51644

Lai, W. C., & Hung, W. H. (2018). *A framework of cloud and AI based intelligent hotel*. Academic Press.

Lau, C. K. H., Chi, F. R. C., & Au, N. (2019). Examination of the adoption of augmented reality: A VAM approach. *Asia Pacific Journal of Tourism Research*, *24*(10), 1005–1020. doi:10.1080/10941665.2019.1655076

Law, R. (2000). Back-propagation learning in improving the accuracy of neural network-based tourism demand forecasting. *Tourism Management*, *21*(4), 331–340. doi:10.1016/S0261-5177(99)00067-9

Law, R., Buhalis, D., & Cobanoglu, C. (2014). Progress on information and communication technologies in hospitality and tourism. *International Journal of Contemporary Hospitality Management*, *26*(5), 727–750. doi:10.1108/IJCHM-08-2013-0367

Laws, E. (1998). Conceptualizing visitor satisfaction management in heritage settings: An exploratory blueprinting analysis of Leeds Castle, Kent. *Tourism Management*, *19*(6), 545–554. doi:10.1016/S0261-5177(98)00056-9

Li, F. (2020). The digital transformation of business models in the creative industries: A holistic framework and emerging trends. *Technovation, 92–93*. https://www.sciencedirect.com/science/article/pii/S0166497217300536 doi:10.1016/j.technovation.2017.12.004

Li, X., Wu, P., Shen, G. Q., Wang, X. Y., & Teng, Y. (2017). Mapping the knowledge domains of Building Information Modeling (BIM): A bibliometric approach. *Automation in Construction*, *84*, 195–206. doi:10.1016/j.autcon.2017.09.011

Loureiro, S., Guerreiro, J., & Ali, F. (2020). 20 years of research on virtual reality and augmented reality in tourism context: A text-mining approach. *Tourism Management, 77*. https://www.sciencedirect.com/science/article/pii/S0261517719302262 doi:10.1016/j.tourman.2019.104028

Lu, Z., Gozgor, G., Lau, C. K. M., & Paramati, S. R. (2019). The dynamic impacts of renewable energy and tourism investments on international tourism: Evidence from the G20 countries. *Journal of Business Economics and Management*, *20*(6), 1102–1120. doi:10.3846/jbem.2019.10181

Manuri, F., & Sanna, A. (2016). A survey on applications of augmented reality. *ACSIJ Advances in Computer Science: An International Journal*, *5*(1), 18–27.

Manzoor, F., Wei, L., Asif, M., Haq, M. Z. U., & Rehman, H. U. (2019). The contribution of sustainable tourism to economic growth and employment in Pakistan. *International Journal of Environmental Research and Public Health*, *16*(19), 3785. doi:10.3390/ijerph16193785 PMID:31597376

Mekni & Lemieux. (2014). Augmented reality: Applications, challenges and future trends. *Applied Computational Science, 20*, 205-214.

Mou, N., Zheng, Y., Makkonen, T., Yang, T., Tang, J. J., & Song, Y. (2020). Tourists' digital footprint: The spatial patterns of tourist flows in Qingdao, China. *Tourism Management*, *81*, 104151. doi:10.1016/j.tourman.2020.104151

Olsson, T., Kärkkäinen, T., Lagerstam, E., & Ventä-Olkkonen, L. (2012). User evaluation of mobile augmented reality scenarios. *Journal of Ambient Intelligence and Smart Environments*, *4*(1), 29–47. doi:10.3233/AIS-2011-0127

Pannu, A. (2015). Artificial intelligence and its application in different areas. *Artificial Intelligence*, *4*(10), 79–84.

Ronaghi, M., Hossein, M., & Ronaghi, M. (2022). A contextualized study of the usage of the augmented reality technology in the tourism industry. *Decision Analytics Journal, 5*. doi:10.1016/j.dajour.2022.100136

Sharma, D., Chaudhary, M., Jaswal, N., & Bhardwaj, B. (2022). Hiding Behind The SWOT: Gender Equality and COVID-19. *Journal of Positive School Psychology*, 730–740.

Singh, N., Tang, Y., Zhang, Z., & Zheng, C. (2020). COVID-19 waste management: Effective and successful measures in Wuhan, China. *Resources, Conservation and Recycling*, *163*, 105071. doi:10.1016/j.resconrec.2020.105071 PMID:32834489

Stroumpoulis, A., Kopanaki, E., & Varelas, S. (2022). Role of artificial intelligence and big data analytics in smart tourism: A resource-based view approach. *WIT Transactions on Ecology and the Environment*, *256*, 99–108. doi:10.2495/ST220091

Thakur, D. J., Verma, P., & Sharma, D. (2019). Influence of Leadership Style: A Review. *International Journal of Advanced Science and Technology*, *28*(20), 945–952.

Topal, İ., & Uçar, M. K. (2018, September). In tourism, using artificial intelligence forecasting with Tripadvisor data: Year of Turkey in China. In *2018 International Conference on Artificial Intelligence and Data Processing (IDAP)* (pp. 1-5). IEEE.

Tuo, Y., Ning, L., & Zhu, A. (2021). How artificial intelligence will change the future of tourism industry: The practice in China. *Proceeding of the ENTER 2021 eTourism Conference,* 83–94. 10.1007/978-3-030-65785-7_7

Tussyadiah, I., & Miller, G. (2019). Nudged by a robot: Responses to agency and feedback. *Annals of Tourism Research*, *78*, 102752. doi:10.1016/j.annals.2019.102752

Van Eck, N., & Waltman, L. (2010). Software survey: VOSviewer, a computer program for bibliometric mapping. *Scientometrics, 84*(2), 523-538.

Vlahakis, V., Ioannidis, M., Karigiannis, J., Tsotros, M., Gounaris, M., Stricker, D., Gleue, T., Daehne, P., & Almeida, L. (2002). Archeoguide: An augmented reality guide for archaeological sites. *IEEE Computer Graphics and Applications*, *22*(5), 52–60. doi:10.1109/MCG.2002.1028726

World Travel and Tourism Council. (2022). *Travel and Tourism Economic Impact 2022, Global Trends*. WTTC.

Xiang, Z. (2020). Tourism in the era of artificial intelligence. *J Tour*, *35*(1), 1–3.

Xie, H., Zhang, Y., Wu, Z., & Lv, T. (2020). A bibliometric analysis on land degradation: Current status, development, and future directions. *Land (Basel)*, *9*(1), 28. doi:10.3390/land9010028

Xu, X., Chen, X., Jia, F., Brown, S., Gong, Y., & Xu, Y. (2018). Supply chain finance: A systematic literature review and bibliometric analysis. *International Journal of Production Economics*, *204*, 160–173. doi:10.1016/j.ijpe.2018.08.003

Yung, R., & Khoo-Lattimore, C. (2019). New realities: A systematic literature review on virtual reality and augmented reality in tourism research. *Current Issues in Tourism*, *22*(17), 2056–2081. doi:10.1080/13683500.2017.1417359

Zhang, Y., & Trubey, P. (2019). Machine learning and sampling scheme: An empirical study of money laundering detection. *Computational Economics*, *54*(3), 1043–1063. doi:10.100710614-018-9864-z

Compilation of References

Aayog, N. I. T. I. (2018). *National Strategy for Artificial Intelligence*. NITI Aayog. https://niti.gov.in/sites/default/files/2019-01/NationalStrategy-for-AI-Discussion-Paper.pdf

Abbas, S., AL-Abrrow, H., Abdullah, H. O., Alnoor, A., Khattak, Z. Z., & Khaw, K. W. (2022). Encountering Covid-19 and perceived stress and the role of a health climate among medical workers. *Current Psychology (New Brunswick, N.J.)*, *41*(12), 9109–9122. doi:10.100712144-021-01381-8 PMID:33519147

Abdeldayem, M. M., & Aldulaimi, S. H. (2020). Trends and opportunities of artificial intelligence in human resource management: Aspirations for the public sector in Bahrain. *International Journal of Scientific and Technology Research*, *9*(1), 3867–3871.

Abdi, H., & Valentin, D. (2007). Multiple Correspondence Analysis. *Encyclopedia of Measurement and Statistics*. https://perso nal. utdal las. edu/ ~Herve/ Abdi- MCA20 07- pretty.

Abdullah, A.G.K., Alzaidiyeen, N., & Aldarabah, I. (2009). Workplace Spirituality and Leadership Effectiveness Among Educational Managers in Malaysia. *European Journal of Soil Science*, *10*, 307–319.

Accenture. (2020). Retrieved from https://www.accenture.com/us-en/insights/capital-markets/wealth-management-artificial-intelligence

Adamska, M., & Minárová, M. (2014). *Role of learning organization in building consumer confidence*. Economics and Management. doi:10.15240/tul/001/2014-1-005

Adeyemo, D. A. (2007). Emotional Intelligence and The Relationship Between Job Satisfaction & Organizational Commitment of the employee in public parastatals in Oyo state, Nigeria, Pakistan. *Journal of Social Sciences*, *4*(2), 324–330.

Aftab, J., Abid, N., Cucari, N., & Savastano, M. (2022). Green human resource management and environmental performance: The role of green innovation and environmental strategy in a developing country. *Business Strategy and the Environment*, *32*(4), 1782–1798. doi:10.1002/bse.3219

Agarwal, R., & Dhar, V. (2014). Editorial—Big data, data science, and analytics: The opportunity and challenge for IS research. *Information Systems Research*, *25*(3), 443–448. doi:10.1287/isre.2014.0546

Aghion, P. (2021). *The Direct and Indirect Effects of Automation on Employment: A Survey of the Recent Literature*. https://www.semanticscholar.org/paper/The-Direct-and-Indirect-Effects-of-Automation-on-%3A-Aghion/006a9a1c0c0784d617b5b946115f9f1c7d884102

Aghion, P., Antonin, C., & Bunel, S. (2020). Artificial Intelligence, Growth and Employment: The Role of Policy. *Economie et Statistique / Economics and Statistics, 510-511-512*, 149–164. doi:10.24187/ecostat.2019.510t.1994

Aguiar-Costa, L. M., Cunha, C. A., Silva, W. K., & Abreu, N. R. (2022). Customer satisfaction in service delivery with artificial intelligence: A meta-analytic study. *RAM. Revista de Administração Mackenzie*, *23*(6), 23. doi:10.1590/1678-6971/eramd220003.en

Ahmadi, S. A. A. (2019). Relationship between emotional intelligence and psychological well-being. In *Relationship Between Emotional Intelligence and Psychological Well Being*. Academic Press.

Ahmad, I., Ullah, K., & Khan, A. (2022). The impact of green HRM on green creativity: Mediating role of pro-environmental behaviors and moderating role of ethical leadership style. *International Journal of Human Resource Management*, *33*(19), 3789–3821. doi:10.1080/09585192.2021.1931938

Ahmed, M., Guo, Q., Qureshi, M. A., Raza, S. A., Khan, K. A., & Salam, J. (2021). Do green HR practices enhance green motivation and proactive environmental management maturity in hotel industry? *International Journal of Hospitality Management*, *94*, 102852. doi:10.1016/j.ijhm.2020.102852

Ahmed, O. (2018). Artificial intelligence in HR. *International Journal of Research and Analytical Reviews*, *5*(4), 971–978.

Ahmed, S., Alshater, M. M., Ammari, A. E., & Hammami, H. (2022). Artificial intelligence and machine learning in finance: A bibliometric review. *Research in International Business and Finance*, *61*(C), 101646. doi:10.1016/j.ribaf.2022.101646

Ahmetoglu, G., Leutner, F., & Chamorro-Premuzic, T. (2011). EQ-nomics: Understanding the relationship between individual differences in Trait Emotional Intelligence and entrepreneurship. *Personality and Individual Differences*, *51*(8), 1028–1033. doi:10.1016/j.paid.2011.08.016

Akanni, A. A., Kareem, D. B., & Oduaran, C. A. (2020). The relationship between emotional intelligence and employee wellbeing through perceived person-job fit among university academic staff: A Structural Equation Modelling Approach. *Cogent Psychology*, *7*(1), 1869376. doi:10.1080/23311908.2020.1869376

Akanni, A. A., Oladejo, O. E., & Oduaran, C. A. (2018). Work-life Balance, Job Insecurity and Counterproductive Work Behaviour among Brewery Workers. *North American Journal of Psychology*, *20*(2).

Akhtar, F., & Das, N. (2020). Investor personality and investment performance: From the perspective of psychological traits. *Qualitative Research in Financial Markets*, *12*(3), 333–352. doi:10.1108/QRFM-11-2018-0116

Akhtar, R., Boustani, L., Tsivrikos, D., & Chamorro-Premuzic, T. (2015). The engageable personality: Personality and trait as predictors of work engagement. *Personality and Individual Differences*, *73*, 44–49. doi:10.1016/j.paid.2014.08.040

Akhund Lotfali, P., Khanneh, H. R., Fallahi Khoshknab, M., & Hosseinzadeh, S. (2011). The Effect of Emotional Intelligence Education on Nurses' JobInteraction. *Health Promotion Management*, *1*(1), 7–16.

Akinkoye, E. Y., & Bankole, O. E. (2020). Effect of Emotional Biases on Investor's Decision Making in Nigeria. *International Journal of Business and Management Future*, *4*(1), 33–39. doi:10.46281/ijbmf.v4i1.548

Akpan, I. J., & Ibidunni, A. S. (2021). Digitization and technological transformation of small business for sustainable development in the less developed and emerging economies: A research note and call for papers. *Journal of Small Business and Entrepreneurship*, 1–7.

Akpan, I. J., Soopramanien, D., & Kwak, D. H. (2021). Cutting-edge technologies for small business and innovation in the era of COVID-19 global health pandemic. *Journal of Small Business and Entrepreneurship*, *33*(6), 607–617. doi:10.1080/08276331.2020.1799294

Al Ali, O. E., Garner, I., & Magadley, W. (2012). An exploration of the relationship between emotional intelligence and job performance in police organizations. *Journal of Police and Criminal Psychology*, *27*(1), 1–8. doi:10.100711896-011-9088-9

Al-Dahan, N. S. H., Hasan, M. F., & Jadah, H. M. (2019). Effect of cognitive and emotional biases on investor decisions: An analytical study of the iraq stock exchange. *International Journal of Innovation. Creativity and Change*, *9*(10), 30–47.

Alex Linley, P., Joseph, S., Harrington, S., & Wood, A. M. (2006). Positive psychology: Past, present, and (possible) future. *The Journal of Positive Psychology*, *1*(1), 3–16. doi:10.1080/17439760500372796

Al-Imam, A., Motyka, M. A., & Jędrzejko, M. Z. (2020). Conflicting opinions in connection with digital superintelligence. *IAES International Journal of Artificial Intelligence (IJ-AI)*, *9*(2), 336. doi:10.11591/ijai.v9.i2.pp336-348

Allport, G. W., & Odbert, H. S. (1936). Trait-names: A psycho-lexical study. *Psychological Monographs*, *47*(1), i–171. doi:10.1037/h0093360

Alola, U. V., & Atsa'am, D. D. (2020). Measuring employees' psychological capital using a data mining approach. *Journal of Public Affairs*, *20*(2), 1–10. doi:10.1002/pa.2050

Al-Omoush, K. S., Simón-Moya, V., & Sendra-García, J. (2020). The impact of social capital and collaborative knowledge creation on e-business proactiveness and organizational agility in responding to the COVID-19 crisis. *Journal of Innovation & Knowledge*, *5*(4), 279–288. doi:10.1016/j.jik.2020.10.002

Alsabban, S., & Alarfaj, O. (2020). An Empirical Analysis of Behavioral Finance in the Saudi Stock Market:Evidence of Overconfidence Behavior. *International Journal of Economics and Financial Issues*, *10*(1), 73–86. doi:10.32479/ijefi.8920

Alsharif, A. H., Salleh, N. Z., Baharun, R., Rami, A., Hashem, E., Alsharif, A. H., Salleh, N. Z., & Baharun, R. (2021). Neuromarketing research in the last five years : A bibliometric analysis. *Cogent Business & Management*, *8*(1), 1978620. Advance online publication. doi:10.1080/23311975.2021.1978620

Alsughayir, A. (2021). The effect of emotional intelligence on organizational commitment: Understanding the mediating role of job satisfaction. *Management Science Letters*, *11*(4), 1309–1316. doi:10.5267/j.msl.2020.11.008

Altbach, P. G. (1970, December). Commitment and Powerlessness on the American Campus: The Case of the Graduate Student. *Liberal Education*, *56*, 562–582.

Alzoubi, H. M., & Aziz, R. (2021). Does emotional intelligence contribute to quality of strategic decisions? The mediating role of open innovation. *Journal of Open Innovation*, *7*(2), 130. Advance online publication. doi:10.3390/joitmc7020130

Amagoh, F. (2009). Leadership development and leadership effectiveness. *Management Decision*, *47*(6), 989–999. doi:10.1108/00251740910966695

Ameen, N., Tarhini, A., Reppel, A., & Anand, A. (2021). Customer experiences in the age of artificial intelligence. *Computers in Human Behavior*, *114*, 106548. doi:10.1016/j.chb.2020.106548 PMID:32905175

Amir Kabiri, A., Hejazi Farz, N., & Ziaei, Z. (2011). Evaluation of the Relationship between Emotional Excitement and Job Satisfaction among Overseer Deputy Officers of IRIB. *Journal of State Administration Mission*, *2*(1), 123–130.

Anantharaman, A. (2019). *How artificial intelligence is enabling financial inclusion in India*. Retrieved from: https://yourstory.com/2019/05/artificial-intelligence-enabling-financial-inclusion

Anarfi, J., Quartey, P., & Agyei, J. (2010). *Key determinants of migration among health professionals in Ghana*. Development Research Centre on Migration, Globalisation and Poverty. Research report. Available from: https://www.gov.uk/dfid-research-outputs/key-determinants-of-migration-among-health-professionals-in-ghana#citation

Andrabi, N. F., & Rainayee, R. A. (2020). Emotional intelligence and innovative work behaviour: A review. *International Journal of Engineering and Management Research*, *10*(4), 10. doi:10.31033/ijemr.10.4.26

Andrew Morris, J., & Daniel, C. (1996). The Dimensions, Antecedents, and Consequences of Emotional Labor. Academy of Management Review, 21(4). doi:10.5465/amr.1996.9704071861

Andries, P., & Hünermund, P. (2020). Firm-level effects of staged investments in innovation: The moderating role of resource availability. *Research Policy*, *49*(7), 103994. doi:10.1016/j.respol.2020.103994

Angrave, D., Charlwood, A., Kirkpatrick, I., Lawrence, M., & Stuart, M. (2016). HR and analytics: Why HR is set to fail the big data challenge. *Human Resource Management Journal*, *26*(1), 1–11. doi:10.1111/1748-8583.12090

Anju. (2000). *A comparative study of Emotional maturity in relation to Intelligence and Sex* [Unpublished M.Ed. dissertation]. Punjab University, Chandigarh.

Anna, S. (2016, November). Measuring the Effects of Self-Awareness: Construction of the Self-Awareness Outcomes Questionnaire. *The Journal of Psychology*, *12*(4), 645–658.

Antonakis, J., & Dietz, J. (2011). Looking for validity or testing it? The perils of stepwise regression, extreme-scores analysis, heteroscedasticity, and measurement error. *Personality and Individual Differences*, *50*(3), 409–415. doi:10.1016/j.paid.2010.09.014

Aqqad, N., Obeidat, B., Tarhini, A., & Masa'deh, R. E. (2019). The relationship among emotional intelligence, conflict management styles, and job performance in Jordanian banks. *International Journal of Human Resources Development and Management*, *19*(3), 225–265. doi:10.1504/IJHRDM.2019.100636

Aria, M., & Cuccurullo, C. (2017). bibliometrix: An R-tool for comprehensive science mapping analysis. *Journal of Informetrics*, *11*(4), 959–975. doi:10.1016/j.joi.2017.08.007

Arntz, M., Gregory, T., & Zierahn-Weilage, U. (2017). Revisiting the risk of automation. *Economics Letters*, *159*(C), 157–160. doi:10.1016/j.econlet.2017.07.001

Arrieta, A. B., Del Ser, J., Bennetot, A., Tabik, S., Barbado, A., Garcia, S., Gil-lopez, S., Molina, D., Benjamins, R., Chatila, R., & Herrera, F. (2019). Explainable Artificial Intelligence (XAI): Concepts, Taxonomies, Opportunities and Challenges toward Responsible AI. *Information Fusion*, *58*, 82–115. doi:10.1016/j.inffus.2019.12.012

Arya, A. (1997). *Emotional Maturity and values of superior children in family. Fourth survey of research in Education* (Vol. 11). NCERT.

Asadi, S., Hadavandi, E., Mehmanpazir, F., & Nakhostin, M. M. (2016). *Hybridization of evolutionary Levenberg-Marquardt neural networks and data pre-processing for stock market prediction*. Academic Press.

Ashkanasy, N. M., & Dorris, A. D. (2017). Emotions in the workplace. *Annual Review of Organizational Psychology and Organizational Behavior*, *4*(1), 67–90. doi:10.1146/annurev-orgpsych-032516-113231

Athey, S., & Luca, M. (2019). Economists (And Economics) in Tech Companies. *The Journal of Economic Perspectives*, *33*(1), 209–230. doi:10.1257/jep.33.1.209

Attila, K., & Edit, B. (2012). Beyond reality: The possibilities of augmented reality in cultural and heritage tourism. *2nd International Tourism and Sport Management Conference,* 5(6).

Atwell, E., & Shawar, B. (2003). Machine learning from dialogue corpora to generate chatbots. *Expert Update Journal*, *6*(3), 25–29.

Atzori, L., Iera, A., & Morabito, G. (2017, October). Understanding the Internet of Things: Definition, potentials, and societal role of a fast evolving paradigm. *Ad Hoc Networks*, *56*, 122–140. doi:10.1016/j.adhoc.2016.12.004

Avdic, S., Elsaman, H. A., & Gernal, L. (2021). COVID-19 Pandemic and Performance: Empirical Study of Integrated Remote Site Management Services in Dubai, United Arab Emirates. JPAIR Multidisciplinary Research, 46(1), 51-75.

Awan, M. I., Shamim, A., & Ahn, J. (2021). Implementing 'cleanliness is half of faith'in re-designing tourists, experiences and salvaging the hotel industry in Malaysia during COVID-19 pandemic. *Journal of Islamic Marketing*, *12*(3), 543–557. doi:10.1108/JIMA-08-2020-0229

Aziz, S., & Dowling, M. (2019). Machine learning and AI for risk management. *Disrupting finance: FinTech and strategy in the 21st century*, 33-50.

Aziz, S., Dowling, M., Hammami, H., & Piepenbrink, A. (2022). Machine learning in Finance: A topic modelling approach. *European Financial Management*, *28*(3), 744–770. doi:10.1111/eufm.12326

Azuma, R. T. (1997). A survey of augmented reality. *Presence (Cambridge, Mass.)*, *6*(4), 355–385. doi:10.1162/pres.1997.6.4.355

Azuma, R., Baillot, Y., Behringer, R., Feiner, S., Julier, S., & MacIntyre, B. (2001). Recent advances in augmented reality. *IEEE Computer Graphics and Applications*, *21*(6), 34–47. doi:10.1109/38.963459

Backhaus, K., Lügger, K., & Koch, M. (2011). The structure and evolution of business-to-business marketing: A citation and co-citation analysis. *Industrial Marketing Management*, *40*(6), 940–951. doi:10.1016/j.indmarman.2011.06.024

Bacon, A. M., & Corr, P. J. (2017). Motivating emotional intelligence: A reinforcement sensitivity theory (RST) perspective. *Motivation and Emotion*, *41*(2), 254–264. doi:10.100711031-017-9602-1

Bag, S., Wood, L. C., Xu, L., Dhamija, P., & Kayikci, Y. (2020). Big data analytics as an operational excellence approach to enhance sustainable supply chain performance. *Resources, Conservation and Recycling*, *153*, 104559. doi:10.1016/j.resconrec.2019.104559

Bahadori, M. (2012). The effect of emotional intelligence on entrepreneurial behaviour: A case study in a Medical Science University. *Asian Journal of Business Management.*, *4*(1), 81–85.

Bailey, W., Kumar, A., & Ng, D. (2011). Behavioral biases of mutual fund investors. *Journal of Financial Economics*, *102*(1), 1–27. doi:10.1016/j.jfineco.2011.05.002

Baker, H. K., Kumar, S., & Pattnaik, D. (2021). Twenty-five years of the Journal of Corporate Finance : A scientometric analysis. *Journal of Corporate Finance, 66*, 101572.

Baker, H. K., Kumar, S., & Goyal, N. (2021). Personality traits and investor sentiment. *Review of Behavioral Finance*, *13*(4), 354–369. doi:10.1108/RBF-08-2017-0077

Baker, H. K., Pandey, N., Kumar, S., & Haldar, A. (2020). A bibliometric analysis of board diversity: Current status, development, and future research directions. *Journal of Business Research*, *108*, 232–246. doi:10.1016/j.jbusres.2019.11.025

Bakker, A. B., & de Vries, J. D. (2021). Job Demands–Resources theory and self-regulation: New explanations and remedies for job burnout. *Anxiety, Stress, and Coping*, *34*(1), 1–21. doi:10.1080/10615806.2020.1797695 PMID:32856957

Balasubramaniam, N., Kauppinen, M., Kujala, S., & Hiekkanen, K. (2020). Ethical guidelines for solving ethical issues and developing AI systems. *Product-Focused Software Process Improvement: 21st International Conference, PROFES 2020, Turin, Italy, November 25–27, 2020 Proceedings*, *21*, 331–346.

Balluerka, N., Aritzeta, A., Gorostiaga, A., Gartzia, L., & Soroa, G. (2013). Emotional intelligence and depressed mood in adolescence: A multilevel approach. *International Journal of Clinical and Health Psychology*, *13*(2), 110–117. doi:10.1016/S1697-2600(13)70014-0

Balluerka, N., Gorostiaga, A., Alonso-Arbiol, I., & Aritzeta, A. (2016). Peer attachment and class emotional intelligence as predictors of adolescents' psychological well-being: A multilevel approach. *Journal of Adolescence*, *53*(1), 1–9. doi:10.1016/j.adolescence.2016.08.009 PMID:27596053

Bande, B., Fernández-Ferrín, P., Varela, J. A., & Jaramillo, F. (2015). Emotions and salesperson propensity to leave: The effects of emotional intelligence and resilience. *Industrial Marketing Management*, *44*, 142–153. doi:10.1016/j.indmarman.2014.10.011

Bankins, S., & Formosa, P. (2020). When AI meets PC: Exploring the implications of workplace social robots and a human-robot psychological contract. *European Journal of Work and Organizational Psychology*, *29*(2), 215–229. doi:10.1080/1359432X.2019.1620328

Bansibihari, P., & Surwade, L. (2006). The Effect of Emotional Maturity in Teacher Effectiveness. Educational Tracks, 6(1).

Bao, W., Yue, J., & Rao, Y. (2017, July 14). A deep learning framework for financial time series using stacked autoencoders and long-short term memory. *PLoS One*, *12*(7), e0180944. doi:10.1371/journal.pone.0180944 PMID:28708865

Barber, B. M., & Odean, T. (2001). Boys will be boys: Gender, overconfidence, and common stock investment. *The Quarterly Journal of Economics*, *116*(1), 261–292. doi:10.1162/003355301556400

Barbuto, J. E. Jr, Gottfredson, R. K., & Searle, T. P. (2014). An examination of emotional intelligence as an antecedent of servant leadership. *Journal of Leadership & Organizational Studies*, *21*(3), 315–323. doi:10.1177/1548051814531826

Barczak, G., Lassk, F., & Mulki, J. (2010). Antecedents of team creativity: An examination of team emotional intelligence, team trust and collaborative culture. *Creativity and Innovation Management*, *19*(4), 332–345. doi:10.1111/j.1467-8691.2010.00574.x

Barley, S. R., Meyerson, D. E., & Grodal, S. (2011). E-mail as a source and symbol of stress. *Organization Science*, *22*(4), 887–906. doi:10.1287/orsc.1100.0573

Barney, J. B., & Arikan, A. M. (2005). The resource-based view: origins and implications. The Blackwell handbook of strategic management, 123-182. doi:10.1111/b.9780631218616.2006.00006.x

Baron, R. A., & Markman, G. D. (2000). Beyond social capital: How social skills can enhance entrepreneurs' success. *The Academy of Management Perspectives*, *14*(1), 106–131. doi:10.5465/ame.2000.2909843

Baron, R. A., & Markman, G. D. (2003). Beyond social capital: The role of entrepreneurs' social competence in their financial success. *Journal of Business Venturing*, *18*(1), 41–60. doi:10.1016/S0883-9026(00)00069-0

Bar-on, R. M. (2006). The Bar-On model of emotional-social intelligence (ESI). *Psicothema*, *18*(1), 13–25. https://dialnet.unirioja.es/servlet/articulo?codigo=4679040&info=resumen&idioma=SPA PMID:17295953

Barreiro, C. A., & Treglown, L. (2020). What makes an engaged employee? A facet-level approach to trait emotional intelligence as a predictor of employee engagement. *Personality and Individual Differences*, *159*, 109892. doi:10.1016/j.paid.2020.109892

Barta, S., Gurrea, R., & Flavi, C. (2023). *Using augmented reality to reduce cognitive dissonance and increase purchase intention*. doi:10.1016/j.chb.2022.107564

Bartlett, S. (2015). *The relationship between emotional intelligence, work engagement, creativity and demographic variables* [Unpublished Master's thesis]. University of South Africa.

Bashir, T., Azam, N., Butt, A. A., Javed, A., & Tanvir, A. (2013). Are behavioural biases influenced by demographic characteristics & personality traits? Evidence from Pakistan. *European Scientific Journal*, *9*(29), 277–293.

Bass, B. M., & Avolio, B. J. (1994). Transformational leadership and organizational culture. *International Journal of Public Administration, 17*(3-4), 541–554. doi:10.1080/01900699408524907

Bass, B. M., Avolio, B. J., Jung, D. I., & Berson, Y. (2003). Predicting unit performance by assessing transformational and transactional leadership. *The Journal of Applied Psychology, 88*(2), 207–218. doi:10.1037/0021-9010.88.2.207 PMID:12731705

Bastian, V. A., Burns, N. R., & Nettlebeck, T. (2005). Emotional intelligence predicts life skills, but not as well as personality and cognitive abilities. *Personality and Individual Differences, 39*(6), 1135–1145. doi:10.1016/j.paid.2005.04.006

Basu, S., Majumdar, B., Mukherjee, K., Munjal, S., & Palaksha, C. (2023). Artificial Intelligence–HRM Interactions and Outcomes: A Systematic Review and Causal Configurational Explanation. *Human Resource Management Review, 33*(1), 100893. doi:10.1016/j.hrmr.2022.100893

Bataineh, M. Z. (2013, January). Academic stress among undergraduate students: The case of education faculty at King Saud University. *International Interdisciplinary Journal of Education, 2*(1), 82–88. doi:10.12816/0002919

Batool, B. F. (2013). Emotional intelligence and effective leadership. *Journal of Business Studies Quarterly, 4*(3), 84.

Bechara, A., & Damasio, A. R. (2005). The somatic marker hypothesis: A neural theory of economic decision. *Games and Economic Behavior, 52*(2), 336–372. doi:10.1016/j.geb.2004.06.010

Becker, A., Deckers, T., Dohmen, T., Falk, A., & Kosse, F. (2012). The relationship between economic preferences and psychological personality measures. *Annual Review of Economics, 4*(1), 453–478. doi:10.1146/annurev-economics-080511-110922

Beck, M., & Libert, B. (2017). The rise of AI makes emotional Intelligence more important. *Harvard Business Review, 15*(1-5).

Bellack, J. P. (1999). Emotional Intelligence: A Missing Ingrethent? *The Journal of Nursing Education, 38*(1), 3–4. doi:10.3928/0148-4834-19990101-03 PMID:9921779

Beloff, B., Tanzil, D., & Lines, M. (2004). Sustainable development performance assessment. *Environmental Progress, 23*(4), 271–276. doi:10.1002/ep.10045

Benartzi, S., & Thaler, R. H. (2001). Naive Diversification Strategies in Defined Contribution Saving Plans, The American Economic Review. *American Economic Association, 91*(1), 79–98.

Benomar, L., Elferjani, R., Hamilton, J., O'Neill, G. A., Echchakoui, S., Bergeron, Y., & Lamara, M. (2022). Bibliometric analysis of the structure and evolution of research on assisted migration. *Current Forestry Reports, 8*(2), 199–213. doi:10.100740725-022-00165-y

Berdiyeva, O., Islam, M. U., & Saeedi, M. (2021). Artificial Intelligence in Accounting and Finance: Meta-Analysis. *International Business Review, 3*(1), 56–79.

Berezina, K., Ciftci, O., & Cobanoglu, C. (2019). Robots, artificial intelligence, and service automation in restaurants. In *Robots*. Artificial Intelligence and Service Automation in Travel, Tourism and Hospitality. doi:10.1108/978-1-78756-687-320191010

Berkovich, I., & Eyal, O. (2015). Educational Leaders and Emotions. *Review of Educational Research, 85*(1), 129–167. doi:10.3102/0034654314550046

Berndt, T. J. (2002). Friendship quality and social development. *Current Directions in Psychological Science, 11*(1), 7–10. doi:10.1111/1467-8721.00157

Bharadiya, J. P. (2023, January 1). The role of machine learning in transforming business intelligence. *International Journal of Computing and Artificial Intelligence*, *4*(1), 16–24. doi:10.33545/27076571.2023.v4.i1a.60

Bhardwaj, B., & Sharma, D. (2022). Migration of skilled professionals across the border: Brain drain or brain gain? *European Management Journal*. ttps:// doi:10.1016/j.emj.2022.12.011

Bhardwaj, B. (2013). Women empowerment: Cracking glass ceiling at the workplace. *International Journal of Management*, *4*(2), 267–272.

Bhardwaj, B. (2017). Migration vulnerability: Role of digital media and internet in stimulating and inhibiting brain drain. *International Journal of Advances in Management and Economics*, *6*(6), 24–32.

Bhardwaj, B. (2021). *Short-term foreign trips correlate with the four factors model of cultural Intelligence*. Rajagiri Management Journal. doi:10.1108/RAMJ-01-2021-0008

Bhardwaj, B., & Kalia, N. (2021). *Contextual and task performance: role of employee engagement and organizational culture in the hospitality industry*. Vilakshan-XIMB Journal of Management. doi:10.1108/XJM-08-2020-0089

Bhardwaj, B., Kalia, N., Chand, M., & Sharma, D. (2023). Engaged Organizational Culture as a precursor to job performance: An evidence from the hospitality industry of Himachal Pradesh. *International Journal of Hospitality and Tourism Systems*, *16*(4), 48–57.

Bhardwaj, B., & Sharma, D. (2022). Migration of skilled professionals across the border: Brain drain or brain gain?. *European Management Journal*. https://doi.org/10.1016/j.emj.2022.12.011

Bharsakhale, R. L. (2013). A Study of Emotional Intelligence among Marathi and English Medium Students in Aurangabad City. *Indian Streams Research Journal*, *3*(5), 1–5. doi:10.9780/22307850

Bhattacharya, C., & Sinha, M. (2022). The Role of Artificial Intelligence in Banking for Leveraging Customer Experience. *Australasian Accounting. Business and Finance Journal*, *16*(5), 89–105.

Bikas, E., Jurevičienė, D., Dubinskas, P., & Novickytė, L. (2013). Behavioural finance: The emergence and development trends. *Procedia: Social and Behavioral Sciences*, *82*, 870–876. doi:10.1016/j.sbspro.2013.06.363

Biswas, S., Carson, B., Chung, V., Singh, S., & Thomas, R. (2020). *AI-bank of the future: Can banks meet the AI challenge*. McKinsey & Company.

Black, J. S., & van Esch, P. (2020). AI-enabled recruiting: What is it and how should a manager use it? *Business Horizons*, *63*(2), 215–226. doi:10.1016/j.bushor.2019.12.001

Blattberg, R. C., Kim, B. D., Neslin, S. A., Blattberg, R. C., Kim, B. D., & Neslin, S. A. (2008). Cross-Selling and Up-Selling. *Database Marketing: Analyzing and Managing Customers*, 515-547.

Bob Johansen. (2013). Leaders make the future: ten new leadership skills for an uncertain world. Berrett-Koehler Publishers. doi:10.5860/CHOICE.50-2757

Bodinson, G. W. (2005). Change healthcare organizations from good to great. *Quality Progress*, *38*(11), 22–29.

Bodtker, A. M., & Katz Jameson, J. (2001). Emotion in conflict formation and its transformation: Application to organizational conflict management. *International Journal of Conflict Management*, *12*(3), 259–275. doi:10.1108/eb022858

Bohlouli, M., Mittas, N., Kakarontzas, G., Theodosiou, T., Angelis, L., & Fathi, M. (2017). Competence assessment as an expert system for human resource management: A mathematical approach. *Expert Systems with Applications*, *70*, 83–102. doi:10.1016/j.eswa.2016.10.046

Bollen, J., Mao, H., & Zeng, X. (2011, March). Twitter mood predicts the stock market. *Journal of Computational Science*, *2*(1), 1–8. doi:10.1016/j.jocs.2010.12.007

Bonnstetter, B. J., & Fry, C. C. (2012). Creating and Assessing a New Class of Entrepreneurially-Minded Engineers. In *VentureWell. Proceedings of Open, the Annual Conference* (p. 1). National Collegiate Inventors & Innovators Alliance.

Borman, W. C., & Motowidlo, S. J. (1997). Task performance and contextual performance: The meaning for personnel selection research. *Human Performance*, *10*(2), 99–109. doi:10.120715327043hup1002_3

Bostrom, N., & Yudkowsky, E. (2011). The ethics of Artificial Intelligence. In K. Frankish (Ed.), *Cambridge Handbook of Artificial Intelligence*. Cambridge University Press.

Boukherouaa, E. B., AlAjmi, K., Deodoro, J., Farias, A., & Ravikumar, R. (2021). Powering the DigitalEconomy: Opportunities and Risks of Artificial Intelligence in Finance, *Departmental Papers*, (24), A001. https://doi.org/doi:10.5089/9781589063952.087.A001

Bouzguenda, K. (2018). Emotional intelligence and financial decision making: Are we talking about a paradigmatic shift or a change in practices? *Research in International Business and Finance*, *44*, 273–284. doi:10.1016/j.ribaf.2017.07.096

Boyatzis, R. E., Goleman, D., & Rhee, K. (2000). Clustering competence in emotional intelligence: Insights from the Emotional Competence Inventory (ECI). Handbook of Emotional Intelligence, 99(6), 343-362.

Boyatzis, R. E. (2006). Using tipping points of emotional intelligence and cognitive competencies to predict financial performance of leaders. *Psicothema*, *18*(SUPPL.1), 124–131. PMID:17295969

Boyatzis, R. E., Good, D., & Massa, R. (2012). Emotional, Social, and Cognitive Intelligence and Personality as Predictors of Sales Leadership Performance. *Journal of Leadership & Organizational Studies*, *19*(2), 191–201. doi:10.1177/1548051811435793

Boyatzis, R. E., & McKee, A. (2005). *Resonant leadership: Renewing yourself and connecting with others through mindfulness, hope, and compassion*. Harvard Business Press.

Boyatzis, R. E., & Sala, F. (2004). Assessing emotional intelligence competencies. *The Measurement of Emotional Intelligence*, *2*, 147.

Boyd, N. G., & Vozikis, G. S. (1994). The influence of self-efficacy on the development of entrepreneurial intentions and actions. *Entrepreneurship Theory and Practice*, *18*(4), 63–77. doi:10.1177/104225879401800404

Božić, V. (n.d.). *Risks of digital divide in using artificial intelligence (AI)*. researchgate.net

Brackett, M. A., & Mayer, J. D. (2003). Convergent, discriminant, and incremental validity of competing measures of emotional intelligence. *Personality and Social Psychology Bulletin*, *29*(9), 1147–1158. doi:10.1177/0146167203254596 PMID:15189610

Brackett, M. A., Rivers, S. E., & Salovey, P. (2011). Emotional intelligence: Implications for personal, social, academic, and workplace success. *Social and Personality Psychology Compass*, *5*(1), 88–103. doi:10.1111/j.1751-9004.2010.00334.x

Brackett, M. A., Rivers, S. E., Shiffman, S., Lerner, N., & Salovey, P. (2006). Relating emotional abilities to social functioning: A comparison of self-report and performance measures of emotional intelligence. *Journal of Personality and Social Psychology*, *91*(4), 780–795. doi:10.1037/0022-3514.91.4.780 PMID:17014299

Bradberry, T., & Greaves, J. (2005). *The Emotional Intelligence Quick Book*. Simon & Schuster.

Brambilla, I., César, A., Falcone, G., & Gasparini, L. (2023). The impact of robots in Latin America: Evidence from local labor markets. *World Development, 170*. doi:10.1016/j.worlddev.2023.106271

Brandstätter, H. (1997). Becoming an entrepreneur — A question of personality structure? *Journal of Economic Psychology, 18*(2-3), 157–177. doi:10.1016/S0167-4870(97)00003-2

Brandstätter, H. (2011). Personality aspects of entrepreneurship: A look at fve meta-analyses. *Personality and Individual Differences, 51*(3), 222–2. doi:10.1016/j.paid.2010.07.007

Bravi, L., Murmura, F., & Santos, G. (2018). Manufacturing labs: Where new digital technologies help improve life quality. *International Journal of Qualitative Research, 12*(4), 957–974. doi:10.18421/IJQR12.04-11

Brit, P. (2020). Overcoming Bias Requires an AI Reboot. Speech Technology, 25(2), 14–17.

Brit, P. (2021). *Tips for battling bias in ai-based personalization.* https://www.destinationcrm.com/Articles/Editorial/Magazine-Features/Tips-for-Battling-Bias-in-AI-Based-Personalization-147143.aspx

Brooks, C., & Williams, L. (2021). The impact of personality traits on attitude to financial risk. *Research in International Business and Finance, 58*, 101501. doi:10.1016/j.ribaf.2021.101501

Broussard, M. (2019). *Artificial Unintelligence: How computers misunderstand the world.* MIT Press.

Brown, B. (2004). Adolescents' relationships with peers. In R. Lerner & L. Steinberg (Eds.). Handbook of adolescent psychology. Wiley. doi:10.1002/9780471726746.ch12

Brown, K. W., & Ryan, R. M. (2003). The benefits of being present: Mindfulness and its role in psychological well-being. *Journal of Personality and Social Psychology, 84*(4), 822–848. doi:10.1037/0022-3514.84.4.822 PMID:12703651

Brun, E., & Milczarek, M. (2007). Expert forecast on emerging psychosocial risks related to occupational safety and heath - European Risk Observatory Report. European Agency for Safety and Health at Work.

Brundtland, G. H. (1987). *Report of the World Commission on Environment and Development: Our Common Future.* Retrieved from chrome-extension://bocbaocobfecmglnmeaeppambideimao/pdf/viewer.html?file=https%3A%2F%2Fsustainabledevelopment.un.org%2Fcontent%2Fdocuments%2F5987our-common-future.pdf accessed on 30/07/2023

Brunetto, Y., Teo, S. T., Shacklock, K., & Farr-Wharton, R. (2012). Emotional intelligence, job satisfaction, well-being and engagement: Explaining organisational commitment and turnover intentions in policing. *Human Resource Management Journal, 22*(4), 428–441. doi:10.1111/j.1748-8583.2012.00198.x

Brynjolfsson, E., & Mitchell, T. (2017). What can machine learning do? Workforce implications. *Science, 358*(6370), 1530–1534. doi:10.1126cience.aap8062 PMID:29269459

Budale, D., & Mane, D. (2013). Predictive analytics in retail banking. *International Journal of Engineering and Advanced Technology, 2*(5), 508–510.

Budhwar, P., Malik, A., De Silva, M. T., & Thevisuthan, P. (2022). Artificial intelligence–challenges and opportunities for international HRM: A review and research agenda. *International Journal of Human Resource Management, 33*(6), 1065–1097. doi:10.1080/09585192.2022.2035161

Buehring, J. H., & Moore, P. (2018). Emotional and social intelligence as 'magic key'in innovation: A designer's call toward inclusivity for all. *Journal of Innovation Management, 6*(2), 6–12. doi:10.24840/2183-0606_006.002_0002

Buganza, T., & Verganti, R. (2006). Life-cycle flexibility: How to measure and improve the innovative capability in turbulent environments. *Journal of Product Innovation Management, 23*(5), 393–407. doi:10.1111/j.1540-5885.2006.00212.x

Bughin J., Eric, H., Susan, L., Peter, D., Anna, W., & Armesh, S. (2018). Skill shift: Automation and the future of the workforce. *McKinsey Global Institute, 3*(84).

Bughin, J., Hazan, E., Ramaswamy, S., Chui, M., Allas, T., Dahlström, P., & Henke, N. (2018). *Artificial intelligence: The next digital frontier?* McKinsey Global Institute.

Bulińska-Stangrecka, H., & Bagieńska, A. (2021). Culture-based green workplace practices as a means of conserving energy and other natural resources in the manufacturing sector. *Energies*, *14*(19), 6305. doi:10.3390/en14196305

Bunjak, A., Bruch, H., & Černe, M. (2022). Context is key: The joint roles of transformational and shared leadership and management innovation in predicting employee IT innovation adoption. *International Journal of Information Management*, *66*, 102516. doi:10.1016/j.ijinfomgt.2022.102516

Buolamwini, J., & Gebru, T. (2018). Gender Shades: Intersectional Accuracy Disparities in Commercial Gender Classification. *Proceedings of Machine Learning Research*, *81*, 77–91.

Burke, R. (2006). Leadership and spirituality. *Foresight*, *8*(6), 14–25. doi:10.1108/14636680610712504

Butler, T., & O'Brien, L. (2019). Artificial intelligence for regulatory compliance: Are we there yet? *Journal of Financial Compliance*, *3*(1), 44–59.

Butts, D. (1999). Spirituality at work: An overview. *Journal of Organizational Change Management*, *12*(4), 328–332. doi:10.1108/09534819910282162

Butts, J. B., & Rich, K. L. (2012). *Nursing ethics*. Jones & Bartlett.

Byggeth Sophie, H., Henrik, N., Johan, W., Göran, B., & Karl-Henrik, R. (2007). Introductory procedure for sustainability-driven design optimization. *Guidelines for a Decision Support Method Adapted to NPD Processes.*

Cabral, C., & Chiappetta Jabbour, C. J. (2020). Understanding the human side of green hospitality management. *International Journal of Hospitality Management*, *88*(April), 102389. doi:10.1016/j.ijhm.2019.102389

Campbell, A., & Ntobedzi, A. (2007). Emotional intelligence, coping and psychological distress: A partial least squares approach to developing a predictive model. Electronic Journal of Applied Psychology: Emotional Intelligence. *Coping and Psychological Distress*, *3*(1), 39–54.

Campbell, J. J., Dunnette, M. D., Lawler, E. E., & Weick, K. E. (1970). *Managerial behavior, performance, and effectiveness*. McGraw-Hill.

Canedo, D., & Neves, A. J. R. (2019). Facial expression recognition using computer vision: A systematic review. *Applied Sciences (Basel, Switzerland)*, *9*(21), 1–31. doi:10.3390/app9214678

Cantzler, I., & Svante, L. (2007). Team-oriented women entrepreneurs: A way to modern. *Journal of Small Business and Enterprise Development*, *14*(4), 732–746. doi:10.1108/14626000710832802

Cardon, M. S., Foo, M. D., Shepherd, D., & Wiklund, J. (2012). Exploring the heart: Entrepreneurial emotion is a hot topic. *Entrepreneurship Theory and Practice*, *36*(1), 1–10. doi:10.1111/j.1540-6520.2011.00501.x

Carless, S. (1998). Assessing the discriminant validity of transformational leader behavior as measured by the MLQ. *Journal of Occupational and Organizational Psychology*, *71*(4), 353–359. doi:10.1111/j.2044-8325.1998.tb00681.x

Carlson, N. R. (2010). *Psychology: The science of behaviour*. Pearson Education Canada.

Carmeli, A. (2003). The relationship between emotional intelligence and work attitudes, behavior and outcomes: An examination among senior managers. *Journal of Managerial Psychology*, *18*(8), 788–813. doi:10.1108/02683940310511881

Carmeli, A., Brueller, D., & Dutton, J. E. (2009). Learning behaviours in the workplace: The role of high-quality interpersonal relationships and psychological safety. Systems Research and Behavioral Science. *The Official Journal of the International Federation for Systems Research*, *26*(1), 81–98.

Carmeli, A., & Josman, Z. E. (2006). The Effects of Cognitive Appraisal and Emotion on Social Motive and Negotiation Behavior : The Critical Role of Agency of Negotiator Emotion. *Human Performance*, *19*(4), 403–419. doi:10.120715327043hup1904_5

Carmeli, A., Yitzhak-Halevy, M., & Weisberg, J. (2009). The relationship between emotional intelligence and psychological wellbeing. *Journal of Managerial Psychology*, *24*(1), 66–78. doi:10.1108/02683940910922546

Carolan, S., Harris, P. R., & Cavanagh, K. (2017). Improving Employee Well-Being and Effectiveness: Systematic Review and Meta-Analysis of Web-Based Psychological Interventions Delivered in the Workplace. *Journal of Medical Internet Research*, *19*(7), e271. doi:10.2196/jmir.7583 PMID:28747293

Caron, M. S. (2019). The transformative effect of AI on the banking industry. *Banking & Finance Law Review*, *34*(2), 169–214.

Carosia, A. E. O., Coelho, G. P., & Silva, A. E. A. (2019, October 31). Analyzing the Brazilian Financial Market through Portuguese Sentiment Analysis in Social Media. *Applied Artificial Intelligence*, *34*(1), 1–19. doi:10.1080/08839514.2019.1673037

Carpenter, T. (2020). Revolutionising the consumer banking experience with artificial intelligence. *Journal of Digital Banking*, *4*(4), 291–300.

Carta, S. M., Consoli, S., Piras, L., Podda, A. S., & Recupero, D. R. (2021). Explainable Machine Learning Exploiting News and Domain-Specific Lexicon for Stock Market Forecasting. *IEEE Access : Practical Innovations, Open Solutions*, *9*, 30193–30205. doi:10.1109/ACCESS.2021.3059960

Cartea, Á., Chang, P., Mroczka, M., & Oomen, R. (2022). AI-driven liquidity provision in OTC financial markets. *Quantitative Finance*, *22*(12), 2171–2204. doi:10.1080/14697688.2022.2130087

Caruso, D. R., Bienn, B., & Kornacki, S. A. (2013). Emotional intelligence in the workplace. *Emotional Intelligence in Everyday Life*, (January), 187–205. doi:10.4324/9780203943397-20

Carvalho, V. R., Ribeiro, A., & Santos, M. Y. (2020). Explainable artificial intelligence: A review of machine learning interpretability methods. *Journal of Ambient Intelligence and Humanized Computing*, *11*(2), 441–471.

Casteleiro-Roca, J. L., Gómez-González, J. F., Calvo-Rolle, J. L., Jove, E., Quintián, H., Martín, J. F. A., ... Méndez-Perez, J. A. (2018). Prediction of the energy demand of a hotel using an artificial intelligence-based model. *Hybrid Artificial Intelligent Systems: 13th International Conference, HAIS 2018, Oviedo, Spain, June 20-22, 2018 Proceedings*, *13*, 586–596.

Castelnovo, A., Crupi, R., Del Gamba, G., Greco, G., Naseer, A., Regoli, D., & Gonzalez, B. S. M. (2020, December). Befair: Addressing fairness in the banking sector. In *2020 IEEE International Conference on Big Data (Big Data)* (pp. 3652-3661). IEEE. 10.1109/BigData50022.2020.9377894

Cavazotte, F., Moreno, V., & Hickmann, M. (2012). Effects of leader intelligence, personality and emotional intelligence on transformational leadership and managerial performance. *The Leadership Quarterly*, *23*(3), 443–455. doi:10.1016/j.leaqua.2011.10.003

Cegarra-Navarro, J. G., Reverte, C., Gómez-Melero, E., & Wensley, A. K. (2016). Linking social and economic responsibilities with financial performance: The role of innovation. *European Management Journal*, *34*(5), 530–539. doi:10.1016/j.emj.2016.02.006

Cekmecelioglu, H. G., Gunsel, A., & Ulutas, T. (2012). Effects of emotional intelligence on job satisfaction: An empirical study on call center employees. *Procedia: Social and Behavioral Sciences*, *58*, 363–369. doi:10.1016/j.sbspro.2012.09.1012

Chakraborty, S., Giri, A., Aich, A., & Biswas, S. (2020). Evaluating influence of artificial intelligence on human resource management using PLS-SEM (Partial least squares-structural equation modeling). *International Journal of Scientific and Technology Research*, *9*(3), 5876–5880.

Chan, D. W. (2002). Emotional Intelligence: Implications for Educational Practice in Schools. *Educational Research Journal*, *17*(2), 183–196.

Chandra, P. (2016). *Behavioral Finance*. McGraw Hill Education.

Chari, R., Chang, C. C., Sauter, S. L., Petrun Sayers, E. L., Cerully, J. L., Schulte, P., Schill, A. L., & Uscher-Pines, L. (2018). Expanding the Paradigm of Occupational Safety and Health: A New Framework for Worker Well-Being. *Journal of Occupational and Environmental Medicine*, *60*(7), 589–593. doi:10.1097/JOM.0000000000001330 PMID:29608542

Chaudhary, M., Jaswal, N., & Bhardwaj, B. (2022). Hiding Behind The SWOT : Gender Equality and COVID-19. *Journal of Positive School Psychology*, *6*(6), 730–740.

Chavali, K., & Mohanraj, M. P. (2016). Impact of demographic variables and risk tolerance on investment decisions–an empirical analysis. *International Journal of Economics and Financial Issues*, *6*(1), 169–175.

Chen, G., & Xiao, L. (2016). Selecting publication keywords for domain analysis in bibliometrics: A comparison of three methods. *Journal of Informetrics*, *10*(1), 212–223. doi:10.1016/j.joi.2016.01.006

Chen, H., Chiang, R. H., & Storey, V. C. (2012). Business intelligence and analytics: From big data to big impact. *Management Information Systems Quarterly*, *36*(4), 1165–1188. doi:10.2307/41703503

Chen, H.-J., Shuai, H.-H., & Cheng, W.-H. (2023, May). A Survey of Artificial Intelligence in Fashion. *IEEE Signal Processing Magazine*, *40*(3), 64–73. doi:10.1109/MSP.2022.3233449

Chen, J. C., Lin, T. L., & Kuo, M. H. (2002). Artificial worlds modeling of human resource management systems. *IEEE Transactions on Evolutionary Computation*, *6*(6), 542–556. doi:10.1109/TEVC.2002.802279

Chen, M., Mao, S., & Liu, Y. (2018). Big data: A survey. *Mobile Networks and Applications*, *19*(2), 171–209. doi:10.100711036-013-0489-0

Chen, Q., Li, S., & Wu, X. (2021). An ensemble method based on random forest and gradient boosting for stock price prediction. *Applied Soft Computing*, *107*, 107476.

Cherniss, C. (1999). The Business Case for Emotional Intelligence Prepared. *Consortium for Research on Emotional Intelligence in Organizations*. www.econsortium.org

Cherniss, C., & Goleman, D. (2000). Emotional intelligence. *Annual meeting of the society for industrial and organizational psychology*. www. eiconsortium. org

Cherniss, C. (2010). Emotional intelligence: Toward clarification of a concept. *Industrial and Organizational Psychology: Perspectives on Science and Practice*, *3*(2), 110–126. doi:10.1111/j.1754-9434.2010.01231.x

Cherniss, C., & Goleman, D. (2001). *The emotionally intelligent workplace: How to select for, measure, and improve emotional intelligence in individuals, groups, and organizations*. John Wiley & Sons.

Cherniss, C., Goleman, D., Emmerling, R., Cowan, K., & Adler, M. (1998). *Bringing emotional intelligence to the workplace*. Consortium for Research on Emotional Intelligence in Organizations, Rutgers University.

Chesley, N. (2014). Information and communication technology use, work intensification and employee strain and distress. *Work, Employment and Society*, *28*(4), 589–610. doi:10.1177/0950017013500112

Chesney, R., & Citron, D. (2019). Deepfakes and the new disinformation war. *Foreign Affairs*, *98*(1), 147–155.

Chew, B. H., & Zain, A. M. (2018). Emotional intelligence as a mediator between emotional labor, job stress, burnout, and turnover intention among clinical nurses. *The Journal of Nursing Research*, *26*(6), 348–354.

Chigeda, F., Ndofirepi, T. M., & Steyn, R. (2022). Continuance in organizational commitment : The role of emotional intelligence, work-life balance support, and work-related stress. *Global Business and Organizational Excellence*, *42*(1), 22–38. doi:10.1002/joe.22172

Chiu, P. S., Chang, J. W., Lee, M. C., Chen, C. H., & Lee, D. S. (2020). Enabling intelligent environment by the design of emotionally aware virtual assistant: A case of smart campus. *IEEE Access : Practical Innovations, Open Solutions*, *8*, 62032–62041. doi:10.1109/ACCESS.2020.2984383

Chlesinger, A., O'Hara, K. P., & Taylor, A. S. (2018). Let's talk about race: identity, chatbots, and AI. *Proceedings of the 2018 CHI ConferenceonHuman Factors in Computing Systems, CHI'18*, 1-14.

Chopra, P. K., & Kanji, G. K. (2010). Emotional intelligence: A catalyst for inspirational leadership and management excellence. *Total Quality Management & Business Excellence*, *21*(10), 971–1004. doi:10.1080/14783363.2010.487704

Chotai, J., Lundberg, M., & Adolfsson, R. (2003). Variations in personality traits among adolescents and adults according to their season of birth in the general population: Further evidence. *Personality and Individual Differences*, *35*(4), 897–908. doi:10.1016/S0191-8869(02)00306-9

Chouldechova, A., Putnam-Hornstein, E., Benavides-Prado, D., Fialko, O., & Vaithianathan, R. (2018). A case study of algorithm-assisted decision making in child maltreatment hotline screening decisions. *Proceedings ofMachine Learning Research*, *81*, 134–148.

Chowdhury, S., Dey, P., Joel-Edgar, S., Bhattacharya, S., Rodriguez-Espindola, O., Abadie, A., & Truong, L. (2023). Unlocking the value of artificial intelligence in human resource management through AI capability framework. *Human Resource Management Review*, *33*(1), 100899. doi:10.1016/j.hrmr.2022.100899

Chui, M., Manyika, J., & Miremadi, M. (2016). *Where machines could replace humans—And where they can't (yet).* https://www.mckinsey.com/business-functions/digital-mckinsey/our-insights/where-machines-couldreplace-humans-and-where-they-can't-yet

Ciarrochi, J. V., Forgas, J. P., & Mayer, J. D. (Eds.). (2006). *Emotional intelligence in everyday life* (2nd ed.). Psychology Press.

Claralabs. (2021). *Clara, can you find a time for us to meet next week?* Clara Labs. https://claralabs.com/

Coetzee, M., & Harry, N. (2014). Emotional Intelligence as a Predictor of employees' career adaptability. *Journal of Vocational Behavior*, *84*(1), 90–97. doi:10.1016/j.jvb.2013.09.001

Collins, C. J., & Clark, K. D. (2003). Strategic human resource practices, top management team social networks, and firm performance: The role of human resource practices in creating organizational competitive advantage. *Academy of Management Journal*, *46*(6), 740–751. doi:10.2307/30040665

Conte, J. M. (2005). A review and critique of emotional intelligence measures. *Journal of Organizational Behavior*, *26*(4), 433–440. doi:10.1002/job.319

Conway, R. A., & Kovacs, K. (2015). New and emerging models of human intelligence. *Wiley Interdisciplinary Reviews: Cognitive Science*, *6*(5), 419–426. doi:10.1002/wcs.1356 PMID:26267702

Copeland, J. (1993). *Artificial Intelligence: A Philosophical Introduction*. John Wiley & Sons.

Cop, S., Alola, U. V., & Alola, A. A. (2020). Perceived behavioral control as a mediator of hotels' green training, environmental commitment, and organizational citizenship behavior: A sustainable environmental practice. *Business Strategy and the Environment*, *29*(8), 3495–3508. doi:10.1002/bse.2592

Coqueret, G., & Guida, T. (2023). *Machine Learning for Factor Investing*. CRC Press. doi:10.1201/9781003121596

Côté, S. (2010). Taking the "Intelligence" in Emotional Intelligence Seriously. *Industrial and Organizational Psychology: Perspectives on Science and Practice*, *3*(2), 127–130. doi:10.1111/j.1754-9434.2010.01211.x

Côté, S. (2014). Emotional intelligence in organizations. *Annual Review of Organizational Psychology and Organizational Behavior*, *1*(1), 459–488. doi:10.1146/annurev-orgpsych-031413-091233

Cote, S., DeCelles, K. A., McCarthy, J. M., Van Kleef, G. A., & Hideg, I. (2011). The Jekyll and Hyde of emotional intelligence: Emotion-regulation knowledge facilitates both prosocial and interpersonally deviant behavior. *Psychological Science*, *22*(8), 1073–1080. doi:10.1177/0956797611416251 PMID:21775654

Cote, S., & Miners, C. T. (2006). Emotional intelligence, cognitive intelligence, and job performance. *Administrative Science Quarterly*, *51*(1), 1–28. doi:10.2189/asqu.51.1.1

Cranmer, E., Dieck, M., & Fountoulaki, P. (2020). Exploring the value of augmented reality for tourism. *Tourism Management Perspectives, 35*. https://www.sciencedirect.com/science/article/pii/S2211973620300398 doi:10.1016/j.tmp.2020.100672

Cristofaro, M. (2019). The role of affect in management decisions: A systematic review. *European Management Journal*, *37*(1), 6–17. doi:10.1016/j.emj.2018.12.002

Cross & Travaglione. (2003). *The untold story: is the entrepreneur of the 21st century defined by emotional intelligence?* Academic Press.

Crudu, R. (2019). The role of innovative entrepreneurship in the economic development of EU member countries. *Journal of Entrepreneurship, Management and Innovation*, *15*(1), 35–60.

D'Amato, A., & Herzfeldt, R. (2008). Learning orientation, organizational commitment and talent retention across generations: A study of European managers. *Journal of Managerial Psychology*, *23*(8), 929–953. doi:10.1108/02683940810904402

Danneels, E. (2011). Trying to become a different type of company: Dynamic capability at Smith Corona. *Strategic Management Journal*, *32*(1), 1–31. doi:10.1002mj.863

Danquah, E. (2014). Analysis of the impact of emotional intelligence on organizational performance: A banking perspective. *British Journal of Marketing Studies*, *2*, 34–50.

Dauda, S. Y., & Lee, J. (2015). Technology adoption: A conjoint analysis of consumers' preference on future online banking services. *Information Systems*, *53*, 1–15. doi:10.1016/j.is.2015.04.006

Davenport, T. H., & Ronanki, R. (2018). Artificial Intelligence for the Real World. *Harvard Business Review*. Retrieved from https://hbr.org/2018/01/artificial-intelligence-for-the-real-world

Davenport, T. H., & Ronanki, R. (2018). Intelligence for the Real World. *Harvard Business Review*, *96*(1), 108–116.

Davenport, T., Guha, A., Grewal, D., & Bressgott, T. (2020). How artificial intelligence will change the future of marketing. *Journal of the Academy of Marketing Science*, *48*(1), 24–42. doi:10.100711747-019-00696-0

Davies, G. B., & Brooks, P. (2014). Risk tolerance: Essential, behavioural and misunderstood. *Journal of Risk Management in Financial Institutions*, *7*(2), 110–113.

Davies, M., Stankov, L., & Roberts, R. D. (1998). Emotional intelligence: In search of an elusive construct. *Journal of Personality and Social Psychology*, *75*(4), 989–1015. doi:10.1037/0022-3514.75.4.989 PMID:9825531

Day, A. L., & Carroll, S. A. (2004). Using an ability-based measure of emotional intelligence to predict individual performance, group performance, and group citizenship behaviours. *Personality and Individual Differences*, *36*(6), 1443–1458. doi:10.1016/S0191-8869(03)00240-X

De Acypreste, R., & Paraná, E. (2022). Artificial Intelligence and employment: A systematic review: Inteligência Artificial e emprego: uma revisão sistemática. *Brazilian Journal of Political Economy. Revista de Economia Política*, *42*(4), 1014–1032. doi:10.1590/0101-31572022-3320

De Cremer, D., & Kasparov, G. (2021). AI should augment human intelligence, not replace it. *Harvard Business Review*, *18*, 1.

De Jong, J. P., & Den Hartog, D. N. (2008). Innovative work behavior: Measurement and validation. *EIM Business and Policy Research*, *8*(1), 1–27.

De Witte, H., Pienaar, J., & De Cuyper, N. (2016). Review of 30 years of longitudinal studies on the association between job insecurity and health and well-being: Is there causal evidence? *Australian Psychologist*, *51*(1), 18–31. doi:10.1111/ap.12176

DeBondt, W., Forbes, W., Hamalainen, P., & Gulnur Muradoglu, Y. (2010). What can behavioural finance teach us about finance? *Qualitative Research in Financial Markets*, *2*(1), 29–36. doi:10.1108/17554171011042371

Deloitte. (2018). *The rise of cognitive intelligence in banking*. Retrieved from https://www2.deloitte.com/content/dam/Deloitte/nl/Documents/financial-services/deloitte-nl-fsi-cognitive-intelligence-in-banking.pdf

Deloitte. (2022). *A blueprint for green workforce transformation*. Accessed from chrome-extension://bocbaocobfecmglnmeaeppambideimao/pdf/viewer.html?file=https%3A%2F%2Fwww2.deloitte.com%2Fcontent%2Fdam%2FDeloitte%2Fuk%2FDocuments%2Fconsultancy%2Fdeloitte-uk-a-blueprint-for-green-workforce-transformation.pdf accessed on 01/06/2023

DePierro, J., Katz, C. L., Marin, D., Feder, A., Bevilacqua, L., Sharma, V., Hurtado, A., Ripp, J., Lim, S., & Charney, D. (2020). Mount Sinai's Center for Stress, Resilience and Personal Growth as a model for responding to the impact of COVID-19 on health care workers. *Psychiatry Research*, *293*, 113426. doi:10.1016/j.psychres.2020.113426 PMID:32861094

Der Foo, M., Elfenbein, H. A., Tan, H. H., & Aik, V. C. (2004). Emotional intelligence and negotiation: The tension between creating and claiming value. *International Journal of Conflict Management*, *15*(4), 411–429. doi:10.1108/eb022920

Dey, S., Kumar, Y., Saha, S., & Basak, S. (2016). *Forecasting to Classification: Predicting the Direction of Stock Market Price Using Xtreme Gradient Boosting*. Working Paper.

Dhamija, P., & Bag, S. (2020). Role of artificial intelligence in operations environment: A review and bibliometric analysis. *The TQM Journal*, *32*(4), 869–896. doi:10.1108/TQM-10-2019-0243

Dhanabalan, T., & Sathish, A. (2018). Transforming Indian Industries Through Artificial Intelligence and Robotics in Industry 4.0. *Editor@iaeme.Com International Journal of Mechanical Engineering and Technology*, *9*(10), 835–845.

Dhanabalan, T., Subha, K., Shanthi, R., & Sathish, A. (2018). Factors influencing consumers car purchasing decision in Indian automobile industry. *International Journal of Mechanical Engineering and Technology*, *9*(10), 53–63.

Dhiman, B., & Raheja, S. (2018). Do personality traits and emotional intelligence of investors determine their risk tolerance? *Management and Labour Studies*, *43*(1-2), 88–99. doi:10.1177/0258042X17745184

Di, A., Palladino, R., Hassan, R., & Escobar, O. (2020). Artificial intelligence and business models in the sustainable development goals perspective : A systematic literature review. *Journal of Business Research*, *121*(January), 283–314. doi:10.1016/j.jbusres.2020.08.019

DiClaudio, M. (2019). People analytics and the rise of HR: How data, analytics and emerging technology can transform human resources (HR) into a profit center. *Strategic HR Review*, *18*(2), 42–46. doi:10.1108/SHR-11-2018-0096

Diener, E. (2000). Subjective well-being: The science of happiness and a proposal for a national index. *The American Psychologist*, *55*(1), 34–43. doi:10.1037/0003-066X.55.1.34 PMID:11392863

Diener, E., Suh, E. M., Lucas, R. E., & Smith, H. L. (1999). Subjective well-being: Three decades of progress. *Psychological Bulletin*, *125*(2), 276–302. doi:10.1037/0033-2909.125.2.276

Digalaki, E. (2020). *The impact of artificial intelligence in the banking sector & how AI isbeing used in 2020*. https://www.businessinsider.in/finance/news/the-impact-of-artificial-intelligence in-the-banking-sector-how-ai-is-being-used-in-2020/article show/728608

Dimitrieska, S., Stankovska, A., & Efremova, T. (2018). Artificial intelligence and marketing. *Entrepreneurship*, *6*(2), 298–304.

Dincer, H., & Orhan, N. (2012). *Relationship between emotional intelligence and innovative work behaviors in Turkish banking sector*. Academic Press.

Divandari, A., Nazari, M., Seyed Javadin, S. R., Haji Karimi, A., & Rayej, H. (2018). Investigating the Effect of Compensation on Individual Performance: A Study on the Mediating Role of Internal Motivation and the Moderating Role of Self-efficacy and Reward Expectancy. *Journal of Business and Management*, *10*(3), 673–694.

Djourova, N. P., Rodríguez Molina, I., Tordera Santamatilde, N., & Abate, G. (2020). Self-Efficacy and Resilience: Mediating Mechanisms in the Relationship Between the Transformational Leadership Dimensions and Well-Being. *Journal of Leadership & Organizational Studies*, *27*(3), 256–270. doi:10.1177/1548051819849002

Domínguez-García, E., & Fernández-Berrocal, P. (2018). The Association Between Emotional Intelligence and Suicidal Behavior: A Systematic Review. *Frontiers in Psychology*, *9*(NOV), 1–12. doi:10.3389/fpsyg.2018.02380 PMID:30555393

Domínguez-Quintero, A. M., González-Rodríguez, M. R., & Paddison, B. (2020). The mediating role of experience quality on authenticity and satisfaction in the context of cultural-heritage tourism. *Current Issues in Tourism*, *23*(2), 248–260. doi:10.1080/13683500.2018.1502261

Donepudi, P. K. (2017). Machine Learning and Artificial Intelligence in Banking. *Engineering International*, *5*(2), 83–86. doi:10.18034/ei.v5i2.490

Donthu, N., Kumar, S., Mukherjee, D., Pandey, N., & Lim, W. M. (2021). How to conduct a bibliometric analysis: An overview and guidelines. *Journal of Business Research*, *133*, 285296. doi:10.1016/j.jbusres.2021.04.070

Donthu, N., Kumar, S., Pandey, N., & Gupta, P. (2021). Forty years of the International Journal of Information Management: A bibliometric analysis. *International Journal of Information Management*, *57*, 102307. doi:10.1016/j.ijinfomgt.2020.102307

Donthu, N., Kumar, S., & Pattnaik, D. (2020). Forty-five years of Journal of Business Research: A bibliometric analysis. *Journal of Business Research, 109*, 1–14. doi:10.1016/j.jbusres.2019.10.039

Dovlo, D. (2007). Migration of nurses from sub-Saharan Africa: A review of issues and challenges. *Health Services Research, 42*(3p2), 1373–1388. doi:10.1111/j.1475-6773.2007.00712.x PMID:17489920

Draft National Tourism Policy. (2022). *Ministry of Tourism, Government of India Economic Survey 2022- 23 (2023).* Finance Ministry, Government of India.

Drucker, P. F. (1999). Knowledge-worker productivity: The biggest challenge. *California Management Review, 41*(2), 79–94. doi:10.2307/41165987

Druskat, V. U., & Wolff, S. B. (2001). Building the emotional intelligence of groups. *Harvard Business Review, 79*(3). PMID:11246926

Duan, Y., Edwards, J. S., & Dwivedi, Y. K. (2019). Artificial intelligence for decision making in the era of bigdata – evolution, challenges and research agenda. *International Journal of Information Management, 48*, 63–71. doi:10.1016/j.ijinfomgt.2019.01.021

Dulewicz, V., & Higgs, M. (2000). Emotional intelligence–A review and evaluation study. *Journal of Managerial Psychology, 15*(4), 341–372. doi:10.1108/02683940010330993

Dulewicz, V., & Higgs, M. (2003). Leadership at the top: The need for emotional intelligence in organizations. *The International Journal of Organizational Analysis, 11*(3), 193–210. doi:10.1108/eb028971

Dumitrescu, B., Băltoiu, A., & Budulan, Ş. (2022). Anomaly detection in graphs of bank transactions for anti money laundering applications. *IEEE Access : Practical Innovations, Open Solutions, 10*, 47699–47714. doi:10.1109/ACCESS.2022.3170467

Durieux, V., & Gevenois, P. A. (2010). Bibliometric indicators: Quality measurements of scientific publication. *Radiology, 255*(2), 342–351. doi:10.1148/radiol.09090626 PMID:20413749

Durlak, J. A., Weissberg, R. P., Dymnicki, A. B., Taylor, R. D., & Schellinger, K. B. (2011). The impact of enhancing students' social and emotional learning: A meta-analysis of school-based universal interventions. *Child Development, 82*(1), 405–432. doi:10.1111/j.1467-8624.2010.01564.x PMID:21291449

Dwivedi, Y. K., Hughes, L., Ismagilova, E., Aarts, G., Coombs, C., Crick, T., Duan, Y., Dwivedi, R., Edwards, J., Eirug, A., Galanos, V., Ilavarasan, P. V., Janssen, M., Jones, P., Kar, A. K., Kizgin, H., Kronemann, B., Lal, B., Lucini, B., ... Williams, M. D. (2021). Artificial Intelligence (AI): Multidisciplinary Perspectives on Emerging Challenges, Opportunities, and Agenda for Research, Practice and Policy. *International Journal of Information Management, 57*, 101994. doi:10.1016/j.ijinfomgt.2019.08.002

Dwivedi, Y. K., Kshetri, N., Hughes, L., Slade, E. L., Jeyaraj, A., Kar, A. K., Baabdullah, A. M., Koohang, A., Raghavan, V., Ahuja, M., Albanna, H., Albashrawi, M. A., Al-Busaidi, A. S., Balakrishnan, J., Barlette, Y., Basu, S., Bose, I., Brooks, L., Buhalis, D., ... Wright, R. (2023). "So what if ChatGPT wrote it?" Multidisciplinary perspectives on opportunities, challenges and implications of generative conversational AI for research, practice and policy. *International Journal of Information Management, 71*, 102642. doi:10.1016/j.ijinfomgt.2023.102642

Dyke, L. S., & Murphy, S. A. (2006). How we define success: A qualitative study of what matters most to women and men. *Sex Roles, 55*(5-6), 357–371. doi:10.100711199-006-9091-2

Dzhaparov, P. (2020). Application of blockchain and artificial intelligence in bank risk management. *Икономика иуправление, 17*(1), 43-57.

Ebadati, E. O. M., & Mortazavi, T. M. (2018). An efficient hybrid machine learning method for time series stock market forecasting. *Neural Network World*, *28*(1), 41–55. doi:10.14311/NNW.2018.28.003

Edelman, P., & van Knippenberg, D. (2018). Emotional intelligence, management of subordinate's emotions, and leadership effectiveness. *Leadership and Organization Development Journal*, *39*(5), 592–607. doi:10.1108/LODJ-04-2018-0154

Edmans, A., Garcia, D., & Norli, Ø. (2007). Sports sentiment and stock returns. *The Journal of Finance*, *62*(4), 1967–1998. doi:10.1111/j.1540-6261.2007.01262.x

Elkins, A. C., Dunbar, N. E., Adame, B., & Nunamaker, J. F. (2013). Are Users Threatened by Credibility Assessment Systems? *Journal of Management Information Systems*, *29*(4), 249–262. doi:10.2753/MIS0742-1222290409

Emdady, M., & Bagheri, N. (2013). The relation between emotional intelligence and job satisfaction. *European Journal of Experimental Biology*, *3*, 554–558.

Emmerling, R. J., & Boyatzis, R. E. (2012). Emotional and social intelligence competencies: Cross cultural implications. *Cross Cultural Management*, *19*(1), 4–18. doi:10.1108/13527601211195592

Etaiwi, W., Biltawi, M., & Naymat, G. (2017). Evaluation of classification algorithms for banking customer's behavior under Apache Spark Data Processing System. *Procedia Computer Science*, *113*, 559–564. doi:10.1016/j.procs.2017.08.280

Eurich, T. (2018). What self-awareness really is (and how to cultivate it). *Harvard Business Review*, 4.

Evans, M. (2019). Build A 5-Star Customer Experience with Artificial Intelligence. *Forbes*.

Extremera, N., & Fernández-Berrocal, P. (2005). Perceived emotional intelligence and life satisfaction: Predictive and incremental validity using the Trait Meta-Mood Scale. *Personality and Individual Differences*, *39*(5), 937–948. doi:10.1016/j.paid.2005.03.012

Extremera, N., Mérida-López, S., Sánchez-Álvarez, N., & Quintana-Orts, C. (2018). How does emotional intelligence make one feel better at work? The mediational role of work engagement. *International Journal of Environmental Research and Public Health*, *15*(9), 1909. doi:10.3390/ijerph15091909 PMID:30200548

Extremera, N., Quintana-Orts, C., Mérida-López, S., & Rey, L. (2018). Cyberbullying victimization, self-esteem and suicidal ideation in adolescence: Does emotional intelligence play a buffering role? *Frontiers in Psychology*, *9*, 367. doi:10.3389/fpsyg.2018.00367 PMID:29623058

Extremera, N., & Rey, L. (2015). The moderator role of emotion regulation ability in the link between stress and well-being. *Frontiers in Psychology*, *6*, 1632. doi:10.3389/fpsyg.2015.01632 PMID:26579017

Ezzaouia, I., & Bulchand-Gidumal, J. (2020). Factors influencing the adoption of information technology in the hotel industry. An analysis in a developing country. *Tourism Management Perspectives*, *34*, 100675. doi:10.1016/j.tmp.2020.100675

Fama, E. F. (1970). Efficient capital markets: A review of theory and empirical work. *The Journal of Finance*, *25*(2), 383–417. doi:10.2307/2325486

Farooq, R., Zhang, Z., Talwar, S., & Dhir, A. (2022). Do green human resource management and self-efficacy facilitate green creativity? A study of luxury hotels and resorts. *Journal of Sustainable Tourism*, *30*(4), 824–845. doi:10.1080/09669582.2021.1891239

Fathali, Z., Kodia, Z., & Ben Said, L. (2022, September 16). Stock Market Prediction of NIFTY 50 Index Applying Machine Learning Techniques. *Applied Artificial Intelligence*, *36*(1), 2111134. Advance online publication. doi:10.1080/08839514.2022.2111134

Fayyad, U., Piatetsky-Shapiro, G., & Smyth, P. (2019). From data mining to knowledge discovery in databases. *AI Magazine*, *17*(3), 37–54.

Fernandez, A. (2019). *Artificial Intelligence in Financial Services* (*SSRN* Scholarly Paper 3366846). doi:10.2139/ssrn.3366846

Fernandez, A. A., & Shaw, G. P. (2020). Academic leadership in a time of crisis: The Coronavirus and COVID-19. *Journal of Leadership Studies*, *14*(1), 39–45. doi:10.1002/jls.21684

Ferrell, O. C., & Ferrell, L. (2021). Applying the Hunt Vitell ethics model to artificial intelligence ethics. *Journal of Global Scholars of Marketing Science*, *31*(2), 178–188. doi:10.1080/21639159.2020.1785918

Fiaidhi, J., Mohammed, S., & Mohammed, S. (2018). The Robotization of Extreme Automation: The Balance Between Fear and Courage. *IT Professional*, *20*(6), 87–93. doi:10.1109/MITP.2018.2876979

Fianko, S. K. Jnr, Jnr, S. A., & Dzogbewu, T. C. (2020). Does the interpersonal dimension of Goleman's emotional intelligence model predict effective leadership? *African Journal of Business and Economic Research*, *15*(4), 221–245. doi:10.31920/1750-4562/2020/v15n4a10

Figueroa-Armijos, M., Clark, B. B., & da Motta Veiga, S. P. (2022). Ethical Perceptions of AI in Hiring and Organizational Trust: The Role of Performance Expectancy and Social Influence. *Journal of Business Ethics*, *186*(1), 179–197. doi:10.100710551-022-05166-2 PMID:33758450

Floridi, L. (2014). Technological Unemployment, Leisure Occupation, and the Human Project. *Philosophy & Technology*, *27*(2), 143–150. doi:10.100713347-014-0166-7

Floridi, L., & Cowls, J. (2022). A Unified Framework of Five Principles for AI in Society. In *Machine Learning and the City* (pp. 535–545). John Wiley & Sons, Ltd. doi:10.1002/9781119815075.ch45

Foltin, A., & Keller, R. (2012). Leading change with emotional intelligence. *Nursing Management*, *43*(11), 20–25. doi:10.1097/01.NUMA.0000421675.33594.63 PMID:23086169

Fountaine, T., McCarthy, B., & Saleh, T. (2019). Building the AI-Powered Organization. *Harvard Business Review*, *97*(4), 62–73.

Frey, C. B., & Osborne, M. A. (2017). The future of employment: How susceptible are jobs to computerisation? *Technological Forecasting and Social Change*, *114*, 254–280. doi:10.1016/j.techfore.2016.08.019

Fuchs, D. J. (2018). The dangers of human-like bias in machine-learning algorithms. *MissouriS&T'sPeerPeer.*, *2*(1), 1.

Gallie, D., Felstead, A., Green, F., & Inanc, H. (2017). The hidden face of job insecurity. *Work, Employment and Society*, *31*(1), 36–53. doi:10.1177/0950017015624399

Gardner, H. (1983). *Frames of mind: The theory of multiple intelligences*. Basic Books.

Gardner, W. L., Cogliser, C. C., Davis, K. M., & Dickens, M. P. (2011). Authentic leadership: A review of the literature and research agenda. *The Leadership Quarterly*, *22*(6), 1120–1145. doi:10.1016/j.leaqua.2011.09.007

GarimaKaneria. (2022). Artificial Intelligence in Banking Industry. *Impact of Artificial Intelligence on Organizational Transformation*, 327-348.

Gartner. (2019). *How AI is transforming the banking industry.* Retrieved from https://www.gartner.com/smarterwithgartner/how-ai-is-transforming-the-banking-industry/

Gay, L. R., Mills, G. E., & Airasian, P. W. (2011). *Educational research: Competencies for analysis and application* (10th ed.). Pearson Education.

Gedam, V. V., Raut, R. D., Lopes de Sousa Jabbour, A. B., Narkhede, B. E., & Grebinevych, O. (2021). Sustainable manufacturing and green human resources: Critical success factors in the automotive sector. *Business Strategy and the Environment, 30*(2), 1296–1313. doi:10.1002/bse.2685

Geetha, R., & Uma, G. (2021). Role of artificial intelligence in banking. *Journal of Computer Science and Technology, 3*(1), 1-7.

George, J. M. (2000). Emotions and leadership: The role of emotional intelligence. *Human Relations, 53*(8), 1027–1055. doi:10.1177/0018726700538001

George, M. (2006). Practical application of spiritual intelligence in the workplace. *Human Resource Management International Digest, 14*(5), 3–5. doi:10.1108/09670730610678181

Gerber, S., & Hiernaux, Q. (2022). Plants as Machines: History, Philosophy and Practical Consequences of an Idea. *Journal of Agricultural & Environmental Ethics, 35*(1), 4. doi:10.100710806-021-09877-w

Gerling, C., & Lessmann, S. (2023). *Multimodal Document Analytics for Banking Process Automation.* arXiv preprint arXiv:2307.11845

Ghaderi, M., & Shamsi, A. (2015). The correlation between emotional intelligence and mental health among students of Jiroft city. *Journal of Healthcare Protection Management, 5*(1), 62–72.

Ghandour, A. (2021). Opportunities and challenges of artificial intelligence in banking: Systematic literature review. *TEM Journal, 10*(4), 1581–1587. doi:10.18421/TEM104-12

Ghoniem, A., Elkhouly, S., Mohsen, G., & Ibrahim, M. (2011). Impact of Emotional Intelligence and Gender on Job Satisfaction among Egyptian Government Sector Employees. *J Soc Sci., 3*(1), 7–22.

Ghosh, B., Daugherty, P. R., Wilson, H. J., & Burden, A. (2019). Taking a Systems Approach To Workplace Learning. *Harvard Business Review.*

Gilbert, N. (1997). A simulation of the structure of academic science. *Sociological Research Online, 2*(2), 91–105. doi:10.5153ro.85

Gilley, A., McMillan, H. S., & Gilley, J. W. (2009). Organizational change and characteristics of leadership effectiveness. *Journal of Leadership & Organizational Studies, 16*(1), 38–47. doi:10.1177/1548051809334191

Goh, S. H., Lee, Y. C., & Chai, S. T. (2020). A deep learning framework for stock market volatility prediction using long short-term memory networks. *Expert Systems with Applications, 152*, 113392.

Gokhan, O. Z. E. R., & Mutlu, U. (2019). The effects of personality traits on financial behaviour. *Journal of Business Economics and Finance, 8*(3), 155–164.

Goleman, D. (2001). An EI-based theory of performance. *The emotionally intelligent workplace: How to select for, measure, and improve emotional intelligence in individuals, groups, and organizations, 1*(1), 27-44.

Goleman, D., & Intelligence, E. (1995). Why it can matter more than IQ. *Emotional Intelligence.*

Goleman, D., Boyatzis, R., & McKee, A. (2009). Primal Leadership: The Hidden Driver of Great Performance. *Discovering Leadership*, 63–72. doi:10.1007/978-1-137-24203-7_6

Goleman, D. (1995). *Emotional Intelligence.* Bantam Book.

Goleman, D. (1998). *Working with emotional intelligence.* Bantam Books.

Goleman, D. (2004). What makes a leader? *Harvard Business Review*, *82*(1), 82–91. PMID:10187249

Goleman, D. (2006). *Emotional intelligence.* Random House LLC.

Goleman, D., Boyatzis, R. E., & McKee, A. (2013). *Primal leadership: Unleashing the power of emotional intelligence.* Harvard Business Press.

Goleman, D., & Intelligence, E. (1995). *Why it can matter more than IQ.* Emotional Intelligence.

Gómez-Leal, R., Holzer, A. A., Bradley, C., Fernández-Berrocal, P., & Patti, J. (2022). The relationship between emotional intelligence and leadership in school leaders: A systematic review. *Cambridge Journal of Education*, *52*(1), 1–21. doi:10.1080/0305764X.2021.1927987

Goode, A. (2018). Biometrics for banking: Best practices and barriers to adoption. *Biometric Technology Today*, *2018*(10), 5–7. doi:10.1016/S0969-4765(18)30156-5

Goodell, J. W., Kumar, S., Lim, W. M., & Pattnaik, D. (2021). Artificial intelligence and machine learning in finance: Identifying foundations, themes, and research clusters from bibliometric analysis. *Journal of Behavioral and Experimental Finance*, *32*, 100577. doi:10.1016/j.jbef.2021.100577

Görgens-Ekermans, G., & Brand, T. (2012). Emotional intelligence as a moderator in the stress–burnout relationship: A questionnaire study on nurses. *Journal of Clinical Nursing*, *21*(15-16), 2275–2285. doi:10.1111/j.1365-2702.2012.04171.x PMID:22788561

Government of India. (2021). *India's climate vision – Success Story.* Author.

Grandey, A. A. (2000). Emotional regulation in the workplace: A new way to conceptualize emotional labor. *Journal of Occupational Health Psychology*, *5*(1), 95–110. doi:10.1037/1076-8998.5.1.95 PMID:10658889

Gravina, D., Khalifa, A., Liapis, A., Togelius, J., & Yannakakis, G. N. (2019, August). Procedural content generation through quality diversity. In *2019 IEEE Conference on Games (CoG)* (pp. 1-8). IEEE.

Grech, A., Mehnen, J., & Wodehouse, A. (2023). An extended AI-experience: Industry 5.0 in creative product innovation. *Sensors (Basel)*, *23*(6), 3009. doi:10.339023063009 PMID:36991718

Green, R. (2018). Mayer and Salovey model of emotional intelligence. The Emotional Intelligence Institute, 1-6.

Gretzel, U. (2011). Intelligent systems in tourism: A social science perspective. *Annals of Tourism Research*, *38*(3), 757–779. doi:10.1016/j.annals.2011.04.014

Grewal, D., Brackett, M., & Salovey, P. (2006). Emotional Intelligence and the Self-Regulation of Affect. In D. K. Snyder, J. Simpson, & J. N. Hughes (Eds.), *Emotion regulation in couples and families: Pathways to dysfunction and health* (pp. 37–55). American Psychological Association. doi:10.1037/11468-002

Guenole, N., & Feinzig, S. (2018). *The Business Case for AI in HR. IBM Corporation. United states of America.* Retrieved from chrome-extension://bocbaocobfecmglnmeaeppambideimao/pdf/viewer.html?file=https%3A%2F%2Fwww.ibm.com%2Fdownloads%2Fcas%2FAGKXJX6M accessed on 16/04/2023

Guerrero, M., Urbano, D., & Gajón, E. (2020). Entrepreneurial university ecosystems and graduates' career patterns: Do entrepreneurship education programmes and university business incubators matter? *Journal of Management Development*, *39*(5), 753–775. doi:10.1108/JMD-10-2019-0439

Gulyani, G., & Sharma, T. (2018, October). Total rewards components and work happiness in new ventures: The mediating role of work engagement. In Evidence-based HRM: A global forum for empirical scholarship (Vol. 6, No. 3, pp. 255-271). Emerald Publishing Limited.

Guni, A., Normahani, P., Davies, A., & Jaffer, U. (2021). Harnessing machine learning to personalize web-based health care content. *Journal of Medical Internet Research*, *23*(10), e25497. doi:10.2196/25497 PMID:34665146

Guo, X., Zhang, X., Li, C., & Xiong, Y. (2021). A review of applications and challenges of artificial intelligence in finance. *Journal of Industrial Information Integration*, *22*, 100168.

Gupta, M. (2021). *Financial institutions using AI*. Academic Press.

Gupta, R., & Jayaraman, R. (2021). Impact of artificial intelligence in banking sector: A systematic review. *Journal of Applied Accounting Research*.

Gupta, P., Fernandes, S. F., & Jain, M. (2018). Automation in Recruitment: A New Frontier. *Journal of Information Technology Teaching Cases*, *8*(2), 118–125. doi:10.105741266-018-0042-x

Gupta, R. K., & Kumari, R. (2017). Artificial intelligence in public health: Opportunities and challenges. *JK Science*, *19*(4), 191–192.

Gu, T.-T., Zhang, S.-F., & Cai, R. (2022). Can Artificial Intelligence Boost Employment in Service Industries? Empirical Analysis Based on China. *Applied Artificial Intelligence*, *36*(1), 1–18. doi:10.1080/08839514.2022.2080336

Gutek, B. A. (1988). Sex segregation and women at work: A selective review. *Applied Psychology*, *37*(2), 103–120. doi:10.1111/j.1464-0597.1988.tb01130.x

Gyanani, T. C., & Kushwaha, S. S. (2001). Emotional Intelligence and Its Development. *Journal of Indian Education, NCERT*, *25*(2), 66–75.

Haan, K. (2023). *How Businesses Are Using Artificial Intelligence In 2023*. https://www.forbes.com/advisor/business/software/ai-in-business/

Hackett, P. P. T., Hortman, J., Hortman, W. J., & Hortman, J. (2008). The Relationship of Emotional Competencies to Transformational Leadership: Using a Corporate Model to Assess the Dispositions of Educational Leaders. *Journal of Educational Research & Policy Studies*, *8*(1), 92–111. http://www.eric.ed.gov/ERICWebPortal/recordDetail?accno=EJ809444%5Cnhttp://search.proquest.com/docview/61945952?accountid=17215

Hadavandi, E., Ghanbari, A., Shahanaghi, K., & Abbasian-Naghneh, S. (2011). Tourist arrival forecasting by evolutionary fuzzy systems. *Tourism Management*, *32*(5), 1196–1203. doi:10.1016/j.tourman.2010.09.015

Haenlein, M., & Kaplan, A. (2019). A Brief History of Artificial Intelligence: On the past, present, and future of artificial intelligence. 1–10. doi:10.1177/0008125619864925

Haghighatjoo Z, Shafigh Pour, M. R, & Anari, H. (2008). The relationship between emotional intelligence and job satisfaction among men and women working for Iran medical sciences universities. *Journal of Nursing and Midwifery Urmia University of Medical Sciences, 6*(4), 159-169.

Hair, J. F., Black, W. C., Babin, B. J., & Anderson, R. E. (2010). *Multivariate Data Analysis* (7th ed.). Pearson.

Hameed, I., Ijaz, M. U., & Sabharwal, M. (2022). The impact of human resources environment and organizational identification on employees' psychological well-being. *Public Personnel Management*, *51*(1), 71–96. doi:10.1177/00910260211001397

Hamouda, M. (2019). Omni-channel banking integration quality and perceived value as drivers of consumers' satisfaction and loyalty. *Journal of Enterprise Information Management*, *32*(4), 608–625. doi:10.1108/JEIM-12-2018-0279

Hannam, K., Butler, G., & Paris, C. M. (2014). Developments and key issues in tourism mobilities. *Annals of Tourism Research*, *44*, 171–185. doi:10.1016/j.annals.2013.09.010

Harms, P. D., & Credé, M. (2010). Emotional intelligence and transformational and transactional leadership: A meta-analysis. *Journal of Leadership & Organizational Studies*, *17*(1), 5–17. doi:10.1177/1548051809350894

Harvey, G., Williams, K., & Probert, J. (2013). Greening the airline pilot: HRM and the green performance of airlines in the UK. *International Journal of Human Resource Management*, *24*(1), 152–166. doi:10.1080/09585192.2012.669783

Harvey, S. B., Modini, M., Joyce, S., Milligan-Saville, J. S., Tan, L., Mykletun, A., Bryant, R. A., Christensen, H., & Mitchell, P. B. (2017). Can work make you mentally ill? A systematic meta-review of work-related risk factors for common mental health problems. *Occupational and Environmental Medicine*, *74*(4), 301–310. doi:10.1136/oemed-2016-104015 PMID:28108676

Hasbullah, S. S., Maynard, D., Chik, R. Z. W., Mohd, F., & Noor, M. (2016, January). Automated content analysis: A sentiment analysis on Malaysian government social media. In *Proceedings of the 10th International Conference on Ubiquitous Information Management and Communication* (pp. 1-6). 10.1145/2857546.2857577

Hashemi, S. K., Mirtaheri, S. L., & Greco, S. (2022). Fraud Detection in Banking Data by Machine Learning Techniques. *IEEE Access : Practical Innovations, Open Solutions*, *11*, 3034–3043. doi:10.1109/ACCESS.2022.3232287

Hassan, M. M., Hossain, M. S., Alelaiwi, A., & Alamri, A. (2019). Real-time and secure IoT-based smart transportation systems: A review. *IEEE Access : Practical Innovations, Open Solutions*, *7*, 6647–6665.

Hastie, T., Tibshirani, R., & Friedman, J. (2009). Unsupervised learning. In *The elements of statistical learning* (pp. 485–585). Springer. doi:10.1007/978-0-387-84858-7_14

Hatzius, J., Briggs, J., Kodnani, D., & Pierdomenico, G. (2023). *The Potentially Large Effects of Artificial Intelligence on Economic Growth* (Global Economics Analyst). Goldman Sachs. https://www.gspublishing.com/content/research/en/reports/2023/03/27/d64e052b-0f6e-45d7-967b-d7be35fabd16.html# doi:10.1001/jamasurg.2020.0839

Havrda, M., & Rakova, B. (2020). Enhanced well-being assessment as basis for the practical implementation of ethical and rights-based normative principles for AI. *2020 IEEE International Conference on Systems, Man, and Cybernetics (SMC)*, 2754–2761. 10.1109/SMC42975.2020.9283137

Hayashi, A., & Ewert, A. (2006). Outdoor leaders' emotional intelligence and transformational leadership. *Journal of Experiential Education*, *28*(3), 222–242. doi:10.1177/105382590602800305

Hernandez-Nieves, E., Hernández, G., Gil-Gonzalez, A. B., Rodríguez-González, S., & Corchado, J. M. (2021). CEBRA: A CasE-Based Reasoning Application to recommend banking products. *Engineering Applications of Artificial Intelligence, 104*, 104327. https://djangostars.com/blog/6-examples-ai-financial-services/

Hess, J. D., & Bacigalupo, A. C. (2011). Enhancing decisions and decision-making processes through the application of emotional intelligence skills. *Management Decision*, *49*(5), 710–721. doi:10.1108/00251741111130805

Higgs, M., & Dulewicz, V. (2016). Coaching and mentoring: A critical text. *Sage (Atlanta, Ga.)*.

Hilovska, K., & Koncz, P. (2012). Application of Artificial Intelligence and Data Mining Techniques to Financial Markets. *Economic Studies & Analyses / Acta VSFS*, *6*(1), 62-76.

Himanshu and Roshan A. (2021). *Ecotourism Market*. Retrieved from Allied Market Research: https://www.allied marketresearch.com/eco-tourism-market-A06364

Hira, T. K. (2012). Promoting sustainable financial behaviour: Implications for education and research. *International Journal of Consumer Studies*, *36*(5), 502–507. doi:10.1111/j.1470-6431.2012.01115.x

Hoecht, A., & Trott, P. (2006). Innovation risks of strategic outsourcing. *Technovation*, *26*(5-6), 672–681. doi:10.1016/j.technovation.2005.02.004

Hoehndorf, R., & Queralt-Rosinach, N. (2017). Data Science and Symbolic AI: Synergies, Challenges and Opportunities. Data Science, 1(1-2), 27-38. doi:10.3233/DS-170004

Horton, J., Cameron, A., Devaraj, D., Hanson, R., & Hajkowicz, S. (2018). *Workplace Safety Futures: The impact of emerging technologies and platforms on work health and safety and workers' compensation over the next 20 years*. https://www.data61.csiro.au/en/Our-Work/Future-Cities/Planning-sustainable-infrastructure/WorkplaceSafety

Hosseinian, S., Yazdi, S. M., Zahraie, S., & Fathi-Ashtiani, A. (2008). Emotional intelligence and job satisfaction. *Journal of Applied Sciences (Faisalabad)*, *8*(5), 903–906. doi:10.3923/jas.2008.903.906

Huang, L. C., Wu, P., & Kuo, R. J. (2001). A neural network modelling on human resource talent selection. *Int. J. Human Resources Development and Management, 1*(2/3/4), 206–219.

Huang, J., & Liu, J. (2019, June 27). Using social media mining technology to improve stock price forecast accuracy. *Journal of Forecasting*, *39*(1), 104–116. doi:10.1002/for.2616

Huang, L. C., Ahlstrom, D., Lee, A. Y. P., Chen, S. Y., & Hsieh, M. J. (2016). High performance work systems, employee well-being, and job involvement: An empirical study. *Personnel Review*, *45*(2), 296–314. doi:10.1108/PR-09-2014-0201

Huang, M. H., & Rust, R. T. (2018). Artificial intelligence in service. *Journal of Service Research*, *21*(2), 155–172. doi:10.1177/1094670517752459

Huang, M. H., & Rust, R. T. (2021). A strategic framework for artificial intelligence in marketing. *Journal of the Academy of Marketing Science*, *49*(1), 30–50. doi:10.100711747-020-00749-9

Huang, X., Chan, S. C. H., Lam, W., & Nan, X. (2010). The joint effect of leader–member exchange and emotional intelligence on burnout and work performance in call centers in China. *International Journal of Human Resource Management*, *21*(7), 1124–1144. doi:10.1080/09585191003783553

Hussain, M., & Khan, S. M. (2016). Leadership Qualities of Administrators in the Light of Seerat-Ul-Nabi (Saw). *Abha'th*, *1*(4), 17.

Hyson, P. (2013). The spirited leader: The potential of spiritual intelligence to improve leadership. *The International Journal of Leadership in Public Services*, *9*(3/4), 109–115. doi:10.1108/IJLPS-10-2013-0028

Iacobucci, T. A., Daly, B. J., Lindell, D., & Griffin, M. Q. (2013). Professional values, self-esteem and ethical confidence of baccalaureate nursing students. *Nursing Ethics*, *20*(4), 479–490. doi:10.1177/0969733012458608 PMID:23166146

IDC. (2020). Retrieved from https://www.idc.com/getdoc.jsp?containerId=US45569118

Imran, R., Alraja, M. N., & Khashab, B. (2021). Sustainable Performance and Green Innovation: Green Human Resources Management and Big Data as Antecedents. *IEEE Transactions on Engineering Management*. Advance online publication. doi:10.1109/TEM.2021.3114256

Inanc–Demir, M., & Kozak, M. (2019). Big data and its supporting elements: Implications for tourism and hospitality marketing. *Big data and innovation in tourism, travel, and hospitality: Managerial approaches, techniques, and applications*, 213-223.

India B2C ecommerce market opportunities report 2023: A $149 billion ... (n.d.). https://www.businesswire.com/news/home/20230321005608/en/India-B2C-Ecommerce-Market-Opportunities-Report-2023-A-149-Billion-Market-by-2028---Social-Commerce-Firms-are-Refocusing-their-Efforts-on-Direct-Sales-Amid-Growing-Competition---ResearchAndMarkets.com

India Tourism Statistics 2022. (2022). Ministry of Tourism, Government of India.

Infante-Moro, A., Infante-Moro, J. C., & Gallardo-Pérez, J. (2019). The importance of ICTs for students as a competence for their future professional performance: The case of the faculty of business studies and tourism of the University of Huelva. *Journal of New Approaches in Educational Research*, *8*(2), 201–213. doi:10.7821/naer.2019.7.434

Ingram, A., Peake, W.O., Stewart, W., & Watson, W. (2017). Emotional Intelligence and Venture Performance. *Journal of Small Business Management*. doi:10.1111/jsbm.12333

Insights, O. (2022). *Government AI Readiness Index 2022*. Oxford Insights.

Iqbal, S., Hussain, N., Latif, M., & Aslam, S. (2013). Investor Type and Financial Market Anomalies: A Comparison of Individual, Institutional and Foreign Investors and Role of Their Behaviors in Investing Decisions. *Middle East Journal of Scientific Research*, *17*, 1591–1596. doi:10.5829/idosi.mejsr.2013.17.11.11787

Ismail, K., Nopiah, Z. M., & Rasul, M. S. (2020). Emotional intelligence and work performance among vocational teachers. *Journal of Technical Education and Training*, *12*(3), 106–117.

Itzkovich, Y., & Dolev, N. (2017). The Relationships between Emotional Intelligence and Perceptions of Faculty Incivility in Higher Education. Do Men and Women Differ? *Current Psychology (New Brunswick, N.J.)*, *36*(4), 905–918. doi:10.100712144-016-9479-2

Jabbour, C. J. C. (2013). Environmental training in organisations: From a literature review to a framework for future research. *Resources, Conservation and Recycling*, *74*, 144–155. doi:10.1016/j.resconrec.2012.12.017

Jain, A. (2017). *Study of Artificial Intelligence (AI) with Augmented Reality(AR)*. www.ijcst.com

Jain, C. (2022). Virtual Fitting Rooms: "A Review of Underlying Artificial Intelligence Technologies, Current Developments, and the Biometric Privacy Laws in the US, EU and India." *Current Developments, and the Biometric Privacy Laws in the US, EU and India.*

Jain, V. (2019). An impact of artificial intelligence on business. *International Journal of Research and Analytical Reviews*, *6*(2), 302–308.

Jakkani, N., & Kodali, R. (2020). A systematic review of artificial intelligence applications in banking. *Journal of Artificial Intelligence and Data Science*, *2*(1), 29–40. doi:10.32628/JAIDS.V2I1.454

James Thomas, K. (2004). Emotional intelligence: The new science of interpersonal effectiveness. *Human Resource Development Quarterly*, *15*(4), 489–495. doi:10.1002/hrdq.1117

James Wilson, H., & Daugherty, P. R. (2018). Collaborative intelligence: Humans and AI are joining forces. *Harvard Business Review*.

Jarrahi, M. H., Lutz, C., & Newlands, G. (2022). Artificial intelligence, human intelligence and hybrid intelligence based on mutual augmentation. *Big Data & Society*, *9*(2). doi:10.1177/20539517221142824

Jena, L. K., & Goyal, S. (2022). Emotional intelligence and employee innovation: Sequential mediating effect of person-group fit and adaptive performance. *European Review of Applied Psychology*, *72*(1), 100729. doi:10.1016/j.erap.2021.100729

Jerman, A., Pejić Bach, M., & Aleksić, A. (2020). Transformation towards smart factory system: Examining new job profiles and competencies. *Systems Research and Behavioral Science*, *37*(2), 388–402. doi:10.1002res.2657

Jerónimo, H. M., Henriques, P. L., de Lacerda, T. C., da Silva, F. P., & Vieira, P. R. (2020). Going green and sustainable: The influence of green HR practices on the organizational rationale for sustainability. *Journal of Business Research*, *112*, 413–421. doi:10.1016/j.jbusres.2019.11.036

Jiang, Z., & Benbasat, I. (2004). Virtual product experience: Effects of visual and functional control of products on perceived diagnosticity and flow in electronic shopping. *Journal of Management Information Systems*, *21*(3), 111–147. doi:10.1080/07421222.2004.11045817

Jia, Q., Guo, Y., Li, R., Li, Y., & Chen, Y. (2018). A Conceptual Artificial Intelligence Application Framework in Human Resource Management. *International Conference on Electronic Business*, 106–114.

Jingen Liang, L., & Elliot, S. (2021). A systematic review of augmented reality tourism research: What is now and what is next? *Tourism and Hospitality Research*, *21*(1), 15–30. doi:10.1177/1467358420941913

Johnson, R. D., Stone, D. L., & Lukaszewski, K. M. (2021). The benefits of eHRM and AI for talent acquisition. *Journal of Tourism Futures*, *7*(1), 40–52. doi:10.1108/JTF-02-2020-0013

Joo, B. A., & Durri, K. (2015). Comprehensive review of literature on behavioural finance. *Indian Journal of Commerce and Management Studies*, *6*(2), 11–19.

Jordan, M., & Mitchell, T. (2015). Machine learning: Trends, perspectives, and prospects. *Science*, *349*(6245), 255–260. doi:10.1126cience.aaa8415 PMID:26185243

Jordan, P. J., Ashkanasy, N. M., Härtel, C. E., & Hooper, G. S. (2002). Workgroup emotional intelligence: Scale development and relationship to team process effectiveness and goal focus. *Human Resource Management Review*, *12*(2), 195–214. doi:10.1016/S1053-4822(02)00046-3

Jordan, P. J., & Troth, A. C. (2004). Managing emotions during team problem solving: Emotional intelligence and conflict resolution. *Human Performance*, *17*(2), 195–218. doi:10.120715327043hup1702_4

Joseph, D. L., Jin, J., Newman, D. A., & O'Boyle, E. H. (2015). Why does self-reported emotional intelligence predict job performance? A meta-analytic investigation of mixed EI. *The Journal of Applied Psychology*, *100*(2), 298–342. doi:10.1037/a0037681 PMID:25243996

Joseph, D. L., & Newman, D. A. (2010). Emotional intelligence: An integrative meta-analysis and cascading model. *The Journal of Applied Psychology*, *95*(1), 54–78. doi:10.1037/a0017286 PMID:20085406

Kahneman, D. (2011). *Thinking, Fast and Slow*. Macmillan.

Kahneman, D., & Tversky, A. (1979). Prospect Theory: An Analysis of Decision under Risk. *Econometrica*, *47*(2), 263–292. doi:10.2307/1914185

Kalia, N., & Bhardwaj, B. (2019). Contextual and Task Performance: Do Demographic and Organizational variables Matter? *Rajagiri Management Journal*, *13*(2), 30–42. doi:10.1108/RAMJ-09-2019-0017

Kalsie, A., & Kalra, J. K. (2015). An empirical study on efficient market hypothesis of Indian capital markets. *Journal of Management Research and Analysis*, *2*(2), 108–114.

Kalyanaraman, V., Kazi, S., Tondulkar, R., & Oswal, S. (2014). *Sentiment analysis on news articles for stocks*. Paper presented at the 2014 8th Asia Modelling Symposium (AMS), Taipei, Taiwan. 10.1109/AMS.2014.14

Kalyanathaya, K. P., Akila, D., & Rajesh, P. (2019). Advances in natural language processing–a survey of current research trends, development tools and industry applications. *International Journal of Recent Technology and Engineering*, *7*(5C), 199–202.

Kanesan, P., & Fauzan, N. (2019). Models of Emotional Intelligence: A Review. *Journal of Social Sciences and Humanities*, *16*(7), 1823–1884.

Kang, Y., Cai, Z., Tan, C. W., Huang, Q., & Liu, H. (2020). Natural language processing (NLP) in management research: A literature review. *Journal of Management Analytics*, *7*(2), 139–172. doi:10.1080/23270012.2020.1756939

Kapoor, R., & Arora, A. (2019). Role of artificial intelligence in business analytics. *Procedia Computer Science*, *165*, 44–51.

Kapoor, S., & Prosad, J. M. (2017). Behavioural finance: A review. *Procedia Computer Science*, *122*, 50–54. doi:10.1016/j.procs.2017.11.340

Kar, A. K., Kar, A. K., Choudhary, S. K., Choudhary, S. K., Singh, V. K., & Singh, V. K. (2022). How can artificial intelligence impact sustainability: A systematic literature review. *Journal of Cleaner Production*, *376*, 134120. doi:10.1016/j.jclepro.2022.134120

Karam, S., & Nagahi, M., Dayarathna, V. L., Ma, J., Jaradat, R., & Hamilton, M. (2020). Integrating systems thinking skills with multi-criteria decision-making technology to recruit employee candidates. *Expert Systems with Applications*, *160*(June), 113585. doi:10.1016/j.eswa.2020.113585

Karatepe, O. M., Hsieh, H., & Aboramadan, M. (2022). The effects of green human resource management and perceived organizational support for the environment on green and non-green hotel employee outcomes. *International Journal of Hospitality Management*, *103*, 103202. doi:10.1016/j.ijhm.2022.103202

Karatop, B., Kubat, C., & Uygun, Ö. (2015). Talent management in manufacturing system using fuzzy logic approach. *Computers & Industrial Engineering*, *86*, 127–136. doi:10.1016/j.cie.2014.09.015

Kasemsap, K. (2015). The role of psychological factors in behavioural finance. In *Handbook of Research on Behavioural Finance and Investment Strategies: Decision Making in the Financial Industry*. IGI Global. doi:10.4018/978-1-4666-7484-4.ch006

Kashyap, A. K., Sahu, I., & Kumar, A. (2022). Artificial Intelligence and Its Applications in E-Commerce – a Review Analysis and Research Agenda. *Journal of Theoretical and Applied Information Technology*, *100*(24), 7347–7365.

Kathpal, S., Akhtar, A., Zaheer, A., & Khan, M. N. (2021). Covid-19 and heuristic biases: Evidence from India. *Journal of Financial Services Marketing*, *26*(4), 305–316. doi:10.105741264-021-00116-x

Kaur, S., & Sharma, R. (2021). Emotion AI: integrating emotional intelligence with artificial intelligence in the digital workplace. In *Innovations in Information and Communication Technologies (IICT-2020) Proceedings of International Conference on ICRIHE-2020, Delhi, India: IICT-2020* (pp. 337-343). Springer International Publishing. 10.1007/978-3-030-66218-9_39

Kaur, D., Sahdev, S. L., Sharma, D., & Siddiqui, L. (2020). Banking 4.0:'The Influence of Artificial Intelligence on the Banking Industry & How AI Is Changing the Face of Modern Day Banks'. *International Journal of Management*, *11*(6). Advance online publication. doi:10.34218/IJM.11.6.2020.049

Kaushal, N., Kaurav, R. P. S., Sivathanu, B., & Kaushik, N. (2023). Artificial intelligence and HRM: Identifying future research Agenda using systematic literature review and bibliometric analysis. *Management Review Quarterly*, *73*(2), 455–493. doi:10.100711301-021-00249-2

Kellner, F., Chew, E., & Turner, J. (2018). Understanding the Relationship Eff ectiveness through Emotional Intelligence : An Integrative. *Performance Improvement Quarterly, 31*(1), 35–56. doi:10.1002/piq.21254

Kim, H. (2022). Historical Sketch of Artificial Intelligence. In H. Kim (Ed.), *Artificial Intelligence for 6G* (pp. 3–14). Springer International Publishing. doi:10.1007/978-3-030-95041-5_1

Kim, K. J., & Han, I. (2000, August). Genetic algorithms approach to feature discretization in artificial neural networks for the prediction of stock price index. *Expert Systems with Applications, 19*(2), 125–132. doi:10.1016/S0957-4174(00)00027-0

Kim, S. (2007). Learning goal orientation, formal mentoring, and leadership competence in HRD A conceptual model. *Journal of European Industrial Training, 31*(3), 181–194. doi:10.1108/03090590710739269

Kim, Y. J., Kim, W. G., Choi, H. M., & Phetvaroon, K. (2019). The effect of green human resource management on hotel employees' eco-friendly behavior and environmental performance. *International Journal of Hospitality Management, 76*, 83–93. doi:10.1016/j.ijhm.2018.04.007

Kirilenko, A. P., Stepchenkova, S. O., Kim, H., & Li, X. (2018). Automated sentiment analysis in tourism: Comparison of approaches. *Journal of Travel Research, 57*(8), 1012–1025. doi:10.1177/0047287517729757

Kirkwood, J. J. (2016). How women and men business owners perceive success. *International Journal of Entrepreneurial Behaviour & Research, 22*(5), 594–615. doi:10.1108/IJEBR-01-2016-0024

Kolnhofer-Derecskei, A., Reicher, R. Z., & Szeghegyi, A. (2017). The X and Y Generations' Characteristics Comparison. *Acta Polytechnica Hungarica, 14*(8), 107–125. doi:10.12700/APH.14.8.2017.8.6

Kołodziej, M. (2017). Virtual reality as the indicator of the modern banking. *Financial Sciences. Nauki o finansach, 2*(31).

Königstorfer, F., & Thalmann, S. (2020). Applications of Artificial Intelligence in commercial banks–A research agenda for behavioral finance. *Journal of Behavioral and Experimental Finance, 27*, 100352. doi:10.1016/j.jbef.2020.100352

Kopka, A., & Grashof, N. (2022). Artificial intelligence: Catalyst or barrier on the path to sustainability? *Technological Forecasting and Social Change, 175*, 121318. Advance online publication. doi:10.1016/j.techfore.2021.121318

Korinek, A., & Stiglitz, J. E. (2019). Artificial Intelligence and Its Implications for Income Distribution and Unemployment. In The Economics of Artificial Intelligence (Issue May, pp. 349–390). University of Chicago Press. doi:10.7208/chicago/9780226613475.003.0014

Kot, S., Hussain, H. I., Bilan, S., Haseeb, M., & Mihardjo, L. W. (2021). The role of artificial intelligence recruitment and quality to explain the phenomenon of employer reputation. *Journal of Business Economics and Management, 22*(4), 867–883. doi:10.3846/jbem.2021.14606

Kotsou, I., Mikolajczak, M., Heeren, A., Grégoire, J., & Leys, C. (2019). Improving Emotional Intelligence: A Systematic Review of Existing Work and Future Challenges. *Emotion Review, 11*(2), 151–165. doi:10.1177/1754073917735902

Koubova, V., & Buchko, A. A. (2013). Life-work balance: Emotional intelligence as a crucial component of achieving both personal life and work performance. *Management Research Review, 36*(7), 700–719. doi:10.1108/MRR-05-2012-0115

Kounavis, C. D., Kasimati, A. E., & Zamani, E. D. (2012). Enhancing the tourism experience through mobile augmented reality: Challenges and prospects. *International Journal of Engineering Business Management, 4*, 10. doi:10.5772/51644

Kramar, R. (2014). Beyond strategic human resource management: Is sustainable human resource management the next approach? *International Journal of Human Resource Management, 25*(8), 1069–1089. doi:10.1080/09585192.2013.816863

Krén, H., & Séllei, B. (2021). The role of emotional intelligence in organizational performance. *Periodica Polytechnica Social and Management Sciences, 29*(1), 1–9. doi:10.3311/PPso.15879

Krishnakumar, S., Hopkins, K., & Robinson, M. D. (2017). When feeling poorly at work does not mean acting poorly at work: The moderating role of work-related emotional intelligence. *Motivation and Emotion*, *41*(1), 122–134. doi:10.100711031-016-9588-0

Kshetri, N., & Voas, J. (2021). AI in Banking: A Research Agenda. *IEEE Software*, *38*(3), 39–46.

Kudyba, S., & Hoptroff, R. (2019). Ethical considerations of artificial intelligence in business analytics: A synthesis and research agenda. *Journal of Business Analytics*, *2*(2), 69-83.

Kulagin, K., Leksashov, A., Bolsunovskaya, M., & Shirokova, S. (2021). Development of a human flow generation module for testing machine learning algorithms. *Transportation Research Procedia*, *54*, 783–792. doi:10.1016/j.trpro.2021.02.134

Kulkarni, C. S., Bhavsar, A. U., Pingale, S. R., & Kumbhar, S. S. (2017). BANK CHAT BOT–an intelligent assistant system using NLP and machine learning. *International Research Journal of Engineering and Technology*, *4*(5), 2374–2377.

Kumar, I., Dogra, K., Utreja, C., & Yadav, P. (2018, April). A comparative study of supervised machine learning algorithms for stock market trend prediction. In *2018 Second International Conference on Inventive Communication and Computational Technologies (ICICCT)* (pp. 1003-1007). IEEE. 10.1109/ICICCT.2018.8473214

Kumar, N., & Kumar, A. (2021). Applications of artificial intelligence in banking sector: A review of literature. *International Journal of Applied Engineering Research: IJAER*, *16*(2), 276–284.

Kumar, P., Khan, A. M., Inder, D., & Sharma, N. (2013). Primary Health Care Providers (Public Sector) job satisfaction in an urban setting. *Journal of Family Medicine and Primary Care*, *2*, 227–233. doi:10.4103/2249-4863.120718 PMID:24479088

Kumar, S., Aishwaryalakshmi, S., & Akalya, A. (2020). Impact and Challenges of Artificial Intelligence in Banking. *Journal of Information and Computational Science*, *10*(2), 1101–1109.

Kumar, S., Lim, W. M., Sivarajah, U., & Kaur, J. (2023). Artificial Intelligence and Blockchain Integration in Business: Trends from a Bibliometric-Content Analysis. *Information Systems Frontiers*, *25*(2), 871–896. doi:10.100710796-022-10279-0 PMID:35431617

Kumar, S., & Nayyar, P. (2019). Artificial intelligence in banking sector: Transforming the way banking is done. *International Journal of Management, Technology, and Social Sciences*, *4*(1), 1–11. doi:10.5281/zenodo.2592248

Kushwaha, A. K., Pharswan, R., Kumar, P., & Kar, K. A. (2022). How do users feel when they use artificial intelligence for decision making? A Framework for Assessing Users' Perception. *Information Systems Frontiers*. Advance online publication. doi:10.100710796-022-

Kwansah, J., Dzodzomenyo, M., Mutumba, M., Asabir, K., Koomson, E., Gyakobo, M., & Snow, R. C. (2012). Policy talk: Incentives for rural service among nurses in Ghana. *Health Policy and Planning*, *27*(8), 669–676. doi:10.1093/heapol/czs016 PMID:22349086

Lai, W. C., & Hung, W. H. (2018). *A framework of cloud and AI based intelligent hotel*. Academic Press.

Laney, D. (2001). 3D Data management: Controlling data volume, velocity and variety. Meta Group. *Lakshen, Guma Abdulkhader*, 1-4.

Langhorn, S. (2004). How emotional intelligence can improve management performance. *International Journal of Contemporary Hospitality Management*, *16*(4), 220–230. doi:10.1108/09596110410537379

Laschinger, H. K. S. (1996). A theoretical approach to studying work empowerment in nursing: A review of studies testing Kanter's theory of structural power in organizations. *Nursing Administration Quarterly*, *20*(2), 25–41. doi:10.1097/00006216-199602020-00006 PMID:8700383

Lau, C. K. H., Chi, F. R. C., & Au, N. (2019). Examination of the adoption of augmented reality: A VAM approach. *Asia Pacific Journal of Tourism Research*, *24*(10), 1005–1020. doi:10.1080/10941665.2019.1655076

Laursen, K., Masciarelli, F., & Prencipe, A. (2012). Regions matter: How localized social capital affects innovation and external knowledge acquisition. *Organization Science*, *23*(1), 177–193. doi:10.1287/orsc.1110.0650

Law, K. S., Wong, C. S., & Song, L. J. (2004). The construct and criterion validity of emotional intelligence and its potential utility for management studies. *The Journal of Applied Psychology*, *89*(3), 483–496. doi:10.1037/0021-9010.89.3.483 PMID:15161407

Lawler, J. J., & Elliot, R. (1993). Artificial intelligence in HRM: An experimental study of an expert system. *Proceedings of the 1993 Conference on Computer Personnel Research*, 473–480. 10.1145/158011.158264

Law, R. (2000). Back-propagation learning in improving the accuracy of neural network-based tourism demand forecasting. *Tourism Management*, *21*(4), 331–340. doi:10.1016/S0261-5177(99)00067-9

Law, R., Buhalis, D., & Cobanoglu, C. (2014). Progress on information and communication technologies in hospitality and tourism. *International Journal of Contemporary Hospitality Management*, *26*(5), 727–750. doi:10.1108/IJCHM-08-2013-0367

Laws, E. (1998). Conceptualizing visitor satisfaction management in heritage settings: An exploratory blueprinting analysis of Leeds Castle, Kent. *Tourism Management*, *19*(6), 545–554. doi:10.1016/S0261-5177(98)00056-9

Lea, R. G., Qualter, P., Davis, S. K., Pérez-González, J. C., & Bangee, M. (2018). Trait emotional intelligence and attentional bias for positive emotion: An eye tracking study. *Personality and Individual Differences*, *128*, 88–93. doi:10.1016/j.paid.2018.02.017

Lee, G. L. (2022). *Pivoting to robo-advisor services in wealth management*. Academic Press.

Lee, H. J. (2021). Relationship between emotional labor and job satisfaction: Testing mediating role of emotional intelligence on South Korean public service employees. *Public Organization Review*, *21*(2), 337–353. doi:10.100711115-020-00490-5

Lee, J. J., & Ok, C. (2012). Reducing burnout and enhancing job satisfaction: Critical role of hotel employees' emotional intelligence and emotional labor. *International Journal of Hospitality Management*, *31*(4), 1101–1112. doi:10.1016/j.ijhm.2012.01.007

Lee, S. M., & Lee, D. (2020). "Untact": A new customer service strategy in the digital age. *Service Business*, *14*(1), 1–22. doi:10.100711628-019-00408-2

Leesakul, N., Oostveen, A. M., Eimontaite, I., Wilson, M. L., & Hyde, R. (2022). Workplace 4.0: Exploring the implications of technology adoption in digital manufacturing on a sustainable workforce. *Sustainability (Basel)*, *14*(6), 3311. doi:10.3390u14063311

Lee, T. K. W., Castilho, A., Cheung, V. C. H., Tang, K. H., Ma, S., & Ng, I. O. L. (2011). CD24+ liver tumor-initiating cells drive self-renewal and tumor initiation through STAT3-mediated NANOG regulation. *Cell Stem Cell*, *9*(1), 50–63. doi:10.1016/j.stem.2011.06.005 PMID:21726833

Lee, Y. H., & Chelladurai, P. (2018). Emotional intelligence, emotional labor, coach burnout, job satisfaction, and turnover intention in sport leadership. *European Sport Management Quarterly*, *18*(4), 393–412. doi:10.1080/16184742.2017.1406971

Leo, M., Sharma, S., & Maddulety, K. (2019). Machine learning in banking risk management: A literature review. *Risks*, *7*(1), 29. doi:10.3390/risks7010029

Li, F. (2020). The digital transformation of business models in the creative industries: A holistic framework and emerging trends. *Technovation, 92–93*. https://www.sciencedirect.com/science/article/pii/S0166497217300536 doi:10.1016/j.technovation.2017.12.004

Li, L., Wu, X., & Yin, X. (2018). Stock price movement prediction using a deep neural network model. In *Proceedings of the 2018 International Conference on Data Mining (DMIN)* (pp. 47-53). Academic Press.

Liden, R. C., Sparrowe, R. T., & Wayne, S. J. (1997). Leader-member exchange theory: The past and potential for the future. *Research in Personnel and Human Resources Management*, *15*, 47–119.

Likert, R. (1961). *New Patterns of Management*. McGraw-Hill.

Li, L., & Zhang, H. (2021). Applications of artificial intelligence in finance: A review. *Journal of Financial Economics*, *42*(3), 49–60.

Limon, D., & Plaster, B. (2022). *Can AI Teach Us How to Become More Emotionally Intelligent?* https://hbr.org/2022/01/can-ai-teach-us-how-to-become-more-emotionally-intelligent

Lin, Q., Li, T., Shakeel, P. M., & Samuel, R. D. J. (2021). Advanced artificial intelligence in heart rate and blood pressure monitoring for stress management. *Journal of Ambient Intelligence and Humanized Computing*, *12*(3), 3329–3340. doi:10.100712652-020-02650-3

Lipe, M. G. (1998). Individual investors' risk judgments and investment decisions. The impact of accounting and market data. *Accounting, Organizations and Society*, *23*(7), 625–640. doi:10.1016/S0361-3682(97)00065-2

Lipton, Z. C., Kale, D. C., & Wetzel, R. (2018). *Learning to diagnose with LSTM recurrent neural networks*. arXiv preprint arXiv:1511.03677.

Li, S., Da Xu, L., & Zhao, S. (2015). The internet of things: A survey. *Information Systems Frontiers*, *17*(2), 243–259. doi:10.100710796-014-9492-7

Li, S., Sun, B., & Wilcox, R. T. (2005). Cross-selling sequentially ordered products: An application to consumer banking services. *JMR, Journal of Marketing Research*, *42*(2), 233–239. doi:10.1509/jmkr.42.2.233.62288

Littunen, H. (2000). Entrepreneurship and the characteristics of the entrepreneurial personality. *International Journal of Entrepreneurial Behaviour & Research*, *6*(6), 295–310. doi:10.1108/13552550010362741

Liu, L., & Duffy, V. G. (2023). Exploring the Future Development of Artificial Intelligence (AI) Applications in Chatbots: A Bibliometric Analysis. *International Journal of Social Robotics*, *15*(5), 703–716. doi:10.100712369-022-00956-0

Li, X., Wu, P., Shen, G. Q., Wang, X. Y., & Teng, Y. (2017). Mapping the knowledge domains of Building Information Modeling (BIM): A bibliometric approach. *Automation in Construction*, *84*, 195–206. doi:10.1016/j.autcon.2017.09.011

Llinares-Insa, L. I., Casino-García, A. M., & García-Pérez, J. (2020). Subjective well-being, emotional intelligence, and mood of parents: A model of relationships. Impact of giftedness. *Sustainability (Basel)*, *12*(21), 8810. doi:10.3390u12218810

Lockey, S., Gillespie, N., Holm, D., & Someh, I. A. (2021). *A review of trust in artificial intelligence: Challenges, vulnerabilities and future directions.* Academic Press.

Lopes, P. N. (2016). Emotional intelligence in organizations: Bridging research and practice. *Emotion Review*, *8*(4), 316–321. doi:10.1177/1754073916650496

Lopes, P. N., Salovey, P., Côté, S., & Beers, M. (2005). Emotion regulation abilities and the quality of social interaction. *Emotion (Washington, D.C.)*, *5*(1), 113–118. doi:10.1037/1528-3542.5.1.113 PMID:15755224

Lopes, P. N., Salovey, P., & Straus, R. (2003). Emotional intelligence, personality, and the perceived quality of social relationships. *Personality and Individual Differences*, *35*(3), 641–658. doi:10.1016/S0191-8869(02)00242-8

Lopetcharat, K., Paredes, D., & Beckley, J. H. (2022). Future Trends and Direction. *Product Innovation Toolbox: A Field Guide to Consumer Understanding and Research*, 509-519.

López de Prado, M. (2018). *Advances in Financial Machine Learning*. Academic Press.

Loureiro, S., Guerreiro, J., & Ali, F. (2020). 20 years of research on virtual reality and augmented reality in tourism context: A text-mining approach. *Tourism Management, 77*. https://www.sciencedirect.com/science/article/pii/S0261517719302262 doi:10.1016/j.tourman.2019.104028

Lucia-Casademunt, A. M., Ariza-Montes, A., & Becerra-Alonso, D. (2013). Exploring emotional involvement in workplace by applying artificial neural networks: European study. *Actual Problems of Economics*, *143*(5), 376–385.

Ludwig, E. (2018). Regulators have their eye on AI. *American Banker*, *183*(130), 1.

Lui, A. K., Lee, M., & Ngai, E. W. (2022). Impact of artificial intelligence investment on firm value. *Annals of Operations Research*, *308*(1), 373–388. doi:10.100710479-020-03862-8

Luthans, F., & Youssef, C. M. (2007). Emerging positive organizational behavior. *Journal of Management*, *33*(3), 321–349. doi:10.1177/0149206307300814

Luu, T. T. (2018). Employees' green recovery performance: The roles of green HR practices and serving culture. *Journal of Sustainable Tourism*, *26*(8), 1308–1324. doi:10.1080/09669582.2018.1443113

Lu, Z., Gozgor, G., Lau, C. K. M., & Paramati, S. R. (2019). The dynamic impacts of renewable energy and tourism investments on international tourism: Evidence from the G20 countries. *Journal of Business Economics and Management*, *20*(6), 1102–1120. doi:10.3846/jbem.2019.10181

Mabekoje, S. O. (2009). Gender differences in job satisfaction among secondary school teachers. *African Journal of Research in Personnel and Counselling Psychology*, *1*, 99–108.

MacCann, C., Erbas, Y., Dejonckheere, E., Minbashian, A., Kuppens, P., & Fayn, K. (2020). Emotional in- telligence relates to emotions, emotion dynamics, and emotion complexity: A meta-analysis and experience sampling study. *European Journal of Psychological Assessment*, *36*, 460. doi:10.1027/1015-5759/a000588

MacCann, C., Fogarty, G. J., Zeidner, M., & Roberts, R. D. (2011). Coping mediates the relationship between emotional intelligence (EI) and academic achievement. *Contemporary Educational Psychology*, *36*(1), 60–70. doi:10.1016/j.cedpsych.2010.11.002

Madanchian, M., Hussein, N., Noordin, F., & Taherdoost, H. (2017). Leadership effectiveness measurement and its effect on organization outcomes. *Procedia Engineering*, *181*, 1043–1048. doi:10.1016/j.proeng.2017.02.505

Maity, S. (2019). Identifying opportunities for artificial intelligence in the evolution of training and development practices. *Journal of Management Development*, *38*(8), 651–663. doi:10.1108/JMD-03-2019-0069

Majumder, S., & Mondal, A. (2021). Are chatbots really useful for human resource management? *International Journal of Speech Technology*, *24*(4), 969–977. doi:10.100710772-021-09834-y

Makridakis, S. (2017). The forthcoming Artificial Intelligence (AI) revolution: Its impact on society and firms. *Futures*, *90*, 46–60. doi:10.1016/j.futures.2017.03.006

Malali, A. B., & Gopalakrishnan, S. (2020). Application of artificial intelligence and its powered technologies in the indian banking and financial industry: An overview. *IOSR Journal Of Humanities And Social Science*, *25*(4), 55–60.

Malik, A., Budhwar, P., Mohan, H., & Srikanth, N. R. (2023). Employee experience –the missing link for engaging employees: Insights from an MNE's AI-based HR ecosystem. *Human Resource Management*, *62*(1), 97–115. doi:10.1002/hrm.22133

Malik, A., Budhwar, P., Patel, C., & Srikanth, N. R. (2022). May the bots be with you! Delivering HR cost-effectiveness and individualised employee experiences in an MNE. *International Journal of Human Resource Management*, *33*(6), 1148–1178. doi:10.1080/09585192.2020.1859582

Malik, M., Haider, Z., & Hussain, A. (2019). Perceived emotional intelligence, work life balance and job satisfaction among healthcare professionals in Pakistan. *International Journal of Pharmaceutical Research & Allied Sciences*, *8*(2), 80–86.

Malinauskas, R., Dumciene, A., Sipaviciene, S., & Malinauskiene, V. (2018). Relationship Between Emotional Intelligence and Health Behaviours among University Students: The Predictive and Moderating Role of Gender. *BioMed Research International*, *2018*, 1–11. doi:10.1155/2018/7058105 PMID:29967780

Malini, A., & Menon, D. G. (2017, December). Technological innovations in the banking sector in India: An analysis. In *2017 International Conference on Technological Advancements in Power and Energy (TAP Energy)* (pp. 1-5). IEEE. 10.1109/TAPENERGY.2017.8397342

Malinowski, J., Weitzel, T., & Keim, T. (2008). Decision support for team staffing: An automated relational recommendation approach. *Decision Support Systems*, *45*(3), 429–447. doi:10.1016/j.dss.2007.05.005

Manafi, M., & Devi Subramaniam, I. (2015). Balancing Performance by Human Resource Management Practices. *Asian Social Science*, *11*(10), 386–400. doi:10.5539/ass.v11n10p386

Mancini, G., Biolcati, R., Joseph, D., Trombini, E., & Andrei, F. (2022). Editorial: Emotional intelligence: Current research and future perspectives on mental health and individual differences. *Frontiers in Psychology*, *13*, 1049431. Advance online publication. doi:10.3389/fpsyg.2022.1049431 PMID:36312187

Mandell, B., & Pherwani, S. (2003). Relationship Between Emotional Intelligence and Transformational Leadership Style: A Gender Comparison. *Journal of Business and Psychology*, *17*(3), 387–404. doi:10.1023/A:1022816409059

Mangal, S. K., & Mangal, S. (2013). *Research methodology in behavioural sciences*. PHI Learning Pvt. Ltd.

Manuri, F., & Sanna, A. (2016). A survey on applications of augmented reality. *ACSIJ Advances in Computer Science: An International Journal*, *5*(1), 18–27.

Manzoor, F., Wei, L., Asif, M., Haq, M. Z. U., & Rehman, H. U. (2019). The contribution of sustainable tourism to economic growth and employment in Pakistan. *International Journal of Environmental Research and Public Health*, *16*(19), 3785. doi:10.3390/ijerph16193785 PMID:31597376

Mapuranga, R., Sharon, C., & Manhimanzi, G. (2022). Emotional intelligence as a conduit for effective business leadership in a volatile, uncertain, complex and ambiguous (VUCA) environment. *Journal of Leadership, Governance and Development*, *1*(1&2).

Maqbool, R., Sudong, Y., Manzoor, N., & Rashid, Y. (2017). The impact of emotional intelligence, project managers' competencies, and transformational leadership on project success: An empirical perspective. *Project Management Journal*, *48*(3), 58–75. doi:10.1177/875697281704800304

Marechal, C., Mikolajewski, D., Tyburek, K., Prokopowicz, P., Bougueroua, L., Ancourt, C., & Wegrzyn-Wolska, K. (2019). Survey on AI-Based Multimodal Methods for Emotion Detection. *High-performance modelling and simulation for big data applications, 11400*, 307-324.

Maree, M., Kmail, A. B., & Belkhatir, M. (2019). Analysis and shortcomings of e-recruitment systems: Towards a semantics-based approach addressing knowledge incompleteness and limited domain coverage. *Journal of Information Science*, *45*(6), 713–735. doi:10.1177/0165551518811449

Margherita, A. (2021). Human resources analytics: A systematization of research topics and directions for future research. *Human Resource Management Review*, *32*(2), 100795. doi:10.1016/j.hrmr.2020.100795

Marković, I. P. (2014). *Stock market trend prediction using support vector machines*. Academic Press.

Marksberry, P., Church, J., & Schmidt, M. (2014). The Employee Suggestion System: A New Approach Using Latent Semantic Analysis. *Human Factors and Ergonomics in Manufacturing*, *24*(1), 29–39. doi:10.1002/hfm.20351

Marr, B. (2021). How Is AI Used In Business – 5 Powerful Real-World Examples. *Forbes*. Retrieved from https://www.forbes.com/sites/bernardmarr/2021/01/25/how-is-ai-used-in-business-5-powerful-real-world-examples/?sh=1901b54f44e0

Martínez-Navarro, J., Bigné, E., Guixeres, J., Alcañiz, M., & Torrecilla, C. (2019). The influence of virtual reality in e-commerce. *Journal of Business Research*, *100*, 475–482. doi:10.1016/j.jbusres.2018.10.054

Martin, G. P., McKee, L., & Dixon-Woods, M. (2015). Beyond metrics? Utilizing 'soft intelligence' for healthcare quality and safety. *Social Science & Medicine*, *142*, 19–26. doi:10.1016/j.socscimed.2015.07.027 PMID:26282705

Martins, A., Ramalho, N., & Morin, E. (2010). A comprehensive meta-analysis of the relationship between Emotional Intelligence and health. *Personality and Individual Differences*, *49*(6), 554–564. doi:10.1016/j.paid.2010.05.029

Maruti Techlabs. (2019). *5 Ways ai is transforming the finance industry*. Retrieved from: https://marutitech.com/ways-ai-transforming-finance/

Mason, E. S. (1995). Gender differences in job satisfaction. *The Journal of Social Psychology*, *135*(2), 143–151. doi:10.1080/00224545.1995.9711417 PMID:7776638

Masum, A. K., Beh, L. S., Azad, A. K., & Hoque, K. (2018). Intelligent human resource information system (i-HRIS): A holistic decision support framework for HR excellence. *The International Arab Journal of Information Technology*, *15*(1), 121–130.

Mattingly, V., & Kraiger, K. (2019). Can emotional intelligence be trained? A meta-analytical. *Human Resource Management Review*, *29*(2), 140–155. doi:10.1016/j.hrmr.2018.03.002

Mayer, J. D., Salovey, P., & Caruso, D. R. (2009). *Psychological Inquiry An International Journal for the Advancement of Psychological Theory*. https://doi.org/ doi:10.1207/s15327965pli1503

Mayer, J. D., Caruso, D. R., & Salovey, P. (1999). Emotional intelligence meets traditional standards for an intelligence. *Intelligence*, *27*(4), 267–298. doi:10.1016/S0160-2896(99)00016-1

Mayer, J. D., Caruso, D. R., & Salovey, P. (2016). The ability model of emotional intelligence: Principles and updates. *Emotion Review*, *8*(4), 290–300. doi:10.1177/1754073916639667

Mayer, J. D., Roberts, R. D., & Barsade, S. G. (2008). Human abilities: Emotional intelligence. *Annual Review of Psychology*, *59*(1), 507–536. doi:10.1146/annurev.psych.59.103006.093646 PMID:17937602

Mayer, J. D., & Salovey, P. (1990). Perceiving affective content in ambiguous visual stimuli: A component of emotional intelligence. *Journal of Personality Assessment*, *54*(3), 772–781. doi:10.120715327752jpa5403&4_29 PMID:2348356

Mayer, J. D., Salovey, P., & Caruso, D. R. (2000). Emotional intelligence as zeitgeist, as personality, and as a mental ability. In R. Bar-On & J. D. A. Parker (Eds.), *The handbook of emotional intelligence: Theory, development, assessment, and application at home, school, and in the workplace* (pp. 92–117). Jossey-Bass/Wiley.

Mayer, J. D., Salovey, P., & Caruso, D. R. (2004). Emotional intelligence: Theory, findings, and implications. *Psychological Inquiry*, *1*(3), 197–215. doi:10.120715327965pli1503_02

Mayer, J. D., Salovey, P., & Caruso, D. R. (2008). Emotional Intelligence: New Ability or Eclectic Traits? *The American Psychologist*, *63*(6), 503–517. doi:10.1037/0003-066X.63.6.503 PMID:18793038

McCann, P., & Soete, L. (2020). *Place-based innovation for sustainability*. Publications Office of the European Union.

McCarthy, J. (2007). *What Is Artificial Intelligence Anyway*. Academic Press.

McCrae, R. R., & Costa, P. T. Jr. (2008). The five-factor theory of personality. In O. P. John, R. W. Robins, & L. A. Pervin (Eds.), *Handbook of Personality: Theory and Research*. The Guilford Press.

McKee, A. (2017). How to be happy at work. *Leader to Leader*, *2017*(86), 47–52. doi:10.1002/ltl.20321

McKinsey Global Institute. (2017). *A Future that Works: Automation, Employment, and Productivity*. McKinsey & Company.

McKinsey. (2022). *Five years in review: AI adoption, impact, and spending*. Author.

McLean, G., & Osei-Frimpong, K. (2019). Hey Alexa… examine the variables influencing the use of artificial intelligent in-home voice assistants. *Computers in Human Behavior*, *99*, 28–37. doi:10.1016/j.chb.2019.05.009

Mehndiratta, N., Arora, G., & Bathla, R. (2023, May). The use of Artificial Intelligence in the Banking Industry. In *2023 International Conference on Recent Advances in Electrical, Electronics & Digital Healthcare Technologies (REEDCON)* (pp. 588-591). IEEE. 10.1109/REEDCON57544.2023.10150681

Mehrizi, M. Z. Z. (2014). Evaluation of emotional intelligence and job satisfaction in employees of Kashan Hospitals. *Nursing and Midwifery Studies*, *3*, e11977. PMID:25414889

Mehrotra, A. (2019, April). Artificial intelligence in financial services–need to blend automation with human touch. In *2019 International Conference on Automation, Computational and Technology Management (ICACTM)* (pp. 342-347). IEEE. 10.1109/ICACTM.2019.8776741

Meißner, M., Pfeiffer, J., Pfeiffer, T., & Oppewal, H. (2019). Combining virtual reality and mobile eye tracking to provide a naturalistic experimental environment for shopper research. *Journal of Business Research*, *100*, 445–458. doi:10.1016/j.jbusres.2017.09.028

Mekni & Lemieux. (2014). Augmented reality: Applications, challenges and future trends. *Applied Computational Science, 20*, 205-214.

Mérida-López, S., Extremera, N., Quintana-Orts, C., & Rey, L. (2019). In pursuit of job satisfaction and happiness: Testing the interactive contribution of emotion-regulation ability and workplace social support. *Scandinavian Journal of Psychology*, *60*(1), 59–66. doi:10.1111jop.12483 PMID:30240014

Mérida-López, S., Sánchez-Gómez, M., & Extremera, N. (2020). Leaving the teaching profession: Examining the role of social support, engagement and emotional intelligence in teachers' intentions to quit. *Intervención Psicosocial*, *29*(3), 141–151. doi:10.5093/pi2020a10

Mhlanga, D. (2020). Industry 4.0 in finance: The impact of artificial intelligence (ai) on digital financial inclusion. *International Journal of Financial Studies*, *8*(3), 45. doi:10.3390/ijfs8030045

Miao, C., Humphrey, R. H., & Qian, S. (2016). Leader emotional intelligence and subordinate job satisfaction: A meta-analysis of main, mediator, and moderator effects. *Personality and Individual Differences, 102*, 13–24. doi:10.1016/j.paid.2016.06.056

Miao, C., Humphrey, R. H., & Qian, S. (2017). A meta-analysis of emotional intelligence and work attitudes. *Journal of Occupational and Organizational Psychology, 90*(2), 177–202. doi:10.1111/joop.12167

Miao, C., Humphrey, R. H., & Qian, S. (2018a). Emotional intelligence and authentic leadership: A meta-analysis. *Leadership and Organization Development Journal, 39*(5), 679–690. doi:10.1108/LODJ-02-2018-0066

Miao, C., Humphrey, R. H., & Qian, S. (2018b). A cross-cultural meta-analysis of how leader emotional intelligence influences subordinate task performance and organizational citizenship behavior. *Journal of World Business, 53*(4), 463–474. doi:10.1016/j.jwb.2018.01.003

Mikalef, P., & Gupta, M. (2021). Artificial intelligence capability: Conceptualization, measurement calibration, and empirical study on its impact on organizational creativity and firm performance. *Information & Management, 58*(3), 103434. doi:10.1016/j.im.2021.103434

Mikhalkina, T., & Cabantous, L. (2015). How to identify the types of risks that "really matter"? *Journal of Risk Research, 18*(3), 298–320.

Mikolajczak, M., & Luminet, O. (2008). Trait emotional intelligence and the cognitive appraisal of stressful events: An exploratory study. *Personality and Individual Differences, 44*(7), 1445–1453. doi:10.1016/j.paid.2007.12.012

Mikolajczak, M., Luminet, O., Leroy, C., & Roy, E. (2007). Psychometric properties of the Trait Emotional Intelligence Questionnaire: Factor structure, reliability, construct, and incremental validity in a French-speaking population. *Journal of Personality Assessment, 88*(3), 338–353. doi:10.1080/00223890701333431 PMID:17518555

Miller, A., & Hosanagar, K. (2020). *Personalized discount targeting with causal machine learning*. Academic Press.

Mills, L. B. (2009). A meta-analysis of the relationship between emotional intelligence and effective leadership. *Journal of Curriculum and Instruction, 3*(2), 22–38. doi:10.3776/joci.2009.v3n2p22

Min, H. (2010). Artificial intelligence in supply chain management: theory and applications. *International Journal of Logistics: Research and Applications, 13*(1), 13–39. https://doi.org/http://dx.doi.org/10.1080/13675560902736537

Misra, A., & Bohra, N. S. (2020). Examining enablers of omni-channel banking in developing countries: An Indian perspective. *International Journal of Management, 11*(4).

Mitchell, M. (2019). Artificial Intelligence: A Guide for Thinking Humans. *Picador.*

Mittal, A., & Goel, A. (2012). *Stock prediction using Twitter sentiment analysis*. Stanford University, CS229.

Mizumoto, K., Yanagimoto, H., & Yoshioka, M. (2012). Sentiment Analysis of Stock Market News with Semi-Supervised Learning. In *2012 IEEE/ACIS 11th International Conference on Computer and Information Science (ICIS)* (pp. 325-328). May. 10.1109/ICIS.2012.97

Modassir & Singh. (2008). Relationship of Emotional Intelligence with Transformational Leadership and Organizational Citizenship Behavior. *International Journal of Leadership Studies, 4*(4), 3–21.

Modassir, A., & Singh, T. (2008). *Relationship of emotional intelligence with transformational leadership and organizational citizenship*. Academic Press.

Mohammadyfar, M. A., Khan, M. S., & Tamini, B. K. (2009). The effect of emotional intelligence and job burnout on mental and physical health. *Journal of the Indian Academy of Applied Psychology, 35*(2), 219–226.

Mohammed, I. A. (2021). The interaction between artificial intelligence and identity and access management: An empirical study. *International Journal of Creative Research Thoughts, 2320*(2882), 668–671.

Moon, C., Lee, J., & Lim, S. (2010). A performance appraisal and promotion ranking system based on fuzzy logic: An implementation case in military organizations. *Applied Soft Computing, 10*(2), 512–519. doi:10.1016/j.asoc.2009.08.035

Moradi, M., Khatouni, M., Zeighami, R., Hashemi Global, H., & Sheikhi, M. R. (2013). *The Relationship between Professional Engagement and Job Satisfaction among Nurses in Governmental Hospitals Affiliated to Qazvin University of Medical Sciences*. Academic Press.

Mou, N., Zheng, Y., Makkonen, T., Yang, T., Tang, J. J., & Song, Y. (2020). Tourists' digital footprint: The spatial patterns of tourist flows in Qingdao, China. *Tourism Management, 81*, 104151. doi:10.1016/j.tourman.2020.104151

Mughal, F., Wahid, A., & Khattak, M. A. K. (2022). Artificial Intelligence: Evolution, Benefits, and Challenges. In S. Garg, G. S. Aujla, K. Kaur, & S. Hassan Ahmed Shah (Eds.), *Intelligent Cyber-Physical Systems for Autonomous Transportation* (pp. 59–69). Springer International Publishing. doi:10.1007/978-3-030-92054-8_4

Müller, J. M., Buliga, O., & Voigt, K.-I. (2021). The role of absorptive capacity and innovation strategy in the design of industry 4.0 business Models - A comparison between SMEs and large enterprises. *European Management Journal, 39*(3), 333–343. doi:10.1016/j.emj.2020.01.002

Muradoglu, G., & Harvey, N. (2012). Behavioural finance: The role of psychological factors in financial decisions. *Review of Behavioral Finance, 4*(2), 68–80. doi:10.1108/19405971211284862

Nabi, G., & Khan, S. (2020). Risk of COVID-19 pneumonia in aquatic mammals. *Environmental Research, 188*, 109732. doi:10.1016/j.envres.2020.109732 PMID:32502685

Naik, N., Hameed, B. M. Z., Shetty, D. K., Swain, D., Shah, M., Paul, R., Aggarwal, K., Ibrahim, S., Patil, V., Smriti, K., Shetty, S., Rai, B. P., Chlosta, P., & Somani, B. K. (2022). Legal and Ethical Consideration in Artificial Intelligence in Healthcare: Who Takes Responsibility? *Frontiers in Surgery, 9*(March), 1–6. doi:10.3389/fsurg.2022.862322 PMID:35360424

Nandan, T., & Saurabh, K. (2016). Big-five personality traits, financial risk attitude and investment intentions: Study on Generation Y. *International Journal of Business Forecasting and Marketing Intelligence, 2*(2), 128–150. doi:10.1504/IJBFMI.2016.078154

Narimani, A., Khaleghi, A., Haedar, H., & Semnani, F. (2021). The use of gamification in evaluating children's emotional intelligence. In *Internet of Things, Infrastructures and Mobile Applications: Proceedings of the 13th IMCL Conference 13* (pp. 806-813). Springer International Publishing. 10.1007/978-3-030-49932-7_75

NASSCOM. (2022). *NASSCOM AI Adoption Index 2022*. https://nasscom.in/system/files/publication/nasscom-ai-adoption-index-2022-upload.pdf

Nazareno, L., & Schiff, D. S. (2021). The impact of automation and artificial intelligence on worker well-being. *Technology in Society, 67*(July), 101679. doi:10.1016/j.techsoc.2021.101679

Nelis, D., Kotsou, I., Quoidbach, J., Hansenne, M., Weytens, F., Dupuis, P., & Mikolajczak, M. (2011). Increasing emotional competence improves psychological and physical well-being, social relationships, and employability. *Emotion (Washington, D.C.), 11*(2), 354–366. doi:10.1037/a0021554 PMID:21500904

Neong, S. C., Isa, Z. M., & Abdul Manaf, M. R. B. H. (2022). Emotional Intelligence And Organisational Culture: A Systematic Literature Review. *Journal of Pharmaceutical Negative Results, 13*(5), 1582–1592. doi:10.47750/pnr.2022.13.S05.249

Newell, A., & Simon, H. (1956). The logic theory machine–A complex information processing system. *IEEE Transactions on Information Theory*, *2*(3), 61–79. doi:10.1109/TIT.1956.1056797

Newman, A., Herman, H. M., Schwarz, G., & Nielsen, I. (2018). The effects of employees' creative self-efficacy on innovative behavior: The role of entrepreneurial leadership. *Journal of Business Research*, *89*, 1–9. doi:10.1016/j.jbusres.2018.04.001

Ngah, R., & Salleh, Z. (2015). Emotional intelligence and entrepreneurs' innovativeness towards entrepreneurial success: A preliminary study. *American Journal of Economics*, *5*(2), 285–290.

Nga, J. K., & Ken Yien, L. (2013). The influence of personality trait and demographics on financial decision making among Generation Y. *Young Consumers*, *14*(3), 230–243. doi:10.1108/YC-11-2012-00325

Nightingale, S., Spiby, H., Sheen, K., & Slade, P. (2018). The impact of emotional intelligence in health care professionals on caring behaviour towards patients in clinical and long-term care settings: Findings from an integrative review. *International Journal of Nursing Studies, 80*, 106–117. doi:10.1016/j.ijnurstu.2018.01.006

Nikoloski, K. (2014). The Role of Information Technology in the Business Sector. *International Journal of Scientific Research*, *3*(12), 12. http://www.ijsr.net/v3i12.php#sthash.x82xSS6g.JbQkpxXM.dpbs

Nishant, R., Kennedy, M., & Corbett, J. (2020). Artificial intelligence for sustainability: Challenges, opportunities, and a research agenda. *International Journal of Information Management*, *53*, 102104. doi:10.1016/j.ijinfomgt.2020.102104

Nopp, C., & Hanbury, A. (2015, September). Detecting risks in the banking system by sentiment analysis. In *Proceedings of the 2015 conference on empirical methods in natural language processing* (pp. 591-600). 10.18653/v1/D15-1071

Noreen, U., Shafique, A., Ahmed, Z., & Ashfaq, M. (2023). Banking 4.0: Artificial Intelligence (AI) in Banking Industry & Consumer's Perspective. *Sustainability (Basel)*, *2023*(15), 3682. doi:10.3390u15043682

Northey, G., Hunter, V., Mulcahy, R., Choong, K., & Mehmet, M. (2022). Man vs machine: How artificial intelligence in banking influences consumer belief in financial advice. *International Journal of Bank Marketing*, *40*(6), 1182–1199. doi:10.1108/IJBM-09-2021-0439

Noughabi, E. A., Naseri, M. R. A., Albadvi, A., & Saeedi, M. (2016). Human resource performance evaluation from CRM perspective: A two-step association rule analysis. *International Journal of Business Performance Management*, *17*(1), 89. doi:10.1504/IJBPM.2016.073340

Nouman, H., & Cnaan, R. A. (2021). Toolbox recommendations for social workers to promote successful social entrepreneurship. *Social Work*, *66*(4), 317–328. doi:10.1093wwab037 PMID:34458923

Nurul, H., Redzuan, M., Hamsan, H., & Noor, H. (2017). Emotional intelligence (self-awareness, self-management, social awareness and relationship management) and leadership behavior (transformational and transactional) among school educator leaders. *International Journal of Educational Studies*, *4*(2), 37–47.

O'Donohue, W., & Torugsa, N. A. (2016). The moderating effect of 'Green' HRM on the association between proactive environmental management and financial performance in small firms. *International Journal of Human Resource Management*, *27*(2), 239–261. doi:10.1080/09585192.2015.1063078

Obeidat, S. M., Al Bakri, A. A., & Elbanna, S. (2020). Leveraging "Green" Human Resource Practices to Enable Environmental and Organizational Performance: Evidence from the Qatari Oil and Gas Industry. *Journal of Business Ethics*, *164*(2), 371–388. doi:10.100710551-018-4075-z

Odame, C., Pandey, M., & Pathak, P. (2020). Emotional Intelligence and Its Importance in Sustainable Development of Human Resources: A Conceptual Model. *Sustainable Human Resource Management: Transforming Organizations, Societies and Environment*, 273-287.

OECD. (2006). *OECD Science, Technology and Industry Outlook 2006*. Organisation for Economic Co-operation and Development. https://www.oecd-ilibrary.org/science-and-technology/oecd-science-technology-and-industry-outlook-2006_sti_outlook-2006-en

Oh, H., Yoon, S. Y., & Shyu, C. R. (2008). How can Virtual Reality reshape furniture retailing? *Clothing & Textiles Research Journal*, *26*(2), 143–163. doi:10.1177/0887302X08314789

Oju, O. (2017). Impact of innovation on the entrepreneurial success in selected business enterprises in South-West Nigeria. In *Driving Innovation and Business Success in the Digital Economy* (pp. 16–25). IGI Global. doi:10.4018/978-1-5225-1779-5.ch002

Olsson, T., Kärkkäinen, T., Lagerstam, E., & Ventä-Olkkonen, L. (2012). User evaluation of mobile augmented reality scenarios. *Journal of Ambient Intelligence and Smart Environments*, *4*(1), 29–47. doi:10.3233/AIS-2011-0127

Oncioiu, I. (Ed.). (2013). *Business innovation, development, and advancement in the digital economy*. IGI Global. doi:10.4018/978-1-4666-2934-9

ORACLE (2019). *AI in Human Resouce: The Time is Now*. Retrieved from chrome-extension://bocbaocobfecmglnme-aeppambideimao/pdf/viewer.html?file=https%3A%2F%2Fwww.oracle.com%2Fa%2Focom%2Fdocs%2Fapplications%2Fhcm%2Foracle-ai-in-hr-wp.pdf accessed on 26/07/2023 doi:10.1016/j.tourman.2018.12.008

Orejarena, H., Zambrano, O., & Carvajal, M. (2019). Emotional intelligence and its influence on organizational leadership in the VUCA world. *Proceedings of the 4th International Conference on Social, Business, and Academic Leadership (ICSBAL 2019), 359*, 185–188. 10.2991/icsbal-19.2019.32

Oswald, F. L., Behrend, T. S., Putka, D. J., & Sinar, E. (2020). Big Data in Industrial-Organizational Psychology and Human Resource Management: Forward Progress for Organizational Research and Practice. *Annual Review of Organizational Psychology and Organizational Behavior*, *7*(1), 505–533. doi:10.1146/annurev-orgpsych-032117-104553

Ovans, A. (2015). How emotional intelligence became a key leadership skill. *Harvard Business Review*, *28*, 3–6.

Özdemir, V., & Hekim, N. (2018). Birth of Industry 5.0: Making Sense of Big Data with Artificial Intelligence, "The Internet of Things" and Next-Generation Technology Policy. *OMICS: A Journal of Integrative Biology*, *22*(1), 65–76. doi:10.1089/omi.2017.0194 PMID:29293405

P., A. (2015). KESHAVA- Holistic Employee Selection Framework in the VUCA World. *SCMS Journal of Indian Management, 12*(4), 5–18. https://search.ebscohost.com/login.aspx?direct=true&db=buh&AN=112038228&site=ehost-live

Paillé, P., Chen, Y., Boiral, O., & Jin, J. (2014). The Impact of Human Resource Management on Environmental Performance: An Employee-Level Study. *Journal of Business Ethics*, *121*(3), 451–466. doi:10.100710551-013-1732-0

Pai, P. Y., & Tsai, H. T. (2011). How virtual community participation influences consumer loyalty intentions in online shopping contexts: An investigation of mediating factors. *Behaviour & Information Technology*, *30*(5), 603–615. doi:10.1080/0144929X.2011.553742

Palmer, B., Walls, M., Burgess, Z., & Stough, C. (2001). Emotional intelligence and effective leadership. *Leadership and Organization Development Journal*, *22*(1), 5–10. doi:10.1108/01437730110380174

Panigrahi, S., Sahoo, M., & Jena, L. K. (2021). A review on artificial intelligence and machine learning applications in banking sector. *Journal of Financial Crime*, *28*(2), 299–310.

Pannu, A. (2015). Artificial intelligence and its application in different areas. *Artificial Intelligence*, *4*(10), 79–84.

Pan, Y., Froese, F., Liu, N., Hu, Y., & Ye, M. (2022). The adoption of artificial intelligence in employee recruitment: The influence of contextual factors. *International Journal of Human Resource Management*, *33*(6), 1125–1147. doi:10.1080/09585192.2021.1879206

Papadakis, S., Garefalakis, A., Lemonakis, C., Chimonaki, C., & Zopounidis, C. (Eds.). (2020). *Machine Learning Applications for Accounting Disclosure and Fraud Detection*. IGI Global.

Parameshwari & Krishnan J. (2015). Personality Traits and Risk Profile Influencing Attitude of Investor. *Paripex – Indian Journal of Research*, *4*(5), 86–89.

Parikh, P. (2017). *Value Investing and Behavioral Finance*. McGraw Hill Education.

Park, J., Konana, P., Gu, B., Kumar, A., & Raghunathan, R. (2010). *Confirmation bias, overconfidence, and investment performance: Evidence from stock message boards*. McCombs Research Paper Series No. IROM-07-10.

Park, B., Knörzer, L., Plass, J. L., & Brünken, R. (2015). Emotional design and positive emotions in multimedia learning: An eyetracking study on the use of anthropomorphisms. *Computers & Education*, *86*, 30–42. doi:10.1016/j.compedu.2015.02.016

Park, H., & Kim, S. (2023). Do augmented and virtual reality technologies increase consumers' purchase intentions? The role of cognitive elaboration and shopping goals. *Clothing & Textiles Research Journal*, *41*(2), 91–106. doi:10.1177/0887302X21994287

Park, J. Y., & Dhanabalan, T. (2019). What Makes Customers Repurchase Grocery Products from Online Stores in Korea. *International Journal of E-Business Research*, *15*(4), 24–39. doi:10.4018/IJEBR.2019100102

Paschen, J., Wilson, M., & Ferreira, J. J. (2020). Collaborative intelligence: How human and artificial intelligence create value along the B2B sales funnel. *Business Horizons*, *63*(3), 403–414. doi:10.1016/j.bushor.2020.01.003

Patel, R. (2023). Artificial intelligence: A tool for enhancement of lending facilities in banking institutions. *EPRA International Journal of Multidisciplinary Research*, *9*(3), 214–217.

Pathak, S., & Muralidharan, E. (2020). A two-staged approach to technology entrepreneurship: Differential effects of intellectual property rights. *Technology Innovation Management Review*, *10*(6), 5–13. doi:10.22215/timreview/1364

Pathak, S., & Muralidharan, E. (2020). Implications of culturally implicit perspective of emotional intelligence. *Cross-Cultural Research*, *54*(5), 502–533. doi:10.1177/1069397120938690

Pattnaik, D., Kumar, S., & Vashishtha, A. (2020). Research on trade credit – a systematic review and bibliometric analysis. *Qualitative Research in Financial Markets*, *12*(4), 367–390. doi:10.1108/QRFM-09-2019-0103

Pau, A. K., & Croucher, R. (2003). Emotional intelligence and perceived stress in dental undergraduates. *Journal of Dental Education*, *67*(9), 1023–1028. doi:10.1002/j.0022-0337.2003.67.9.tb03685.x PMID:14518841

Payne, W. L. (1985). *A Study of Emotion: Developing Emotional Intelligence; Self-Integration; Relating to Fear, Pain and Desire*. Union for Experimenting Colleges and Universities. https://www.scirp.org/(S(351jmbntvnsjt1aadkozje))/reference/referencespapers.aspx?referenceid=2979927%0Ahttps://books.google.com.eg/books/about/A_Study_of_Emotion.html?id=9EhKAQAACAAJ&redir_esc=y

Pereira, V., Hadjielias, E., Christofi, M., & Vrontis, D. (2021). Human Resource Management Review A systematic literature review on the impact of artificial intelligence on workplace outcomes : A multi-process perspective. *Human Resource Management Review*, *100857*(July), •••. doi:10.1016/j.hrmr.2021.100857

Pérez-Fuentes, M. D. C., Molero Jurado, M. D. M., Gázquez Linares, J. J., & Oropesa Ruiz, N. F. (2018). The role of emotional intelligence in engagement in nurses. *International Journal of Environmental Research and Public Health, 15*(9), 1915. doi:10.3390/ijerph15091915 PMID:30177621

Pessach, D., Singer, G., Avrahami, D., Chalutz Ben-Gal, H., Shmueli, E., & Ben-Gal, I. (2020). Employees recruitment: A prescriptive analytics approach via machine learning and mathematical programming. *Decision Support Systems, 134*(March), 113290. doi:10.1016/j.dss.2020.113290 PMID:32501316

Peters, M. A. (2017). Technological unemployment: Educating for the fourth industrial revolution. *Educational Philosophy and Theory, 49*(1), 1–6. doi:10.1080/00131857.2016.1177412

Petrides, K. V. (2011). Ability and trait emotional intelligence. In T. Chamorro-Premuzic, S. von Stumm, & A. Furnham (Eds.), *The Wiley-Blackwell handbook of individual differences* (pp. 656–678). Wiley Blackwell. doi:10.1002/9781444343120.ch25

Petrides, K. V., & Furnham, A. (2000). On the dimensional structure of emotional intelligence. *Personality and Individual Differences, 29*(2), 313–320. doi:10.1016/S0191-8869(99)00195-6

Petrides, K. V., & Furnham, A. (2003). Trait emotional intelligence: Behavioural validation in two studies of emotion recognition and reactivity to mood induction. *European Journal of Personality, 17*(1), 39–57. doi:10.1002/per.466

Petrides, K. V., Pérez-González, J. C., & Furnham, A. (2007). On the criterion and incremental validity of trait emotional intelligence. *Cognition and Emotion, 21*(1), 26–55. doi:10.1080/02699930601038912

Petrides, K. V., Pita, R., & Kokkinaki, F. (2007). The location of trait emotional intelligence in personality factor space. *British Journal of Psychology, 98*(2), 273–289. doi:10.1348/000712606X120618 PMID:17456273

Pham, N. T., Chiappetta Jabbour, C. J., Vo-Thanh, T., Huynh, T. L. D., & Santos, C. (2020). Greening hotels: Does motivating hotel employees promote in-role green performance? The role of culture. *Journal of Sustainable Tourism, 31*(4), 951–970. doi:10.1080/09669582.2020.1863972

Pham, N. T., Vo Thanh, T., Tučková, Z., & Thuy, V. T. N. (2020). The role of green human resource management in driving hotel's environmental performance: Interaction and mediation analysis. *International Journal of Hospitality Management, 88*(August), 102392. Advance online publication. doi:10.1016/j.ijhm.2019.102392

Pietikäinen, M., & Silven, O. (2022). *Challenges of Artificial Intelligence-From Machine Learning and Computer Vision to Emotional Intelligence.* arXiv preprint arXiv:2201.01466.

Pillai, R., & Sivathanu, B. (2020). Adoption of artificial intelligence (AI) for talent acquisition in IT/ITeS organizations. *Benchmarking, 27*(9), 2599–2629. doi:10.1108/BIJ-04-2020-0186

Polizzi, C. P., & Lynn, S. J. (2021). Regulating emotionality to manage adversity: A systematic review of the relation between emotion regulation and psychological resilience. *Cognitive Therapy and Research, 45*(4), 1–21. doi:10.100710608-020-10186-1

Pompian, M. M. (2006). *Behavioral Finance and Wealth Management – How to Build Optimal Portfolios That Account for Investor Biases*. John Wiley and Sons Inc. Retrieved from http://library.perbanas.ac.id/images/book/behavioralfinance.pdf

Por, J., Barriball, L., Fitzpatrick, J., & Roberts, J. (2011). Emotional intelligence: Its relationship to stress, coping, well-being and professional performance in nursing students. *Nurse Education Today, 31*(8), 855–860. doi:10.1016/j.nedt.2010.12.023 PMID:21292360

Powell, B. A. (2020). Detecting malicious logins as graph anomalies. *Journal of Information Security and Applications, 54*, 102557. doi:10.1016/j.jisa.2020.102557

Power, B. A. S. (2022). *Intelligent Automation.* Author.

Pradhan, I. P., & Saxena, P. (2023). Reskilling workforce for the Artificial Intelligence age: Challenges and the way forward. In The Adoption and Effect of Artificial Intelligence on Human Resources Management, Part B (pp. 181-197). Emerald Publishing Limited.

Prentice, C., Dominique Lopes, S., & Wang, X. (2020). Emotional Intelligence or artificial Intelligence–an employee perspective. *Journal of Hospitality Marketing & Management*, *29*(4), 377–403. doi:10.1080/19368623.2019.1647124

Prikshat, V., Islam, M., Patel, P., Malik, A., Budhwar, P., & Gupta, S. (2023). Technological Forecasting & Social Change AI-Augmented HRM : Literature review and a proposed multilevel framework for future research. *Technological Forecasting and Social Change*, *193*(May), 122645. doi:10.1016/j.techfore.2023.122645

Priya, G. J., & Saradha, S. (2021). Fraud Detection and Prevention Using Machine Learning Algorithms: A Review. *7th International Conference on Electrical Energy Systems (ICEES),* 564-568. 10.1109/ICEES51510.2021.9383631

Provost, F., & Fawcett, T. (2013). Data science and its relationship to big data and data-driven decision making. *Big Data*, *1*(1), 51–59. doi:10.1089/big.2013.1508 PMID:27447038

Psilopanagioti, A., Anagnostopoulos, F., Mourtou, E., & Niakas, D. (2012). Emotional intelligence, emotional labor, and job satisfaction among physicians in Greece. *BMC Health Services Research*, *12*(1), 1–12. doi:10.1186/1472-6963-12-463 PMID:23244390

PTI. (2017). *Indian robot made in China steals the show at IT event.* IBEF. Retrieved from: https://www.ibef.org/news/indianrobot-made-in-china-steals-the-show-at-it-event

Pulakos, E. D., Arad, S., Donovan, M. A., & Plamondon, K. E. (2000). Adaptability in the workplace: Development of a taxonomy of adaptive performance. *The Journal of Applied Psychology*, *85*(4), 612–624. doi:10.1037/0021-9010.85.4.612 PMID:10948805

Purificato, E., Lorenzo, F., Fallucchi, F., & De Luca, E. W. (2023). The use of responsible artificial intelligence techniques in the context of loan approval processes. *International Journal of Human-Computer Interaction*, *39*(7), 1543–1562. doi:10.1080/10447318.2022.2081284

PwC. (2017). *Artificial Intelligence and Robotics 2017: Leveraging artificial intelligence and robotics for sustainable growth.* Retrieved from:https://www.pwc.in/publications/2017/artifcial-intelligence-and-robotics-2017.html

PwC. (2018). https://www.pwc.com/m1/en/publications/potential-impact-artificial-intelligence-middle-east.html

Qamar, Y., Agrawal, R. K., Samad, T. A., & Jabbour, C. J. C. (2021). When technology meets people: The interplay of artificial intelligence and human resource management. *Journal of Enterprise Information Management*, *34*(5), 1339–1370. doi:10.1108/JEIM-11-2020-0436

Qiu, M., & Song, Y. (2016, May 19). Predicting the Direction of Stock Market Index Movement Using an Optimized Artificial Neural Network Model. *PLoS One*, *11*(5), e0155133. doi:10.1371/journal.pone.0155133 PMID:27196055

Qiu, M., Song, Y., & Akagi, F. (2016, April). Application of artificial neural network for the prediction of stock market returns: The case of the Japanese stock market. *Chaos, Solitons, and Fractals*, *85*, 1–7. doi:10.1016/j.chaos.2016.01.004

Quach, K. C. (2022). Types of artificial intelligence (AI) in marketing management. In Artificial Intelligence for Marketing Management. Routledge.

Quarteroni, S. (2018). Natural Language Processing for Industry. *Informatik Spektrum*, *41*(2), 105–112. doi:10.100700287-018-1094-1

Racine, E., Boehlen, W., & Sample, M. (2019). Healthcare uses of artificial intelligence: Challenges and opportunities for growth. *Healthcare Management Forum, 32*(5), 272–275. doi:10.1177/0840470419843831 PMID:31234654

Radonjić, A., Duarte, H., & Pereira, N. (2022). Artificial intelligence and HRM: HR managers' perspective on decisiveness and challenges. *European Management Journal.* Advance online publication. doi:10.1016/j.emj.2022.07.001

Rafiei, M. (2017). The effect of emotional quotient on organizational citizenship behavior in some Iranian hospitals. *Kybernetes, 46*(7), 1189–1203. doi:10.1108/K-01-2017-0001

Rahman, M., Ming, T. H., Baigh, T. A., & Sarker, M. (2021). Adoption of artificial intelligence in banking services: an empirical analysis. *International Journal of Emerging Markets.*

Rajah, R., Song, Z., & Arvey, R. D. (2011). Emotionality and leadership: Taking stock of the past decade of research. *The Leadership Quarterly, 22*(6), 1107–1119. doi:10.1016/j.leaqua.2011.09.006

Rajamohan, S., & Dhanabalan, T. (2014). Beneficiaries" opinion towards the mahatma Gandhi national rural employment guarantee scheme. *International Journal of Retailing & Rural Business Perspectives, 3*(4), 1256.

Ramalingam, H., & Venkatesan, V. P. (2019, October). Conceptual analysis of Internet of Things use cases in Banking domain. In TENCON 2019-2019 IEEE Region 10 Conference (TENCON) (pp. 2034-2039). IEEE. doi:10.1109/TENCON.2019.8929473

Rampersad, G. (2020). Robot will take your job: Innovation for an era of artificial intelligence. *Journal of Business Research, 116*, 68–74. doi:10.1016/j.jbusres.2020.05.019

Rana, S., Mahavidyalaya, K., Rathore, D., & Chadha, N. K. (2017). Emotional intelligence in the workplace. *Indian Journal of Positive Psychology, 8*(2), 162–165.

Ravi, V., & Kamaruddin, S. (2017). Big data analytics enabled smart financial services: opportunities and challenges. *Big Data Analytics: 5th International Conference, BDA 2017, Hyderabad, India, December 12-15, 2017 Proceedings, 5*, 15–39.

Rayson, P., Garside, R., & Sawyer, P. (2000). Assisting requirements engineering with semantic document analysis. In *Content-based multimedia information access RIAO 2000 (Recherche d'Informations Assistie par Ordinateur, Computer-Assisted Information Retrieval) International Conference* (pp. 1363-1371). Academic Press.

Reddin, W. J. (1970). *Managerial Effectiveness.* McGraw-Hill.

Rehman Khan, S. A., Ahmad, Z., Sheikh, A. A., & Yu, Z. (2022). Digital transformation, smart technologies, and eco-innovation are paving the way toward sustainable supply chain performance. *Science Progress, 105*(4). Advance online publication. doi:10.1177/00368504221145648 PMID:36573795

Renwick, D. W., Redman, T., & Maguire, S. (2013). Green human resource management: A review and research agenda. *International Journal of Management Reviews, 15*(1), 1–14. doi:10.1111/j.1468-2370.2011.00328.x

Richter, Y., Naveh, Y., Gresh, D. L., & Connors, D. P. (2008). Optimatch : Applying constraint programming to workforce management of highly skilled employees. *Int. J. Services Operations and Informatics, 3*(3/4), 258–270. doi:10.1504/IJSOI.2008.021338

Riederer, J. P., Baier, M., & Graefe, G. (2005). Innovation management–An overview and some best practices. *C-Lab Report, 4*(3), 1-58.

Riggio, E. R., Murphy, S., & Pirozzolo, F. (2002). Multiple Intelligences and Leadership. Lawrence Erlbaum Associates. doi:10.4324/9781410606495-8

Rinfret, N., Laplante, J., Lagacé, M. C., Deschamps, C., & Privé, C. (2020). Impacts of leadership styles in health and social services: A case from Quebec exploring relationships between emotional intelligence and transformational leadership. *International Journal of Healthcare Management, 13*(1), 329–339. doi:10.1080/20479700.2018.1548153

Ritter, J. (2003). Behavioral finance. *Pacific-Basin Finance Journal, 11*(4), 429–437. doi:10.1016/S0927-538X(03)00048-9

Robbins, S. P., & Coulter, M. (2005). *Management* (8th ed.). Pearson.

Robins, R. W., & Pals, J. L. (2002). Implicit self-theories in the academic domain: Implications for goal orientation, attributions, affect, and self-esteem change. *Self and Identity, 1*(4), 313–336. doi:10.1080/15298860290106805

Rockstuhl, T., Seiler, S., Ang, S., Van Dyne, L., & Annen, H. (2011). Beyond general intelligence (IQ) and emotional intelligence (EQ): The role of cultural intelligence (CQ) on cross-border leadership effectiveness in a globalized world. *The Journal of Social Issues, 67*(4), 825–840. doi:10.1111/j.1540-4560.2011.01730.x

Rodgers, W., Murray, J. M., Stefanidis, A., Degbey, W. Y., & Tarba, S. Y. (2022). An artificial intelligence algorithmic approach to ethical decision-making in human resource management processes. *Human Resource Management Review.* Advance online publication. doi:10.1016/j.hrmr.2022.100925

Rodriguez, A., & Rodriguez, Y. (2015). Metaphors for today's leadership: VUCA world, millennial and "Cloud Leaders.". *Journal of Management Development, 34*(7), 854–866. doi:10.1108/JMD-09-2013-0110

Rodríguez, D., Busco, C., & Flores, R. (2015). Information technology within society's evolution. *Technology in Society, 40*, 64–72. doi:10.1016/j.techsoc.2014.08.006

Ronaghi, M., Hossein, M., & Ronaghi, M. (2022). A contextualized study of the usage of the augmented reality technology in the tourism industry. *Decision Analytics Journal, 5.* doi:10.1016/j.dajour.2022.100136

Rozell, E. J., Pettijohn, C. E., & Parker, R. S. (2004). Customer-oriented selling: Exploring the roles of emotional intelligence and organizational commitment. *Psychology and Marketing, 21*(6), 405–424. doi:10.1002/mar.20011

Ruiz-Aranda, D., Extremera, N., & Pineda-Galan, C. (2014). Emotional intelligence, life satisfaction and subjective happiness in female student health professionals: The mediating effect of perceived stress. *Journal of Psychiatric and Mental Health Nursing, 21*(2), 106–113. doi:10.1111/jpm.12052 PMID:23578272

Ruiz-Aranda, D., Salguero, J. M., Cabello, R., Palomera, R., & -Berrocal, P. F. (2012). Can an Emotional Intelligence Program Improve Adolescents' Psychosocial Adjustment? Results from the Intemo Project. *Social Behavior and Personality, 40*(8), 1373–1379. doi:10.2224bp.2012.40.8.1373

Russell, S. J., & Norvig, P. (2010). *Artificial Intelligence A Modern Approach.* Pearson Education Inc. https://pubs.aip.org/ajp/article/56/1/18/1053122/E-mc2

Russell, S. (2019). *Human compatible: Artificial Intelligence and the problem of control.* Penguin.

Russell, S. J., & Norvig, P. (2010). *Artificial intelligence: A modern approach* (3rd ed.). Prentice Hall.

Russell, S. J., & Norvig, P. (2016). *Artificial Intelligence: A modern approach.* Pearson Education Limited.

Russo-Netzer, P., & Shoshani, A. (2019). Becoming teacher leaders in Israel: A meaning-making model. *Cambridge Journal of Education, 49*(3), 369–389. doi:10.1080/0305764X.2018.1533524

Rydzik, A., & Kissoon, C. S. (2022). Decent work and tourism workers in the age of intelligent automation and digital surveillance. *Journal of Sustainable Tourism, 30*(12), 2860–2877. doi:10.1080/09669582.2021.1928680

Ryff, C. D. (1989). Happiness is everything, or is it? Explorations on the meaning of psychological well-being. *Journal of Personality and Social Psychology*, *57*(6), 1069–1081. doi:10.1037/0022-3514.57.6.1069

Sabri, M. F., Wijekoon, R., & Rahim, H. A. (2020). The influence of money attitude, financial practices, self-efficacy and emotion coping on employees' financial well-being. *Management Science Letters*, *10*(4), 889–900. doi:10.5267/j.msl.2019.10.007

Sadiq, M. N., & Khan, R. A. A. (2019). Impact of personality traits on investment intention: The mediating role of risk behaviour and the moderating role of financial literacy. *Journal of Finance and Economics Research*, *4*(1), 1–18. doi:10.20547/jfer1904101

Sadok, H., Sakka, F., & El Maknouzi, M. E. H. (2022). Artificial intelligence and bank creditanalysis: A review. *Cogent Economics & Finance*, *10*(1), 2023262. doi:10.1080/23322039.2021.2023262

Safadel, P., & White, D. (2019). Facilitating molecular biology teaching by using Augmented Reality (AR) and Protein Data Bank (PDB). *TechTrends*, *63*(2), 188–193. doi:10.100711528-018-0343-0

Saha, S., Das, R., Lim, W. M., Kumar, S., Malik, A., & Chillakuri, B. (2023). Emotional intelligence and leadership: Insights for leading by feeling in the future of work. *International Journal of Manpower*, *44*(4), 671–701. doi:10.1108/IJM-12-2021-0690

Salanova, M., Agut, S., & Peiró, J. M. (2005). Linking organizational resources and work engagement to employee performance and customer loyalty: The mediation of service climate. *The Journal of Applied Psychology*, *90*(6), 1217–1227. doi:10.1037/0021-9010.90.6.1217 PMID:16316275

Salguero, J. M., Palomera, R., & Fernández-Berrocal, P. (2012). Perceived emotional intelligence as predictor of psychological adjustment in adolescents: A 1-year prospective study. *European Journal of Psychology of Education*, *27*(1), 21–34. doi:10.100710212-011-0063-8

Salminen-Tuomaala, M. H. (2020). Developing emotional intelligence and situational awareness through simulation coaching. *Clinical Nursing Studies*, *8*(2), 13. doi:10.5430/cns.v8n2p13

Salovey, P., & Grewal, D. (2005). The science of emotional intelligence. *Current Directions in Psychological Science*, *14*(6), 281–285. doi:10.1111/j.0963-7214.2005.00381.x

Salovey, P., & Mayer, J. (1989). Emotional Intelligence. *Imagination, Cognition and Personality*, *9*(3), 185–211. doi:10.2190/DUGG-P24E-52WK-6CDG

Samadi, A., & Keyvan, N. (2013). A study on emotional intelligence of teachers in establishing the effective communication. *Governmental Management*, *1*, 129–148.

Sanchez-Álvarez, N., Extremera, N., & Fernández-Berrocal, P. (2016). The relation between emotional intelligence and subjective well-being: A meta-analytic investigation. *The Journal of Positive Psychology*, *11*(3), 276–285. doi:10.1080/17439760.2015.1058968

Sánchez-López, M. T., Fernández-Berrocal, P., Gómez-Leal, R., & Megías-Robles, A. (2022). Emotional Intelligence and Risk Behaviour: A Risk Domain-Dependent Relationship. *Psicothema*, *34*(3), 402–409. doi:10.7334/psicothema2021.527 PMID:35861002

Sánchez-Núñez, M. T., Patti, J., & Holzer, A. (2015). Effectiveness of a Leadership Development Program that Incorporates Social and Emotional Intelligence for Aspiring School Leaders. *Journal of Educational Issues*, *1*(1), 65. doi:10.5296/jei.v1i1.7443

Sarin, A. B. (2019). *Behavioral Factors affecting Investment Decisions and Performance: An Empirical Study of Investors in Delhi*. Ph.D., Lingayas Vidhyapeeth.

Sarin, A. B. (2021). Emotional Bias in Investment Decision Making. In M. Cristofaro (Ed.), *Emotion, Cognition, and Their Marvellous Interplay in Managerial Decision-Making. Cambridge Scholars Publishing.*

Sarin, A. B. (2023). Behavioral Finance and Cryptocurrency Market. In K. Mehta, R. Sharma, & P. Yu (Eds.), *Revolutionizing Financial Services and Markets Through FinTech and Blockchain* (pp. 217–236). IGI Global. doi:10.4018/978-1-6684-8624-5.ch014

Sarin, A. B., & Chowdhury, J. K. (2018). Understanding behavioral biases influencing investment decisions: An exploratory study. *International Research Journal of Management and Commerce*, *1*, 584–596.

Sarkar. (2017). *Robotic process automation in insurance industry*. Nalashaa. Retrieved from: https://www.nalashaa.com/robotic-processautomation-insurance-industry/

Sarwar, D., Sarwar, B., Raz, M. A., Khan, H. H., Muhammad, N., Azhar, U., & Kasi, M. K. (2020). Relationship of the big five personality traits and risk aversion with investment intention of individual investors. *The Journal of Asian Finance. Economics and Business*, *7*(12), 819–829.

Schiff, D., Ayesh, A., Musikanski, L., & Havens, J. C. (2020). IEEE 7010: A New Standard for Assessing the Well-being Implications of Artificial Intelligence. *Conference Proceedings - IEEE International Conference on Systems, Man and Cybernetics*, 2746–2753. 10.1109/SMC42975.2020.9283454

Schutte Nicola, S., & John, M. (2001). Emotional Intelligence and Interpersonal Relations. *The Journal of Social Psychology*, *141*(4), 523–536. doi:10.1080/00224540109600569 PMID:11577850

Schutte, N. S., & Loi, N. M. (2014). Connections between emotional intelligence and workplace flourishing. *Personality and Individual Differences*, *66*, 134–139. doi:10.1016/j.paid.2014.03.031

Schutte, N. S., & Malouff, J. M. (2011). Emotional intelligence mediates the relationship between mindfulness and subjective well-being. *Personality and Individual Differences*, *50*(7), 1116–1119. doi:10.1016/j.paid.2011.01.037

Schutte, N. S., Malouff, J. M., Thorsteinsson, E. B., Bhullar, N., & Rooke, S. E. (2007). A meta-analytic investigation of the relationship between emotional intelligence and health. *Personality and Individual Differences*, *42*(6), 921–933. doi:10.1016/j.paid.2006.09.003

Schutte, N. S., Schuettpelz, E., & Malouff, J. M. (2001). Emotional intelligence and task performance. *Imagination, Cognition and Personality*, *20*(4), 347–354. doi:10.2190/J0X6-BHTG-KPV6-2UXX

SchwantesM. (2020). Retrieved from https://www.inc.com/marcel-schwantes/research-says-you-can-earn-way-more-money-by-boosting-your-emotional-intelligence-here-are-4-ways-to-do-it.html

Segal, J. (2002). Good leaders use" emotional intelligence". Emotionally intelligent leadership is a skill that can be learned and taught throughout life. *Health Progress (Saint Louis, Mo.)*, *83*(3), 44–46. PMID:12038009

Seltzer, J., & Bass, B. M. (1990). Transformational leadership: Beyond initiation and consideration. *Journal of Management*, *16*(4), 693–703. doi:10.1177/014920639001600403

Serrat, O (2017). Understanding and developing emotional intelligence. *Knowledge solutions: Tools, methods, and approaches to drive organizational performance*, 329-339.

Sethi, N., & Paliwal, M. S. Moblie Banking Security. *International Journal of Engineering Research & Technology, 4*(9).

Sewell, M. (2007). *Behavioural finance*. London: University College London.

Sexton, R. S., McMurtrey, S., Michalopoulos, J. O., & Smith, A. M. (2005). Employee turnover: A neural network solution. *Computers & Operations Research*, *32*(10), 2635–2651. doi:10.1016/j.cor.2004.06.022

Seymour, M., Yuan, L., Dennis, A., & Riemer, K. (2020). *Facing the artificial: Understanding affinity, trustworthiness, and preference for more realistic digital humans*. Academic Press.

Shahhosseini, V., & Sebt, M. H. (2011). Competency-based selection and assignment of human resources to construction projects. *Scientia Iranica*, *18*(2), 163–180. doi:10.1016/j.scient.2011.03.026

Shah, S. Z. A., Ahmad, M., & Mahmood, F. (2018). Heuristic biases in investment decision-making and perceived market efficiency: A survey at the Pakistan stock exchange. *Qualitative Research in Financial Markets*, *10*(1), 85–110. doi:10.1108/QRFM-04-2017-0033

Shambira, L. (2020). Exploring the adoption of artificial intelligence in the Zimbabwe banking sector. *European Journal of Social Sciences Studies*, *5*(6). Advance online publication. doi:10.46827/ejsss.v5i6.942

Sharma, D., Chaudhary, M., Jaswal, N., & Bhardwaj, B. (2022). Hiding Behind The SWOT: Gender Equality and COVID-19. *Journal of Positive School Psychology*, 730–740.

Sheng, Q. Z., Zeadally, S., & Kumar, S. (2018). Edge computing in the big data era: From the Internet of Things to genuine intelligence. *IEEE Communications Magazine*, *56*(2), 21–27.

Shenkar, O. (1990). Managing in a Robotic Age. *Human Systems Management*, *9*(2), 107–114. doi:10.3233/HSM-1990-9206

Sheth, J. N., Jain, V., Roy, G., & Chakraborty, A. (2022). AI-driven banking services: The next frontier for a personalised experience in the emerging market. *International Journal of Bank Marketing*, *40*(6), 1248–1271. doi:10.1108/IJBM-09-2021-0449

Shih, H.-A., & Susanto, E. (2010). Conflict management styles, emotional intelligence, and job performance in public organizations. *International Journal of Conflict Management*, *21*(2), 147–168. doi:10.1108/10444061011037387

Shi, Y., Prentice, C., & He, W. (2014). Linking service quality, customer satisfaction and loyalty in casinos, does membership matter? *International Journal of Hospitality Management*, *40*, 81–91. doi:10.1016/j.ijhm.2014.03.013

Shojaei, M., & Siuki, M. (2014). A study of relationship between emotional intelligence and innovative work behavior of managers. *Management Science Letters*, *4*(7), 1449–1454. doi:10.5267/j.msl.2014.6.021

Shooshtarian, Z., Ameli, F., & Amini Lari, M. (2013). The effect of labor's emotional intelligence on their job satisfaction, job performance and commitment. *Iranian Journal of management studies, 6*(1), 27-43. Golparvar, M., & Nadi, M. (2010). Cultural values and overall fairness. *Journal of Iranian Cultural Research*, *3*(1), 207–228.

Shorey, H. S., & Chaffin, J. S. (2018). Leader – Follower Attachment : Implications for Personality Assessment in Organizational Contexts Leader – Follower Attachment : Implications for Personality Assessment. *Journal of Personality Assessment*, *100*(5), 1–11. doi:10.1080/00223891.2018.1472100 PMID:29897260

Shujahat, M., Sousa, M. J., Hussain, S., Nawaz, F., Wang, M., & Umer, M. (2019). Translating the impact of knowledge management processes into knowledge-based innovation: The neglected and mediating role of knowledge-worker productivity. *Journal of Business Research*, *94*, 442–450. doi:10.1016/j.jbusres.2017.11.001

Shukla, R., & Nagar, D. (2013). Impact of gender and managerial levels on emotional intelligence and job performance of Indian revenue service officers. *Indian Journal of Health and Wellbeing, 4*(1), 83.

Siadati, H., & Memon, N. (2017, October). Detecting structurally anomalous logins within enterprise networks. In *Proceedings of the 2017 ACM SIGSAC Conference on Computer and Communications Security* (pp. 1273-1284). 10.1145/3133956.3134003

Simoes, M., Elmusrati, M., Vartiainen, T., Mekkanen, M., Karimi, M., Diaba, S., . . . Lopes, W. (2023). *Enhancing data security against cyberattacks in artificial intelligence based smartgrid systems with crypto agility.* arXiv preprint arXiv:2305.11652.

Singh, S. K., Giudice, M. Del, Chierici, R., & Graziano, D. (2020). Green innovation and environmental performance: The role of green transformational leadership and green human resource management. *Technological Forecasting and Social Change, 150*, 119762. https://doi.org/ doi:10.1016/j.techfore.2019.119762

Singh, G., Garg, V., & Tiwari, P. (2019). Application of Artificial Intelligence on Behavioral Finance. *International Conference on Information Technology and Applied Mathematics.*

Singh, N., Tang, Y., Zhang, Z., & Zheng, C. (2020). COVID-19 waste management: Effective and successful measures in Wuhan, China. *Resources, Conservation and Recycling, 163*, 105071. doi:10.1016/j.resconrec.2020.105071 PMID:32834489

Singh, S. K., Pradhan, R. K., Panigrahy, N. P., & Jena, L. K. (2019). Self-efficacy and workplace well-being: Moderating role of sustainability practices. *Benchmarking, 26*(6), 1692–1708. doi:10.1108/BIJ-07-2018-0219

Singh, T. (2016). Relating emotional intelligence and organisational commitment though moderated mediation of psychological well being and work life balance: A study on teachers of NGOs. *Rupkatha Journal on Interdisciplinary Studies in Humanities, 8*(2), 28–42. doi:10.21659/rupkatha.v8n2.04

Singh, T., & Pathak, N. (2020). Emerging role of artificial intelligence in Indian banking sector. *Journal of Critical Reviews, 7*(16), 1370–1373.

Singh, V., Chen, S. S., Singhania, M., Nanavati, B., Kar, A. K., & Gupta, A. (2022). How are reinforcement learning and deep learning algorithms used for big data based decision making in financial industries–A review and research agenda. *International Journal of Information Management Data Insights, 2*(2), 100094. doi:10.1016/j.jjimei.2022.100094

Sivarajah, U., Kamal, M. M., Irani, Z., & Weerakkody, V. (2017). Critical analysis of Big Data challenges and analytical methods. *Journal of Business Research, 70*, 263–286. doi:10.1016/j.jbusres.2016.08.001

Slaski, M., & Cartwright, S. (2003). Emotional intelligence training and its implications for stress, health and performance. *Stress and Health, 19*(4), 233–239. doi:10.1002mi.979

Smith, R., Killgore, W. D., Alkozei, A., & Lane, R. D. (2018). A neuro-cognitive process model of emotional intelligence. *Biological Psychology, 139*, 131–151. doi:10.1016/j.biopsycho.2018.10.012 PMID:30392827

Sniezek, J. A., Wilkins, D. C., Wadlington, P. L., & Baumann, M. R. (2002). Training for crisis decision-making: Psychological issues and computer-based solutions. *Journal of Management Information Systems, 18*(4), 147–168. doi:10.1080/07421222.2002.11045704

Soh, C., & Connolly, D. (2021). New Frontiers of Profit and Risk: The Fourth Industrial Revolution's Impact on Business and Human Rights. *New Political Economy, 26*(1), 168–185. doi:10.1080/13563467.2020.1723514

Sokmen, Y., & Sarikaya, İ. (2022). The mediating role of self-efficacy between emotional intelligence and job satisfaction of primary school teachers. *European Review of Applied Psychology, 72*(4), 100779. doi:10.1016/j.erap.2022.100779

Solymossy, E. (1997). Push/pull motivation: Does it matter in venture performance. *Frontiers of Entrepreneurship Research, 17*(5), 204-217.

Somani, B., Tyagi, G., Mukul, M., Gaurav, M., & Preetham, A. (2022). Automation in Onboarding of Customer in Banking. *International Journal of Research in Engineering and Science, 10*(6), 1424-1428.

Soni, V. D. (2019). Role of artificial intelligence in combating cyber threats in banking. *International Engineering Journal For Research & Development*, *4*(1), 7–7.

Sosik, J. J., & Megerian, L. E. (1999). Understanding Leader Emotional Intelligence and Performance: The Role of Self-Other Agreement on Transformational Leadership Perceptions. *Group & Organization Management*, *24*(3), 367–390. doi:10.1177/1059601199243006

Spearman, C. (1927). *The abilities of man*. Macmillan.

Spence, G., Oades, L. G., & Caputi, P. (2004). Trait emotional intelligence and goal self-integration: Important predictors of emotional well-being? *Personality and Individual Differences*, *37*(3), 449–461. doi:10.1016/j.paid.2003.09.001

Spiegel, M., & Tookes, H. (2022). All or nothing? Partial business shutdowns and COVID-19 fatality growth. *PLoS One*, *17*(2), e0262925. doi:10.1371/journal.pone.0262925 PMID:35139100

Stars, D. (2019). *6 examples of ai in financial services*. Retrieved from: https://djangostars.com/blog/6-examples-ai-financial-services/

Stein, S. J., Papadogiannis, P., Yip, J. A., & Sitarenios, G. (2009). Emotional intelligence of leaders: A profile of top executives. *Leadership and Organization Development Journal*, *30*(1), 87–101. doi:10.1108/01437730910927115

Sternberg, R. J., & Zhang, L.-f. (Eds.). (2001). *Perspectives on thinking, learning, and cognitive styles*. Lawrence Erlbaum Associates Publishers.

Stratton, E., Lampit, A., Choi, I., Calvo, R. A., Harvey, S. B., & Glozier, N. (2017). Effectiveness of eHealth interventions for reducing mental health conditions in employees: A systematic review and meta-analysis. *PLoS One*, *12*(12), 1–23. doi:10.1371/journal.pone.0189904 PMID:29267334

Strohmeier, S., & Piazza, F. (2015). Artificial Intelligence Techniques in Human Resource Management — A Conceptual Exploration. *Intelligent Techniques in Engineering Management: Theory and Applications*, 149–172. doi:10.1007/978-3-319-17906-3_7

Strohmeier, S., & Piazza, F. (2013). Domain driven data mining in human resource management: A review of current research. *Expert Systems with Applications*, *40*(7), 2410–2420. doi:10.1016/j.eswa.2012.10.059

Stroumpoulis, A., Kopanaki, E., & Varelas, S. (2022). Role of artificial intelligence and big data analytics in smart tourism: A resource-based view approach. *WIT Transactions on Ecology and the Environment*, *256*, 99–108. doi:10.2495/ST220091

Subrahmanyam, A. (2008). Behavioural finance: A review and synthesis. *European Financial Management*, *14*(1), 12–29.

Suhel, S. F., Shukla, V. K., Vyas, S., & Mishra, V. P. (2020, June). Conversation to automation in banking through chatbot using artificial machine intelligence language. In *2020 8th international conference on reliability, infocom technologies and optimization (trends and future directions)(ICRITO)* (pp. 611-618). IEEE. 10.1109/ICRITO48877.2020.9197825

Suh, K. S., & Lee, Y. E. (2005). The effects of virtual reality on consumer learning: An empirical investigation. *Management Information Systems Quarterly*, *29*(4), 673–697. doi:10.2307/25148705

Sun, T. Q., & Medaglia, R. (2019). Mapping the challenges of artificial intelligence in the public sector:Evidence from public healthcare. *Government Information Quarterly*, *36*(2), 368–383. doi:10.1016/j.giq.2018.09.008

Swapna, M. (2018). *Ethics of Using Artificial Intelligence in Financial Banking Industry.* Available at https://medium.com/datadriveninvestor/ethics-of-using-ai-in-thefinancial-banking-industry-fa93203f6f25

Sy, T., Tram, S., & O'Hara, L. A. (2006). Relation of employee and manager emotional intelligence to job satisfaction and performance. *Journal of Vocational Behavior, 68*(3), 461–473. doi:10.1016/j.jvb.2005.10.003

Szczygieł, D., & Mikolajczak, M. (2017). Why are people high in emotional intelligence happier? They make the most of their positive emotions. *Personality and Individual Differences, 117*, 177–181. doi:10.1016/j.paid.2017.05.051

Tambe, P., Cappelli, P., & Yakubovich, V. (2019). Artificial intelligence in human resources management: Challenges and A path forward. *California Management Review, 61*(4), 15–42. doi:10.1177/0008125619867910

Tan, C. Y. (2018). Examining school leadership effects on student achievement: The role of contextual challenges and constraints. *Cambridge Journal of Education, 48*(1), 21–45. doi:10.1080/0305764X.2016.1221885

Tanphan, I., Pongsamran, S., Saounpong, R., Visitnitikija, C., Yeesoontes, W., & Mahamud, T. (2022). Lessons from Entrepreneurs Covid-19 Affecting in Resource Work in Business Digital Approach. *Journal of Positive School Psychology*, 6182–6191.

Tarafdar, M., Tu, Q., & Ragu-Nathan, T. S. (2010). Impact of Technostress on End-User Satisfaction and Performance. *Journal of Management Information Systems, 27*(3), 303–334.

Tawira, L., & Ivanov, A. (2023). Leveraging personalization and customization affordances of virtual try-on apps for a new model in apparel m-shopping. *Asia Pacific Journal of Marketing and Logistics, 35*(2), 451–471. doi:10.1108/APJML-09-2021-0652

Tayarani, N. M. H. (2021). Applications of artificial intelligence in battling against covid-19: A literature review. *Chaos, Solitons, and Fractals, 142*, 110338. doi:10.1016/j.chaos.2020.110338 PMID:33041533

Taylor, C., Harrison, J., Haimovitz, K., Oberle, E., Thomson, K., Schonert-Reichl, K., & Roeser, R. W. (2016). Examining ways that a mindfulness-based intervention reduces stress in public school teachers: A mixed-methods study. *Mindfulness, 7*(1), 115–129. doi:10.100712671-015-0425-4

Taywade. (2023, July 29). *AI-powered VR: How machine learning is enhancing the virtual reality experience*. https://community.nasscom.in/

Teece, D. J. (2018). Dynamic capabilities as (workable) management systems theory. *Journal of Management & Organization, 24*(3), 359–368. doi:10.1017/jmo.2017.75

Thakur, D. J., Verma, P., & Sharma, D. (2019). Influence of leadership style: A review. *International Journal of Advanced Science and Technology, 28*(20), 945–952.

Thakur, D. J., Verma, P., & Sharma, D. (2019). Influence of Leadership Style: A Review. *International Journal of Advanced Science and Technology, 28*(20), 945–952.

Thakur, D. J., Verma, P., & Sharma, D. (2019). Influence of Leadership Style: A Review. International. *Journal of Advanced Science and Technology, 28*(20), 945–952.

Thaler, R. (2005). Advances in Behavioral Finance II. Princeton University Press.

The CFM Surveys. (2023). *Artificial Intelligence and the Economy*. https://cfmsurvey.org/surveys/artificial-intelligence-and-economy

Thirumalesh Madanaguli, A., Kaur, P., Bresciani, S., & Dhir, A. (2021). Entrepreneurship in rural hospitality and tourism. A systematic literature review of past achievements and future promises. *International Journal of Contemporary Hospitality Management, 33*(8), 2521–2558. doi:10.1108/IJCHM-09-2020-1121

Thowfeek, M. H., Samsudeen, S. N., & Sanjeetha, M. B. F. (2020). Drivers of artificial intelligence in banking service sectors. *Solid State Technology*, *63*(5), 6400–6411.

Tischler, L., Biberman, J., & McKeage, R. (2002). Linking emotional intelligence, spirituality and workplace performance: Definitions, models and ideas for research. *Journal of Managerial Psychology*, *17*(3), 203–218. doi:10.1108/02683940210423114

Todd, P., & Benbasat, I. (1991). An experimental investigation of the impact of computer based decision aids on decision making strategies. *Information Systems Research*, *2*(2), 87–115. doi:10.1287/isre.2.2.87

Topal, İ., & Uçar, M. K. (2018, September). In tourism, using artificial intelligence forecasting with Tripadvisor data: Year of Turkey in China. In *2018 International Conference on Artificial Intelligence and Data Processing (IDAP)* (pp. 1-5). IEEE.

Townsend, A. M., DeMarie, S. M., & Hendrickson, A. R. (1998). Virtual teams: Technology and the workplace of the future. *The Academy of Management Perspectives*, *12*(3), 17–29. doi:10.5465/ame.1998.1109047

Tripathy, A., Agrawal, A., & Rath, S. K. (2014, December). Requirement analysis using natural language processing. In *Fifth International Conference on Advances in Computer Engineering* (*Vol. 26*, p. 27). Academic Press.

Tripathy, N. T. (n.d.). *Stock price prediction using support vector machine approach*. Academic Press.

Trujillo-Gallego, M., Sarache, W., & de Sousa Jabbour, A. B. L. (2022). Digital technologies and green human resource management: Capabilities for GSCM adoption and enhanced performance. *International Journal of Production Economics*, *249*, 108531. doi:10.1016/j.ijpe.2022.108531

Tuo, Y., Ning, L., & Zhu, A. (2021). How artificial intelligence will change the future of tourism industry: The practice in China. *Proceeding of the ENTER 2021 eTourism Conference,* 83–94. 10.1007/978-3-030-65785-7_7

Turing, A. M. (1950). Computing machinery and intelligence. *Mind*, *59*(236), 433–460. doi:10.1093/mind/LIX.236.433

Tussyadiah, I., & Miller, G. (2019). Nudged by a robot: Responses to agency and feedback. *Annals of Tourism Research*, *78*, 102752. doi:10.1016/j.annals.2019.102752

Tyson, L. D., & Zysman, J. (2022). Automation, AI & Work. *Daedalus*, *151*(2), 256–271. doi:10.1162/daed_a_01914

Umamaheswari, S., & Valarmathi, A. (2023). Role of Artificial Intelligence in The Banking Sector. *Journal of Survey in Fisheries Sciences*, *10*(4S), 2841–2849.

Umbrico, A., Cesta, A., Cortellessa, G., & Orlandini, A. (2020). A holistic approach to behavior adaptation for socially assistive robots. *International Journal of Social Robotics*, *12*(3), 617–637. doi:10.100712369-019-00617-9

UNCTAD. (Ed.). (2017). *Digitalization, trade and development*. United Nations.

UNIDO. (2010). *A Greener Footprint for Industry: opportunities and challenges of sustainable industrial development.* Accessed from https://www.greenpolicyplatform.org/research/greener-footprint-industry-opportunities-and-challenges-sustainable-industrial-development

Upadhyay, A. K., & Khandelwal, K. (2018, October 8). Applying arti fi cial intelligence : Implications for recruitment. *Strategic HR Review*, *17*(5), 255–258. Advance online publication. doi:10.1108/SHR-07-2018-0051

Utami, A. M., & Septivani, M. D. (2022). Regulatory Technology (RegTech): The Solution to Prevent Money Laundering in Indonesia. *Telaah Bisnis*, *23*(1), 86–98. doi:10.35917/tb.v23i1.288

Vaidya, R. W., Prasad, K., & Mangipudi, M. R. (2020). Mental and emotional competencies of leader's dealing with disruptive business environment - A conceptual review. *International Journal of Management, 11*(5), 366–375. doi:10.34218/IJM.11.5.2020.036

Valodkienė, G., & Snieška, V. (2012). Tarptautinis konkurencingumas ir jį lemiantys veiksniai ekonomikos nuosmukio laikotarpiu. *Economics and Management, 17*(2), 602-608.

Van Dijk, J. A. (2006). Digital divide research, achievements and shortcomings. *Poetics, 34*(4-5), 221-235.

Van Eck, N., & Waltman, L. (2010). Software survey: VOSviewer, a computer program for bibliometric mapping. *Scientometrics, 84*(2), 523-538.

Van Rooy, D. L., & Viswesvaran, C. (2004). Emotion intelligence: A meta-analytic investigation of predictive validity and nomological net. *Journal of Vocational Behavior, 65*(1), 71–95. doi:10.1016/S0001-8791(03)00076-9

Vardiman, P. D., Houghton, J. D., & Jinkerson, D. L. (2006). Environmental leadership development: Toward a contextual model of leader selection and effectiveness. *Leadership and Organization Development Journal, 27*(2), 93–105. doi:10.1108/01437730610646606

Varma, A., Dawkins, C., & Chaudhuri, K. (2023). Artificial intelligence and people management: A critical assessment through the ethical lens. *Human Resource Management Review, 33*(1), 100923. doi:10.1016/j.hrmr.2022.100923

Varsha, P. S. (2023). How can we manage biases in artificial intelligence systems – A systematic literature review. *International Journal of Information Management Data Insights, 3*(1). Advance online publication. doi:10.1016/j.jjimei.2023.100165

Varsha, P. S. (2023). How can we manage biases in artificial intelligence systems–A systematic literature review. *International Journal of Information Management Data Insights, 3*(1), 100165.

Varshney, D., & Varshney, N. K. (2020). Workforce agility and its links to emotional intelligence and workforce performance : A study of small entrepreneurial firms in India. *Global Business and Organizational Excellence, 39*(5), 1–11. doi:10.1002/joe.22012

Vasudevan, H. (2013). The influence of emotional intelligence and creativity on employee's work commitment and performance. *International Journal of Management and Business Research, 3*(3), 233–255.

Vega, A., Cabello, R., Megías-Robles, A., Gómez-Leal, R., & Fernández-Berrocal, P. (2022). Emotional Intelligence and Aggressive Behaviors in Adolescents: A Systematic Review and Meta-Analysis. *Trauma, Violence & Abuse, 23*(4), 1173–1183. doi:10.1177/1524838021991296 PMID:33568015

Velay, M., & Daniel, F. (2018). *Stock chart pattern recognition with deep learning*. Academic Press.

Vidhya, A. (2023). *How to Use AI and ML Tools for HR Management in 2023?* Retrieved from https://www.analyticsvidhya.com/blog/2023/03/ai-and-ml-tools-for-hr/

Vidyarthi, P. R., Anand, S., & Liden, R. C. (2014). Do emotionally perceptive leaders motivate higher employee performance? The moderating role of task interdependence and power distance. *The Leadership Quarterly, 25*(2), 232–244. doi:10.1016/j.leaqua.2013.08.003

Vieira, A., & Sehgal, A. (2017). How banks can better serve their customers through artificial techniques. In *Digital marketplaces unleashed* (pp. 311–326). Springer Berlin Heidelberg.

Vijai, C. (2019). Artificial intelligence in Indian banking sector: challenges and opportunities. *International Journal of Advanced Research, 7*, 1581-1587. . doi:10.21474/IJAR01/8987

Villanueva, L., Prado-Gascó, V., & Montoya-Castilla, I. (2022). Longitudinal analysis of subjective well-being in pre-adolescents: The role of emotional intelligence, self-esteem and perceived stress. *Journal of Health Psychology*, *27*(2), 278–291. doi:10.1177/1359105320951605 PMID:32830558

Villar, A. S., & Khan, N. (2021). Robotic process automation in banking industry: A case study on Deutsche Bank. *Journal of Banking and Financial Technology*, *5*(1), 71–86. doi:10.100742786-021-00030-9

Villasenor, J. (2019). *Artificial intelligence and bias: Four key challenges*. Academic Press.

Vlahakis, V., Ioannidis, M., Karigiannis, J., Tsotros, M., Gounaris, M., Stricker, D., Gleue, T., Daehne, P., & Almeida, L. (2002). Archeoguide: An augmented reality guide for archaeological sites. *IEEE Computer Graphics and Applications*, *22*(5), 52–60. doi:10.1109/MCG.2002.1028726

Von Krogh, G. (2018). Artificial Intelligence in Organizations: New Opportunities for Phenomenon-Based Theorizing. *Academy of Management Discoveries*, *4*(4), 404–409. doi:10.5465/amd.2018.0084

Von Solms, J. (2021). Integrating Regulatory Technology (RegTech) into the digital transformation of a bank Treasury. *Journal of Banking Regulation*, *22*(2), 152–168. doi:10.105741261-020-00134-0

Votto, A., & Liu, C. Z. (2023). *Transparent Artificial Intelligence and Human Resource Management: A Systematic Literature Review*. Academic Press.

Votto, A. M., Valecha, R., Najafirad, P., & Rao, H. R. (2021). Artificial Intelligence in Tactical Human Resource Management: A Systematic Literature Review. *International Journal of Information Management Data Insights*, *1*(2), 100047. doi:10.1016/j.jjimei.2021.100047

Vrontis, D., Christofi, M., Pereira, V., Tarba, S., Makrides, A., & Trichina, E. (2022). Artificial intelligence, robotics, advanced technologies and human resource management: A systematic review. *International Journal of Human Resource Management*, *33*(6), 1237–1266. doi:10.1080/09585192.2020.1871398

Wach, D., Stephan, U., & Gorgievski, M. (2016). More than money: Developing an integrative multi-factorial measure of entrepreneurial success. *International Small Business Journal*, *34*(8), 1098–1121. doi:10.1177/0266242615608469

Wagner, M. (2013). "Green" Human Resource Benefits: Do they Matter as Determinants of Environmental Management System Implementation? *Journal of Business Ethics*, *114*(3), 443–456. doi:10.100710551-012-1356-9

Walker, E. A., & Webster, B. J. (2007). Gender, age and self-employment: Some things change, some stay the same. *Women in Management Review*, *22*(2), 122–135. doi:10.1108/09649420710732088

Walmsley, A., Partington, S., Armstrong, R., & Goodwin, H. (2019). Reactions to the national living wage in hospitality. *Employee Relations*, *41*(1), 253–268. doi:10.1108/ER-02-2018-0044

Walsh, W. B., & Betz, N. E. (1995). *Tests and assessment* (3rd ed.). Prentice-Hall, Inc.

Walter, O., Shenaar-Golan, V., & Routray, S. (2021). Cross-Cultural Comparison of How Mind-Body Practice Affects Emotional Intelligence, Cognitive Well-Being, and Mental Well-Being. *Frontiers in Psychology*, *12*(July), 1–8. doi:10.3389/fpsyg.2021.588597 PMID:34335347

Wang, D., Zhang, Z., Zhang, L., & Li, P. (2021). Data intelligence for decision support in business: A bibliometric analysis and research agenda. *Information Processing & Management*, *58*(2), 102408.

Wang, J., Li, C., Han, S., Sarkar, S., & Zhou, X. (2017). Predictive maintenance based on event-log analysis: A case study. *IBM Journal of Research and Development*, *61*(1), 11–121. doi:10.1147/JRD.2017.2648298

Wang, L., Owens, B. P., Li, J. J., & Shi, L. (2018). Exploring the affective impact, boundary conditions, and antecedents of leader humility. *The Journal of Applied Psychology*, *103*(9), 1019–1038. doi:10.1037/apl0000314 PMID:29781636

Wang, L., Wang, W., & Zhou, L. (2020). Artificial intelligence in business intelligence: A bibliometric analysis. *Information Systems Frontiers*, *22*(2), 389–404.

Wang, X., & Dong, B. (2022). Emotional Intelligence and Knowledge Hiding Behaviors: The Mediating Role of Job Stress. *Frontiers in Psychology*, *13*(May), 845782. Advance online publication. doi:10.3389/fpsyg.2022.845782 PMID:35645869

Watkins, D., Earnhardt, M., Pittenger, L., Roberts, R., Rietsema, K., & Cosman-Ross, J. (2017). Thriving in complexity: A framework for leadership education. *Journal of Leadership Education*, *16*(14), 148–163. doi:10.12806/V16/I4/T4

Webb, T. L., Miles, E., & Sheeran, P. (2012). Dealing with feeling: A meta-analysis of the effectiveness of strategies derived from the process model of emotion regulation. *Psychological Bulletin*, *138*(4), 775–808. doi:10.1037/a0027600 PMID:22582737

Wechsler, D. (1943). Non-intellective factors in general intelligence. *Journal of Abnormal and Social Psychology*, *38*(1), 101–103. doi:10.1037/h0060613

Wehrmeyer, W. (Ed.). (2017). *Greening people: Human resources and environmental management*. Routledge. doi:10.4324/9781351283045

Weiss, R. P. (2000). Promoting Emotional Intelligence in Organizations: Making Training in Emotional Intelligence Effective. *Training & Development, 54*(8), 67. link.gale.com/apps/doc/A64705693/AONE?u=anon~4491e680&sid=googleScholar&xid=83fe5508

Werdayani, D., & Widiaty, I. (2021). Virtual fitting room technology in fashion design. *IOP Conference Series. Materials Science and Engineering*, *1098*(2), 022110. doi:10.1088/1757-899X/1098/2/022110

Whitmore, A., Agarwal, A., & Da Xu, L. (2015). The Internet of Things—A survey of topics and trends. *Information Systems Frontiers*, *17*(2), 261–274. doi:10.100710796-014-9489-2

Winick, E. (2020, April 2). *Every Study We Could Find on What Automation Will Do to Jobs, in One Chart*. MIT Technology Review. www.technologyreview.com/2018/01/25/146020/every-study-we-could-find-on-what-automation-will-do-to-jobs-in-one-chart/

Wolff, S. B., Pescosolido, A. T., & Druskat, V. U. (2002). Emotional intelligence as the basis of leadership emergence in self-managing teams. *The Leadership Quarterly*, *13*(5), 505–522. doi:10.1016/S1048-9843(02)00141-8

Wong, C. S., & Law, K. S. (2017). The effects of leader and follower emotional intelligence on performance and attitude: An exploratory study. In Leadership Perspectives (Vol. 13). doi:10.4324/9781315250601-10

Wong, C. S., Foo, M. D., Wang, C. W., & Wong, P. M. (2007). The feasibility of training and development of EI: An exploratory study in Singapore, Hong Kong and Taiwan. *Intelligence*, *35*(2), 141–150. doi:10.1016/j.intell.2006.04.008

Wong, C. S., & Law, K. S. (2002). The effects of leader and follower emotional intelligence on performance and attitude: An exploratory study. *The Leadership Quarterly*, *13*(3), 243–274. doi:10.1016/S1048-9843(02)00099-1

Wong, C.-S., & Law, K. S. (2002). *Wong and Law Emotional Intelligence Scale (WLEIS)* [Database record]. APA PsycTests.

World Economic Forum. (2023). *Future of Jobs Report, 2023* [Insight Report]. https://www3.weforum.org/docs/WEF_Future_of_Jobs_2023.pdf

World Travel and Tourism Council. (2022). *Travel and Tourism Economic Impact 2022, Global Trends*. WTTC.

Xiang, Z. (2020). Tourism in the era of artificial intelligence. *J Tour*, *35*(1), 1–3.

Xiao, J. J., Ahn, S. Y., Serido, J., & Shim, S. (2014). Earlier financial literacy and later financial behaviour of college students. *International Journal of Consumer Studies*, *38*(6), 593–601. doi:10.1111/ijcs.12122

Xie, H., Zhang, Y., Wu, Z., & Lv, T. (2020). A bibliometric analysis on land degradation: Current status, development, and future directions. *Land (Basel)*, *9*(1), 28. doi:10.3390/land9010028

Xingzhou, L., Hong, R., & Yujun, Z. (2019, July). Predictive modeling of stock indexes using machine learning and information theory. In *Proceedings of the 2019 10th International Conference on E-business, Management and Economics* (pp. 175-179). 10.1145/3345035.3345087

Xu, M., David, J. M., & Kim, S. H. (2018). The Fourth Industrial Revolution: Opportunities and Challenges. *International Journal of Financial Research*, *9*(2), 90. doi:10.5430/ijfr.v9n2p90

Xu, S., Stienmetz, J., & Ashton, M. (2020). How will service robots redefine leadership in hotel management? A Delphi approach. *International Journal of Contemporary Hospitality Management*, *32*(6), 2217–2237. doi:10.1108/IJCHM-05-2019-0505

Xu, X., Chen, X., Jia, F., Brown, S., Gong, Y., & Xu, Y. (2018). Supply chain finance: A systematic literature review and bibliometric analysis. *International Journal of Production Economics*, *204*, 160–173. doi:10.1016/j.ijpe.2018.08.003

Xu, X., Pang, W., & Xia, M. (2021). Are emotionally intelligent people happier? A meta-analysis of the relationship between emotional intelligence and subjective well-being using Chinese samples. *Asian Journal of Social Psychology*, *24*(4), 477–498. doi:10.1111/ajsp.12445

Yadav, A., & Vishwakarma, D. K. (2020). Sentiment analysis using deep learning architectures: A review. *Artificial Intelligence Review*, *53*(6), 4335–4385. doi:10.100710462-019-09794-5

Yammarino, F. J., Spangler, W. D., & Bass, B. M. (1993). Transformational leadership and performance: A longitudinal investigation. *The Leadership Quarterly*, *4*(1), 81–102. doi:10.1016/1048-9843(93)90005-E

Yang, Y., Liu, K., & Guo, H. (2020). Ethical considerations of artificial intelligence in banking. *Journal of Financial Services Marketing*, *25*(2), 61–71.

Yao, S., Wang, X., Yu, H., & Guchait, P. (2019). Effectiveness of error management training in the hospitality industry: Impact on perceived fairness and service recovery performance. *International Journal of Hospitality Management*, *79*, 78–88. doi:10.1016/j.ijhm.2018.12.009

Yarmohammadi Monfared, S., Hemmati NezhadTouli, M., & Ramazani, R. (2010). The relationship between emotional intelligence and job satisfaction in physical education teachers. *Sport Management Journal*, *2*(6), 47–111.

Yeğin, T. (2020). The place and future of artificial intelligence in marketing strategies. *Ekev Akademi Dergisi*, (81), 489–506.

Yitshaki-Hagai, R., & Rothstein, M. (2011). Does entrepreneurs' emotional intelligence impact performance? The mediating role of managerial style and social capital (interactive paper). *Frontiers of Entrepreneurship Research*, *30*(4), 15.

Yong, J. Y., Yusliza, M. Y., Ramayah, T., Chiappetta Jabbour, C. J., Sehnem, S., & Mani, V. (2020). Pathways towards sustainability in manufacturing organizations: Empirical evidence on the role of green human resource management. *Business Strategy and the Environment*, *29*(1), 212–228. doi:10.1002/bse.2359

Yu, C. S., Sardessai, R. M., Lu, J., & Zhao, J. H. (2006). Relationship of emotional intelligence with conflict management styles: An empirical study in China. *International Journal of Management and Enterprise Development, 3*(1–2), 19–29. doi:10.1504/IJMED.2006.008240

Yukl, G. A. (2002). *Leadership in Organizations* (5th ed.). Prentice Hall.

Yung, R., & Khoo-Lattimore, C. (2019). New realities: A systematic literature review on virtual reality and augmented reality in tourism research. *Current Issues in Tourism, 22*(17), 2056–2081. doi:10.1080/13683500.2017.1417359

Yu, W., Chavez, R., Feng, M., Wong, C. Y., & Fynes, B. (2020). Green human resource management and environmental cooperation: An ability-motivation-opportunity and contingency perspective. *International Journal of Production Economics, 219*, 224–235. doi:10.1016/j.ijpe.2019.06.013

Zainurin, M. Z. L., Haji Masri, M., Besar, M. H. A., & Anshari, M. (2023). Towards an understanding of metaverse banking: A conceptual paper. *Journal of Financial Reporting and Accounting, 21*(1), 178–190. doi:10.1108/JFRA-12-2021-0487

Zapata, A. (2015). The Emotional Stability and Emotional Maturity of Fourth Year Teacher Education Students of the Bulacan State University. *Journal of Social Sciences & Humanities Research., 1*(2), 1–5.

Zeidner, M., Matthews, G., & Roberts, R. D. (2004). Emotional Intelligence in the Workplace: A Critical Review. *Applied Psychology, 53*(3), 371–399. doi:10.1111/j.1464-0597.2004.00176.x

Zeidner, M., Matthews, G., & Roberts, R. D. (2012). The emotional intelligence, health, and well-being nexus: What have we learned and what have we missed? *Applied Psychology. Health and Well-Being, 4*(1), 1–30. doi:10.1111/j.1758-0854.2011.01062.x PMID:26286968

Zhang, D., & Deng, J. (2011). The Data Mining of the Human Resources Data Warehouse in University Based on Association Rule. *Journal of Computers, 6*(1), 139–146. doi:10.4304/jcp.6.1.139-146

Zhang, J., Cui, S., Xu, Y., Li, Q., & Li, T. (2018). A novel data-driven stock price trend prediction system. *Expert Systems with Applications, 97*, 60–69. doi:10.1016/j.eswa.2017.12.026

Zhang, L., Cao, T., & Wang, Y. (2018). The mediation role of leadership styles in integrated project collaboration: An emotional intelligence perspective. *International Journal of Project Management, 36*(2), 317–330. doi:10.1016/j.ijproman.2017.08.014

Zhang, M. J., Law, K. S., & Wang, L. (2021). The risks and benefits of initiating change at work: Social consequences for proactive employees who take charge. *Personnel Psychology, 74*(4), 721–750. doi:10.1111/peps.12423

Zhang, X., & Bartol, K. M. (2010). Linking empowering leadership and employee creativity: The influence of psychological empowerment, intrinsic motivation, and creative process engagement. *Academy of Management Journal, 53*(1), 107–128. doi:10.5465/amj.2010.48037118

Zhang, Y., & Liu, Q. (2021). Customer Relationship Management in the Banking Industry: A Literature Review and Future Directions. *International Journal of Financial Research, 12*(4), 188–199.

Zhang, Y., & Trubey, P. (2019). Machine learning and sampling scheme: An empirical study of money laundering detection. *Computational Economics, 54*(3), 1043–1063. doi:10.100710614-018-9864-z

Zheng, N., Liu, Z., Ren, P., Ma, Y., Chen, S., Yu, S., Xue, J., Chen, B., & Wang, F. (2017). Hybrid-augmented intelligence: Collaboration and cognition. *Frontiers of Information Technology and Electronic Engineering, 18*(2), 153–179. doi:10.1631/FITEE.1700053

Zhou, N., Zhang, Z., Nair, V. N., Singhal, H., Chen, J., & Sudjianto, A. (2021). *Bias, Fairness, and Accountability with AI and ML Algorithms.* arXiv preprint arXiv:2105.06558.

Zhou, H., & Bojica, A. M. (2017). The role of emotional intelligence in entrepreneurs' perceptions of success: An exploratory study. *International Review of Entrepreneurship, 15*(3), 341–360.

ZhouH.EstradaI.BojicaA. (n.d.). The role of emotional intelligence on entrepreneurs' perception of success. doi:10.2139/ssrn.2436333

Zhou, J., & George, J. M. (2003). Awakening employee creativity: The role of leader emotional intelligence. *The Leadership Quarterly, 14*(4-5), 545–568. doi:10.1016/S1048-9843(03)00051-1

Zhou, N., Zhang, Z., Nair, V. N., Singhal, H., & Chen, J. (2022). Bias, fairness and accountability with artificial intelligence and machine learning algorithms. *International Statistical Review, 90*(3), 468–480. doi:10.1111/insr.12492

Zimmerer, T. W., Scarborough, N. M., & Wilson, D. (2007). *Essentials of entrepreneurship and small business management* (5th ed.). Pearson Prentice Hall.

Zohar, D., & Marshall, I. (2000). *Spiritual Intelligence: The Ultimate Intelligence*. Bloomsburry.

Zvobgo, V., Abraham, R., & Sabharwal, M. (2022). Faking Versus Feeling Emotions: Does Personality–Job Fit Make a Difference. *Public Personnel Management, 51*(1), 125–148. doi:10.1177/00910260211034213

About the Contributors

Bhawana Bhardwaj is a faculty member at the School of Commerce and Management Studies, at Central University of Himachal Pradesh, India. She has 18 Years of postgraduate teaching and research experience. Throughout her education, she has been recognised for her merit and has received merit scholarships. She has contributed to the academic field as a dedicated academician and prolific writer by raising numerous social and organizational issues. She has over 35 research papers and book chapters published in prestigious refereed national and international journals with worldwide publishers such as Elsevier, Emerald, and others. She has presented papers as well as acted as a resource person in more than 34 National and International conferences. She has also attended and organized numerous faculty development programs and workshops. As a resource person, she has been immensely appreciated by the organisers for her pedagogy and content. She has been conferred with "The Young Researcher Award" and National Budding Researcher Award and the "Education Excellence Award in Human Resource Management." Currently, she is working on Book projects related to Contemporary issues such as AI, Emotional Intelligence and Conflict Management. Her research interest includes AI, GHRM, Skilled Migration and Organizational Ambidexterity.

Dipanker Sharma is a faculty at Central University of Himachal Pradesh in the School of Commerce and Management Studies. He has total work experience of eighteen years and his area of interests are Human Resource Management and Organisational Behaviour. With an illustrious industrial experience of over a decade as a Corporate Trainer with many renowned MNCs, his contribution to academia is unparalleled. Dr. Sharma's academic career has been extraordinary. He has three patents in his name and has published more than two dozens of research articles in nationally and internationally acclaimed journals. He has presented research papers in more than 30 national and international conferences and he has received National and International awards for his work. He has done short assignments in Asian countries like Hong Kong, Dubai, Bhutan, and Singapore and has taken up many research projects on women empowerment and related issues. His area of research includes migration studies, Brain Circulation of Human Capital, Leadership, Work-life Balance, Workforce Diversity and Knowledge Management.

Mohinder Chand Dhiman is currently Professor, School of Tourism, Travel and Hospitality Management, Central University of Himachal Pradesh. Dharamshala, H.P., India. He joined CUHP on 1-11-2022 after serving 29 years in the Department of Tourism and Hotel Management, Kurukshetra University, Kurukshetra, India. Dr. Mohinder's teaching interests have been in Travel Agency Management, Research Methodology, HRM in Hospitality and Tourism, Business Management, Hospitality Finance & Accounting, and Hospitality Strategic Management. As a part of his research program, Dr Mohinder has guided

20 PhD students and 8 M.Phil. students, Dr. Mohinder has published more than 108 research papers in Tourism and Hospitality journals and other management Journals & books of international repute Dr. Mohinder has authored/ co-authors / co-edited 12 books such as International Tourism and Hospitality in Digital Age (2015) IGI-publication USA, Opportunities and Challenges for Tourism and Hospitality in The BRIC Nations (2016) IGI-publication USA, and International Travel Agency and Tour Operation Management (2019)- IGI- Global publication USA. Presently, he is editor of International Journal of Hospitality and Tourism Systems (Scopus Indexed). Dr. Mohinder is also serving as Editorial Board member of various international and national journals. He is Vice –President, Indian Tourism and Hospitality Congress (ITHC) and also General Secretary of Indian Hospitality Congress (IHC).

* * *

Yashpal Azad is working as an Assistant Professor in the department of Psychology, Akal College of Arts and Social Science, Eternal University, Baru Sahib, District- Sirmaur, Himachal Pradesh, India. He formerly has worked with ICFAI National College-Shimla, IIPS (Indigrow Institute of Professional Studies-Shimla), EBEL (Everonn Business Education Ltd- Shimla), Bahra University-Waknaghat, Shimla Hill having 11 years of teaching (UG and PG), and research experience along with 3 years of corporate experience in business development and resource person for various organizations. His area of research interest is organizational behavior, Cognitive development, School Psychology, Subjective well-being, Academic performance, Prolonged deprivation, Stress, Anxiety, Depression, Spirituality, Life span development, Indigenous Psychology, PCT, Fuzzy Cognitive mapping, Management task, SWT, Industrial and Organizational Psychology. He has published research papers and book chapters in national and international journals and books.

Asheetu Bhatia Sarin is an Assistant Professor (Management) at Vivekananda Institute of Professional Studies affiliated to GGSIPU, Delhi. She is having around 9+ years of teaching experience in the field of Commerce and Management. She has done Ph.D. in Behavioral Finance, did her post-graduation (MBA) from ICFAI Business School in Finance and Marketing, and earned her graduate degree in B.Com (H) from Delhi University. She is a lifetime member of the Indian Commerce Association and has to her credit many national and International publications.

Rachna Bhopal is an engineering graduate with post-graduation from NMIMS Mumbai. Currently she is a research scholar in HPKVBS, department of Management at Central University of Himachal Pradesh availing the ICSSR Doctoral Fellowship. Prior to joining as research scholar, she has worked as software engineer in Infosys.

Puneet Bhushan is presently working as an Assistant Professor at Himachal Pradesh University Business School, Shimla. He is a Ph.D. in management. He has more than 15 Years of academic and research experience. Prior to joining HP University, he served as a faculty member in Jaypee University of Information Technology, Waknaghat. He is also actively engaged in guiding Ph. D. research scholars and teaching various PG & Ph. D. level courses. He has published more than 30 papers in reputed journals and attended more than a dozen conferences in India and abroad. He has a good working knowledge of SPSS and been a resource person in many workshops relating to the analysis of data through SPSS. Besides this, he has attended more than 30 Seminars/Webinars, workshops, refresher courses, Short Term

Courses, Faculty Development Programmes. He is also actively engaged in delivering expert lectures in different business management institutions of India. He has completed two major research projects and one minor research project.

Ankita Chaudhary is an MBA from the Central University of Himachal Pradesh, India. Her area of specialization is HRM.

Meena Chaudhary is a research scholar at HPKVBS, Central University of Himachal Pradesh, India. Her area of interest is knowledge management and contemporary issues in HRM.

Vinay Chauhan is a Professor and Director of the Business School in the University of Jammu, India. He has done MTM, Ph.D., and SCHE from Switzerland. His area of Research include Research Methodology, Strategic management, and Marketing.

Rita Devi currently working as Assistant Professor at HPKV Business School, Central University of Himachal Pradesh. Her area of Specialization is HRM and OB. She has 7 Years of teaching and research experience. She has been meritorious throughout her studies and was awarded JRF for pursuing her Ph.D. degree. She has published various research papers in peer reviewed/UGC listed journals. She has participated in different national and international conferences. She has also attended numerous faculty development programs along with workshops. Her research interest area is leadership, organization development, cross-cultural management and emotional intelligence and entrepreneurship.

Saloni Devi is an Assistant Professor at Business School, University of Jammu. Her area of research includes Organizational Behaviour and Human Resource Management.

Rozy Dhanta is Associate Professor Economics is a Belt & Road Fellow in International Relations at the Institute of South Asian Studies, Sichuan University, China. Dr. Dhanta has a Ph.D. in Economics from Shoolini University, India, with her thesis titled "Crop Diversification in Western-Himalayan State of Himachal Pradesh, India." She has also completed her Master of Arts (Economics) and Bachelor of Arts (Economics) from Himachal Pradesh University, India.

Yashwant Kumar Gupta is a senior professor of Accounts and Finance in HPUBS, he also remained as a director of HPUBS and dean of Faculty of Commerce and Management at HPU. He has guided more than 10 PHD scholars and has various publications to his credit. He has attended more than 2 dozen conferences in India as well as abroad.

Nidhi Jaswal is a research scholar at HPKVBS, Central University of Himachal Pradesh, India. Her area of interest is Work-family conflict and contemporary issues in HRM.

Reejo Joseph has eleven years of teaching experience in various government colleges under Collegiate Education Department, Government of Kerala. He has authored one book on Competitive Geography and co-authored one book on Tribal Affairs. He has published a number of articles in edited books and reputed journals on Sustainable tourism. He specializes in the area of Tourism Geography and Environment Geography.

Tanveer Kajla is an engineering graduate with doctorate in Tourism Analytics, presently working in NALSAR University of Law, Hyderabad, India. He worked as Assistant Professor with Lovely Professional university. Prior to that he also worked as Research Associate under ICSSR-IMPRESS Major Project at Punjabi University, Patiala (IN). He has published and presented papers in globally acclaimed conferences and Journals. He has been instrumental delivering expert talks on subjects like Business Analytics, Big Data Analytics, Microsoft Excel, R and Hadoop in academic institutions. His area of research includes Social Network Analysis, Sentiment Analysis, Twitter and Facebook analysis, Text Classification.

Anil Kumar Kashyap is an associate professor at HPKV Business School of Central University of Himachal Pradesh. Before joining the Central University of Himachal Pradesh, he was Assistant Professor at Dr. Harisingh Gour Vishwavidyala (Central University) Sagar. He has been an assistant professor at the National Institute of Fashion Technology and an academic associate at the Indian Institute of Management, Ahmedabad. He has specialisation in marketing more specifically retail marketing, global marketing, consumer behaviour and social media marketing. He holds a degree of Ph.D. And MBA in Marketing from The University of Lucknow. He did his graduation from Rohilkhand University Bareilly with foreign trade and economics. He has hold various administrative responsibilities including placement coordinator, assistant proctor and warden Boys Hostel. He has been the coordinator for various certificate and diploma programmes including social and digital media marketing, retail management, fashion design and international business and export management. On research front he has published more than 15 research articles in Scopus and web of Science, and UGC care indexed journals. He is working as a mentor for startups and consulted various marketing problems for Tihar Prison and Kamuna Agro Pvt ltd. He has conducted ministry of Rural Development sponsored project to evaluate Sansad Adarsh Gram Yojana and currently working in ICSSR sponsored project. He has attended national and international conferences and delivered talk and lectures in various institutions across the country. He loves to serve society and is a member of Rotary International.

Kapil Kathuria is a Professor at Dr. Y.S.P. University of Horticulture and Forestry, India. His Area of Specialization is marketing and contemporary issues in management. He comes with a unique blend of industry and academic experience. In His 20 years in academics, he has worked in the area of marketing, consumer behaviour and strategic management.

Anupriya Kaur is Professor in the Department of Humanities and Social Sciences at Jaypee University of Information Technology, Waknaghat, India. Her research interests include service marketing, customer relationship management, and consumer behavior.

Mayura Kemkar is an Assistant Professor at Govt. Engineering College of Indore and is an alumnus of IMI Delhi. Prior to this, she did her B.E from Pune. She has more than 10 years of experience and specializes in the area of Indian Knowledge system, Compensation Management and women entrepreneurship. She has conducted several workshops and conferences in Women's entrepreneurship and actively works in this area. She did her Ph.D. from Devi Ahilya University, Indore and has several research papers of repute under her name.

Amit Kumar is an Assistant Professor at Akal College of Economics, Commerce and Management, Eternal University, Baru Sahib and currently pursuing Ph.D. from Jaypee University of Information Technology, Waknaghat, His research interests include the areas of service marketing, customer relationship management, and consumer behavior.

Devesh Kumar is working as an Associate Professor in the School of Commerce and Management Studies, Central University of Himachal Pradesh, Dharamshala, India. He has completed his PhD in Information Systems. He has more than 23 years of experience in academics and industry. He has published several research papers in cloud computing, innovation diffusion, e-learning and information systems. He has also presented papers at many conferences in India and abroad. His teaching interests include business analytics, predictive modelling, machine learning and information systems.

Pyare Lal is working as Assistant Professor, in the Department of Economics at Rajiv Gandhi Government Degree College, Chaura Maidan, Shimla – 4 affiliated to Himachal Pradesh University, Shimla – 5. He is having more than 20 years of teaching and research experience in the area of economics. He has done Ph.D. in Economics from Himachal Pradesh University, Shimla – 5 in the subject of Economics. He has edited one book, published 9 research articles in various journals of national and international repute and 6 chapters in various books on economics. He has presented research papers in 16 national and internal seminars/conferences.

Mohit Lohani is an Associate Professor in the area of Marketing at Lal Bahadur Shastri Institute of Management, Delhi (LBSIM). He has 14 years of corporate experience in Marketing, Retail, IT & Ecommerce. He completed his BE in Chemical Technology from Delhi College of Engineering (Delhi University), PGDM from IIM Lucknow and PhD from Devi Ahilya University, Indore in Service Quality of E-commerce in India. He has 3 conference paper presentations to his credit in e-commerce and has conducted sessions in MDP programs in Digital Marketing at IIM Rohtak in 2021-22.

Vaniki Joshi Lohani is an Assistant Professor at Management School in JNU and has more than 10 years of experience. Prior joining to JNU she worked as an Assistant Director at AICET and handled several key positions. She has also taught at IIM Indore and DAV University of Indore. Prior to coming into academics, she was a business analyst at Nomura Securities. She has several research projects under her name. Her area of study is women's entrepreneurship, socio-entrepreneurship, Financial Literacy, and Derivatives Management. She has several publications under her name. She did her B. Tech from IIIT Allahabad and MBA from IIM Indore and Ph.D. from Devi Ahilya University, Indore.

Monica Negi is a research scholar in Dr. Y.S.P. University of Horticulture and Forestry, India.

Vinod Negi is working as Associate Professor in Himachal Pradesh University Business School (HPUBS), Shimla, India. He holds a Ph.D. degree in management from Himachal Pradesh University Shimla. He has served in corporate sector for about 4.5 years (with esteemed organizations like Bajaj Electricals Ltd. and HDFC Standard Life now (HDFC Life). He started his academic journey with ICFAI National College, Shimla and later on also worked with Everon IIPS and Bahra University. He has total 16 years of experience in academics and specializes in Consumer Behavior, Rural Marketing and Services Marketing.

Shabnam Pangtu is a scholar at Dr. Y.S.P. University of Horticulture and Forestry, India.

Chandni Rani is a Commerce graduate with a doctorate in Human Resources, currently working at Baba Farid College, Bathinda (Punjab), India. She worked as an Assistant Professor at Gian Jyoti Institute of Management and Technology. With a profound passion for Human Resource, Finance, Artificial Intelligence and, She has dedicated her academic career to advancing knowledge in this field through rigorous research, innovative teaching, and active engagement in academic communities. Dr. Chandni Rani is a distinguished author renowned for her profound insights and expertise in the world of financial services and markets. She has published and presented numerous papers in globally acclaimed conferences and Journals. Her area of research includes Systematic literature Review and bibliometric analysis.

Ekam Riar has done MBA from Eternal University, Baru Sahib. Her interest area includes Behavioral Finance and consumer behavior.

Dimple Roy is a Ph. D Scholar at ICFAI University, Jaipur, India. She is a personality development trainer and an author.

Ity Sahu is a research scholar in the Department of Business Management at Dr. Harisingh Gour Vishwavidyala (A Central University) Sagar. Her are of research is AI intervention in e-commerce. She has published articles in Scopus-indexed journals and book chapters in edited book. She has been a meritorious student and a gold medallist in her MBA programme.

Anshima is a research scholar, HPKV Business School, School of Commerce and Management studies. Currently, she is working on Green Human Resource management and her area of interest is Human Resource Management & Organizational behaviour.

Nidhi Sharma is a scholar at Dr. Y.S.P. University of Horticulture and Forestry, India.

Rohan is a dedicated researcher and a trainee at the School of Core Engineering and Management, as well as the Office of International Affairs at Shoolini University, India. He specializes in the fields of optical fibre communication, general management, and photonics and optoelectronics.

Shivangi Sharma is from Delhi University. Her fervent interest in Finance has set her on an exceptional trajectory in academics. Her other interest areas are entrepreneurship management and organization behavior.

Anu Sohal is a research scholar in HPKVBS, Central University of Himachal Pradesh, India. Her area of interest is mental well-being and contemporary issues in HRM.

Dahlak Daniel Solomon is a distinguished researcher at Adma Sciences Technology University in Ethiopia and pursuing a Ph.D. scholar from Shoolini University, India. His primary areas of expertise include the Internet of Things (IoT), MATLAB, and contemporary and general management issues.

Shantnu Sood is a dedicated researcher and a passionate scholar in the field of finance. Currently pursuing a Ph.D. in Finance at Himachal Pradesh University Business School, he is deeply committed to advancing knowledge and understanding in the realm of financial markets and investments. With a strong academic background and a keen interest in emerging technologies, Shantnu's research focuses on the application of artificial intelligence and machine learning techniques in stock market prediction and financial decision-making.

Sonali Vaid is a Research Scholar at the Business School, University of Jammu, India. Her area of research is Human Resource Management and Marketing.

Pooja Verma is an Associate Professor in Shoolini University, Solan, India. Her research area includes Human Resource Management, IPRs and organisational behaviour.

Index

A

B

C

D

E

P

R

S

T

V

W

www.ingramcontent.com/pod-product-compliance
Lightning Source LLC
LaVergne TN
LVHW062112300926
849161LV00010B/2438
* 9 7 9 8 3 6 9 3 0 4 1 8 1 *